Business Research Methods

The Irwin Series in Information and Decision Sciences

Consulting Editors:

Robert B. Fetter
Yale University

Claude McMillan
University of Colorado

Business Research Methods

C. William Emory
Washington University

1985   Third Edition

Homewood, Illinois   60430

ISBN 0-256-03009-X

Library of Congress Catalog No. 84–81416

Printed in the United States of America

3 4 5 6 7 8 9 0 K 2 1 0 9 8 7 6

To Jean

Preface

Managers can face a "make-or-buy" research situation. They often meet this dilemma inadequately equipped either to (1) perform the data gathering and analysis job themselves or (2) judge whether they are getting good value when others do the research for them. For either situation, a manager needs an understanding of the processes of research design and implementation.

The study of research methodology in business schools is often restricted to the area of marketing research. Students may develop research competence in their other functional area courses, but usually the focus there is on the subject content of accounting, finance, management, or whatever. Some schools are recognizing that knowledge of research methods and skill in their use are competencies of high value to managers and future managers, regardless of their functional area of concentration.

This book is a response to the perceived need for a cross-discipline text on research methods in business schools as well as a reference manual for managers. Its content, organization, and coverage have been guided by the following objectives:

1. Students and managers should be exposed to the set of conceptual tools and techniques that will enable them to:
    a. Understand the nature of scientific method as it applies in a business setting.
    b. Evaluate the worth of research proposals and studies from a design and execution point of view.
    c. Do a good amateur job of planning and executing a research project.
2. Professors should be provided with a book that will:
    a. Qualify as the basic text for a challenging course in business research methods.
    b. Cover the subject of research methods in sufficient breadth and depth to free them from methodological detail so they can concentrate on the more creative aspects of their teaching.

Every book is a compromise between conflicting objectives, and this one is no exception. One such compromise has been between length and coverage. The length was set as an initial constraint to assure that reading assignments would be short enough to leave students time for doing research. The length restriction also disciplined the author in balancing detail against breadth of coverage. The aim has been to "cover the territory" of the fundamentals but seldom to venture beyond the minimum needed to plan and execute relatively simple designs.

A second compromise was between what one might call traditional and modern orientations. The latter is identified with the development of sophisticated multivariate analysis tools. The author has tended to the more traditional emphasis for three reasons. In the first place, good research is a generic reasoning approach that is more or less divorced from specific tools and techniques. Secondly, only a limited number of students will master the more sophisticated analysis techniques, but a much larger number should have a grounding in research thinking. Finally, sophisticated techniques and complex research designs can be more effectively learned if the student has first mastered the fundamentals.

The book is organized into five sections. Section 1 consists of two chapters which cover the nature of business research and the notions of concepts, operational definitions, hypotheses, theories, and research reasoning. Section 2 includes chapters on research design, measurement, and experimental design.

Section 3 includes four chapters largely concerned with data collection. Included are discussions on effective library searching, questionnaire design, scaling, and field operations. Section 4 consists of a chapter on sampling and an appendix on complex probability sampling. Section 5 consists of three chapters on data analysis and one on research reporting.

In addition, Appendix A consists of an extensive reference on library research sources, while Appendix B provides the necessary tables for the various statistical tests cited in the book.

A number of people deserve a special word of thanks. For the first edition, my colleagues Walter Nord and Francis Connelly were especially helpful. Robert Fetter, Claude McMillan, and Alexander Voloatta all read the original manuscript and suggested improvements. J. Paul Peter, Phillip Beukema, and Steward E. Fleige provided useful critiques that guided the revision for the second edition.

This third edition has profited from insightful comments and recommendations from: Donald R. Cooper, Florida Atlantic University; Harold F. Rahmlow, The American College; Alan D. Carey, Bloomsburg State College; Richard A. Wald, New Mexico State University; and J. K. Bandyopadhyay, Central Michigan University.

Finally, I would like to express my deep appreciation and thanks to Mrs. Ruth Scheetz who has typed all of the versions of all three editions with great skill and good humor.

C. William Emory

Contents

SECTION 4
SAMPLING   273

SECTION 5
ANALYSIS AND REPORTING   317

APPENDIXES   439

FOUNDATIONS
OF RESEARCH

1. Research and management

WHO NEEDS IT?

Where will you be a decade from now? You could be putting your career on the line as the manager of a plant where productivity lags behind other plants in the company. Or, you could be responsible for deciding what company your firm should acquire. Or, you could be charged with investing millions in new products, or leading a breakthrough in labor relations. Any of these challenges will tax your talent and demand your best decision-making efforts.

Tomorrow's managers (you) will need to know more than any managers in history. You will need to deal with more variables, use longer planning horizons, and operate on a larger scale than your predecessors. To perform well in such an environment, you should be certain that what you know, and what you believe, are firmly grounded in fact and logic. Yet down through history, managers have often based decisions on beliefs that were not well founded. Indeed, it is easy to base our thinking and beliefs on suggestions alone. Too many of our opinions are held because we have been so bombarded with a certain viewpoint that we accept it without challenge.

Another way we develop beliefs, or learn to know, is by accepting the word of an "authority." Yet, all too often such authority depends on status or position rather than true expertise. Such authorities are often wrong, so it is wise to accept their views cautiously. Even the experts can be mistaken and predictions are especially subject to error, as economists demonstrate regularly.

We can also depend on our own experience. This can be a good source of knowledge but it suffers from two major weaknesses. Often a decision has to be made in an area where we have had little or no first-hand knowledge. Another difficulty is that much of what we believe from experience is based on inferences rather than fact. We can easily fail to differentiate between the two. What we know too often turns out to be assumptions, inferences, or

3

guesses. The general semanticist urges us to guard constantly against confusing what we know (fact) with what we infer (assume or conclude).

The best way to gain knowledge, as you might have guessed, is by conducting research. One can carry out a specific study to gather the information needed to better understand a certain problem or to make a decision. If this information is gathered by persons schooled in research methodology, the chances of getting valid and useful answers are indeed enhanced.

THE VALUE OF RESEARCH STUDY

Since the 1920s, many colleges and universities have offered courses in marketing research. Business research courses, of more recent origin, are a recognition that students in all management areas need training in the scientific method and its application to decision making. This broadening of interest in a more scientific approach has been stimulated by two factors: (1) the manager's increased need for more and better information, and (2) the availability of improved techniques and tools to meet this need.

The trend toward large, complex business operations has increased the risks associated with business decisions, making it more important for each to have a sound information base. Increased complexity means that there are more variables to consider. The competition is more vigorous and expansion adds unfamiliar markets. Workers, stockholders, customers, and the general public are all better informed and more sensitive to their self-interest. Government continues to show concern with all aspects of our society. Each of these factors demands that managers have more and better information upon which to base decisions.

At the same time, there has been an increase in the number and power of the tools that one can use to conduct research. The scientific method is now taking hold in all fields of management. We have begun to build better theories. The computer has given us a quantum leap in the ability to deal with problems. New techniques of quantitative analysis take advantage of this electronic power; communication and measurement techniques have also been enhanced. These trends reinforce each other and are having a massive impact on business management.

Management-researcher roles. Even if your major interest is in other aspects of management, there are at least four situations in which you can profit by having research skills. First, a manager often needs more information before making certain decisions. Your options are limited if there is no one to whom you can delegate this task; you either do not gather the information, or gather it yourself, it is hoped, with some reasonable level of skill. It is obvious which option is the better.

In a second instance, you may be called upon to do a research study for a higher-level executive. Such an opportunity is especially likely to occur in your early career years; it can be just the chance you need to make a favorable impression on that executive. A third reason why having research skills is valuable is that you may need to buy research services from others, or at least evaluate research done by others. If you can understand the research design used, and adequately judge its quality, your decisions will be the better for it.

A fourth reason for you to study research methods is that you may find a career position as a research specialist. As a specialized function it offers attractive career opportunities, especially in the areas of financial analysis, marketing research, and operations research. Job opportunities in other fields of management also exist but are not as widespread as in these three areas.

WHAT IS RESEARCH?

Textbook writers usually are prompt to supply definitions about the major concepts they are discussing. Here, it would be appropriate to address the question, "What is research in a managerial setting?" Just this once, however, let's try a different approach. Let's begin with a few examples of management problems in which information-gathering is involved. From these, we can abstract the essence of research, how it is carried out, what it can do, and what it should not be expected to do.

Case 1. The management of your company is preparing for labor negotiations. The vice-president of industrial relations asks you to provide some estimates of living costs in Chicago, where the company has its headquarters and major plant. Other plants are located in Atlanta, Los Angeles, and New York, and the vice-president would like similar data for these cities. You consult different sources and eventually find that the U.S. Bureau of Labor Statistics publishes periodic statistics on the costs of living in various major metropolitan areas. You find the latest of these reports in the documents section of the local university library, write a memorandum showing the requested figures, and submit the report to the vice-president. Is this research?

Case 2. You work in the treasurer's office in a corporation and have been asked to investigate six companies that are potential acquisition candidates. You are to gather pertinent data and make a comparative study of the merger attractiveness of all six. Because of the delicate nature of such an inquiry, you confine your search to published sources. You gather copies of each company's annual reports for a number of years, examine what financial analysts have said about them, and read everything else you can find about each company. After an extensive analysis, you submit a report which emphasizes the potential problems and opportunities that acquisition of each company would present. Is this research?

Case 3. Beginning in fiscal year 1984 (October 1, 1983–September 30, 1984) the federal government initiated a payment system by which hospitals would be directly reimbursed for charges of Medicare patients. Suppose you were a junior administrator at Saint Elsewhere Hospital when this new reimbursement system took effect. The administrator has asked you to gather the available cost data and determine how well the hospital will do receiving payments under the new federally mandated rules. Is this research?

Case 4. Management at General Electric conducted a survey among some of their workers and found that more than half were unhappy, dissatisfied with the information and recognition they received, as well as with their opportunities for advancement.[1] As a result, management began a number of monthly meetings, brought in experts to answer questions, and started a newsletter. A year later, when a second survey was taken, the number of unhappy workers had dropped from 50 to 20 percent. Is this research?

Case 5. A paint manufacturer is having trouble maintaining profits. The executive vice-president feels that inventory management is one of the weaker areas of the company's operations. In this industry, the many colors, types of paint, and container sizes make it easy for a firm to accumulate large inventories and still be unable to fill customer orders. You are asked to make recommendations.

You look into the present warehousing and shipping operations and find what appear to be excessive sales losses and delivery delays because of out-of-stock conditions. An informal survey among customers confirms your impression. You conclude that the present inventory reporting system does not provide the prompt, usable information needed for appropriate production decisions.

Your experience and reading of the literature on the latest inventory management techniques indicate to you what a new system should provide. You collect data on one major product class and simulate the effect of various reporting and replenishment practices on sales and costs. You take an inventory and monitor incoming orders to secure information about the ordering patterns, the average order size, and other pertinent data. You consider several designs for information reporting systems and the types of replenishment and production cycles that might be employed. After developing estimates of costs, you build and operate a simulation model of the inventory process. You choose the most profitable model and extrapolate its results to all product classes. You recommend to the executive vice-president that the company adopt the procedure and cite the expected dollars profits and savings that should accrue. Is this research?

Case 6. The Michigan Bell Telephone Company wants to increase the use of its long-distance service by household consumers. The company has reduced rates during off hours to stimulate traffic, but still the growth has not absorbed equipment capacities. The company engages the Survey Research Center of the University of Michigan to study why people make long

---

[1] "A Productive Way to Vent Employee Gripes," *Business Week*, October 16, 1978, p. 168 ff.

distance calls. The research project is to answer the following three questions.

1. What social and economic factors influence the number of social long distance calls a person will make?
2. What feelings and attitudes about the telephone influence social long distance calls?
3. What personality characteristics influence social long distance calling?

The project leaders devised a working theory to guide the research. This theory is illustrated in the diagram below.

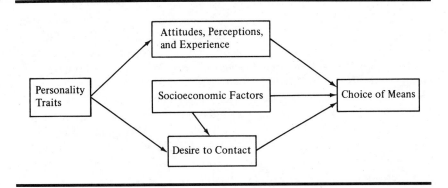

[The] diagram, obviously oversimplified, can be translated into language. Whether a person habitually phones depends on the presence of some factors which make him desire to contact others frequently. How often this desire is present depends on his personality characteristics and upon socioeconomic factors. . . . The desire to contact is undoubtedly influenced by external conditions, such as emergencies or the sudden need for more information. The emphasis in this study, however, is upon those more or less permanent personality characteristics which might influence the strength of the desire to be in contact with friends and relatives. . . . Once the desire to contact is present, whether he uses the telephone or not depends on other socioeconomic factors, as well as certain of his attitudes, his perceptions, and his previous experience with phoning.[2]

With this theoretical model in mind, the investigators conducted 400 interviews, divided equally among households that made a large number of long distance calls and households that made almost no calls. They wrote a report of their findings, which generally confirmed the specifics of their theory. Is this research?

[2]*Motives, Attitudes and Long Distance Calls* (Ann Arbor, Mich.: Survey Research Center, University of Michigan, April 1956), p. 10.

Is research always problem based?

In these six cases, studies were undertaken in direct response to problems that needed solving. The practical problem-solving emphasis is a critical feature of applied research, and one should expect such studies to be closely related to action or policy needs. In this respect, all six examples appear to qualify as applied research. Pure research is also problem solving, but in a different sense. It is aimed at solving perplexing questions (that is, problems) of a theoretical nature that have little direct impact on action or policy decisions. Thus, both applied and pure research are problem-based, but applied research is directed much more to making decisions.

Some authorities equate research with pure, or scientific, investigations and would reject all six examples. History shows, however, that science typically had its beginnings in pragmatic problems of real life. Interest in pure research comes much later, after knowledge in the field has been developed. Research is too narrowly defined if restricted to the pure variety.

One respected author defines scientific research as a "systematic, controlled, empirical, and critical investigation of hypothetical propositions about the presumed relations among natural phenomena."[3] Terms in this definition, such as "systematic, controlled, empirical, and critical . . ." describe characteristics that distinguish good from bad research of all types. These qualities are apparently much of what Kerlinger means by "scientific." Whether research needs to be an "investigation of hypothetical propositions about presumed relationships" is debatable.

The classical concept of pure research does call for a hypothesis, but in applied research such a narrow definition omits at least two types of investigations that are highly valued.[4] First is the exploratory study in which the investigators know so little about the area of study that hypotheses have not yet emerged.[5] An equally, if not more, important area of study is that which the purists call, "merely descriptive." It deals with the discovery of answers to the who, what, when, where, how questions rather than the why questions. The defense of descriptive research as a legitimate enterprise is well made by Dubin:[6]

> There is no more devastating condemnation that the self-designated theorist makes of the researcher than to label his work *purely descriptive*. There is an implication that associates "purely descriptive" research with empty-headedness; the label also implies that as a bare minimum every

---

[3]Fred W. Kerlinger, *Foundations of Behavioral Research*, 2d ed. (New York: Holt, Rinehart, & Winston, 1973), p. 11.

[4]A hypothesis is a statement that is advanced for the purpose of testing its truth or falsity.

[5]An exploratory study describes an investigation when the final research problem has not yet been clearly fixed. Its aim is to provide the insights needed by the researcher to develop a more formal research design.

[6]Reprinted with permission of Macmillan Publishing Co., Inc. from *Theory Building*, rev. ed. 1978, by Robert Dubin. Copyright © 1969 by The Free Press, a division of the Macmillan Co.

healthy researcher has at least an hypothesis to test, and preferably a whole model. This is nonsense.

In every discipline, but particularly in its early stages of development, purely descriptive research is indispensable. Descriptive research is the stuff out of which the mind of man, the theorist, develops the units that compose his theories. The very essence of description is to name the properties of things: you may do more, but you cannot do less and still have description. The more adequate the description, the greater is the likelihood that the units derived from the description will be useful in subsequent theory building.

In answer to the question posed at the beginning of this section, "Is research always problem based?" the answer is yes. Whether pure or applied, simple or complex, all research should provide an answer to some question.

What is the study purpose?

The six cases presented earlier can be classified by their immediate communication objectives. At the most elementary level, an inquiry may be made only to report some data, perhaps statistics. The task may be quite simple and the data readily available. At other times, the information may be difficult to find and the assignment calls for knowledge and skill with information sources. Usually there is little inference or conclusion drawing. Purists claim that this should not be called research even though carefully gathered data can have great value. Does the design have to be complex and require inferences for a project to be called research? Are any of the six cases primarily a reporting exercise?

The next level of investigation is the descriptive study. The researcher seeks to make a profile of a group of problems, persons, or events. Such studies may be only one variable frequency distributions, or they may involve bivariate or multivariate relationships. The descriptive study is popular in business research. It may have a high order of inference drawing or it may not. Which of the previous cases are examples of descriptive research?

A third type of investigation calls for making a prediction. It is something of a hybrid in that it may be largely a descriptive study with the step of prediction added on. Prediction is found especially in studies conducted to evaluate specific courses of action. Prediction involves explicit inference drawing. Do any of the cases involve prediction?

The fourth and most challenging type of study, at least in a conceptual sense, is the explanatory study. Here one tries to account for the forces that caused a certain phenomenon to occur. Theories, or at least hypotheses, are advanced and tested.[7] This type of study often calls for a high order of

---

[7]For now, let's define a theory as a set of hypotheses proposed to explain certain phenomena (facts).

inference and may also include prediction. Is there any explanatory research among the six example cases?

Any of these four types of studies—reporting, description, prediction, or explanation—can properly be called research. Yet does this suggest that any kind of report, no matter how crude or simple, is research? What about an explanatory study that is shallow, carelessly done, and obviously biased?

Let's conclude that *research is a systematic inquiry aimed at providing information to solve problems.* This is the bare minimum that an effort must meet to be called research. All six of the case histories meet this definition, but they suggest different stages of scientific development. A rough measure of the development of science in any field is the degree to which prediction and explanation have replaced reporting and description as research objectives. By this standard, business research is in a relatively primitive stage of scientific development.

Our definition above says nothing about what constitutes high-quality research. Let's go further and consider what is meant by good research.

WHAT IS GOOD RESEARCH?

Good research can be thought of as that which uses the scientific method. One widely accepted view suggests that good research should meet the following tests:

1. *The purpose of the research, or the problem involved, should be clearly defined and sharply delineated in terms as unambiguous as possible.*

   The statement of the research problem should include analysis into its simplest elements, its scope and limitations, and precise specifications of the meanings of all words significant to the research. Failure of the researcher to do this adequately may raise legitimate doubts in the minds of readers as to whether the researcher has sufficient understanding of the problem to make a sound attack upon it.

2. *The research procedures used should be described in sufficient detail to permit another researcher to repeat the research.*

   Excepting when secrecy is imposed in the national interest, research reports should reveal with candor the sources of data and the means by which they were obtained. Omission of significant procedural details makes it difficult or impossible to estimate the validity and reliability of the data and justifiably weakens the confidence of the reader in research.

3. *The procedural design of the research should be carefully planned to yield results that are as objective as possible.*

   When a sampling of the population is involved, the report should include evidence concerning the degree of representativeness of the sample. A questionnaire ought not to be used when more reliable evidence is available from documentary sources or by direct observation. Bibliographic searches should be as thorough and complete as possible.

Experiments should have satisfactory controls. Direct observations should be recorded in writing as soon as possible after the event. Efforts should be made to minimize the influence of personal bias in selecting and recording data.

4. *The researcher should report, with complete frankness, flaws in procedural design and estimate their effect upon the findings.*

   There are very few perfect research designs. Some of the imperfections may have little effect upon the validity and reliability of the data; others may invalidate them entirely. A competent researcher should be sensitive to the effects of imperfect design and his experience in analyzing the data should give him a basis for estimating their influence.

5. *Analysis of the data should be sufficiently adequate to reveal its significance; and the methods of analysis used should be appropriate.*

   The extent to which this criterion is met is frequently a good measure of the competence of the researcher. Twenty years of experience in guiding the research of graduate students leads the writer to conclude that adequate analysis of the data is the most difficult phase of research for the novice.

   The validity and reliability of data should be checked carefully. The data should be classified in ways that assist the researcher to reach pertinent conclusions. When statistical methods are used, the probability of error should be estimated and the criteria of statistical significance applied.

6. *Conclusions should be confined to those justified by the data of the research and limited to those for which the data provide an adequate basis.*

   Researchers are often tempted to broaden the basis of inductions by including personal experiences not subject to the controls under which the research data were gathered. This tends to decrease the objectivity of the research and weakens confidence in the findings.

   Equally undesirable is the all-too-frequent practice of drawing conclusions from a study of a limited population and applying them universally. Good researchers specify the conditions under which their conclusions seem to be valid. Failure to do so justifiably weakens confidence in the research.

7. *Greater confidence in the research is warranted if the researcher is experienced, has a good reputation in research, and is a person of integrity.*

   Were it possible for the reader of a research report to obtain sufficient information about the researcher, this criterion perhaps would be one of the best bases for judging the degree of confidence a piece of research warrants. For this reason, the research report should be accompanied by more information about the qualification of the researcher than is the usual practice.

   Some evidence pertinent to estimates of the competence and integrity of the researcher may be found in the report itself. Language that is restrained, clear, and precise; assertions that are carefully drawn and hedged with appropriate reservations; and an apparent effort to achieve maximum objectivity tend to leave a favorable impression of the researcher. On the other hand, generalizations that outrun the evidence upon which they are based, exaggerations, and unnecessary verbiage tend to leave an unfavorable impression.[8]

These seven criteria provide an excellent summary of what is desirable in scholarly research. Ideally, they should also be applied in business research, but circumstances often force adjustments. Criterion 1 calls for specifying what will be done, but in many exploratory studies, it is just not possible to be that precise. It certainly is important, however, to state the nature of the research problem clearly and unambiguously.

Criterion 2 calls for complete disclosure of methods and procedures used in the research study. This also is highly desirable. It enables others to test the findings through replication, and this openness to scrutiny has a positive effect on the quality of research. However, the motivation for many business research studies is to secure competitive advantage. To disclose the methodology and findings of a research study, or sometimes even its existence, would be considered unwise.

Criteria 3 through 7 should guide all research studies. While these criteria sometimes use vague phraseology such as "unambiguous as possible," this only recognizes the realities of research work. The aim is always to be objective, yet we are all subjective. We must also recognize that research designs have flaws even though calling attention to them in our work may be painful.

The threat of bias is mentioned under criterion 3, but it should be given more emphasis. One difficulty is that the business researcher often knows from the beginning what results the sponsor would like to have. To combat this potentially biasing influence, it may be necessary before the study to have an understanding that the purpose of the research is to uncover reality—whatever that may be.

A final consideration not adequately covered in the seven criteria concerns the question of ethics. Business research often involves human subjects and this raises important ethical issues. In recent years, much greater attention has been given to such issues in research. One source classifies 10 categories of questionable practices in research that can raise ethical concerns:[9]

1. Involving people in research without their knowledge or consent.
2. Coercing people to participate.
3. Withholding from the participant the true nature of the research.
4. Deceiving the research participant.
5. Leading the research participants to commit acts which diminish their self-respect.

---

[8]James Harold Fox, "Criteria of Good Research," *Phi Delta Kappan* 39 (March 1958), pp. 285–86.

[9]Claire Selltiz, Lawrence S. Wrightsman, and Stuart W. Cook, *Research Methods in Social Relations*, 3d ed. (New York: Holt, Rinehart & Winston, 1976), p. 202.

6. Violating the right to self-determination: research on behavior control and character change.
7. Exposing the research participant to physical or mental stress.
8. Invading the privacy of the research participant.
9. Withholding benefits from participants in control groups.
10. Failing to treat research participants fairly and to show them consideration and respect.

For a penetrating discussion of these points, read the entire source cited. Briefly, researchers have a responsibility to guard the welfare of their subjects. Careful consideration should be given to the possibilities for exploitation, loss of dignity, invasion of privacy, and physical or psychological discomfort. The researcher should carefully weigh the potential for adverse effects against the need for the research. Often other approaches can be used or substitute procedures can be devised. When in doubt, seek the counsel of others more objective than yourself. Another source of guidance are the statements of ethical practice issued by such professional organizations as the American Psychological Association and the American Marketing Association.

How scientific is business research?

It is generally claimed that the development of scientific method in business research has lagged behind the physical sciences. This is a fair assessment. Physical scientists have been more rigorous in their concepts and research procedures. They are much more advanced in their theory development than are business scientists. Business researchers should not despair, however. There are several major reasons why the task of scientific development is more difficult in business research.

A major factor in the slower development of science in business research has already been mentioned. Much physical research has been carried on in the public domain, some of it for hundreds of years. Governments have allocated billions of dollars to support such research, driven by the motivation to overcome disease or to improve the human condition. Nations driven by threat of war and national pride have also played a major role in the advance of physical science. A large part of the findings of this research is in the public domain and has been widely disseminated and replicated by others.

Business research is of much more recent origin and has been largely supported by business organizations in the hope of achieving a competitive advantage. Research methods and findings cannot be patented, and to share results is seen as a loss of competitive advantage. In fact, the more valuable the research result is, the greater the value in keeping it a secret. Under such conditions, access to findings is obviously restricted. Even though there is a growing amount of academic business research, it receives meager support when compared to physical research.

Business research operates in a less favorable environment in other ways, too. Physical research is normally conducted under controlled laboratory conditions. Business research seldom is. Business research normally deals with such topics as human attitudes, behavior, and performance. People think they already know a lot about these topics. They do not easily accept research findings that differ from their opinions.

Even with these handicaps, business researchers are making great strides in the scientific arena. New techniques are being developed, and rigorous research procedures are advancing rapidly. The development of computers and powerful quantitative analytical methods have contributed to this movement, but even more important has been the greater understanding of the basic principles of sound research. This improvement in scientific sophistication is expected to continue.

One important outcome of these trends is that research-based decision making will be more widely used in the future than it has in the past. Managers who are not prepared for this change will be at a severe disadvantage.

THE MANAGER-RESEARCHER RELATIONSHIP

Information gathering is an integral part of any manager's job. So, it is not surprising that many managers do their own research, at least part of the time. When they lack either research time or talent, managers may delegate the task to a staff assistant or a research specialist. This delegation of responsibility can result in more relevant results, especially if the research is decision-driven and each party makes a full contribution to the joint venture.

Decision-driven research. Applied research has an inherent value to the extent that it can assist management in making decisions. Interesting information about consumers, employees, or competitors might be pleasant to have, but its value is limited. If a study does not help management to select more efficient, less risky, or more profitable alternatives than otherwise would be the case, its use should be questioned. The important point is: *Applied research in a business environment finds its justification in the contribution it makes to the decision-maker's task.*

Participant contributions. Both managers and researchers have important obligations in making a research study successful. The obligation of managers is to specify their problems and provide to researchers adequate background information relating to them. It is usually more effective if managers state their problems in terms of the decisions they must make rather than to specify the information they think they need. If this is done, both manager and researcher can jointly determine the kinds of information needed.

Researchers also have obligations. They are expected to develop a creative research design that will provide answers to important business questions. Not only should researchers provide data analyzed in terms of the problem specified, but they should also point out the implications that flow from the results. In the process, conflict may arise between what the decision maker wants and what the researcher can provide. The decision maker wants certainty and simple, explicit recommendations, while the researcher often can offer only probabilities and hedged interpretations. This conflict is inherent in their respective roles and has no simple resolution. However, a workable balance can usually be found if each party is sensitive to the demands and restrictions imposed on the other.

The problem of client relations. In an organizational setting, the researcher should look on the manager as a client. An effective working relationship between researcher and manager is not easily achieved unless several critical barriers can be overcome. Some of these can be traced to management's limited exposure to research. Managers seldom have had either formal training in research methodology or research expertise gained through experience.

In addition, managers often see research people as threats to their personal status. They still view management as the domain of the "intuitive artist" who is the master in this area. They may feel that a request for research assistance implies that they are inadequate to the task. These fears may often be justified. The researcher's function is to test old ideas as well as new ones. The insecure manager may see the researcher as a potential rival.

The researcher will inevitably have to consider the political situations that develop in any organization. Members strive to maintain their niches and may seek ascendency over their colleagues. Coalitions tend to form, and people engage in various self-serving activities, both overt and covert. As a result, research is blocked or the findings or objectives of the research are distorted for an individual's self-serving purposes. To allow one's operations to be probed with a critical eye may be to invite trouble from others competing for promotion, resources, or other forms of organizational power.

Another problem reflects the explosive growth of research technology in recent years. A knowledge gap has developed between manager and research specialist as model building and more sophisticated investigative techniques have come into use. The manager must now put his or her faith in the research specialist and hope for the best.

A fifth source of client-related stress for researchers is their frequent isolation from managers. Researchers tend to draw back into their specialty and communicate only among themselves. This problem is compounded by management's lack of understanding. The research department thus becomes an isolated, technical job shop. These problems have caused some people to advocate the use of a "research generalist." Such a person would head the research activity, help managers detail their research needs, and translate these needs into research problems. He or she would also facilitate the flow of information between manager and research specialist that is so important for bringing the researcher into the decision-making process. While this is an attractive idea, it does not appear to be taking hold.

The objective of this text is to address these problems. In the chapters that follow, we discuss scientific research procedures and show how they can be applied to the pragmatic problems of the business manager. At a minimum, the objective is to make you a more intelligent consumer of research products.

SUMMARY

The managers of tomorrow will need to know more than any managers in history. And, research will be a major contributor to that knowledge. There are a number of situations where managers will find knowledge of research methods to be of value. They may need to conduct research either for themselves or others. As buyers of research services, they will need to be able to judge research quality. Finally, they may become research specialists themselves.

Research is any organized inquiry carried out to provide information for solving problems. It includes reporting, as well as descriptive, predictive, and explanatory studies; only the last three are treated in this book.

What characterizes good research? Generally speaking, one expects good research to be purposeful, its goals to be clearly defined, the procedures defensible and replicable, and the objectivity of the researcher clearly evident. The reporting of procedures—their strengths and weaknesses—should be complete and honest. Appropriate analytical techniques should be used; conclusions drawn should be limited to those clearly justified by the findings. If the investigator has an established reputation for quality work, so much the better.

The manager-researcher relationship is an important one. Both share the obligation of making a project meaningful. A number of factors complicate this relationship. Among these are ethical considerations and the political environment.

SUPPLEMENTAL READINGS

1. Churchill, Gilbert A. *Marketing Research* 3d ed. Hinsdale, Ill.: Dryden Press, 1983. Chapter 1 discusses the marketing manager's role and the role of marketing research. It also covers the position of market research in the company organization.
2. Freeman, Howard E. and Clarence C. Sherwood. *Social Research and Social Policy.* Englewood Cliffs, N.J.: Prentice-Hall, 1970. Chapter 2 discusses the contribution of research to social policy.
3. Random, Matthew. *The Social Scientist in American Industry.* New Brunswick, N.J.: Rutgers University Press, 1970. A research report of experiences

of social scientists employed in industry. Chapter 9 presents a summary of findings.

DISCUSSION QUESTIONS

1. What is research? Why should there be any question about the definition of research?
2. Managers who wish to have information on which to base a decision face a make or buy situation. What are the problems they face in selecting either of these alternatives?
3. You are manager of the midwestern division of a major corporation, supervising five animal-feed plants scattered over four states. Corporate headquarters asks you to conduct an investigation to determine whether any of these plants should be closed, expanded, moved, or reduced. Is there a possible conflict between your roles as an investigator and manager? Explain.
4. Advise each of the following persons on the specific research studies which he or she might find useful. Classify each proposed study as reporting, description, explanation, or prediction.
   a   Manager of the men's furnishings department at a Sears store.
   b   Plant manager at a Ford auto assembly plant.
   c   Director of admissions at a large state university.
   d   Investment analyst at Merrill Lynch, Pierce, Fenner, and Smith.
   e   Director of personnel at a large metropolitan hospital.
   f   Product manager for Crest toothpaste at Procter & Gamble.
5. The new president of an old, established company is facing a problem. The company is currently unprofitable and is, in the president's opinion, operating inefficiently. The company sells a wide line of equipment and supplies to the dairy industry. Some items it manufactures, and many it wholesales to dairies, creameries, and similar plants. Because the industry is changing in several ways, survival will be more difficult in the future. In particular, many equipment companies are bypassing the wholesalers and selling directly to dairies. In addition, many of the independent dairies are being taken over by large food chains. How might research help the new president to make the right decisions? In answering this question, consider the areas of marketing and finance as well as the whole company.
6. The president of Bleu Jeans Manufacturing has assigned you the task of collecting data for use in making the long-range strategic plan for the company. In particular, you are to investigate critical environment areas involving technologial changes, sociocultural changes, and legal/political factors. What kinds of data would you seek? Where and how might you gather such data?
7. You have received a research report done by a consultant for your firm—a life insurance company. The study is a survey of morale in the home office, and covers the opinions of about 500 secretaries and clerks plus about 100 executives and actuaries. You are asked to comment on its quality. What would you look for?

2. The research process

"Staring at a blank sheet of paper is hard work when you are trying to be creative," thought Mary Kirk as she pondered the problem before her. She had just come from the research team meeting where she had been given a new assignment.

Her task was to lead the team in developing a first draft proposal for a new research client, a major telephone company. The client's management wanted to increase the use of long-distance telephone service by its household customers. It was felt that a research study into the sociologic, psychologic, and economic factors affecting long-distance phone usage might help the firm to increase their sales to this public.

Mary had already decided that she should first do some fundamental thinking about the client's problem and how to translate it into research terms. After several false starts, she came up with three questions that she knew needed to be answered. They were:

1. What is the problem facing the client and how does this translate into a research problem?
2. What are the major research concepts that will have to be dealt with in this study and how can they be defined?
3. What should the basic theory underlying this project be and what major hypotheses should flow out of this theory?

We will return to Mary's problem shortly, but first let's discuss these questions in more general terms.

THE ORIGIN OF RESEARCH NEED

The point has already been made, but bears repeating, that any research project should be a response to a need for information in order to solve a problem. This is true in academic as well as business research.

18

Academic research. Academic research ranges from scholarly theoretical work to mundane student projects. For the scholar, the problem might be to understand how two theories of motivation do or do not explain worker performance. The student's research can be to answer the question, "How do freshmen and seniors differ in political attitudes?" In these situations, the researcher's objective is to answer a particular question or solve a problem.

Applied management research. In a business context, the research project originates in the needs of the manager. It would be impossible here to recount all the possible types of management problems for which research is useful. We can, however, define decision making into three problem types.

One type of problem involves management's choice of purposes or objectives. The general question is, "What do we want to achieve?" At the company level this might be, "Should we reconsider our basic corporate objectives as they concern our public image?" In a more narrow sense, we might see a management question on objectives that asks, "What goals should we try to achieve in our next labor negotiations?"

A specific question can lead to many studies. Concern for the company's image might lead to a survey among various groups to ascertain their attitudes toward the company. A question might suggest research into what other companies are doing in this regard; another question might call for a forecast of expected changes in social attitudes. The question concerning labor negotiation objectives might prompt research into what recent settlements in the industry have been. Alternatively, it might involve a survey among workers to determine how well we have been meeting their concerns about quality of work life.

Another set of management decisions involves the generation and evaluation of solutions. The general question is, "How can we achieve the ends we seek?" Research projects in this class usually deal with concrete problems that managers quickly recognize as being useful. Such projects can involve such strategic questions as, "How can we achieve our five-year goal of doubled sales and net profits?" At a more tactical level, the questions may be as specific as, "Which of three approaches is the most effective way to organize the shipping department?"

A final class of management problems concerns the troubleshooting or control situation. The problem usually involves monitoring or diagnosing various ways in which an organization appears to be failing to achieve its established goals. This group includes such questions as, "Why is Department A the high-cost department?" and, "How well is our program meeting its goals?"

The business researcher also finds substantial opportunity in the environment in which an organization functions. These external concerns include such topics as prospective acquisition candidates, the nature and trend of government regulations, cultural changes, and new technology developments.

No matter how the management question is defined, there often are many research directions that can be taken. It is the joint responsibility of the researcher, in collaboration with the manager, to choose the most productive project. This task can be best approached using a question hierarchy.

The question hierarchy

A useful way to approach the research process is to state the basic problem that prompts the research. From this, try to develop other questions by progressively breaking down the original question into more specific ones. We can think of this as the hierarchy of questions.

The process begins at the most general level with the management question. *The management question represents a decision that a manager must make and is the problem prompting the research.* Since the definition of the management problem sets the research task, it follows that a poorly defined management problem or question will misdirect research efforts.

For example, a research consultant was asked to help the new management of a bank. The president was concerned about erosion of the bank's profitability and wanted to turn this situation around. The Center City Bank was the oldest and largest of three banks in a city of about 50,000 population. Profits had stagnated in recent years. The president and the consultant discussed the problem facing the organization and settled on the management question as "How can we improve our profit picture?"

Note that the management question does not specify what kind of research to be done. This question is strictly managerial in thrust. It implies that the bank's management faces the task of developing a strategy for increasing deposits and therefore profits. The question is broad. As a starting point, this is good, although we may want to break such a broad question down into more specific subquestions.

In this case, further discussion between the bank president and the research consultant indicated that there were really two questions to be answered. The problem of low deposit growth was linked to concerns of a competitive nature. While lowered deposits directly affected profits, another part of the profit weakness seemed to be associated with negative factors that were within the organization itself. This separation of the management problem into two subproblems grew out of the discussion between the consultant and the manager.

The research question. Once the researcher has a clear statement of a manager's question, she must translate it into a research problem, i.e., an information-gathering problem. As pointed out above, there are probably a number of different ways to address any management problem. This is the point at which the insight and expertise of the researcher come into play. It is also the point at which the manager's decision is most important. A choice of wrong research for the right problem can be dangerous.

It is important to remember, however, that a manager's motivations for seeking research are not always obvious. Managers might express a genuine need for specific information on which to base a decision. This is the ideal. Sometimes, however, a research study may not really be desirable, but is authorized anyway, chiefly because its presence may win approval for a certain manager's pet idea. At other times, research may be authorized as a measure of personal protection for a decision maker in case he or she is criticized later. In these less than ideal cases, the researcher may find it more difficult to win the client's interest and support for a sound study design.

Let's assume, however, that the manager's needs for sound research are sincere. Our task then is to formulate a research question that fits this need. *A research question is the single question or hypothesis that best states the objective of the research study.* On occasion, it may be more than one question, but often, it is just one. A study that answers the question provides the manager with the desired information.

For example, the Center City Bank, mentioned earlier, had done no research in the past. It had little specific information about competitors or customers, and had not analyzed its internal operations. The client and consultant agreed that there were two research subquestions which should be addressed simultaneously. They were:

1. What are the major factors contributing to the bank's failure to achieve a stronger growth rate in deposits?
2. How well is the bank doing with regard to
    a Quality of its work climate?
    b Efficiency of operations compared to industry norms?
    c Financial condition compared to industry norms?

The research consultant took on the responsibilities of conducting a study of the competition and the bank's market structure, as well as conducting a climate survey of its employees. Other studies were undertaken by the bank's accounting firm. Our discussion, however, is concerned only with the consultant's assignment.

Investigative questions.   Once the general research question(s) has been selected, the thinking moves to a more specific level, that of investigative questions. *Investigative questions are those that the researcher must answer in order to satisfactorily answer the general research question.* Our purpose is to take a more general research question and break it down into more specific questions about which we need to gather data. This fractionating process can continue down through several levels of progressively more specific questions. These are all questions which a researcher must ask and answer for herself. They guide the development of the research direction.

For example, continuing with the Center City bank project, the research consultant developed two major investigative questions for studying the market, plus a number of subquestions under each. These were to provide insight into the lack of deposit growth. They were as follows:

1. *What is the public's position with regard to financial services and their use?*
   a What specific financial services are used?
   b How attractive are various services?
   c What factors influence a person's use of a particular service?
2. *What is the bank's competitive position?*
   a What are the geographic patterns of our customers and of our competitors' customers?
   b What is indicated by demographic differences among our customers and those of our competitors?
   c How aware is the public of the bank's promotional efforts?
   d What general opinions does the public hold of the bank and our competitors?
   e How does growth in services compare among competing institutions?

Similarly, investigative questions were developed to guide the organizational climate study.

Measurement questions.   Measurement questions constitute the fourth and final level of fractionation. In surveys, the measurement questions are those that we actually ask the respondents. They appear on the questionnaire. In an observation study, measurement questions are those that observers must answer about each subject studied. In the case of the Center City Bank, a survey was conducted among local residents. The questionnaire contained a number of measurement questions seeking information that provided answers to the investigative questions. Interviews were completed with about 200 residents. The information collected was used to guide a reorientation of the bank's strategy.

Summary.   How one structures the research sets the direction of the project. Using the research question hierarchy is a good way to do this. Think of the hierarchy as four sequential stages moving from the general to the specific. While this suggests four discrete levels, it is actually more of a continuum. The investigative question stage, in particular, may involve several levels of questioning before you reach satisfactory measurement questions.

At this stage, the research is basically a thinking process. With it comes a number of definition problems to resolve in order to make our measurement more precise. Research question fractionation also requires inference drawing. Let's review these topics to assure that our research thinking is precise and our logic correct.

RESEARCH TRAINING

When doing research, we try to learn "what is" before trying to predict, explain, or understand. For example, one might want to answer the question, "What will be the employee reaction to the new pension plan proposal?" Or, "Why did the stock market go up so much when major indicators suggested it would go down?" When dealing with such questions, we must all agree on basic definitions. For example, which employees? What kind of reaction? What pension plan proposal? How is stock market defined? How much higher is so much higher? What are the major indicators? These questions require the use of concepts.

Concepts

If one is to understand and communicate information about objects and events, there must be a common ground on which to do it. Concepts are used for this purpose. A concept is a bundle of meanings or characteristics associated with certain events, objects, conditions, situations, and the like.[1] We abstract such meanings from reality and use words as labels to designate them. For example, we see a man passing and think "He is running, walking, skipping, crawling, or hopping." These movements all represent concepts. We also have abstracted certain visual elements by which we identified that the moving object was a he not a she or a truck or horse. We obviously use large numbers of concepts daily in our thinking, conversing, and other activities.

Sources of concepts. Concepts that are in frequent and general use have been developed over time through shared usage. We have acquired them through personal experience. If we lived in another society, we would hold many of the same concepts (although in a different language). Some concepts, however, are unique to a particular culture and are not readily translatable into another language.[2]

Ordinary concepts make up the bulk of communication even in research, but we can often run into difficulty trying to deal with an uncommon concept or a newly advanced idea. One way to handle this problem is to borrow from other languages (for example, *gestalt*) or to borrow from other fields. For example, the concept of "gravitation" is borrowed from physics and used in marketing in an attempt to explain why people shop where they do. The concept of "distance" is used in attitude measurement to describe degrees of difference between the attitudes of two or more persons. "Threshold" is used effectively to describe a concept in perception studies, while "velocity" is a term borrowed by the economist from the physicist.

---

[1] Another definition, "Concepts are terms that refer to the characteristics of events, situations, groups and individuals that we are studying . . . ." is from Claire Selltiz, Lawrence S. Wrightsman, and Stuart W. Cook, *Research Methods in Social Relations*, 3d ed. (New York: Holt, Rinehart & Winston, 1976), p. 16.

[2] "In Lithuanian there is a word for gray when you speak of eyes, another when you speak of hair, a third when you speak of ducks and geese, several others for other purposes, but no word for gray in general." See Rudolph Flesch, *The Art of Clear Thinking* (New York: Crowell-Collier Publishing, 1962), p. 59.

Borrowing is not always practical, so we need to (1) adopt new meanings for words (make a word cover a different concept) or (2) develop new labels (words) for concepts. The recent broadening of the meaning of "model" is an example of the first instance, while the development of concepts such as "sibling" and "status stress" are examples of the second. When we adopt new meanings or develop new labels, we begin to develop a specialized jargon or terminology. Researchers in medicine, the physical sciences, and related fields frequently use terms that are unintelligible to outsiders. Jargon no doubt contributes to efficiency of communication among specialists, but excludes everyone else.

Importance to research.   Concepts are basic to all thought and communication, yet we pay too little attention to what they are, and the problems encountered in their use. These considerations alone would not justify considering the subject here if it were not that there are special problems in research that grow out of the need for concept precision and inventiveness. We design hypotheses using concepts. We devise measurement concepts by which to test these hypothetical statements. We gather data using these measurement concepts. We may even invent new concepts to express ideas. The success of research hinges on (1) how clearly we conceptualize; and (2) how well others understand the concepts we use. For example, when we survey people on the question of tax equity, the questions we use need to tap faithfully the attitudes of the respondents. Attitudes are abstract, yet we must attempt to measure them using carefully selected concepts.

The challenge is to develop concepts that others will clearly understand. We might, for example, ask respondents for an estimate of their family's total income. This may seem to be a simple, unambiguous concept, but we will receive varying and confusing answers unless we restrict or narrow the concept by specifying (1) time period, such as weekly, monthly, or annually; (2) before or after income taxes; (3) for head of family only or for all family members; and (4) for salary and wages only, or also for dividends, interest, and capital gains. (How about income in kind such as free rent, employee discounts, food stamps?)

Problems in concept use.   The use of concepts presents difficulties that are accentuated in a research setting. First, people differ in the meanings that they include under the particular label. This problem is so great in normal human communication that we often see cases where people use the same language but do not understand each other. We might all agree to the meaning of such concepts as dog, table, electric light, money, employee, and wife. We may encounter more difficulties, however, when we communicate concepts such as household, retail transaction, dwelling unit, regular user, debit, and wash sale. Still more challenging are concepts that are familiar but not well understood, such as leadership, motivation, IQ, social class, and fiscal policy.

These sets of concepts represent progressive levels of abstraction, i.e., the degree to which the concept does or does not have objective referents.

Table is an objective concept in that we can point to tables and we can conjure up in our mind images of tables. An abstraction like social class is much more difficult to visualize. Furthermore, there is no objective thing called "social class." Such abstract concepts are often called "constructs."

Definition

Confusion about the meaning of the concepts can destroy a research study's value, without the researcher or client even knowing it. If words have different meanings to the parties involved then they are not communicating on the same wavelength. Definitions are one way to reduce this danger.

While there are various types of definitions, the most familiar are dictionary definitions. In these, a concept is defined with a synonym. For example, a customer is defined as a patron; a patron, in turn, is defined as a customer or client of an establishment; a client is defined as one who employs the services of any professional man . . . , also, loosely, a patron of any shop.[3] Circular definitions such as these may be adequate for general communication, but not for research. Here we must measure concepts and this requires a more rigorous definition.

Operational definitions. *An operational definition is one stated in terms of specific testing criteria or operations.* These terms must have empirical referents (that is, we must be able to count, measure, or in some other way gather the information through our senses). Whether the object to be defined is physical, e.g., a machine tool, or highly abstract, e.g., achievement motivation, the definition must specify the characteristics to study and how they are to be observed. The specifications and procedures must be so clear that any competent person using them would classify the objects in the same way.

Suppose college undergraduates are to be classified by class. No one has much trouble understanding such terms as freshman, sophomore, and so forth. The task may not be that simple if you must determine which students fall in each class. To do this, you need an operational definition.

Operational definitions may vary depending on your purpose and the way you choose to measure them. Here are two different situations requiring different definitions of the same concepts.

1. You conduct a survey among students and wish to classify their answers by their class levels. You merely ask them to report their class status and you record it. In this case, class is freshman, sophomore, junior, or senior and you accept the answer each respondent gives as correct. This is a rather casual definition process but nonetheless an operational definition. It is probably adequate in this case even though some of the respondents report inaccurately.

---

[3]Webster's *New Collegiate Dictionary* (Springfield, Mass.: G. & C. Merriam, 1961), pp. 205, 617, 154, respectively.

2. Or, you make a tabulation of the class level of students for the university registrar's annual report. The measurement task here is more critical so your operational definition needs to be more precise. You decide to define class levels in terms of semester hours of credit completed and recorded in each student's record in the registrar's office. Thus:

Freshman	—less than 30 hours credit
Sophomore	—30 to 59 hours credit
Junior	—60 to 89 hours credit
Senior	—over 90 hours credit

These examples deal with relatively concrete concepts, but operational definitions are even more critical for treating abstract ideas. For example, suppose one tries to measure the construct of "organizational commitment." We may intuitively understand what this means, but to attempt to measure it among workers is a difficult task. We would probably develop a "commitment" scale or we may use a scale that has already been developed and validated by someone else.

While operational definitions are needed in research, they also present some problems. There is the ever-present danger of thinking that a concept and the operational definition are the same thing. We forget that our definitions provide only limited insight into what a concept or construct really is. In fact, the operational definition may be quite narrow and not at all the same as that which someone else would use when researching the same topic. When measurements by two different definitions correlate well, it supports the view that they are measuring the same concept.

The problems of operational definitions are particularly difficult when dealing with constructs. In this case, there are few empirical referents by which to confirm that an operational definition really measures what we hope it does. In this case correlation between two different definition formulations strengthens the belief that you are measuring the same thing. On the other hand, if there is little or no correlation, it may mean we are tapping several different partial meanings of a construct. It may also mean that one or both of the definitions are not true labels.

Whatever the form of definition, its purpose in research is basically the same—to provide an understanding and measurement of concepts. We may need to provide operational definitions for only a few critical concepts, but these will almost always be the ones used to develop the relationships found in hypotheses and theories.

Hypotheses

In the literature of research, there are disagreements about the meanings of the terms "proposition" and "hypothesis." We *define a proposition as a statement about concepts which may be judged as true or false if it refers to observable phenomena. When a proposition is formulated for empirical test-ing, we call it a hypothesis.* These declarative statements are of a tentative and conjectural nature.

Hypotheses have also been described as statements in which we assign variables to cases. A "case" is defined in this sense as the entity or thing the hypothesis talks about. The variable is the characteristic, trait, or attribute which, in the hypothesis, is imputed to the case.[4] For example, we might form the hypothesis, "Executive Jones (case) has a higher than average achievement motivation (variable)." If our hypothesis was based on more than one case, it would be a *generalization.* For example, "Executives in Company Z (cases) have higher than average achievement motivation (vari-able)." Both of these hypotheses are examples of *descriptive hypotheses.*

Descriptive hypotheses. *These are propositions that typically state the existence, size, form, or distribution of some variable.* For example, "The current unemployment rate in Detroit exceeds 6 percent of the labor force." In this example, the case is Detroit and the variable is unemployment. Examples of other simple descriptive hypotheses are: "American cities are experiencing budget difficulties," and "Eighty percent of Company Z stock-holders favor increasing the company's cash dividend." In the first illustra-tion, "city" is the case and "budget problem" is the variable. In the second example, "Company Z" is the case and "stockholder attitude toward in-creased dividends" is the variable.

Researchers will often use a research question rather than a descriptive hypothesis. Thus, in place of the above hypothesis, we might use the follow-ing questions: "What is the unemployment rate in Detroit?" "Are American cities experiencing budget difficulties?" "Do stockholders of Company Z favor an increased cash dividend?" Either format is acceptable, but the hy-pothesis has several advantages. It encourages researchers to crystallize their thinking about the likely relationships to be found; it further encourages them to think beyond the mere quantity or to form expectations to their implications if the hypothesis is supported or rejected. Finally, the hypoth-esis is especially useful for testing statistical significance (to be discussed in Chapter 12). The research question is less frequently used with the second type of situation—the one calling for *relational hypotheses.*

Relational hypotheses. *These are statements that describe a relation-ship between two variables with respect to some case.* For example, "Foreign cars are perceived by American consumers to be of better quality than domestic cars." In this instance, the case is "consumer" and the variables are "country of origin" and "perceived quality." The nature of the relationship between the two variables is not specified. Is there only an implication that the variables occur in some predictable relationship, or is one variable some-how responsible for the other? The first interpretation indicates a *correla-*

---

[4]William N. Stephens, *Hypotheses and Evidence* (New York: Thomas Y. Crowell, 1968), p. 5.

tional relationship while the second indicates an *explanatory*, or *causal*, relationship.

Correlational relationships state merely that the variables occur together in some specified manner without implying that one causes the other. Such weak claims are often made when we believe that there are more basic causal forces that affect both variables, or when we have not developed enough evidence to claim a stronger linkage. Sample correlational hypotheses are: (1) young machinists (under 35 years of age) are less productive than those who are 35 years or older; (2) the height of women's hemlines varies directly with the level of the business cycle; or (3) people in Atlanta give the president a more favorable rating than do people in St. Louis.

By labeling these as correlational hypotheses, we make no claim that one variable causes the other to change or take on different values. Other persons, however, may view one or more of these hypotheses as reflecting cause and effect relationships.

With explanatory or causal hypotheses, there is an implication that the existence of, or a change in, one variable causes or leads to an effect on the other variable. The causal variable is typically called the *independent variable* (IV) and the other the *dependent variable* (DV). "Cause" means roughly to "help make happen." That is, the IV need not be the sole reason for the existence of, or change in, the DV. Examples of explanatory hypotheses are:

1. An increase in family income leads to an increase in the percentage of income saved.
2. Exposure to the company's messages concerning industry problems leads to more favorable attitudes by production workers toward the company.
3. Loyalty to a particular grocery store increases the probability of purchasing the private brands sponsored by that store.

In proposing or interpreting causal hypotheses, the researcher must consider the direction of influence. In many cases, the direction is obvious from the nature of the variables. Thus, in example 1, one would assume that family income influences savings rate rather than the reverse case. In example 2, our ability to identify the direction of influence depends on the research design. If the message clearly precedes the attitude measurement, then the direction of exposure to attitude seems clear; if information about both exposure and attitude were collected at the same time there might be justification for saying that different attitudes led to selective message exposure or nonexposure. Loyalty to a store may increase the probability of buying the store's private brands, but the use of private brands may also lead to greater store loyalty. In this hypothesis, the variables appear to be interdependent.

The role of the hypothesis. In research, a hypothesis serves several important functions. The most important is that it guides the direction of the study. A frequent problem in research is the proliferation of interesting information. Unless the urge to include additional elements is curbed, a study can be diluted by trivial concerns that do not answer the basic questions posed. The virtue of the hypothesis is that, if taken seriously, it limits what shall be studied and what shall not. It identifies facts that are relevant and those that are not; in so doing, it suggests which form of research design is likely to be most appropriate. A final role of the hypothesis is to provide a framework for organizing the conclusions that result.

To consider specifically the role of the hypothesis in determining the direction of the research, suppose we use this: "Husbands and wives agree in their perceptions of their respective roles in purchase decisions." The hypothesis specifies who shall be studied, in what context they shall be studied (their consumer decision making), and what shall be studied (their individual perceptions of their roles).

The nature of this hypothesis and the implications of the statement suggest that the best research design is probably a survey. We have at this time no other practical means to ascertain perceptions of people except to ask about them in one way or another. In addition, we are interested only in the roles that are assumed in the purchase or consumer decision-making situation. The study should clearly, therefore, not involve itself in seeking information about other types of roles which husband and wife might play. Another suggestion that might flow from a reflection upon this hypothesis is that we might find that husbands and wives do disagree on their perceptions of roles but that these differences may be explained in terms of additional variables, such as age, social class, background, personality differences, and other factors not associated with their differences of sex.

What is a good hypothesis? A good hypothesis should fulfill three conditions. The most elementary requirement is that it be *adequate for its purpose*. For a descriptive hypothesis, this means that it clearly states the condition, size, or distribution of some variable in terms of values meaningful to the research task. If it is an explanatory hypothesis, it must explain the facts that gave rise to the need for explanation. Using the hypothesis, plus other known and accepted generalizations, one should be able to deduce the original problem condition.

A second major condition is that the hypothesis must be *testable*. A hypothesis is not testable if it calls for techniques that are not available with the present state of the art. A hypothesis is also untestable if it calls for an explanation which defies known physical or psychological laws. Explanatory hypotheses are also untestable if there are no consequences or derivatives that can be deduced for testing purposes.

For explanatory hypotheses, there is another major condition: The hypothesis must be *better than its rivals*. Generally speaking, the better hypothesis has a greater range; it explains more facts and a greater variety of facts than do others. The better hypothesis is also the one which informed judges accept as being the most likely. Their opinions can be highly subjective but depend chiefly on their judgment of which hypothesis fits best with other information. Finally, the better hypothesis is the simple one requiring few conditions or assumptions.

Hypotheses play an important role in the development of theory. While theory development has not historically been an important aspect of business research, it is likely to become more so in the future.

Theory

The term "theory" is often used by the layman to express the opposite of fact. In this sense, theory is viewed as being speculative or ivory-tower. One hears that Professor X is too theoretical, that managers need to be practical, or that some idea will not work because it is too theoretical. This is an incorrect picture of the relationship between fact and theory.

When you are too theoretical, it means that your basis of explanation or decision is not sufficiently attuned to specific empirical conditions. This may be so, but it does not prove that theory and fact are opposites. The truth is that fact and theory are each necessary for the other to be of value. Our ability to make rational decisions, as well as to develop scientific knowledge, is measured by the degree to which we combine fact and theory.

We all operate on the basis of theories we hold. In one sense, theories are the generalizations we make about variables and the relationships among them. We use these generalizations to make decisions and predict outcomes. For example, it is midday and you note that the outside natural light is dimming, dark clouds are moving rapidly in from the west, the breeze is freshening, and the air temperature is cooling. Would your understanding of the relationship among these variables (your weather theory) lead you to a prediction of what else will probably occur in a short time?

Consider another situation where you are called on to interview two persons for possible promotion to the position of department manager. Do you have a theory about what characteristics such a person should have? Suppose you interview Ms. A and observe that she answers your questions well, openly, and apparently sincerely. She also expresses thoughtful ideas about how to improve departmental functioning and is articulate in stating her views. Ms. B, on the other hand, is guarded in her comments and reluctant to advance ideas for improvements. She answers questions by saying what "Mr. General Manager wants." She is also less articulate and seems less sincere than Ms. A. You would probably choose A, based upon the way you combine the concepts, definitions, and propositions mentioned into a theory of managerial effectiveness. It may not be a good theory because of the variables we have ignored, but it illustrates the point that we all use theory to guide our decisions, predictions, and explanations.

A theory is a set of systematically interrelated concepts, definitions, and propositions that are advanced to explain and predict phenomena (facts). In this sense, we have many theories and use them continually to explain or predict what goes on around us. To the degree that our theories are sound, and fit the situation, we are successful in our explanations and predictions. Thus, while a given theory and a set of facts may not fit, they are not opposites. Our challenge is to build better theory and to be more skillful in fitting theory and fact together.

A point which may also cause some confusion is that of how theory differs from hypothesis. One person may advance an explanation and call it a theory while another may call it a hypothesis. It may be difficult to distinguish one from the other since both involve concepts, definitions, and relationships among variables. The basic differences are in the level of complexity and abstraction. Theories tend to be abstract and involve multiple variables, while hypotheses tend to be simple, two-variable propositions involving concrete instances.

In this book, we make the general distinction that the difference between theory and hypothesis is one of degree of complexity and abstraction. At times these may be confused, but it should not make much practical research difference.

Theory and research. It is important for researchers to recognize the pervasiveness and value of theory. Theory serves us in many useful ways. First, as orientation, it narrows the range of facts that we need to study. Any problem may be studied in a number of different ways, and theory suggests which ways are likely to yield the greatest meaning. Theory may also suggest a system for the researcher to impose on data in order to classify them in the most meaningful way. Theory also summarizes what is known about an object of study and states the uniformities that lie beyond the immediate observation; what it does so, theory can also be used to predict further facts which should be found.

Models. The term "model" has gained such popularity that it threatens to become an all-purpose word for relationships among concepts. Many writers have attempted to define the term more narrowly but with little success to date. For example, one writer defines a model as "anything used to represent something else—a map used to represent a section of countryside is a model, and so is a chart used to represent concurrent changes in fuel oil sales and temperature."[5] Another view is: "Since the purpose of the model is the representation of relationships between or among concepts, the prerequisite for any model is a conceptual scheme. . . . Sources of conceptual schemes for model building are theories, laws, hypotheses, and principles. . . . Models are not substitutes for conceptual schemes, principles, hypotheses, or theories but rather are devices to depict their concepts and the relationships which are involved. . . ."[6] Still another writer holds that models

---

[5]Robert D. Buzzell, *Mathematical Models and Marketing Management* (Boston: Graduate School of Business Administration, Harvard University, 1964), p. 9.

[6]Paul H. Rigby, *Conceptual Foundations of Business Research* (New York: John Wiley and Sons, 1965), p. 112.

are simulations, and a fourth source says that "Models are created by speculating about processes that could have produced the observed facts."[7]

In view of this confusion, we will continue to use such traditional terms as proposition, hypothesis, theory, law, and so forth. However, the popularity of model assures that it will creep into the discussion at times; when it does, it will be used as a general synonym for any of the above-mentioned terms.

The inference process

To draw a conclusion that we think logically follows from one or more statements is to make an inference, in other words, to reason. We use the inference process to relate concepts by introducing propositions and building theories. We might, for example, devise a series of propositions between various concepts such as work output, incentive pay, working conditions, job satisfaction, and style of management. We might then relate these propositions into a management theory on how work output is affected by the other four concepts and how they affect each other.

There are two major types of inference-making processes—induction and deduction. Both are important in research and are briefly described here.

Induction. *To induce is to draw a conclusion from one or more particular facts or pieces of evidence.* The conclusion explains the facts and the facts support the conclusion. To illustrate, suppose you push the light switch in your room and the light fails to go on. This is a fact—the light does not go on when you pushed the switch. Under such circumstances, we ask, "Why doesn't the light go on?"

One likely answer to this question is a conclusion that the light bulb has burned out. This conclusion is an induction because we know from experience that (1) the light should go on when you push the switch; and (2) if the bulb is burned out, the light will not function. The nature of induction, however, is that the conclusion is only a hypothesis. It is one explanation, but there are others that fit the fact just as well. For example, it could be that the electrical power is off in the neighborhood, or it might mean that the switch is malfunctioning.

In this example, we see the essential nature of inductive reasoning. The inductive conclusion is an inferential jump beyond the evidence presented. That is, while one conclusion explains the fact of no light, other conclusions can explain the fact also. It may even be that none of the three conclusions we have advanced correctly explains the failure of the light to go on.

Deduction. This is the other form of making inferences. *To deduce is to reason in such a way that the conclusion reached must necessarily follow*

---

[7] See, respectively, Paul Davidson Reynolds, *A Primer in Theory Construction* (Indianapolis, Ind.: The Bobbs-Merrill Company, 1971), p. 111, and Charles A. Lave and James G. March, *An Introduction to Models in the Social Sciences* (New York: Harper & Row, 1975), p. 19.

from the premises: the conclusion must be true if the premises are true.[8]
Deduction in some ways can be thought of as the reverse of induction.
Deduction moves from the general to the specific and from explanation to
fact, while induction moves from specific case to generalizations and from
facts to explanation.

To illustrate deductive reasoning, we use the lighting example again. Let's
begin with the normally accepted premise:

(premise)   If the bulb is burned out when you push the switch, there is
             no light.

(premise)   The bulb is burned out.

(conclusion)   There is no light.

This conclusion must follow if our premises are true.

Let's compare the nature of induction and deduction again by using the
problem of John Lacey, salesman for the Square Box Company. John has one
of the poorest performance records in the company. His unsatisfactory performance prompts the question, "Why is he doing so poorly?" The answer to
this question is a conclusion or hypothesis advanced to explain his poor
record. The conclusion is that John is not diligent in his work; in a word, he
is lazy. The reasoning flow is like this:

(premise/fact)   (conclusion/explanation)
John has a poor ———————→ John is lazy
performance

This is only one of a number of hypotheses by which to explain John's poor
record. Others might be, "Business is bad for all salesmen," or "John has a
poor territory with little sales potential." One, or two or all three of these
conclusions may be true or false since this is an inductive conclusion.

Now suppose someone asked you what your conclusion would be about a
salesman named John, if you were told that John is lazy. Among other things
you might say, "John will have a poor sales record." You would deduce this
specific conclusion from your general premise:

(premise)   If a salesman is lazy, he or she will have a poor performance
             record.

(premise)   John is lazy.

(conclusion)   John will have a poor performance record.

Induction and deduction are both reasoning processes, but they differ in
the nature of the relationship between premise and conclusion. An inductive
conclusion is a conjectural explanation of events or conditions and cannot,

---

[8]There is much more to the understanding of deductive reasoning than presented here.
In particular, for a deduction to be correct, it is necessary that it be both true and valid.
That is, the premises (reasons) must agree with the real world (be true). In addition, the
premises must be arranged in such a form that the conclusion will necessarily follow from
the premises. A deduction has a valid form if it is impossible for the conclusion to be false
when the premises are true.

FIGURE 2–1   Why doesn't the light go on?

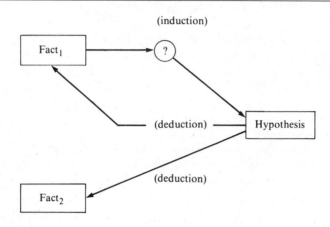

Fact₁ = Pushing the light switch results in no light.

Fact₂ = Inserting a new bulb brings light when switch is pushed.

by the power of its process, be proven. That is, no matter how many times you push the light switch and get no light from a bad bulb, there is no proof that the next time there is no light, it will also mean a burned out bulb.

With deduction, on the other hand, a conclusion is the necessary outcome of the reasons or premises. This is because the conclusion in a deduction is, in a sense, "contained in" the premises used. Thus, if a bulb is burned out, you can be certain that pushing the light switch will produce no light.

The induction-deduction sequence

The induction and deduction processes are used in research reasoning in a sequential manner. This has been described by John Dewey as the "double movement of reflective thought."[9] Induction occurs when we observe a fact and ask "Why is this?" In answer to this question we advance a tentative explanation (hypothesis). The hypothesis is plausible if it explains the event or condition (fact) which prompted the question. Deduction is the process by which we test whether the hypothesis is capable of explaining the fact. The process is:

1. You push the light switch and find no light.
2. You ask the question, "Why no light?"

[9]John Dewey, *How We Think* (Boston: D. C. Heath, 1910), p. 79.

3. You induce a conclusion hypothesis to answer the question and explain the fact that the bulb is burned out.
4. You use this hypothesis to conclude (deduce) that the light will not go on when we push the switch. We know from experience that a burned-out bulb will not light.

This example is only an exercise in circular reasoning, but it does point out that one must be able to deduce the initiating fact from the hypothesis advanced to explain that fact. This is illustrated in Figure 2–1. A second critical point is also illustrated in Figure 2–1. That is, in order to test a hypothesis, one must be able to deduce other facts from it that can be then investigated. This is what classical research is all about. We must deduce other specific facts or events from the hypothesis and then gather information to see if the deductions are true. In the light example, we deduce:

5. A new bulb put in the lamp will result in a light when the switch is pushed.
6. We put in the new bulb and push the switch. The light goes on.

How would the double movement of reflective thought work when applied to John Lacey's problem? The process is illustrated in Figure 2–2. The

---

FIGURE 2–2   Why is John Lacey's performance so poor?

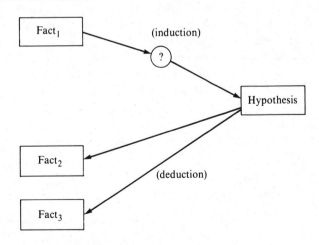

Fact₁ = Poor performance record

Fact₂ = Late to work regularly

Fact₃ = Fewer calls per day than average performance

initial fact$_1$ leads to hypothesis$_1$ that John is lazy. We deduce several other facts from the hypothesis. These are shown as fact$_2$ and fact$_3$. We use research to find out if fact$_2$ and fact$_3$ are true. If they are found to be true, they confirm our hypothesis. If we do not, our hypothesis is not confirmed and we must look for another explanation.

In most research, the process is more complicated than these simple examples suggest. For instance, we often develop multiple hypotheses by which to explain the phenomenon in question. Then we design a study to test all the hypotheses at once. Not only is this more efficient, it is also a good way to reduce the attachment (and potential bias) of the researcher for any given hypothesis.

In this chapter, we have introduced a number of ideas in the abstract. Do they really have value in a research study?

The Telephone Company Study[10]

Recall that Mary Kirk had been given an assignment to prepare a draft project proposal. As we left her, she was staring at the sheet of paper, wondering just where to start. Then she remembered the admonition of her research professor to begin with the management problem. So she began:

> *What is management's problem?* The management of the telephone company has excess long-distance capacity that it would like to utilize. The excess is heavily concentrated in the evening hours and on weekends, suggesting that a solution will involve social calling rather than business calling.

The client's representatives indicated that they were interested in knowing more about why some people are relatively heavy users of long-distance calling, while others seldom place long-distance social calls. Comments in the planning meeting had indicated that information in this area would be useful in management's strategy development. After some false starts, Mary settled on the following research question:

> *The basic research question*—Why do some people make a large number of long-distance calls for social purposes while others do not? What are the factors that influence social long distance calling?

Further thought about the problem, and a search of the literature on consumer behavior led her to break the general research question into the following investigating questions.[11]

1. What social and economic factors influence the number of social long-distance calls a person will make?

---

[10]This fictionalized account is based on *Motives, Attitudes, and Long Distance* (Ann Arbor, Mich.: University of Michigan, Survey Research Center, 1956).

[11]*Motives, Attitudes, and Long Distance*, p. 7.

2. What feelings and attitudes about the telephone influence social long-distance calling?

3. What personality characteristics influence social long distance calling?

While these investigative questions imply that all influences will be analyzed, it was quickly apparent that only a selection of socioeconomic attitudes, and personality influences could be used. This decision eventually led to the following breakdown of each of the investigative questions:

1. Socioeconomic factors:
   a   What is the influence of friends or relatives living far away?
   b   How does the stage in the family "life cycle" affect social long-distance calling?
   c   What is the influence of family income?
   d   What is the influence of "who in the family makes the call"?
2. How do the following affect attitudes toward calling?
   a   Nature and frequency of phone use by family members.
   b   Relationship of attitudes toward calling and other forms of communication.
   c   Difficulties of placing a call.
   d   Degree to which people enjoy calling.
   e   Factors causing a reluctance to call.
   f   Motives for social calling.
   g   Trouble hearing on a telephone.
   h   Attitudes toward rates.
3. How do the following personality factors affect social long-distance calling?
   a   Security-insecurity feelings.
   b   Need affiliation.
   c   Underlying attitudes toward money.

Concepts and definitions.   It is obvious from the above questions that a number of concepts and constructs require operational definition. In considering the research design further, it was decided that the best design would be to study intensively two distinct groups: people who make a large number of long distance calls and people who make almost none.

While the complexities of this study called for a number of operational definitions only a few are included here. Obviously one of the first tasks is to define low callers and high callers. The following operational definitions are used:

Low callers—Families with long-distance phone bills of x amount of dollars and under for the six-month period used in the study.

High callers—Families with long-distance phone bills of over x amount of dollars for the six-month period.

The amounts are the total bill for calls from these phones. Some business calls may be included, especially for self-employed persons.

It is important next to classify respondents on the basis of personality dimensions. A special scale for security-insecurity was developed consisting of seven items, such as: "You have often lost sleep over your worries" or "You sometimes avoid social contacts for fear of doing the wrong thing." Respondents answer yes or no to each statement. A yes answer is to be scored as a 1 and a no answer as a 0. Total scores of 4 or more represent an insecure person, while individuals scoring 3 or less are judged to be secure.

Hypotheses development. Obviously, the variations in the use of long-distance calling involve a number of relationships. The first question is, "Why do some families have a higher usage rate for long distance calling than other families?" Here Mary can use the Double Movement of Reflective Thought as illustrated in Figure 2–3. One hypothesis is, "High-call families

---

FIGURE 2–3 The double movement of reflective thought

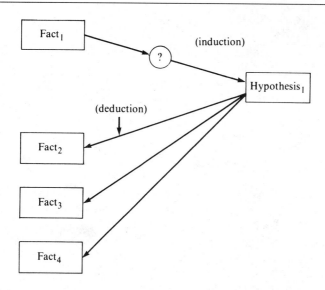

$Fact_1$ = Some families have higher long distance call rates.

$Fact_2$ = High desire callers have more friends and relatives who live at a distance.

$Fact_3$ = High desire callers have higher need affiliations.

$Fact_4$ = High desire callers make more local calls.

have a greater desire to call others by long-distance telephone." From this hypothesis other "facts" can be deduced.

Certain socioeconomic factors should probably affect the incidence of long-distance calling. Drawing on knowledge of how socioeconomic factors typically affect consumption one arrives at the following deductions:

—Families with relatively high income will have high call rates.

—Families with higher education will have high call rates.

—Families in the young and old life cycle stages should be more frequent callers than those in middle-year stages.

—Families in which the placing of long distance calls was viewed as man's work should make fewer calls.

—Families classified as free spenders would tend to be high callers.

Theory. Using these and other conclusions, Mary can begin to construct a theory of social long-distance telephone calling. The theory (as finally used in the study) is shown in Figure 2–4. In section A, the theoretical relationships are shown. The lines between the various construct labels indicate the proposed relationships and the direction of influence. These relationships indicate that a number of variables affect call usage through two intervening variables—desire to contact and choice of means.

All the concepts and constructs shown were operationally defined using the approaches listed in column B of Figure 2–4. For example, consider the testing of the group of circled concepts Attitudes, Perceptions, and Experiences. This testing included making operational definitions of concepts such as frequency of communication (regardless of medium), local phone usage practices as a measure of perception of the phone and its uses, experience in using phones at work, and feelings when using the phone. Information on these points was collected using direct questions, observations of callers, and in some cases, attitude scales.

There was also an exploratory question about an imaginary phone user. It was hypothesized that people who made frequent phone calls, who used the phone for visiting and chatting, who were frequent communicators regardless of the medium, who used the phone at work, and who reported pleasant feelings when making long-distance calls, would all be frequent long-distance callers. A projective question was used probing attitudes further but was not the source of a hypothesis.

The theory about social long-distance calling as it stands may be persuasive, but is it true? Is it possible that some parts and true and others false? The researchers needed to develop means (sector B in Figure 2–4) for testing the relationships. They developed and used attitude scales, projective techniques, and a detailed survey questionnaire. They also observed persons making calls and inspected telephone company records. By developing specific operational definitions, they related empirical reality (column C, Figure 2–4) to their theory (column A).

To summarize, the development of the underlying theory provided the blueprint by which the research was planned and carried out. The theory

FIGURE 2–4   Relating a theory of social long-distance telephone calling to empirical reality

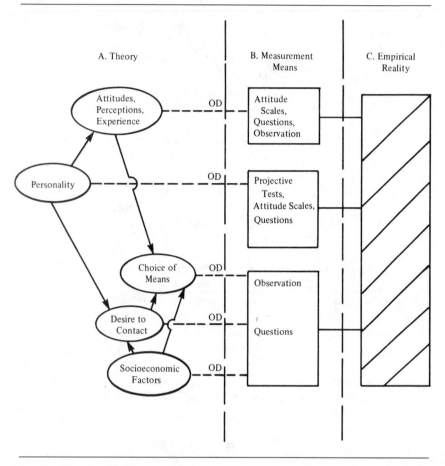

OD = Operational definition.
Source: Adapted from *Motives, Attitudes, and Long Distance Calls* (Ann Arbor, Mich.: Survey Research Center, University of Michigan, 1956).

itself drew heavily on prior knowledge from other disciplines (chiefly psychology and economics), the experiences of the company, and the research experiences of the investigators. Constructs, concepts, descriptive definitions, operational definitions, and hypotheses were combined in the development of a theory, which was then tested by the application of various research tools and techniques to empirical reality.

SUMMARY

In business, the research need originates where management must make a decision. A manager needs specific information to assist in setting objectives, defining tasks, finding the best strategy by which to carry out the tasks, and finally, judging how well the strategy is being implemented.

Researchers must think of their task as an orderly process. They may, for instance, view project development as a hierarchical sequence of questions. At the initial and most general level is the management question. This is translated into a research question—the major objective of the study. In turn, the research question is fractionated into one or more investigative questions. These questions may be posed on several levels of generality, but the researcher must answer all of them. At the most specific level are measurement questions, those answered by respondents in surveys or answered for each subject in an observational study.

Scientific methods and thinking are based on concepts, the symbols that we attach to bundles of meanings we hold and share with others. We invent concepts in order to be able to think about and communicate abstract meanings. We also use constructs—more highly abstract concepts invented for specific explanatory purposes. Concepts and constructs may be defined descriptively or operationally. Operational definitions, which are especially significant in research, are stated in terms of specific testing criteria or operations. Good operational definitions must adequately specify the empirical information needed, how it will be collected, and have the proper scope or fit for the research problem at hand.

Of great interest in research are propositions, describing relationships between or among variables. When we advance a proposition to explain tentatively some phenomenon, we are hypothesizing. A good hypothesis is one that can explain what it claims to explain, is testable, and has greater range, probability, and simplicity than its rivals. Sets of interrelated concepts, definitions, and propositions advanced to explain phenomena are theories.

The inference process is used in the development and testing of various propositions largely through the double movement of reflective thinking. This is a sequencing of induction-deduction processes by which one seeks inductively to explain (by a hypothesis) a puzzling condition. In turn, the hypothesis is used in the deduction of further facts, which can be sought to confirm or deny the truth of the hypothesis.

SUPPLEMENTAL READINGS

1. Beardsley, Monroe. *Practical Logic.* Englewood Cliffs, N.J.: Prentice-Hall, 1961, chapters 7 and 15. A lucid discussion of deduction and induction as well as excellent coverage of argument analysis.
2. Kerlinger, Fred N. *Foundations of Behavioral Research.* 2d ed. New York: Holt, Rinehart & Winston, 1973. An excellent and comprehensive book on

most aspects of research methodology. Chapters 2 and 3 are on hypotheses, definitions, and constructs.

3. Lave, Charles A., and James G. March. *An Introduction to Models in the Social Sciences.* New York: Harper & Row, 1975. The first three chapters are especially recommended. They concern model-building, which roughly equates here to hypothesis formation. Some interesting examples.

4. Phillips, Bernard S. *Social Research.* 2d ed. New York: Macmillan, 1971. Chapter 2 is a good summary of the elements of inquiry.

5. Selltiz, Claire; Lawrence S. Wrightsman; and Stuart W. Cook. *Research Methods in Social Relations.* 3d ed. New York: Holt, Rinehart & Winston, 1976. Chapters 1 and 2 present a good research process example and a discussion on formulating a research problem.

DISCUSSION QUESTIONS

1. What are some management and accompanying research questions that might be useful to the following executives?
   a The production manager of a shoe factory.
   b The president of First National Bank.
   c The vice-president of labor relations for an auto manufacturer.
   d The chief of police in a major city.
2. What are some of the important reasons why a research project will fail to make an adequate contribution to the solution of management problems?
3. The vice-president of administration calls you into her office and states that the computer programming department is not functioning well because there is excessive turnover among the programmers. She suggests that you conduct a survey among other major companies in the region to learn how they handle the problem of high programmer turnover.
   a What do you think of this problem assessment and research suggestion?
   b How, if at all, could you improve on the vice-president's formulation of the research problem?
4. Distinguish among the following sets of terms and suggest the significance of each in a research context.
   a Concept and construct.
   b Deduction and induction.
   c Operational definition and dictionary definition.
   d Fact and theory.
5. Here are some terms commonly found in a management setting. Are they concepts or constructs? Give two different operational definitions for each.
   first line supervisor   leadership
   employee morale   price-earnings ratio
   assembly line   union democracy
   overdue account   ethical standards
   line management
6. In your company's management development program, recently there was a heated discussion between some people who claimed that "theory is impractical and thus no good" and others who claimed that "good theory is the most practical approach to problems." What position would you take and why?
7. You wish to study a condition that you have observed to the effect that, "Some workers seem to be much more diligent than others."

a Propose at least three concepts and three constructs you might use in such a study.

b How might any of these concepts and/or constructs be related to explanatory hypotheses?

8. In a metal stamping plant, the production manager has suddenly been faced with a problem of quality. The production process is one of forming large sheets of metal into auto fenders using large stamping machines. Suddenly, yesterday, the quality of the stamped fenders deteriorated. This problem began in department A but quickly spread to the other departments. At a meeting to deal with this problem, the assistant plant manager reported that yesterday on the first shift, the foreman in department A caught a worker drinking on the job and summarily fired him. This man had been a problem in the past and it was reported that he and the foreman had often argued. The workers in department A were angered by this treatment of one of their popular coworkers. The shop steward claimed that the firing was unfair and violated the union contract. As a result, there was considerable negative reaction among the workers.

a Propose several hypotheses that might account for the sudden surge in poor quality output.

b Using the double movement of reflective thought, show how you would test these hypotheses.

9. You have been approached by the editor of *Gentlemen's Magazine* to carry out a research study. The magazine has been unsuccessful in attracting shoe manufacturers as advertisers. When the sales force tried to secure advertising from shoe manufacturers, they were told that men's clothing stores are a small and dying segment of their business. Since *Gentlemen's Magazine* goes chiefly to men's clothing stores, the manufacturers reasoned that it was, therefore, not a good vehicle for their advertising.

The editor believes that a survey (via mail questionnaire) of men's clothing stores in the United States will probably show that these stores are important outlets for men's shoes and that they are not declining in importance as shoe outlets. He asks you to develop a proposal for the study and submit it to him. Develop research questions or hypotheses of various levels that will enable you to develop a specific proposal.

APPENDIX   THE VALUE OF RESEARCH INFORMATION

Conceptually, the value of applied research is not difficult to determine. In a business situation the research should produce added revenues or reduce expenses in much the same way as any other investment of resources. One source suggests that the value of research information may be judged in terms of "the difference between the results of decisions made with the information and the results that would be made without it."[1] While such a criterion is simple to state, its actual use presents some difficult measurement problems.

---

[1] Robert D. Buzzell, Donald F. Cox, and Rex V. Brown, *Marketing Research and Information Systems* (New York: McGraw-Hill, 1969), p. 595.

Ex post facto evaluation. If there is any measurement of the value of research, it is usually an after-the-fact event. Twedt reported on one such effort, an evaluation of marketing research done at a major corporation.[2] He secured "an objective estimate of the contribution of each project to corporate profitability." He reported that most studies were intended to help management determine which one of two (or more) alternatives was preferable. He guessed that in 60 percent of the decision situations, the correct decision would have been made *without* the benefit of the research information. In the remaining 40 percent of the cases, the research led to the correct decision. Using these data, he estimated that the return on investment in marketing research in this company was 351 percent for the year studied. However, he acknowledges that the "return on investment" figure was inflated because only the direct research costs had been included.

This effort at cost-benefit analysis is commendable, even though it is only a tentative first step. One may be able to judge after the fact whether the research study was justified, given certain assumptions. While the results come too late to guide the current research decision, such analysis may sharpen the manager's ability to make judgments about future research proposals. However, the critical problem remains, that of project evaluation *before the study is done*.

Prior evaluation. The challenge to effective research evaluation is the inability of the evaluator to measure or forecast the benefits and costs of the project. For example, a proposal to conduct a thorough management audit of operations in a company may be a worthy one, but neither its costs nor its benefits are easily estimated in advance. Such projects are sufficiently unique that managerial experience seldom provides much aid in evaluating such a proposal either.

Even in these complex situations, however, managers often can make some useful judgments. They may be able to determine that a management audit is needed because the company is in dire straits and management does not understand the scope of its problems. The management information need may be so great as to assure that the research is approved. In such cases they may decide to control the research expenditure risk by doing a study in stages. They can then review costs and benefits at the end of each step and give or withhold further authorization. Typical of this approach is the two-stage study discussed later.

Option analysis. Some progress has been made in the development of methods for assessing the value of research when management has a choice between well-defined options. Each alternative can be judged in terms of estimated costs and benefits associated with it and a formal analysis can be conducted, but managerial judgment still plays a major role.

---

[2]Dik Warren Twedt, "What Is the 'Return on Investment' in Marketing Research?" *Journal of Marketing* 30 (January 1966), pp. 62–63.

While both costs and benefits present major estimating problems, the development of the cost side of the equation is normally the easiest. If the research design can be stated clearly, one can estimate an approximate cost. The critical task is to quantify the benefits from the research. At best, estimates of benefits are crude and largely reflect a more orderly way to estimate outcomes under uncertain conditions. To illustrate how the contribution of research is evaluated in such a decision situation, we must digress briefly into the rudiments of decision theory.

Decision theory approach

To compare two or more alternatives, a manager must estimate the expected outcome of each alternative. The case of two choices will be discussed here, although the same approach can be used with more than two choices. Two possible actions (A_1 and A_2) may represent two different ways to organize a company, to provide financing, to produce a product, and so forth. We need not specify the nature of the alternatives in order to describe the approach.

When there are alternatives from which to choose, a rational way to approach the decision is to try to assess the outcomes of each course of action; then one can choose the outcome which best meets the criterion established for judging alternatives. This criterion is a combination of a *decision rule* and a *decision variable*. For example, the decision variable might be "direct dollar savings," "contribution to overhead and profits," "time required for completion of the project," and so forth.

Usually the decision variable is expressed in dollars, representing sales, costs, or some form of profits or contribution. The decision rule may be "choose the course of action with the lowest loss possibility" or perhaps "choose the alternative which provides the greatest annual net profit." The alternative selected depends on the decision variable chosen and the decision rule used. The evaluation of alternatives requires that (1) they may be explicitly stated; (2) a decision variable be defined by the outcome which may be measured; and (3) a decision rule be determined by which outcomes may be compared.

For example, Mr. White, the manager, may be trying to decide whether to make a major equipment change in a production department. The new equipment can be leased for five years and will replace several old machines, the operation of which requires constant attention. The problem facing him is, "Shall I lease the new machine, with its attendant efficiencies, reduced labor input, and high lease charges, or shall I continue to use the older equipment?"

The decision situation has been precipitated by information that the firm might secure several large orders from companies that have not previously been customers. With this added volume, he expects that his departmental profit contribution will go up substantially if he has the new equipment. For this decision, he adopts as the decision variable "average annual departmental profit contribution."[3] He adopts as a decision rule, "Choose that course of action that will provide the highest average annual contribution to departmental profits."

Table 2A–1 indicates the results of the evaluation of the two available courses of action. Under the conditions cited, it is obvious that course A_1 is preferred.

TABLE 2A–1   Payoff under conditions of certainty

Course of action	Average annual department profit contribution
A_1—Lease new equipment	$20,000
A_2—Retain old equipment	12,000

Conditions of certainty.   Table 2A–1 presents the case with the assumption that the anticipated new business will materialize. It therefore represents, in decision theory terminology, *decision making under conditions of certainty*. It has been assumed that the payoffs are certain to occur if the particular course of action is chosen and that the probability of the additional business being secured is 1.0.[4] The decision to choose course of action A_1 is obvious under these conditions with the given payoff data and decision rule.

Conditions of uncertainty.   In a more realistic situation, the outcome is less than certain. The new business may not materialize, and then the department might be left with costly excess capacity. The union may resist the introduction of the new equipment because it replaces a worker. The new equipment may not perform as anticipated. For these or other reasons, the decision maker may be uncertain about the consequences (for instance, that course A_1 will result in a $20,000 contribution).

Suppose that Mr. White gives these other possible outcomes some consideration and concludes that the one serious uncertainty is that the new business may not be forthcoming. For purposes of simplicity, he concludes

---

[3] Recall that the decision variable is the unit of measurement used in the analysis. At this point we need not be concerned with how this measure is calculated or whether it is the appropriate decision variable. Assume for purposes of this illustration that it is appropriate.

[4] A probability is a measure between 1.0 and 0.0 which expresses the likelihood of an event occurring. For example, the probability of a "head" on a toss of a coin is 0.5. Under conditions of certainty, the forecasted outcome is assumed to have a probability of 1.0 even though we might agree that we normally cannot know the future with certainty. In most forecasting where a specific amount is named, there is an implicit assumption of certainty.

that one of two conditions will exist in the future—either the new business will be secured as expected (O_1) or the new business will not materialize (O_2). In the first case, the expected payoffs would be the same as in Table 2A–1; but if the new business is not secured, then the addition of the new equipment would give the department costly excess capacity, with fixed lease changes. The payoff table may now be revised as in Table 2A–2.

TABLE 2A–2   Payoff under conditions of uncertainty

	Average annual departmental profit contribution		Expected monetary value
	New business (O_1)	No new business (O_2)	
A_1—Lease new equipment	$20,000	$5,000	$14,000
A_2—Retain old equipment	12,000	9,000	10,800

Under these conditions, the original decision rule does not apply. That rule said, "Choose that course of action which will provide the highest average annual departmental profit contribution." Under the conditions in Table 2A–2, action A_1 would be better if the new business is secured, but A_2 would be the better choice if the new business is not secured. If Mr. White can delay his decision until the new order question is resolved, he can escape his dilemma. However, because of lead times, he may have to make the equipment decision first.

When faced with two or more possible outcomes for each alternative, Mr. White can adopt one of two approaches. He may conclude that he cannot judge the likelihood that the company will receive the new business. Even so, he may still make a rational decision by adopting an appropriate decision rule. For example, he may use the rule, "Choose that course of action for which the minimum payoff is the highest." This is known as the *maximin criterion* because it calls for maximizing the minimum payoff. In Table 2A–2 the minimum payoff for alternative A_1 is shown as $5,000, and the minimum payoff for A_2 is $9,000. According to the *maximin* rule, the choice would be A_2 because it is the best of the worst outcomes. This decision is a "cut your losses" strategy.

The second approach is for Mr. White to use subjective judgment to estimate the probability that either O_1 or O_2 will take place.[5] When the

---

[5]There are three types of situations into which concepts of probability enter. In the classical situation, each possible outcome has a known chance of occurrence. For example,

assumption was decision under certainty, he tacitly assumed that only one event was possible (had a probability of 1.0). Now, however, he uses his experience and information from other sources to conclude that there is a less-than-certain chance of the new business materializing and that he should incorporate this doubt into the decision.

He might estimate that there is a 0.6 chance that the new business will be secured and a 0.4 chance that it will not. With this or any other set of similar probabilities, Mr. White can now arrive at an overall evaluation of the two courses of action. One approach is to calculate an *expected monetary value (EMV)* for each alternative.[6]

The decision flow diagram. The decision problem already has been summarized in a payoff table, but further illustration in the form of a decision flow diagram (or decision tree) may be helpful. The decision tree for the equipment problem is shown in Figure 2A–1. The diagram may be seen as a sequential decision flow. At the square node on the left, Mr. White must choose between A_1 and A_2. After he chooses one of these courses of action, a chance event will take place—either the new business will be received by the company (O_1) or it will not be receied (O_2). At the right extremity of the branches are listed the conditional payoffs that will occur for each combination of decision and chance event. On each chance branch is placed the expected probability of that chance event occurring. Keep in mind that these are subjective probability estimates by Mr. White, expressing his degree of belief that such a chance event will occur.

Having set up this series of relationships, he calculates back from right to left on the diagram by an *averaging out* and *folding back* process. At each decision juncture, he selects the path which yields the best alternative to the decision rule. In this case, the *EMV* for A_1 averages out to $14,000, while the *EMV* for A_2 is $10,800. The double slash line on the A_2 branch

---

a coin tossed in the air has a 0.5 chance of landing heads up; a spade card has a 0.25 chance of being drawn from a well-mixed deck.

In the same type of situation, probabilities are thought of in terms of "relative frequency." Even if the probability is not known from the structure of the problem (as it is in the classical case), it can still be estimated if there is a body of empirical evidence. For example, experience may show that about 1 in 50 products produced is defective. From this statistic, one can estimate that there is a 0.02 chance that any given product will be defective.

If there is no direct empirical evidence, one can still assess probability on the basis of opinion, intuition, and/or general experience. In such cases, uncertainty is expressed in terms of a subjectively felt "degree of confidence" or "degree of belief" that a given event will occur. The discussions in this chapter are cases in point. For more information on probability concepts, see any modern statistics text.

[6] One calculates an *EMV* for an alternative by weighting each conditional value (for example, $20,000 and $5,000 for A_1) by the estimated probability of the occurrence of the associated event (for example, 0.6 probability of the $20,000 being made).

$$EMV = P_1\ (\$20,000) + P_2\ (\$5,000)$$
$$= 0.6\ (\$20,000) + 0.4\ (\$5,000)$$
$$= \$14,000$$

FIGURE 2A–1   Decision tree for equipment problem

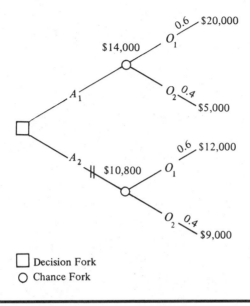

Decision Fork
Chance Fork

indicates that it is the inferior alternative and should be dropped in favor of A_1.

The contribution of research.   At this point, the contribution of research can be assessed. Recall that the value of research may be judged as "the difference between the results of decisions made with the information and the results that would be made without it." In this example the important research need is to determine whether the new business will be secured. This is the major uncertainty which, if known, would make a perfect forecast possible. Just how much is a perfect forecast worth in this case?

Consider Figure 2A–1 once again. What would happen if Mr. White had information by which he could accurately predict whether the new business orders would be secured? He would choose A_1 if the research indicated that the orders would be received, and A_2 if research indicated that the orders would not be received. However, at the decision point (before the research is undertaken) the best estimate is that there is a 0.6 chance that the research will indicate the O_1 condition and 0.4 that the condition will be O_2. The decision flow implications of the use of research are illustrated in Figure 2A–2.

The decision sequence begins with the decision fork at the left. If Mr. White chooses to do research (R), he comes to the first chance fork, where

FIGURE 2A–2   The value of perfect information

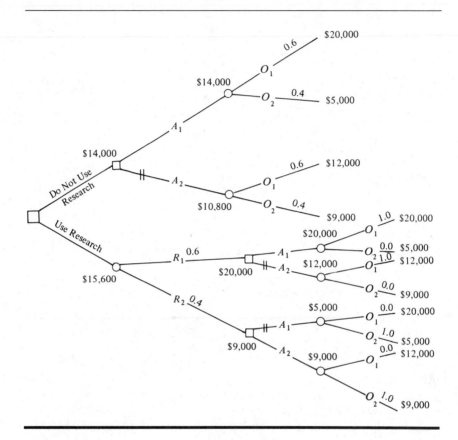

one of two things will occur. Research indicates either that the orders will be received (R_1), or the orders will not be received (R_2). Before he does the research, the best estimate of the probability of R_1 taking place is the same as the estimate that O_1 will occur (0.6). In like manner, the best estimate that R_2 will occur is 0.4.

After Mr. White learns R_1 or R_2, he moves on to a second decision fork; shall he take A_1 or A_2? After the A_1–A_2 decision, there is a second chance fork (O_1 or O_2), which indicates whether or not the actual orders were received. Note, however, that the probabilities at O_1 and O_2 have now changed from 0.6 and 0.4, respectively, to 1.0 and 0.0, or to 0.0 and 1.0, depending upon what was learned at the research stage. This change occurs because we have evaluated the effect of the research information on our original O_1 and O_2 probability estimates by calculating *posterior probabilities*. These are revisions of our prior probabilities that result from the assumed research findings. The posterior probabilities (for example, $P(O_1|R_i)$ and $P(O_2|R_i)$ are calculated by using Bayes' theorem.[7]

Research outcomes	States of nature		Marginal probabilities	Posterior probabilities	
	O_1	O_2		$P(O_1|R_i)$	$P(O_2|R_i)$
R_1	0.6	0.0	0.6	1.0	0.0
R_2	0.0	0.4	0.4	0.0	1.0
Marginal probabilities	0.6	0.4			

Mr. White is now ready to average out and fold back the analysis from right to left in order to evaluate the research alternative. Clearly, if R_1 is found, he will choose A_1 with its EMV of \$20,000 over the A_2 alternative of \$12,000. In like fashion, if R_2 is reported, then A_2 is more attractive. However, prior to the research, the probabilities of R_1 and R_2 being secured must be incorporated by a second averaging out. The result is an EMV of \$15,600 for the research alternative versus an EMV of \$14,000 for the no-research path. The conclusion then is this: Research that would enable Mr. White to make a perfect forecast regarding the potential new orders would be worth up to \$1,600. If the research costs more than \$1,600, he would decline to buy it because the net EMV of the research alternative would be less than the EMV of \$14,000 of the no-research alternative.

Imperfect information. The analysis up to this point assumes that research on decision options will give a perfect prediction of the future states of nature O_1 and O_2. Perfect prediction seldom occurs in actual practice. Sometimes research indicates one condition when later evidence shows something else to be the case. Thus, we need to consider that the research in the machinery decision example will provide less than perfect information and is, therefore, worth less than the \$1,600 calculated in Figure 2A–2.

Suppose that the research in that example involves interviews with the customers' key personnel as well as some of the customers' executives. They might all answer our questions to the best of their ability but still predict imperfectly what will happen. Consequently, we might judge that the chances of their predictions being correct are no better than 3 to 1; or 0.75. If we accept that our research results may provide imperfect information in this manner, we need to factor this into our research evaluation decision. We do this by averaging out and folding back again. The results are shown in Figure 2A–3. The revised EMV, given research judged to be 75 percent reliable, is \$14,010. This revised EMV is only \$10 higher than the \$14,000 EMV using no research and would seem to be hardly worth consideration.

---

[7]Bayes' theorm with two states of nature is:

$$P(O_1|R_i) = \frac{P(R_i|O_1) \times P(O_1)}{P(R_i|O_1) \times P(O_1) + P(R_i|O_2) \times P(O_2)}$$

$$= \frac{1.0 \times 0.6}{(1.0 \times 0.6) + (0.0 \times 0.4)}$$

$$= 1.0$$

FIGURE 2A–3 The value of imperfect information

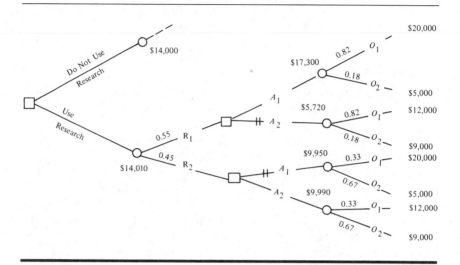

Pragmatic complications. This discussion, while simplified, contains the basic concepts for a determination of the value of research. However, practical difficulties complicate the use of these concepts. First, the situation with two events and two alternatives is artificial. Problems with more choices and events are common, and the chief complication is the increased number of calculations.

Research outcomes	States of nature		Marginal probabilities	Posterior probabilities	
	O_1	O_2		$P(O_1|R_i)$	$P(O_2|R_i)$
R_1	0.45	0.1	0.55	0.82	0.18
R_2	0.15	0.3	0.45	0.33	0.67
Marginal probabilities	0.60	0.40			

A more serious problem is posed by the measurement of outcomes. In the example, we assumed that we could assess the various courses of action in terms of an umambiguous dollar value, but often we cannot. It is very difficult to place a dollar value on outcomes related to morale or public image, for example.

An allied problem lies in the exclusive use of *EMV* as the criterion for decision. This approach is correct in an actuarial sense and implies that each decision maker has a linear system of evaluation. In truth, we often use another evaluation system. For example, the person who accepts *EMV* as a criterion sees that an even bet of $20 between two people on the toss of a fair coin is a fair bet. Many people, however, may not be willing to make such a bet because they fear the loss of $20 more than they value the gain of $20. They may need to be offered a chance, say, to win $20 but to lose only $10 before they would be willing to bet. These persons have a nonlinear decision scale. The "utility" concept is more relevant in this case.

The development of more precise methods of evaluating the contribution of research is now only at the pioneer stage. In the meantime, continued emphasis on improvement of our understanding of the researcher's task and the research process will make research more valuable when it is conducted.

DISCUSSION QUESTIONS

1. What are the major problems in the evaluation of a business research study?
2. Using such concepts as maximin and expected monetary value, suggest appropriate decision rules and variables in each of the following cases:
   a Whether to switch to a new supplier of raw materials.
   b Whether to invest in project A or B.
   c Whether to make a product or buy it from another company.
3. You are considering whether to produce and market a new product. Your choices are:
   a A_1—Produce and market the new product.
   b A_2—Do not produce and market it.
   c A_3—Market test the product to determine whether it should be marketed.
      You are uncertain about what to do, but the research department has proposed a market test. They estimate that it will cost $75,000 but will predict the product's chances for success. On the basis of your experience, you estimate that the product could be very profitable; if it receives strong market acceptance, the company should make about $500,000 in incremental profits over the product's life. However, if the acceptance is poor, there would be an incremental loss of perhaps $300,000. Your best judgment now is that there is a 40-percent chance that acceptance will be poor, and a 60-percent chance that it will be strong.
   a Assuming you use the EMV criterion, should you launch this product even if you do not test market?
   b You are confident of your conditional profit and loss estimates but question your outcome probability estimates. How low could your success probability estimate be and still produce a positive EMV?
   c Would research be a worthwhile action, assuming that it gives a perfect success-failure prediction?
   d Suppose research of this type is accurate in its prediction only 80 percent of the time. Would it then be worth doing?
   e How might your answers to the above questions be affected by the fact that your company's net worth is $1 million?
4. Assume that you are the president of a large bank and are considering whether to form a consortium of banks to introduce electronic funds transfer (EFT). To do this, your bank will have to invest substantial resources in developing the project but will gain a substantial profit if the project succeeds. The techno-

logical problems have been solved, consumer acceptance does not seem to be overly difficult, but there are regulatory problems. Some smaller banks are attempting to block *EFT* through the bank regulatory agencies; if that fails, they will go to the courts. It is considered certain that *EFT* will come eventually, but it may be delayed by legal problems for as long as five years.

You and your executives, in trying to assess the project, conclude that one of three conditions will occur: (1) the project will go forward as scheduled; (2) regulatory problems will delay the project by a year if you launch it now; and (3) legal and regulatory problems will stop the project for five years if you launch it now. You estimate that the probabilities are 0.30, 0.40, and 0.30, respectively. Two alternatives are open to your bank—either take the lead now in forming the consortium, or withdraw and allow a competing bank to become the leader. In either case, it will be launched soon. If you withdraw, your bank can still participate in the project but with much less profit opportunity and less risk. You ask your staff to develop conditional profit estimates for various combinations of actions and states of nature and to convert these estimates to present-value terms. These results are shown in the accompanying table.

	States of nature		
	EFT goes ahead	EFT delay 1 year (millions of dollars)	EFT delay 5 years
Our bank leads	9.0	4.5	−12.0
Our bank follows	2.0	2.1	−1.5

a   Draw a decision tree for this decision.

b   Assume the maximin decision criterion. Which course of action would you recommend?

c   Based on an *EMV* criterion, which course of action would you take?

d   Assume that someone comes to you with a proposal to do research which will enable you to predict correctly which state of nature will occur. How much would such research be worth?

e   Even if the *EMV* suggests one course of action, what other considerations might cause you to decide against this course?

RESEARCH DESIGN

3. Research design

Glenn Detrick had just finished revising the employee morale study for the Big Store Company when the phone rang. It was Ed Byldor, a local contractor, whom Glenn had met at the Rotary Club meeting recently. Ed is active in the development of subdivisions in Northridge, an old town now becoming a high-growth suburb. He and his partners had purchased substantial acreage there for future development, but now the local planning board is threatening to rezone the land. If rezoning goes through, it will virtually eliminate any chance for profitable development. Ed is preparing to fight the planning board proposal and feels a need for some quick research help. Glenn made an appointment to meet him the next day to talk it over.

Glenn was experienced enough to anticipate the major concerns Ed would have. Clients usually expect to learn immediately what research needs to be done, how it should be done, how much it will cost, and how quickly it can be completed. Instant answers to these questions are generally not possible, but useful answers should be in the research design statement that results from following an orderly research procedure.

THE RESEARCH PROCESS

We tend to view the research process as a linear sequence of clearly defined steps. Yet no one really believes that the process moves in a clearly defined order, each step completed before going on to the next. Recyclings and skips do occur. Some steps are begun out of sequence and some may even be omitted. In spite of these variations, the concept of sequence is useful when we try to develop a project.

It all begins much like Ed's call. Some management problem develops that triggers a need for information. In this case, Ed and his partners are threatened with substantial losses and might see their problem as follows:

Management problem: Take appropriate actions to get the planning board to reverse its preliminary stand. At least, this is how the problem now looks to Glenn. After a talk with Ed, he will have a better picture of the situation. For now, however, he might conjecture a little about what procedure he will follow if he gets the assignment. In general, he would follow the classical research procedure. This includes these steps:

1. Exploration—A relatively unstructued investigation in which the researcher attempts to define the problem more specifically, and determine how the research task will be carried out. It is at this stage that the researcher learns the dimensions of the research problem. Exploration ends either when it is decided to go no further, or when the design for the formal study is drafted.
2. Data collection—The actual data gathering may range from a relatively simple observation at one location to a national survey involving thousands of interviews in a succession of waves over several months or years. Data collection requires substantial resources but probably not as large a part of the budget as most readers would expect. Field workers must be paid, and research and other expenses are incurred, but this stage often takes no more than one third of the total research budget.
3. Analysis and interpretations of results—After the field work, Glenn will still need to analyze the data, derive various measures, and study the relationships that he finds. He must then interpret these findings in the light of the client's specific problem. Finally, he develops the report and transmits his findings to the client.

While all research studies go through these steps, one must also develop a research design that is appropriate for the study at hand.

WHAT IS RESEARCH DESIGN?

Many definitions of "research design" have been advanced, but no one definition imparts the full range of important aspects. Several examples from leading authors can be cited:

> The research design constitutes the blueprint for the collection, measurement, and analysis of data. It aids the scientist in the allocation of his limited resources by posing crucial choices: Is the blueprint to include experiments, interviews, observation, the analysis of records, simulation, or some combination of these? Are the methods of data collection and the research situation to be highly structured? Is an intensive study of a small sample more effective than a less intensive study of a large sample? Should the analysis be primarily quantitative or qualitative?[1]
>
> Research design is the plan, structure, and strategy of investigation conceived so as to obtain answers to research questions and to control variance.

---

[1]Reprinted with permission of Macmillan Publishing from Bernard S. Phillips, *Social Research Strategy and Tactics*, 2d ed., p. 93. Copyright © 1971 by Bernard S. Phillips.

The plan is the overall scheme or program of research. It includes an outline of what the investigator will do from writing the hypotheses and their operational implications to the final analysis of the data. The *structure* of the research is . . . the outline, the scheme, and paradigm of the operation of the variables. . . . *Strategy* . . . includes the methods to be used to gather and analyze the data. In other words, strategy implies *how* the research objectives will be reached and *how* the problems encountered in the research will be tackled.[2]

These definitions differ in detail, but together they give the essentials of a good research design. First, the design is a plan that specifies the sources and types of information relevant to the research question. Second, it is a strategy or blueprint specifying the approaches to be used for gathering and analyzing data. For example, what specific techniques will be used to gather the desired data? What kind of sampling, if any, will be used? How will variables be related? Finally, since most business research studies have time and cost constraints, both are typically included.

Classification of designs

Early in any research study, one faces the task of selecting the specific design to use. There are a number of different design approaches, but unfortunately there is no simple classification system that defines all the variations that must be considered. Research design is a complex concept that may be viewed from at least seven different perspectives.

1. The degree to which the research problem has been crystallized (the study may be either exploratory or formal).
2. The method of data collection (studies may be observational or survey).
3. The power of the researcher to affect the variables under study (the two major types of research are the experimental and the ex post facto).
4. The purpose of the study (research studies may be descriptive or causal).
5. The time dimension (research may be cross-sectional or longitudinal).
6. The topical scope—breadth and depth—of the study (a case or statistical study).
7. The research environment (most business research is conducted in a field setting, although laboratory research is not unusual; simulation is another category, somewhat similar to laboratory research).

A brief discussion of these perspectives illustrates their nature and contribution to research. Several are considered in more detail later in the chapter, the remainder are reserved for later chapters.

Degree of problem crystallization. A study may be viewed as exploratory or formal. The essence of the distinction between these two is the

---

[2]Fred N. Kerlinger, *Foundations of Behavioral Research*, 2d ed. (New York: Holt, Rinehart & Winston, 1973), p. 300.

degree of structure and the immediate objective of the study. Exploratory studies tend to be loosely structured with an objective of learning what the major research tasks are to be. In fact, the immediate purpose of exploration is usually to develop hypotheses or questions for further research. The formal study begins where the exploration leaves off—it begins with a hypothesis or question and involves precise procedures and data source specifications. The goal of a formal research design is to test the hypotheses or answer the research questions posed.

The method of data collection. This classification distinguishes between observational and survey data collection processes. In the first, the researcher monitors and records information about subjects without questioning them. A traffic count at an intersection, a search of a library collection, watching and recording the actions of a group of decision makers—all are examples of observation.

In a survey design, the researcher interrogates subjects and collects their responses. Studies of this type may be further classified by the communication medium used—mail, telephone, or personal interview. The term *survey* is often used to describe what is more properly called an *ex post facto design*, described below.

Researcher control of variables. In terms of the researcher's ability to manipulate variables, we differentiate between experimental and ex post facto designs. In an experiment, the researcher attempts to control and/or manipulate the variables in the study. It is enough that we can cause variables to be changed or held constant in keeping with our research objectives. Experimental design is appropriate when one wishes to determine whether certain variables affect other variables in some way. Experimentation provides the most powerful support possible for a hypothesis of causation.

With an ex post facto design, investigators have no control over the variables in sense of being able to manipulate them. They can only report what has happened or what is happening. In fact, it is important in this design that the researchers not influence the variables; to do so is to introduce bias. The researcher is limited to holding factors constant by judicious selection of subjects according to strict sampling procedures and by statistical manipulation of findings.

The purpose of the study. The essential difference between descriptive and causal studies lies in their objectives. If the research is concerned with finding out who, what, where, when, or how much, then the study is descriptive. If it is concerned with learning why, i.e., how one variable affects another, it is causal. For example, research on crime is descriptive when it measures the types of crime committed, how often, when, where, and by whom. In a causal study, we try to explain relationships among variables— for instance, why the crime rate is higher in city A than in city B.

The nature of descriptive/causal studies is sometimes confused with that of experimental/ex post facto studies. This confusion comes from the fact that experimental studies are concerned with causation questions. In addition, descriptive studies are normally ex post facto. But ex post facto designs must also be used to determine causation. It would be unlikely, for example, that we could use experimental techniques to determine the causes of variation in crime rates between city A and city B. We would need to use an ex post facto design and try to infer causation by correlating city crime rates with other variables.

The time dimension. In terms of time coverage, we classify research designs as either cross-sectional or longitudinal. Cross-sectional studies are carried out once, while the longitudinal are repeated. The longitudinal study allows one to study changes over time. The panel study is one type of longitudinal study that is widely used to study changes in a particular group of subjects.

The topical scope. Along this dimension, studies may be statistical or case designs, although the difference between the two is one of degree. In the statistical study, we sample a cross section of data with the emphasis on breadth of coverage. We are interested in the frequency with which certain characteristics or instances occur. If we were using a case-study approach, we would emphasize the detailed analysis of a limited number of events or conditions and their interrelationships. Case-study analysis is concerned more with interactive processes.

A study of attitudes toward labor-management problems furnishes a good example of these approaches. In a statistical study, we might administer a questionnaire to the managers and workers in a plant; tabulate the answers; and calculate typical attitudes by department, type of workers, and the like. We might cross-tabulate responses to infer relationships between variables.

If the research were being done as a case study, we might examine several departments in depth. The study would focus on labor-management attitudes from a variety of perspectives. Systematic interviewing would be used to elicit the reciprocal perceptions and attitudes of workers, supervisors, shop stewards, department managers, and so forth. Stress would be placed on these interrelationships and how they might affect attitudes of the various parties.

The research environment. Designs also differ as to whether they take place under actual environmental conditions or under artificial or simulated conditions. These are called field and laboratory studies, respectively. The main distinction hinges on whether the study is of subjects under normal conditions for the problem being studied.

To simulate is to replicate the essence of a system or process. Simulations are being used more and more in research, especially in operations research. The major characteristics of various conditions and relationships in actual situations are often represented in mathematical models. Role playing and other behavioral activities may also be viewed as simulations.

Exploratory, descriptive, and causal research designs are discussed in the sections which follow. Other design aspects are covered in later chapters.

EXPLORATION

Exploration should generally be the first major step in research. It is useful because the researcher often does not have a clear idea of the problems that will surface in the study. This was clearly Glenn's situation, mentioned earlier. He was only vaguely familiar with the controversy between the Northridge planning board and the Byldor's group.

Exploration serves several purposes. In the first place, the area of investigation may be so new or so vague that a researcher needs to perform an exploration just to learn something about the problems. Also, the researcher may explore to be sure that it is practical to do a study in the area. For example, one federal government agency proposed that research be done on how executives in a given industry made decisions about raw material purchases. Specifically involved were questions about how and at what price spreads was one raw material substituted for another in certain manufactured products. A critical prerequisite to this study was an exploration to determine whether industry executives would divulge adequate information about their decision making on this topic.

In spite of its obvious value, however, researchers and managers alike give the matter of exploration too little attention. There are often strong pressures for quick answers to research problems. Too often it is "obvious" that exploration is "stalling around" when urgent projects could be done. A wiser view is that exploration saves time and money and should not be slighted.

Methods of exploration

Literature search. An obvious first step in an exploratory study is to do a literature search. It is inefficient to discover anew through original research what has been done by others already. There are literally tens of thousands of periodicals and hundreds of thousands of books on all aspects of business and business lines. Writers often publish research results or other useful information. There are special catalogs and subject guides available in most libraries that will help in this search. Much more is said on this topic in Chapter 6.

A literature search can provide excellent background on the areas of interest and will supply a number of good leads if one is creative. If we confine the investigation to obvious subjects in these bibliographic sources, we will often miss much of the best information. For example, suppose we are interested in estimating the outlook for the copper industry over the next 10 years. The obvious first step would be to search through the literature for information on copper production and consumption. However, a search restricted to these two topics would miss more than it finds. When a creative search of the copper industry was undertaken, useful information was turned up under the following reference headings: mines and minerals;

nonferrous metals; forecasting; planning; econometrics; such consuming industries as automotive, communications; particular countries where copper is produced, such as Chile; and companies prominent in the industry, such as Anaconda, Kennecott, and others.

Experience survey. While published data are a valuable resource, seldom is more than a fraction of the existing knowledge in a field put into writing. Then, too, even if more is published, it may be difficult to find. Thus we will profit by seeking information from persons experienced in the area of study. Such persons can help us secure an insight into relationships between variables. To get an accurate picture of the current situation we need to solicit the views of those believed to know what is going on. The amount of exploration needed depends on what is being learned. If the last interviews taken turn up some new information of value, then we have not gone far enough. We should keep going until our findings duplicate what we know.

When we interview persons in an experience survey, we should seek their ideas on which are the important issues or aspects of the subject. The investigative format we use should be flexible enough so that we can explore various avenues that emerge during the interview. We seek to learn what is being done. What has been tried in the past without success? What are the change-producing elements of the situation? How have things changed over time? What problem areas and barriers can be seen? Who is involved in decisions, and what roles do they play? What are the costs of various aspects of the processes under study? Who can we count on to assist and/or participate in the research? What are the priority areas? Many similar questions might be posed, but these give the general drift of the process.

The product of such questioning may be a new hypothesis, a discarding of old hypotheses, or information about the practicality of doing the study. Probing may indicate whether certain facilities are available for study, what factors need to be controlled, which can be controlled and how, and who will cooperate in the study.

Discovery is more easily carried out if the researcher can analyze cases that provide special insight. Typically in exploration, we are less interested in getting a representative cross-section view than in getting information from those sources that might provide especially "insight-stimulating." Assume that we are called on to study an automobile assembly plant which has a recent history of declining productivity, increasing costs, and growing numbers of quality defects. People who might provide such insightful information include the following:

1. Newcomers to the scene—new employees or personnel who may have recently been transferred to this plant from similar plants.
2. Marginal or peripheral individuals—persons whose jobs place them on the margin between contending groups. For example, first-line super-

visors and lead workers are often neither management nor workers but
something in between.

3. Individuals in transition—recently promoted employees who have been
   transferred to new departments.

4. Deviants and isolates—those in a given group who hold a different
   position from the majority—workers who are happy with the present
   situation, highly productive departments and workers, loners of one sort
   or another.

5. "Pure" cases or cases that show extreme examples of the conditions
   under study—the most unproductive departments, the most antagonis-
   tic workers, and so forth.

6. Those who fit well and those who do not—the workers who are well
   established in their organizations versus those who are not, those executives who fully reflect management views and those who do not.

7. Those who represent different positions in the system—unskilled workers, assemblers, superintendents, and so forth.[3]

The end of exploration

The end of an exploratory study comes when the researchers are convinced that they have found the major dimensions of the research task. They
may have defined a set of subsidiary investigative questions which can be
used as specific guides to a detailed research design. Or they may have
developed a number of potential hypotheses about possible causes of a specific problem situation. They may also have determined that certain other
hypotheses are such remote possibilities that they can be safely ignored in
any subsequent study. Finally, researchers may end exploration because
they feel that additional research is either not needed or is not feasible.

Two-stage approach. One useful way to design a research study is to
visualize it as a two-stage project. Under this approach, break out the exploration as a separate first stage with the limited objectives of (1) more clearly
defining the research problem, and (2) developing the research design. Under these conditions, the exploration can be a preliminary study of limited
scope and budget.

In arguing for a two-stage approach, we are recognizing that there is much
about the problem that is not known and such information should be known
before a major commitment of effort and resources is made. In these circumstances, one is operating in unknown areas, where it is difficult to predict
the problems and costs of the study. The two-stage proposal is particularly
useful when the research is on a fixed-cost basis and the complications and
problems that will be encountered are difficult to anticipate. A limited exploration for a specific, modest cost carries little risk for both parties and often

---

[3]This classification is suggested in Selltiz, Wrightsman, and Cook, *Research Methods*,
pp. 99–101.

uncovers information that reduces the total research cost. Sometimes the evidence uncovered in the exploration indicates that a major study is unnecessary. The amount of exploration should depend on the researchers' general level of knowledge of the subject under study.

Development of the formal design

At this point, the development of the formal research design begins. The research questions are set, and the general-level investigative questions have been derived. These may be stated in the form of hypotheses to be tested or questions to be answered. The classical form, of course, is the hypothesis.

The steps involved in designing a study depend to some extent on the nature of the specific project. As a general procedure, however, the following are common:

1. The major concepts or constructs to be used in the study are defined. Further operational definitions emerge as the design process continues.
2. The investigative questions are reviewed and typically need to be further broken down into more specific second- and third-level questions. In effect, this is the process of determining what evidence must be collected to test the major hypotheses or to answer the questions.
3. At this point, the general direction of the research has probably made clear which of the various research or design types is most appropriate. For example, it may be decided that a survey, or an experiment, or some other design should be used.
4. The next task is the construction of the measurement instruments. For a survey, the interview guide or questionnaire is written, and the way in which the survey is to be carried out is specified. For an observational study, the specific form and conditions of the observation and the types of recording processes to be used must be determined.
5. When both the design and the measurement specifics have been determined, a test is needed to assure that they are feasible for the purposes intended. Almost certainly deficiencies requiring revisions and additional testing will be found at this stage.
6. At this point, a plan for the analysis of the data is available. Planning may go as far as the development of a set of dummy tables for the expected statistical data. Such detailed planning is not always found in business research projects, but it does help assure that data relevant to the hypotheses or questions will be secured.
7. The final stage of project development is preparation of specific instructions and other arrangements (such as training sessions) to assure that the data will be collected efficiently.

At the end of this series of design steps, the researchers can compile the *formal research plan*. In many commercial projects, no formal document is prepared, especially when the projects are relatively routine, carried out under severe time pressures, or limited by a modest budget. If the study is relatively small, the formal plan is often eliminated in the interest of cost saving.

DESIGNING A RESEARCH STUDY

Glenn Detrick learned much from his luncheon meeting with Ed Byldor. Latest counts indicate that 40,000 people live in the Northridge area and that the population is growing rapidly. Ed reports that most of the homes being built in the area are tract homes designed to appeal to a wide range of white-collar and blue-collar families. Home construction for recent years has showed an upgrading in size and cost with the typical price of a new three-bedroom home in the moderate range.

At this meeting, it was agreed that Glenn would undertake some exploration immediately to familiarize himself with the problem. The two men agreed to meet again in a few days.

Glenn immediately went to the university library to do some research on the economics of suburban housing development and land use. One reference led to a long-distance phone call to the Washington, D.C. headquarters of the National Association of Home Builders. That organization was able to supply valuable information about the economics of land use in residential areas. Glenn quickly concluded that there would be no problem in developing the estimates to compare the economic impacts of different land-use patterns.

A visit to the local planning office provided some material on the issues and copies of statements that had been presented to the commission. A review of recent newspaper stories on the proceedings of the planning commission was also informative. At the next meeting, Ed had also done some thinking and was prepared to express his views about the problem.

The problem as the client sees it. Ed and his associates have purchased a substantial quantity of land for future development. He now faces a possible rezoning of this land that will virtually eliminate his existing plans for profitable development. In cooperation with several other builders, Ed is beginning to mount a broad campaign against the planning commission's position. The commission has proposed that current zoning, which calls for residential development on lots of 7,500 to 10,000 square feet, be changed to require a minimum of one acre and sometimes two acres for each building site.

The first task that Ed suggests is the development of an economic argument showing how much more municipal revenue the greater building density will bring, how many more stores and shopping centers will be developed, and how many jobs will be generated with the increased population. In addition, Ed feels the need to show that the people who are living in his other developments like the area and want to stay there.

After further exploration, including some in-depth interviews with Northridge residents, Glenn arranged another meeting with his client. By this time, he had determined that an economic argument could be developed from published studies and data available from local sources. But his view was that the argument, while useful, would not meet the objections of the local planning commission.

The problem as Glenn sees it. The general nature of the commission's position suggests a need for research among the people of the area to test the major points that the planning commission is making. None of the commission's five members is considered an expert in planning. A majority of them believe that the present development of the city is inadequate. They are backed in this view by a few long-time residents living on large estates directly in the path of the population movement. Further analysis of the commission majority's argument indicates that an entirely different research direction is called for.

The argument presented by the planning commission and its backers is that existing development of the area is leading to three deficiencies:

1. Aesthetic—Residential development is creating a definite problem of unsightly urban sprawl. Commercial development is being accomplished by area strip zoning, which brings about further urban ugliness.
2. Social—The area is primarily a working-class neighborhood. The city must attract more affluent people to provide future civic leadership. One way of doing so would be the provision of acre-or-more land plots on which more expensive homes could be built.
3. Economic—The school system, although growing rapidly, is chronically overcrowded. Further dense housing development would continue to put pressures on the school system. A decrease in the density of residential development would lessen school population pressures.

An analysis of these arguments suggests that a study of residents should provide useful information concerning the first two arguments (the third is answered by an economic analysis). The investigative questions are stated in terms of the following descriptive hypotheses.

1. The population of the city represents a broad cross section that includes many college-educated, concerned citizens who are potential civic leaders.
2. A large share of the population is composed of young families who have been attracted by the lifestyles and environment in this city.
3. These satisfied residents see the city as their permanent home and do not expect to leave the area, even if they buy larger homes.
4. While the residents desire environmental improvements, they do not want any drastic changes in present plans for residential use.

The research hypotheses are translated into specific research requirements. For example, hypothesis 2 concerns attitudes of the people toward their area as a place to live and raise a family. To test this, the researcher has to learn the basis for the residents' original attraction to the area; their opinions about schools, churches, shopping, and convenience to work; their satisfaction with their specific neighborhood and neighbors; and their views on the adequacy of their homes and lot size.

The exploratory in-depth interviews with residents give the researcher a better understanding of the types of people and their responses. From these interviews, a questionnaire is developed. Glenn tests it, revises it, and tests it again. Dummy tables are drawn up to suggest the ways in which the final data will be analyzed. These tables and their probable contents are then compared against the specific research requirements to be certain the objectives will be met.

Sampling reliability is determined to be a critical matter. At the same time, the research budget suggests that the sample size must be limited. These restrictions, plus the fact that the area of study is clearly defined and geographically limited, lead to the use of probability sampling methods. All addresses in the study areas are listed and a random sample drawn.

After the successful pilot test, the project is released to a field interviewing organization, which places a substantial number of interviewers in the field. They complete their study in a few days. The results are then tabulated and analyzed and the final report presented to the client. The schedule for this project is approximately as follows:

> July 15—Initiate contact with the client.
> July 24—Decide to go ahead with the study.
> July 26–Aug. 10—Seek background data on economic aspects and conduct some exploratory interviews.
> Aug. 11—Begin the development of specific research design and questionnaire.
> Aug. 24—Meet client and set final go-ahead.
> Aug. 30—Begin field interviewing.
> Sept. 3—Begin coding and tabulation.
> Sept. 13—Begin analysis of results.
> Sept. 21—Complete report.

FORMAL STUDIES

Formal research studies are typically structured with clearly stated hypotheses or investigative questions. These studies serve a variety of research objectives, among which are (1) descriptions of phenomena or characteristics associated with a subject population, (2) estimates of the proportions of a population that have these characteristics, (3) discovery of associations among different variables, and finally (4) discovery and measurement of cause-and-effect relationships among variables. The first three objectives are normally associated with descriptive studies, while the fourth calls for studies of causal relationships.

Descriptive studies

The objective in a descriptive study is to learn the who, what, when, where, and how of a topic. The study may be simple or complex; it may be done in a laboratory or in the field. It can also be described in terms of the other dimensions we have discussed. Whatever the form, however, a descriptive study can be just as demanding of research skills as the more idealized causal study, and we should insist upon the same high standards for design and execution.

The simplest descriptive study concerns a univariate question or hypothesis in which we ask about, or state something about, the size, form, distribution, or existence of a variable. For example, in an account analysis at a savings and loan association, we might be interested in developing a profile of savers. We may want first to locate them in relation to the association office. In this case the question might be, "What percent of the savers live within a two-mile radius of the office?" Using the hypothesis format, we might predict that, "Sixty percent or more of the savers live within a two-mile radius of the office."

We may also be interested in securing information about such other variables as:

1. The relative size of accounts.
2. The number of accounts for minors.
3. The number of accounts opened within the last six months.
4. The amount of activity (number of deposits and withdrawals per year) in accounts.

Data on each of these variables, by themselves, may have value for management decisions. Bivariate relationships between these or other variables may be of even greater interest. Cross-tabulations between distance from the branch and account activity, for example, may suggest that differential rates of activity are related to location of account. A cross-tabulation of account size and sex of account owner may also show interrelation. Such correlative relationships as these may not necessarily imply a causal relationship in a strict sense.

Descriptive studies are often much more complex than this example. One study of savers began as described and then went into much greater depth. Part of the study included an observation of account records, which indicated a concentration of nearby savers. Their accounts were typically larger and more active than those whose owners lived at a distance. A sample survey of savers provided information on stage in the family life cycle, attitudes toward savings, family income levels, and other matters. Correlation of this information with known savings data indicated that accounts in women's names tended to be larger. Further investigation suggested that women with larger accounts were often widowed or working single women and were older than the average account holder. Information about their attitudes and savings practices led to some revised business strategies at the savings and loan association.

Some of the evidence collected suggested causal relationships. For example, the correlation between nearness to the office and the probability of having an account at the office suggested the question, "Why would people who live at some distance from the office have an account there?" It is this type of question situation where hypothesizing makes its greatest contribution by pointing out directions that the research might follow. In this example it might be hypothesized that:

1. Distant savers (operationally defined as those with addresses more than two miles from the office) have accounts at the office because they once lived near the office; they were "near" when the account decision was made.
2. Distant savers actually live near the office, but the address on the account is, for some unknown reason, located at a place outside the two-mile radius; they are "near," but the records do not show this.
3. Distant savers work near the office; they are "near" by virtue of their work location.
4. Distant savers are not normally near to the office but responded to a promotion that encouraged savers to use the mail system; this is another form of "nearness" in which this concept is transformed into one of "convenience."

When these hypotheses were tested, it was determined that a substantial portion of the distant savers could be accounted for by hypotheses 1 and 3. It was concluded that nearby location was closely related to saving at a given association. The determination of cause is not so simple, however.

Causal studies

The correlation between location and probability of account holding at a savings and loan association looks like strong evidence to many, but the researcher with a more scientific disposition will argue that this correlation is not causation. Who is right? The essence of the disagreement seems to lie in the concept of "cause."

One writer asserts that, *"there appears to be an inherent gap between the languages of theory and research* which can never be bridged in a completely satisfactory way. One *thinks* in terms of theoretical language that contains notions such as causes, forces, systems, and properties. But one's tests are made in terms of covariations, operations, and pointer readings."[4] The essential element in the theoretical concept of cause is that A "produces" B or A "forces" B to occur. Empirically, however, we can never demonstrate

---

[4]Hubert M. Blalock, Jr., *Causal Inferences in Nonexperimental Research* (Chapel Hill, N.C.: University of North Carolina Press, 1964), p. 5.

such certainty. To meet the ideal standard of causation would require that one factor always causes another, and that no other factor has the same causal effect. When one realizes that even the physicist in the laboratory cannot achieve such control, it is apparent that we will not achieve it in a business setting.

The experiment is the ideal form of causal analysis because it allows us to arrange and manipulate variables. To determine causal relationships in a nonexperimental situation is even more difficult. However, causal inferences are going to be made, and we must make them as best we can if we are to have more scientific decision making. Recognizing this caveat, let's look further at the process of causal inference.

Causal inference

Our concern in causal analysis is with the study of how one variable affects, or is "responsible for," changes in another variable. The stricter interpretation of "causation," found in experimentation, is that some external factor "produces" a change in the dependent variable. In much business research, however, we are interested in cases in which the cause-effect relationship is less explicit. In fact, we are more interested in understanding, explaining, predicting, and controlling relationships between variables than we are with determining causes per se.

If we consider the possible relationships that can occur between two variables, we can conclude that there are three possibilities. The relationships may be reciprocal, symmetrical or asymmetrical.[5] A symmetrical relationship is one in which two variables fluctuate together but we assume that the changes in neither variable are due to changes in the other. Symmetrical conditions are most often found when the two variables are alternative indicators of some other cause or independent variable. We might conclude that a correlation between low work attendance and active participation in a company camping club are both the result of (dependent on) some other factor such as a hedonistic lifestyle.

A reciprocal relationship exists when two variables mutually influence or reinforce each other. This could occur if the readings of an advertisement leads to the use of a brand of product. The usage, in turn, sensitizes the person to notice and read more of the advertising of that particular brand.

Asymmetrical relationships. The major relationships of interest to the research analyst are those which are *asymmetrical*. With these relationships we postulate that one variable (the independent variable, or *IV*) is responsible for another variable (the dependent variable, or *DV*). The identification of the *IV* and *DV* is often obvious, but there are times when the choice is not clear. In these latter cases we evaluate them on the basis of (1) the fixity or alterability of each variable and (2) the time order between them. For

---

[5]Morris Rosenberg, *The Logic of Survey Analysis* (New York: Basic Books, 1968), p. 3.

example, since age, social class, climate, world events, present manufacturing technology, and the like are relatively unalterable we normally choose them as independent variables. In addition, when we can determine a time order we usually find that the *IV* precedes the *DV.*

Types of asymmetrical relationships. In business research, we are concerned chiefly with the asymmetrical relationships of which the most common forms are the following:

1. Stimulus-response relationship. This represents an event or force that results in a response from some object. For example, a price rise results in fewer unit sales; a change in work rules leads to a higher level of worker output; or, a change in government economic policy restricts corporate financial decisions. Experiments usually involve stimulus-response relationships.

2. Property-disposition relationship. A property is a relatively enduring characteristic of a subject that does not depend upon circumstances for its activation. For example, age, sex, family status, religious affiliation, ethnic group, and physical condition are personal properties.

A disposition is a tendency to respond in a certain way under certain circumstances. Dispositions include attitudes, opinions, habits, values, drives, and the like. Examples of property-disposition relationships would be the effect of our age on our attitudes about saving, our sex and its effect on our attitudes toward certain social issues, or our social class and our opinion about right-to-work laws. Properties and dispositions are major concepts used in business and social science research.

3. Disposition-behavior relationship. Behavior responses include consumption practices, work performance, interpersonal acts, and other kinds of performance. Examples of relationships between dispositions and behavior include opinions about a brand and its purchase, job satisfaction and work output, moral values and tax cheating. Much of ex post facto causal research involves relationships between properties, dispositions, and behaviors.

4. Property-behavior relationship. Examples include such relationships as the stage of the family life cycle and purchases of furniture, social class and family savings patterns, and age and sports participation.

When thinking about possible causal relationships or proposing causal hypotheses, one must state the expected positions of the variables relative to each other, i.e., which is cause and which is effect.

Positional relationships

In dealing with asymmetrical relationships between variables, one can view each variable as being either an explanatory or an extraneous variable.

Explanatory variables. There is at least one independent variable (IV) and a dependent variable (DV) in each asymmetrical relationship. It is normally hypothesized that in some way the IV "causes" the DV to occur. For simple relationships, all other variables are considered extraneous and are ignored. Thus, we might be interested in a study of the effect of the four-day work week on office productivity and hypothesize the following:

> The introduction of the four-day work week (IV) will lead to increased office productivity per worker-hour (DV).

In actual study situations, however, such a simple one-on-one relationship needs to be conditioned or revised to take other variables into account. Often one uses another type of explanatory variable of value here—the moderating variable (MV). A moderating variable is a second independent variable that is included because it is believed to have a significant contributory or contingent effect on the originally stated IV-DV relationship. For example, one might hypothesize that:

> The introduction of the four-day work week (IV) will lead to higher productivity (DV), especially among younger workers (MV).

In this case, there is a differential pattern of relationship between the four-day week and productivity that is the result of age differences among the workers.

Whether a given variable is treated as an independent or a moderating variable depends on the hypothesis. If you are interested in studying the impact of length of work week, you would make the length of week the IV. If you were focusing on the relationship of age of worker and productivity, you might use work week length as a moderating variable.

Extraneous variables. An almost infinite number of variables exists that might conceivably affect a given asymmetrical relationship. Several of these can be treated as independent or moderating variables, but most of them must either be assumed or excluded from the study. Fortunately, the infinite number of variables has little or no effect on a given situation. Most can be safely ignored. Others may be important, but their impact occurs in such a random fashion as to have little effect.

Using the example of the effect of the four-day work week, one would normally think that the imposition of a local sales tax, the election of a new mayor, a three-day rainy spell, and thousands of similar events and conditions would have little effect on work week and office productivity.

However, there may be other extraneous variables to consider as possible confounding variables to our hypothesized IV-DV relationship between length of work week and office productivity. For example, one might think that the kind of work being done would have an effect on any work week length impact on office productivity. This might lead to our introducing a control variable (CV) as follows:

> In routine office work (CV), the introduction of a four-day work week (IV) will lead to higher productivity (DV), especially among younger workers (MV).

In this example, we attempt to control for type of work by studying the effects of the four-day week within groups performing different types of work.

Intervening variables. The variables mentioned with regard to causal relationships are concrete, clearly measurable, and can be seen, counted, or observed in some way. Sometimes, however, one may not be completely satisfied by the explanations they give. Thus, while we may recognize that a four-day work-week results in higher productivity, one might think that this is not the full explanation—that work-week length affects some intervening variable which, in turn, results in higher productivity. An intervening variable is a conceptual mechanism through which the IV and MV might affect the DV. Tuckman defines the intervening variable as "that factor which theoretically affects the observed phenomenon but cannot be seen, measured, or manipulated: its effect must be inferred from the effects of the independent and moderator variables on the observed phenomenon."[6]

In the case of the work week hypothesis, one might view the intervening variable (IVV) to be job satisfaction, giving a hypothesis as:

> The introduction of a four-day work week will lead to higher productivity by increasing job satisfaction (IVV).

Examples. Here are additional examples illustrating the relationships involving independent, moderating, controlled extraneous, and dependent variables. The management of a savings & loan company wishes to study the effect of promotion on savings. It might advance the following hypothesis:

> A promotion campaign (IV) will increase savings activity (DV), especially when free prizes are offered (MV), but chiefly among smaller savers (CV). The results come from enhancing the motivation to save (IVV).

Or, suppose you are studying a situation involving the causes of defective parts production. We might hypothesize the following:

> Changing to worker self-inspection (IV) will reduce the number of defective parts (DV), when the part can be identified with its producer (MV), in electronic assembly work (CV), by stimulating the worker's sense of responsibility (IVV).

TESTING CAUSAL HYPOTHESES

While no one can ever be certain that variable A causes variable B to occur, one can gather some evidence that increases the belief that A does, in fact, lead to B. We seek three types of evidence to do this:

1. Is there a predicted covariation between A and B? That is, do we find that A and B occur together in the way hypothesized? When A does not

---

[6]Bruce Tuckman, *Conducting Educational Reserch* (New York: Harcourt Brace Jovanovich, 1972), p. 45.

occur, is there also an absence of B? Or, when there is more or less of A, does one also find more or less of B? When such conditions of covariation exist, it is an indication of a possible causal connection.

2. Is the time order of events moving in the hypothesized direction? That is, does A occur before B? If we find that B occurs before A, we can have little confidence that A causes B.

3. Is it possible to eliminate other possible causes of B? That is, can one determine that C, D, E, and so forth do not covary with B in a way that suggests possible causal connections?

Causation and experimental design. Here is a demonstration of how these three factors are used to determine causation. Assume that you wish to conduct a survey among the alumni of Big University to enlist their support for a new program. There are two different appeals, one largely emotional in nature and the other much more logical in its approach. Before mailing out appeal letters to 50,000 alumni, you decide to conduct an experiment to see whether the emotional or the rational appeal will draw the greater response.

You choose a sample of 300 names from the list of alumni and divide them into two groups of 150 each. One of these groups is designated as the experimental group; they get the emotional appeal. The other group is the control group and it receives the rational appeal. Note that either group can be designated as experimental and the other as control. One group must be the basis for comparison, however.

Covariation in this case is expressed by the percentage of alumni who respond in relation to the appeal used. For example, suppose that 50 percent of those who receive the emotional appeal respond, while only 35 percent of those receiving the rational appeal respond. We would conclude that response probability is enhanced by using the emotional appeal.

In this case, the sequence of events is not a problem. Obviously, alumni did not respond until they received the appeal letter, so there could be no chance that the alumni support led to sending the letter requesting support.

The major problem, however, is that of making sure that other variables have not confounded the results. That is, could some factor other than the nature of the appeal have produced the same results? One can anticipate that certain factors are particularly likely to confound the results. One can control some of these variables to assure that they do not have this confounding effect. For example, the proposal under study may be one which is of major concern only to alumni who attended the university as undergraduates. Thus, persons who came only to graduate school are not concerned and you would want to make sure that answers from these people did not distort the results. The control would be achieved by excluding graduate students from the survey.

A second approach to control uses a matching process. For example, there might be reason to believe that different ratios of support will come from students in various age groups. To control by matching, we need to be sure that the age distribution of alumni is the same in both groups. In a similar way, control could be achieved by matching alumni from engineering, liberal arts, business, and other schools.

Even after using such controls, however, there are other possible confounding variables that one cannot match or exclude. These are dealt with through randomization.

Randomization is the basic method by which equivalence between experimental and control groups is determined. At the heart of experimental design is the assumption that experimental and control groups can be established in such a way that they are equal. Matching and controlling are useful, but they still leave an infinite number of unknowns unaccounted for. The best procedure is to assign subjects either to experimental or control groups at random (this is not to say haphazardly—randomness must be secured in a carefully controlled fashion according to strict rules of assignment). If the assignments are made randomly, each group should receive its fair share of different factors. The only deviation from this fair share would be that which results from random variation (luck of the draw). The possible impact of these unknown extraneous variables on the dependent variables should also vary at random. The researcher, using tests of statistical significance, can estimate the probable effect of these chance variations on the *DV* and can then compare this estimated effect of extraneous variation to the actual differences found in the *DV* in the experimental and control groups.

It is important to emphasize that random assignment to experimental and control groups is the *basic technique* by which the two groups can be made equivalent. Matching and other control forms are supplemental ways of improving the quality of measurement. In a sense, matching and controls reduce the extraneous "noise" in the measurement system and in this way improve the sensitivity of measurement of the hypothesized relationship.

Causation and ex post facto design.   Most research studies cannot be carried out experimentally by manipulating variables. Yet we still are interested in the question of causation. Instead of manipulating and/or controlling exposure to an experimental variable, we are forced back to other ways of studying different subjects which have been exposed to the independent factor and those which have not.

Consider a situation in which a number of workers in our plant have developed a pattern of absenteeism on Mondays. In searching for hypotheses to explain this phenomenon, we discover that a number of these workers are also members of a camping club which was formed a few months ago. Could it be that membership in the club caused increased absenteeism? It is not practical to try to set up an experiment. This would require us to assign persons to join the club and then determine whether this affected their work attendance.

The better approach would be to get the list of the club's membership and review the absence record of workers, concentrating on their record of work attendance on the Mondays after a camping event. In like fashion, we would take a sample of employees who are not members of the club and calculate their Monday absence rates. The results might look something like that found in Table 3–1.

TABLE 3–1   Data on employee absenteeism

	Camping club member?	
Absences	Yes	No
High	40	70
Low	10	280

The data suggest that membership in the camping club might well be a cause of higher Monday absenteeism. Certainly the covariation evidence is consistent with this conclusion; but what other evidence will give us an even greater confidence in our conclusion?

We would also like some evidence of time order of events. It is logical to expect that, if club membership causes higher absenteeism, there will be a temporal relationship between these two facts. If the high absenteeism was found only on the Monday immediately following a camping trip, it would be good evidence in support of our hypothesis. If absences from work occur before the camping trip, the time order does not support our hypothesis as well.

Of course, there are many other factors that could be causing the high absenteeism among the club members. Here again, use control techniques to improve the ability to draw firm conclusions. First, in drawing a sample of nonmembers of the club, it is important that a random sample be chosen from the files of all employees. In this way, one can be more confident that there is a fair representation of average worker absence experiences.

We cannot use assignment of subjects in ex post facto research as we did in experimentation. However, we can gather information about potentially confounding factors and use these data to make cross classification comparisons. In this way, we can determine whether or not there appears to be a relationship between club membership, absenteeism, and these other factors. For example, assume that we also gather age data on the employees under study and introduce this as a cross classification variable; the results might look like those in Table 3–2. These data indicate that age is also a factor. Younger people are more likely to be among the high absentees. Part of the high absenteeism rate among club members seems to be associated

TABLE 3–2 Data on employee absenteeism

	Club member		Nonclub member	
Age	High absentee	Low absentee	High absentee	Low absentee
Under 30 years	36	6	30	48
30 to 45	4	4	35	117
45 and over	0	0	5	115

with the fact that most club members are under 30 years of age. On the other hand, within age groups, it is also apparent that club members have substantially higher incidence of excessive absenteeism than nonclub members of the same age. By such comparisons as these, one can employ the strong inference approach of testing to eliminate multiple factors as potential causes. More will be said about the analysis of crossbreak data and the interpretation of relationships in later chapters.

The post hoc fallacy. While researchers must necessarily use ex post facto research designs to address causal questions, a word of warning is in order. Because persons with high absentee records are members of a certain club is weak evidence for claiming a causal relationship. In like manner, the covariation found between any variables must be interpreted carefully when the relationship is based on ex post facto analysis. The term "post hoc fallacy" has been used to describe these frequently unwarranted conclusions.

Ex post facto design is widely used in business research and often is the only approach feasible. In particular, one seeks causal explanations between variables that are impossible to manipulate. Not only can the variables not be manipulated, but the subjects usually cannot be assigned to treatment and control groups on an a priori basis. Then too, we often find that there are multiple causes rather than a single one. The careful researcher using the ex post facto design should approach causal conclusions cautiously; in addition, one should seek to test and falsify multiple hypotheses, and try to control the confounding impact of extraneous variables.

THE RESEARCH PROPOSAL

A written proposal is often required when a study is being suggested. It assures that the parties understand the project's purpose and proposed methods of investigation. Cost and time budgets are often spelled out, as are other responsibilities and obligations. Depending upon the needs and desires of the client, there may also be substantial background detail and elaboration of proposed techniques.

The length and complexity of research proposals range widely. A graduate student may present a doctoral dissertation proposal that runs 50 pages or more. Applicants for foundation or government research grants typically file a proposal request of a few pages, often in a standardized format specified by the granting agency. Business research proposals normally range from perhaps one to five pages.

Proposal contents.   Every proposal, regardless of length, should include two basic sections. First is the problem statement. In the brief memo type of proposal, the problem statement may be only a paragraph setting out the situation and stating the specific task that the research is going to undertake.

Examples of such problem statements are:

1. The Center City Bank is currently the leading bank in the city but recently has not been growing as fast as its major competitors. Before developing a long-range plan to enhance the bank's competitive position, it is important to determine the bank's present competitive status, its major advantages and opportunities, and its major deficiencies. The major objective of this proposed research is to develop a body of benchmark information about the Center City Bank, its major competitors, and the Center City metropolitan area as a market for banking services.

2. Management is faced with a problem of locating a new plant to serve eastern markets. Before this location decision is made, it is proposed that a feasibility study be conducted to determine, for each of five sites, the estimated:

   a Costs of serving existing customers.

   b Building, relocation, tax, and operating costs.

   c Availability of local labor in the six major crafts used in production.

   d Attractiveness as a living environment for professional and management personnel.

The above statements give the problem facing the respective managements and point out, in a general way, the nature of the research that will be undertaken. Other problem statements might begin with issues raised by behavioral or other theories and state a number of hypotheses for testing. Such statements would usually be more detailed than the examples cited.

A second necessary section of the proposal includes a statement of what will be done. In the bank example cited, the researcher might propose:

> Personal interviews will be conducted with a minimum of 200 residents of the area to determine their knowledge of, use of, and attitudes toward local banks. In addition, information will be gathered about their banking and financing practices and preferences. Other information of an economic or demographic nature will also be gathered from published sources and public agencies.

Often proposals will be much more detailed and may include specific measurement devices that will be used, time and cost budgets, sampling plans, and many other details.

The formal research plan. Another format, still essentially a proposal, is the formal research plan. It is found both in student and business research situations, especially when a two-stage project is needed. Exploration is undertaken to determine the dimensions of the problem before the proposal is made for the major study. Under these circumstances, it is reasonable to expect a written proposal that is more detailed than proposals suggested to this point. Formats will vary, but one set of sample instructions used for student research projects includes the following:

Research plan outline

1. Statement of research objective. A clear sentence or two are needed that tell exactly what you plan to do. If the objective is to test a hypothesis, then so state. In many cases, the objective will be a question. For example, you may be interested in studying why a local Red Cross chapter has not met its quota for blood collection. This might be stated as, "Why has the local Red Cross blood donor drive been unsuccessful?"
2. Statement of the procedures that you expect to use. When research is exploratory, and when hypotheses will be the result rather than the beginning of your research, you should state this. Identify the major dimensions of your planned study. Is it a cross-section? Is it descriptive? Other?
3. If the research design goes beyond exploration, specify the research problem or hypotheses to be tested. A good way to do this is to state investigative questions for each of the major research questions or hypotheses. For example, you might hypothesize that the unsuccessful blood donor drive could be explained by one or more of three hypotheses.
   a People failed to donate blood because they were unaware of the blood donor campaign.
   b People failed to donate blood in the campaign because they did not believe it was important for them to do so (i.e., no real need was recognized).
   c People failed to donate blood in the campaign because they had fears about the experience which have not been relieved.
4. For each hypothesis, you might list several investigative questions. To illustrate, for Hypothesis A, you might be interested in the following:
   a Did they know about the campaign?
   b Do they know about the regular need for blood donors?
   c Did they know what they needed to do and where and when they needed to do it?
5. Present all measurement instruments as well as results of pilot testing of such instruments.
6. Describe the sampling plan to be used. For example, specify if it is going to be a probability sample or not? How large? How drawn?

7. Present the dummy tables to show the major tests of the hypotheses or questions advanced.
8. Prepare time-and-cost budgets.

SUMMARY

If the direction of a research project is not clear, it is often wise to follow a two-step research procedure. The first stage is largely exploratory, aimed at formulating hypotheses and developing the specific research design. The general research process contains three major stages:

1. Exploration of the situation.
2. Collection of data.
3. Analysis and interpretation of results.

A research design is the strategy for a study as well as the plan by which the strategy is to be carried out. It specifies the methods and procedures for the collection, measurement, and analysis of data. Unfortunately, there is no simple classification of research designs which covers the variations found in practice. Some of the major perspectives on designs are:

Exploratory versus formalized.

Observational versus survey.

Experimental versus ex post facto.

Descriptive versus causal.

Cross-sectional versus longitudinal.

Case versus statistical.

Field versus laboratory versus simulation.

Exploratory research is appropriate for the total study in subject areas where the developed data are limited. In most other studies, exploration is the first stage of a project and is used to orient the researcher and the study. The objective of exploration is the development of hypotheses, not testing. Formalized studies are those with substantial structure and with specific hypotheses to be tested or research questions to be answered.

Descriptive studies are those used to describe phenomena associated with a subject population or to estimate the proportions of the population that have certain characteristics. Causal studies seek to determine what effect one variable has on others or why certain conditions obtain.

The theoretical ideal of causation can never be demonstrated because of the need for many simplifying assumptions. We can never prove beyond doubt, because the techniques of inductive inference are tools of limited power.

The relationships that occur between two variables may be reciprocal, symmetrical, or asymmetrical. The form of greatest interest to the research analyst, the asymmetrical, takes one of the following forms:

1. Stimulus-response
2. Property-disposition
3. Disposition-behavior
4. Property-behavior

To identify causal connections between variables, the researcher must also recognize and deal effectively with the positional relationships among variables. Those relationships may be classified as:

1. Explanatory variables.
   a Independent variable.
   b Dependent variable.
   c Moderating variables.
2. Extraneous variables.
   a Controlled variables.
   b Uncontrolled variables.
      (1.) Confounding variables.
      (2.) Random variables.
3. Intervening variables.

We test causal hypotheses by seeking to do three things. We (a) measure the covariation among variables; (b) determine the time order relationships among variables; (c) assure that other factors do not confound the explanatory relationships.

The problems of achieving these aims differ somewhat in experimental and ex post facto studies. Where possible, we try to achieve the ideal of the experimental design with its random assignment of subjects, matching of subject characteristics, and manipulation and control of variables. Using these methods and techniques, we measure relationships as accurately and objectively as possible.

SUPPLEMENTAL READINGS

1. Fox, David J. *The Research Process in Education.* New York: Holt, Rinehart & Winston, 1969. Chapter 2 includes a research process model somewhat different from the one in this chapter. Chapter 1 presents a case study in research design.
2. Kerlinger, Fred N. *Foundations of Behavioral Research,* 2d ed. New York: Holt, Rinehart & Winston, 1973. Chapters 22–24 discuss various types of research.
3. Selltiz, Claire; Lawrence S. Wrightsman; and Stuart M. Cook. *Research Methods in Social Relations.* 3d ed. New York: Holt, Rinehart & Winston, 1976. Chapters 4 and 5 discuss various types of research design.
4. Tuckman, Bruce W. *Conducting Educational Research.* New York: Harcourt Brace Jovanovich, 1972. An excellent discussion of the relationships between variables.

DISCUSSION QUESTIONS

1. Distinguish between:
   a   Formal and exploratory studies.
   b   Case and statistical studies.
   c   Field and laboratory studies.
   d   Cross-sectional and longitudinal studies.
   e   Observational and survey studies.
   f   Experimental and ex post facto studies.
   g   Descriptive and causal studies.
2. You have been asked to determine how large corporations go about preparing for contract negotiations with labor unions. Since you know relatively little about this subject, how would you go about finding out? Be as specific as possible.
3. You are the administrative assistant of a division chief in a large manufacturing organization. You and the division chief have just come from the general manager's office, where you were informed that worker morale was unsatisfactory. You had sensed the tension among the workers but had not considered it unusual. The division chief calls you into the office after the meeting and instructs you to investigate morale. Suggest at least three different types of research that might be appropriate in this situation.
4. Using yourself as the subject, give an example of each of the following asymmetrical relationships:
   a   Stimulus-response.
   b   Property-disposition.
   c   Disposition-behavior.
   d   Property-behavior.
5. Classify the relationships between the following variables as symmetrical, asymmetrical, or reciprocal.
   a   Education and income.
   b   Opinion about and purchase of brand X.
   c   Job satisfaction and existence of a company suggestion system.
   d   Sales of product Y and dollars spent advertising product Y.
6. In a causal analysis, how can you tell which variable should be the independent variable and which should be the moderating variable? Why not use more control variables rather than depend on randomization as the means of controlling extraneous variables?
7. Propose one or more hypotheses for each of the following variable pairs, specifying which is the IV and which the DV. Then elaborate the basic hypothesis to include at least one moderating variable, an intervening variable, and one or more extraneous variables.
   a   The Index of Consumer Confidence and the business cycle.
   b   Level of worker output and closeness of supervision of the worker.
   c   Degree of personal friendship between customer and salesperson and the frequency of sales calls on the customer.
8. Researchers seek causal relationships by either experimental or ex post facto research designs.
   a   In what ways are these two approaches similar?
   b   In what ways are they different?

4.   Measurement

Ron Gribbins, assistant plant manager, walked out of the plant manager's office and headed for the coffee machine. He had just been given an assignment that sounded interesting, but he had no idea how to go about it. After getting a cup of coffee, he went into his office, closed the door, and reviewed the situation.

Import competition had been getting stronger, but his employer, the Acme Machine Company, had still been able to do well until recently. Now, however, word had come down from corporate headquarters that productivity at the plant must be improved. Local management was told to assess their situation and make specific improvement proposals within 30 days. Ron was made the chairman of the task force to do this.

The next day, Ron convened his group of four managers and opened the discussion with the questions, "What should we do and what should come first?" Mike Phelps, the industrial engineer, suggested that first they needed a better measurement of their plant's productivity. Wendy Miller, the assistant personnel manager, suggested that they should probably survey their employees to learn more about their morale, job satisfaction, and job motivation. After some discussion, they agreed that some measurement of these factors should be done. All agreed that with the short time they had, it would be necessary to find existing measurement devices that they could use with confidence.

After the meeting, Ron went back to his office, got out his old research methods text and began to reread the chapter on measurement. He believed that he understood the general concept rather well. In everyday usage, one measures when one uses some established yardstick to determine the height, weight, or some other feature of a physical object. One also measures when one judges how well one likes a song, a painting, or the personalities of friends. In a dictionary sense, to measure is "to ascertain the extent, dimensions, quantity, capacity of, especially by comparison with a standard."

One can measure in a rather casual way in daily life, but in research, the requirements are rigorous. As a result, research measurement can be a complex and demanding task.

THE NATURE OF MEASUREMENT

Research measurement is the process by which one tests hypotheses and theories. Researchers deduce from a hypothesis that certain conditions should exist in the real world; then they are measured for these conditions. If found, they lend support to the hypothesis; if they are not found, we conclude that the hypothesis is faulty. An important question at this point is, "Just what does one measure?"

What is measured?

Concepts used in research may be classified as objects or as properties. Objects include the things of ordinary experience, such as tables, people, books, and automobiles. Objects also include things that are not as concrete, for example, genes, attitudes, neutrons, and peer-group pressures. Properties, on the other hand, are the characteristics of the objects. For example, a person's physical properties may be stated in terms of weight, height, posture; psychological properties include attitudes, intelligence; and social properties include leadership ability and class affiliation or status. These and many other properties of that individual can be of measurement interest in a research study.

In a literal sense, researchers do not actually measure objects or properties. They measure indicants of the properties.[1] Thus, researchers actually measure indicants of the properties of objects. Some might feel that this distinction is just an effort to make a simple topic more complex. So it might seem when you are dealing with objective and observable properties. It is easy to observe that A is taller than B and that C participates more than D in a group process. The indicants in these cases are so accepted that one considers the properties to be observed directly. The task is different with such properties as motivation, attitude, creativity, and market potential. Since these cannot be measured directly, one must infer their presence or absence by observing some indicant or pointer measurement. When you begin to make these inferences, you get into an area where not everyone agrees.

Suppose you are analyzing members of a sales force of several hundred people to determine what personal properties make for sales success. Properties such as age, years of experience, number of calls made per week, and so forth, can be measured directly. In contrast, it is not easy to measure

---

[1]Kerlinger views an indicant as "merely a convenient word used to mean something that points to something else." See Fred N. Kerlinger, *Foundations of Behavioral Research*, 2d ed. (New York: Holt, Rinehart & Winston, 1973), p. 432.

properties like motivation to succeed, ability to stand stress, problem-solving ability, and persuasiveness. Not only is it a challenge to measure such constructs, but the researcher may also find little agreement that these are even the proper ones to study. The quality of a study depends on the adequacy of the research design and the appropriateness of the measuring concepts and procedures.

Assume that you are conducting a study of persons who attend an auto show where all of the year's new models are on display. We are interested in learning the male-to-female ratio among attendees. You observe those who enter the show area. If a person appears to be female we record a 1 and if male a 2. Any other symbols such as f and m or # and @ could have been used as long as we know what group the symbol identified.

Researchers might also want to measure the acceptability of the styling of the new Belchfire 8. They interview a sample of visitors and assign their opinions according to the following scale.

What is your opinion of the styling of the Belchfire 8?

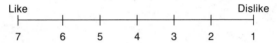

All measurement theorists would call the above opinion rating scale a form of measurement, but some would challenge the male-female classification. Their argument is that measurement must involve quantification. For example, one definition of measurement is "the assignment of numbers to objects to represent amounts or degrees of a property possessed by all of the objects."[2] Here we shall accept the more general view that numbers reflect qualitative as well as quantitative concepts. Researchers strive for quantitative measurement, which is more powerful statistically, but there are different types of scales, each of which is appropriate under given circumstances.

MEASUREMENT SCALES

In measuring, one devises some form of scale and then transfers the observation of property indicants onto this scale. Several types of scales are possible in this situation; the appropriate choice depends on what you assume about the rule of correspondence. Each scale has its own set of underlying assumptions about how the numerals correspond to the real world observations.

Scale classifications employ the characteristics of the real numbers system. The most accepted scale conceptualization is based on the following three characteristics:

1. Numbers are ordered. One number is greater than, less than, or equal to another number.

---

[2]W. S. Torgerson, *Theory and Method of Scaling* (New York: John Wiley & Sons, 1958), p. 19.

2. Differences between numbers are ordered. The difference between any pair of numbers is greater than, less than, or equal to the difference between any other pair of numbers.
3. The number series has a unique origin indicated by the number zero.

Combinations of these characteristics of order, distance, and origin provide the following widely used classification of measurement scales:

Type of scale	Characteristics of scale	Basic empirical operation
Nominal	No order, distance, or origin.	Determination of equality.
Ordinal	Order but no distance or unique origin.	Determination of greater or lesser values.
Interval	Both order and distance but no unique origin.	Determination of equality of intervals or differences.
Ratio	Order, distance, and unique origin.	Determination of equality of ratios.

Nominal scales

Some purists would argue that the use of a nominal scale does not qualify as measurement. In the social sciences and business research, however, nominal scales are probably more widely used than any others. When you use a nominal scale, you partition a set into subsets or categories that are mutually exclusive and collectively exhaustive. For example, in the camping club illustration used in Table 3–1 persons were classified into four unique categories through cross-classification of club membership and degree of absenteeism. Each employee could be placed in one and only one of the four cells.

The counting of members in each group is the only possible arithmetic operation when a nominal scale is employed. If numbers are used the numerals are recognized as labels only and have no quantitative value. Nominal classifications may consist of any number of separate groups so long as the groups are mutually exclusive and collectively exhaustive. Thus, one might class the residents of a city according to their expressed religious preferences in many ways. Classification set "A" given in the accompanying table is not a sound nominal scale because it is neither mutually exclusive nor collectively exhaustive. Set "B" meets these minimum requirements, although the classification may not be the most useful for a given research purpose.

Religious preferences	
A	B
Baptist	Catholic
Catholic	Jewish
Jewish	Protestant
Lutheran	Other
Methodist	None
Presbyterian	
Protestant	

Nominal scales are the least powerful of the four types. They indicate no order or distance relationship and have no arithmetic origin. The scale wastes any information about varying degrees of attitude, skills, understandings, and so on.

Since the only quantification is the number count of cases in each subset, one is restricted to the use of the mode as the measure of central tendency.[3] You can conclude which class has the most members, but that is all. There is no generally used measure of dispersion for nominal scales. Several tests for statistical significance may be utilized, the most common being the chi-square test. For measures of correlation, the contingency coefficient C or one of several other measures may be appropriate. These and other significance tests and measures of association are presented in Chapter 12.

While nominal scales are weak, they are still useful. If one cannot use any other scale, one can almost always classify one set of properties into a set of equivalent classes. This scale is especially valuable in exploratory work, the objective of which is to uncover relationships rather than secure precise measurements. These scales are also widely used in survey and other ex post facto research when data are being classified by major subgroups of the population. Responses may vary with respondents' age, sex, political persuasion, exposure to a certain experience, and so on. Cross-partitions of these and other factors can provide insight into important data patterns.

Ordinal scales

These scales include the characteristics of the nominal scale plus an indicator of order. Ordinal measurement is possible when the transitivity postulate is justified. This postulate states: If a is greater than b and b is greater than c, then a is greater than c.[4] The use of an ordinal scale implies a statement of "greater than" or "less than" (an equality statement is also acceptable) without stating how much greater or less. It is like a rubber yardstick that can stretch varying amounts at different places along its length. Thus, the real difference between ranks "1" and "2" may be more or less than the difference between ranks "2" and "3."

An ordinal concept can be generalized beyond the simple illustration of $a > b > c$. For example, any number of cases can be ranked. While ordinal measurement speaks of "greater than" and "less than" measurements, other relationships may be used—for example, "superior to," "happier than," or

---

[3]It is assumed that the reader has had an introductory statistics course in which measures of central tendency such as the arithmetic mean, median, and mode have been treated. Similarly, we assume that the student is familiar with measures of dispersion such as the standard deviation, range, and interquartile range. For a review of these concepts, refer to almost any introductory statistics text.

[4]While this might intuitively seem to be the case, consider that one might prefer a over b, b over c, yet prefer c over a. These results cannot be scaled ordinally because there is apparently more than one dimension involved.

"above." A third extension of the simple ordinal concept occurs when more than one property is of interest. For example, tasters may be asked to rank varieties of carbonated soft drink by flavor, color, and carbonation as well as a combination of these characteristics. We can secure the combined ranking either by asking the respondent to make such a ranking or by doing our own combining of the individual rankings. The simplest approach is to ask the respondent to make the overall judgment. To develop an overall index, the researcher typically has to add and average ranks for each of the three dimensions. This procedure is technically incorrect and, especially for a given respondent, may yield misleading results. When the number of re-spondents is large, however, these errors tend to "average out." A more sophisticated way to combine a number of dimensions into a total index is to use a multidimensional scale.

The researcher faces another difficulty when combining the rankings of a number of respondents. Here again, it is not uncommon for weighted sums of rank values to be used to provide a combined index. If there are a number of observations, this approach will probably give adequate results, though it is not theoretically correct. A more sophisticated approach is to convert the ordinal scale into an interval scale, the values of which can then be added and averaged. One well-known example is Thurstone's *Law of Comparative Judgment*.[5] The simplest conceptualization of Thurstone's procedure is that the distance between scale positions of two objects A and B depends on the percentage of judgments in which A is preferred to B. This would seem to be a reasonable assumption to make.

Examples of regularly used ordinal scales include opinion and preference scales. The widely used paired-comparison technique also uses an ordinal scale. Because the numbers of this scale have only a rank meaning, the appropriate measure of central tendency is the median. A percentile or quartile measure is used for measuring dispersion. Correlations are re-stricted to various rank-order methods. Measures of statistical significance are technically restricted to that body of methods known as nonparametric methods.[6]

Researchers in the behavioral sciences differ as to whether the more powerful parametric significance tests are appropriate with ordinal mea-sures. One position is that this use of parametric tests is incorrect on both theoretical and practical grounds. This view was strongly argued by Siegel,

> If the measurement is weaker than that of an interval scale, by using parametric methods tests the researcher would "add information" and

---

[5]L. L. Thurstone, *The Measurement of Values* (Chicago: University of Chicago Press, 1959).

[6]Parametric tests are appropriate when the measurement is interval or ratio, and when we can accept certain assumptions about the underlying distribution of the data with which we are working. Nonparametric tests usually involve much weaker assumptions about mea-surement scales (nominal or ordinal), and the assumptions about the underlying distribution of the population are fewer and less restrictive. More on these tests is found in Chapter 13.

thereby create distortions. . . . Moreover, the assumptions which must be made to justify the use of parametric tests usually rest on conjecture and hope. . . .[7]

At the other extreme, some behavioral scientists argue that parametric tests are usually acceptable for ordinal scales on both practical and theoretical grounds. On this point Anderson has written,

> Regarding practical problems, it was noted that the difference between parametric and rank-order tests were not great insofar as significance level and power were concerned. However, only the versatility of parametric statistics meets the everyday needs of psychological research. It was concluded that parametric procedures are the standard tools of psychological statistics although nonparametric procedures are useful minor techniques.
>
> Under this heading of measurement theoretical considerations . . . It was thus concluded that the type of measuring scale used had little relevance to the question of whether to use parametric or nonparametric tests.[8]

Another view, somewhat between these extremes, recognizes that there are risks in using parametric procedures on ordinal type data but these risks are usually not great. Kerlinger expresses this view,

> The best procedure would seem to be to treat ordinal measurements as though they were interval measurements but to be constantly on the alert to the possibility of gross inequality of measurement.[9]

The approach in this book on this controversy is one of neutrality with a tilt toward conservatism. Nonparametric tests are confusingly abundant, but most are simple to calculate, have good power efficiencies, and do not force the researcher to accept the assumptions of parametric testing. On the other hand, parametric tests (for example, analysis of variance) are so versatile, accepted, and understood that they will continue to be used with ordinal data when they seem to approach interval scales in nature.

Ordinal scale with origin. Some properties or dimensions, especially when measuring attitudes and preferences, appear to have natural origins on an ordinal scale. On a scale, the values in the range might be:

$+2$ Strongly like
$+1$ Like somewhat
0 Indifferent
-1 Dislike somewhat
-2 Strongly dislike

---

[7] Sidney Siegel, *Nonparametric Statistics for the Behavioral Sciences* (New York: Mc-Graw-Hill, 1956), p. 32.

[8] Norman A. Anderson, "Scales and Statistics: Parametric and Nonparametric," *Psychological Bulletin*, 58, no. 4, pp. 315–16.

[9] Kerlinger, *Foundations*, p. 441.

In this case, the center of the scale represents a natural origin of zero preference. This form of ordinal scale is treated statistically in the same way as other ordinal scales.

Interval scales

The interval scale has the powers of nominal and ordinal scales plus one additional strength: It incorporates the concept of equality of interval (the distance between 1 and 2 equals the distance between 2 and 3). Calendar time is such a scale. For example, the elapsed time between 3 and 6 A.M. equals the time between 4 and 7 A.M. On the other hand, one can not say that 6 A.M. is twice as late as 3 A.M. because "zero time" is an arbitrary origin. Centigrade and fahrenheit temperature scales are other examples of classical interval scales. With both, there is an arbitrarily determined zero point.

Many attitude scales are presumed to be interval, although such claims are often challenged. Thurstone's differential scale was an early effort to develop such a scale.[10] Users also often treat intelligence scores, semantic differential scales, and many other multipoint scales as being interval in nature. When contentions arise about this practice, it is that the critics believe that the scales should be treated as ordinal. Obviously the data does not know what scale it is, so whether a particular scale is interval or ordinal often is a matter of judgment. The question of scale type affects both the interpretation of results and the form of statistical analysis used. As has been mentioned in the discussion on ordinal scales, there often appears to be little difficulty if one uses parametric statistics on ordinal data.

When a scale is interval, you can use the arithmetic mean as the measure of central tendency. For example, you can compute the average time of first arrival of trucks at a warehouse in the morning, or the average attitude value of union workers versus nonunion workers on certain questions. In like fashion, one uses the standard deviation as the measure of dispersion for arrival times or worker opinions. Product moment correlation, analysis of variance, and the use of the parametric t-tests and F-tests are the statistical procedures of choice.[11]

Ratio scales

These scales incorporate all of the powers of the previous ones plus the concept of absolute zero or origin. The ratio scale represents the actual amounts of a variable. Measures of physical dimensions such as weight, height, distance, and area are examples. In the behavioral sciences, few

---

[10]See Chapter 9 for a discussion of the differential scale.

[11]See Chapter 12 for a discussion of these procedures.

situations satisfy the requirements of the ratio scale—the area of psycho-physics offering some exceptions. In business research, we do find ratio scales in a number of areas. For example, we find money values, population counts, distances, return rates, and amounts of time in a time-period sense.

All statistical techniques mentioned up to this point are usable with ratio scales. In addition, all other manipulations that one can carry out with real numbers can also be carried out with ratio-scale values. Thus, multiplication and division can be used with this scale but not with the others mentioned. Geometric and harmonic means can be used as measures of central tend-ency, and coefficients of variation may also be calculated.

SOURCES OF MEASUREMENT DIFFERENCES

The ideal study should be designed and controlled for precise and unam-biguous measurement of the variables of interest. Since attainment of this ideal is unlikely, we must recognize the sources of potential error and try to eliminate, neutralize, or otherwise deal with them. Much potential error is systematic (results from a bias) while the remainder is random (occurs in an erratic fashion). One authority has pointed out a number of major sources from which measured differences can come.[12]

Assume that you are conducting an ex post facto survey of the residents of a major city. The study concerns the Prince Corporation, a large manufac-turer with headquarters and several major plants located in the city. The objective of the study is to determine the public's opinions about the com-pany and the origin of any generally held adverse opinions.

Ideally, any variation of scores among the respondents would reflect true differences in their opinions about the company. Attitudes toward the firm as an employer, as an ecologically sensitive organization, or as a progressive corporate citizen would be accurately expressed. However, four major error sources may contaminate the results. These sources are the respondent, the situation, the measurer, and the instrument.

The respondent as an error source. Opinion differences will come from relatively stable characteristics of the respondent which affect the scores. Typical of these are employee status, ethnic group membership, social class, and nearness to plants. Many of these dimensions will be anticipated in the design, but others of a less obvious nature will not be. Typical of these latter are specific traumatic experiences which a given respondent may have had with the Prince Corporation or its personnel. The respondent may be reluc-tant to express strong negative feelings or may have little knowledge about Prince but be reluctant to admit ignorance. This reluctance can lead to an interview of "guesses."

---

[12]Selltiz, Wrightsman, and Cook, *Research Methods*, pp. 164–69.

Respondents may also suffer from temporary factors like fatigue, boredom, or anxiety about some other matter; these limit the ability to respond accurately and fully. Hunger, impatience at having been interrupted, or general variations in mood may also have an impact.

Situational factors. These potential problem areas are legion. Any condition that places a strain on the interview can have serious effects on the interviewer-respondent rapport. If another person is present, that person can distort responses by joining in, by distracting, or merely by being present. If the respondents feel that anonymity is not assured, they may be reluctant to express certain feelings. Curbside interviews are unlikely to elicit elaborate responses while in-home interviews more often do.

The measurer as an error source. The interviewer can distort responses by rewording, paraphrasing, or reordering questions. Stereotypes in appearance and action introduce bias. Inflections of voice and conscious or unconscious prompting with smiles, nods, and so forth, may encourage or discourage certain replies. Careless mechanical processing—checking of the wrong response or failure to record full replies—will obviously distort findings. In the data-analysis stage, further errors may be introduced by incorrect coding, careless tabulation, and faulty statistical calculation.

The measurement instrument as an error source. A defective instrument can distort in two major ways. First, it can be too confusing and ambiguous. The use of complex words and syntax beyond respondent comprehension is typical. Leading questions, ambiguous meanings, mechanical defects such as inadequate space for replies, response choice omissions, and poor printing suggest the range of problems.

Another and more elusive type of instrument deficiency is poor sampling of the universe of items of concern. Seldom does the instrument explore all of the potentially important issues. The Prince Corporation study might treat company image in areas of employment and ecology but omit the company management's civic leadership posture, its support of local education programs, or its position on various minority issues. Even if the general issues are studied, the questions may not cover enough aspects of each area of concern. While we might study the Prince Corporation's image as an employer in terms of salary and wage scales, promotion opportunities, and work stability, perhaps such topics as working conditions, company management relations with organized labor, and retirement and other benefit programs should also be included.

Many of the remaining chapters in this book deal with specific measurement problems, but at this point it might be useful to discuss the general requirements for good measurement. While discussion will revolve around the research instrument, it is recognized that successful measurement depends on successfully meeting all of the problems that have just been covered.

THE CHARACTERISTICS OF SOUND MEASUREMENT

What are the characteristics of a good measurement tool? An intuitive answer to this question is that the tool should be an accurate counter or indicator of what we are interested in measuring. In addition, it should be easy and efficient to use. These criteria hold up well when compared to the more scholarly statements of criteria which have been advanced. One view is that there are three major considerations we should use in evaluating a measurement tool. They are *validity, reliability,* and *practicality.* They are described thus:

> Validity refers to the extent to which a test measures what we actually wish to measure. Reliability has to do with the accuracy and precision of a measurement procedure. . . . Practicality is concerned with a wide range of factors of economy, convenience, and interpretability.[13]

In the following sections, we discuss the nature of these qualities and how the researcher can achieve them in his or her measurement procedures.

Validity

Many concepts of validity are mentioned in the research literature, and the number grows as we expand the concern for more scientific measurement. In this text, there are only two major forms—external and internal validity.[14] The external validity of research findings refers to their ability to be generalized across persons, settings, and times; more will be said about this form in Chapters 5 and 10.[15] In this chapter, only internal validity or the ability of a research instrument to measure what it is purported to measure is discussed. That is, does the instrument really measure what its designer claims it does? In this discussion, internal validity will be referred to merely as validity.

Validity is the extent to which differences found with a measuring tool reflect true differences among those being tested. The difficulty in meeting this test is that usually one does not know what the true differences are; if one did, one would not do the measuring in the first place. In the absence of direct knowledge of the dimension being studied, you must face the question, "How can one determine validity without direct confirming knowledge?" A quick answer is to seek other relevant evidence that confirms the

---

[13]Robert L. Thorndike and Elizabeth Hagen, *Measurement and Evaluation in Psychology and Education,* 3d ed. (New York: John Wiley & Sons, 1969), p. 5.

[14]Examples of some of the other concepts of validity are convergent validity, factorial validity, job-analytic validity, synthetic validity, rational validity, and statistical conclusion validity.

[15]Thomas D. Cook and Donald T. Campbell, "The Design and Conduct of Quasi Experiments and True Experiments in Field Settings," which is published as chapter 7 of Marvin D. Dunnette (ed.), *Handbook of Industrial and Organizational Psychology* (Chicago: Rand McNally, 1976), p. 223.

answers found with the measurement device, but this answer leads to a second question, "What constitutes 'relevant evidence'?" There is no quick answer this time. What is relevant depends on the nature of the research problem and the researcher's judgment. One way to approach this question is to organize the answer according to types of internal validity. One widely accepted classification consists of three major forms: *content, criterion-related,* and *construct.*[16]

Content validity.   The *content validity* of a measuring instrument is the extent to which it provides adequate coverage of the topic under study. If the instrument contains a representative sample of the universe of subject matter of interest, then content validity is good. To evaluate the content validity of an instrument, one must first agree on what elements constitute adequate coverage of the problem. In the Prince Corporation study, for example, one must decide what knowledge, attitudes, and opinions are relevant to the measurement of corporate public image. Then determine what forms of these opinions constitute relevant positions on these topics. If the questionnaire adequately covers the topics which have been defined as the relevant dimensions, we conclude that the instrument has good content validity.

The determination of content validity is judgmental and can be approached in several ways. First, the designer may determine the validity through a careful definition of the topic of concern, the items to be scaled, and the scales to be used. This logical process is somewhat intuitive and is unique to each research designer. In fact, the research question hierarchy discussed in Chapter 2 has as its aim the orderly fractionation of the major research question into specific questions that have content validity. A second way to determine content validity is to use a panel of persons to judge how well the instrument meets the standards.

It is important *not* to define "content" too narrowly. For example, if you secure only superficial expressions of opinion in the Prince Corporation public opinion survey it would probably not have adequate content coverage. The research should also probably delve into the processes by which these opinions came about. How did the respondents come to feel as they did, and what is the intensity of feeling?

Criterion-related validity.   This form of validity reflects the success of measures used for some empirical estimating purpose. You may want to predict some outcome or estimate the existence of some current behavior or condition. These cases involve *predictive and concurrent validity,* respectively. They differ only in a time perspective. An opinion questionnaire which correctly forecasts the outcome of a union election has predictive validity. An observational method which correctly categorizes families by current income class has concurrent validity. While these examples appear

---

[16]*Standards for Educational and Psychological Tests and Manuals* (Washington, D.C.: American Psychological Association, 1974), p. 26.

to have rather simple and unambiguous validity criteria, there are difficulties in estimating validity. Consider the problem of estimating family income. There clearly is a knowable true income for every family. However, we may find it difficult to secure this figure. Thus, while the criterion is conceptually clear, it may be unavailable.

In other cases, there may be several criteria, none of which is completely satisfactory. Consider again the problem of judging success in a sales force. A researcher may want to develop a preemployment test that will predict sales success. For this, there may be a number of possible criteria, none of which tells the full story. For example, total sales per salesperson may not adequately reflect territory market potential, competitive conditions, or the different profitability rates of various products. One might rely on the sales manager's overall evaluation, but how unbiased and accurate are those impressions? The researcher must assure that the validity criterion used is itself "valid." One source suggests that any criterion measure must be judged in terms of four qualities: relevance, freedom from bias, reliability, and availability.[17]

A criterion is *relevant* if it is defined and scored in the terms we judge to be the proper measures of salesperson success. For example, if you believe that sales success is adequately measured by dollar sales volume achieved per year, then this is the relevant criterion. If you believe that success must also include a high level of penetration of large accounts, then sales volume alone is not fully relevant. In making this relevance decision, you are eventually thrown back to your judgment in deciding what partial criteria are appropriate indicants of salesperson success.

Freedom from bias is attained when the criterion gives each salesperson an equal opportunity to score well. The sales criterion would be biased if it did not show adjustments for differences in territory potential and competitive conditions.

A *reliable* criterion is stable or reproducible. An erratic criterion (highly variable sales performances from month to month) can hardly be considered a reliable standard by which to judge performances on a sales employment test.

Finally, the information specified by the criterion must be *available*. If not available, how much will it cost and how difficult will it be to secure? The amount of money and effort that should be spent on development of a criterion depends on the importance of the problem for which the test is used.

Once there are test and criterion scores, the problem becomes one of relating them in some way. The usual approach is to correlate them. For example, you might correlate test scores of 40 salespeople who have newly joined the company with first-year sales achievements adjusted to reflect differences in territorial selling conditions.

---

[17]Thorndike and Hagen, *Measurement*, p. 168.

Construct validity. One may also wish to measure or infer the presence of abstract characteristics for which no empirical validation seems possible. Attitude scales and aptitude and personality tests generally concern concepts that fall in this category. Even though this validation situation is much more difficult, there still needs to be some assurance that the measurement has an acceptable degree of validity.

In attempting to determine *construct validity* we associate a set of other propositions with the results received from using the measurement tool. If measurements on the devised scale correlate in a predicted way with these other propositions, we then conclude that there is some construct validity.

In the Prince Corporation study, you may be interested in securing a judgment of "how good a citizen" the corporation is. Variations in respondent ratings may be drastically affected if the respondents have substantial differences in opinion about what constitutes proper corporate citizenship. Respondent Barbara Schoen, for example, may feel that any company is an economic organization designed to make profits for its stockholders. She sees relatively little role for corporations in the wide-ranging social issues of the day. Respondent John Lapp is at the other end of the continuum. He views the corporation as an organization that must become a leader in solving social problems, even at the cost of profits.

Each of these respondent types might clearly understand Prince's role in the community but judge it quite differently in light of their views about what that role should be. If these different views are held, you would theorize that other information about these respondents would be logically compatible with their judgments. You might expect Mrs. Schoen to oppose high corporate taxes, to be critical of increased involvement of government in family affairs, and to believe that a corporation's major responsibility is to its stockholders. Mr. Lapp would be more likely to favor high corporate income taxes, to opt for more governmental involvement in daily life, and to believe that a corporation's major responsibility is a social one.

Respondents may not be consistent on all of these questions because the measurements may be crude and the "theory" may be deficient in some way. When these hypothesized tests do not confirm the measurement scale, you are faced with a two-edged question: Is our measurement instrument invalid, or is our theory invalid? Answers to this question call for more information and/or exercise of judgment.

The three forms of validity have been discussed separately, but they are interrelated, both theoretically and operationally. For example, predictive validity is obviously important for a test designed to predict employee success. In developing such a test, however, you would probably first postulate the factors (constructs) that provide the basis for useful prediction. That is, you would advance a theory about the variable in employee success—an area for construct validity. Finally, in developing the specific items for inclusion in the success prediction test, you would be concerned with how well the specific items sample the full range of each construct (a matter of content validity).

In the corporate image study for the Prince Corporation, both content and construct validity considerations have already been discussed, but how about criterion-related validity? The criteria are less obvious than in the employee success prediction, but there will be judgments made of the quality of evidence about the company's image. The criteria used may be subjective (does the evidence agree with what we believe?) as well as objective (does the evidence agree with other research findings?).

Reliability

The concept of reliability means many things to many people, but in most formulations, the notion of consistency emerges. A measure is reliable to the degree that it supplies consistent results. Reliability is a contributor to validity and is a necessary but not sufficient condition for validity. The relationship between reliability and validity can be simply illustrated with the use of a bathroom scale. If the scale measures your weight correctly (using a concurrent criterion such as a scale known to be accurate) then it is both reliable and valid. If it consistently overweighs you by six pounds, then the scale is reliable but not valid. If the scale measures erratically from time to time, then it is not reliable and therefore cannot be valid.

Reliability is concerned with estimates of the degree to which a measurement is free of random or unstable error. It is not as valuable as validity determination, but it is much easier to assess. It is also often the only one which we can assess. Reliable instruments can at least be used with some confidence that a number of transient and situational factors are not interfering. Reliable instruments are robust; they work well at different times under different conditions. This distinction of time and condition is the basis for two frequently used perspectives on reliability—stability and equivalence.

Stability. A measure is said to be stable if you can secure consistent results with repeated measurements of the same person with the same instrument. For example, an observation procedure would be stable if it gives the same reading on a particular person when repeated one or more times. It is often possible to repeat observations on a subject and to compare them for consistency. The major problem with this approach is that when there is much time between measurements, there is a chance for situational factors to change, thereby affecting the observations. This would appear incorrectly as a drop in reliability of the measurement process.

Stability measurement in survey situations is more difficult and less attractive than for observation studies. While you can observe a certain action repeatedly, you usually can resurvey only once. This leads to a test-retest arrangement—with comparisons between the two tests to determine how reliable they are. Two difficulties occur, in addition to the time delay mentioned with observation study. First, if the retest is given too quickly, the respondent will remember the answers already given and repeat them. This will result in a biased higher reliability indication than is justified. On the other hand, the test-retest process itself may introduce bias. For example, the respondent may become savvy about the testing purpose and procedure or at least exhibit less anxiety on the retest. Another condition might be that the first test sensitizes the respondent to the subject, who may then go on to learn more or form new and different opinions before the retest. Then, too, it may just happen that the opinions change from situational influence between the test and the retest. In all of these cases, the tendency is to produce a downward bias in the stability scores.

A suggested approach for reducing these distortions of test-retest results is to extend the time interval between test and the retest in order to reduce the effect of the initial measurement. In psychological testing, the suggested delay is from two weeks to a month. While this may help in one respect, it hinders in another. The longer the time span, the more the chance that outside factors will contaminate the measurement and distort the stability score. The result of all of these problems is that stability measurement through the test-retest approach is less well regarded in research circles than it once was. More interest has centered on equivalence.

Equivalence. A second perspective on reliability considers how much error may be introduced by different investigators (in observation) or different samples of items being studied (in questioning or scales). Thus, while stability is concerned with personal and situational fluctuations from one time to another, equivalence is concerned with variations at one point in time among observers and samples of items. A good way to test for the equivalence of measurements by different observers is to compare their scoring of the same event.

The test items to be included in any instrument are limited in number and chosen in a somewhat arbitrary fashion. The major interest typically is not how respondents differ from item to item but how well a given set of items will categorize individuals. That is, there may be many differences in response between two samples of items, but if a person is classified the same way by each test, then our tests have a good equivalency.

One tests for item sample equivalence by using alternative or *parallel tests* administered to the same persons at roughly the same time. The results of the two tests are then correlated. A second method, the *split-half* technique can be used when the measuring tool has a number of similar questions or statements to which the subject can respond. The instrument is administered to the subject, and then the results are separated by item into two randomly selected halves. These are then compared. If the results are similar, the instrument is said to have high reliability in an equivalence sense; however, the longer the test length in the split-half test, the higher the reliability. The Spearman-Brown correction formula is used to adjust for the effect of test length and to measure the split-half equivalence.

Another approach to the problem of equivalence holds that random rather than split halves should be used. This view emphasizes internal consistency and *homogeneity*. The two most widely used homogeneity indexes are Cronbach's Coefficient Alpha and the Kuder-Richardson Formula 20. Both give average split-half correlation for all possible ways of dividing the test into two parts.

Improving reliability. One can improve reliability if external sources of variation are minimized. For example, one can standardize the conditions under which the measurement takes place. You can achieve enhanced equivalence through improved investigator consistency by using only well-trained, supervised, and motivated persons to conduct the research. Much can be done to improve equivalence by broadening the sample of items used. You can do this by adding similar questions to the questionnaire or adding more observers or occasions to an observation study.

With measurement instruments such as achievement, attitude, or employment tests, we can often increase equivalence by improving the internal consistency of the test. This approach requires the assumption that a high total score reflects high performance and a low total score low performance. One selects the extreme scorers, say the top 20 percent and bottom 20 percent, for individual analysis. By this process, you can distinguish those items that differentiate high and low scorers. Items that have little discriminatory power can then be dropped from the test.

Researchers decide whether reliability is or is not adequate in terms of the objectives and the basic variability of the data. In terms of the objectives, are you interested in some rough ordering of subjects? If so, then a relatively crude instrument will probably suffice. For more precise estimation, reliability standards must be more demanding. In a relatively homogeneous population, a crude measure appears to be reliable because variations in the data are limited. Hence, any reliable instrument should score higher on reliability than would be the case in a heterogeneous population.

Practicality

The scientific requirements of a project call for the measurement process to be reliable and valid, while the operational requirements call for it to be practical. Thorndike and Hagen define practicality in terms of economy, convenience, and interpretability.[18] While they are referring chiefly to the development of educational and psychological tests, their conclusions hold for other measurement instruments as well.

Economy. Some tradeoff is usually needed between the ideal research project and that which the budget can afford. Instrument length is one area where economic pressures are quickly felt. More items give more reliability, but in the interest of limiting the interview or observation time (therefore costs), we hold the item number down. The choice of data collection method is also often dictated by economic factors. The use of long-distance telephone surveys, for example, has been strongly influenced by the rising costs of

---

[18]Thorndike and Hagen, *Measurement*, p. 199.

personal interviewing. In standardized tests, the cost of test materials alone can be such a significant expense that it encourages multiple reuse. Add to this the need for fast and economical scoring, and we see why computer scoring on special answer sheets is so attractive.

Convenience. A measuring device passes the *convenience* test if it is easy to administer. For instance, a questionnaire with a set of detailed but clear instructions, with examples, is substantially easier to complete correctly than one that lacks these features. In a well-prepared study, it is not uncommon for the interviewer instructions to be several times longer than the interview guide. Naturally, the more complex the concepts being dealt with, the greater the need for clear and complete instructions. We can also make the instrument easier to administer by giving close attention to the layout of the measuring instrument. Too numerous are the instrument formats that are the designer's dream and the user's nightmare. Crowding of material, poor reproductions of illustrations, and the carryover of items from one page to the next all make completion of the instrument more difficult.

Interpretability. This consideration is particularly important when persons other than the designers of the test must interpret the results. This situation is usually but not exclusively found with standardized tests. In such cases there is a need for a number of aids such as the following:

1. A statement of the functions which the test was designed to measure and of the general procedures by which it was developed.
2. Detailed instructions for administering the test.
3. Scoring keys and specific instructions for scoring the test.
4. Norms for appropriate reference groups.
5. Evidence about the reliability of the test.
6. Evidence on the intercorrelations of subscores.
7. Evidence on the relationship of the test to other evidence.
8. Guides for using the test and interpreting results.

THE DEVELOPMENT OF MEASUREMENT TOOLS

Many concepts in business are easy to measure. For example, if you study wages and worker-benefit payments, you find they are stated in dollar amounts and accurate records are kept on such matters. In other instances, however, researchers want to measure such concepts as motivation, sales effectiveness, and the like. This is not as easy and these concepts must be operationally defined by developing a special measurement procedure. One authority suggests that this process involves four steps: (1) imagery; (2) concept specification; (3) selection of indicators; and (4) formation of indexes.[19]

---

[19]Paul F. Lazarsfeld, "Evidence and Inference in Social Research," in David Lerner, *Evidence and Inference* (Glencoe, Ill.: The Free Press, 1950), pp. 108–117.

Image. The first task is to conceive of the constructs of interest, probably somewhat vague at the beginning. For example, when thinking about the Prince Corporation's image, researchers will have some notion that it concerns the company's reputation among various groups. But what aspects might make up such an image? In developing these thoughts, one must enumerate the specific ways the corporation may be involved with various groups and what the nature of each of these involvements is.

Concept specification. The second task is to break down the original image into its various components. For example, in the Prince Corporation study, the concept of "corporate image" might be divided into four parts:

1. The corporate citizen—i.e., how well Prince is thought of as a contributor to the communities in which it has establishments.
2. Ecological responsibility—i.e., how well Prince disposes of its waste products and protects the environment.
3. The employer—i.e., how well Prince is regarded as a place in which to work.
4. The supplier of consumer needs—i.e., how Prince products and services are viewed by consumers.

In place of this more or less intuitive approach, factor analysis or similar statistical techniques can be used to determine concept components. One such study, using cluster analysis, concluded that there are six major dimensions of company image: product reputation, employer role, customer treatment, corporate leadership, defense contribution, and concern for individuals.[20]

Indicator selection. Once the dimensions have been set, the indicators by which to measure each concept must be developed. Since there is seldom a perfect or absolute measure of a concept, several possibilities should be considered. Indicators can be questions, statistical measures, or other scoring devices.

With the Prince Corporation example, measurement of "corporate citizenship" could be achieved by asking a cross section of the general public a single question such as:

> Which of the following best describes the reputation of the Prince Corporation as a corporate citizen in our community? (Please check one)
> _____ The company is a leader in these activities.
> _____ The company is a strong supporter, but not a leader in these activities.
> _____ The company is an average supporter of these activities.
> _____ The company is a below average supporter of these activities.

This question is a single-scale index of Prince's corporate citizenship. Single-scale indexes are often criticized as being less reliable than multiple factor

---

[20]Reuben Cohen, "The Measurement of Corporate Images," in John W. Riley, Jr., ed., *The Corporation and its Publics* (New York: John Wiley & Sons, 1963), pp. 48–63.

indexes. This is often a fair criticism, since one item may not capture the variety of dimensions that could be included in a term. Even when using the total concept of "corporate citizenship" in the question, it is not unusual to find people thinking of one dimension or another, for example, charity support, political activity, or the like. It is more desirable to specify the number of dimensions to be included in "corporate citizenship" and then combine them into a summary index.

To develop such a summary index, first construct scales to measure each aspect of corporate citizenship. For example, ask a cross section of the public to rate the Prince Corporation on the following:

How would you rate the Prince Corporation as a:

	Good				Poor
			(please check)		
1. Supporter of civic fund drives	————	————	————	————	————
2. Supporter of higher education	————	————	————	————	————
3. Supporter of good local government	————	————	————	————	————
4. Supporter of civic development projects	————	————	————	————	————

Formation of indexes. When there are several dimensions of a concept, or different measures for each dimension, it may be desirable to combine them into a single index. Lazarsfeld points out that each "individual indicator has only a probability relation to what we really want to know."[21] That is, any single indicator may not be a fair representation of what is being measured. Use of more than one indicator lends stability to the scores and probably improves their validity, too.

One simple way to achieve such improvements is to provide scale values to the responses and then combine the scores. For example, combine the four scale items on the Prince Corporation as a corporate citizen into a single index. One way would be to assign a value to each response possibility ranging from 1 for a poor evaluation to a 5 for a good response. An average of these scores would give a more reliable, and probably a more valid, measure of the company's citizenship image than would the single question.

Additional sets of scales can be devised to measure how the Prince Corporation is viewed on ecological responsibility, employer image, and as a supplier of consumer needs. These sets of scales could also be combined into summary scores. Finally, these summary measures for the four dimensions of corporate image might be again combined, and even weighted, to arrive at an overall score which could be called the corporate image index. Such an index, as well as its various subscores, might be compared to indexes of other corporations which have been similarly measured.

---

[21]Lazarsfeld, "Evidence and Inference," p. 112.

Back at Acme Machine Company

Earlier, Ron Gribbins was pondering on how or where to find some useful tools by which to measure employee morale, job satisfaction, and motivation at Acme Machine. In reviewing his old business research book he came across a reference to this publication:

> Martin Patchen, *Some Questionnaire Measures of Employee Motivation and Morale*, Monograph No. 41 (Ann Arbor, Mich.: Institute for Social Research, University of Michigan, 1965).

This looked like just what he needed so he went to the university library and found the monograph. The table of contents indicated that the monograph included indexes on:

Interest in Work Innovation.

Job Motivation.

Acceptance of Job Changes.

Willingness to Disagree with Supervisors.

Identification with the Work Organization.

These looked interesting enough that Ron checked out the book for further study. The research that formed the basis for the Patchen study had been conducted at five geographically separate units of the Tennessee Valley Authority, three divisions of an electronics company, and five departments of an appliance manufacturing company. The procedure for developing the measures was first to hold a number of informal interviews with supervisory and nonsupervisory employees. From the knowledge acquired in this way, the researchers constructed a number of questions. These were then pretested and revised twice on separate groups of TVA employees. Out of this process came a six-item questionnaire on interest in work innovation shown in Figure 4–1. This instrument as well as the others were completed by employees of the three companies. Reliability of the Index of Interest in Work Innovation was measured by a test-retest of individual questions. The retest was made about one month after the first test. Correlating the test-retest scores question-by-question gave the following results:

Question	r
Q1	.72
Q2	.72
Q3	.64
Q4	.67
Q5	.54
Q6	.85

The researchers measured criterion-based validity by comparing worker scores on the six questions to ratings of the same workers by their supervisors. For example, supervisors were asked to "think of specific instances where employees in their units had suggested new or better ways of doing

FIGURE 4–1   Interest in work innovation index*

1. In your kind of work, if a person tries to change his usual way of doing things, how does it generally turn out?

   (1)_____Usually turns out worse; the tried and true methods work best in my work.
   (3)_____Usually doesn't make much difference.
   (5)_____Usually turns out better; our methods need improvement.

2. Some people prefer doing a job in pretty much the same way because this way they can count on always doing a good job. Others like to go out of their way in order to think up new ways of doing things. How is it with you on your job?

   (1)_____I always prefer doing things pretty much in the same way.
   (2)_____I mostly prefer doing things pretty much in the same way.
   (4)_____I mostly prefer doing things in new and different ways.
   (5)_____I always prefer doing things in new and different ways.

3. How often do you try out, on your own, a better or faster way of doing something on the job?

   (5)_____Once a week or more often.
   (4)_____Two or three times a month.
   (3)_____About once a month.
   (2)_____Every few months.
   (1)_____Rarely or never.

4. How often do you get chances to try out your own ideas on the job, either before or after checking with your supervisor?

   (5)_____Several times a week or more.
   (4)_____About once a week.
   (3)_____Several times a month.
   (2)_____About once a month.
   (1)_____Less than once a month.

5. In my kind of job, it's usually better to let your supervisor worry about new or better ways of doing things.

   (1)_____Strongly agree.
   (2)_____Mostly agree.
   (4)_____Mostly disagree.
   (5)_____Strongly disagree.

6. How many times in the past year have you suggested to your supervisor a different or better way of doing something on the job?

   (1)_____Never had occasion to do this during the past year.
   (2)_____Once or twice.
   (3)_____About three times.
   (4)_____About five times.
   (5)_____Six to ten times.
   (6)_____More than ten times had occasion to do this during the past year.

*Numbers in parentheses preceding each response category indicate the score assigned to each response.

Source: Martin Patchen, *Some Questionnaire Measures of Employee Motivation and Morale,* Monograph No. 41 (Ann Arbor, Mich.: Institute for Social Research, The University of Michigan, 1965), pp. 15–16.

the job. They then ranked employees they personally knew on 'looking out for new ideas.' "[22] The median correlation between index scores and the supervisor ratings was about .35. At TVA, where there was an active suggestion system in operation, they also found that the index scores of suggestors were significantly higher than those of nonsuggestors.

TABLE 4–1 Relation of scores on interest in work innovation index* to scores on other job-related variables,† for 90 work groups at TVA (Pearson product-moment correlation coefficient, r)

Variable name

1. Job Difficulty	.44‡
2. Identification with Own Occupation	.39‡
3. Control over Work Methods	.29‡
4. Perceived Opportunity for Achievement	.28‡
5. Feedback on Performance	.19
6. Control Over Goals in Work	.13
7. Need for Achievement§	.06
8. Pressure from Peers to Do a Good Job	−.05
9. General Job Motivation	.36‡
10. Willingness to Disagree with Supervisors	.36‡
11. Acceptance of Changes in Work Situation	.12
12. Identification with TVA	.00
13. Overall Satisfaction (with pay, promotion, supervisors, and peers)	.21‖

*The shorter three-item Index B was used for these correlations.
†Variables listed are all indices; each index is composed of several specific questions.
‡$p < .01$, 2-tailed t-test.
§This is the Achievement Risk Preference Scale developed by P. O'Conner and J. W. Atkinson (1960).
‖$p < .05$, 2-tailed t-test.

Source: Patchen, *Some Questionnaire Methods*, p. 24.

Construct validity was evaluated by comparing scores on the Interest in Work Innovation Index to other job-related variables. Group means on the Index were computed for 90 work groups at TVA. These means were then correlated with group scores on other variables which were hypothesized to relate to interest in innovation. The results are shown in Table 4–1.

---

[22]Patchen, *Some Questionnaire Methods*, p. 17.

The researchers concluded that, "the Index of Interest in Work Innovation, while a rough one, shows adequate reliability and sufficient evidence of validity to warrant its use in making rough distinctions among groups of people (or among units)."[23] In addition they tested a short version of the Index (items 1, 5, and 6) and found its validity to be almost equal to that of the longer form.

Job motivation. While Ron Gribbins felt that the University of Michigan's Interest in Work Innovation Index would be useful, he was also interested in other questions about the workers. In particular, he wanted to get some indication of worker motivation. Motivation is sometimes inferred from other evidence such as productivity data. Often, however, it is difficult if not impossible to measure motivation in this manner. Then some direct effort at assessing one's job motivation may be helpful.

In the Michigan study, three variations of an Index of Job Motivation were developed, using two, three, and four questions respectively. The questions used are shown in Figure 4–2. Test-retest reliability calculations were conducted in the same way as described with the work innovation index. Criterion-related validity was tested by correlating job absenteeism (negative) with supervisory ratings (positive). Construct validity was evaluated by comparisons in much the same way as with the Innovation Index. In summary, Patchen concluded, ". . . the data show that the indices of job motivation have fairly good ability to distinguish among individuals or groups when there is considerable variation in index scores and/or on the criteria being predicted. The indices show less ability to detect fine differences within units where job motivation is relatively homogeneous."[24] For example, there was less discrimination between scores of workers in repetitive production jobs than with those found in engineering departments.

Having reviewed Patchen's Michigan research study with its derived indexes, Ron's task is to decide whether to use what he has found, search for more, or develop his own measurement devices. There is a strong tendency for managers and researchers to assume that they need a device tailored to their unique situation, and that there is no alternative but to devise their own. This approach suffers from several weaknesses. First, it is costly and time consuming if one does the job properly. Then, too, there is a tendency to ignore questions of reliability and validity. Too often people accept conclusions of face validity only. That is, one looks over the instruments and judges intuitively that they will be satisfactory. Finally, with unique measurements, there is no comparative evidence from other studies by which to calibrate the findings.

If Ron searches further, he will find that there are a number of established measurement devices that might fit his needs. Most of these are copyrighted and available from commercial sources.

---

[23]Patchen, *Some Questionnaire Methods*, p. 25.

[24]Patchen, *Some Questionnaire Methods*, p. 39.

FIGURE 4–2   Job motivation index

1. On most days on your job, how often does time seem to drag for you?

    (1)_____About half the day or more
    (2)_____About one-third of the day
    (3)_____About one-quarter of the day
    (4)_____About one-eighth of the day
    (5)_____Time never seems to drag

2. Some people are completely involved in their job—they are absorbed in it night and day. For other people, their job is simply one of several interests. How involved do you feel in your job?

    (1)_____Very little involved; my other interests are more absorbing
    (2)_____Slightly involved
    (3)_____Moderately involved; my job and my other interests are equally absorbing to me
    (4)_____Strongly involved
    (5)_____Very strongly involved; my work is the most absorbing interest in my life

3. How often do you do some extra work for your job which isn't really required of you?

    (5)_____Almost every day
    (4)_____Several times a week
    (3)_____About once a week
    (2)_____Once every few weeks
    (1)_____About once a month or less

    (This question was used in the electronics company and in the appliance company, but not at TVA)

4. Would you say you work harder, less hard, or about the same as other people doing your type of work at (name of organization)?

    (5)_____Much harder than most others
    (4)_____A little harder than most others
    (3)_____About the same as most others
    (2)_____A little less hard than most others
    (1)_____Much less hard than most others

    (This question was used in the electronics company and in the appliance company, but not at TVA)

SUMMARY

While people measure things in a rather casual way in daily life, research measurement is more precise and controlled. To measure things, one settles for measuring properties of the objects rather than the objects themselves. For example, an event is measured in terms of its duration. What happened during it, who was involved, and the like, are all properties of the event. To be more precise, what are measured are indicants of the properties. Thus, for duration, one measures the number of hours and minutes recorded. For what happened, one uses some system to classify types of activities that occurred. When involved in measurement, we typically use some sort of scale to classify or quantify the data collected.

There are four major scale types. In increasing order of power, they are nominal, ordinal, interval, and ratio. Nominal scales merely classify without indicating either order, distance, or unique origin. Ordinal scales indicate magnitude relationships of more than and less than but indicate no distance or unique origin. Interval scales have both order and distance value but no unique origin. Ratio scales have all of these features.

Instruments may yield incorrect readings of an indicant for a number of reasons. These may be classified according to major error sources: (1) the respondent or subject; (2) situational factors; (3) the measurer; and (4) the instrument.

Sound measurement must meet the tests of validity, reliability, and practicality. Validity is the most critical and indicates the degree to which an instrument measures what it is supposed to measure. Three major forms of validity are often mentioned. Content validity exists to the degree that a measure provides an adequate reflection of the topic under study. Its determination is primarily judgmental and intuitive. Criterion-related validity relates to our ability to predict some outcome or estimate the existence of some current condition. Construct validity is the most complex and abstract. A measure has construct validity to the degree that it conforms to predicted correlations with other theoretical propositions.

A measure is reliable if it provides consistent results. It is a partial contributor to validity, but a measurement tool may be reliable without being valid. Two major forms of reliability are stability and equivalence. A measure meets the third criterion, practicality, if it is economical, convenient, and interpretable.

Development of measurement tools can be viewed as a four-stage process of (1) concept development; (2) specification of concept dimensions; (3) selection of observable indicators; and (4) combination of these indicators into indexes.

SUPPLEMENTAL READINGS

1. Dunnette, Marvin D., ed. *Handbook of Industrial and Organizational Psychology.* Chicago: Rand McNally, 1976. Chapter 7, by Thomas D. Cook and Donald T. Campbell, is entitled, "The Design and Conduct of Quasi-Experiments and True Experiments in Field Settings." It is especially recommended to the serious student of measurement.

2. Kerlinger, Fred N. *Foundations of Behavioral Research,* 2d ed. New York: Holt, Rinehart & Winston, 1973. Chapters 25, 26, and 27 cover the nature of measurement as well as reliability and validity.

3. Lazarsfeld, Paul F.; Ann K. Pansanella; and Morris Rosenberg. *Continuities in the Language of Social Research.* New York: The Free Press, 1972. Section

I consists of 14 papers concerned with concepts, indexes, classification, and typologies.

4. Leege, David C., and Wayne L. Francis. *Political Research.* New York: Basic Books, 1974. Chapter 6 has a good discussion on index construction.
5. Thorndike, Robert L., and Elizabeth Hagen. *Measurement and Education in Psychology and Education.* 3d ed. New York: John Wiley & Sons, 1969. Thorough discussion of measurement as it applies to the development of educational tests.

DISCUSSION QUESTIONS

1. What do we measure when we measure? What can we measure about the four objects listed below? Be as specific as possible.
   a   Laundry detergent.
   b   Employees.
   c   Factory output.
   d   Job satisfaction.
2. a   What are the essential differences among nominal, ordinal, interval and ratio scales?
   b   How do these differences affect the statistical analysis techniques we can use?
3. Below are listed some objects of varying degrees of abstraction. Suggest properties of each of these objects that can be measured by each of the four basic types of scales.
   a   Store customers.
   b   Voter attitudes.
   c   Hardness of steel alloys.
   d   Preference for a particular common stock.
   e   Profitability of various divisions in a company.
4. What are the four major sources of measurement error? Illustrate by example how each of these might affect measurement results in a face-to-face interview situation.
5. Do you agree or disagree with the following statements? Explain.
   a   Validity is more critical to measurement than is reliability.
   b   Content validity is the most difficult type of validity to determine.
   c   A valid measurement is reliable but a reliable measurement may not be valid.
   d   Stability and equivalence are essentially the same thing.
6. You have been asked to design an instrument by which students can evaluate the quality and value of their various courses. How might you try to assure that your instrument has:
   a   Stability.
   b   Equivalence.
   c   Content validity.
   d   Predictive validity.
   e   Construct validity.
7. A new book entitled, *The 100 Best Companies to Work for in America* has just been published. In their study of companies, the authors chose five dimensions and rated each company on them, giving one to five stars to a firm on

each dimension. What five dimensions would you use if you had designed their rating system?

8. You have been asked to develop an index of student morale at your school.
   a What constructs or concepts might you employ?
   b Choose several of the major concepts and specify their dimensions.
   c Select observable indicators that you might use to measure these dimensions.
   d How would you compile these various dimensions into a single index?
   e How would you judge the reliability and/or validity of these measurements?

APPENDIX 'MUSHINESS INDEX' DEVISED FOR SURVEYS ON FOREIGN POLICY (By Jeffrey H. Birnbaum)
Staff Reporter of THE WALL STREET JOURNAL

NEW YORK—A lot of public opinion polls are mostly mush.

A leading survey group doesn't only acknowledge this, but proposes to quantify it. Yankelovich, Skelly & White Inc., a public attitude research concern here, has devised a new polling method that it says will show how firm or "mushy" a person's opinion is. It's called the "mushiness index."

Pollsters have for years conceded that the people they question are quick to offer an opinion, but sometimes are equally quick to change it. "They flip-flop like a fish," Daniel Yankelovich, chairman, says. The new index, in effect, is designed to ferret out "closet undecideds."

Yankelovich will apply the index, which comprises four questions, to all foreign and some domestic policy surveys. The questions, answered on a scale of one to six, determine how well informed, personally affected, deeply considered and generally stable is an interviewee's opinion on a particular issue.

Americans generally are mushier on topics that affect them indirectly and about which they have limited knowledge. A test poll last December found that 63% of the 1,000 people queried were firm in their views about making abortions illegal except when a woman's life is endangered. But 63% were "mushy" or "very mushy" about whether to sign an arms limitation treaty with the Soviet Union unless the Russians withdraw from Afghanistan. "There are some people who don't know where Afghanistan is," said Florence Skelly, president.

The most tantalizing potential use for the index is in preelection polling. Although mushiness questions haven't yet been developed for the purpose, Yankelovich believes the concept can and probably will be applied when the right questions are prepared and tested. The company has spent $150,000 and two years researching the current four-question mushiness index alone.

Other pollsters are enthusiastic about the index. Robert Teeter, a Republican pollster from Detroit, says he intends to use it "right away. If the index is good then it ought to be used for a lot of things," he said in an interview.

Mr. Yankelovich believes that in two to five years, measurements of mushiness might become a staple for many kinds of surveys.

Some doubt, however, that the index will catch on so widely. Everett Ladd of the Roper Center for Public Opinion Research, a library for polls at the University of Connecticut, says: "It will be relatively rare that any commercial polling operation will employ the index." The reason is the extra cost of expanding the survey length. All four index questions would be asked after each policy query.

Yankelovich argues that the additional expense for the index is marginal, although polls might need to be shortened to leave room for the mushiness questions. A full-scale national telephone survey can cost between $50,000 and $70,000. The addition of the index might bring that cost closer to $70,000 than $50,000 and might force the elimination of one out of 16 questions, an official of Yankelovich, a unit of Reliance Group Inc., says.

The mushiness index will aid policy makers to analyze poll results. In a survey on establishing diplomatic relations with Cuba, the true sentiment of the population appears to be belied by a simple "favor" or "opposed" question.

In the December survey, 47% favored establishing ties with Cuba compared to 39% opposed. Of those who were firm in their convictions, those opposing diplomatic relations outnumbered those favoring the issue by two to one. In addition, the very mushy group tended to favor diplomatic relations. Therefore, Yankelovich concludes, very compelling evidence must be produced to move the country to support the ties, even though a plurality say they favor the ties.

Concern about the volatility of opinion isn't new. In 1947 George Gallup, founder of the Gallup poll, criticized surveys for failing to distinguish between snap and others that are deeply held. Some polls, particularly about consumer product preferences, ask probing, open-ended questions to solve this problem. But such polls are very costly and rarely are applied to public policy questions. The mushiness index is a cheaper shorthand substitute for this complex test.

If the mushiness index works, it might boost the image of pollsters that was tarnished during the 1980 presidential contest. Most polls showed the election neck and neck just days before the Reagan landslide victory. Mr. Yankelovich says misperception of the number of truly undecided voters is "casting some ambiguity over the creditability of the (polling) field."

---

5. Experimentation

Betty White thought about her new assignment as she drove home that Tuesday evening. She had gone to work at Big Top Food Corporation directly from graduate school a year ago. She had now finished her training assignments and had just been made the director of research for the company. This was a new position that John Paxon, president of the company, had just established.

As she was telling her husband, Jed, about her interview with Mr. Paxon she recalled, "Paxon is trained in the physical sciences like you are, Jed. He feels that business management should become more scientific and he is making a number of moves to change the company culture in that direction."

"What do you think Paxon expects from you?" asked Jed.

"Well, as he explained it to me, I should search out research findings on any topic that might help our managers make better decisions. I should also encourage managers to ask for research help so they can improve the quality of their decisions. I should also design much of the research, although most of the studies will be done by outside suppliers."

"Have you thought about doing experimental research?" asked Jed.

"I don't think experiments are very practical in business and the social sciences. We can not control things like you can in the laboratory," was Betty's reply.

"I disagree, Betty. All of us experiment all the time. When you went shopping last Saturday, you tried on a number of dresses before you bought one. You were experimenting. Any time we try out new ideas we are experimenting. I admit these are casual experiments without scientific controls; but we can make them more scientific, and experimental results are usually more valid than results from other designs. It certainly is more useful to do research that measures actual sales impact than it is to ask people what they think the impact might be."

Next morning, Betty recalled Jed's words when she began planning for her next interview with Mr. Paxon. "Maybe I ought to look into experimentation. Jed could be right," she thought. That afternoon she went to the university library to do some reading on experimentation. Following is a summary of what she learned.

WHAT IS EXPERIMENTATION?

Experiments are studies whose implementation involves intervention by the researcher beyond that required for measurement. The usual intervention is to manipulate some variable in a setting and observing how it affects the subjects being studied, e.g., people or physical entities. The researcher manipulates the independent or explanatory variable and then observes whether the hypothesized dependent variable is affected by the intervention.

An example of such an intervention is the study of bystanders and thieves.[1] In this experiment, students were asked to come to an office where they had an opportunity to see a fellow student steal some money from a receptionist's desk. The stealing, of course, was done by a confederate of the experimenter. The major hypothesis concerned the question of whether persons observing a theft would be more likely to report it (1) if they observed the crime alone, or (2) in the company of someone else. The independent or explanatory variable, therefore, was the state of either being alone when observing the theft or being in the company of another person. The dependent variable was whether or not the subjects reported observing the crime. The results indicated that bystanders were more likely to report the theft if they observed it alone rather than in another person's company.

Conclusion drawing. On what grounds did the researchers conclude that persons who were alone were more likely to report crimes observed than people in the company of others? Three types of considerations formed the basis for this conclusion. First, there must be an agreement between independent and dependent variables. The presence or absence of one is associated with the presence or absence of the other. Thus, more reports of the theft (DV) came from alone observers (IV_1) than from paired observers (IV_2).

Beyond this correlation of independent and dependent variables, the time order of the occurrence of the variables must be considered. The dependent variable should not precede the independent variable. They may occur more or less simultaneously or the independent variable must occur before the dependent variable. This requirement is of little concern in this

---

[1]Bibb Latane and J. M. Darley, *The Unresponsive Bystander: Why Doesn't He Help?* (New York: Appleton-Century-Crofts, 1970) pp. 69–77. Research into the responses of bystanders who witness crimes has been stimulated by an incident of some years ago when a young New York woman, Kitty Genovese, was chased, attacked, and stabbed to death in the presence of at least 38 witnesses who refused to come to her aid or even promptly summon authorities.

experiment since it is unlikely that persons could report a theft prior to observing it.

The third and important support for the conclusion comes when researchers are confident that *other extraneous variables did not influence the dependent variable.* The major method of assuring that these other variables are not the source of influence is to control their ability to confound the planned comparison. Under laboratory conditions, standardized conditions as a means of control can be arranged. For example, the crime observation experiment was carried out in an office actually set up as a laboratory. The entire event was staged without the observers' knowledge. The receptionist whose money was to be stolen was instructed to speak and act in a specific way. Only the receptionist, observers, and the "criminal" were in the office. The same process was repeated with each run of the experiment.

While such controls are important, further precautions are needed to assure that the results achieved reflect the influence of the independent variable alone on the dependent variable. Readers may recognize this as the problem of validity already discussed in Chapter 4.

Validity and experimentation

Even when an experiment is the ideal research design, it is not without problems. There is always a question about whether the results are true. We have previously defined validity in terms of whether a measure does what is claimed for it. While there are a number of different types of validity, here only the two major varieties are considered. *Internal validity*—do the conclusions we draw about a demonstrated experimental relationship truly imply cause? *External validity*—does an observed causal relationship generalize across persons, settings, and times?[2] In each of these types of validity, there are a number of specific subspecies which we need to guard against.

Internal validity. While there are many threats to internal validity we will consider seven major ones here.

1. History. During the time that an experiment is taking place, some events may occur that confuse the relationship being studied. In many experimental designs, we take a control measurement (O_1) of the dependent variable before introducing the manipulation (X). After the manipulation, take an after measurement (O_2) of the dependent variable. Then take the difference between O_1 and O_2 as the change that the manipulation has brought about. For example, Big Top Company management may wish to find the best way to educate its workers about the financial condition of the company before this year's labor negotiations. To assess the value of such an effort, give employees a test on their knowledge about the company's finances (O_1). Then present the educational campaign (X) to these employees,

---

[2]Donald T. Campbell and Julian C. Stanley, *Experimental and Quasi-Experimental Designs for Research* (Chicago: Rand McNally, 1963), p. 5.

after which again measure this knowledge level (O_2). This particular design, known as a preexperiment because it is not a very strong design, can be diagrammed as follows:

$$O_1 \qquad\qquad X \qquad\qquad O_2$$
Pretest   Manipulation   Post-test

Between O_1 and O_2, however, a number of events might occur that could confound the effects of the education effort. A newspaper article might appear about companies with financial problems, a union meeting might be held at which this topic is discussed, or some other occurrence could distort the effects of the company's education test.

2. *Maturation.* Changes may also take place within the subject which are a function of the passage of time and are not specific to any particular event. These are of special concern when the study covers a long period of time, but may also be a factor in tests which are as short as an hour or two. For example, a subject can become hungry, bored, or tired in a short time and this can affect response results.

3. *Testing.* The process of taking a test can affect the scores of a second testing. The mere experience of taking the first test can have a learning effect that influences the results on the second test.

4. *Instrumentation.* This is a threat to internal validity that results from changes between observations, in measuring instrument or observer. Using different questions at each measurement is an obvious source of potential trouble, but using different observers or interviewers is also a validity threat. There can even be an instrumentation problem if the same observer is used for all measurements. Observer boredom, fatigue, experience, or anticipation of results can all distort the results of separate observations.

5. *Selection.* One of the more important threats to internal validity is the differential selection of subjects to be included in experimental and control groups. Validity considerations require that the groups be equivalent in every respect. If subjects are randomly assigned to experimental and control groups, this selection problem can be largely overcome. Additionally, however, the equivalence of the groups can be enhanced by matching the members of the groups on key factors.

6. *Statistical regression.* This factor operates especially when study groups have been selected on the basis of their extreme scores. For example, suppose that we measure the output of all workers in a certain department for a few days prior to an experiment, and then choose to conduct the experiment only with those who are in the top 25 percent and bottom 25 percent of the productivity groups. No matter what is done between O_1 and O_2 there is a strong tendency for the average of the high scores at O_1 to decline at O_2, and the low scores at O_1 to increase. This tendency results from imperfect measurement which, in effect, records some persons abnormally high and abnormally low at O_1. In the second measurement, members of both groups tend to score more closely to their long-run mean scores.

7. *Experiment mortality.* This occurs when the composition of the study groups changes during the test. Attrition is especially likely in the experimental group, and with each dropout the makeup of that group changes. Members of the control group, because they are not affected by the testing situation, are less likely to withdraw. In a compensation incentive study, for example, some employees might not like the change in compensation method and withdraw from the test group; this could distort the comparison with the control group which has continued working under the established system, perhaps without knowing that a test is underway. All of the threats mentioned to this point are generally, but not always, dealt with adequately in experiments by random assignment. In addition, however, there are five added threats to internal validity that are independent of whether one randomizes.[3] Three of these have the effect of equalizing experimental and control groups. They are:

1. *Diffusion or imitation of treatment*—If people in the experimental and control groups communicate, then those in the control group may learn of the treatment, eliminating the difference between the groups.
2. *Compensatory equalization*—Where the experimental treatment is much more desirable, there may be an administrative reluctance to deprive the control group members. In this case, some compensatory actions for the control groups may confound the experiment.
3. *Compensatory rivalry*—This may occur when members of the control group know that they are the control group. This may generate competitive pressures, causing the control group members to try harder. In addition, there are two other possible forces which may threaten internal validity and whose effects are to create a spurious difference. They are:
4. *Resentful demoralization of the disadvantaged*—When the treatment is desirable and the experiment is obtrusive, the control group may become resentful of their deprivation and lower their cooperation and output.
5. *Local history*—The regular history effect already mentioned impacts both experimental and control groups alike. However, when one assigns all experimental persons to one group session and all control people to another session, there is a chance for some idiosyncratic event to confound results. This problem can be handled by administering treatments to individuals or small groups that are randomly assigned to experimental or control sessions.

External validity. Internal validity factors cause confusion about whether the experimental factor (X) or extraneous factors are the source of

---

[3]Thomas D. Cook and Donald T. Campbell, "The Design and Conduct of Quasi-Experiments and True Experiments in Field Settings," in Marvin D. Dunnette (ed.), *Handbook of Industrial and Organizational Psychology* (Chicago; Rand McNally, 1976), p. 223.

observation differences. In contrast, external validity is concerned with the interaction of the experimental stimulus (X) with other factors and the resulting impact on abilities to generalize to (and across) times, settings, or persons. Among the major threats to external validity are the following interactive possibilities.

1. *The reactivity of testing on X.* In terms of external validity, the reactive effect is one of sensitizing subjects by the pretest so that they respond to the experimental stimulus in a different way. For example, a before-measurement of the level of knowledge about the ecology programs of a certain company will often sensitize the subject to the various experimental communication efforts that might then be made about that company. This before-measurement effect can be particularly significant in attitude studies.

2. *Interaction of selection and X.* The process by which test subjects are selected for an experiment may be a threat to external validity. The population from which one actually selects subjects may not be the same as the population to which one wishes to generalize results. For example, you might use a selected group of workers in one department for the test of the piecework incentive system, but the question may remain as to whether you can extrapolate the results to all production workers. Or consider a study in which you ask a cross section of a population to participate in an experiment, but a substantial number refuse. If you do the experiment only with those who agree to participate can the results be generalized to the total population?

3. *Other reactive factors.* The experimental settings themselves may have a biasing effect on a subject's response to X. An artificial setting can obviously give results that are not representative of larger populations. Or, suppose that the group of workers who is given the incentive pay is moved to a different work area in order to separate them from the control group. These new conditions alone could create a strong reactive condition.

If the subject knows he or she is participating in an experiment, there may be a tendency to role-play in such a way as to distort the effects of X. Another reactive effect is the possible interaction between X and subject characteristics. For example, an incentive pay proposal may be more effective with persons in one type of job, with a certain skill level, personality trait, and the like.

Problems of internal validity are amenable to solution by the careful design of experiments, but this is less true for external validity. External validity is largely a matter of generalization and, in a logical sense, this is an inductive process of extrapolating beyond the data collected. In generalizing, estimate the factors that can be ignored and that will interact with the experimental variable. Assume that the closer two events are in time, space, and measurement the more likely they are to follow the same laws. As a general approach, first seek internal validity. Try to secure as much external validity as is compatible with the internal validity requirements by making experimental conditions as similar as possible to conditions under which to apply our results.

Ethics and experimentation

There is a growing concern for protecting the rights of the subjects used in research projects. This is a problem in all studies using human beings as subjects, but it is of special concern in experiments because the subject is exposed to manipulation. To carry out the experiment, the researcher often deceives the subject as to the purpose, nature, and possible personal repercussions from the study. Such actions can lead to embarrassment or invasion of privacy, and in other ways run counter to a subject's rights and interests as a member of a free society.

A good general rule is *not* to deceive subjects in a research study, but strict adherence to this rule often destroys any chance of conducting a study. For example, one cannot hope to secure valid results in a study of the effect of distasteful situations, malfunctioning products, and stressful interpersonal events on a subject who is fully on guard. Therefore, if there is to be research involving human beings, there is a need to weigh the values of the study against the risks to the subjects. Fortunately, business research studies are largely innocuous in their impact, and a relatively harmless cover story can be used to satisfy the subject's curiosity. If there is reason to believe that the rights of the subject may be infringed upon, the researcher can consider several courses of action. If there is substantial risk to the subject, the project may be abandoned or drastically revised. Such revision may call for securing the subject's prior consent after a thorough briefing on the project. At a minimum, the subject should be debriefed after the experiment is completed.[4]

EXPERIMENTAL RESEARCH DESIGNS

There are many experimental designs and they vary widely in terms of their power to control contamination of the relationship between independent and dependent variables. The most widely accepted designs are based on this characteristic of control: (1) preexperiments, (2) true experiments, and (3) quasiexperiments.

Preexperimental designs

All three preexperimental designs are weak in terms of their scientific measurement power. That is, they fail adequately to control the various

---

[4]For a more detailed discussion of this topic as well as a discussion of debriefing techniques, see E. Aronson and J. M. Carlsmith, "Experimentation in Social Psychology," in G. Lindzey and E. Aronson, eds., *The Handbook of Social Psychology* (Reading, Mass.: Addison-Wesley, 1968), pp. 29–36.

threats to internal validity. This is especially the case with the one-shot case study.

One-shot case study. This may be diagrammed as follows:[5]

$$X \qquad\qquad O$$

X	O	
Treatment or	Observation or	
manipulation of	measurement of	(1)
independent	dependent variable	
variable		

An example of such a study would be to conduct an employee education campaign about the company's financial condition without a prior measurement of employee knowledge. Results would reveal only how much the employees know after the education campaign, but there was no way to judge the effectiveness of the campaign. How well do you think this design would meet the various threats to internal validity?

The one-group pretest-post-test design. This is the design used earlier in the educational example. It meets the various threats to internal validity

O	X	O	
Pretest	Manipulation	Post-test	(2)

better than the one-shot case study, but it is still a weak design. How well does it control for history? maturation? testing effect? the others?

The static-group comparison. This design provides for two study groups, one of which receives the experimental stimulus while the other serves as a control.

$$X \qquad O_1$$
$$\text{---------------}$$
$$O_2 \qquad\qquad (3)$$

The addition of a comparison group makes this a substantial improvement over the other two designs. Its chief weakness is that there is no way to assure that the two groups really are comparable. To overcome this difficulty, true experiments need to be used.

True experimental designs

The major deficiency of the previous designs is that they fail to provide comparison groups that are truly equivalent. The way to achieve the equiv-

---

[5]An X represents the introduction of an experimental stimulus to a group. It is the stimulus whose effects are of major interest. O identifies a measurement or observation event. The Xs and Os in a design diagram are read from left to right. Xs and Os vertical to each other indicate that the stimulus and/or observation take place simultaneously. R indicates that the group members have been selected randomly. Parallel rows unseparated by dashes indicate comparison groups chosen randomly, while parallel rows separated by a dashed line indicate comparison groups which have not been selected by randomization.

alency has already been discussed in Chapter 3—random assignment to groups.[6] Matching is also a useful device by which to make improvements in equivalency, but the basic safeguard is random assignment. With randomly assigned study groups, one cam employ tests of statistical significance of the observed differences.

It is common to indicate an X for the test stimulus and a blank for the existence of a control situation. This is an oversimplification of what really occurs. In the more typical case, there is actually an X_1 and an X_2, and sometimes more. The X_1 identifies one specific independent variable while X_2 is another independent variable that has been chosen, often arbitrarily, as the control case. Different levels of the same independent variable may also be used with one level serving as the control.

Pretest-post-test control group design. This design consists of (1) adding a control group to the design number 2 (one group pretest-post-test) and (2) assigning the subjects to either of the groups by a random procedure. The diagram is:

$$R \qquad O_1 \qquad X \qquad O_2 \tag{4}$$
$$R \qquad O_3 \qquad \qquad O_4$$

The effect of the experimental variable is

$$E = (O_2 - O_1) - (O_4 - O_3)$$

In this design, the seven major internal validity problems are dealt with fairly well, although there are still some difficulties. For example, local history may occur in one group and not the other. Also, if communication exists between people in test and control groups, there can be rivalry and other internal validity problems.

Maturation, testing, and regression are handled well because one would expect them to be felt equally in experimental and control groups. Mortality, however, can be a problem if there are different dropout rates in the study groups. Selection is adequately dealt with by random assignment.

The record of this design is not as good on external validity. There is a chance for a reactive effect from testing. This might be a substantial influence in attitude change studies where pretests introduce unusual topics and content. Nor does this design insure against reaction between selection and the experimental variable. Even random selection may be defeated by a high decline rate by subjects. This would result in using a disproportionate share of persons who are essentially volunteers and who may not be typical of the population. If this occurs we will need to replicate the experiment a number of times with other groups under other conditions before we can be confident of external validity.

---

[6]See page 76. A distinction should be made between random selection and random assignment. The former concerns the drawing of a representative sample from a population and is of concern in external validity. Random assignment concerns the equating of experimental and control groups and is chiefly of concern to internal validity.

Post-test-only control group design.. In this design the pretest measurements are omitted. These pretests are well-established in classical research design but are not really necessary when it is possible to randomize. The design is:

$$
\begin{array}{ccc}
R & X & O_1 \\
R & & O_2
\end{array}
\tag{5}
$$

The experimental effect is measured by the difference between O_1 and O_2. The simplicity of this design makes it more attractive than the pretest-post-test control group design. Internal validity threats from history, maturation, selection, and statistical regression are adequately controlled by random assignment. Since the subjects are measured only once, the threats of testing and instrumentation are reduced, but differential mortality between experimental and control groups continues to be a potential problem. In terms of external validity, this design reduces the problem of testing interaction effect, although other problems remain.

Extensions of true experimental designs

The true experimental designs have been discussed in their classical forms, but researchers normally use an operational extension of the basic design. These extensions differ from the classical design forms in terms of (1) the number of different experimental stimuli that are considered simultaneously by the experimenter; and (2) the extent to which assignment procedures are used to increase precision.

Before considering the types of extensions some terms that are commonly used in the literature of applied experimentation are introduced. *Factor* is widely used to denote an independent variable. Factors are divided into *levels*, which represent various subgroups. A factor may have two or more levels such as (1) male and female; (2) large, medium, and small; or (3) no training, brief training, and extended training. These levels should be operationally defined.

Factors may also be classed as to whether the experimenter can manipulate the levels to be associated with the subject. *Active factors* are those the experimenter can manipulate by causing a given subject to receive one level or another. *Treatment* is used to denote the different levels of active factors. With the second type, the *blocking factor*, the experimenter can only identify and classify the subject on the basis of an existing level. Sex, age group, customer status, and organizational rank are examples of blocking factors because the subject comes to the experiment with a given level of each.

Up to this point, the assumption is that experimental subjects are persons, but this is often not the case. A better term for subject is *test unit*; it can refer equally well to an individual, organization, geographic market, animal, machine type, mix of materials, and innumerable other entities.

Completely randomized design. The basic form of the true experiment is also called a completely randomized design. To illustrate its use, as well as that of more complex designs, take a decision now facing the pricing manager at the Big Top Company. He would like to know what the ideal differential in price should be between Big Top's private brand of canned vegetables and the national brands such as Del Monte and Stokely's.

It is possible to set up an experiment on price differentials for canned green beans. The 18 company stores are used for the study and three price spreads (treatments) of one cent, three cents, and five cents between the company brand and national brands are selected. Six of the stores are assigned randomly to each of the treatment groups. The price differentials are maintained for a period of time and then a tally is made of the sales volumes and gross profit of the canned green beans category for each group of stores.

This design can be diagrammed as follows:

$$
\begin{array}{cccc}
R & O_1 & X_1 & O_2 \\
R & O_3 & X_3 & O_4 \\
R & O_5 & X_5 & O_6
\end{array}
\qquad (6)
$$

In this case, O_1, O_3, and O_5, represent the total gross profits for canned green beans in the treatment stores for the month before the test. X_1, X_3, and X_5 represent the one-cent, three-cent, and five-cent treatments, while O_2, O_4, and O_6 are the gross profits for the month after the test started.

In this example, it is assumed that the randomization of stores to the three treatment groups was sufficient to make the three store groups equivalent. Where there is reason to believe that this is not so we must use a more complex design.

Randomized block design. When there is a single major extraneous variable, the randomized block design is used. Random assignment is still the basic way to assure equivalency among treatment groups, but something more is desired for two reasons. The more critical reason is that the sample being studied may be so small that it is risky to depend upon random assignment alone to assure equivalency. Small samples, such as the 18 stores in the example, are typical in field experiments because of high costs or because few test units are available. Another reason for blocking is to learn whether treatments bring different results among various groups of subjects.

Consider again the canned green beans pricing experiment. Assume that there is reason to believe that lower income families are more sensitive to price differentials than are higher income families. Such a factor could seriously distort our results unless we stratify the stores by customer income. On this basis, each of the 18 stores is assigned to one of three income blocks and then randomly assigned, within blocks, to the price difference treatments. The design is shown in the accompanying table.

In this design, one can measure both *main effect* and *interaction effect*. Main effect is the average direct influence that a particular treatment has independent of other factors. Interaction is the influence of one factor on

Active factor—Price difference		Blocking factor—Customer income			
		High	Medium	Low	
1 cent	R	X_1	X_1	X_1	
3 cents	R	X_2	X_2	X_2	(7)
5 cents	R	X_3	X_3	X_3	

Note that the Os have been omitted. The horizontal rows no longer indicate a time sequence, but various levels of the blocking factor. However, there are before-and-after measurements associated with each of the treatments.

the effect of another. The main effect of each price differential is secured by calculating the impact of each of the three treatments averaged over the different blocks. An interaction effect occurs if you find that different customer income levels have a pronounced influence on the customer reactions to the price differentials.

Whether this design improves the precision of the experimental measurement depends upon how successfully the design minimizes the variance within blocks and maximizes the variance between blocks. That is, if the response patterns are about the same in each block when there is little value to the more complex design. In fact, blocking may be counterproductive.

Latin square design. The Latin square may be used when there are two major extraneous factors. To continue with the pricing example, assume that we decide to block on the size of store as well as on customer income. It is convenient to consider these two blocking factors as forming the rows and columns of a table. Each factor is divided into three levels to provide nine groups of stores, each representing a unique combination of the two blocking variables. Treatments are then randomly assigned to these cells so that a given treatment appears only once in each row and column. Because of this restriction a Latin square must have the same number of rows, columns, and treatments. The design looks like the accompanying table.

Store size	Customer income			
	High	Medium	Low	
Large	X_3	X_1	X_2	
Medium	X_2	X_3	X_1	(8)
Small	X_1	X_2	X_3	

Treatments can be assigned by using a table of random numbers to determine the order of treatment in the first row. For example, the pattern may be 3, 1, 2 as shown above. Following this the other two cells of the first column are filled in a similar manner and the remaining treatments are then assigned to meet the restriction that there can be no more than one treatment type in each row and column.

The experiment is carried out, sales results are gathered, and the average treatment effect calculated. From this, one can determine the main effect of the various price spreads on the sales of company and national brands. With cost information, one can determine which price differential produces the greatest margin.

A major limitation of the Latin square is that one must assume that there is no interaction between treatments and blocking factors. Therefore, you cannot determine how store size, customer income, and price spreads interrelate. This limitation exists because there is not an exposure of all combinations of treatments, store sizes, and customer income groups. To do so would take a table of 27 cells, while this one has only 9. This can be accomplished by replicating the experiment twice in order to furnish the number needed to provide for every combination of store size, customer income, and treatment. On the other hand, when one is not especially interested in interaction the Latin square is much more economical.

Factorial design. One misconception that many have about experiments is that you can manipulate only one variable at a time. This is not true; with *factorial designs*, you can deal with more than one treatment simultaneously. Consider again the pricing experiment. The president of the chain might also be interested in determining the effect of posting unit prices on the shelf to aid shopper decision making. The accompanying table can be used to design an experiment to include both the price differentials and the unit pricing.

Unit price information?	Price spread		
	1 Cent	3 Cents	5 Cents
Yes	X_1Y_1	X_1Y_2	X_1Y_3
No	X_2Y_1	X_2Y_2	X_2Y_3

(9)

This is known by a 2 by 3 factorial design in which we use two factors: one with two levels and one with three levels of intensity. The version shown here is completely randomized with the stores being randomly assigned to one of six treatment combinations. With such a design, it is possible to estimate the main effects of each of the two independent variables as well as the interactions between them. The results can give answers to the following questions.

1. What are the sales effects of the different price spreads between company and national brands?
2. What are the sales effects of using unit price marking on the shelves?
3. What are the sales effect interrelations between price spread and the presence of unit price information?

Covariance analysis. Up to this point, we have discussed direct controlling for extraneous variables through blocking. It is also possible to apply some degree of indirect statistical control on one or more such variables through analysis of covariance. For example, even with randomization, one may find that the "before" measurement shows an average knowledge level difference between experimental and control groups. With covariance analysis, one can adjust statistically for this "before" difference. Another application might occur if the canned green beans pricing experiment was carried out with a completely randomized design, only to find that there is a contamination effect from differences in average customer income levels. With covariance analysis, one can still do some "statistical blocking" on average customer income even after the experiment has been run.

Quasiexperiments[7]

Under actual field conditions, one often cannot control enough of the variables to use a true experiment design. Under such conditions, use quasiexperiments. In a quasiexperiment, equivalent experimental and control groups cannot be established through random assignment. Often one cannot even determine when or to whom to expose the experimental variable. Usually, however, one can determine when and whom to measure.

A quasiexperiment is inferior to a true experiment design, but is usually superior to available nonexperimental approaches. There are many quasiexperiment designs but here we will consider only several of the most common.

Nonequivalent control group design. This is one of the strongest and most widely used quasiexperimental designs. It differs from experimental design (4) because the test and control groups are not randomly assigned. The design is diagrammed as follows:

$$O_1 \quad X \quad O_2$$
$$\text{---------------------------} \tag{10}$$
$$O_3 \qquad O_4$$

There are two varieties of this design. One is the *intact equivalent design* in which the membership of the experimental and control groups is naturally assembled. For example, one may use different classes in a school, membership in similar clubs, customers from similar stores, and the like. Ideally, the two groups should be as alike as possible. This design is especially useful when any type of individual selecting process would be reactive.

A second variation, the *self-selected experimental group design*, is weaker because volunteers are recruited to form the experimental group, while nonvolunteer subjects are used for control. Such a design is likely when a number of subjects believe that it would be interesting or in their interest to be a subject in an experiment—say, an experimental training program.

---

[7]For an in-depth discussion of many quasiexperiment designs and their internal validity, see Cook and Campbell, "Design and Conduct," pp. 246–98.

Comparison of pretest results $(O_1 - O_3)$ is one indicator of the degree of equivalency between test and control groups. If the pretest results are significantly different there is a real question as to the groups' comparability. On the other hand, if pretest observations are similar between groups, there is more reason to believe that internal validity of the experiment is good.

Separate sample pretest-post-test design. This design is most applicable in those situations where we cannot determine when and to whom to introduce the treatment but can determine when and whom to measure. The basic design is:

$$R \quad\quad O_1 \quad\quad (X) \quad\quad\quad\quad\quad\quad\quad\quad (11)$$
$$R \quad\quad\quad\quad\quad X \quad\quad Q_2$$

The bracketed treatment (X) is irrelevant to the purpose of the study but is shown to indicate that the experimenter cannot control the treatment.

This is not a strong design because a number of threats to internal validity are not handled adequately. For example, history can confound the results, and about the only way to overcome this is to repeat the study at other times in other settings. In contrast, this design is considered to be superior to true experiments in external validity. This strength results from it being a field experiment in which the samples are usually drawn from the population to which we wish to generalize our results.

This design is more appropriate when the population is large, a before-measurement is probably reactive, and there is no way to restrict the application of the treatment. For example, suppose that Big Top Company is planning an intense campaign to change its employees' attitudes toward energy conservation. It might draw two random samples of employees, one of which is interviewed regarding energy use attitudes prior to the information campaign. After the campaign the other group is interviewed.

Group time-series design. This design, which introduces repeated observations before and after the treatment, allows subjects to act as their own controls. The single treatment group design has before-after measurements as the only controls. There is also a multiple design with two or more comparison groups as well as the repeated measurements in each treatment group.

The time series format is especially useful where regularly kept records are a natural part of the environment and are unlikely to be reactive. The time-series approach is also a good way to study unplanned events in an ex post facto manner. For example, if the federal government would suddenly institute price controls, one could still study the effects of this action at a later date if one had regularly collected records for a period of time before and after the advent of price control.

The major internal validity problem for this design is history. To reduce this risk, one can keep a record of possible extraneous factors during the period of the experiment and attempt to adjust the results to reflect their influence.

A job enrichment quasiexperiment.[8]   One theory of job attitudes holds
that "hygiene" factors, which include working conditions, pay, security,
status, interpersonal relationships, and company policy can be a major
source of dissatisfaction among workers but have little positive motivational
power. This theory holds that the positive motivator factors are intrinsic to
the job; they include achievement, recognition for achievement, the work
itself, responsibility, and growth or advancement.[9]

One study of the value of job enrichment as a builder of job satisfaction
was carried out with laboratory technicians or "experimental officers" (EOs)
in a British chemical company. The project was a multiple group time-series
quasiexperiment. The project can be diagrammed as:

$$O \quad O \quad O \quad X \quad O \quad O \quad O \quad O \quad O \quad O \quad O \quad O \quad O \quad O \quad O$$

$$O \quad O \quad O \quad O \quad O \quad O \quad O \quad O \quad X \quad O \quad O \quad O \quad O \quad O \quad O$$

$$O \quad O \quad O \quad O \quad O \quad O \quad O \quad O \quad O \quad O \quad O \quad O \quad O \quad O \quad O$$

Two sections of the department acted as experimental groups and two as
control groups. It is not clear how these were chosen, but there was no
mention of random assignment. One of the experimental groups and one of
the control groups worked closely together, while the other two groups were
separated geographically, and were engaged on quite different research.
Hygiene factors were held constant during the period of the research, and
the studies were kept confidential in order to avoid the tendency on the part
of participants to act in artificial ways.

A before-measurement was made using a job reaction survey instrument.
This indicated that the EOs typically had low morale and many wrote of
their frustrations. All EOs were asked to write monthly progress reports,
and these were used to assess the quality of their work. The assessment was
made against eight specifically defined criteria by a panel of three managers
who were not members of the department. These assessors were never told
which laboratory technicians were in the experimental group and which
were in the control group.

The study extended over a year, with the treatments being introduced in
the experimental groups at the start of the 12 months study period. Changes
were made to give experimental group EOs important chances for achievement; these changes also made the work more challenging. Recognition of
achievement was given, authority over certain aspects was increased, new
managerial responsibilities were assigned to the senior EOs, added advance-
ments were given to others, and the opportunity for self-initiated work was
provided. After a period of about six months these same changes were insti-

---

[8]William J. Paul, Jr., Keith B. Robertson, and Frederick Herzberg, "Job Enrichment
Pays Off," *Harvard Business Review* (March–April 1969), pp. 61–78.
[9]Frederick J. Herzberg, "One More Time: How Do You Motivate Employees?" *Harvard
Business Review* (January–February 1968), pp. 53–62.

tuted with one of the control groups, while the remaining group continued for the entire period as a control. Several months of *EO* progress reports were available as a prior base line for evaluation. The results of this project are shown in Figure 5–1.

FIGURE 5–1   Assessment of *EO*s monthly reports

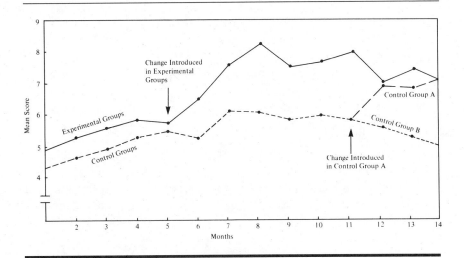

An evaluation of experimentation

There are clearly some positives and some negatives with this approach. Experimentation is often difficult to do, and it is expensive. All experiments are artificial to some degree and it is often difficult to design an experiment for field conditions. If we do not control the extraneous factors, there is a question of validity that cannot be fully answered. Then, too, there are ethical problems in manipulating people.

However, there is no other method that can approach power of experimentation to determine causal relationships between variables. Albeit imperfectly, we can control contamination from extraneous variables more effectively than with other designs. Advances in research will depend heavily upon the ability to do more and better experimental research. These arguments are so powerful that they have led one scholar to write, ". . . I think it is essential that we always keep in mind the model of the controlled experiment, even if in practice we may have to deviate from an ideal model."[10]

---

[10]Samuel A. Stouffer, "Some Observations on Study Design," *American Journal of Sociology* 4 (January 1950), pp. 355–61.

The decision at Big Top Company

Betty White got up from her desk and walked over to the water cooler. She thought:

> There are going to be many situations where experiments are not going to be feasible or even desirable. But my job is to help our managers make better decisions and this often means that they must try out ideas, test alternatives, or test to see if a strategy will work. This must call for some kind of experimentation. Sure, some will be crude studies and not very scientific, but we can make them better. We won't always get a good answer, but we can move closer to the truth.

As she sat back down at her desk, the phone rang. It was Jed.

"How's your analysis going? Have you come to a decision yet? What are you going to tell Paxon?" were his questions.

"I've just made up my mind," was her reply. "I'm going to make a strong pitch for using experiments where we can. It's obvious that the marketing people can do a lot in this area, but I see applications elsewhere in the organization, too. The warehouse is an ideal place to try out some different ways to operate; even in our personnel activities we should be trying different approaches to recruiting, training, and supervision. I'm really enthused about this and I think Mr. Paxon will be too. Thanks, Jed, for giving me such a good argument."

SUMMARY

Experiments are studies whose implementation involves intervention by the researcher beyond that required for measurement. The usual intervention is to manipulate some variable (the independent variable) and observe how it affects the subjects being studied (the dependent variable).

We can judge various types of manipulative research designs by how well they meet the tests of internal and external validity. An experiment has high internal validity if one has confidence that the experimental treatment has, in fact, been the source of change in the dependent variable. More specifically, a design's internal validity is judged by how well it meets seven threats. These are history, maturation, testing, instrumentation, selection, statistical regression, and experimental mortality.

External validity is high when the results of an experiment are judged to apply to some larger population. Such an experiment is said to have high external validity with regard to that population. There are three potential threats to external validity. They are testing reactivity, selection interaction, and other reactive factors.

Experimental research designs can be classified into three major groups: (1) preexperiments, (2) true experiments, and (3) quasiexperiments. The main distinction among these types is the degree of control that the researcher can exercise over validity problems.

Three preexperimental designs are presented. These represent the crudest form of experimentation and are only undertaken when nothing else stronger is possible. Their major weakness is the lack of an equivalent comparison group, and as a result, they fail to meet many internal validity criteria. The three preexperimental designs are (1) one-shot study; (2) one-group pretest-post-test design; (3) static-group comparison.

Two forms of the true experiment are also presented. Their central characteristic is that they provide a means by which we can assure equivalence between experimental and control groups through random assignment to the groups. These designs are (1) pretest-post-test control group; (2) post-test-only control group.

The classical two-group experiment can be extended to multigroup designs in which different levels of the test variable are used as controls rather than the classical nontest control. In addition, the true experimental design is extended into more sophisticated forms that make use of blocking. Two such forms, the randomized block and the Latin square, are discussed. Finally, the factorial design is discussed in which two or more independent variables can be accommodated.

Between the extremes of preexperiments, with little or no control, and true experiments, with random assignment, there is a gray area in which are found quasiexperiments. These are useful designs when some variables can be controlled, but equivalent experimental and control groups usually cannot be established by random assignment. There are many quasiexperimental designs, but only three are discussed in this chapter. They are (1) nonequivalent control group design; (2) separate sample pretest-post-test design; (3) group time-series design.

SUPPLEMENTAL READINGS

1. Banks, Seymour. *Experimentation in Marketing*. New York: McGraw-Hill, 1965. The pioneering book on the application of experimentation to marketing research. Excellent discussion with good examples.
2. Campbell, Donald T., and Julian C. Stanley. *Experimental and Quasi-Experimental Designs for Research*. Chicago: Rand McNally, 1963. The almost universally quoted discussion of experimental designs in the social sciences.
3. Cook, Thomas D., and Donald T. Campbell. "The Design and Conduct of Quasi-Experiments and True Experiments in Field Settings," in Dunnette, Marvin D. (ed.). *Handbook of Industrial and Organizational Psychology*. Chicago: Rand McNally, 1976. A major authoritative work on both true and quasiexperiments and their design. It is already a classic reference.
4. Dayton, C. Mitchell. *The Design of Educational Experiments*. New York: McGraw-Hill, 1970. This book is "designed to provide a workable compromise between exhaustive coverage of designs and the practical facts of their utility." Each chapter includes summaries of actual experiments.
5. Edwards, Allen l. *Experimental Design in Psychological Research*, 4th ed. New York: Holt, Rinehart & Winston, 1972. A thorough treatment of experi-

mental design with illustrative examples. Requires only elementary statistical analysis and a working knowledge of algebra.

DISCUSSION QUESTIONS

1. Distinguish between:
   a Internal and external validity.
   b Preexperiment and quasiexperiment.
   c History and maturity.
   d Contribution of randomization and matching to experimentation.
   e Active and blocking factors.
2. What are the essential characteristics that distinguish a true experiment from other research designs?
3. Why would a noted social science researcher say, "It is essential that we always keep in mind the model of the controlled experiment, even if in practice we have to deviate from an ideal model"?
4. What ethical problems do you see in conducting experiments with human beings? What ethical guidelines should we follow?
5. Suggest at least two specific situations, each, in marketing, finance, and production, in which you think an experiment would be an appropriate research design. Which of the various designs would you recommend for each of the situations? What specific internal and/or external validity threats would you face with your suggested designs?
6. You are asked to develop an experiment for a study on the effect that compensation has upon the response rates secured from personal interview subjects. This study will involve 300 people who will be assigned to one of the following conditions: (1) no compensation, (2) $1 compensation, and (3) $3 compensation. A number of sensitive issues will be explored concerning various social problems, and the 300 persons will be drawn from the adult population.

   Describe how your design would be set up if it were a completely randomized design, randomized block design, Latin square, factorial (suggest another active variable to use). Which would you use? Why?
7. What type of experimental design would you recommend in each of the following cases? Suggest in some detail how you would design each study:
   a A test of three methods of compensation of factory workers. The methods are hourly wage, incentive pay, and weekly salary. The dependent variable is direct labor cost per unit of output.
   b The effects of various levels of advertising effort and price reduction on the sale of specific branded grocery products by a retail grocery chain.
   c The Ajax Auto Company is expecting to announce soon the largest profits in the company's history and the largest bonuses ever awarded to their executives. Company management is concerned about the effect of these acts on public attitudes toward retaining or dropping quotas on the importation of foreign cars into the United States.
   d It has been claimed that the use of fast-paced music played over a store's P.A. system will speed up the shopping rate of customers without any adverse effect on the amount spent per customer.

DATA COLLECTION

6. Secondary data sources

Every study is a search for information about some topic. If one taps all of the relevant sources, one can be more confident of the quality of the findings. This chapter concerns the problems and techniques of finding and using data already collected by others. More specifically, the chapter covers the nature of these data sources and how to use them. While some of the major tools are mentioned here, Appendix A contains a more detailed listing of important indexes, guides, and other reference tools for secondary sources.

THE NATURE OF SECONDARY DATA SOURCES

One can classify information sources into primary and secondary types. Primary data come from the original sources and are collected especially for the task at hand. Thus, you collect primary data when you observe certain production operations and measure their cost. Studies made by others for another purpose, represent secondary data.

Primary and secondary sources each have strengths and weaknesses. For example, with primary sources, one can collect precisely the information he or she wants. One usually can specify the operational definitions used and can eliminate, or at least monitor and record, the extraneous influences on the data as they are gathered. But secondary sources also have their merits.

Advantages of secondary data. Secondary sources can usually be found more quickly and cheaply. Collection of primary data can be so costly and time-consuming as to be impractical. We cannot hope to gather primary information comparable to Census reports and industry statistics at any cost. These collections are not only voluminous and detailed, but their collection is provided for by law. Most research on past events also has to rely on secondary data sources. In like manner, data gathered about distant places often can be collected more cheaply through secondary sources.

Disadvantages of secondary data. The most important limitation with secondary sources is that the information often does not meet one's specific needs. This is source material that has been collected by others for their own purpose. Definitions will differ, units of measure are different, and different time periods may be involved. It is difficult to assess the accuracy of the information because one knows little about the research design or the conditions under which the research took place. Finally, secondary information is often out of date. A study made five years ago may not be relevant today.

The search task. Research using secondary sources is a special case of information retrieval. One must search through a vast inventory of information stored in books, pamphlets, periodicals, microfilm, computer files, and other media. One must use the indexing files of information storage systems to find that which is needed. Do this by searching the files (classifying and cataloging devices) and extracting those index codes (key words or descriptions of the material) that appear relevant. In this process, information requirements are matched to the indexing statements in the files.

One of the major sources of information are the research libraries typically found in large cities and at universities. Company libraries and general public libraries present the same resources, but have fewer of the indexing and documents resources required for specific research.

USES OF SECONDARY DATA

Secondary data is used for three research purposes. First, it fills a need for a specific reference on some point. Examples would be the estimated U.S. production of sulfuric acid last year, the population of Atlanta in 1980, or the current rate of return on government bonds. We may also seek reference benchmarks against which to test other findings. For example, from a sample survey, one could estimate that a certain percentage of the population has certain age and income characteristics. These estimates could then be checked against census data.

Another major use of secondary data is as an integral part of a larger research study. Research procedures typically call for at least a minimum amount of early exploration to learn if the past can make a contribution to the present study. In essence, the researcher tries to keep from "reinventing the wheel." Data from secondary sources helps one to decide what further research needs to be done, and can be a rich source of hypotheses.

Finally, secondary data may be used as the sole basis for a research study. The historical method is the classical example, but by no means the only one. Retrospective research often requires the use of past published data. In many research situations, one cannot conduct primary research because of physical, legal, or cost limitations. The federal government, for example, publishes massive amounts of data each year that no one else can provide.

TYPES OF SECONDARY SOURCES

One way to classify data sources is to label them either as internal (organization) or external sources of information. Internal organization sources are so varied that there is little in a general way that can be said about their use. The collection methods used are unique to the specific situation, and collection success depends on our knowing just where and how to look. Internal data sources may be the only source of information for many studies. Examples are departmental reports, production summaries, financial and accounting reports, marketing and sales studies, and a host of other types.

External sources. These are more varied than internal sources, but we have defined better methods for the search. This discussion is restricted to printed sources, although it is recognized that for specific cases other sources of information may be useful.

Published sources of data can be classified into four categories. An obvious category is that of books. It is estimated that more than 42,000 books were published in the United States in 1980, of which about 95 percent were nonfiction.[1] A second major source of secondary data is periodicals. The 21st edition of *Ulrich's International Periodicals Directory* lists approximately 65,000 in-print periodicals published throughout the world. A third major source of materials for secondary research is government documents. *The Monthly Catalog* of U.S. Government publications had almost 15,000 listings in 1981, and this represented only a fraction of the total government output.

The fourth major source of published information consists of a variety of materials. First, there are many reference books, each a compendium of a wide range of information. A second group includes university publications, of which the major categories are master's theses, doctoral dissertations, and research records. A third important category includes company publications such as financial reports, company policy statements, speeches by prominent executives, sales literature, product specifications, and many others. There are miscellaneous information sources consisting of the productions of various trade, professional, and other associations. These organizations often publish statistical compilations, research reports, and proceedings of meetings. Finally, there are personal documents. These often are used in historical and other social science research but less frequently in business studies.

Data are classified as either statistical or nonstatistical in nature. Government documents and company and association publications are often statistical in nature, while periodicals and books tend to be nonstatistical. Before going on to the general problem of good library search procedure, here is an outline of some of the important statistical sources for the business researcher.

---

[1] *The Bowker Annual of Library and Book Trade Information*, 27th ed. (New York: R. R. Bowker, 1982), p. 385.

STATISTICAL SOURCES

There are many statistical sources with a wealth of data, yet it is often difficult to find the specific information needed. There are guides, however, that can help locate the major statistical sources or provide descriptions of the various statistical publications. Two such sources are mentioned here, while more are given in Appendix A in the back of the book.

Statistical sources. 7th ed. Detroit: Gale Research, 1981. This volume identifies primary sources of statistical data on a large number of subjects. Most of the titles listed are issued by the government, but some are published by private agencies such as commercial and trade associations. The sources are arranged alphabetically by subject.

Office of Management and Budget. *Statistical Services of the United States Government*, rev. ed. Washington, D.C.: U.S. Government Printing Office, 1975. This handbook describes (1) the relation of the federal statistical programs to those of other governmental and private organizations; (2) the methods of collection and presentation; and (3) the principal series collected by government agencies. There are two appendixes; one describes each agency's area of responsibility, and the other gives an annotated bibliography of its principal statistical publications.

The guides mentioned above are directories to the location of the various types of statistics and do not themselves present statistical data. There are, however, several widely available statistical reference books. The most important of these is: U.S. Bureau of the Census. *Statistical Abstract of the United States*. Washington, D.C.: U.S. Government Printing Office, 1879 to date. This is an annual compendium of summary statistics on the political, social, industrial and economic life of the United States. It should be the starting point in gathering statistical data on most topics. The *Statistical Abstract* has two particular values to the business researcher. First, it is the most comprehensive and up-to-date compilation of statistics covering wide areas of our national life. Second, even if the specific figures or detail needed are not presented, the source notes for the tables and appended bibliography of sources of statistics are useful guides for further research.

There are several major supplements to the *Statistical Abstract of the United States*. *The County and City Data Book* provides recent figures for county, city, standard metropolitan area, and urbanized area data on population, vital statistics, industry, voting records and many other items. The *Congressional District Data Book* presents a similar variety of information by congressional district. Finally, the *Historical Statistics of the United States* brings together historical series of wide general interest from colonial times to 1962.

There are four major monthly governmental periodicals that provide the majority of the current statistics available on our economy and its operation. The *Survey of Current Business* contains about 2,500 statistical series on income, expenditures, production and prices of commodities, and many other aspects of the economy. Historical figures for the statistical data published in the *Survey of Current Business* are available in a supplement entitled *Business Statistics*, published in odd-numbered years. A second major statistical source is the *Federal Reserve Bulletin*. It publishes a large volume of national economic data with emphasis upon financial statistics. The third major governmental publication is the *Monthly Labor Review* which publishes data on work and labor conditions, wage rates, consumer price indexes, and the like. The fourth is the *Business Conditions Digest* which contains about 600 economic time series in a form convenient for forecasters and business analysts.

Many other government periodicals contain regular statistical information about transportation, agriculture, health, education, welfare and other areas. Hundreds of privately published periodicals also provide statistical information.

Census data. One of the basic statistical data sources in the United States are the periodic censuses conducted by the U.S. government. The oldest of these censuses is the *Census of Population* first taken for the year 1790; it has been taken at 10-year intervals since then. Over the years, there have been substantial additions to the type of information collected in this census. Today, one can secure detailed breakdowns of population by ethnic, economic, social, and occupational characteristics. Many of these data are available by state, county, metropolitan area, city and census tract (a relatively small homogeneous urban area that consists of a few hundred to a few thousand people). In addition, special enumerations of data may be purchased for smaller areas or for special combinations of variables selected for a particular project.

In recent decades, a *Census of Housing* has been conducted in conjunction with the population census. It provides information about the cost of housing, rental values, quality of housing, size of homes, occupancy rates and other information. In some metropolitan areas, housing data are available down to as small a geographic unit as a single city block.

A number of business and industrial censuses have been taken at varying intervals. One is the *Census of Manufactures*, which was first taken for the year 1809, but has been published at frequent intervals only since 1929. Another major census is the *Census of Business*. It was first published for 1929 and has been published since then at intervals of four or five years. The *Census of Business* is divided into three units, the "Census of Retail Trade," the "Census of Wholesale Trade," and the "Census of Selected Services." There are also major censuses taken in agriculture, transportation, government, construction industries, and mining and mineral industries.

Several of the most useful statistical compilations of economic data for small geographic areas in our economy are provided by private sources. One of these is *Sales and Marketing Management* magazine which publishes annually (usually in July) a "Survey of Consumer Buying Power." It provides current estimates of population, income, retail sales, and a variety of other statistics for every county and standard statistical metropolitan area in the United States, and for most cities of about 10,000 population or more.

This brief coverage of statistical publications includes only the major sources of the most readily available statistical data. In each case, only those that specialize in statistics are given. In addition, many statistics of value will be found in publications that are primarily nonstatistical in nature. It is to these more general data sources and the problems of their use that we now turn.

DATA SEARCH PROCEDURE

Joan Marsh must conduct a library research; she has a problem that breaks down into two parts. First, she much search out the appropriate information sources. For this she matches her information needs against the library's indexing systems. When she has matched and listed the sources she is ready to extract the specific information and organize it into an appropriate form. This collection can be carried out more efficiently if she first does a thorough search job.

Library search procedure

If Joan is unfamiliar with her topic she should first acquire some background in the subject. One approach is to look into general sources such as appropriate encyclopedias. Elementary textbooks in the field are also useful sources, and their perusal will help evaluate the more technical references.

Good search technique moves from the general to the specific, and from a wide-screen search for sources to a narrow in-depth study of specifics. The exact sequence and importance of individual sources will vary depending upon the subject and Joan's knowledge. One general approach might follow the flow diagram in Figure 6–1.

Search for bibliography. Assuming that she has some knowledge in the field, Joan should first develop a bibliography. This makes the entire research project more efficient because the investigator quickly acquires an inventory of the materials on the subject. By inspecting titles, authors, dates and other indexing information, she can select the priority sources for further study. She sees the development of the subject over time, discovers the authoritative sources, and can be more assured of covering the full range of material on the subject. Every search turns up only a sampling of the available information, but it is important that Joan secure an adequate sample.

The logical first step is for her to determine whether someone else has already prepared a bibliography on the subject. Bibliographies frequently accompany articles and books, and it is waste to duplicate such effort. Hence, the first step may be to go to the *Bibliographic Index: A Cumulative Bibliography of Bibliographies*. New York: H. W. Wilson, 1937 to date. This publication, organized by subject, is an index to books, magazine articles

FIGURE 6–1 Library search flow diagram

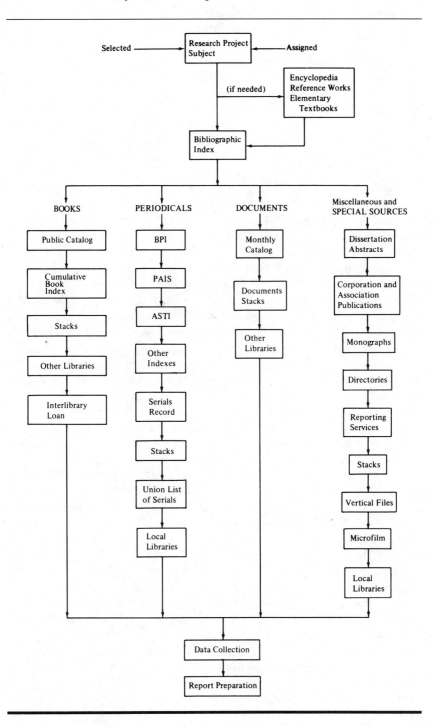

and other printed materials which include a bibliography. Thus, Joan may find publications in which the authors have listed their own reference sources on her subject.

Searching the public catalog may also turn up books that are primarily bibliographies although the subjects treated tend to be rather general. For example, there are bibliographies on business topics such as accounting, marketing, operations research, and many others. Many of these bibliographies have subsections that cover more specific topics.

Books as a source.   Joan may continue the search along one of the major investigative channels indicated in Figure 6–1. The first of these may be to seek information about books on the topic. The obvious first place to look is the public catalog in the library. This is the general bibliography of books in the library. Cards for these books are filed under author, title and subject. An example of a title card is shown in Figure 6–2. Joan will save time and effort if she can recognize the information found on this typical catalog card. It gives the title of the book; authors' names; publisher; date of publication; notes on special features such as illustrations, maps, or bibliographies; and sometimes notes listing contents. In addition, the card shows that the same publication is cataloged under three subject headings (those mentioned with arabic numerals near the bottom of the card) and under both authors' names. In the upper left corner is the call number and a notation that the book is in the Business School branch library.[2]

Searching by use of subject headings is usually the easiest, but can also present a confusing problem. If Joan does not happen to think of the same exact subject heading statement as that used by the library she may miss some good sources altogether. One way to deal with this problem is to refer to: U.S. Library of Congress. Subject Cataloging Division. *Subject Headings Used in the Dictionary Catalog of the Library of Congress.* 9th ed. Washington, D.C.: U.S. Government Printing Office, 1980. This reference indicates the headings used in any public catalog following the Library of Congress system. In addition, it suggests related subjects which she might consult. If the subject matter is specialized or narrow in scope, very new, or if relatively little has been published on it, there may not be a reference in the catalog.

It is often a shock to inexperienced researchers when they find no references to their subject in the library's public catalog. This may result from one of three circumstances: (1) a library can have only a small percentage of the publications that are produced; (2) the topic may be so narrow that it is not the subject of a full book or pamphlet in the library collection; (3) the material on the subject may be in the library in one of the collections not listed in the public catalog.

The holdings of a particular library are always restricted by the limited funds with which to purchase materials, and by the interests of those people

---

[2]This book is cataloged according to the Library of Congress system. In some libraries, the Dewey decimal call number system is used.

FIGURE 6–2   Typical title card

```
            Stein, Barry A.
Bus
HD 58    Life in organizations : workplaces as
.7           people experience them / Rosabeth
L 53         Moss Kanter and Barry A. Stein,
             editors. New York : Basic Books,
             c1979.
             xvi, 444 p. ; 24 cm.
             Bibliography: p. [429]-431.
             Includes index.


             1. Organizational behavior--Case
         studies.   2. Industrial sociology--Case
         studies.   3. Occupations--Social
         aspects--Case studies.   I. Kanter,
         Rosabeth Moss.   II. Stein, Barry A.


MoSW                             WTUNdc        77-20413
```

who choose books for the library. In a university library, the holdings reflect the importance of various fields of study in the university and the specific interests of the faculty members who order books.

There is still a good chance that there may be books published on the topic even though they are not available in that library. One can track down these references by going to one of a number of guides to published books. One good guide to use is: *Cumulative Book Index: World List of Books in the English Language.* New York: H. W. Wilson, 1928—to present. This guide includes books published in the English language in the United States and, since 1930, in other parts of the world. Books are recorded by author, title, and subject. Other guides are listed in Appendix A.

The second type of failure to find a reference in the public catalog occurs when the topic is not the subject of a separate publication. However, it may be included in some work that covers a more general topic. For example, information on executive bonus systems may not be found in a card catalog. A search under the broader subject of management will show many publications which may include coverage of bonus arrangements.

A third possibility is that the library has holdings on the subject that are not listed in the card catalog. This is the case with most U.S. government publications. The U.S. government is one of the largest publishers in the world. Each month it produces a vast array of materials on a wide variety of subjects. These publications range from a single mimeographed page to sets of books running into the thousands of pages. The volume of this output is so great that the cost of cataloging them is prohibitive. As a result, most research libraries have large collections of "documents" which are not listed in the public catalog.

Many state and local government publications are also not cataloged. In addition, libraries have vertical files with many pamphlets, speeches, bulletins, annual reports of companies, bank reports, and similar items which may be of current interest to the business researcher. Usually these are not recorded in the public catalog.

Documents as a source. The topics covered in documentary publications range widely. The best technique for searching U.S. government publications is to use: U.S. Superintendent of Documents. *United States Government Publications: Monthly Catalog.* Washington, D.C.: U.S. Government Printing Office, 1893 to date. Materials issued by all branches of the U.S. government are listed by name of the issuing office. There are monthly and annual subject indexes which are valuable to the investigator.

On looking through the listings in the *Monthly Catalog,* one will often notice a heavy black dot placed in the margin next to an entry. The dot identifies that item as a publication that is available to depository libraries. Depository libraries have been designated by the U.S. government to hold a collection of major government documents. This program is designed to assure widespread dissemination of government literature. A list of depository libraries is given in the September issue of the *Monthly Catalog.* Even the largest depository library will not have every depository marked item. In fact, a library usually selects only that part of the designated publications that fits with the interests of its patrons. A metropolitan library, for example, may choose few of the agricultural items. With each entry in the *Monthly Catalog* is a special Superintendent of Documents classification number. Library holdings of documents are often, but not always, shelved by this number.

Government publications are good sources of information in many topic areas. Obviously, the entire area of economics statistics is one of these areas. There are also important documents concerning many scientific fields, government relations to business and business operations. The various congressional committee reports frequently have testimony about business operations which is seldom available any place else. The documents literature of agricultural marketing contains many pioneering field experiment research studies.

Periodicals as a source. Periodicals are often the best single source of information for the business researcher. There are thousands of publications covering almost any subject imaginable. Many of them may have little value for research purposes, but one is often amazed at the richness of this data source when some way is found to tap it. Periodicals are especially useful in providing the most current information.

Libraries have indexes by which the investigator may quickly review the contents of many periodicals without actually going to the publications themselves. The most widely known of these indexes is the *Reader's Guide to Periodical Literature*. This is a subject guide to about 180 general-interest magazines such as *Time, Newsweek, Business Week, Fortune, Scientific American, Vogue,* and others. It is useful for topics of general interest but also includes many articles on business and technological matters.

Four widely available indexes are germane to business topics. They are:

1. *Business Periodicals Index.* New York: H. W. Wilson, 1958 to date.
2. *Applied Science and Technology Index.* New York: H. W. Wilson, 1958 to date.
3. Public Affairs Information Service, *Bulletin.* New York: 1915 to date.
4. *F. & S. Index of Corporations and Industries.* Detroit: Funk & Scott, 1960 to date.

The *Business Periodicals Index (BPI)* is a subject index of articles from approximately 260 business and economics periodicals. It is quite useful as a guide to materials concerning the practical aspects of business operations and for specific industries and businesses. A companion index is the *Applied Science and Technology Index (ASTI)*. The ASTI catalogs those periodicals that concentrate on scientific and technological subjects, but many articles on nontechnical subjects are also included in these periodicals. It is organized by subject and indexes approximately 300 publications.

The third major index of value to the business researcher is the Public Affairs Information Service *Bulletin* (PAIS). Its coverage overlaps the *BPI* to some extent, but it also includes a more wide-ranging list of English-language publications from around the world. In addition, many books, government publications, and pamphlets are also indexed by subject. It covers many nonperiodical publications that become available from time to time.

The *F. & S. Index of Corporations and Industries* indexes articles in periodicals as well as other references on U.S. corporations and industries. Currently, this index covers about 750 publications. Through 1966, coverage also included the same topics for Canada, Great Britain, and Japan. Since 1966, there has been a companion volume called the *F. & S. Index International* which covers companies, industries, and countries outside the United States.

The *New York Times, The Wall Street Journal,* and *Fortune* are also indexed and will frequently provide excellent information. *The Wall Street Journal Index,* for example, is a monthly index divided into two sections, one for corporate news arranged by the name of the firm, and one for general news arranged by subject. Thee are also many other indexes and bibliographies available. Suggestive of this range are the *Psychological Abstracts*, the *Art Index, Biological & Agricultural Index,* and the *Education Index.*

While these periodical indexes are invaluable, they may still prove to be inadequate for a specific research study. This may occur because the indexes cover such a small portion of the periodicals published. There are many publications with valuable information which are not indexed in any of the guides mentioned. It is more difficult, but by no means impossible, to find material from these other sources. An example will illustrate one approach to this problem.

Assume for the moment that you are interested in conducting research into the use of paint by the American consumer. You are interested in such information as (1) how frequently families paint their homes; (2) how many rooms they paint at one time; (3) how much paint they use, and similar information. Such information would be useful as a basis for estimating the consumption of paint.

Obviously, you could interview consumers to obtain answers to these questions. On the other hand, it may be more efficient and less expensive to obtain information from other research studies. A review of the *BPI, PAIS,* and *ASTI* provides relatively little concrete information on these questions. There are two possible reasons for the lack of information. One is that there is just no information available on this subject. In this case, you will have no choice but to do field research if you want the answers to your questions. The other explanation is that such information is available in publications which are not indexed in the guides.

One way to check would be to determine whether paint-oriented periodicals are indexed. A look at the coverage of the traditional periodical indexing services indicates that they do not cover specific paint-oriented magazines. There are several references to which one can go to identify the magazines associated with the painting industry.

One which is available in most libraries is: *Ayer Directory of Publications.* Philadelphia: Ayer Press, 1980 to date. This is an annual list of American newspapers and periodicals, arranged by state and city of publication; it gives detailed information about each title. It also has an alphabetical list of titles and a classified list of trade, technical and professional journals. Reference to it indicates that there are at least six periodicals published in the United States that are concerned with some aspect of the paint history. With this information we can take one of two courses of action.

One course would be to contact the publishers of these magazines and seek help from them. They often know of specific articles in their own publications or may have a file on the subject which they may make available. A second approach is to continue the library search route by locating the nearest library which has copies of the newly discovered magazines. The best source for this is: *Union List of Serials in Libraries of the United States and Canada.* 3d ed. 5 vols. New York: H. W. Wilson, 1965. It is the most comprehensive list of periodicals available and indicates which American libraries hold each publication listed. It is updated by *New Serial Titles.*

Washington, D.C.: Library of Congress, 1953 to date. This paint illustration is from an actual case known to the author in which the researcher used both approaches cited. The direct contact with a publisher turned out to be most fruitful. The inquiry brought copies of a half-dozen specific articles and research studies which dealt with paint use practices. This information answered the major research questions satisfactorily without the need to go to expensive field research.

Miscellaneous sources. A final category listed in Figure 6–1 is the miscellaneous sources. Among these are many reference works, some of which have already been mentioned. Others are listed in Appendix A at the back of the book. Data published by business associations may be listed in the public catalog, or the material may be in vertical files kept by the library. Company annual reports and other similar materials are also more likely to be found in uncataloged collections, especially in microfilm or microfiche collections.

One major miscellaneous source is the publications from colleges and universities. Doctoral dissertations are one such source that is particularly valuable if one is investigating subjects at the frontiers of knowledge. The dissertations of persons receiving their doctorate at a given university will usually be cataloged in that university's library only. To meet the need for information about dissertations from other universities there are: *American Doctoral Dissertations.* Ann Arbor, Mich.: Xerox University Microfilms, 1957 to date. *Dissertation Abstracts International.* Ann Arbor, Mich.: Xerox University Microfilms, 1938 to date. The first publication provides "a complete listing of all doctoral dissertations accepted by American and Canadian universities." The abstracts typically run a few hundred words in length and may be enough for the reader to determine whether to order a copy of the entire dissertation. Another excellent reference for tracking down university research publications is: Associated University Bureaus of Business and Economic Research. *Index of Publications of Bureaus of Business and Economic Research.* 1950–1956. Eugene, Ore.: 1957 to date. This is an index to the reports, bulletins and monographs published by university bureaus of business research. Supplements include some articles appearing in periodicals published by these bureaus.

A sample search. A summary of the process of searching a library for information by describing an actual investigation is in order. Assume that a higher executive in your organization requests that you prepare a report for her on technological forecasting. She wants to know what it is, how it is carried out, who is doing it and so on. This executive must decide whether or not the organization should engage in this type of effort.

She is uninformed about the topic, and you are equally uninformed. You are fortunate, however, in knowing something about proper research methods, so are confident about the assignment. With this thought in mind, you begin the search. The path leads to the library of a local university, and the sequence followed is illustrated in a general way by the flow diagram in Figure 6–1.[3]

Since you are unfamiliar with the term "Technological forecasting," you look in the *Encyclopaedia Britannica* and the *International Encyclopedia of the Social Sciences*. These are usually good sources for some quick information about a topic; but in this case, there is no mention of technological forecasting. This is likely to happen if a topic or its terminology is rather new.

Next, try two guides to business reference materials. These provide lists of bibliographies, handbooks, textbooks and manuals which are often helpful. These sources are: Coman, Edwin T., *Sources of Business Information*, and Harvard University, *Selected Business Reference Sources*. In the Coman book, there are nine books listed on forecasting, but nothing that specifically mentions technological forecasting. It also lists a bibliography on business forecasting.

While putting Coman back on the shelf, serendipity takes over. One of the skills that researchers need to cultivate is a certain sensitivity that enables them to find things by luck. On the shelf, about two books away from the Coman book, is a 152-page bibliography, dated 1965, entitled, *Business Trends and Forecasting*, published as *Management Information Guide No. 9* by the Gale Research Company. This turns out to be an excellent annotated bibliography. In fact, the annotations are so complete that a study of the contents shows that there was virtually nothing on technological forecasting in business forecasting books up to 1965. While this is negative information, it is useful. You decide to restrict your search to the period since 1965.

With the preliminary steps not paying off, you decide to go directly to the *Bibliographic Index (BI)*. In the *Index* for 1966–1968, you find two entries listing bibliographies on technological forecasting. Search of earlier indexes back to 1960 turns up nothing further. The *BI* for 1969 has no mentions, while the April 1970 *Index* has one reference. Moving now to the public catalog, you learn that the library has only one of the two books mentioned in the *BI*, but does list two other books on technological forecasting and one published proceedings of a conference on the subject. Three out of four of these items come from Européan sources. Their cards in the public catalog indicate that three books have bibliographies ranging from 3 to 40 pages in length.

While finding four books on the subject in the card catalog is encouraging, you search further by going to the *Library of Congress Subject Catalog*. This is rewarded by finding four more books listed there. Now, you have identified eight English-language books that have been published on technological forecasting from 1967 to 1970. Some of these new discoveries may

---

[3]This example is based on an actual study done in 1970.

be in one of the local libraries, or you might choose to buy one or more of them.

Periodical search.   Since the topic includes the word "technological," you decide first to investigate the *Applied Science and Technology Index.* You review entries from 1963 to June 1970 and find one entry on the subject in the 1966 volume. There are three entries in 1967, five in 1968, four in 1969, and one in 1970. From 1966 to mid–1970, you find total of 14 entries in *ASTI* referencing articles about technological forecasting. A search of *PAIS* for the same time period turns up 11 more references to articles on technological forecasting, while *BPI* produces 19 which do not duplicate any of the ones found in the other two indexes.

Other sources.   With an inventory of eight book references and 44 periodical references, there is not much incentive to look further, but for sake of completeness, you search through the annual subject indexes of the *Monthly Catalog* of the U.S. Superintendent of Documents. From 1968 through mid–1970, there are eight references to published government documents on technological forecasting. All of them concern technological forecasting in the Soviet Union. None of them is on the depository list.

A search of the retrospective and annual subject indexes of *Dissertation Abstracts International* does not indicate any dissertations on technological forecasting. In total, then, after several hours of search, you have a set of bibliography cards which include:

> Eight books specifically about technological forecasting, at least four of which have extensive bibliographies to check.
>
> Forty-four periodical references.
>
> Eight government document references.

With this list, the reference search is well launched. The problem now is to find the references, weed out those which do not hold promise, and extract information that is appropriate to the task from the remainder. This extraction process is the subject of the next section.

EXTRACTING INFORMATION

Gathering and recording information from printed sources are often viewed as simple chores within the competence of anyone. This may be true, but it is also a task which is often done poorly. The task has three aspects which are worthy of consideration. First, you are faced with the job of selecting which information to record. That is, which information is useful and which is not, which is a net addition to our collection and which is mere repetition. These decisions are not easy to make, but in general, be guided by the research purpose. Set up an outline of the topic as quickly as possible, even knowing that it will probably change as you gather more information.

The idea that "I'll gather all of the material and then decide how to organize it" is inefficient. There is much interesting information that will turn up on many subjects which is diversionary in nature. It take self-discipline to ignore these interesting sideshows of information in order to concentrate on the main task; an a priori outline is helpful.

The second task is to determine how to record what you extract from the published material. Should you report it verbatim, paraphrase it, or outline it? More often than not, outlining is the most efficient method. For specific important decisions or statements, you will wish to record them verbatim. In a few other instances, a paraphrase statement of the author's position is suitable.

The third task is to develop an orderly recording system. With it, one can have the extracted information available when needed, have a ready reference source for checking, and have maximum flexibility in organizing the information.

Note taking. The first requirement is to use some orderly system that is also comfortable. Many use cards upon which to record both bibliographic references and the notes taken from these references. Putting notes on cards allows for flexible handling and organizing of the data. Some even advocate putting a single fact or idea on each individual card; this obviously promotes maximum flexibility, but is also fragments the information. The single idea per card concept is probably more desirable in those cases where the researcher does not have a fairly clear idea of subject organization.

One method of note taking uses two sets of cards and an outline of the key elements or questions regarding the topic. While the outline may change as the researcher acquires further insight into the subject, it is a help in deciding which information is needed and how various bits of information should be related.

One set of cards (probably 3- × -5 cards) is used for bibliographic references, and the second set (probably 5- × -8 cards) is used for the actual note-taking. The 3- × -5 cards should be set up in proper bibliographic format, one reference per card, so that they can be used later for footnote statements and for the drafting of the bibliography. These cards can be coded by a simple system that may be used to identify specific passages on the note cards. One useful coding system employs a combination letter and number (F1, F2, and so forth) to identify each author whose last name begins with "F."

The 5- × -8 note cards (some prefer to use regular 8½- × -11 note paper) provide more adequate space for writing information. On the note card margins, the bibliography reference codes may be entered to provide a ready source reference for each idea. Allied ideas from different sources may be placed on the same card without losing the ability to track each reference back to its source. This use of this note-taking system will enable you to develop a substantial set of notes, readily sortable into new patterns of

FIGURE 6–3   A note card example

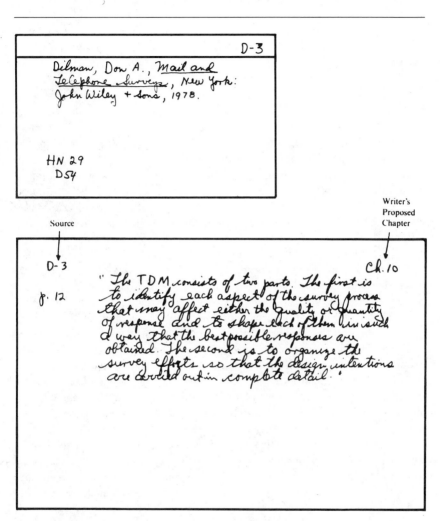

Source

Writer's
Proposed
Chapter

organization, and with each idea referenced back to the source. Figure 6–3 illustrates such cards.

Having gathered a data set of this type, you are ready to prepare your own analysis. One of the first steps of this analysis, one that you have probably been doing unconsciously along the line, is the evaluation of the quality of information found.

EVALUATING SECONDARY DATA

While the value of secondary data sources and their use has been stressed, there is still the task of evaluating the data which are found. This evaluation takes two forms; first, how well does the data fit the research needs; and, second, what confidence can you put in the accuracy and legitimacy of the data?

Data pertinency. Paramount in any consideration of secondary data is the inescapable fact that the data were not originally collected for our needs. Do you understand the definitions and classifications employed? Are their meanings consistent with your own? Of particular importance are the measurements used and the coverage of their data in terms of topic and time.

Data quality. The question of data quality is, first of all, a question of data accuracy. It is good research technique to go to the original source of the information rather than use an intermediate source which has quoted from the original. This enables you to catch any errors in transcription as well as review the cautionary and other comments that went along with the original data; finally, it may uncover revisions that have been made in the data since the intermediate source used it.

Another aspect of data accuracy concerns its completeness; that is, how much does the reported material actually cover? Is it based upon a narrow sample, a large population or what? Answers to these questions may indicate that the data are not appropriate for the problem. Another aspect of data quality concerns the capability of the source of the data. In this context, there are two concerns; first, are the persons who conducted the study people in whom you can have confidence? Are they highly regarded? Is their organization well regarded? A second aspect of source capability concerns the original source itself; that is, could the respondent actually answer this question? What are the chances that the respondent would know and be willing to give such information under the study conditions?

A concern that any investigator has in studying the quality of secondary data is to determine the degree to which they accurately reflect reality. A confounding factor here is the question of possible bias. The study has conducted for some purpose which may have dictated a particular orientation or flavor. Here again, the question of who did the study, whether the findings promote a special interest, and how the study itself was conducted are all important clues. One must especially be on guard when a study does not report the methodology and sampling design. These and other factors are of prime concern in determining if the secondary data are adequate for the investigator's research purposes.

SUMMARY

The use of secondary data sources for research presents some unique problems. The collection of data from within one's own organization, in particular, defies generalized description. Published data, on the other hand, are cataloged and coded so as to facilitate their use (if one understands library systems and has some facility with search tools).

Literature sources may be classed into three major groups, plus a fourth catch-all group. Books are usually the basic source for general coverage and for established topics of breadth or depth. Periodicals are a second major source and are especially valuable for current information and for topics of limited scope. Documents from governmental organizations are a third major source of literature. Finally, there are miscellaneous materials produced by private organizations, universities, and references services.

In using secondary data sources, researchers have two jobs. First, they must define their research needs so as to be able to use the coding systems that have been developed to make printed information more accessible. This calls for the researchers to have a clear knowledge and understanding of major reference tools available, as well as some skill in their use. Their second job is to secure adequate usable data from the information storage system. This calls for skill in extracting information efficiently, and the ability to judge how much confidence to place in the data.

Research based on secondary sources may constitute the sole input in some cases but is often significant only in the exploratory phases of a study. Just what role secondary sources play is a function of the study's research design.

SUPPLEMENTAL READINGS

1. Barzun, Jacques, and Henry F. Graff. *The Modern Researcher*. rev. ed. New York: Harcourt, Brace & World, 1970, pts. I and II. Chapters 4 and 5 treat the processes of fact gathering and verification.
2. Harvard University, Graduate School of Business. *Current Periodical Publications in Baker Library*. Boston, Mass. Includes magazines, journals, newspapers, bulletins, statistical annuals, yearbooks, conference proceedings, directories, government agency annual reports, and loose-leaf business services.
3. Helppie, Charles E.; James R. Gibbons; and Donald W. Pearson. *Research Guide in Economics*. Morristown, N.J.: General Learning Press, 1974. Designed to meet the "need in economics for a practical guide to research for the student."
4. Johnson, H. Webster. *How to Use the Business Library*. 4th ed. Cincinnati: South-Western Publishing Company, 1972. Useful suggestions on the use of a business library.

For other references, see Appendix A at back of book.

DISCUSSION QUESTIONS

1. Some researchers find that their sole sources are secondary data. Why might this be? Name some management research situations where secondary data sources are probably the only ones feasible.

2. While card catalogs of libraries are useful, what problems do you see if a researcher depends only on the catalog for information sources?

3. Many managements gather and analyze statistical data for small geographic areas. For what types of businesses do you think these data might be important? For what purposes might they want such information? What types of data might they use? Where might they secure such information from secondary sources?

4. Assume that you are asked to investigate the use of mathematical programming in accounting applications; you decide to depend upon secondary data sources. What search tools might you use? Which do you think would be the most fruitful? Sketch a flow diagram of your search sequence.

5. What are the problems of secondary data quality that researchers must face? How can they deal with them?

6. Secure a recent copy of the *Statistical Abstract* and determine what information is available on the following topics:

   a Coal mining.

   b Consumer credit.

   c Advertising expenditures.

   d Labor unions.

   e Social welfare expenditures.

   f Hospitals in the United States.

   g Law enforcement.

7. Choose a line of trade and determine what data are available for that line at a state and local level in the *Census of Business*.

8. Choose a two-digit industry classification from the *Census of Manufactures*, and determine the type of information that is available for it. How much information is available at more detailed (for example, four-digit) levels?

9. Below are a number of requests that a young staff assistant might receive. What specific tools or services would you expect to use to find the requisite information? (Appendix A may be helpful.)

   a The president wants a list of perhaps six of the best references that have appeared on executive compensation during the last 10 years.

   b Has the FTC published any recent statements (within the last year) concerning their position regarding quality stabilization?

   c A man at a western university is said to have completed his Ph. D. dissertation last year on competition problems in our industry. Can we find out whether or not this is true? How can we get a copy?

   d I need a list of the major companies that are located in Springfield, Missouri.

   e Please get me a list of the directors of General Motors, Dial Finance, and American Investment Company.

   f A new book has recently come out concerning technological forecasting. Can you get the reference for me?

   g We are looking at a man named Franklin T. Pierce who is a senior VP of the Harris Trust Company in Chicago. Can you get some biographical data on him for me?

   h Is there a trade magazine that specializes in the flooring industry?

   i I need a copy of the *Journal of the Oil Chemist's Society*, but our library does not have it. Where is the closest place I could go to look at it?

j The Fuji Bank of Tokyo, Japan, has issued a special study in their December 1984 *Fuji Bank Bulletin*. Where can I get a copy?

k I would like to track down a study of small-scale service franchising that was recently published by a Bureau of Business Research at one of the southern universities. Can you help me?

7. Primary source data collection

Ken Lane stopped to admire the new brass plate that had been mounted on the wall by the entrance to his offices. It read,

> **Lane Research, Inc.**

Just seeing it there gave him a feeling of pride and achievement. In two years his firm had grown from a one-man shop to six full-time professional employees, three clericals, and a large number of part-time field workers. "Not bad," he muttered as he opened the door and entered.

He was looking forward to this morning's staff meeting where they would review four new projects on which they have been invited to bid. Never before had they had so many projects to consider at one time. An important task would be to decide just what type of data collection method they should use. Once this was decided, they could better estimate the costs and resources that each study would take. He ran quickly over the proposed projects in his mind. The first was a request from a major foundation for a nationwide study of American public opinion and attitudes about business and government.

The second project was a request by the U.S. Occupational Safety and Health Administration (OSHA) for private research firms to propose regional studies on safety conditions in small manufacturing plants. The third proposal would go to a major teaching hospital located in the city. It was for an in-depth study of the work practices of floor nurses in the hospital. The fourth project was a proposal to test the consumer acceptance of a new food product. Each project represented a challenging design problem, but to have four at one time was enough to boggle one's mind. They could not hope to do more than two and even this would require that they choose every aspect of the research design carefully.

As Ken sat down at his desk he glanced at the clock. He had 30 minutes until the meeting in which to think again about the various primary data collection method options for each project.

PRIMARY DATA COLLECTION METHODS

One of the ways research designs can be classified is by the communication method used to gather primary source data. There are really only two alternatives. First, we might *observe* conditions, events, subjects or what have you. Secondly, we might *survey* or *question* persons about various topics. We take up each briefly, discussing characteristics, advantages, and disadvantages in turn.

Observation

Much of what one knows comes from observation. You notice such things as the weather, what is going on about you, how people react to events, and a host of other activities and conditions. While such observation may be the basis for knowledge, the collection processes are often haphazard. For research one needs to improve the quality of observation, and this begins with understanding the strengths and weaknesses of this method.

Strengths.   There are vast areas of information for which observation is the only method available. Obviously the study of records, mechanical processes, and lower animals fall into this category. Most small children cannot be questioned very successfully.

Another value of observation is that one can collect the original data at the time it occurs. One need not depend upon reports by others. Every respondent filters the information no matter how well-intentioned he or she is. Forgetting occurs, and there are reasons why the respondent may not want to report fully and fairly. Observation overcomes many of these deficiencies of questioning.

A third strength is that one can secure information that most participants would ignore either because it is so common and expected or because it is not seen relevant. For example, if you are observing buying activity in a store there may be conditions important to the research study but which the shopper would not notice. Such questions as: What is the weather? the day of the week? the time of day? customer traffic at the time? promotional activity in competing stores? and the like. One can expect to learn only a part of the answers to these questions from most respondents.

Another strength of observation is that only with this method can one capture the whole event as it occurs. You may be interested in all of the conditions surrounding a confrontation at a bargaining session between union and management representatives. These sessions may extend over a period of time, and any effort to study the unfolding of the negotiation process is greatly facilitated by the use of observation. Questioning could seldom provide the insight of observation for many of the aspects of the negotiation process.

Finally, subjects seem to accept an observational type of intrusion better than questioning. It is less demanding of them and normally has less biasing effect on their conduct than does questioning. In addition, it is also possible to conduct disguised and unobtrusive observation studies much more easily than disguised questioning.

Weaknesses. There are also some severe research limitations of the observational method. A major problem is that the observer normally must be at the scene of the event when it takes place. Yet it is often impossible to predict where and when the event will occur. One way to guard against missing an event is to observe for prolonged periods until it does occur, but this brings up a second disadvantage. Observation is a slow and expensive process that requires either human observers or some type of costly surveillance equipment.

A third limitation of observation is that its most reliable results are restricted to data that can be determined by overt action or surface indicators. To go below the surface, the observer must make inferences from surface indicators. Two observers will probably agree on the nature of various surface events, but the inferences they draw from such data are much more variable.

Finally, observation is limited as a way to learn of the past. It is limited in a similar manner as a method by which to learn what is going on at present at some distant place. It is also difficult to gather information on such topics as intentions, attitudes, opinions, or preferences.

Any consideration of the merits of observation indicates that it is a valuable research tool when used with care and understanding. The use of observation will be treated later in this chapter.

Surveying

To survey is to question persons and record their responses as the data for analysis. This is the second major technique for gathering information and also has its special strengths and weaknesses.

Strengths. The great strength of questioning as a data collecting technique is its versatility. It does not require that there be a visual or other objective perception of the sought information by a researcher. Indeed, abstract information of all types can be gathered only by questioning others. One can seldom learn much about opinions and attitudes except by questioning. The same can be said for intentions and expectations. Information about past events is often available only through questioning of persons who remember the events.

Surveys tend to be more efficient and economical than observation. For example, information can be gathered by a few well-chosen questions which would take much more time and effort to gather by observation. Surveying, using the telephone or the mail as a medium of communication, can expand geographic coverage at a fraction of the cost and time required by observation.

Weaknesses. The questioning technique has its shortcomings. The major weakness is that the quality of information secured depends heavily on the ability and willingness of respondents to cooperate. Often, people will refuse an interview or fail to reply to a mail survey. There may be many reasons for this unwillingness to cooperate. Certain people at certain times fail to see any value in participation; they also may fear the interview experience for some personal reason; or they may view the topic as too sensitive.

Even if respondents do participate, they may not have the knowledge sought, or even have an opinion on the topic of concern. Under these circumstances, their proper response should be "don't know" or "have no opinion." Too often, what actually happens is that respondents feel obliged to express some opinion even if they do not have one. In those cases, it is difficult for researchers to know how true or reliable answers are.

Another problem is that a respondent may interpret a question or concept differently from what was intended by the researcher. In this frame of reference, the respondent is answering a question different from the one being asked. Finally, a respondent may intentionally mislead the researcher by giving false information. It is quite difficult for a researcher to identify these occasions. Thus, it becomes important to keep in mind that survey responses must be accepted for what they are—statements by others which may be true or untrue. In spite of these weaknesses, surveying is much more widely used in business research than is observation.

The use of questioning. The versatility of surveying has already been pointed out. Almost any topic can be investigated by asking questions about it. Obviously, the most appropriate applications are those where conditions indicate that respondents are uniquely qualified to provide the desired information. We should expect that such facts as age, income, immediate family situation, and so forth would be appropriate topics on which one would expect to get good data. However, if we ask the respondent to report on events that have not been personally experienced, we need to assess the replies carefully. If the purpose is to learn what the respondent understands to be the case, it is quite legitimate to accept the answers given. On the other hand, if the intent is to learn what the event or situation was, we should recognize that the respondent is reporting second-hand data and the expected accuracy of the information declines. One should not depend on these sources if a more direct source can be found. For example, a family member should be asked about another family member's experience only when there is no other way to get the information directly.

Questions can be used to inquire also about subjects that are exclusively internal to the respondent. We include here such items as attitudes, opinions, expectations, and intentions. Such information can be made available to the researcher if the right questions are asked of respondents. It becomes, finally, a matter of whether to ask direct or indirect questions in order to collect the most meaningful data. More is said about this topic in Chapter 8.

In addition to the considerations mentioned above, there is a variety of methods by which to interview respondents. Questioning can be carried out by face-to-face interviewing, by telephone, by mail, or by a combination of these. While there are many commonalities among these approaches, there are many considerations unique to each. For this reason, each is discussed separately.

Personal interviewing

Personal interviewing, i.e., face-to-face, is a two-way conversation initiated by an interviewer to obtain information from a respondent. The differences in roles of interviewer and respondent are pronounced. They are typically strangers and the topics and pattern of discussion are generally dictated by the interviewer. The consequences of the event are usually minimal to the respondent. The respondent is asked to provide information with little hope of receiving any immediate or direct benefit from this cooperation. Yet if the interview is carried off successfully, it is an excellent data collection technique.

Pros and cons. There are real advantages as well as clear limitations to personal interviewing. The greatest value lies in the depth and detail of information that can be secured. It far exceeds the information secured from telephone and mail surveys. The interviewer can also do more things to improve the quality of the information received than with other methods. Interviewers can note conditions of the interview, probe with additional questions, and gather supplemental information through observation.

The interviewers also have more control than with other kinds of interrogation. They can prescreen to assure that the correct respondent is reply-

FIGURE 7–1   Opposing motivation levels affecting a respondent in an interview

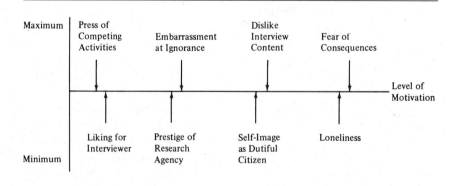

Source: Kahn and Cannell, "Interviewing," David L. Sills, ed., *International Encyclopedia of the Social Sciences,* vol. 8, p. 153. Copyright © 1968 by Crowell Collier and Macmillan, Inc.

ing and can set up and control interviewing conditions. They can use special scoring devices, visual materials, and the like. Finally, interviewers can make adjustments to the language of the interview because they can observe the problems and effects that the interview is having on the respondent.

With such advantages, why would anyone want to use any other survey method? Probably the greatest reason is that the method is costly, both in money and time. A personal interview can cost anywhere from a few dollars to $100 or more for an interview with a hard-to-reach person. Costs are particularly high if the study covers a wide geographic area or has stringent sampling requirements.

Costs have risen rapidly in recent years because changes in the social climate have made personal interviewing more difficult. Many people are reluctant to talk with strangers who visit their homes. Interviewers are reluctant to visit unfamiliar neighborhoods alone, especially for evening interviewing. Finally, results of personal interviews can be affected adversely by interviewers who alter the questions asked, or in other ways, bias the results. More about this is discussed later in the chapter. If we are to overcome these deficiencies we must appreciate the conditions necessary for interview success.

Success requirements. Three broad conditions must be met to have a successful personal interview. They are (1) availability of the needed information from the respondent; (2) an understanding by the respondent of his or her role; and (3) adequate motivation by the respondent to cooperate. The interviewer can do relatively little about the respondent's information level. That is why there should be screening questions to qualify respondents when there is doubt about their ability to answer. This is the study designer's responsibility.

There are a number of ways that interviewers can influence respondents. For example, an interviewer can explain what kind of answer is sought, how complete it should be, and in what terms it should be expressed. Interviewers even do some coaching in the interview although this can be a biasing factor.

Respondent motivation is certainly a responsibility of the interviewer. Studies of reactions to a number of surveys indicate that respondents can be motivated to participate in personal interviews and, in fact, can even enjoy the experience. In one study, more than 90 percent of respondents said that the interview experience was interesting, and three-fourths reported that they were willing to be interviewed again.[1]

Kahn and Cannell point out that there are a variety of forces that affect respondent motivation in an interview. Many of these involve the interviewer. A graphic way to represent these various forces is presented in Figure 7–1.

---

[1]Robert L. Kahn and Charles F. Cannell, *The Dynamics of Interviewing* (New York: John Wiley & Sons, 1957), pp. 45–51.

Interviewing technique[2]

At first, it may seem easy to ask another person questions about various topics, but research interviewing is not so simple. What we do or say as interviewers can make or break a study. Respondents often react more to their feelings about the interviewer than to the content of the questions. It is also important that the interviewer ask the questions properly, record the responses accurately, and probe meaningfully. To achieve these aims, the interviewer must be trained to carry out those procedures that foster a good interviewing relationship.

Increasing respondent's receptiveness. The first goal in an interview is to establish a friendly relationship with the respondent. Three factors will help to bring about respondent receptiveness. The respondent must (1) feel that the experience will be pleasant and satisfying; (2) believe that the survey is important and worthwhile; and (3) have any mental reservations satisfied. Whether the experience will be pleasant and satisfying depends heavily upon the interviewer. Typically, respondents will cooperate with an interviewer who is understanding and accepting.

The respondent must also think that the survey is important and worthwhile. This typically requires some explanation of the study, although the amount will vary. It is the interviewer's responsibility to determine what explanation is needed and to supply it. Usually, the interviewer should state the purpose of the study, tell how the information will be used, and suggest what is expected of the respondent. Respondents should feel that their cooperation will be meaningful both to themselves and to the survey results. When this is achieved, more respondents will express their views willingly. Respondents often have reservations about being interviewed that must be overcome. They may suspect that the interviewer is a disguised salesperson, bill collector, or the like. In addition, they may also feel inadequate, or fear that they will be embarrassed by the questioning. What follows are techniques for successful interviewing of respondents in their homes.

The introduction. The respondent's first reaction to the request for an interview is at best a guarded one. Interviewer appearance and action are critical in forming a good first impression. Interviewers should immediately identify themselves by name and organization, showing any special identification. Introductory letters or other information can demonstrate the study's legitimacy. In this brief period, the interviewer must demonstrate friendly intentions and stimulate the respondent's interest.

The interviewer's introductory explanations should be no more detailed than necessary. Too much information can introduce a bias. However, some respondents will demand more detail. For them, the interviewer might explain the objective of the study, its background, how the respondent was

---

[2]One of the top research organizations in the world is the Survey Research Center of the University of Michigan. The material in this section draws heavily upon the *Interviewer's Manual* (Ann Arbor, Mich.: Survey Research Center, University of Michigan, 1969).

selected, the confidential nature of the interview (if it is such), and the beneficial values of the research findings. Be prepared to deal with such questions as:

"How did you happen to pick me?"

"Who gave you our name?"

"I don't know enough about this. Why don't you go next door?"

"Why are you doing this study?"[3]

The home interview typically involves two stages. The first occurs at the door when the introductory remarks are made, but this is not a satisfactory location for many interviews. In trying to secure entrance, it is considered more effective to suggest the desired course of action rather than to ask permission. It is argued that "May I come in?" can be easily countered with a respondent's "No," while "I would like to come in and talk with you about X," is more successful.

If the respondent is busy or away. If it is obvious that the respondent is busy, it may be a good idea to give a general introduction and try to stimulate enough interest to arrange an interview at a later date. If the designated respondent is not at home, the interviewer should briefly explain the proposed visit to the person who is contacted. It is desirable to establish good relations with intermediaries since their attitudes can help in contacting the proper respondent.

The good interviewing relationship. In the successful interview, there is rapport, meaning that a relationship of confidence and understanding exists between interviewer and respondent. Interview situations are often new to respondents and they need help in defining their roles. The interviewer can help by conveying the fact that the interview is confidential and important, and that the respondent can discuss the topics with freedom from censure, coercion, or pressure. Under such conditions, the respondent can obtain much satisfaction in "opening up" without pressure being exerted.

Gathering the data. To this point, the communication aspects of the interviewing process have been stressed. Having completed the introduction and established initial rapport, the interviewer turns to the technical task of gathering information. The interview centers around the prearranged questioning sequence. The technical task is well-defined in studies with a structured questioning procedure (in contrast to an exploratory interview situation). The interviewer should follow the exact wording of the questions, ask them in the order presented, and ask every question that is specified. When questions are misunderstood or misinterpreted, they should be repeated.

One of the most difficult tasks in interviewing is to make certain that the answers adequately satisfy the question objectives. To do this, the inter-

---

[3]Survey Research Center, *Interviewer's Manual*, pp. 3–4.

viewer must learn the objectives of each question from a study of the survey instructions or by asking the project director. It is important to have this information well in mind because many first responses are inadequate even in the best-planned studies.

The technique of stimulating respondents to answer more fully and relevantly is termed *probing*. Since it presents a great potential for bias, a probe should be neutral and appear as a natural part of the conversation. There are a number of different probing styles:

1. A brief assertion of understanding and interest. With comments such as "I see" or "yes" or "uh-huh" the interviewer can tell the respondent that the interviewer is listening and is interested in more.
2. An expectant pause. The simplest way to suggest to the respondent to say more is a pause along with an expectant look or a nod of the head. This approach must be used with caution. Some respondents have nothing more to say and frequent pausing could give them some embarrassing silences.
3. Repeating the question. This is particularly useful when the respondent appears not to understand the question or has strayed from the subject.
4. Repeating the respondent's reply. This can be done while writing it down and often serves as a good probe. Hearing thoughts restated often prompts revisions or further comments.
5. A neutral question or comment. Such comments make a direct bid for more information. Examples are: "How do you mean? Can you tell me more about your thinking on that? Why do you think that is so? Anything else?"[4]

Another valuable technique is to ask for clarification. This approach is particularly effective when the answer is unclear or is inconsistent with something already said. In this case the interviewer suggests that he or she failed to understand fully. Typical of such probes is, "I'm not *quite* sure I know what you mean by that—could you tell me a little more?" or "I'm sorry, but I'm not sure I understand. Did you say previously that . . . ?" It is important that the interviewer take the blame for failure to understand so as not to appear to be cross-examining the respondent.

A specific type of response that requires persistent probing is the "I don't know." This is a satisfactory response if the respondent actually does not know. But, too often, "I don't know" means that the respondent (1) does not understand; (2) says this to get time to think; or (3) is trying to evade the question. The interviewer can best probe this type of reply by using the expectant pause or by some reassuring remark such as "We are interested in your ideas about this."[5]

Recording the interview. While the methods used in recording will vary, the interviewer usually writes down the answers of the respondent. There are some guidelines to make this task more efficient. First, it is important to record responses as they take place. If you wait until later you

---

[4] Survey Research Center, pp. 5–2.

[5] Survey Research Center, *Interviewing*, pp. 5–3.

lose much of what is said. If hard pressed for time during the session, the interviewer should use some system of shorthand that will preserve the essence of the respondent's replies without converting them into an interviewer's paraphrases. Abbreviating words, leaving out articles and prepositions, using only key words, and the like, are good ways to do this.

Another technique is for the interviewer to repeat the response while writing it down. This helps to hold the respondent's interest during the writing and checks the interviewer's understanding of what the respondent has said. Normally the interviewer should start the writing as soon as the respondent begins to reply. The interviewer should also record all probes and other comments on the questionnaire in parentheses to set them off from responses.

Personal interview problems

In personal interviewing, the researcher must deal with two major problems, bias and cost. While each is discussed separately, they are closely interrelated. Biased results grow out of three types of error: sampling error, nonresponse error, and response error. Sampling error is discussed in Chapter 10.

Nonresponse error. This error occurs when you are not able to find those whom you are supposed to study. It is an especially difficult problem when one is using a probability sample of subjects. In such a case, there are predesignated persons to be interviewed; the task is to find these respondents. If one is forced to interview substitutes, an unknown but possibly substantial bias is introduced. In one study of nonresponse, it was found that only 31 percent of all first calls (and 20 percent of all first calls in major metropolitan areas) were completed. The best first-call rate of 52 percent was for rural male respondents contacted after 6 P.M. on a weekday.

The most reliable solution to nonresponse problems is to make callbacks. If enough attempts are made, it is usually possible to contact most target respondents, although unlimited callbacks are expensive.[6] An original contact plus three callbacks should usually secure about 85 percent of the target respondents. Yet in one study, 36 percent of central city residents still were not contacted after three callbacks.[7] One way to improve the productivity of callbacks is to vary them by time of day and day of the week. Sometimes, neighbors can suggest the best time to call.

A method that has been used with success is, after a limited number of callbacks, to treat all remaining nonrespondents as a new subpopulation. A

---

[6]In one study, 5.5 percent of white respondents and 11 percent of nonwhite respondents remained uncontacted after six calls. See W. C. Dunkleberg and G. S. Day, "Nonresponse Bias and Callbacks in Sample Surveys," *Journal of Marketing Research* 10 (May 1973), Table 3.

[7]Ibid.

random sample is then drawn from this group and every effort is made to complete this sample with 100-percent response. These findings can then be weighted into the total population estimate.

Another approach is to adjust the results secured by weighting.[8] For example, in a survey in which central city residents are underrepresented we can weight the results of the interviews that are secured in order to give them full representation in the results. The weakness of this approach is that weighted returns often differ from those that would be secured if callbacks were made. Weighting for nonresponse after only one contact attempt will probably not overcome nonresponse bias, but respondent characteristics do tend to converge on their population values after two to three callbacks.[9]

A third way to deal with this nonresponse problem is to substitute someone else for the missing respondent, but this is a dangerous practice. "At home" respondents are likely to differ from "not at home" persons in systematic ways. One study indicates that "not at home" persons tend to be younger, better educated, more urban, and have a higher income than the average.[10]

If one must substitute, it is better for the interviewer to query others in the household about the designated respondent. This approach has worked reasonably well "when questions are relatively objective, when informants have a high degree of observability with respect to respondents, when the population is homogeneous, and when the setting of the interview provides no clear-cut motivation to distort responses in one direction or another . . . ."[11]

Response error. This occurs when the data reported differ from the actual data. There are many ways that such errors can happen. One is errors made in the processing and tabulating of data. Discussion of these is reserved for Chapter 11. Another important source of error is the respondent who fails to report fully and accurately. In one study, it was found that liquid asset holdings are typically underreported by as much as 25 to 50 percent. Other data, such as income and purchases of consumer durables, are more accurately reported. It has already been pointed out that respondents have difficulty in reporting fully and accurately on topics that are sensitive or involve ego matters. Consistent control or elimination of such respondent bias is a problem that has yet to be solved. The best advice is to use trained interviewers who are knowledgeable about such problems.

The interviewer is also a major source of response bias. Perhaps the most insidious source of interviewer bias is cheating. Surveying is difficult work,

---

[8]C. H. Fuller, "Weighting to Adjust for Survey Nonresponse," *Public Opinion Quarterly* 38 (Summer 1974), pp. 239–46.

[9]W. C. Dunkleberg and G. S. Day. "Nonresponse Bias," Table 3.

[10]Ibid., pp. 160–168.

[11]Eleanore Singer, "Agreement between Inaccessible Respondents and Informants," *Public Opinion Quarterly* 36 (Winter 1972–73), pp. 603–11.

often done by part-time employees, usually with only limited training, and under little direct supervision. Under such conditions, falsification of an answer to an overlooked question is an easy, harmless first step that can be followed by more pervasive forgery. It is not known how much of this goes on, but it should be of constant concern to research directors.

It is also obvious that an interviewer can distort the results of any survey by inappropriate suggestions, word emphasis, tone of voice, and question rephrasing. Such activities, whether premeditated or merely due to care-lessness are widespread. Schyberger investigated this problem with a rela-tively simple structured questionnaire and using planted respondents to report on the interviewers. His conclusion was "the high frequency of devia-tions from instructed behavior are alarming. . . ."[12]

In addition to these factors, there are many other ways that interviewers can influence respondents. For example, older interviewers are often seen as authority figures by young respondents who modify their responses ac-cordingly. Some research indicates that perceived social distance between interviewer and respondent has a distorting effect, although the studies do not fully agree on just what this relationship is.[13]

There have been a large number of studies on the various aspects of interviewer bias, most of which support the conclusion that it is a major problem area. However, many of the findings are at odds on the exact dimensions of this bias and the conditions under which it occurs. In the light of this confusion, the safest course for research directors is to recognize that there is a constant potential for response error. They should select interview-ers carefully and preferably use trained personnel whose age, sex, social status, and ethnic origin conform to that of the population being studied. When the study is a cross-section of the general population, this matching is not possible. In such a case, the typical interviewer, a middle-aged, middle-class woman, is probably the best choice. Respondents generally perceive such an interviewer as being accepting, understanding, and nonthreatening.

Costs. While professional interviewers' wage scales are typically not high, interviewing is costly and these costs continue to rise. Much of the cost results from the substantial interviewer time taken up with administra-tive and travel tasks. Respondents are often geographically scattered and this adds to the cost. In recent years, some professional research organiza-tions have attempted to gain control of these spiraling costs. Interviewers have typically been paid on an hourly rate, but Sudman suggests that this method rewards the inefficient interviewers and often results in field costs

---

[12]Bo W:son Schyberger, "A Study of Interviewer Behavior," *Journal of Marketing Research* 4 (February 1967), p. 35.

[13]B. S. Dohrenwend, J. A. Williams Jr., and C. H. Weiss, "Interviewer Biasing Effects: toward a Reconciliation of Findings," *Public Opinion Quarterly* 33 (Spring 1969), pp. 121–29.

exceeding budgets.[14] The U.S. Bureau of the Census and The National Opinion Research Center have experimented with production standards and a formula pay system that provides an incentive for efficient interviewers. It is reported that this approach has cut field costs by about 10 percent and has improved the accuracy of the forecasts of field work costs.

A second approach to the reduction of field costs has been to use the telephone to schedule personal interviews. Telephone calls to set up appointments for interviews are reported to reduce personal calls by 25 percent without reducing cooperation rates.[15] Telephone screening is also valuable when a study is concerned with a rare population. In one such case, where blind persons were sought, it was found that telephone screening of households by telephone was only one third the cost of screening on a face-to-face basis.[16]

A third approach to the problem of high field costs is to use self-administered questionnaires. In one study, a personal interview was conducted in the household with a self-administered questionnaire left for one or more other members of the household to complete. In this study, the cost per completed case was reduced by about one half when compared to personal interviews. A comparison between a personal interview and a self-administered questionnaire seeking the same data indicated that there was generally sufficient similarity of answers to enable them to be combined.[17]

Another study compared the use of a "drop off" delivery of a self-administered questionnaire to a mail survey.[18] Under the drop-off system, a lightly trained survey taker personally delivered the questionnaires to target households and returned in a couple of days for the completed instrument. Response rates for the drop-off system were typically above 70 percent—much higher than for comparable mail surveys. At the same time, the cost per completed questionnaire was from 18 to 40 percent lower than the mail surveys.

In addition to a higher rate and lower cost per response, the drop-off method gives greater control over sample design, permits more complete identification of the respondents' geographic location, and allows the researcher to eliminate those persons who fall outside of a predefined sample frame (persons of the wrong age, income, or other characteristics). Additional information can also be gathered by observation on the visits. However, the cost advantage of this method is probably restricted to those studies where the respondents can be reached with relatively little travel.

---

[14]Seymour Sudman, *Reducing the Costs of Surveys* (Chicago: Aldine Publishing, 1967), p. 67.

[15]Ibid., p. 59.

[16]Ibid., p. 63.

[17]Ibid., p. 53.

[18]C. H. Lovelock, Ronald Stiff, David Cullwick, and Ira M. Kaufman, "An Evaluation of the Effectiveness of Drop-Off Questionnaire Delivery," *Journal of Marketing Research* 13 (November 1976), pp. 358–64.

Training. Field interviewers receive varying degrees of training, ranging from brief written instructions to extensive sessions. Commercial market research studies tend to the former level of training, while governmental, educational, and similar research organizations tend to provide more extensive training.

Written instructions should be provided in all studies. Such instructions should cover at least the general objectives of the study, something on the problems which have been encountered in tests of the interview procedure, and how they were solved. In addition, most questions should be discussed separately, giving the interviewer some insight into the purpose of the question, examples of adequate and inadequate responses, and other suggestions such as how to probe for more information. Definitions should be included so that the interviewer can explain and interpret in a standardized manner.

Those who believe in the value of training have some evidence to support their views. In one widely cited study, intensive training produced significant improvements in interviewer performance. The training effect was so great that performances of individual interviewers before training were poor predictors of post-training performance.[19] Cannell and Kahn suggest that a training program for interviewers should include the following:

1. Provide the new interviewers with the principles of measurement, give them an intellectual grasp of the data-collection function and a basis for evaluating interviewing behavior.
2. Teach the techniques of interviewing.
3. Provide the opportunity for practice and evaluation by actually conducting interviews under controlled conditions.
4. Offer careful evaluation of interviews, especially at the beginning of actual data collection. Such evaluation should include review of interview protocols.[20]

TELEPHONE INTERVIEWING

The telephone can be helpful in setting up personal interviews and screening large populations for rare respondent types. Studies have also shown that one can use the telephone to improve the response rates of mail surveys by making prior notification calls.[21] However, the telephone's greatest contribution in survey work is as a mode of communication.

Telephone strengths. Of all the advantages of telephone interviewing, probably none ranks higher than its moderate cost. One study reports that

---

[19]S. A. Richardson, B. S. Dohrenwend, and D. Klein, *Interviewing: Its Forms and Functions* (New York: Basic Books, 1965), pp. 328–58.

[20]Reprinted by special permission from Cannell–Kahn, "Interviewing," in *The Handbook of Social Psychology*, 2d ed., vol. 2, edited by Lindzey–Aronson (Reading, Mass.: Addison-Wesley, 1968).

[21]Marvin A. Jolson, "How to Double or Triple Mail-Survey Response Rates," *Journal of Marketing* 41 (October 1977), pp. 78–81.

sampling and data collection costs for telephone surveys can run from 45 to 64 percent lower than comparable personal interviews.[22] Much of the savings comes from cuts in travel costs and administrative economies in training and supervision. All calls are made from a single location, enabling the researcher to use fewer, yet more skilled interviewers. Telephones are especially economical when there are callbacks and respondents are widely scattered. Since the advent of WATS lines it is possible to interview nationally at a reasonable cost.

With the widespread use of computers, one can now combine telephone interviewing with immediate entry of the responses into a computer file using cathode ray terminals. This brings added savings in time and money. When compared to either personal interviews or mail surveys, the use of telephones brings a faster completion of a study, sometimes taking only a day or so for the field work. When compared to personal interviewing, it is also likely that interviewer bias is reduced by using telephones.

Limitations. There are also limitations to using the telephone for research. The obvious first limitation is that the respondent must be available by phone. In the past, this has been a major problem, but this deficiency has been receding year by year. It is now estimated that about 90 percent of U.S. households, and almost all businesses, have telephones. The usage rates are not as high in rural areas, among lower-income groups, or among young households, and these variations can be a source of bias.[23]

Because about 20 percent of American householders move each year, there are always a large number of obsolete numbers as well as new households for which numbers have not yet been published. In addition, it is estimated that about 22 percent of all household phone numbers are unlisted.[24] Another source indicates that the highest incidence of nonlisting is in the West, in large metropolitan areas, among nonwhites, and persons between 18 to 34 years of age.[25] Several methods have been developed to overcome this deficiency of directories; among them are techniques for choosing phone numbers by using random digit dialing or combinations of directories and random dialing.[26] Random dialing procedures normally call

---

[22]Robert M. Groves and Robert L. Kahn, *Surveys by Telephone* (New York: Academic Press, 1979), p. 223.

[23]D. A. Leuthold and R. Scheele, "Patterns of Bias in Samples Based on Telephone Directories," *Public Opinion Quarterly* 35 (Summer 1971), pp. 249–57.

[24]R. W. Graves, "An Empirical Comparison of Two Telephone Sample Designs," *Journal of Marketing Research* 15 (November 1978), p. 622.

[25]G. J. Glasser and G. D. Metzger, "National Estimates of Nonlisted Telephone Households and Their Characteristics," *Journal of Marketing Research* 12 (August 1975), p. 360.

[26]G. J. Glasser and G. D. Metzger, "Random Digit Dialing as a Method of Telephone Sampling," *Journal of Marketing Research* 11 (February 1972), pp. 59–64, and S. Sudman, "The Uses of Telephone Directories for Survey Sampling," *Journal of Marketing Research* 10 (May 1973), pp. 204–07.

for choosing exchanges or exchange blocks and then generating random numbers within these blocks for calling.[27]

Limits on the length of interview is another disadvantage of the telephone, but the degree of this limitation depends on the respondent's interest in the topic. Ten minutes or so has generally been thought of as the maximum, but interviews of 20 minutes or more are not uncommon. Interviews ran as long as 1½ hours in one long-distance survey.[28]

In telephone interviewing, it is not possible to use budgets, maps, illustrations, or complex scales. The medium also limits the complexity of the questioning and the use of sorting techniques. One rather ingenious solution to the scale deficiency, however, has been to employ a nine-point scaling approach and to ask the respondent to visualize this by using the telephone dial.[29]

Some studies indicate that the response rate in telephone studies is lower than for comparable face-to-face interviews. One reason for this is that respondents find it easier to terminate an interview. It has also been found that telephone surveys can result in less complete responses and that those interviewed by phone find the experience to be less rewarding to them than a personal interview. Respondents report less rapport with telephone interviewers than with personal interviewers. Given the growing costs and difficulties of personal interviews, it is likely that an even higher share of surveys will be by telephone in the future. Thus, it behooves the business researcher using telephone surveys to attempt to improve the enjoyment of the interview. One authority suggests:

> We need to experiment with techniques to improve the enjoyment of the interview by the respondent, maximize the overall completion rate, and minimize response error on specific measures. This work might fruitfully begin with efforts at translating into verbal messages the visual cues that fill the interaction in a face-to-face interview: the smiles, frowns, raising of eyebrows, eye contact, etc. All of these cues have informational content and are important parts of the personal interview setting. We can perhaps purposefully choose those cues that are most important to data quality and respondent trust and discard the many that are extraneous to the survey interaction.[30]

INTERVIEWING BY MAIL

The self-administered questionnaire has been mentioned as a substitute for the personal interview, but its more frequent use is in mail surveys. In

---

[27]A block is defined as an exchange group composed of the first four or more digits of a seven-digit number such as 721–0, 721–1, and so forth.

[28]S. Sudman, *Reducing the Cost of Surveys*, p. 65.

[29]J. J. Wheatley, "Self-Administered Written Questionnaires or Telephone Interviews," *Journal of Marketing Research* 10 (February 1973), pp. 94–95.

[30]Groves and Kahn, *Survey by Telephone*, p. 223.

this section, the merits of the mail questionnaire, its special problems, and techniques for using it successfully are discussed.

Evaluation of mail surveys

Advantages. Mail surveys are typically lower in cost than personal interviews. Telephone and mail costs are in the same general range although in specific cases, either may be lower. The more dispersed the sample, the more likely it is that mail will be the low-cost method. One reason for the cost advantage of a mail study is that it is often a one-person job. Another value in using mail is that we can contact respondents who might otherwise be inaccessible. Persons such as major corporate executives are difficult to reach in any other way. When the researcher has no specific person to contact, say in a study of corporations, the mail survey often will be routed to the appropriate respondent.

In a mail survey, the respondent can take more time to collect facts, talk with others, or consider replies at length than is possible with either the telephone or personal interview. Finally, mail surveys are typically perceived as being more impersonal, providing more anonymity than the other communication modes.

Disadvantages. The major weakness of the mail survey is nonresponse. Many studies have shown that the better educated and those more interested in the topic tend to answer mail surveys. A high percentage of those who reply to a given survey have usually replied to others, while a large share of those who do not respond are habitual nonrespondents.[31] Mail surveys with a return of 30 percent or so are often considered satisfactory, but there are instances of more than 70 percent response.[32] In either of these cases, there is a substantial number of nonresponders and we usually know nothing about how those who answer might differ from those who do not answer.

The second major limitation of mail surveys concerns the type and amount of information that can be secured this way. We normally do not expect to secure large amounts of information, and cannot probe deeply into questions. It is generally believed that respondents will refuse to cooperate with a long and/or complex mail questionnaire. Returned mail questionnaires with many questions left unanswered testify to this problem, but there are also many exceptions. One general rule of thumb is that the respondent should be able to answer the questionnaire in no more than 10 minutes. On the other hand, Dillman reports on a study of the general population in which he secured more than a 70-percent response to a questionnaire calling for 158 answers.[33]

---

[31]D. Wallace, "A Case for and against Mail Questionnaires," *Public Opinion Quarterly* 18 (Spring 1954), pp. 40–52.

[32]D. A. Dillman, "Increasing Mail Questionnaire Response in Large Samples of the General Public," *Public Opinion Quarterly* 36 (Summer 1972), pp. 254–57.

[33]Don A. Dillman, *Mail and Telephone Surveys* (New York: John Wiley & Sons, 1978), p. 6.

Improving mail-survey returns

The research literature is filled with studies addressing the problems of improving mail survey returns. Seemingly every possible variable has been studied. Dillman reports that well over 200 methodological articles have been published on efforts to improve mail response rates. From such an outpouring, one would expect that the problems of improving mail research response rates have largely been solved. Unfortunately, this is not true. In 1975, two major review articles appeared in the literature.[34] Both concluded that there were relatively few variables that consistently showed positive response rates. The conclusions of Kanuk and Berenson were:[35]

A number of tentative conclusions can be drawn on the basis of the empirical studies reported here. Unfortunately, there is so little evidence on which to base conclusions that those which follow, though valid, appear to be weak.

Follow-ups

Follow-ups, or reminders, are almost universally successful in increasing response rates. Since each successive follow-up results in added returns, the very persistent (and well-financed) researcher can potentially achieve an extremely high total response rate. However, the value of additional information thus obtained must be weighed against the costs required for successive contacts.

Preliminary Notification

The evidence indicates that advance notification, particularly by telephone, is effective in increasing response rates; it also serves to accelerate the rate of return. However, follow-ups appear to be a better investment than preliminary notification.

Concurrent Techniques

1. *Questionnaire Length.* Despite the fact that common sense suggests that short questionnaires should obtain higher response rates than longer questionnaires, research evidence does not support this view.

2. *Survey Sponsorship.* There is little experimental evidence concerning the influence of survey sponsorship on response rates; however, the sparse evidence that does exist indicates that official or "respected" sponsorship tends to increase response.

3. *Return Envelopes.* The one study which tested the hypothesis that return envelopes increase response rates suggests that the inclusion of a stamped, return envelope does encourage response because it facilitates questionnaire return.

4. *Postage.* Though a number of tests regarding postage are reported in the literature, few studies have tested the same variables. The existing evidence indicates that special delivery is very effective in increasing response rates. . . . Findings do not show a significant advantage for first class over third class, for commemorative stamps over ordinary postage, for stamped mail over metered mail, or for multiple small denomination stamps over single larger denomination stamps.

---

[34]Leslie Kanuk and Conrad Berenson, "Mail Surveys and Response Rates: A Literature Review," *Journal of Marketing Research* (November 1975), pp. 440–53; and Arnold S. Linsky, "Stimulating Responses to Mailed Questionnaires: A Review," *Public Opinion Quarterly* 39 (1975), pp. 82–101.

[35]Kanuk and Berenson, "Mail Surveys," p. 450. Reprinted from the *Journal of Marketing Research*, published by the American Marketing Association.

5. *Personalization.* Empirical evidence indicates that personalization of the mailing has no clear-cut advantage in terms of improved response rates. For example, neither personal inside addresses nor individually signed cover letters significantly increased response rates; personally typed cover letters proved to be somewhat effective in most cases cited, but not in all. The one study which tested the use of a titled signature versus one without a title did show a significant advantage in favor of the title.

6. *Cover Letters.* The influence of the cover letter on response rates has received almost no experimental attention, despite the fact that the cover letter is an integral part of the mail survey. The cover letter appears to be the most logical vehicle for persuading individuals to respond, yet the very few studies which are reported offer no insights as to its formulation.

7. *Anonymity.* Experimental evidence indicates that the promise of anonymity to respondents—either explicit or implied—has no significant effect on response rates.

8. *Size, Reproduction, and Color.* The few studies which examined the effects of questionnaire size, method of reproduction, and color found no significant differences in response rates.

9. *Money Incentives.* A number of studies indicate that a . . . [monetary] incentive sent with the questionnaire is very effective in increasing response rates. Larger sums tend to bring in added response, but at a cost that may exceed the value of the added information.

10. *Deadline Dates.* The few studies which tested the impact of deadline dates found that they did not increase the response rate; however, they did serve to accelerate the rate of questionnaire return.

Dillman argues that these ambiguous results occur because "the manipulation of one or two techniques independently of all others may do little to stimulate response."[36] He believes that efforts should be directed toward the more important question of maximizing the overall probability of response. He proposes the Total Design Method (TDM) to meet this need. The TDM consists of two parts.[37] First, one must identify the aspects of the survey process that may affect the response rate, either qualitatively or quantitatively. Each aspect must be shaped to obtain the best response. The second part consists of organizing the survey efforts so that the design intentions are carried out in detail. He reports the results achieved with the TDM in 48 surveys. Response rates ranged from 50 to 94 percent, with the median response rate of 74 percent.[38]

Implementing the mail survey

In the TDM approach, explicit attention is given to each point of the survey process at which the response may break down. For example:[39]

---

[36]Dillman, *Mail and Telephone Surveys*, p. 8.

[37]Ibid., p. 12.

[38]Ibid., pp. 22–24.

[39]Dillman, *Mail and Telephone Surveys*, pp. 160–61.

1. The wrong address and a low-class postage can result in nondelivery plus nonreturn.
2. The letter may look like junk mail and be discarded without opening.
3. Lack of proper instructions as to who should complete it leads to nonresponse.
4. The wrong person opens letter but fails to call it to attention of the right person.
5. Respondent finds no convincing explanation as to why survey should be completed so discards it.
6. Respondent temporarily lays questionnaire aside and fails to complete it.
7. Return address is lost so questionnaire can not be returned.

The efforts to overcome these problem areas will vary according to the circumstances, but some general suggestions can be made.

The process. In addition to a questionnaire, a cover letter and a return envelope are sent. Incentives, such as a quarter, are often attached to the letter in commercial studies. Follow-ups are usually needed to get the maximum response. There are differences in opinion as to how many follow-ups are needed and how they should be timed. Some researchers mail the first follow-up only several days after the original mailing. Dillman, in his TDM approach, suggests these follow-ups:

1. One week later—a preprinted postcard to all recipients thanking them for returns and reminding others to complete and mail the questionnaire.
2. Three weeks after the original mailout—a new questionnaire plus a letter telling nonrespondents that questionnaire has not been received and including a repetition of the basic appeals of the original letter.
3. Seven weeks after original mailing. A third cover letter and questionnaire are sent by certified mail to the remaining nonrespondents.

The appeal. The appeal to make to respondents may be an altruistic one or it may be a more powerful stimulus. The former is often found when the questionnaire is short, easy to complete, and does not require much effort from a respondent. Anonymity may or may not be mentioned. A brief letter emphasizes the "Would you do me a favor?" approach. Often some token (for example, a quarter) is sent along as a show of appreciation.

However, in many cases, the approach is not powerful enough. What is needed is an appeal that tells how important the problem is to a group with which the respondent can identify. The cover letter should also convey that the respondent's help is needed to solve the problem. The researchers are portrayed as reasonable persons making a reasonable appeal for help. They are identified as intermediaries between the person asked to help and an important problem. Some simple phrases describe how the respondent can help to solve the problem.

The TDM approach depends heavily on personalization as the vehicle for conveying to the respondents that they are important to the study. Such a personalized approach requires much more than just putting the respondent's name on the cover letter and using a real signature. The total effect must be personalized and should include typing of names and addresses on the envelope rather than on labels, signing the researchers' names in a contrasting color, and using first-class mail. Another strong element of personalization is available on the follow-ups when the respondent can be told, "as of today we have not received your questionnaire." Other techniques such as computer printing enables one to make personal references to respondents within the body of the letter. The standard is to make the appeals comparable in appearance and content to that which one would expect in a business or professional letter.

THE USE OF OBSERVATION

Some people restrict the concept of observation to "watching," but this is too narrow a view; it also involves listening and reading. Behavioral scientists tend to define observation in terms of animal or human behavior, but this is also too narrow. As used in this text, observation includes the full range of monitoring behavioral and nonbehavioral activities and conditions, which can roughly be classified into the following types:

1. Nonbehavioral observation.
    a Record analysis.
    b Physical condition analysis.
    c Physical process analysis.
2. Behavioral observation.
    a Nonverbal analysis.
    b Linguistic analysis.
    c Extralinguistic analysis.
    d Spatial analysis.

Nonbehavioral observation.   One of the more prevalent forms of observation research is *record analysis*. Such analysis may involve historical or current records, public or private records. They may be written, printed, sound-recorded, photographic, or videotaped. Historical statistical data are often the only sources used for a study. Analysis of current financial records and economic data also provides a major data source for studies. Other examples of this type of observation are the content analysis of competitive advertising and the analysis of personnel records.

Physical condition analysis is typified by store audits to determine availability of merchandise, studies of plant safety compliance, analysis of inventory conditions, and the analysis of the financial statements of organizations. *Process or activity* studies include time/motion studies of manufacturing processes, traffic flows in a distribution system, paperwork flow in an office, and the study of financial flows in our banking system.

Behavioral observation. The observational study of persons can be classified into four major categories.[40] *Nonverbal behavior* is the most prevalent of these and includes body movement, motor expressions, and even exchanged glances. At the gross body movement level one might study how a salesperson travels a territory. At a narrower level, one can study the body movements of a worker assembling a product, or time sample the activity of a department's work force to determine the share of time each spends in various ways. At a more abstract level, one can study body movement as an indicator of interest or boredom, anger or pleasure in a certain environment. Motor expressions such as facial movements can be observed as a sign of emotional states. Eyeblink rates are studied as indicators of interest in advertising messages. Finally, exchanged glances might be of interest in studies of interpersonal behavior.

Linguistic behavior is a second frequently used form of behavior observation. One simple type, familiar to most students, is the tally of "ahs" (or other annoying sounds or words) that a professor makes during a class. More serious applications are to the study of sales presentation content, or the study of what, how, and how much information is conveyed in a training situation. A third form of linguistic behavior involves interaction processes that take place between two persons or in small groups. Bales has proposed one widely used system for classifying such linguistic interactions.[41]

Behavior may also be analyzed on an *extralinguistic* level. Sometimes this is as important a means of communication as the linguistic. One author has suggested that there are four dimensions to extralinguistic activity.[42] They are (1) vocal, including pitch, loudness, and timbre; (2) temporal, including rate of speaking duration of utterance and rhythm; (3) interaction, including the tendencies to interrupt, dominate, or inhibit; and (4) verbal stylistic, including vocabulary and pronunciation peculiarities, dialect, and characteristic expressions. These dimensions could add substantial insight to the linguistic content of the interactions between supervisors and subordinates or salespeople and customers.

A fourth type of behavior study involves *spatial relationships*, especially as to how one relates physically to others. One form of this study, proxemics, concerns how people organize the territory about them as well as how they maintain discrete distances between themselves and others. A study of how salespeople physically approach customers or a study of the effects of crowding in a workplace are examples of this type of observation.

---

[40]K. E. Weick, "Systematic Observational Methods," in G. Lindzey and E. Aronson, *The Handbook of Social Psychology*, vol. 2 (Reading, Mass.: Addison-Wesley, 1968). p. 360.

[41]R. Bales, *Interaction Process Analysis* (Reading, Mass.: Addison-Wesley, 1951).

[42]Weick, "Systematic Observational Methods," p. 381.

Often in a given study, one will be interested in two or more of these types of information. This will require more than one observer. In all of these forms of behavior study, it is also important to consider the relationship between observers and subjects.

The observer-subject relationship

In interrogation, there is a clear opportunity for interviewer bias. The problem is less pronounced with observation but is still real. The relationship between observer and subject may be viewed from three perspectives: (1) whether the observation is direct or indirect; (2) whether the observer's presence is known or unknown to the subject; and (3) what role the observer plays.

Directness of observation. The direct method describes the situation in which the observer is physically present and personally monitors what takes place. This approach is very flexible because it allows the observer to react to and report subtle aspects of events and behavior as they occur. He or she is also free to shift places, change the focus of the observation, or concentrate on unexpected events if they should occur. A weakness of this approach is that the observers' perception circuits may become overloaded as events move quickly; they are left with the alternative of later trying to reconstruct what they were not able to record. Then, too, observer fatigue, boredom, and distracting events can reduce the accuracy and completeness of such observation.

Indirect observation is the term used to describe studies in which the recording is done by mechanical, photographic, or electronic means. For example, a special motion picture camera that takes one frame every second is mounted in a department of a large store to study customer and employee movement. Such methods are less flexible than direct observation, but they are much less biasing and may be less erratic in accuracy. Another advantage of such indirect systems is the permanent record that can be reanalyzed to include many different aspects of an event. Electronic recording devices, which have improved in quality and declined in cost, are being used more frequently in observation research.

Observer concealment. A second decision affecting the observer-subject relationship concerns whether the presence of the observer should be known to the subject. When the observer is known, there is a risk of atypical activity by the subjects. The famous Hawthorne experiments are the classic example of this effect.[43] The initial entry of an observer into a situation often

---

[43]This study concerned the measurement of varying conditions of illumination on factory worker output. No matter how the illumination was varied, an improvement in output was secured. It was concluded that the *fact of being observed* was itself a stronger variable than any degree of illumination. Apparently the workers reacted to the unaccustomed attention they were receiving by working harder. See F. J. Roethlisberger and W. J. Dickson, *Management and the Worker* (Cambridge, Mass.: Harvard University Press, 1939).

tends to upset activity patterns of the subjects, but this influence can usually be dissipated rather quickly. This is especially so when subjects are engaged in some absorbing activity and/or the presence of observers offers no potential threat to the subjects' self-interest. The potential bias from subject awareness of observers is always a matter of concern, however.

In some situations, observers are concealed by using one-way mirrors, hidden cameras, or microphones. These methods reduce the risk of observer bias but bring up a question of ethics. Hidden observation is a form of spying, and the propriety of this action must be determined by each researcher.

A modified approach involves partial concealment. In this case, the presence of the observer is not concealed, but her objectives and content of interest are. For example, a study of selling methods may be carried out by sending an observer with a salesperson who is making calls on customers. However, the observer's real purpose may be hidden from both the salesperson and the customer. For example, she may pretend that she is analyzing the display and layout characteristics of the stores they are visiting.

Observer participation. A third decision concerns whether the observer should participate in the situation while observing. The more involved arrangement, *participant observation,* exists when the observer enters into the social setting and acts both as an observer and a participant. Sometimes he or she is known as an observer to some or all of the participants, while at other times the true role is concealed. This again raises the ethical problem but reduces the potential for bias.

Another problem of participant observation is the dual demand made on the observer. Recording can interfere with participation, and participation can, in turn, interfere with observation. In addition, there is the problem of the influence that the observer's role has on the way others act. Because of these problems, participant observation is less used in business research than, say, in anthropology or sociology. It is typically restricted to those cases where nonparticipant observation is not practical, for example, a study of the functioning of a traveling auditing team.

Observation design

The decision to observe. Obsevation is found in almost all research studies, at least in the exploratory stage. Such data collection is often known as *simple observation.* Its practice is not very standardized, as befits the heuristic nature of exploratory reserch. Participant studies are also usually classed as simple observation because participant roles do not permit systematic observing. *Systematic observation,* on the other hand, employs standardized procedures, training of observers, schedules for recording, and other devices to control the observer and sometimes even the subject. Clearly some systemization is valuable in research observation, but the situation often limits what can be done.

The decision of whether to use observation as the major data collection method may be made as early as the moment the researcher moves from research questions to the investigative questions. The latter specify the outcomes of the study—the specific questions that the researcher must answer with the collected data. In a time sampling study of workers in department X, the outcome may be a judgment as to how well the department is being supervised. In a study of sales presentations, the research outcome may be a judgment of a given salesperson's effectiveness, or the effectiveness of different types of selling messages.

Content specification. When a specification of outcomes suggests an observational study, we move on to observation content—those specific conditions, events, and/or activities that we want to observe. These content specifics, when incorporated into an observational reporting system, correspond to the measurement questions already discussed. To specify the observation content, one should include both the major variables of interest and any other variables that may affect them. From this cataloging, one then selects those items which one plans specifically to observe. For each variable chosen, you must define it operationally if there is any question of concept agreement or special meanings.

Even if the concept is a common one, you must make certain that all agree upon the measurement terms by which to record results. For example, you may agree that variable W will be reported by count, while variable Y will be counted and the effectiveness of its use judged qualitatively.

Observation may be at either a *factual* or an *inferential* level. For example, in the study of a salesperson's presentation one might specify the following data as being of interest:

Factual	*Inferential*
Identification of salesperson and customer.	Salesperson's degree of enthusiasm for the interview.
Day of week and time of day.	Welcoming attitude of customer.
Products presented.	Customer acceptance of selling points per product.
Selling points presented per product.	Effectiveness of salesperson rebuttal attempts.
Customer objections raised per product.	General evaluation of sales presentation skill.
Salesperson rebuttal attempts.	
Salesperson attempt to secure order.	
Customer purchase decision.	
Environmental factors interfering with interview.	
Length of interview.	

This listing is suggestive only; it does not include many other variables which might be of interest. Data on customer purchase history, company, industry, and general economic conditions, the order in which sales arguments are presented, and specific words used to describe certain product characteristics are illustrations of still other items that might be included. The particular content of observation will also be affected by the nature of the observation setting.

The observation setting. Variations in the observation environment present another dimension that somewhat parallels the simple-systematic dichotomy. Settings may be viewed as being either *natural* or *contrived*. Field observation tends to be in a natural setting and laboratory study in a contrived setting, but the distinctions are not this simple. A natural setting generally exists when no controls are placed on the subject, the environment is the normal one for the event to occur, and no changes or controls have been introduced into that environment. For example, the observation of workers by time sampling of normal departmental work activities involves a natural setting. On the other hand, a degree of contrivance exists if certain events are introduced into the setting to see how various workers respond.

The observer. The selection and training of observers are typically given too little attention. There are a few general rules to guide the selection. First, the observer must have sufficient concentration powers to function in settings full of distractions. In addition, ability to remember details of an experience is an asset. There is also the need to select persons who will be unobtrusive in the situation. For example, an attractive young female observer would introduce an obvious distraction in some settings, but be ideal in other cases. The same can be said for persons of other ages, ethnic groups, and the like.

If observation is at the surface level and involves a few relatively simple concepts, then experience is less important. Inexperience may even be an advantage if there is some risk that experienced observers may bring preset convictions about the topic. On the other hand, experience is valuable if the observer must work under trying conditions with inferential level content. In any event, it is important that the observer be thoroughly versed in the requirements of the specific study.

Each observer should be informed of the specific outcomes sought and the precise content elements to be studied. Ample opportunity for questions should be provided in training sessions. This should be followed by practice, evaluation, correction, and more practice until all observers show a high degree of reliability in their observations. Included should be substantial practice in a simulated study setting. Where there are interpretative differences between observers, they should be discussed and reconciled.

Data collection plan. Data collection plans specify the details of the task. In essence they answer the question of who, what, where, when, and how. Who are the targets? What qualifies a subject to be observed? Are they randomly selected—every fifth person who passes, as in a traffic survey? Must each one meet a given criterion—those who initiate a specific action? Who are the contacts to reach if conditions change or trouble develops? Who has the responsibility for various aspects of the study?

What? This question has already been mentioned in the discussion on content, but additional specifics are called for. For example, the dimension of the basic observational unit must be set. This may be specified both in terms of a time dimension and in "act" terms. In the former case, the observer is instructed to observe for some period of time, say 10 minutes out of each hour. Such time sampling can give a good estimate of the total pattern of activities over a period of time if a number of time samples are drawn randomly.

Dimensions of importance often have to be defined in "act" terms. The concept of an act is affected by the needs of the given study. It is the basic unit of observation such as (1) a single expressed thought; (2) a physical movement; (3) a facial expression; (4) a transaction; (5) a type of behavior, or the like. While these must be defined, they will often continue to present difficulties to the observer. For example, in a single statement a salesperson may include several different thoughts, such as product advantages B and C, a rebuttal of objection K, and some remark about competitor X. The observer is hard pressed to sort out each thought, decide whether it represents a separate unit of observation, and then record it quickly enough to be able to follow continued statements.

When? Is the time of study important or can any time be used? For example, in a study of out-of-stock conditions in a supermarket, the exact times of observation may be important. Inventory is shipped to the store on certain days only, and buying peaks occur on other days. The likelihood of a given product being out-of-stock is a function of both of these time-related activities.

How? Shall the data be directly observed? If there is more than one observer, how shall they divide the task? How shall the results be recorded for later analysis? How shall the observers deal with various situations which may occur—when expected actions do not take place, or when the observer is challenged by someone in the setting?

The number of possible variations of conditions that faces an observer is unlimited. Fortunately, most of these problems do not occur at one time. When the plans are carefully laid, and the observers well-trained, observation research can be successful.

Unobtrusive measures. Up to this point, observation has been considered as a relatively traditional approach to data collection. Sometimes, however, such staightforward methods are not adequate. Webb and his colleagues have given us an insight into new dimensions of innovative observation called unobtrusive measures.[44] Suggestive of such approaches are natural erosion measures such as measuring the frequency of replacement of vinyl tile in front of various museum exhibits as an indicator of their popularity, and the study of wear and tear on book pages as a measure of library

---

[44]E. J. Webb, D. T. Campbell, R. D. Schwartz, and L. Sechrest, *Unobtrusive Measures; Nonreactive Research in the Social Sciences* (Chicago: Rand McNally, 1966).

book use. Examples also include natural accretion measures such as determining the advertising listenership of various radio stations by observing car radio settings as autos are brought to service garages. Another type of unobtrusive study includes estimating liquor and magazine consumption by collecting and analyzing family trash. For many other interesting approaches to unobtrusive observation research, the reader is urged to consult Webb et al.

LANE RESEARCH, INC.

The staff meeting at Lane Research had been going on for about 30 minutes when Ken said, "O.K., let's summarize our thinking on these projects. First, we agree that a mail survey is the right approach for the Study of American Opinion for the National Foundation. The great variety of questions they want to ask make it infeasible to use the telephone and the need for it to be nationwide means it cannot be personal interview."

"Right," agreed Craig Bell, "but do you think we should even try for the bid on this one? We have not yet established ourselves as national mail surveyors, and I have heard that Opinion Research, Inc. and Gallup Poll have both been invited to bid. Wouldn't we be wiser to go for one or two of the others?"

"What do you think, Jean?" asked Ken.

"I disagree with Craig," was Jean's response. "We will never get a reputation unless we bid and win projects of this type. I say we should try."

Craig's response was quick. "That's well and good, Jean, but we are a young, small research group which needs to establish itself on a local and regional basis first. Also, don't forget that we need certainty of revenue right now because we are about to finish the last big project we have. We need to bid where we have a better chance of winning."

"I guess I agree with you, Craig," said Ken. "Our cash flow forecast is bleak and both the OSHA project and the hospital study are right down our alley. Even the marketing research study is something we could handle easily. Let's discuss what would be the best research approaches on these projects."

What do you recommend?

SUMMARY

The major advantages of personal interviewing are the ability to explore topics in great depth, to achieve a high degree of interviewer control, and to provide maximum interviewer flexibility for meeting unique situations. However, this method is costly and time-consuming and the flexibility can result in excessive interviewer bias.

A successful interview requires that we seek information that the respondent can provide, that the respondent understands the role, and is motivated to play this role. Motivation, in particular, is a task for the interviewer. Good rapport with the respondent should be quickly established and then the technical process of collecting data should be begun. The latter often calls for skillful probing to supplement the answers volunteered by the respondent.

There are two major problems of bias in interviewing. One is the "non-response" problem; it is of major concern with all types of surveys. Some studies show that first calls will often secure as few as 20 percent of the designated respondents. Various methods are useful for increasing this representation, the most effective being the making of callbacks until we secure adequate numbers of completed interviews. Another major personal interviewing problem is that of "response error" in which the respondent fails to give a complete answer. The interviewer can make a major contribution to the correction of this problem.

Telephone interviewing has become much more popular in recent years because of the widespread adoption of the telephone in American households, and the low cost of this method compared with personal interviewing. Long-distance telephone interviewing is also growing in use. There are also disadvantages to telephone interviewing. Many phone numbers are unlisted, and directory listings become obsolete quickly; there is also a limit on the length and depth of interviews using the telephone.

Mail surveys are another widely used low-cost method, especially when the population is scattered geographically. Replying to a mail survey calls for some overt action by the respondent. As a result, the response rates for mail surveys tend to be low, although there are many techniques by which respondents can be motivated to participate.

Observation is about the only feasible type of research in those cases where we are studying records, mechanical processes, lower animals, small children, or complex interactive processes. We can gather data as the event occurs, and can come closer to capturing the whole event than with interrogation. On the other hand, we have to be present to catch the event or have some recording device on the scene to do the job.

Observation includes a variety of monitoring situations which can be classified as nonbehavioral or behavioral observation. We can also look at observation in terms of the observer-subject relationship. This relationship may be viewed from three perspectives: (1) Is the observation direct or indirect? (2) Is the observer's presence known or unknown? (3) Is the observer a participant or nonparticipant?

The design of an observation study follows the same general procedure as other research. When the researcher has specified the outcomes desired (the investigation questions), it often becomes apparent that the best way to secure the desired data is by observation. The researcher then must define the content of the study, determine what the observation settings will be, develop and test a specific data collecting plan, secure observers, train them, and launch the study.

SUPPLEMENTAL READINGS

1. Dexter, Louis A. *Elite and Specialized Interviewing.* Evanston, Ill.: Northwestern University Press, 1970. Discusses the techniques and problems of interviewing "people in important or exposed positions."
2. Dillman, Don A. *Mail and Telephone Surveys.* New York: John Wiley & Sons, 1978. A practical book on mail and telephone survey projects. Entire book recommended. Extensive bibliography.
3. Gorden, Raymond L. *Interviewing: Strategic Techniques and Tactics.* rev. ed. Homewood, Ill.: The Dorsey Press, 1975. A comprehensive coverage of interviewing for survey planners and supervisors as well as field workers.
4. Richardson, S. A.; B. S. Dohrenwend; and, D. Klein. *Interviewing: Its Forms and Functions.* New York: Basic Books, 1965. An excellent coverage of the interview process including a consideration of the roles of interviewers and respondents.
5. Survey Research Center. *Interviewer's Manual.* rev. ed. Ann Arbor, Mich.: Institute for Social Research, University of Michigan, 1976. An excellent guide for interviewers. Also discusses sampling procedures and survey administrative procedures used by the Survey Research Center.
6. Webb, E. J.; D. T. Campbell; R. D. Schwartz; and, L. Sechrest. *Unobtrusive Measures: Nonreactive Research in the Social Sciences.* Chicago: Rand McNally, 1966.

DISCUSSION QUESTIONS

1. Distinguish:
   a Response and nonresponse error.
   b Relative values of questioning and observation.
   c Nonverbal, linguistic, and extralinguistic analysis.
   d Factual and inferential observation.
2. Assume that you are planning to interview women in a shopping center about their views on increased food prices and what the federal government should do about them. In what different ways might you try to motivate them to cooperate in your survey?
3. In recent years, the conduct of in-home personal interviews has grown more costly and more difficult to complete. Suppose, however, that you have a project in which you need to talk with women in the home. What might you do to hold down the costs and increase the response rate?
4. How do environmental factors affect response rates in personal interviews? How can we overcome these environmental problems?
5. In the following situations, would you use a personal interview, telephone survey, or mail survey? Give your reasons.
   a A survey of the residents of a new subdivision on why they happened to select that particular area in which to live. You also wish to secure some information about what they like and do not like about life in the subdivision.
   b A poll of students at Cranial University on their preferences among three candidates who are running for the presidency of the student government.

   c   A survey of 58 wholesale grocery companies, scattered over the eastern United States, on their personnel management policies for warehouse personnel.

   d   A survey of financial officers of the *Fortune* top 500 corporations to learn their prediction for the economic outlook in their industries for next year.

   e   A survey of pharmacists in the state of Illinois to secure their opinions concerning a proposed state law to permit the advertising of prescription drugs.

6. You decide to take a telephone survey sample of 40 families in the 721-exchange area. You would like this sample to be an excellent representation of all subscribers in the exchange area. Explain how you would draw this sample and how you would carry out the sampling process.

7. You plan to conduct a mail survey of the traffic managers of 1,000 major manufacturing companies across the country. The study concerns their company policies regarding the payment of moving expenses for employees who are transferred. What might you do to improve the response rate of such a survey?

8. The observer-subject relationship is an important consideration in the design of observational studies. What kind of relationship would you recommend in each of the following cases?

   a   Observation of professorial conduct in the classroom by the student author of a course evaluation guide.

   b   Observation of retail shoppers by a researcher who is interested in determining the customer purchase time, by type of good purchased.

   c   Observation of a focus group interview by a client.

   d   Effectiveness of individual farm worker organizers in their efforts to organize employees of grape growers.

9. Assume that you are to set up an observational study in which we will observe five students engaging in a discussion of the question "How should students conduct themselves so as to profit most from college experience?"

   a   What are the varieties of information which might be observed in such a setting?

   b   Select a limited number of content areas for study and operationally define the observation "acts" that should be measured.

   c   Develop a recording form to be used by observers in the study.

   d   Determine how many observers you need and assign each to a specific observation task.

10. You wish to analyze the pedestrian traffic that passes a given store in a major shopping center. You are interested in determining how many shoppers pass by this store, and you would like to classify these shoppers on various relevant dimensions. Any information you secure should be obtainable from observation alone.

   a   What other information might you find useful to observe?

   b   How would you decide what information to collect?

   c   Devise the operational definitions you would need.

   d   What would you say in the way of instructions to the observers you plan to use?

   e   How might you sample this shopper traffic?

APPENDIX MARKETING CONCEPTS INC. (MCI)[1]

Early in 1977, the author received the letter shown in Figure 7A–1. It was printed on an executive size letterhead (7- × -10½ inches) and had the printed signature of R. G. Robertson, president of the organization. It was

---

FIGURE 7A–1   First letter, study of American opinion project

---

MARKETING CONCEPTS INCORPORATED

1235 N Avenue, Nevada, Iowa 50201

Dear Reader:

In the next several days, you will receive an invitation to participate in a national survey that is being conducted by mail. This "Study of American Opinion" is designed to measure opinions and attitudes of the American people toward business and the government.

This survey is a major undertaking -- one of the most significant studies yet undertaken in these critical public opinion areas.

We hope that you will agree to participate in the study by filling out the questionnaire you will receive in a few days. They are being sent to a mathematically selected cross section of the nation's household heads. As in any study, the reliability of the findings depends heavily on the coopera-tion of each person in the sample.

Your name will not be divulged -- individual answers will be used only in a composite report of American opinion.

We will greatly appreciate your cooperation.

Sincerely,

R. G. Robertson

---

[1]Used with the kind permission of R. G. Robertson, president of Marketing Concepts Incorporated.

sent by first-class mail and stated that the recipient would be receiving "an invitation to participate in a national survey that is being conducted by mail." The letter stressed the importance of the study, asked for participation, pointed out why each reply was important, and assured the reader that names and replies would be kept confidential.

Several days later, a large envelope (8¾- × -11¼ inches) arrived by first-class mail. The envelope carried commemorative stamps rather than being metered and "first class" was printed on the front in large red type. Inside were four items. The cover letter was printed on an 8½- × -11 letterhead with the same R. G. Robertson signature (see Figure 7A–2). No effort was made to personalize the letter. The text again stressed those items which are believed to motivate respondents to participate. In addition, a small plastic envelope with a new quarter in it was attached to the letter. Enclosed also was a prepaid postcard by which the respondent could request a free summary report. The third enclosure was a return envelope addressed to R. G. Robertson, President of MCI. It had a regular first-class stamp (not a commemorative).

The final enclosure, of course, was the questionnaire entitled, "The Study of American Opinion, 1977." It was a booklet eight pages long and covered a variety of subjects on economic, political, and social topics, shown in Figure 7A–3. The respondent could easily reply by checking appropriate boxes. The paper stock of the questionnaire and reply postcard were both cream-colored while all other materials were white. At the bottom of the last page of the questionnaire was typed "Study F1382." Since this represented the only nonprinted item in the entire set of materials, it probably was the respondent's identification code rather than the project identification.

The author, interested in the process of the study, decided not to reply in order to see if there were follow-ups. Three weeks later, he received another large envelope from MCI. It included a second questionnaire, a return postcard, and a reply envelope. There was also a cover letter with a second quarter attached (see Figure 7A–4). The letter writer (again the president) thanked the respondent if he or she had already answered, urged the laggards to reply, and stressed the need for all respondents to participate in order to make the study reliable. Again, the author decided to wait and see what else would occur. The second time nothing further happened.

About a year later, a request was made for permission to use the Marketing Concepts, Inc. materials in this book. Along with the permission letter came a copy of their study results. They reported that they had secured a 52-percent response in this survey.

FIGURE 7A–2   Cover letter, study of American opinion project

MARKETING CONCEPTS INCORPORATED
1235 N Avenue, Nevada, Iowa 50201

> Is the person to whom this letter was addressed the HEAD OF THE
> HOUSEHOLD -- that is, the person whose income is the chief source
> of support of the household? If not, will you please give the
> letter and questionnaire to the person who is the household head
> and ask him/her to complete the questionnaire for us?

Dear Household Head:

A few days ago we wrote to you asking for your participation in a major study
of American opinions and attitudes. You will find the questionnaire for this
"Study of American Opinion" enclosed. We would greatly appreciate your
cooperation in providing your answers to the questions asked.

This is one of the most significant studies yet undertaken on the attitudes
and opinions of the American people toward business and government. Your
answers will make a most important contribution to the project.

It will take you a little time and some thought to answer the questions.
However, we have tried to make it as convenient as possible for you to answer,
by asking you simply to check your answers to most questions. In a few cases,
we hope you will take the time to write in your answers -- and, of course, if
you would like to add a comment to <u>any</u> of your answers, we will be very much
interested in what you have to say.

Your answers and opinions are extremely important to us, <u>even if you do not
have opinions on some of the questions asked</u>. Questionnaires are being mailed
only to a representative sample of household heads. The reliability of the
findings depends heavily on our receiving a response from each person in the
sample. Responses from all participants will be combined to form a composite
interpretive report on American opinion.

The attached shiny new quarter is simply to tell you that we appreciate your
help. It is not, of course, intended to reimburse you for your time, but
merely to say "thank you".

A postage-paid self-addressed envelope is enclosed for your convenience in
returning the questionnaire. Thank you very much for your help.

                                              Sincerely,

                                              R. G. Dawton

P.S.: If you would like a FREE Summary report of the study, simply fill in
       and return the self-addressed, postage-paid card provided. Maybe you
       would like to compare your opinions and attitudes with those of your
       fellow Americans.

FIGURE 7A–3   The MCI questionnaire

Please be sure that this questionnaire is filled out by the HEAD OF THE HOUSEHOLD—that is, the person whose income is the chief source of support of the household.

THE STUDY OF AMERICAN OPINION, 1977

We will greatly appreciate your assistance in this major study. Your answers are of particular importance since you have been selected as part of a "sample" representative of America today. Under no circumstances will your individual answers be divulged —they will be used only in combination with those of other people responding to the study. For most of the questions, your answers can be given simply by checking the appropriate box or boxes. Please disregard the numbers before the boxes—they are for tabulation purposes only. THANK YOU.

> If you would like a FREE Summary Report of this study, simply return the business reply card enclosed. A copy will be sent as soon as possible after completion of the survey.

1. Please check whether you are: ¹☐ Male   ²☐ Female

2. Please check whether you are: ¹☐ Married   ²☐ Single   ³☐ Widowed   ⁴☐ Divorced, separated

3. What is _your_ approximate age? _(Please check.)_

¹☐ Under 18   ³☐ 25-34   ⁵☐ 45-49   ⁷☐ 55-64
²☐ 18-24   ⁴☐ 35-44   ⁶☐ 50-54   ⁸☐ 65 or older

4. Please check the _highest_ level of education achieved by you. _(Please check ONLY _one_ box.)_

¹☐ Post graduate degree
²☐ Post graduate work, no PG degree
³☐ Graduate of 4-year college
⁴☐ Graduate of 2-year (junior) college
⁵☐ Completed 1-3 years college, not a graduate

⁶☐ Completed less than 1 year of college
⁷☐ High school graduate
⁸☐ Trade or technical school graduate
⁹☐ Did not graduate from high school, or from trade or technical school

5a. Have you ever taken any courses in economics?   ¹☐ Yes   ²☐ No

b. If yes, were these courses taken in: ¹☐ College   ²☐ High school   ³☐ Other

6. Do you consider _yourself_ a Democrat, a Republican or an Independent?

¹☐ Democrat   ²☐ Independent   ³☐ Republican   ⁴☐ Other _____   ⁵☐ None
                                                                (Please specify)

7a. Generally speaking, do you consider yourself a conservative, a liberal, or somewhere between the two?

¹☐ Conservative   ²☐ Liberal   ³☐ Somewhere in-between

b. If "somewhere in-between", would you say you tend to lean more toward the conservative or the liberal point of view?

¹☐ Conservative   ²☐ Liberal   ³☐ Neither

8. Are _you personally_ now registered to vote?   ¹☐ Yes   ²☐ No

9. Did you vote in the LAST presidential election?   ¹☐ Yes   ²☐ No

FIGURE 7A–3   *(continued)*

10. Which (if any) of these things have you <u>personally</u> done in the past 12 months? *(Please check as many as apply.)*

¹☐ Written to the editor of a newspaper or magazine
²☐ Attended a stockholders' meeting
³☐ Written to an elected official or government agency
⁴☐ Worked in support of a political candidate

⁵☐ Served as an officer or on a committee of a community, civic or professional group
⁶☐ Signed a petition
⁷☐ Attended a public meeting at which local affairs were discussed

⁸☐ Participated in a parade or demonstration about a public issue
⁹☐ Engaged in picketing
⁰☐ Joined an organization advocating consumerism
ˣ☐ NONE of these

11. For <u>each</u> of the statements listed below, would you please indicate the degree of your agreement or disagreement? *(Please check ONE box for <u>each</u> statement.)*

	Strongly Agree	Mildly Agree	No Opinion	Mildly Disagree	Strongly Disagree
Monopoly is growing in the U.S.	¹☐	²☐	³☐	⁴☐	⁵☐
The government should set a limit on the amount of profit any company can make	¹☐	²☐	³☐	⁴☐	⁵☐
Business should be required to have public members on Boards of Directors	¹☐	²☐	³☐	⁴☐	⁵☐
Cost to taxpayers of regulating business is well worth it	¹☐	²☐	³☐	⁴☐	⁵☐
The more government regulation there is, the <u>less</u> efficiently companies can operate	¹☐	²☐	³☐	⁴☐	⁵☐
Large companies have a major influence on the government agencies regulating them	¹☐	²☐	³☐	⁴☐	⁵☐
Government regulation is the best way to ensure safe products	¹☐	²☐	³☐	⁴☐	⁵☐
Competition is better than government regulation to make sure that the public gets what it pays for	¹☐	²☐	³☐	⁴☐	⁵☐
Government regulation is needed to maintain safe working conditions	¹☐	²☐	³☐	⁴☐	⁵☐
Business should be required to publish more information on profits for each product manufactured	¹☐	²☐	³☐	⁴☐	⁵☐
Business is <u>mostly</u> to blame for inflation	¹☐	²☐	³☐	⁴☐	⁵☐
Government is <u>mostly</u> to blame for inflation	¹☐	²☐	³☐	⁴☐	⁵☐
Labor unions are <u>mostly</u> to blame for inflation	¹☐	²☐	³☐	⁴☐	⁵☐
The general public is <u>mostly</u> to blame for inflation	¹☐	²☐	³☐	⁴☐	⁵☐

12a. Just as a rough guess, <u>out of every sales dollar</u> a typical MANUFACTURING COMPANY receives for its products about how much of that sales dollar do you think the manufacturer is able to <u>keep as profit</u> (after all costs and taxes are paid)? *(Please check.)*

¹☐ 1 or 2 cents   ⁴☐ 10-14 cents   ⁷☐ 25-29 cents   ⁹☐ 40-49 cents
²☐ 3 or 4 cents   ⁵☐ 15-19 cents   ⁸☐ 30-39 cents   ⁰☐ 50 cents or more
³☐ 5-9 cents   ⁶☐ 20-24 cents

2

FIGURE 7A–3 *(continued)*

b. About how much of the sales dollar do you think the manufacturer <u>should</u> be able to keep as profit? *(Please check.)*

¹☐ 1 or 2 cents   ⁴☐ 10-14 cents   ⁷☐ 25-29 cents   ⁹☐ 40-49 cents
²☐ 3 or 4 cents   ⁵☐ 15-19 cents   ⁸☐ 30-39 cents   ⁰☐ 50 cents or more
³☐ 5-9 cents   ⁶☐ 20-24 cents

13a. During the past year, did you personally return anything you bought <u>to the place where you bought</u> it because the item was unsatisfactory?

                 ¹☐ Yes   ²☐ No

b. In general, were you satisfied or dissatisfied with the way your complaint was handled?

                      ¹☐ Satisfied   ²☐ Dissatisfied

14a. During the past year, did you personally complain to a manufacturer about the quality of his product, <u>either in writing or by telephone?</u>

                 ¹☐ Yes   ²☐ No

b. In general, were you satisfied or dissatisfied with the way your complaint was handled?

                      ¹☐ Satisfied   ²☐ Dissatisfied

15a. During the past year, did you personally register a complaint with <u>a local, state or federal government agency</u> about (governmental) delays, errors, poor service, etc.?

                 ¹☐ Yes   ²☐ No

b. In general, were you satisfied or dissatisfied with the way your complaint was handled?

                      ¹☐ Satisfied   ²☐ Dissatisfied

16. Below is a list of functions of the American business system along with a rating scale. *(The higher the number, the higher the rating—1 is a "poor" rating and 7 is "excellent".)*
For <u>each</u> function, please check the rating for business which you feel <u>best</u> describes your feeling on the job business is doing for that function.

RATING OF AMERICAN BUSINESS SYSTEM

	Poor Job 1	2	3	4	5	6	Excellent Job 7
Providing products and services that meet people's needs	¹☐	²☐	³☐	⁴☐	⁵☐	⁶☐	⁷☐
Producing safe products	¹☐	²☐	³☐	⁴☐	⁵☐	⁶☐	⁷☐
Paying good wages	¹☐	²☐	³☐	⁴☐	⁵☐	⁶☐	⁷☐
Providing value for the money	¹☐	²☐	³☐	⁴☐	⁵☐	⁶☐	⁷☐
Improving the standard of living	¹☐	²☐	³☐	⁴☐	⁵☐	⁶☐	⁷☐
Controlling pollution	¹☐	²☐	³☐	⁴☐	⁵☐	⁶☐	⁷☐
Dealing with shortages	¹☐	²☐	³☐	⁴☐	⁵☐	⁶☐	⁷☐
Maintaining strong competition	¹☐	²☐	³☐	⁴☐	⁵☐	⁶☐	⁷☐
Providing steady work	¹☐	²☐	³☐	⁴☐	⁵☐	⁶☐	⁷☐
Conserving natural resources	¹☐	²☐	³☐	⁴☐	⁵☐	⁶☐	⁷☐
Developing new products	¹☐	²☐	³☐	⁴☐	⁵☐	⁶☐	⁷☐
Hiring members of minority groups	¹☐	²☐	³☐	⁴☐	⁵☐	⁶☐	⁷☐
Being honest in what they say about their products	¹☐	²☐	³☐	⁴☐	⁵☐	⁶☐	⁷☐
Being interested in customers	¹☐	²☐	³☐	⁴☐	⁵☐	⁶☐	⁷☐
Helping solve social problems	¹☐	²☐	³☐	⁴☐	⁵☐	⁶☐	⁷☐
Communicating with: Employees	¹☐	²☐	³☐	⁴☐	⁵☐	⁶☐	⁷☐
Stockholders	¹☐	²☐	³☐	⁴☐	⁵☐	⁶☐	⁷☐
Customers	¹☐	²☐	³☐	⁴☐	⁵☐	⁶☐	⁷☐
General Public	¹☐	²☐	³☐	⁴☐	⁵☐	⁶☐	⁷☐

3

FIGURE 7A–3   *(continued)*

17. Whether or not people deal with a particular type of business, they frequently have some opinion of the job that business is doing.

   For **each** of the types of business listed below, will you please give us **two** different ratings—even if that rating is based on no more than just a general feeling? *(Again—1 is the lowest rating, 7 the highest.)*

   FIRST—how would you rate **each** type of business on the **over-all job** it is doing?

   SECOND—how would you rate **each** in **providing the customer with enough information** about its products and services to enable the customer to make a sound decision when buying those products or services?

HOW WOULD YOU RATE EACH BUSINESS ON:

	I: The Over-All Job It Does?	**II: Providing Enough Product Information?**
	Poor 1 2 3 4 5 6 7 Excellent	Poor 1 2 3 4 5 6 7 Excellent
Airlines	☐☐☐☐☐☐☐	☐☐☐☐☐☐☐
Aluminum companies	☐☐☐☐☐☐☐	☐☐☐☐☐☐☐
Appliance manufacturers	☐☐☐☐☐☐☐	☐☐☐☐☐☐☐
Appliance repair services	☐☐☐☐☐☐☐	☐☐☐☐☐☐☐
Automobile dealers	☐☐☐☐☐☐☐	☐☐☐☐☐☐☐
Automobile insurance companies	☐☐☐☐☐☐☐	☐☐☐☐☐☐☐
Automobile manufacturers	☐☐☐☐☐☐☐	☐☐☐☐☐☐☐
Banks	☐☐☐☐☐☐☐	☐☐☐☐☐☐☐
Building materials companies	☐☐☐☐☐☐☐	☐☐☐☐☐☐☐
Chemical companies	☐☐☐☐☐☐☐	☐☐☐☐☐☐☐
Electric utilities	☐☐☐☐☐☐☐	☐☐☐☐☐☐☐
Food manufacturers	☐☐☐☐☐☐☐	☐☐☐☐☐☐☐
Forestry companies	☐☐☐☐☐☐☐	☐☐☐☐☐☐☐
Gas utilities	☐☐☐☐☐☐☐	☐☐☐☐☐☐☐
Gasoline service stations	☐☐☐☐☐☐☐	☐☐☐☐☐☐☐
Large department stores	☐☐☐☐☐☐☐	☐☐☐☐☐☐☐
Life insurance companies	☐☐☐☐☐☐☐	☐☐☐☐☐☐☐
Liquor distillers	☐☐☐☐☐☐☐	☐☐☐☐☐☐☐
Medical/hospitalization insurance cos.	☐☐☐☐☐☐☐	☐☐☐☐☐☐☐
Non-prescription drug manufacturers	☐☐☐☐☐☐☐	☐☐☐☐☐☐☐
Oil & gasoline companies	☐☐☐☐☐☐☐	☐☐☐☐☐☐☐
Plastics companies	☐☐☐☐☐☐☐	☐☐☐☐☐☐☐
Prescription drug manufacturers	☐☐☐☐☐☐☐	☐☐☐☐☐☐☐
Property/casualty insurance companies	☐☐☐☐☐☐☐	☐☐☐☐☐☐☐
Railroads	☐☐☐☐☐☐☐	☐☐☐☐☐☐☐
Retail food chains	☐☐☐☐☐☐☐	☐☐☐☐☐☐☐
Savings & loan associations	☐☐☐☐☐☐☐	☐☐☐☐☐☐☐
Steel manufacturers	☐☐☐☐☐☐☐	☐☐☐☐☐☐☐
Telephone companies	☐☐☐☐☐☐☐	☐☐☐☐☐☐☐
Tire manufacturers	☐☐☐☐☐☐☐	☐☐☐☐☐☐☐
Wine producers	☐☐☐☐☐☐☐	☐☐☐☐☐☐☐

4

FIGURE 7A–3   *(continued)*

18. For **each** of the statements listed below, would you please indicate the degree of your agreement or disagreement? *(Please check ONE box for each statement.)*

	Strongly Agree	Mildly Agree	No Opinion	Mildly Disagree	Strongly Disagree
The government should <u>ban the sale</u> of products shown in any laboratory tests to have caused cancer in animals	¹☐	²☐	³☐	⁴☐	⁵☐
Having completely clean air and water is worth paying whatever <u>higher prices</u> and <u>higher taxes</u> are needed	¹☐	²☐	³☐	⁴☐	⁵☐
Keeping <u>inflation</u> under control is necessary even if it results in <u>higher unemployment</u>	¹☐	²☐	³☐	⁴☐	⁵☐
A new federal agency should be set up to be the "<u>voice of the consumer</u>"	¹☐	²☐	³☐	⁴☐	⁵☐
A <u>balanced</u> Federal budget is essential, even if it means <u>lower government benefits</u> or <u>higher taxes</u>	¹☐	²☐	³☐	⁴☐	⁵☐
The government should require the <u>ultimate</u> in product safety standards, regardless of the cost to the customer	¹☐	²☐	³☐	⁴☐	⁵☐

19. For **each** of the statements listed below, would you please indicate the degree of your agreement or disagreement? *(Please check ONE box for each statement.)*

	Strongly Agree	Mildly Agree	No Opinion	Mildly Disagree	Strongly Disagree
Buyers should get a rebate when they buy a new car that gets <u>high</u> miles-per-gallon	¹☐	²☐	³☐	⁴☐	⁵☐
More nuclear power plants should be built right now	¹☐	²☐	³☐	⁴☐	⁵☐
The government should permit increased strip-mining because of the country's need for coal	¹☐	²☐	³☐	⁴☐	⁵☐
Preserving the national parks is <u>more</u> important than making lumber available for construction, paper products, etc.	¹☐	²☐	³☐	⁴☐	⁵☐
The government should increase taxes on <u>gasoline</u> to discourage driving and conserve energy	¹☐	²☐	³☐	⁴☐	⁵☐
The government should increase taxes on <u>new cars</u> that get <u>low</u> miles-per-gallon	¹☐	²☐	³☐	⁴☐	⁵☐

20. How serious do you feel the energy crisis is?

¹☐ Extremely serious   ³☐ Not very serious
²☐ Serious, but not <u>very</u> bad   ⁴☐ Not at all serious

21. If a sudden <u>new</u> energy problem were to come up and differing reasons for its cause were given by business, by environmentalists and by the government, which of these three groups would you be MOST likely to believe? *(Please check ONLY one box.)*

¹☐ Business   ²☐ Environmentalists   ³☐ Government

FIGURE 7A–3   *(continued)*

---

22. For *each* of the statements listed below, would you please indicate the degree of your agreement or disagreement? *(Please check ONE box for each statement.)*

	Strongly Agree	Mildly Agree	No Opinion	Mildly Disagree	Strongly Disagree
There should be <u>no mandatory retirement age</u> so long as a person is healthy and doing a good job	¹☐	²☐	³☐	⁴☐	⁵☐
Business and government should increase efforts to end discrimination against <u>women</u> in employment, training and promotions	¹☐	²☐	³☐	⁴☐	⁵☐
Business and government should increase efforts to end discrimination against <u>minorities</u> in employment, training and promotions	¹☐	²☐	³☐	⁴☐	⁵☐
The Federal government should make it <u>easier</u> for unions to organize workers	¹☐	²☐	³☐	⁴☐	⁵☐
Where a company has a union, it is all right if new workers are required to join the union to keep their jobs	¹☐	²☐	³☐	⁴☐	⁵☐

23. Below is a list of various groups and institutions, along with two qualities that each group possesses in one degree or another. For *each* of these two qualities, please rate *each* of the groups by checking a score from 1 (the lowest rating) to 7 (the highest).

HOW WOULD YOU RATE EACH GROUP IN:

	I: Honesty, Dependability, Integrity? Poor (1) to Excellent (7)	II: Ability to "Get Things Done"? Poor (1) to Excellent (7)
The White House	¹☐ ²☐ ³☐ ⁴☐ ⁵☐ ⁶☐ ⁷☐	¹☐ ²☐ ³☐ ⁴☐ ⁵☐ ⁶☐ ⁷☐
House of Representatives	¹☐ ²☐ ³☐ ⁴☐ ⁵☐ ⁶☐ ⁷☐	¹☐ ²☐ ³☐ ⁴☐ ⁵☐ ⁶☐ ⁷☐
Senate	¹☐ ²☐ ³☐ ⁴☐ ⁵☐ ⁶☐ ⁷☐	¹☐ ²☐ ³☐ ⁴☐ ⁵☐ ⁶☐ ⁷☐
Supreme Court	¹☐ ²☐ ³☐ ⁴☐ ⁵☐ ⁶☐ ⁷☐	¹☐ ²☐ ³☐ ⁴☐ ⁵☐ ⁶☐ ⁷☐
Regulatory Agencies	¹☐ ²☐ ³☐ ⁴☐ ⁵☐ ⁶☐ ⁷☐	¹☐ ²☐ ³☐ ⁴☐ ⁵☐ ⁶☐ ⁷☐
Federal Bureaucracy	¹☐ ²☐ ³☐ ⁴☐ ⁵☐ ⁶☐ ⁷☐	¹☐ ²☐ ³☐ ⁴☐ ⁵☐ ⁶☐ ⁷☐
Politicians	¹☐ ²☐ ³☐ ⁴☐ ⁵☐ ⁶☐ ⁷☐	¹☐ ²☐ ³☐ ⁴☐ ⁵☐ ⁶☐ ⁷☐
Republican Party	¹☐ ²☐ ³☐ ⁴☐ ⁵☐ ⁶☐ ⁷☐	¹☐ ²☐ ³☐ ⁴☐ ⁵☐ ⁶☐ ⁷☐
Democratic Party	¹☐ ²☐ ³☐ ⁴☐ ⁵☐ ⁶☐ ⁷☐	¹☐ ²☐ ³☐ ⁴☐ ⁵☐ ⁶☐ ⁷☐
U.S. Military	¹☐ ²☐ ³☐ ⁴☐ ⁵☐ ⁶☐ ⁷☐	¹☐ ²☐ ³☐ ⁴☐ ⁵☐ ⁶☐ ⁷☐
Postal Service	¹☐ ²☐ ³☐ ⁴☐ ⁵☐ ⁶☐ ⁷☐	¹☐ ²☐ ³☐ ⁴☐ ⁵☐ ⁶☐ ⁷☐
State & Local Government	¹☐ ²☐ ³☐ ⁴☐ ⁵☐ ⁶☐ ⁷☐	¹☐ ²☐ ³☐ ⁴☐ ⁵☐ ⁶☐ ⁷☐
Educators	¹☐ ²☐ ³☐ ⁴☐ ⁵☐ ⁶☐ ⁷☐	¹☐ ²☐ ³☐ ⁴☐ ⁵☐ ⁶☐ ⁷☐
Organized Religion	¹☐ ²☐ ³☐ ⁴☐ ⁵☐ ⁶☐ ⁷☐	¹☐ ²☐ ³☐ ⁴☐ ⁵☐ ⁶☐ ⁷☐
Legal Profession	¹☐ ²☐ ³☐ ⁴☐ ⁵☐ ⁶☐ ⁷☐	¹☐ ²☐ ³☐ ⁴☐ ⁵☐ ⁶☐ ⁷☐
Medical Profession	¹☐ ²☐ ³☐ ⁴☐ ⁵☐ ⁶☐ ⁷☐	¹☐ ²☐ ³☐ ⁴☐ ⁵☐ ⁶☐ ⁷☐
Science and Technology	¹☐ ²☐ ³☐ ⁴☐ ⁵☐ ⁶☐ ⁷☐	¹☐ ²☐ ³☐ ⁴☐ ⁵☐ ⁶☐ ⁷☐
Labor Union Leaders	¹☐ ²☐ ³☐ ⁴☐ ⁵☐ ⁶☐ ⁷☐	¹☐ ²☐ ³☐ ⁴☐ ⁵☐ ⁶☐ ⁷☐
Large Business	¹☐ ²☐ ³☐ ⁴☐ ⁵☐ ⁶☐ ⁷☐	¹☐ ²☐ ³☐ ⁴☐ ⁵☐ ⁶☐ ⁷☐
Small Business	¹☐ ²☐ ³☐ ⁴☐ ⁵☐ ⁶☐ ⁷☐	¹☐ ²☐ ³☐ ⁴☐ ⁵☐ ⁶☐ ⁷☐
Business Executives	¹☐ ²☐ ³☐ ⁴☐ ⁵☐ ⁶☐ ⁷☐	¹☐ ²☐ ³☐ ⁴☐ ⁵☐ ⁶☐ ⁷☐
<u>Broadcast</u> News Media (TV news, radio news)	¹☐ ²☐ ³☐ ⁴☐ ⁵☐ ⁶☐ ⁷☐	¹☐ ²☐ ³☐ ⁴☐ ⁵☐ ⁶☐ ⁷☐
<u>Print</u> News Media (News magazines, newspapers)	¹☐ ²☐ ³☐ ⁴☐ ⁵☐ ⁶☐ ⁷☐	¹☐ ²☐ ³☐ ⁴☐ ⁵☐ ⁶☐ ⁷☐
Consumer groups	¹☐ ²☐ ³☐ ⁴☐ ⁵☐ ⁶☐ ⁷☐	¹☐ ²☐ ³☐ ⁴☐ ⁵☐ ⁶☐ ⁷☐
Environmentalist groups	¹☐ ²☐ ³☐ ⁴☐ ⁵☐ ⁶☐ ⁷☐	¹☐ ²☐ ³☐ ⁴☐ ⁵☐ ⁶☐ ⁷☐

FIGURE 7A–3   *(continued)*

24a. How would you describe the dwelling in which you live all or most of the time?

- ¹☐ Single family house
- ²☐ Apartment
- ³☐ Multi-family house
- ⁴☐ Other _____
  (Please specify)

b. What type of energy is used as the primary source for heating that dwelling?

¹☐ Oil   ²☐ Gas   ³☐ Coal   ⁴☐ Electricity   ⁵☐ Other _____
(Please specify)

c. Do you have any type of solar heating or solar air conditioning for your home?   ¹☐ Yes   ²☐ No

25. Below is a list of TV shows. Will you please check those where you personally watched the most recent program?

- ¹☐ ABC Evening News *(Reasoner & Walters)*
- ²☐ ABC Sunday Night Movie
- ³☐ ABC Tuesday Night Movie
- ⁴☐ Barnaby Jones
- ⁵☐ Barney Miller

- ⁶☐ CBS Evening News *(Cronkite)*
- ⁷☐ CBS Wednesday Night Movie
- ⁸☐ Charlie's Angels
- ⁹☐ Face the Nation
- ⁰☐ Hawaii Five-0

- ¹☐ Issues and Answers
- ²☐ M•A•S•H
- ³☐ Meet the Press
- ⁴☐ NBC Monday Night Movie
- ⁵☐ NBC Nightly News *(Chancellor & Brinkley)*

- ⁶☐ NBC Saturday Night Movie
- ⁷☐ NFL Monday Night Football
- ⁸☐ NFL Sunday Football
- ⁹☐ 60 Minutes
- ⁰☐ Wide World of Sports

26. For EACH of the magazines listed below, will you please check:

(a) Whether or not you personally read the most recent issue?
(b) Whether or not you personally read the issue before that one?

	DID YOU READ THE MOST RECENT ISSUE? *(Please check "Yes" or "No" for EACH)*		DID YOU READ THE ISSUE BEFORE THAT ONE? *(Please check "Yes" or "No" for EACH)*	
	Yes	No	Yes	No
Atlantic	¹☐	²☐	¹☐	²☐
Business Week	¹☐	²☐	¹☐	²☐
Forbes	¹☐	²☐	¹☐	²☐
Fortune	¹☐	²☐	¹☐	²☐
Harper's	¹☐	²☐	¹☐	²☐
National Geographic	¹☐	²☐	¹☐	²☐
Newsweek	¹☐	²☐	¹☐	²☐
Reader's Digest	¹☐	²☐	¹☐	²☐
Sports Illustrated	¹☐	²☐	¹☐	²☐
Time	¹☐	²☐	¹☐	²☐
U.S.News & World Report	¹☐	²☐	¹☐	²☐

7

FIGURE 7A–3 *(concluded)*

27. What title or position do you now hold? *(If you hold more than one position, please check only the highest position held.)*

¹☐ Company officer *(President, Vice President, Secretary, Treasurer, etc.)*
²☐ Assistant company officer
³☐ General manager
⁴☐ Owner or partner
⁵☐ Department head

⁶☐ Manager or supervisor
⁷☐ Technical specialist
⁸☐ Salesman
⁹☐ Craftsman
⁰☐ Clerical

¹☐ Laborer

²☐ Lawyer
³☐ Doctor or dentist
⁴☐ Professor or teacher
⁵☐ Other professional _____
    (Please specify)

⁶☐ NOW in the armed forces
⁷☐ Housewife
⁸☐ Student
⁹☐ Retired *(do not work either full or part-time)*
⁰☐ Other _____
    (Please specify)

28. Do you—or does anyone else in your immediate household—belong to a labor union?

¹☐ <u>Yes</u>, I personally belong to a labor union
²☐ <u>Yes</u>, another member of my household belongs to a labor union
³☐ <u>No</u>, no one in my household belongs to a labor union

29. Are you the head of the household—that is, <u>the person whose income is the chief source of support of the household?</u>

¹☐ Yes   ²☐ No

30. Would you please check the approximate combined yearly income *(before income taxes and any other payroll deductions)* **from all sources of all those in your immediate household?** *(Please include income from salaries, investments, dividends, rents, royalties, bonuses, commissions, etc.)* **Please remember that your individual answers will not be divulged.**

¹☐ Less than $4,000
²☐ $4,000 - $4,999
³☐ $5,000 - $5,999
⁴☐ $6,000 - $6,999
⁵☐ $7,000 - $7,499
⁶☐ $7,500 - $7,999

¹☐ $8,000 - $8,999
²☐ $9,000 - $9,999
³☐ $10,000 - $12,499
⁴☐ $12,500 - $14,999
⁵☐ $15,000 - $19,999
⁶☐ $20,000 - $24,999

¹☐ $25,000 - $29,999
²☐ $30,000 - $39,999
³☐ $40,000 - $49,999
⁴☐ $50,000 - $74,999
⁵☐ $75,000 - $99,999
⁶☐ $100,000 or more

31a. Do you personally own corporate stocks?   ¹☐ Yes   ²☐ No

b. Do you own stocks in the corporation for which you work?—Do you own them in a corporation for which you do <u>not</u> work?
(Please check as many as apply.)

Own <u>STOCK</u> in: ¹☐ Company for which I work   ²☐ Other Company

THANK YOU VERY MUCH FOR YOUR COOPERATION
If you would like to make any comments on any of the
subjects covered in this study, please use the space below:

Marketing Concepts, Inc. • 1235 N Avenue • Nevada, Iowa 50201
Study F1382

FIGURE 7A–4   Second cover letter, study of American Opinion project

---

MARKETING CONCEPTS INCORPORATED
1235 N Avenue, Nevada, Iowa 50201

> If you (the addressee) are not the head of the household,
> will you please ask the person who is the head to complete
> and return the questionnaire? By "household head", we mean
> the person whose income is the chief source of support of
> the household.

Dear Household Head:

A short time ago, you received from us a questionnaire relating to
"The Study of American Opinion", a major research project concerning
the attitudes and opinions of the American people toward business and
government.

If you have already returned the questionnaire, please ignore this letter
and accept our thanks for your cooperation. But in case you misplaced
the original questionnaire, we are enclosing another one. We would
sincerely appreciate your filling it out and returning it to us in the
enclosed stamped envelope.

We hope that you will agree to spend the time and thought necessary to
answer the questions, since your response will be an important contribution to the success of the study. Questionnaires are being sent only to
a representative sample of household heads, and the reliability of the
findings depends heavily on the response of each individual in the sample.

It may also be of interest to you to see a composite report on the
findings -- if so, please simply fill in and return the enclosed self-
addressed postage-paid card.

A token pocket-piece, in the form of a shiny quarter, is attached as a
small measure of our appreciation for your participation in the study.

Many thanks for your help.

                                    Sincerely,

                                    R. G. Robertson, President
                                    /am

8. Survey instrument design

"It's a good team," thought Lisa as she read the names that Professor Emory had posted on the bulletin board. The four members of "A" team were: Brad Fuller, Lisa Kaplan, Margie Morton, Conrado Santiago. Their assignment from Professor Emory was to develop a survey instrument by which to conduct a survey of career prospects in product management. Lisa knew that everyone in her group was interested in product management careers, so this could be an excellent learning experience if they did a good job.

The next day the "A" team held its first meeting. As a first order of business, Lisa was elected captain. She immediately took charge.

"Where do we start?" was her opening question.

"Why don't we each draft 10 questions to ask product managers?" chimed in Brad. "The sooner we get on this, the sooner we'll get it done."

Conrado disagreed. "I think we are getting ahead of ourselves. We need to establish the research question first and then translate that into some investigative questions. Then we can start writing up the questions."

"O.K.," replied Margie, "but we also need to give some serious thought to our general survey strategy before we start writing questions. Don't you remember the lecture we had the other day?"

"That's a good idea," said Lisa. "Before we rush into specific actions, let's review what Professor Emory told us in that lecture."

THE INSTRUMENT DEVELOPMENT PROCESS

Researchers-to-be often want to draft questions immediately. They are reluctant to go through the many preliminary phases that make for survey success. The nature of these preliminary phases was pointed out in Chapter 2, but their importance is reviewed here.

199

Question hierarchy

The process of moving from the general management objective or problem to specific measurement questions goes through four major question levels:

1. The management question—that problem which the manager must answer.
2. The research question—that basic information question or questions which the researcher must answer in order to contribute to the solution of the management question.
3. The investigative questions—those specific questions which the researcher must ask in order to answer the research question. Within this level, there may be several questions as the researcher moves from the general to the specific.
4. The measurement questions—those questions which respondents must answer if the researcher is to gather the needed information.

Procedure example. The process of moving from management question to measurement questions is an exercise in analytical reasoning. The example presented in Chapter 3 might be worth review. Here is a second illustration that involves a relatively simple descriptive survey problem.

> *Gentlemen's Magazine*
>
> The editor of *Gentlemen's Magazine* has asked you to carry out a research study. The magazine has been unsuccessful in attracting advertising revenue from shoe manufacturers. The shoe manufacturers claim that men's clothing stores are a small and declining segment of the men's shoe business. Since *Gentlemen's Magazine* is sold chiefly to men's clothing store managements, the manufacturers have reasoned that it is therefore not a good advertising medium for their shoes.
>
> The editor disagrees about the size and importance of shoe marketing through men's clothing stores. Neither side has much direct evidence on the matter, so the editor asks you to carry out a study to determine the facts about these stores as a channel of distribution for men's shoes. You agree to do so and proceed with the first structuring of the problem.
>
> 1. *Management Question.* The problem facing the magazine management is that of trying to expand their advertising revenue. There are a number of ways that this might be done and research might help in many of them. In this case, however, the management has already decided that the management's problem is to secure more advertising from the shoe industry. The researcher accepted the problem definition as stated.
> 2. *Research Question.* The research question was defined as "Are the actual or potential sales of men's shoes in men's wear stores large enough to represent an advertising opportunity to shoe manufacturers?"
> 3. *Investigative Questions.* Three major investigative questions were proposed:

a   Are shoe sales important to men's wear stores?

b   Have shoe sales been growing in importance in men's wear stores and are they expected to grow in the future?

c   Does the situation in men's wear stores present an advertising opportunity for shoe manufacturers.[1]

It was agreed that the only feasible research design which could be carried out within the available budget was a national mail survey. Because of the limited scope of the study and the problems of population estimation from a mail survey, it was agreed that the research study would be concerned chiefly with the first two questions. The third question would be approached within the limits of the research design, but a full answer to this question would require information not available to the researcher.

To answer the major investigative questions posed above it was necessary to secure information on a number of much more specific points. These represent investigative subquestions which we must know to answer the three major questions. Parenthetical statements attached to them suggest the rationales for including the questions in the study.

A.   Are shoe sales important to men's wear stores?
   1.   What percent of men's wear stores carry men's shoes? (One important measure of this channel of distribution and an indicator of the importance of shoes to retailers.)
   2.   What percent of men's wear store sales come from shoes? (A measure of the importance of shoes to total store operation.)
   3.   How do shoe gross margins compare with total store gross margins? (Another measure of shoe importance to the store and an indicator of whether or not shoes are likely to secure store management attention.)
   4.   How do space/sales ratios compare between shoe departments and the total store? (Another measure of the contribution of shoes to the total store volume. Also a measure of how secure shoes might be as a part of the store product mix.)
   5.   How important are shoes as traffic builders, extra sales, or extra business from those who do not buy other merchandise at the time? (Another measure of the value of shoes to store success and an indicator of the mix security of shoes.)
B.   Have shoe sales been growing in importance in men's wear stores and are they expected to grow in the future?
   1.   What percent of the stores have added, expanded, dropped, or reduced shoe operations in the last five years? (A measure of the changes in importance of shoes in men's wear stores in recent years.)
   2.   Have shoe sales grown or declined in absolute dollars in recent years? As a percent of total store sales? (Measures of the changes that have taken place in men's wear stores concerning shoes.)

---

[1]In descriptive surveys, the research and investigative questions may be stated either as questions or as hypotheses.

3. What are store managements expecting in the next few years concerning shoes? Add or drop? Reduce or enlarge? (A measure of store operator expectations concerning shoes.)

C. Does the situation in men's wear stores present an advertising opportunity for shoe manufacturers?

1. What percent of the men's shoe volume is sold through men's wear stores? (A very crude measure of the importance of this channel to the manufacturer. This estimate will be carefully hedged since there is little hope that the survey can provide an unbiased estimate of total sales of men's shoes.)

2. How important are leased departments in men's shoes operations in men's wear stores? (A measure of the need for shoe manufacturers to contact individual store managements to secure distribution, or whether the approach to a few central buying firms might suffice.)

3. What price lines are carried, and what are their relative importance? (A measure of the type of demand for men's shoes represented in this channel.)

4. What is the importance of casual shoes versus dress shoe sales? (Another measure of the type of shoe demand that prevails in this channel.)

5. What brands are carried and what are their relative importance? (A measure of the penetration by various manufacturers as well as a measure of the product characteristics that are popular in this channel.)

4. *Measurement Questions.* The 13 investigative questions listed under the three major questions were translated into about 20 specific measurement questions that were finally asked of the respondents. There were six additional classification-type questions. They differed from the investigative questions chiefly in wording and format so as to aid the respondent in replying with a minimum of difficulty and a maximum of reliability.

Survey strategy

One should first develop a clear idea of the type of investigative questions to ask. Then, one needs to consider the survey strategy before getting down to instrument design particulars. Prominent among these strategy concerns are:

1. What communication mode will be used?
2. How much structure should be placed on the question-and-answer processes?
3. Should the questioning approach be disguised, and if so, to what degree?

Communication mode. It has already been pointed out that surveys may be conducted by personal interview, mail, telephone, or some combination of these. Clearly the decision on which method to use will affect the design of the instrument. For example, in personal interviewing, it is possible to use graphics and other questioning tools more easily than by mail or phone.

Process structure.   The interviewing experience can vary from one that is essentially unstructured to one with a great deal of structure. At the unstructured extreme are in-depth interviews during which the interviewer's task is largely to encourage the respondent to talk about a set of topics. In these situations, one uses a minimum of prompts and guiding questions.

With more focused in-depth interviews, the researcher provides additional guidance by using a set of questions to promote discussion and elaboration by the respondent. In such interviews, the researcher guides the topical direction and coverage. Whether structured or unstructured, the aim is to provide a relaxed environment in which the respondent will open up and discuss topics in depth. Such questioning is often used in exploratory research or where the investigator is dealing with complex topics that do not lend themselves to structured interviewing. For example, if one were doing case research among various participants in a major event, a substantial portion of the questioning would be unique to each respondent.

There is also a focused-group interview widely used in marketing research. In this setting, a group of 8 to 12 persons are brought together to discuss a certain topic such as new product ideas, reactions to certain consumer problems, and the like. The interviewer generally has a list of specific points which he or she would like to see discussed and these are used to prompt discussion. As long as the discussion stays within fairly broad bounds, however, the interviewer lets the group continue their interaction.

Even if the questioning process is quite structured, we must still decide whether to use structured or unstructured response formats.

Objective disguise.   Another consideration in survey instrument design is whether or not the purpose of the study should be disguised. Some degree of disguise is often present in surveys, especially as to the sponsor of the study. It is believed that this knowledge can bias the results. Here we are concerned with the more general problem. Shall one disguise the objectives of the questions? The accepted wisdom is that often one must do this or abandon the research efforts. The decision as to when to use disguised questioning may be made easier by identifying four interview situations relevant to this problem.

1. Ask for information from respondents who know it at a conscious level and are willing to provide it. For example, ask whether they have attended a certain movie.

2. Ask for information from respondents who know it at a conscious level but are unwilling to provide it. For example, ask for an opinion on some topic for which they hold a socially unacceptable view.

3. Ask for information that is knowable at a conscious level but which the respondents do not know. For example, ask why their actions differ

from those of others when the reason lies outside their knowledge and experience.

4. Ask for information which the respondents do not know at a conscious level although they have the information at some deeper level. For example, seek insight into the basic motivations underlying their consumption practices.

Type 1 situations seldom need disguised questions, but in type 2, respondents may not give their true feelings or may give stereotyped answers. The researcher can encourage more accurate answers by phrasing the questions in a hypothetical way, or by asking how "people around here feel about this topic?" The assumption is that responses to these questions will indirectly reveal the respondent's opinions.

In another form of a type 2 situation, respondents reply with stereotyped answers because they may not have given the subject much thought. This problem may also be approached in an indirect manner. In one corporate image study, the buyers of control instruments were asked for the ". . . five characteristics which a control manufacturer must have if he wants your business." The five highest ranked from a list of more than 20 possible descriptors are given in List A.[2]

The buyers were also asked to choose the descriptions that best characterized each of the six major suppliers in the industry. These responses were then analyzed to determine which words best differentiated each buyer's preferred supplier from the others. This quite different ranking is shown in List B. Further interviewing indicated that List B descriptions much more accurately reflected the real factors that led to choosing one supplier over another.

Rank	List A Most important characteristics	List B Best differentiators
1	Quality products	Diversified line
2	Dependable	Leader
3	Cooperative	Pioneer
4	Quality conscious	Dependable
5	Accurate	Accurate

Indirect questioning and analysis may often be needed to achieve the research objective in the type 3 situation. A classic example is a study of government bond buying during World War II.[3] A survey was undertaken

---

[2]Louis Cohen, "The Differentiation Ratio in Corporate Research," *Journal of Advertising Research* 4 (September 1967), pp. 34–35.

[3]Dorwin Cartwright, "Some Principles of Mass Persuasion," *Human Relations* 2 (1948), p. 266.

to determine why some people bought more war bonds than others with equal ability to buy. It was found that heavy buyers tended to be those who had been personally solicited to buy bonds. No direct "why" question to respondents could have provided the answer to this question because respondents did not know that they were receiving a different solicitation approach.

Type 4 situations represent an in-depth study that may or may not be disguised. Projective and other types of tests can be given that thoroughly disguise the study objective, but they are often quite difficult to interpret.

Schedule design

The procedure to follow in developing a survey varies from case to case, but a useful approach consists of four major steps. While this suggests a linear process, there is always a good deal of cycling and recycling as one works through it.

Information need determination. The research question hierarchy is a major part of this first step. This fractionation process develops chiefly out of the researcher's perception of the project. In many studies, an exploratory investigation is necessary to assure that one understands the full dimensions of the subject. In the *Gentlemen's Magazine* project, there was only limited exploration because the concepts were not complicated and the researcher had substantial experience in the industry. In the Prince Corporation image study (Chapter 4), a number of exploratory interviews were needed to assure that the investigative subquestions covered the areas of relevance to the population being studied.

Researchers are concerned both with adequate coverage of the topic and with securing the information in its most usable form. A good way to test how well the study plan meets these needs is to develop "dummy" tables in which to display the data one expects to secure. This step is a good check on whether the plan meets the data needs.

Data gathering process decisions. At this stage, one must choose the manner by which to gather the data. First, which communication process or combination of processes are most appropriate? Personal or impersonal? Telephone or face-to-face? In-home or at other sites? In the *Gentlemen's Magazine* case, this decision was easy. The wide dispersion of respondents, nature of the data, and budget limitations all dictated a mail survey. In the Prince Corporation, there was a desire to use telephone interviews because of cost savings. However, the study objectives called for data that could not easily be collected by telephone.

The degree of question- and response-structure must also be determined. Question structure is affected largely by the communication mode chosen. Response structure decisions depend more on the content and objectives of specific questions. In the mail survey, it was necessary to use structured questions. Most of the responses were also structured. In the exploratory stages of the Prince study, both questions and responses were unstructured, but in the final project both were largely structured.

The degree of disguise is the third decision needed. In the *Gentlemen's Magazine* study, the questions were direct and the specific information sought was genereally undisguised. However, both the purpose of the study and its sponsorship were disguised. In the Prince Corporation study, the questions concerned only a small number of companies, giving the sponsor only a limited disguise. Many of the questions sought direct answers, but in some cases, indirect questioning was used to (1) seek answers on sensitive topics or to (2) counter the tendency of respondents to give stereotyped answers to general questions.

Instrument drafting. You begin actual instrument design by drafting specific measurement questions. In doing this, consider both the subject content and the wording of each question. As these question formulations are developed, you need also to establish some logical question sequences. Often the content in one question assumes that certain questions have already been asked. You must also consider the psychological order of the questions. For example, questions that are more interesting, easier to answer, and less threatening usually are placed early in the sequence to encourage response and promote rapport.

Instrument testing. Once a draft of the instrument has been developed, it must be put through a series of tests. The first testing can be done by designers. There will be many differences of opinion and suggestions for improvement. Usually at least two or three drafts can be profitably developed in-house by bringing colleagues into the questionnaire development process. Then comes field testing in which the questionnaire is taken or sent to persons typical of the designated target respondents. These respondents, in most cases, should not know that the interrogation is only for testing purposes. Yet, it is very helpful to quiz test survey respondents further about their understanding and interpretation of the questions asked. Such quizzing provides an invaluable guide for instrument revision.

One approach that usually works well after completing the questionnaire is for the interviewer to tell the respondent that "we are just beginning the survey and would appreciate your additional help in evaluating how effective the questions are." This approach will usually elicit cooperation and many useful insights into how well the respondents understood and were able to deal with the questions posed. Such additional discussions about the "questions that were confusing" and the understandings and frames of reference used by the respondents almost always prompt further instrument revision.

It is important in testing to simulate field conditions as much as possible. One situation where testing differs somewhat is with mail surveys. Test mailings are useful, but it is often faster to use a substitute procedure. For example in the *Gentlemen's Magazine* case, several stores were visited and the managers were asked to complete the questionnaire. The interviewers left and returned later for them. Upon their return, they went over the questions with the manager. It was explained that the study was just beginning and that they wanted the manager's reactions on question clarity and ease of answering. This appeal for advice typically elicited cooperation. After several such interviews, the questionnaire was revised and the testing process repeated with new respondents. On the third trial, there appeared to be only minor need for further revision, so the questionnaire was reproduced and mailed.

The importance of the test-revise-retest cycle cannot be overstressed. The failure to take this imporant step is one of the greatest causes of poor survey results. Testing is the hallmark of the scientific researcher.

QUESTION CONSTRUCTION

Survey instruments normally include three types of information. The most important of these is the *sought data* such as facts, attitudes, preferences, and expectations about the central topic. A second type concerns the respondent characteristics needed for *classification and analysis.* Included are a large variety of items such as sex, age, family life cycle stage, family income, social class, and attitudes toward topics allied to the study's subject. The specific classification (or face-sheet) data sought depends on the particular study and its research objectives. A third type of information is *administrative.* It includes respondent identification, interviewer identification, date, place, and conditions of the interview, and the like.

You are ready to begin question drafting once you have decided on the information needed and the collection processes to use. In developing a survey instrument there are four major decision areas. These are (1) question content, (2) question wording, (3) response form, and (4) question sequence. These will be discussed in order, although in practice the process is not linear. In the following discussion, it is also assumed that the questions are structured.

Question content

Should this question be asked? Questions that merely produce "interesting information" cannot be justified on either economic or research grounds. One should challenge each question's function. Does it contribute significant information toward answering one of the investigative questions? Will it hurt if we do not have this information? Is it possible that we can infer the answer from some other question?

Is the question of proper scope? Next, consider each question's coverage. Does it include so much content that it should be broken into two questions? Minimizing the number of questions is highly desirable, but don't try to ask two questions in one. An obvious example might be to ask men's wear retailers whether this year's shoe sales and gross profits were higher than last year's. It is better to break this into separate questions. Less obvious problems occur when we ask for a family's TV station preference, when a better question would be to ask the station preference of each family member.

Another test of question content is, "Does it ask all that needs to be asked?" For example, we ask for the respondent's income when we really want to know the family's income. We sometimes ask "why" when this simple question will not adequately cover the range of causal relationships we want to explore. For example, perhaps two questions on product use by the heavy consumer should be asked while one question would do for the light user.

Questions are also inadequate if they do not provide the information needed to interpret responses fully. If you ask about the Prince Corporation's image as an employer, have you recognized that different classes of employees may have different reactions? Do you need to ask the question about other companies so that you can evaluate relative attitudes?

Can the respondent answer adequately? While the question may concern important content, and adequately cover the territory, does the respondent know the answer? Respondents typically want to cooperate in interviews, but they often assume that giving some answer is being more helpful than denying knowledge of a topic. In addition, their desire to impress the interviewer may encourage them to give answers based on no information. A classic illustration of this problem was the pattern of responses to the following question:[4]

"Which of the following statements most closely coincides with your opinion of the Metallic Metals Act?"

	Answers	*Responses*
1.	It would be a good move on the part of the U.S.	15%
2.	It would be a good thing but should be left to the individual states	41
3.	It is all right for foreign countries but should not be required here	11
4.	It is of no value at all	3
5.	Have no opinion	30

The response pattern indicates that 70 percent of those interviewed had a fairly clear opinion of the Metallic Metals Act; however, *there is no such act.* The respondents apparently assumed that if a question is asked then they should give it an answer. Give them some reasonable sounding choices and they will select one even if they know nothing about the topic.

Beware of assuming that respondents have prior knowledge or understanding of a subject. The risk is getting many answers that have little basis in fact. The Metallic Metals Act illustration may be challenged as an unusual case, but Payne cites a Gallup report where 45 percent of the persons surveyed did not know what a "lobbyist in Washington" was, and 88 percent

---

[4]Sam Gill, "How Do You Stand on Sin?" *Tide*, March 14, 1947, p. 72.

could not give a correct description of "jurisdictional strike."[5] However, you can probably get opinions on these topics from most respondents.

There is another side to this problem. In some studies, the degree of respondent expertise can be substantial, and simplified explanations are inappropriate. For example, in asking the general public about gross margins in men's wear stores, make sure that the respondent understands the nature of gross margin. In a survey of merchants, however, such explanations are not needed. The question designer should consider the respondent information level when determining the content and appropriateness of a question.

The adequacy problem also occurs when one asks questions that overtax the respondent's recall ability. Most cannot recall much that has happened in the past, except when it had some dramatic quality. You might well remember the first brand of cigarettes you smoked, and much about the circumstances of the event, yet be unable to recall much about later brand changes. If the events surveyed are of incidental interest to respondents, they will probably be unable to recall them correctly even a short time later. Boyd and Westfall report that an unaided recall question, "What radio programs did you listen to last night?" might locate as little as 10 percent of those who actually listened to a program.[6]

The adequacy of answers also depends on achieving the proper balance between generality and specificity. One often asks questions in terms too general and detached from respondent experiences. Is asking for average annual consumption making an unrealistic demand for generalization on persons who do not think in these terms? Would it be wiser to ask how many times the product was used last week or last month? Too often respondents are asked to recall individual use experiences over an extended period of time and to average them for us. This is asking interviewees to do your work and can only encourage substantial response errors. It may also discourage participation in the study.

There is also the danger of being too specific. One may ask about movie attendance for the last week when this is too short a time span on which to base attendance estimates. It may be better to ask about attendance, say, for the last month. There are no firm rules about this generality-specificity problem. Developing the right level of generality depends upon the situation and the art and experience of the question designer.

The ability of respondents to answer adequately is also often distorted by questions whose content is biased by what is included or omitted. The question may explicitly mention only the positive or negative aspects of the

---

[5]Stanley Payne, *The Art of Asking Questions* (Princeton, N.J.: Princeton University Press, 1951), p. 18.

[6]Unaided recall gives respondents no clues as to possible answers, while aided recall gives them a list of radio programs which played last night and then asks them which ones they had heard. See Harper W. Boyd, Jr., and Ralph Westfall, *Marketing Research*, 3d ed. (Homewood, Ill.: Richard D. Irwin, 1972), p. 293.

topic, or make unwarranted assumptions about the respondent's position. Consider, for an example, an experiment in which the following two forms of a question were asked:

A. What is your favorite brand of ice cream? _____

B. Some people have a favorite brand of ice cream while others do not have a favorite brand. In which group are you? (please check)

_____ I have a favorite brand of ice cream.

_____ I do not have a favorite brand of ice cream.

What is your favorite (if you have a favorite)? _____
_____.

Fifty-seven randomly chosen graduate business students answered version A, and 56 answered version B. Their responses are shown in the accompanying table.

Response	Version A	Version B
Named a favorite brand	77%*	39%*
Named a favorite flavor rather than a brand	19	18
Had no favorite brand	4	43
Total	100%	100%
	$n = 57$	56

*Significant difference at the 0.001 level.

The probable cause of the wide difference in brand preference is that A is a leading question. It assumes, and by this assumption suggests, that everyone has a favorite brand of ice cream and will report it. Version B indicates that the respondent need not have a favorite.

A deficiency in both versions is that about one respondent in five misinterpreted the meaning of "brand." This misinterpretation cannot be attributed to low education, low intelligence, or nonexposure to the topic. The subjects were students who had studied at least one course in marketing in which branding was prominently treated. Word confusion difficulties are discussed in a later section.

Will the respondents answer adequately? Even if respondents have the information, they may be unwilling to give it. Some topics are considered too sensitive to discuss with strangers. These will vary from person to person, but one study suggests that the most sensitive topics concern money matters and family life.[7] More than one fourth of those interviewed men-

_____
[7]Gideon Sjoberg, "A Questionnaire on Questionnaires," *Public Opinion Quarterly* 18 (Winter 1954), p. 425.

tioned these as the topics about which they would be "least willing to answer questions." Respondents of lower socioeconomic status also included political matters in this "least willing" list. Respondents may also be unwilling to give correct answers for ego reasons. Many tend to exaggerate their incomes, number of cars owned, social status, and the amount of high-prestige literature they read. They minimize their ages and the amount of low-prestige literature they read. Many respondents are also reluctant to make an effort to give an adequate response. Often this will occur when they see the topic as irrelevant to their own interests or to their perception of the survey's purpose. They participate halfheartedly, often answer with "don't know," give negative replies, refuse to be interviewed, or give stereotyped responses.

The researcher's challenge is to develop approaches to overcome these trouble areas. In general, three approaches can be used to secure more complete and truthful information: (1) motivate the respondent to provide appropriate information; (2) change the design of the questioning process, or (3) use methods other than questioning to secure the data.

Motivation. The first requirement for increasing motivation is to build good rapport with the respondent. Most information can be secured by direct undisguised questioning if rapport has been developed. Good rapport is particularly useful in building respondent interest in the project, and the more interest respondents have, the more cooperation they will give. One can also overcome respondent unwillingness to providing some material compensation for cooperation. This approach has been especially successful in mail surveys.

One can also increase respondents' motivations by assuring them that their answers are confidential. One approach is to give discreet assurances, both by question wording and interviewer comments and actions, that all types of behavior, attitudes, and positions on controversial or sensitive subjects are acceptable and normal. Where it can be said truthfully, you can also assure the respondents that their answers will be used only in combined statistical totals. In addition, if they are convinced that their replies contribute to some important purpose, they are more likely to be candid, even with taboo topics.

Redesign. You can also redesign the questioning process to improve the quality of the answers. For example, we might demonstrate that confidentiality is a fact by using a group administration of questionnaires, accompanied by some sort of ballot box collection procedure. Even in face-to-face interviews, the respondent may fill in a part of the questionnaire containing the sensitive information, and then seal the entire instrument in an envelope. While this approach does not guarantee confidentiality, it does suggest it. You can also develop appropriate questioning sequences that will more adroitly lead a respondent from "safe" questions gradually to those that are more sensitive.

Indirect questioning is one of the most widely used approaches by which opinions on sensitive topics are secured. The respondents are asked how "other people" or "people around here" feel about a topic. It is assumed that the respondents will reply in terms of their own attitudes and experiences, but this is by no means certain. For example, it may give a good measure of the majority opinion on a topic but fail either to reflect the views of the respondent or of minority segments.

With certain topics, it may be possible to secure answers by using a sort of proxy code. For example, when we seek family income classes we can hand the respondent a card with income brackets like:

A	Under $10,000 per year
B	$10,000 to $19,999 per year
C	$20,000 to $29,999 per year
D	$30,000 and over per year

The respondent is then asked to report the appropriate bracket as either A, B, C, or D. For some reason, respondents are more willing to provide such an obvious proxy measure than to give actual dollar values.

Other approaches.   Finally, it may be determined that questioning will not secure the information needed. A classic example in the literature concerns a survey to determine magazines read by respondents. An unusually high rate was reported for prestige magazines and an unusually low rate was reported for pulp magazines. The study was revised so that, instead of being interviewed, the subjects were asked to contribute their older magazines to a charity drive. This collection gave a much more realistic estimate of readership of both types of magazines.[8] A classic work on the use of similar unobtrusive measures cites many other types of research situations where a variety of techniques have been used to secure more valid information than was possible from a survey.[9]

Question wording

The difficulties brought about by the problems of question wording exceed most other sources of distortion in surveys. They have led one social scientist to conclude,

> To many who worked in the Research Branch it soon became evident that error or bias attributable to sampling and to methods of questionnaire administration were relatively small as compared with other types of variations—especially variation attributable to different ways of wording questions.[10]

---

[8]Percival White, *Market Analysis* (New York: McGraw-Hill, 1921).

[9]Eugene J. Webb, Donald T. Campbell, Richard D. Schwartz, and Lee Sechrest, *Unobtrusive Measures: Nonreactive Research in the Social Sciences* (Chicago: Rand McNally, 1966).

[10]S. A. Stouffer et al., *Measurement and Prediction, Studies in Social Psychology in World War II*, vol. 4 (Princeton, N.J.: Princeton University Press, 1950), p. 709.

While it is impossible to say which wording of a question is best, we can point out a number of problem areas that cause respondent confusion and measurement error. The diligent question designer will put a given question through many revisions before it satisfies the following six challenges.[11]

1. Is the question stated in terms of a shared vocabulary?
2. Is the question clear?
3. Are there unstated or misleading assumptions?
4. Is there biased wording?
5. Is there the right degree of personalization?
6. Are adequate alternatives presented?

Shared vocabulary. A survey is an exchange of ideas between interviewer and respondent.[12] Each must understand what the other says, and this is possible only if the vocabulary used is common to both parties. Two types of problems arise in this context. First, the words must be simple enough to allow adequate communication with persons of limited education. This is dealt with by reducing the level of word difficulty to basic English; more is said about this in the section on word clarity.

The second problem is one of technical language. Even highly educated respondents are at a loss to answer questions stated in unfamiliar technical terms. A second facet of the technical language problem concerns possible deficiencies on the part of the interviewer. In one study of how corporation executives handled various financial problems, it was necessary for interviewers to be able to talk in technical financial terms. This presented the researcher with two alternatives—hire persons knowledgeable in finance and teach them interviewing skills, or teach financial concepts to experienced interviewers.[13]

Question clarity. It is a frustrating experience when one finds that people misunderstand a question that has been painstakingly written. This is partially a problem of the shared vocabularies already mentioned. Beyond this, however, are the problems of understanding long and complex sentences and involved phraseology. The other requirements of question design (need to be explicit, to present alternatives, and to explain meanings) all contribute to longer and more involved sentences.[14]

Payne suggests that one of the great difficulties in question wording is in the choice of words to use. He argues that questions to be asked of the general public should be restricted to the most common 2,000 words in the

---

[11]An excellent example of the question revision process is presented in Stanley Payne, *The Art of Asking Questions*, pp. 214–25. This example illustrates that a relatively simple question can go through as many as 41 different versions before being judged satisfactory.

[12]Robert L. Kahn and Charles F. Cannell, *The Dynamics of Interviewing* (New York: John Wiley & Sons, 1957), p. 108.

[13]Ibid., p. 110.

[14]More will be said on the general problems of readability in Chapter 14.

English language.[15] Even the use of simple words is not enough. Many of these words have vague references or meanings which must be determined from their context. A question was asked of radio repairmen, "How many radio sets did you repair last month?" This may appear to be an unambiguous question, but respondents interpreted it in two ways. Some viewed it as a question of them alone, while others interpreted it as a more inclusive "you," indicating the total output of the shop. Typical of the many problem words are "any," "could-would-should," "fair," "near," "often," and "average." Payne recommends that, after we have stated a question as precisely as possible, we should test each word with the following six challenges:

1. Does it mean what we intend?
2. Does it have other meanings?
3. If so, does the context make the intended meaning clear?
4. Does the word have more than one pronunciation?
5. Is there any word or similar pronunciation that might be confused?
6. Is a simpler word or phrase suggested?[16]

Assumptions. Many problems of question wording can be traced to making unwarranted assumptions. The difficulties from assuming that the respondents know or understand key words or phrases have already been mentioned. In the Prince Corporation study, what percentage of the population would understand the term "conglomerate," or "multinational company"? We cause other problems when we use "blab" words—abstract concepts that have many overtones and emotional qualifications.[17] Unless words have concrete referents, their meanings are too vague for the researcher's needs. Examples of such words are "business," "government," and "society." Suppose that in the Prince Corporation study we asked the question, "How involved is business in the affairs of our society?" What is meant by "involved"? What parts of "society"? Is there such a thing as "business" per se?

Inherent in word meaning problems is also the matter of frame of reference. Each of us understands concepts, words, and expressions in the light of our own experience. A classic example of the problems this can bring appeared in research conducted by the U.S. Bureau of Census to determine the number of people in the labor market. To learn whether a person was employed, they asked the question, "Did you do any work for pay or profit last week?" The researchers erroneously assumed that there would be a common frame of reference between interviewer and respondents on the meaning of "work." Unfortunately, many persons viewed themselves primarily as housewives, students, or such. They failed to report that they also worked at a job during the week. This difference in frame of reference

---

[15]Payne, *The Art of Asking Questions*, p. 140.

[16]Ibid., p. 141.

[17]Ibid., p. 149.

resulted in a consistent underestimation of the number of persons working in the United States.

The single question was replaced by two questions, the first of which sought a statement on the respondent's major activity during the week. If the respondent gave a nonwork classification, a second question was asked to determine if he or she had done any work for pay in addition to this major activity. This revision increased the estimate of total employment by more than one million persons, with about one half of them working 35 hours or more per week.[18]

Controlling the frame of reference can be approached in two ways. First, the interviewer may seek to learn the frame of reference used by the respondent. For example, when asking respondents to evaluate their reasons for judging a labor contract offer, it is necessary to learn the frames of reference they use. Is the labor offer being evaluated in terms of the specific offer being made, the failure of a management to respond to other demands, the personalities involved, or the personal economic pressures that have resulted from a long strike?

It may be wise to specify the frame of reference for the respondent. For example, in asking for an opinion about the new labor contract offer, we might specify that the question concerns the size of the wage offer, the sincerity of management's offer, or whatever other frames of reference are of interest.

Biased wording.   Bias is the distortion of responses in one direction. It can result from many of the other problems already discussed, but word choice is often a major source. Obviously such words as "communist," "American," and the like must be used with great care. Strong adjectives can be particularly distorting. One alleged opinion survey, concerned with the subject of preparation for death, included the following question: "Do you think that decent, low-cost funerals are sensible?" Who could be against anything that is "decent" or "sensible"? There is a question as to whether this was a legitimate survey or a burial service sales campaign, but it shows how suggestive an adjective can be.

One can also strongly bias the respondent by using prestigious names in a question. For example, in a survey on whether the War and Navy Departments should be combined into a single Defense Department, one form said, "General Eisenhower says the Army and Navy should be combined," while the other version omitted his name. In the first version (name included), 49 percent of the respondents approved of having one department, while in the second version, only 29 percent favored one department.[19]

---

[18]Gertrude Bancroft and Emmett H. Welch, "Recent Experiences with Problems of Labor Force Measurement," *Journal of the American Statistical Association* 41 (1946), pp. 303–12.

[19]National Opinion Research Center, *Proceedings of the Central City Conference on Public Opinion Research* (Denver, Colo.: University of Denver, 1946), p. 73.

Other ways that one can bias response include the use of superlatives, slang expressions, and fad words. These are best excluded unless they are critical to the objective of the question. Ethnic references should also be stated with care.

Personalization. How personalized should a question be? Should we ask, "What would *you* do about . . . ?" or should we ask, "What would *people* do about . . . ?" The effect of personalization is shown by an example reported by Cantril.[20] A split test was made of a question concerning people's attitudes about the expansion of our armed forces in 1940.

> Should the United States do any of the following at this time?
> (A) Increase our army further, even if it means more taxes.
> (B) Increase our army further, even if you have to pay a special tax.

Eighty-eight percent of those answering question A felt we should increase the army, while only 79 percent of those answering question B were in favor of increasing the army.

These and other examples show that responses are changed by personalizing questions, but it is not clear whether this is for better or for worse. We often cannot tell which answer is superior. Perhaps the best that can be said is that when either form is acceptable, we should choose that which appears to present the issues more realistically. If there are doubts, then split versions should probably be used.

Adequate alternatives? Have we adequately expressed the alternatives with respect to the point of the question? It is usually wise to express each alternative explicitly in order to avoid bias. Payne illustrates this problem well with a pair of questions which were asked of matched samples of respondents.[21] The forms used were:

> (A) Do you think most manufacturing companies that lay off workers during slack periods could arrange things to avoid layoffs and give steady work right through the year?
> (B) Do you think most manufacturing companies that lay off workers in slack periods could avoid layoffs and provide steady work right through the year, or do you think layoffs are unavoidable?

	A	B
Company could avoid layoffs	63%	35%
Could not avoid layoffs	22	41
No opinion	15	24

Toward better questions. There is no substitute for a thorough understanding of question wording problems. Beyond this, however, there are several things to do to help improve survey results. At the original question

---

[20]Hadley Cantril, ed., *Gauging Public Opinion* (Princeton, N.J.: Princeton University Press, 1944), p. 48.

[21]Payne, *The Art of Asking Questions*, pp. 7–8.

drafting, try developing positive, negative, and neutral versions of each question. This practice dramatizes the problems of bias. Sometimes, use one of the extreme versions. For example, if we ask people about their children, we want our opinion statement to *encourage* the mention of all children.

Once you have developed a set of questions (including some with the same purpose), then test and revise them. Inexperienced researchers normally underestimate the need for this sequence of design-test-revise. Revising a question five or more times is not unusual. Finally, if there is still some doubt as to which version of a question is the more appropriate, we should use different question versions that go to matched or random selections of the respondents.

Response structure

A third major decision area in question design is the degree and form of structure imposed on responses. The options range from open (free choice of words) to closed (specified alternatives). Free responses, in turn, range from those in which the respondents express themselves extensively to those in which the freedom is to choose one word in a "fill-in" question. Closed responses typically are categorized as dichotomous or multiple choice.

Situational determinants. Kahn and Cannell suggest that five situational factors affect the decision of whether or not to use open or closed response questions.[22] They are:

1. Objectives of the interview.
2. Respondent's level of information about the topic.
3. Degree respondent has thought through the topic.
4. Ease of communication and motivation of respondent to talk.
5. Degree to which the above respondent factors are known to the interviewer.

If the objective of the question is only to classify the respondent on some stated point of view, then the closed form will serve well. For example, if you are interested only in whether a respondent approves or disapproves of a certain corporate policy, a closed response form will provide this answer. Such a response would ignore the full scope of the respondent's opinion and its antecedents. If the objective was to explore this wider territory, then an open response form would be more desirable.

As mentioned earlier, open-response questions are appropriate when the objective is to discover opinions and degrees of knowledge. They are also appropriate when the interviewer seeks sources of information, dates of events, suggestions, or when probes are used to secure more information.

When the topic of a question is likely to be outside of the respondent's experience, the open-end question may be the better way to learn his or her

---

[22]Kahn and Cannell, *Dynamics of Interviewing*, p. 132.

level of information. Open-end questions also help to determine certainty of feelings and expressions of intensity, although well-designed closed questions can do the same.

If a respondent has developed a clear opinion on the topic, a closed response question does well. If this process of thinking out an answer has not been done, the open-end question may give the respondent a chance to think over a reply, and to elaborate and revise it.

Experience has shown that closed questions typically take less motivation and the process of answering is less threatening to respondents. In contrast, the response alternatives sometimes suggest which answer is appropriate; in this sense, it may be biasing.

Finally, it may be better to use open-end questions when the interviewer does not have a clear idea of respondent frame of reference or level of information. Such conditions are likely to occur in exploratory research or at the pilot stage of a study. Closed-response questions are better when there is a clear frame of reference, the respondent's level of information is predictable, and the researcher believes the respondent understands the topic.

Two-way questions. While the open-response question has many advantages, closed questions are generally preferable in large surveys. They reduce the variability of response, make fewer demands on interviewer skills, are less costly to administer, and are much easier to code and analyze. In addition, after adequate exploration and testing, we can often develop closed questions that will perform as effectively as open questions in many situations. In fact, experimental studies suggest that closed questions are equal to or superior to open-response questions in many more applications than is commonly believed.[23]

Should a closed question call for a two-way or multiple-choice response? Often this is a simple decision dictated by the nature of the problem. For example, there may be a clearly dichotomous topic: Something is a fact or it is not, a respondent can either recall or not recall information. In many two-way questions, however, there are potential alternatives beyond the stated two. For example, the respondent may answer "don't know," "no opinion," or even "in-between." In other cases, there are two opposing or complementary choices, but there may also be a qualified choice ("yes, if X doesn't occur," or "sometimes yes and sometimes no," or "about the same"). Thus, two-way questions often become multiple choice, in fact, and these additional responses should be included.

One may omit the middle ground response if interested in which direction the respondent is leaning. One may also omit the middle answer when the topic is one about which people tend to retreat to a safe middle ground, if it is available. Dichotomous questions suggest opposing responses, but this is not always the best arrangement. One response may be so unlikely

---

[23]Barbara Snell Dohrenwend, "Some Effects of Open and Closed Questions on Respondents' Answers," *Human Organization* 24 (Summer 1965), pp. 175–84.

that it would be better to adopt the middle ground alternative as one of the two choices. For example, if you ask respondents whether they are underpaid or overpaid, you are not likely to get many agreements with the latter choice. The choices might better be underpaid and paid about right.

Multiple-choice questions. Multiple-choice questions are clearly appropriate in those cases where there are more than two alternatives, or where one seeks gradations of preference, interest, or agreement. Multiple-choice questions can be efficient, but they also present some unique design problems. One vexing problem is that the list of choices may not be exhaustive. Respondents may want to give an answer that is not one of the alternatives. This can occur when the desired response is one that combines two or more of the listed individual alternatives. For example, we might ask whether mine safety rules should be determined by the (1) mine companies, (2) miners, (3) federal government, or (4) state government. Many people may believe that such rules should be set by two or more of these groups acting jointly, but the question does not include this response option.

A second problem occurs when some response category has not been anticipated. For example, the "union" has not been mentioned in the alternatives on mine safety laws. Many respondents would lump this alternative with "miners," but others will view it as a separate category. Some respondents may feel that certain rules should be set by a federal agency, others by industry-national union negotiation, and still others through local management-worker shop committees. When the researcher tries to provide for all possible options, the list can become exhausting as well as exhaustive. We can guard against this proliferation by determining the major specific choices through pretesting. Then we add the category "other (please specify) _____" to provide for all other options.

Another problem in alternative selection occurs when the choices are not mutually exclusive (the respondent sees two or more responses as overlapping). For example, in a multiple-choice question asking students why they went to a certain college, the following response alternatives might be listed about the chosen school:

1. Good academic reputation.
2. Specific program of study desired.
3. Enjoyable campus life.
4. Many friends from home attend.
5. High quality of the faculty.

It is likely that items (1) and (5) will be viewed as overlapping, and some may see items (3) and (4) in the same way.

It is also important to seek a fair balance in choices. One study has shown that an off-balance presentation of alternatives biases results in favor of the more heavily offered side.[24] For example, if there are four gradations of

---

[24]Cantril, *Gauging Public Opinion*, p. 31.

alternatives on one side of a question and two on the other side, there will be a tendency to bias responses toward the better represented side.

A common problem in multiple-choice questions is the assuring that all alternatives are reasonable. This is particularly the case when choices are numbers or identifications. For example, if we asked, "Which of the following numbers is closest to the number of students enrolled in American colleges and universities today?" the following choices might be presented:

1.   75,000.
2.   750,000.
3.   7,500,000.
4.   25,000,000.
5.   75,000,000.

It should be obvious to most respondents that at least three of these choices are not reasonable in the light of our general knowledge about the population of the United States.

The order of the choices given can also be a problem. Numbers are normally presented in order of magnitude. This reasonable practice tends to introduce a bias. The respondent assumes that if there is a list of five numbers, the correct answer will lie somewhere in the middle of the group. This is not an unreasonable assumption. Researchers often add a couple of incorrect numbers on each side of the correct one. The obvious way to counteract this bias is to put the correct number at one of the extremes more often.

Order bias with nonnumeric data leads to a tendency to choose first or last alternatives over the middle ones. This bias can be counteracted by using the split-ballot technique. A simple way to carry this out, in face-to-face interviews, is to list the alternatives on a card to be handed to the respondent when asking the question. Cards with different choice orders can be alternated to assure positional balance. It is better to leave the choices unnumbered on these cards so that respondents reply by giving the choice itself rather than its identifying number. It is probably a good practice to use cards in this manner any time that there are question alternatives of four or more. It saves interviewer reading time and assures a more valid answer by keeping the full range of choices in front of the respondent.

In most multiple-choice questions, there is also a problem of assuring that the choices represent a unidimensional scale. That is, the alternatives all represent different aspects of the same *conceptual dimension*. To illustrate, the foregoing suggested list for choosing a college included features associated with a college that might be attractive to a student. This list, while not exhaustive, illustrated aspects of the concept of "college attractiveness." But it did not mention other concepts which might affect a school attendance decision. Parents and peer advice, local alumni efforts, and school adviser suggestions may influence the decision, but these represent a conceptual dimension different from "school attractiveness."

All types of response styles have their advantages and disadvantages. All forms are often found in the same questionnaire, and the situational factors mentioned earlier are the major guides in this matter. There is a tendency, however, to use closed-response forms in preference to the more flexible open-response type.

Question sequence

The design of survey questions is also strongly affected by the need to relate each question to the others in the instrument. Question sequencing is particularly important. The basic principle to guide sequence decisions is: *The nature and needs of the respondent must determine the sequence of questions and the organization of the schedule.* Certain guides may be suggested by which to implement this principle of respondent orientation. Some of the major ones are:

1. The question process must quickly awaken interest and motivate the respondent to participate in the interview.
2. The respondent should not be confronted by early requests for information that might be considered personal or ego threatening.
3. The questioning process should begin with simple items and move to the more complex, and from general items to the more specific.
4. Changes in frame of reference should be minimal and should be clearly pointed out.

The interviewer's first challenge is to awaken the respondent's interest in the study and motivate participation. We try to bring this about by choosing early-interview questions that are attention-getting and not controversial in subject or thrust. If the questions have human interest value, so much the better. It is possible that the early questions will contribute hard data to the major study objective, but their major task is to overcome the motivational barrier.

The second rule concerns the inappropriate requesting of information too early in the interview. Two forms of this error are common. There is usually a need to ask for personal classification information about respondents. They normally will provide this data, but the request should be made at the end of the interview. If sought immediately, it often causes respondents to feel threatened, dampening their interest and motivation to continue. It is also a dangerous practice to ask any question at the start that might appear to be personal or private. For example, respondents in one survey were asked whether they suffered from insomnia. When the question was asked immediately after the interviewer's introductory remarks, about 12 percent of those interviewed admitted to having insomnia. When a matched sample was asked the same question after two buffer questions (neutral questions designed chiefly to establish rapport with the respondent), 23 percent admitted having insomnia.[25]

[25] Frederick J. Thumin, "Watch for These Unseen Variables," *Journal of Marketing* 26 (July 1962), pp. 58–60.

A third rule is to place simpler questions first and to move progressively to more complex ones. Even simple questions that require much thought should be deferred until later. These recommendations can help reduce the number of "don't know" responses that are so prevalent in the early part of interviews.

The procedure of moving from general to more specific questions is sometimes called the "funnel approach." The objectives of this procedure are to learn the respondent's frame of reference and to extract the full range of desired information while limiting the distortion effect of earlier questions on later ones. Cannell and Kahn illustrate this process with the following series of questions:

1. How do you think this country is getting along in its relations with other countries?
2. How do you think we are doing in our relations with Russia?
3. Do you think we ought to be dealing with Russia differently than we are now?
4. *(If yes)* What should we be doing differently?
5. Some people say we should get tougher with Russia and others think we are too tough as it is; how do you feel about it?[26]

The first question introduces the general subject and provides some insight into the respondent's frame of reference. The second question narrows the concern to a single country, while the third and fourth seek views on how the United States should deal with Russia. The fifth question illustrates a specific opinion area and would be asked only if this particular point of toughness had not been covered in earlier responses.

In addition to the problem of general-specific sequencing, there is also a risk of interaction whenever two or more questions are related. Cantril reports on a survey with this problem. The two questions shown in the table were asked in a national survey at the start of World War II:[27]

Question	Percent answering yes	
	A asked first	*B asked first*
A. Should the United States permit its citizens to join the French and British Armies?	45%	40%
B. Should the United States permit its citizens to join the German Army?	31%	22%

Apparently, if respondents first endorsed enlistments with the Allies, some felt obliged to extend this same privilege to joining the Germans. Where

---

[26]Charles F. Cannell and Robert L. Kahn, "The Collection of Data by Interviewing," Chapter 8, in Leon Festinger and Daniel Katz, eds., *Research Methods in the Behavioral Sciences* (New York: Holt, Rinehart & Winston, 1953), p. 349.

[27]Cantril, *Gauging Public Opinion*, p. 28.

the decision was first made against joining the German Army, a percentage of the respondents felt constrained from approving the option to join the Allies.

Finally, questions should be arranged so that there is a minimum of shifting in subject matter and frame of reference. Respondents often interpret questions in the light of earlier questions and will miss shifts of perspective or subject unless they are clearly stated. Respondents fail to listen carefully and frequently jump to conclusions about the import of a given question before it is even completely stated. In such cases, their answers are strongly influenced by the frame of reference which they have been holding. Any change in subject by the interviewer may not register with them unless made strong and obvious.

REASON ANALYSIS

Questions to determine "reasons for" present a difficult challenge to the question designer. A simple "why?" to determine the causes of an action or opinion is easy to use, but it throws the conceptualization and definition task to the respondent. The resulting answers typically are partial, from various frames of reference, and often not germane to the researcher's objectives. There are more effective approaches by which causal relationships in surveys may be determined. One approach is cross classification and other forms of correlation; these are discussed in Chapters 11 and 13. A second approach is *reason analysis* which is defined as "a set of procedures used in survey research to construct a causal explanation for the actions, decision, or intentions of individuals."[28] Reason analysis is uniquely appropriate for many research situations. Kadushin suggests that

> If one wants to know how an action came to be—what steps were taken and what the key choices were; what the actor thought he was doing and how he felt about it; what influences were present and what triggered the action; and, finally, what outcomes the actor expected—then no technique other than reason analysis can be used.[29]

Zeisel suggests that the process of reason analysis involves five steps:

1. Formulation of the problem in terms of specific research purposes.
2. Selecting the type of action.
3. Development of the accounting scheme.
4. Interviewing for reasons.
5. Statistical assessment and interpretation.[30]

---

[28]Reprinted with permission of Macmillan Publishing Co., Inc. from "Reason Analysis" by Charles Kadushin in David L. Sills, ed., *The International Encyclopedia of the Social Sciences*, vol. 13, p. 338. Copyright © 1968 by Crowell Collier and Macmillan, Inc.

[29]Ibid., p. 338.

[30]Hans Zeisel, *Say It with Figures*. 4th ed. (New York: Harper & Row, 1957), p. 136.

The discussion which follows draws heavily upon Zeisel's analysis, but only the first three of these steps will be discussed.

Problem formulation. The first step facing the researcher is to determine the relevant range of factors to include in the study. The major source for this decision is the study's research objective. For example, when studying reasons for the purchase of snack foods, one concentrates on certain areas of consumption and conditions of use if the objective is to provide input for an advertising campaign. In this case, you will be more interested in the immediate factors that precipitate brand choice. If you were interested in improving nutritional levels, the direction of questioning would be quite different. In this latter case, for example, you might be much more interested in biographical or historical determinants that have fostered basic habits.

Selecting the type of action. The preliminary analysis of actions, opinions, or intentions often will indicate that there are various types of respondents who need to be dealt with differently. In a study of snack-food eaters, one may find that there are people who eat snacks selectively as to time, occasion, and product; others may be habitual consumers who eat snacks often, in volume, and with little discrimination to product, time, or occasion. While one may be interested in analyzing the reasons behind actions and decisions in both groups, they may be so different as to require different sets of reason questions. In such a case, a filter question or two should be used to identify the classification of snack eater, followed by separate questioning sets for the different classes of respondents.

Developing the accounting scheme. To employ reason analysis, develop an *accounting scheme*—an organized list of factors that are believed to be relevant causes or influences upon some action, opinion, or intention. Zeisel refers to these factors as "dimensions of the action or attitude under study. . . . As long as specific reasons have in common the defining feature of such a single dimension, they are to be treated together, separate from reasons in another dimension."[31] He illustrates a simple accounting concept with a survey designed to find out why women used a particular face cream. From the answers secured, he was able to extract three logical dimensions which were relevant for this study. They were:

1. To the respondent—special skin conditions or certain preferences, prejudices, and so forth.
2. To the product—its qualities, its supposed effects, its prices.
3. To the source through which the respondent learned of the product or its qualities.[32]

From this and similar studies, Zeisel generalized that most simpler purchase propositions can be adequately analyzed with a three-dimension ac-

---

[31]Zeisel, *Say It with Figures*, p. 138.
[32]Ibid., p. 139.

counting scheme. The dimension of *respondent's condition* he generalizes to embrace all of the respondent's motives prior to the decision to buy. The second major dimension concerns *attributes of the product or object*, while the third reflects *influences* that affect the course of the decision. These influences, in turn, consist of the *channel* and *content of communication* subdimensions.[33] An accounting scheme suggested for a study of the purchase decisions of major appliances included similar elements; they were (1) line of rejection (includes reasons why the product was not selected); (2) lines of acceptance (includes those factors which led to the preference for a given brand); and (3) channels of influence (includes the sources of information which led either to rejection or acceptance.[34]

As an example of how the dimensions chosen must reflect the particular problem under study, four major categories were used in a study of reasons for choosing trial with or without jury. In this study, the major dimensions were (1) ultimate advantage aimed at; (2) influences on decisions; (3) expected differences between judge and jury trial; and (4) the case.[35]

Selltiz, Wrightsman, and Cook suggest that accounting schemes often include as many as five broad classes of considerations. They suggest (1) the history of the act or feeling; (2) the characteristics in a given entity that provoke a given reaction; (3) the supports for the beliefs, feelings, and so forth, about a given entity; (4) the personal desires, motives, values, or interests involved in a given reaction; and (5) the specific situations and circumstances in which a given reaction occurs.[36]

Whatever the accounting scheme developed, it must reflect the specific objectives of the study as well as the specific topic of concern. It will also often be necessary to incorporate the time element into the scheme to recognize that individual influences and motives have different impacts at various stages in the decision process. To illustrate the detail that might result from the accounting scheme approach, consider a study reported in the pioneering work on reason analysis.[37] This survey was made of people who attended movies. Preliminary study indicated that there were two types of movie attenders—those who were habitual moviegoers and those who attended because of a desire to see a particular movie. The questionnaire developed to account for these two types and to provide adequate information for the accounting scheme is as follows:

> Do you go primarily (I) just to go to a movie, or (II) because of a certain picture?
>
> I_____   II_____   Both_____

[33]Zeisel, *Say It with Figures*, pp. 141–42.

[34]Ibid., pp. 142–43.

[35]Ibid., p. 143.

[36]Claire Selltiz, Lawrence S. Wrightsman, and Stuart W. Cook, *Research Methods in Social Relations*. 3d ed. (New York: Holt, Rinehart & Winston, 1976), p. 308.

[37]Paul F. Lazarsfeld, "The Art of Asking Why," *National Marketing Review* 1, no. 1 (Summer 1935), pp. 26–38.

If I or both:
1. When did you decide to go to a movie?
2. Why and under what circumstances did you decide?
3. (If not yet inserted) When and how was your company chosen?
4. As to the special theater or show: (Check.)
   a Was it proposed by someone in the company?_____
   b Did you have it in mind yourself?_____
   c Did you look for or get special advice or information?_____
      If (b), how did you know about it?_____
      If (c), where did you look for advice or information?_____
5. How many pictures were taken into consideration?
6. Which was more conducive?: (Check.)
   a the theatre_____
   b the picture_____
   c do not know_____
   Remarks for Interviewers; If b or c, ask question 7 first. If a, ask question 8 first. But ask both questions in any case.
7. What interested you in the picture? (Please try to remember all the details.)
8. What made the theater suitable to your choice?

If II:
1a. When did you learn about this picture?
2a. How did you learn about it?
3a. What interested you in it when you heard about it? (Please try to remember all the details.)
4a. (If not yet inserted) When and how was your company chosen?

In all cases:
1b. (If not yet inserted) When and under what circumstances was the final decision made? Why did you go at this particular time?
2b. What other uses of the time and money spent in seeing the movie were considered?

PRODUCT MANAGER STUDY

After some discussion, the student research team agreed that they would first define the research objective of their study and then get it approved by Professor Emory. They stated their research objective as: Provide an inventory of major U.S. manufacturers who use the product management system, gather descriptive data on the nature and degree of product management, and collect information on how product managers are recruited, selected, and prepared for their responsibilities.

Lisa and Conrado met with Professor Emory and presented their research statement. He approved it and then asked, "Who are you going to study?"

"We are going to request some financial support from the student research fund to survey the major corporations listed in *Fortune's* top *1,000* manufacturing companies," was Lisa's reply.

Conrado chimed in, "We have considered several approaches but have decided that we can do something rather special if we conduct a mail survey. We expect to use a screening question at the beginning of the questionnaire to determine which companies use product managers. If a company does not use product managers, only one question needs to be answered."

"Have you devised your investigative questions yet?" was the professor's next query.

"Yes we have," said Lisa. "Here is a list of five that we have come up with."

1. What is the incidence of use of the product manager system? Included are:
    a To what degree is it presently being used?
    b Has it been used in the past and dropped?
    c Was it considered and not adopted?
    d What are future expectations regarding its use?
2. How are product managers recruited and selected?
3. What are the qualifications for employment as a product manager?
4. How does the product manager function in your company?
5. Classification information by which to analyze the above questions.

"These look pretty good. Go ahead with the development of your project. I will recommend that the student research fund give you some support financially in doing this study," was Professor Emory's concluding comment.

What did they do? For the answer, see the Appendix to this chapter.

SUMMARY

The versatility of the survey method is its greatest strength. It is usually the only practical way to gather opinions, intentions, knowledge, and similar private behaviors. Its dependency upon the respondent's verbal behavior is its greatest weakness. Not only may intentionally false information be given, but verbal behavior can also be dramatically changed by a wide variety of factors.

There are a number of choices to be made in designing a survey instrument. Survey research can be a face-to-face interview or it can be much less personal, using indirect media and self-administered questionnaires. The questioning process can be unstructured as with depth interviewing and similar approaches, or the questions can be clearly structured. Responses may be unstructured with open-ended respondent answers or structured with the respondent choosing an answer from a set of listed possibilities. Finally, there is a decision as to the degree to which to disguise the objectives and intent of the question.

The development of a survey instrument is too often slighted by inexperienced researchers who feel that just about anyone can do it. Question development will be easier if the designer follows the research question hierarchy concept. The logical process is usually a fractionation that begins with the management question, then moves on to the research question, the investigative questions, and, finally, to the measurement questions themselves.

Three general classes of information are generally obtained. The most important is the information of major topical concern. A second class is data concerning respondent characteristics and other information used chiefly for classification and analysis purposes. Finally, certain administrative information is needed.

Question construction has four critical decision areas. They are (1) question content, (2) question wording, (3) response form, and (4) question sequence. Question content should pass the following tests:

1. Should the question be asked?
2. Is the question of proper scope?
3. Can the respondent answer adequately?
4. Will respondents answer adequately?

Question wording difficulties exceed most other sources of distortion in surveys. Each question should pass the following six tests on wording:

1. Is the question stated in terms of a shared vocabulary?
2. Is the question clear?
3. Are there unstated or misleading assumptions?
4. Is there biased wording?
5. Is there the right degree of personalization?
6. Are adequate alternatives presented?

In response form, the third major decision area, situational determinants are major choice factors. Five such determinants are:

1. Objectives of the interview.
2. Respondent's level of information about the topic.
3. Degree respondent has thought through the topic.
4. Ease of communication and motivation of respondent to talk.
5. Degree to which the above respondent factors are known to the interviewer.

Both two-way and multiple-choice questions have their values and their deficiencies, but on balance, the latter tend to be preferred if only because few questions have only two possible answers.

Question sequence can drastically affect respondent willingness to cooperate and the quality of responses received. Generally, the sequence should begin with efforts to awaken the respondent's interest in continuing the interview. Early questions should be simple rather than complex, easy rather than difficult, nonthreatening, and obviously germane to the announced objective of the study. Frame-of-reference changes should be minimal and questions should be sequenced in such a way that earlier questions do not distort the replies of later ones.

A special problem in question design is that of learning the reasons for actions or opinions. A simple "why" question is too often used and almost as often fails to secure the needed information. To measure reasons why, the researcher needs first to analyze the research objectives and the type of actions or opinions under study. In the context of this analysis, an accounting scheme should be used. This is an organized list of factors believed to be relevant causes or influences upon the actions, attitudes, or intentions under study. When done in this manner, substantial causal information can be secured.

SUPPLEMENTAL READINGS

1. Berdie, Douglas R., and John F. Anderson. *Questionnaires: Design and Use.* Metuchen, N.J.: The Scarecrow Press, 1974. Chapters 3 and 4 are on questionnaire design. Appendixes have four sample questionnaires. Also extensive bibliography.
2. Dillman, Don A. *Mail and Telephone Surveys.* New York: John Wiley & Sons, 1978. Chapters 3, 4, and 6 are on question construction and questionnaire design. Extensive bibliography.
3. Kahn, Robert L., and Charles F. Cannell. *The Dynamics of Interviewing.* New York: John Wiley & Sons, 1957. Chapters 5 and 6 cover questionnaire design.
4. Parten, Mildred. *Surveys, Polls, and Samples.* New York: Harper & Row, 1950. Chapter 6 is on questionnaire design.
5. Payne, Stanley L. *The Art of Asking Questions.* Princeton, N.J.: Princeton University Press, 1951. An enjoyable book on the many problems found in developing useful survey questions. It is a classic.
6. Selltiz, Claire; Lawrence S. Wrightsman; and Stuart W. Cook. *Research Methods in Social Relations.* 3d ed. New York: Holt, Rinehart & Winston, 1976. Appendix B is an especially well-organized set of guides for the questionnaire designer.
7. Zeisel, Hans. *Say It with Figures.* 5th ed. New York: Harper & Row, 1968. Chapter 6 presents a thorough discussion of the concept of an accounting scheme.

DISCUSSION QUESTIONS

1. Distinguish between:
   a Direct and indirect questions.
   b Open and closed questions.
   c Research, investigative, and measurement questions.
   d Question and response structure.
2. Why is the survey technique so popular? When is it not appropriate?
3. What special problems do open-ended questions have? How can these be minimized? In what situations is the open-end question most useful?

4. Why might a researcher wish to disguise the questioning objective of a study?

5. One of the major reasons that survey research may not be effective is because the survey instruments are less useful than they should be. What would you say are the four major faults of the survey instrument designer?

6. Why is it desirable to pretest survey instruments? What information can you secure from such a pretest? How can one go about finding the best wording for a question on a questionnaire?

7. One design problem in the development of survey instruments concerns the sequence of questions. What suggestions would you give to persons who are designing their first questionnaire?

8. One of the major problems facing the designer of a survey instrument is the assumptions made. What are the major "problem assumptions"?

9. Below are six questions that might be found on questionnaires. Comment on each as to whether or not it is a good question. If not, tell why. (Assume that no lead-in or screening questions are required for these. That is, judge the question on its own merits.)

   a Do you read the *National Geographic Magazine* regularly?

   b What percent of your time is spent asking for information from others in your organization?

   c When did you first start chewing gum?

   d How much discretionary buying power do you have each year?

   e Why did you decide to attend to attend Big State University?

   f Do you think the president is doing a good job now?

10. Develop an accounting scheme to determine why people attend business school. Using this accounting scheme, develop a short questioning instrument by which to interview persons who have gone to business school.

11. One student class project was to develop a brief self-administered questionnaire by which students might quickly evaluate a professor. One student submitted the following instrument. Evaluate the questions asked and the format of the instrument.

Professor Evaluation Form

1. Overall, how would you rate this professor?

   _____good; _____fair; _____poor;

2. Does this professor:

   a have good class delivery? _____

   b know the subject? _____

   c have a positive attitude toward the subject? _____

   d grade fairly? _____

   e have a sense of humor? _____

   f use audiovisuals, case examples, or other classroom aids? _____

   g return exams promptly? _____

3. What is the professor's strongest point? _____

4. What is the professor's weakest point? _____

5. What kind of class does the professor teach? _____

6. Is this course required? _____

7. Would you take another course from this professor? _____

12. Below is a copy of the letter and mail questionnaire received by a professor who is a member of the American Society of Training Directors. Please evaluate the usefulness and tone of the letter and the questions and format of the instrument.

Dear ASTD Member:

In partial fulfillment of Master's Degree work, I have chosen to do a descriptive study of the industrial trainer in our area. Using the roster of the ASTD as a mailing list, your name came to me. I am enclosing a short questionnaire and a return envelope. I hope you will take a few minutes and fill out the questionnaire as soon as possible, as the sooner the information is returned to me, the better.

Sincerely,

Questionnaire
Directions: Please answer as briefly as possible.
1. With what company did you enter the field of training? _____
2. How long have you been in the field of training? _____
3. How long have you been in the training department of the company with which you are presently employed? _____
4. How long has the training department in your company been in existence? _
5. Is the training department a subdivision of another department? _____
   If so, what department? _____
6. For what functions (other than training) is your department responsible? __
   _____
7. How many people, including yourself, are in the training department of your company? (Local plant or establishment) _____
8. What degrees do you hold, and from what institutions? _____
   Major_____ Minor_____
9. Why were you chosen for training? What special qualifications do you have that prompted your entry into training? _____
   _____

10. What experience would you consider necessary for an individual to enter into the field of training with your company? Include both educational requirements and actual experience. _____
    _____
    _____
    _____

APPENDIX   PRODUCT MANAGER STUDY

Questionnaire development. The team members from Professor Emory's class developed the following procedure for designing the questionnaire. Having agreed upon the investigative questions, each member attempted to write measurement questions aimed at tapping the essence of each investigative question. Each measurement question was written on a 5- × -8 card in order to facilitate comparisons, revisions, additions, and deletions. At a meeting of the team, all questions were reviewed, duplicates eliminated, and a general winnowing took place. After this process, the remaining 31 questions were included in questionnaire draft 1, shown in Figure 8A–1. In this first questionnaire draft, there was no effort to place questions in sequence or to present them graphically as they would eventually be seen by respondents.

FIGURE 8A–1   Preliminary questionnaire, product manager study—draft 1

1. What is your position in the company?
2. Is your company engaged primarily in industrial products, consumer products, or both?
3. Does your company use product managers?
4. How many product managers does the company have?
5. How many products are assigned to one PM?
6. Would you please give or include a job description of your company's PM position?
7. How many brands does your company have?
8. Approximately what percentage of your company's brands have product managers?
9. What percentage of sales volume do the brands in question 8 account for as a whole?
10. How long have product managers been used in your company?
11. Has a PM system been used and dropped in your company? If yes, why was it dropped?
12. Has a PM system ever been considered but never adopted in your company? If yes, why was it not adopted?
13. Are there any plans for the adoption of a PM system in the future?
14. What percentage of your product managers come *directly* from each of the following sources? Campuses, within the company, other companies, other (list).

After some discussion, the team members concluded that the questionnaire would probably need to be three pages in length. In addition, a covering letter would require a page. They decided to use a printed cover letter and to incorporate it as the first page of the questionnaire. The combination would be printed on both sides of an 11- × -17 inch sheet of paper, folded in booklet form to 8½- × -11 size.

Each team member was assigned the individual task of translating draft 1 into a draft 2. In this new draft, the questions should be in planned sequence, have response formats chosen, and graphic arrangements selected. These individual drafts were submitted to a subcommittee of Brad and Margie who used them as the basis for developing questionnaire draft 2. This is shown in Figure 8A–2.

FIGURE 8A–1   *(concluded)*

---

15. If PMs come from within the company, what department or departments do they come from? Sales, marketing, production, advertising, other (list)?

16. If PMs come from outside the company (other than campuses), what department or deprtments do they come from? Product manager, sales, marketing, production, advertising, other (list)?

17. If PMs are recruited directly from campuses, what, if any, are typical degrees required?

18. Rank on a scale from 1 to 5 the relative importance of each of the following qualifications for a PM (1 denotes the greatest importance). Education, age, work experience, personality, creativity.

19. If PMs are recruited from within the company, what is the average age, length of work experience (with the company), and educational background?

20. If PMs are recruited from outside the company (not including campuses), what is the average age, length of work experience, and educational background?

21. What functions (e.g., advertising, pricing, etc.) does the PM actually perform in day-to-day activities, and what percentage of time is spent on each?

22. Of those functions listed in 21, which, if any, does the PM have *final* authority over?

23. To whom does the PM report?

24. Does your company have a structured training program for product management? If yes, please explain.

25. On the basis of which of the following is the PM evaluated? Market share, ROI, sales volume, profits, other (list)?

26. What were the objectives of the company in instituting the PM concept?

27. How successful has the PM concept been in fulfilling the objectives set for it?

28. What were the characteristics of the PM concept which contributed to the fulfillment of these objectives?

29. What elements, if any, of the PM system did not adequately contribute to the fulfillment of the objectives?

30. What specific actions, if any, have been taken to deal with the inadequacies listed in 29?

31. If your company is currently planning any broad revisions in the present PM program, please describe.

Draft 2 was reproduced and submitted to some other members of the research class for critique. In particular, comments and challenges were sought on (1) sources of confusion and vagueness; (2) question value (what useful information does the question provide? Not provide?); (3) appropriateness of the proposed response formats and suggestions for improvement; and (4) gaps in question coverage.

After this critique session, a second subcommittee of the team was asked to revise the questionnaire. This resulted in questionnaire draft 3 not pre-

FIGURE 8A–2   Product manager questionnaire—draft 2

1. Does your company now use product managers? yes _____ no _____ If no, please go to question 17.
2. Would you please send a copy of your job description?
3. How many product managers does your company have? _____
4. What percentage of your total sales are accounted for by product managers? _____%
5. How long have product managers been used by your company? _____ years
6. What percentage of your personnel enter the product management program from the following sources?

    campuses _____ %
    within the company _____ %
    from elsewhere _____ %

7. If product managers come from within the company or elsewhere, what department(s) do they come from?

    sales _____ %
    marketing _____ %
    production _____ %
    advertising _____ %
    other product management programs _____ %
    advertising agencies _____ %
    elsewhere _____ %

8. If product managers are recruited directly from campuses, please rank the following degrees from 1 to 6, with 1 being the most desirable, 2 the next most desirable, and so forth.

    BS _____ areas _____
    AB _____ areas _____
    BSBA (BBA) _____ areas _____
    MA _____ areas _____
    MBA _____ areas _____
    PhD _____ areas _____

9. Briefly state what you consider to be an appropriate profile of a product manager recruited directly from the campus.

    age

    work experience (length and type)

    personal traits, i.e., personality, creativity, aggressiveness, etc.

    education

10. What do you consider to be an appropriate profile for a product manager recruited from within or from another company?

    age

    work experience (length and type)

    personal traits, i.e., personality, creativity, aggressiveness, etc.

    education

FIGURE 8A–2   *(concluded)*

---

11. To whom does the product manager report? _____

12. What percentage of his time does the product manager spend in various functionary areas, such as production, advertising, pricing, etc.? Please list.

13. Please rank the following on a scale of 1 to 5 (1 is most important), the criteria used in evaluating a product manager?
    - _____ market share
    - _____ return on investment
    - _____ sales volume
    - _____ profits
    - _____ other (please explain) _____

14. Does the company have a structured training program? yes _____ no _____ If yes, please describe.

15. What prompted your firm to initiate the product manager system?

16. Is your company currently planning any future revisions in the product manager system?
    yes _____ no _____ If yes, please explain.

17. Is your company primarily engaged in:
    - industrial goods _____ %
    - food products _____ %
    - consumer package goods _____ %
    - consumer durable goods _____ %
    - automotive products _____ %
    - other (list)
      - _____ _____ %
      - _____ _____ %

18. What is your company's total sales volume? $_____
    If you answered the first question yes, you have completed the questionnaire. If your answer was no, please answer question 19. Thank you for your cooperation.

19. Please check which of the following best describes your company's use of product managers.
    - _____ have never considered product managers
    - _____ have considered, but never adopted product management
    - _____ have used previously and discontinued
    - _____ presently considering adoption of the system in the future

---

sented here. The draft was again reviewed by the full team and some modest changes made to produce draft 4.

By this time, the team members were anxious to test the questionnaire with real respondents. Arrangements were made to have several local corporate executives complete the questionnaire. Team members arranged to pick up the completed questionnaires and to interview the executives about their answers as well as any comments they had about the questions or the

FIGURE 8A–3   Product manager questionnaire—final draft

WASHINGTON UNIVERSITY

ST. LOUIS, MISSOURI 63130

GRADUATE SCHOOL
OF BUSINESS ADMINISTRATION

Inside Address

Dear Sir:

We at the Washington Business School are interested in learning more about the actual recruitment and use of product or brand managers. Our objective is to help expand the body of knowledge about this important area of marketing.

To do this, of course, means going to someone such as yourself who *knows*. Your help with the few questions on the attached pages will take only a few minutes and will make a real contribution to the accuracy and success of this study.

Your reply will be treated in strict confidence and will be available only to my research staff and myself. Any publication will be only of statistical totals for groups of companies.

Your assistance will be greatly appreciated and will help us to know more about product management and to teach about it in a more relevant and effective manner.

Sincerely,

William Emory
Professor of Marketing

We define a *product manager* (also called brand manager) as one who is responsible for the integration and planning of a broad range of marketing functions (e.g., pricing, distribution, and so forth) for a specific product, brand, or homogeneous group of products. The position usually has limited or no line authority, especially over the sales force.

1. Please indicate which of the following best describes your company/division's use of product managers.

_____ we are currently using product managers.
_____ we have previously used product managers, but discontinued.
_____ we have considered the system, but never implemented it.
_____ presently considering adoption of the system in the future.
_____ we have never considered product managers.

If you are currently using product managers, please continue. If *you are not* currently using product managers you have completed the questionnaire. Thank you for your cooperation.

FIGURE 8A–3   *(continued)*

(please check)

2. Will you be answering the following for: _____ your company
                                            _____ your division

3. How many product managers (include all levels such as
   Group PM, PM, Assoc. PM, and Assistant PM) does your
   company/division employ?   _____

4. How long have product managers been used by your com-
   pany/division?   _____ years

5. What percentage of your company/division total sales are
   accounted for by products controlled by product managers?   _____ %

6. From the following, please indicate whether the position exists in your com-
   pany/division. Then, indicate the source from which the personnel at the
   various levels were obtained to fill that position. If you have a similar position, but with a different name, please indicate that position in the blank.

(please check)
Major Sources

	Do You Have?		Campuses	Within Company		Other Companies
	Yes	No	Campuses	Other PM Jobs	Other Jobs	
Group PMs	____	____	____	____	____	____
PMs	____	____	____	____	____	____
Assoc. PMs	____	____	____	____	____	____
Asst. PMs	____	____	____	____	____	____
Other (specify)	_____	____	____	____	____	____

7. What is the typical age of your:
     group product managers _____ years
   product managers _____ years
   associate PMs _____ years
   assistant PMs _____ years

8. Of the following personal traits, would you please indicate the degree of
   importance in the evaluation of a candidate for a product management
   position.

(please check)

	Not Important	Desirable	Very Desirable	Essential
Leadership	____	____	____	____
Creativity	____	____	____	____
Aggressiveness	____	____	____	____
Analytical Ability	____	____	____	____
Communications Skill	____	____	____	____
Ability to work with others	____	____	____	____
Other _____	____	____	____	____

FIGURE 8A–3 *(continued)*

9. *(If you recruit directly from campus)* Please indicate the importance of the following traits of a product manager candidate.

(please check)

	Not Important	Desirable	Very Desirable	Essential
Business Experience	_____	_____	_____	_____
High Grade Point Avg.	_____	_____	_____	_____
Extra Curricular Activities	_____	_____	_____	_____
MBA	_____	_____	_____	_____
Master's, technical	_____	_____	_____	_____
Bachelor's, technical	_____	_____	_____	_____
Bachelor's, business	_____	_____	_____	_____
Other (specify) _____	_____	_____	_____	_____

10. If you recruit into your PM group from other jobs (either from your company or other companies), please indicate the importance of the following experiences (please check).

(please check)

Experience:	Not Important	Desirable	Very Desirable	Essential
Sales	_____	_____	_____	_____
Other Product Manager Programs	_____	_____	_____	_____
Other Marketing Positions	_____	_____	_____	_____
Production	_____	_____	_____	_____
Ad Agencies	_____	_____	_____	_____
Undergraduate Degree	_____	_____	_____	_____
Graduate Degree	_____	_____	_____	_____
Other (specify) _____	_____	_____	_____	_____

11. Please indicate the percentage of time a typical product manager spends in the following activities:

Advertising	_____%
Pricing	_____
Distribution	_____
Packaging	_____
Product Development	_____
Marketing Research	_____
Production Liaison	_____
Finance and budgeting	_____
Other (specify) _____	_____
Other (specify) _____	_____
Total _____	100%

FIGURE 8A–3   (concluded)

12. Please indicate which of the following criteria are used in evaluating product managers in your company/division.

   a. _____ market share
       _____ return on investment
       _____ sales volume
       _____ dollar profits
       _____ other (please specify) _____
   b. which one is most important? _____

13. Does your company/division have a structured training program for product managers? yes _____ no _____ (If yes, please describe.)

   _____

   _____

   _____

   _____

14. Is your company/division currently planning any revision in its product manager system? yes _____ no _____ (If yes, please describe.)

   _____

   _____

   _____

   _____

15. Judging from your company's experience, what do you feel is the major problem facing the product management system? _____

   _____

   _____

   _____

   _____

16. It would be most valuable to our studies, if you could supply a sample job description of your product manager positions.
   Are such available?
       _____ yes, examples enclosed
       _____ yes, examples set under separate cover
       _____ not available

   Thank you for your assistance

17. If you would like a summary of the results of this survey please check here.

   _____

study. These experiences led to a revised draft 5. This testing process was repeated twice more with other executives, finally ending with draft 7 shown here as Figure 8A–3. The limitations of time and money led the team to depend upon local product managers for testing rather than a full-scale dress rehearsal by mail. This decision limited the value of the pretesting but was accepted as a limitation of a student project.

The survey was sent to the top 1,000 manufacturing companies in the form described. Only one mailing was made because of time and money limitations. Usable returns numbered 492 at the cutoff point. Approximately 50 companies sent job descriptions of their product management positions.

9. Scaling

A major business research measurement problem is that the available tools are often crude, while the concepts to be measured are complex and abstract. One wants a valid measurement, but one often gets a difference between the *true score* and the *test score*. If the object is a concrete concept, and the measurement tools well-standardized, the variation between the test and true scores will be small. For example, one should expect high accuracy in measuring a length of pipe with a yardstick. On the other hand, if the concept is abstract (attitudes toward various institutions) and the measurement tools not standardized (questions about attitudes), then you are less confident that the test results reflect true scores.

In this chapter, procedures that can help to measure abstract concepts more accurately are considered. It concentrates on the problems of measuring attitudes and opinions, but the same problems are found when measuring physical concepts, psychological concepts, such as intelligence, or institutional concepts, such as organizational effectiveness.

THE NATURE OF SCALING

Scaling defined

Scaling is defined as a "procedure for the assignment of numbers (or other symbols) to a property of objects in order to impart some of the characteristics of numbers to the properties in question."[1] Thus, one assigns a number scale to the various levels of heat and cold and call it a thermometer.

What is scaled?   A more correct definition would be that one assigns numbers to *indicants* of the properties of objects. You want to measure the temperature of the air, you know that a property of temperature is that its

---

[1]Bernard S. Phillips, *Social Research Strategy and Tactics*, 2d ed. (New York: Macmillan, 1971, p. 205.

variation leads to an expansion or contraction of materials such as mercury. You devise a glass tube arrangement with mercury. It provides you with an indicant of the temperature by the rise and fall of the mercury column in the tube as temperatures change.

In another context, you might devise a scale by which to measure the durability (property) of paint. You secure a machine with an attached scrub brush that applies a predetermined amount of pressure as it scrubs. You then count the number of brush strokes that it takes to wear through a 10-mil thickness of paint. The scrub count is the indicant of the paint's durability. Or, you may judge a person's supervisory capacity (property) by asking a peer group to rate that person on various questions (indicants) that you devise.

Scales may be easy to construct, but it is difficult to assure that they measure reliably. It is even more of a challenge to determine scale validity.

Scale classification

Scales may be classified in many ways, but the discussion here is restricted to those approaches that are of greatest value for business research purposes.[2] Even with such a limited objective, six different approaches can be identified.

Study objective. A scale may be designed to (1) measure the characteristics of the respondents who complete it; or (2) use these respondents as judges of the objects or stimuli presented to them. For example, you might present people with a series of scale items about government regulatory programs and ask them to express their approval or disapproval of each program. If you are interested in measuring the respondent's attitudes, you will combine each person's answers to form an indicator of that person's conservatism, political position, and so forth. In this case, the emphasis is on measuring differences among the people, and their responses to specific stimuli (scale items) are of only incidental concern. In the second case, you use the same data but are interested in how people view different government programs. Now there is little concern for how respondents vary among themselves in their answers. The concern is the variation in public attitudes among different programs.

Response scales. Scales may also be classified as *categorical* and *comparative*. These approaches are also known as *rating* and *ranking*, respectively. Categorical (rating) scales are used when respondents score some object without direct reference to other objects. For example, they may be asked to rate the beauty of styling of new autos on a five-point scale. In the comparative (ranking) scaling, the respondents are asked to choose which one of various pairs of cars has more beautiful styling.

---

[2]For a discussion of various scale classifactions, see W. S. Torgerson, *Theory and Methods of Scaling* (New York: John Wiley & Sons, 1958), chap. 3.

Degree of preference. Scaling approaches may also involve *preference* measurement or *nonpreference* evaluation. In the first case, respondents are asked to choose the object each favors or solution each would prefer. In the second case, they are asked to judge which object has the most of some characteristic or which solution takes the most resources, without reflecting any personal preference toward object or solutions.

Scale properties. Scaling approaches may also be viewed in terms of the scale properties possessed by each. The discussion in Chapter 4 pointed out that scales may be classified as nominal, ordinal, interval, or ratio. Their characteristics need not be treated further, except to note again that the assumptions underlying each scale property type determine how the scale may be used statistically.

Number of dimensions. Scales are either *unidimensional* or *multidimensional*. With a unidimensional scale, one seeks to measure only one attribute of the respondent or object. Thus, one measures employees as to promotability, assuming that it is a single dimension. One may use several items by which to measure this dimension, but one can combine them into a single measure and place employees along a linear continuum called "promotability." Multidimensional scaling recognizes that an object might be better described by the concept of an attribute space of n dimensions rather than a unidimensional continuum. For example, you might recognize that employee promotability might be better expressed by two distinct dimensions—managerial performance and technical performance. Most of this chapter deals with unidimensional scaling.

Scale construction. Scales may also be classified by the method used to build them. According to one view, there are five major scale design techniques.[3] One is the *arbitrary* approach in which the scale is developed on an ad hoc basis. One assumes that such scales measure the concepts for which they have been designed, but we have little evidence to support this assumption. Even so, this is probably the most widely used technique.

A second approach is the *consensus* scale. A panel of judges evaluates the items chosen for inclusion in the instrument in terms of whether they are (1) relevant to the topic area and (2) unambiguous in implication. A third technique is the *item analysis* approach. Individual items are developed into a test which is given to a group of respondents. After administering the test, total scores are calculated. Individual items are then analyzed to determine those that discriminate between persons or objects with high total scores and those with low scores.

Cumulative scales are chosen on the basis of their conforming to some ranking of items with ascending and descending discriminating power. For example, in such a scale the endorsement of an item representing an ex-

---

[3]E. A. Suchman and R. G. Francis, "Scaling Techniques in Social Research," in J. T. Doby, ed., *An Introduction to Social Research* (Harrisburg, Pa.: The Stackpole Company, 1954), pp. 126–29.

treme position should result also in the endorsement of all items indicating a less extreme position. Finally, *factor* scales may be constructed on the basis of intercorrelations of items that indicate that a common factor accounts for the relationships between items. This relationship is typically measured through factor analysis or another clustering method.

The following sections of this chapter are organized along the lines of two of these classifications: response methods and scale construction techniques. Other classification bases are considered when appropriate.

RESPONSE METHODS

In Chapter 8, it was pointed out that the asking of questions is a widely used method for measuring concepts. For example, a manager may be asked to state his or her views concerning a certain employee. The respondent may give replies such as "good machinist," "a troublemaker," "union activist," "reliable," or a "fast worker with a poor record of attendance." These answers appear to represent different frames of reference by which the worker is perceived. Such a variety in responses is often of limited research value.

Two approaches are used to improve the usefulness of such replies. First, various properties may be separated out and the respondent asked to judge each specific facet. In this manner, one substitutes several questions for a single question. The second approach is to establish structured patterns by which to guide responses. In this approach, we substitute structuring devices for the free response reply pattern. When one wishes to quantify dimensions that are essentially qualitative, one does this structuring by using rating and/or ranking scales.

Rating scales

One can use rating scales to judge properties of objects without reference to other similar objects. These ratings may be in such forms as "like-dislike," "approve-indifferent-disapprove," or other classifications using even more categories. Whether to use a two-point scale, three-point scale, or scales with more points is a subject which is debated; there is little conclusive support for any particular scale length. One argument is that more points on a scale provide an opportunity for greater sensitivity of measurement. However, the most widely used scales range from three to seven points, and it does not seem to make much difference which number is used.[4]

The *graphic rating scale* is a common and simple form to use. The judge checks his or her responses or evaluation along a continuum. An example of

---

[4]A study of research literature in 1940 found that more than three fourths of the attitude scales used were of the five-point type. A cursory examination of more recent literature suggests that the five-point scale is still quite common but there also seems to be a growing use of longer scales. For the 1940 study, see Daniel D. Day, "Methods in Attitude Research," *American Sociological Review* 5 (1940), pp. 395–410.

one element of such a scale is the statement found in an employee evaluation form:

"How well does the employee get along with co-workers?"
(Please check)

| Always gets along well | Sometimes has trouble | Often has trouble | Always at odds with someone |

This scale illustrates the graphic principle but is not a good scale for several reasons. One defect is that only three of the four positions are likely to be used. It will be the rare situation when the choice "always at odds with someone" will be used. In effect, then, it is a three-point scale. Another deficiency concerns the vagueness of "sometimes" and "often." The meaning of these terms depends upon each judge's frame of reference so completely that the statement might be challenged in terms of its equivalency, and perhaps its stability. At the other extreme is "always" which implies no exceptions. A final problem is that the graphics are set up at such a way that respondents may check at almost any position along the line. This increases the difficulty of analysis.

Several other rating scale variants are presented next; illustrated also are various lengths of rating scales.

Variation 1. Boxes replace the line and make it more certain that respondents will choose only one of four points.

☐ | ☐ | ☐ | ☐
Always gets along well | Sometimes has trouble | Often has trouble | Always at odds with someone

Variation 2. Two polar positions shown with a number scale used to show degree of opinion.

Gets along well ☐ ☐ ☐ ☐ ☐ Has trouble
 1 2 3 4 5

Other Variations. Listed below are some of the common phrasing examples used to indicate degrees of judgment in surveys.[5]

Three-point scales

Greater _____	Equal _____	Less _____
Yes _____	Depends _____	No _____
Above average _____	Average _____	Below average _____

---

[5]Mildred Parten, *Surveys, Polls, and Samples: Practical Procedures* (New York: Harper & Row, 1950), pp. 190–92.

Four-point scales

Many _____   Some _____   Few _____   None _____

Excellent _____   Good _____   Fair _____   Poor _____

Highest _____   Next highest _____   Next lowest _____   Lowest _____

Five-point scales

Strongly approve _____   Approve _____   Un-decided _____   Dis-approve _____   Strongly dis-approve _____

Much greater _____   Somewhat greater _____   Equal _____   Somewhat less _____   Not at all _____

Like very much _____   Like somewhat _____   Neutral _____   Dislike somewhat _____   Dislike very much _____

Longer scales

(Semantic differential)   Good   : : : : : :   Bad

Modern   : : : : : :   Old-fashioned

(Stapel)   ☐ ☐ ☐ ☐ ☐ ■ ■ ■ ■ ■

\+   Taste   −

A second form, the *itemized scale*, presents a series of statements from which respondents select one as best reflecting their evaluation. These judgments are ordered progressively in terms of more or less of some property. It is typical to use five to seven categories, with each being defined or illustrated in words. An example is:

> How well does the employee get along with coworkers?
> _____Almost always involved in some friction or argument with a coworker.
> _____Often at odds with one or more coworkers. The frequency of involvement is clearly above that of the average worker.
> _____Sometimes gets involved in friction. The frequency of involvement is about equal to that of the average worker.
> _____Infrequently becomes involved in friction with others, definitely less often than most workers.
> _____Almost never gets involved in friction situations with other workers.

This form is more difficult to develop, and the statements may not say exactly what the respondent would like to express. On the other hand, it provides more information and meaning to the rater; itemized scales probably increase reliability because the more detailed statements help respondents to develop and hold the same frame of reference as they fill out the form.

Even with rating scales, there must be some criterion that the subject uses to judge that one object is attractive and a second less attractive. This criterion is typically not explicit, allowing for each person's subjective judgment. In the *comparative rating scale*, this criterion is made explicit. The subject is asked to compare against some experience standard. Job evaluation rating forms use the concept of a standard job as the basis for rating others. Job interview analysis forms might specify that the rater compare the interviewee with the typical recruit that the company has hired in the past.

Problems in using rating scales. The value of rating scales for measurement purposes depends upon the assumption that a person can and will make good judgments. Before one accepts respondent's ratings, we should consider the tendencies to make errors. Three of the most common are the errors of *leniency, central tendency,* and *halo effect.*[6]

The error of leniency occurs when certain persons are either "easy raters" or "hard raters," the latter being an error of negative leniency. It has been found that raters tend to rate those people higher whom they know well and with whom they are ego-involved. There is also the contrary of this situation—the case where one rates those acquaintances lower because one is aware of the leniency danger and attempts to counteract it. One way to deal with the tendency to positive leniency, the most common form, is to design the rating scale to anticipate it. An example might be an asymmetrical graphic scale which has only one unfavorable descriptive term and four favorable terms (poor–fair–good–very good–excellent). In this case, the scale designer expects that the mean ratings will be near "good" and that there will be a more or less symmetrical distribution about that point.

Raters are reluctant to give extreme judgments, and this fact accounts for the error of central tendency. This is most often seen where the rater does not know the person being rated. Efforts to counteract this error are to (1) adjust the strength of descriptive adjectives; (2) space the intermediate descriptive phrases further apart in graphic scales; (3) provide smaller differences in meaning between steps near the ends of the scale than between the steps near the center; and (4) use more points in the scale.

A major problem concerns the halo effect—the systematic bias that the rater introduces by carrying over a generalized impression of the subject from one rating to another. One tends to expect the student who does well on question 1 of an examination also to do well on question 2. In other cases, you conclude that a report is good because one likes its form, or one believes someone is intelligent because one agrees on something. Halo is one of the most pervasive errors; it is especially difficult to avoid when the property being studied is not clearly defined, not easily observed, not frequently discussed, involves reactions with others, or is a trait of high moral impor-

---

[6]J. P. Guilford, *Psychometric Methods* (New York: McGraw-Hill, 1954), pp. 278–79.

tance.[7] One way to counteract the halo effect is to rate one trait at a time for all subjects or to have one trait per page rather than one subject per page.

Advantages of rating scales.   Rating scales are now widely used in business research and generally deserve their popularity. While careless use is common, the results obtained with careful use compares favorably with alternative methods. Rating scales typically require less time, are interesting to use, and have a wider range of application than most other methods. In addition, they may be used with a large number of properties or variables.

Ranking scales

In ranking methods, the subject directly compares two or more objects and makes choices among them. Widely encountered is the situation where the respondent is asked to select one as the "best" or the "preferred." When dealing with only two choices, this approach is satisfactory, but it may often result in the "vote-splitting" phenomenon, when more than two choices are found. This may occur in the situation when the respondent is asked to select the most preferred among three or more models of a product. Assume that 40 percent choose model A, 30 percent choose model B, and 30 percent choose model C. The question is, "Which is the preferred model?" The analyst would be taking a risk to suggest that A is most preferred. Perhaps such an interpretation is correct, but 60 percent of the respondents chose some model other than A. It may be that all B and C voters would place A last, preferring either B or C to it. This ambiguity can be avoided by using paired comparisons or rank-ordering techniques.

Method of paired comparisons.   With this technique, the respondent can express attitudes in an unambiguous manner by making a choice between two objects. Typical of such a situation would be a product-testing study where a new flavor of soft drink is tested against an established brand. Another example might be to compare two bargaining proposals available to union negotiators. In the general situation, there are often many more than two stimuli to judge, resulting in a potentially tedious task for respondents. The number of judgments required in a paired comparison is:

$$N = \frac{n(n-1)}{2}$$

where

N = Number of judgments and
n = Number of stimuli or objects to be judged.

For example, if there are 15 suggestions for bargaining proposals available to a union, there are 105 paired comparisons that can be made with them.

---

[7] P. M. Synonds, "Notes on Rating," *Journal of Applied Psychology* 9 (1925), pp. 188–95.

With paired comparing, there is a risk that the respondents will tire to the point that they give ill-considered answers or even refuse to continue. Opinions differ as to what the upper limit is, but five or six stimuli are not unreasonable when the respondent has other questions to answer. If the interview consists only of comparisons, as many as 15 stimuli may be compared.

One can lighten this burden by reducing the number of comparisons per respondent without reducing the number of objects being studied. One approach is to present each respondent with only a sample of the stimuli. If one uses this method one must assure that each pair of objects is compared an equal number of times. A second approach is to choose a few objects which are believed to cover the range of attractiveness at about equal intervals. All other stimuli are then compared to these few standard objects. For example, there may be 36 employees to be judged. Four may be selected as standards and the others divided into four groups of eight each. Within each group, the eight are compared to each other. Then the 32 are individually compared to each of the 4 standard persons. This reduces the number of comparisons from 630 to 240.

Paired-comparison data may be treated in several ways. If there is substantial consistency we will find that, if A is preferred to B, and B to C, then A will consistently be preferred to C. This condition of transitivity need not always be true but should occur most of the time. When this is so, one may take the total number of preferences among the comparisons as the score for that stimulus. For example, assume that there are five major demand proposals which a union bargaining committee is considering. The committee would like to know how the union membership ranks these proposals. One way to determine this would be to ask a sample of the members to pair-compare the personal suggestions. A sample of 200 members might express the views shown by the hypothetical data found in Table 9–1.

By a crude comparison of the total number of preferences stated for each option, it is apparent that B is the most popular. The rank order for the suggestions is shown.

While a paired comparison provides ordinal data, Thurstone has developed a method by which such data may be converted into an interval scale. Known as the Law of Comparative Judgment, it involves the conversion of frequencies of preferences (such as in Table 9–1) into a table of proportions which are then transformed into a Z matrix by referring to the table of areas under the normal curve.[8] Guilford has presented a procedure which is computationally much easier than Thurstone's and secures essentially the same results. It is called the *composite-standard* method and is illustrated here.[9]

---

[8] See L. L. Thurstone, "A Law of Comparative Judgment," *Psychological Review* 34 (1927), pp. 273–86.

[9] From *Psychometric Methods* by J. P. Guilford. Copyright 1954, McGraw-Hill Book Company. Used with permission of McGraw-Hill Book Company.

TABLE 9–1   Response patterns of 200 union members' paired comparisons of five suggestions for union bargaining proposal priorities

	Suggestion				
	A	B	C	D	E
A	—	164*	138	50	70
B	36	—	54	14	30
C	62	146	—	32	50
D	150	186	168	—	118
E	130	170	150	82	—
Total	378	666	510	178	268
Rank order	3	1	2	5	4
M_p	0.478	0.766	0.610	0.278	0.368
Z_j	−0.06	0.73	0.28	−0.59	−0.34
R_i	0.53	1.32	0.87	0.00	0.25

*Read 164 members preferred suggestion B (column) to suggestion A (row).

With the composite-standard method we can develop an interval scale from paired comparisons by the following steps. First, using the data in Table 9–1, we calculate the column means using the equation:

$$M_p = \frac{C + 0.5N}{nN} = \frac{378 + 0.5(200)}{5(200)} = 0.478$$

where

M_p = The mean proportion of the columns, and

C = The total number of choices for a given suggestion.

Guilford points out, "The correction 0.5N in the numerator is for the assumed number of choices the stimulus would have received if it had been compared with itself. . . . It is assumed that the standard is the composite of all the stimuli in the series and that M_p is the proportion of times any given stimulus is chosen in preference to that standard."[10] These calculated means are shown in Table 9–1.

The Z values for M_p are secured from the normal curve tables. When the proportion (M_p) is less than 0.5, the Z value is negative, while all proportions over 0.5 are positive.[11] These values are also shown in Table 9–1 as Z_j. Since

---

[10]Guilford, *Psychometric Methods*, p. 170.

[11]The Z values in this transformation are associated with a given proportion of the *total area* under the normal curve, while Appendix Table B–1 gives the area for one side (or one

this scale is an interval scale the zero is an arbitrary value. We can eliminate negative scale values by giving the value of zero to the lowest scale value and then adding the absolute value of this lowest scale value to all other scale items. This scale (R_j) is shown in Figure 9–1.

FIGURE 9–1 Interval scale derived from paired-comparison data using the composite-standard method

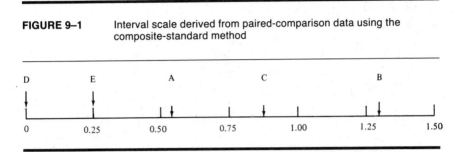

Method of rank order. Another comparative scaling approach is to ask respondents to rank their choices. This method is faster than paired comparisons and is usually easier and more motivating to the respondent. For example, with 7 items, it takes 21 pair comparisons to complete the task while the simple ranking of 7 is easier. With ranking, there is no transitivity problem where A is preferred to B, B to C, but C preferred to A.

On the negative side, there is some question as to how many stimuli may be handled by this method. Less than five objects can usually be ranked easily, but respondents may grow careless in ranking, say, 10 or more items. In addition, the rank ordering is still an ordinal scale with all of its limitations.

There are several simple ways to combine rankings into an overall index. Means cannot properly be calculated, but it is possible to compute medians. Some suggest that the sum of rank values will probably give the best simple indication of composite ranking of stimuli.[12] If there are a substantial number of respondents, it is possible also to translate ordinal rank data into an interval scale. Two general methods are the *normalized-rank* and the *comparative-judgment*.[13] The latter is similar to scaling from paired comparisons. Guilford also suggests a *composite-standard* approach similar to that already discussed.[14]

---

half) of the normal curve. To use Appendix Table B–1 in this calculation we must subtract all M_p values which exceed 0.5 from 1.0 to secure the value with which to enter Table B–1. For example, $1.0 - 0.766 = 0.234$. Entering the body of Table B–1 with this number we find the nearest value is 0.2327, which gives a Z_j of approximately 0.73; recall that all M_p values of less than 0.5 will give Z_j values which are negative.

[12]Guilford, *Psychometric Methods*, pp. 179–80.

[13]Ibid, p. 180.

[14]Ibid, p. 186.

A complete ranking is sometimes not needed or involves too many stimuli. We may secure more cooperation by asking only that the first k ranks be selected. For example, respondents may be asked to judge 25 different automobile designs by ranking only their first five choices. To secure a simple ranking of all designs, we merely total rank values received by each model. We can also develop an interval scale of these data by using either a paired comparison or composite-standard solution.[15]

The method of successive intervals. Neither the paired-comparison nor the rank-order method is particularly attractive when there are a large number of items. Under these circumstances, the method of successive intervals is sometimes used. In this method, the subject is asked to sort the items (usually one per card) into piles or groups representing a succession of values. From these sortings, an interval scale can be developed.[16]

Both rating and ranking scales are used for stimulus-centered scaling, while respondent-centered studies typically use the rating response form. Rating scales are also the response form of choice with all types of scale construction technique.

SCALE CONSTRUCTION TECHNIQUES

Arbitrary scales

One can design arbitrary scales by collecting a number of items that we believe are unambiguous and appropriate to a given topic. We choose some of these items for inclusion in our instrument. To illustrate, consider the problem of conducting a company image study among the general public. We choose a sample of items that we believe are the components of company image. Some of the items are:

How do you regard *(name)* Company's reputation
1. As a place to work?   Bad ____ ____ ____ ____ ____ Good
2. As a sponsor of civic projects? Bad ____ ____ ____ ____ ____ Good
3. For ecological concern?   Bad ____ ____ ____ ____ ____ Good
4. As an employer of minorities? Bad ____ ____ ____ ____ ____ Good

One might score each of these from 0 to 4 depending upon the degree of favorableness reported. The results may be studied in several ways. Totals may be made by individual items, by company, to determine how various companies rate as places to work, for ecological concern, and so on. Or totals

---

[15]For details on these methods see Guilford, *Psychometric Methods*, pp. 188–90.

[16]See Milton A. Saffir, "A Comparative Study of Scales Constructed by Three Psychophysical Methods," *Psychometrica* 11, no. 3 (September 1937), pp. 179–98.

for each company, by individual, may be calculated to determine how each company compares to the others in an overall sense. Based on a total for these four items, each company would be scored from 0 to 16 by each respondent. While not a company-image orientation, these data may also be analyzed from a respondent-centered point of view. Thus, you might use the attitude scores of each individual as a basis for studying differences among the individuals.

Pros and cons. Arbitrary scales are easy to develop and can be designed to be highly specific to the case and content of interest. They are developed quickly and inexpensively. They can provide much useful information, and can be adequate if developed by one who is skilled in scale design. These are all practical benefits and account for the widespread use of arbitrary scales.

There are also some weaknesses. A major one is that this approach is based solely upon the designer's subjective logic. If this logic is good, then the scale can be good. The only assurance we have that the items chosen are a representative sample of the universe of content (the totality of what constitutes "company image") is the researcher's insight and ability. We have no objective evidence that all items will be viewed by respondents from the same frame of reference.

While arbitrary scales are often used, there has been a great effort in the behavioral sciences to develop scale construction techniques that overcome some of the deficiencies cited above. One of the earliest of these was consensus scaling.

Consensus scaling

In this approach, the selection of items is made by a panel of judges who evaluates a proposed scale item as to (1) its relevance to the topic area; (2) its potential for ambiguity; and (3) the level of attitude it represents. A widely known form of this approach is the Thurstone Differential Scale.

Differential scales. This approach, known also as the Method of Equal Appearing Intervals, was an effort to develop an interval rating scale for attitude measurement. Whether this goal was achieved is still debated. The standard development approach is to ask a large number of judges (often 50 or more) to evaluate a large number of statements. These statements express different degrees of favorableness toward an object and are presented one per card. The judges are asked to sort each card into 1 of 11 piles representing their evaluation of the degree of favorableness that the statement expresses. The judge's agreement or disagreement with the statement is not involved. Three of the 11 piles are identified to the judges by labels of "favorable" and "unfavorable" at the extremes, and "neutral" at the midpoint. The eight intermediate piles are unlabeled to encourage the judges to view them as being at equal-appearing intervals between the three labeled positions.

The scale position for a given statement is determined by calculating its median score when placement in the least favorable pile is scored as 1, in the most favorable pile as 11, and in the other piles according to their place in the order. A measure of dispersion, usually the interquartile range, is calculated for each statement.[17] If a given statement has a large interquartile range, it is judged to be too ambiguous to be used in the final scale. The selection of statements to be included in the final attitude scale is made by taking a sample of statements whose median scores are spread evenly from one extreme to the other and whose interquartile ranges are small. Duplicate scales may be constructed and are sometimes used to provide greater score reliability.

The scale is administered to respondents by asking them to read the 20 or so statements and to select those items with which they agree. The mean or median value of the chosen scale items is then calculated as the measure of the respondent's attitude. Below is an example of part of a 50-item scale which was designed to determine the attitude of employees of a company toward their employer. The scale values are shown here but would not be on the instrument when it is used.[18]

Scale Value

10.4	I think this company treats its employees better than any other company does.
8.9	A man can get ahead in this company if he tries.
8.5	The company is sincere in wanting to know what its employees think about it.
5.4	I believe accidents will happen no matter what you do about them.
5.1	The workers put as much over on the company as the company puts over on them.
4.1	Soldiering on the job is on the increase.
2.9	My boss gives all the breaks to his lodge and church friends.
2.5	I think the company goes outside to fill good jobs instead of promoting men who are here.
1.5	In the long run this company will "put it over" on you.
1.0	The pay in this company is terrible.

In the actual instrument, the statements are arranged in random order of scale value. If the values are valid, and if the questionnaire deals with only one attitude dimension, the typical respondent will choose one or several contiguous items (in terms of scale values). At times, however, divergences will occur because a statement appears to tap a different attitude dimension. In the example above, it is possible that the statement, "I think accidents will happen no matter what you do about them" may evoke an entirely different frame of reference than will "company treatment of its employees"

---

[17]The interquartile range is a measure of dispersion that includes the middle 50 percent of the items in a distribution.

[18]R. S. Uhrbrock, "Attitudes of 4,430 Employees," *Journal of Social Psychology* 5 (1934), pp. 367–68.

which pervades the other items. A person may honestly select the accident statement (with a 5.4 score) and then choose either lower or higher scored items.

Differential scales have been used more widely in sociological studies than in business research. An important deterrent to their use has been the cost and effort required to construct them. This approach has also been criticized on the grounds that the values assigned to various statements by the judges may reflect their own attitudes. Some studies have indicated the statement evaluations are independent of the judges' personal attitudes, but other studies indicate the opposite. This was found with questions on topics about which the judges held extreme positions. Even here, however, the rank order of the various evaluations was the same among judges with different attitudes. A final criticism of the differential method is that some other scale designs give more information about the respondent's attitude.

Using a panel of judges to evaluate scale items is better than relying on the researcher's opinion, but the method is costly, time consuming, and ultimately involves the same subjective decision process although repeated by 50 or more different individuals. There is a different logic underlying the scale construction techniques yet to be discussed. They rely upon the analysis of actual responses to the items as the basis for determining item acceptability. The first of these is the Item Analysis technique.

Item analysis

In this procedure, a particular item is evaluated on the basis of how well it discriminates between those persons whose total score is high and those whose score is low. The most popular type using this approach is the summated scale.

Summated scale. This consists of statements which express either a favorable or unfavorable attitude toward the object of interest. The respondent is asked to agree or disagree with each statement. Each response is given a numerical score to reflect its degree of attitude favorableness, and the scores are totaled to measure the respondent's attitude.

The most frequently used form is the Likert scale. With this scale the respondent is asked to respond to each statement in terms of five degrees of agreement (three-point and seven-point scales are also used). An example from a job satisfaction scale is:[19]

I consider my job rather unpleasant.

Strongly Agree (1)	Agree (2)	Undecided (3)	Disagree (4)	Strongly Disagree (5)

---

[19]See A. H. Brayfield and H. F. Rothe, "An Index of Job Satisfaction," *Journal of Applied Psychology* 35 (October 1951), pp. 307–11.

The numbers indicate the value to be assigned to each possible answer with 1 indicating the least favorable degree of job satisfaction and 5 the most favorable. These values are normally not printed on the instrument but are shown here to indicate the scoring system. The full Brayfield and Rothe Index includes 18 statements, making it possible for a respondent to score from 18 to 90, with 54 points being equivalent to a neutral position. If respondents score near 18, it is clear that they hold an unfavorable job attitude; likewise, if the score is quite high, one concludes that there is a high degree of job satisfaction. But the interpretation of scores nearer the middle of the scale is less clear if the objective is to describe the respondent in any absolute sense. For example, a score of 60 is slightly over in the "favorable" side, but it may actually represent a relatively poor job attitude score when compared to those of other workers.

Summated scales are most useful when it is possible to compare one person's score with a distribution of scores from some well-defined group. They are also very useful when we expect to conduct an experiment, undertake a program of change or improvement, and the like. One can use the scales to measure attitudes before and after the experiment, or to judge whether our efforts have had the desired effects. Furthermore, if one wishes to correlate scores on the scale to other measures, it can also be done without concern for the absolute value of what is "favorable" and what is "unfavorable."

Likert-type scales are relatively easy to develop as compared to the differential scales.[20] The first step is to collect a large number of statements that meet two criteria: (1) Each statement is believed to be relevant to the attitude being studied, and (2) each is believed to reflect a favorable or unfavorable position on that attitude. A group of persons, similar to those who are going to be studied, are asked to read each statement and to state the level of their agreement with it, using a five-point scale. For example, a scale value of 1 might indicate a strongly unfavorable attitude and 5 a strongly favorable attitude.

Each person's response values are then added to secure a total score per person. The next step is to array these total scores and select some part of the highest and lowest *total scores*, say, the top 25 percent and the bottom 25 percent. These two extreme groups are interpreted to represent the most favorable and least favorable attitudes toward the topic being studied. They are used as criteria by which to evaluate individual statements. That is, through a comparative analysis of response patterns to each statement by members of these two groups, we determine which statements consistently correlate with low favorability and which with high favorability attitudes.

---

[20]One study reported that the construction of a Likert scale took only half the time required to construct a Thurstone scale. See A. L. Thurstone and K. K. Kenney, "A Comparison of the Thurstone and Likert Techniques of Attitude Scale Construction," *Journal of Applied Psychology* 30 (1946), pp. 72–83.

One approach to item analysis involves calculating the mean scores for each scale item among the low scorers and high scorers. The item means between the high-score group and the low-score groups are then tested for significance by calculating t values. Finally, the 20 to 25 items which have the greatest t values (significant differences between means) are selected for inclusion in the final scale.[21]

This procedure can be illustrated in the following manner. In evaluating response patterns of the high and low groups to the statement, "I consider my job rather unpleasant," we might secure the results shown in Table 9–2.

TABLE 9–2   Evaluating a scale statement by item analysis

Response categories	Low total score group				High total score group			
	X	f	fX	fX²	X	f	fX	fX²
Strongly agree	5	3	15	75	5	22	110	550
Agree	4	4	16	64	4	30	120	480
Undecided	3	29	87	261	3	15	45	135
Disagree	2	22	44	88	2	4	8	16
Strongly disagree	1	15	15	15	1	2	2	2
Total		73	177	503		73	285	1,183
		n_L	ΣX_L	ΣX_L^2		n_H	ΣX_H	ΣX_H^2

$$\bar{X}_L = \frac{177}{73} = 2.42 \qquad\qquad \bar{X}_H = \frac{285}{73} = 3.90$$

$$\Sigma(x_L - \bar{X}_L)^2 = 503 - \frac{(177)^2}{73} \qquad \Sigma(X_H - \bar{X}_H)^2 = 1,183 - \frac{(285)^2}{73}$$

$$= 73.84 \qquad\qquad\qquad = 70.33$$

$$t = \frac{\bar{X}_H - \bar{X}_L}{\sqrt{\dfrac{\Sigma(X_H - \bar{X}_H)^2 + \Sigma(X_L - \bar{X}_L)^2}{n(n - 1)}}}$$

$$= \frac{3.90 - 2.42}{\sqrt{\dfrac{70.33 + 73.84}{73(73 - 1)}}}$$

$$= 8.92$$

After finding the t values for each statement, we rank order them and select those statements with the highest t values. As a crude indicator of a statement's discrimination power, Edwards suggests using only those statements whose t value is 1.75 or greater, provided there are 25 or more subjects in each group.[22] As an added safeguard against response-set bias,

---

[21]Allen L. Edwards, *Techniques of Attitude Scale Construction* (New York: Appleton-Century-Crofts, 1957), pp. 152–54.

[22]Ibid, p. 153.

we should select approximately one half of the statements to be favorable and the other half unfavorable.

The Likert scale has many advantages that account for its popularity. It is easy and quick to construct. Each item that is included has met an empirical test for discriminating ability. Since respondents answer each item, it is probably more reliable than the Thurstone scale, and it provides a greater volume of data than does the Thurstone scale. It is easy to use this scale both in respondent-centered and stimulus-centered studies. That is, one can study how responses differ between people, and how responses differ between various stimuli.

In these discussions, it has been implied that the Thurstone and Likert scales can be developed only by using the consensus and item analysis methods, respectively. This is not the case. One can develop scales of these types in an arbitrary manner; this is common practice, especially with the Likert scale. Such scales have the same validity problems as all arbitrary scales. The classic procedure for developing the Likert and Thurstone scales is as described in this chapter.

The Likert scale is ordinal only, while the Thurstone scale designers claim it to be an interval scale. With the Likert scale, we can report respondents are more or less favorable to a topic, but we cannot tell how much more or less favorable they are. Another potential problem is that a given total score can be secured by a wide variety of answer patterns, bringing the meaning of the total score into question. This particular problem can be addressed by using a cumulative scale.

Cumulative scales

Total scores on cumulative scales have the same meaning. Given a person's total score, it is possible to estimate which items were answered positively and which negatively. The major scale of this type is the Guttman *scalogram*. Scalogram analysis is a procedure for determining whether a set of items forms a unidimensional scale as defined by Guttman.[23] A scale is said to be unidimensional if the responses fall into a pattern in which endorsement of the item reflecting the extreme position results also in endorsing all items which are less extreme.

Assume that we are surveying opinions regarding a new style of fortesary (a hypothetical product). We have developed a preference scale of 4 items as follows:

1. Style X is a very attractive fortesary.
2. I will insist on a style X fortesary next time because it is so beautiful.
3. The appearance of style X fortesary is acceptable to me.
4. I prefer style X fortesaries to other styles.

---

[23]Louis Guttman, "A Basis for Scaling Qualitative Data," *American Sociological Review* 9 (1944), pp. 139–50.

Respondents are asked to express themselves on each item by indicating whether they agree or disagree. If these items form a unidimensional scale the response patterns will approach the ideal configuration shown in Table 9–3:

TABLE 9–3   Ideal scalogram response pattern

Item				Respondent score
2	4	1	3	
X	X	X	X	4
—	X	X	X	3
—	—	X	X	2
—	—	—	X	1
—	—	—	—	0

X = Agree.
— = Disagree.

A score of 4 indicates that all statements are agreed to, and represents the most favorable attitude. Persons with a score of 3 should disagree with item 2, but agree with all others, and so on. According to scalogram theory, this pattern confirms that the universe of content (attitude toward the appearance of this fortesary) is scalable.

In developing a scalogram, one first defines the universe of content. Assume that you are interested in determining the attitudes of people toward television advertising. We might define the universe of content as "viewer attitudes toward TV advertising." The second step is to develop items which can be used in a pretest to determine whether this topic is scalable. Guttman suggests that a pretest should include 12 or more items, while the final scale may have only 4 to 6 items. Pretest respondent numbers may be small, say 20 or 30, but final scale use should involve 100 or more respondents.[24]

Take the pretest results and order the respondents from top to bottom—from those with the most favorable total score to the least favorable. Then order the statements from left to right from the most favorable to the least favorable. The next step is to discard those statements that fail to discrimi-

_____

[24]For details on construction procedure, see Louis Guttman, "The Cornell Technique for Scale and Intensity Analysis," *Educational and Psychological Measurement* 7 (1947), pp. 247–80.

nate well between favorable and unfavorable respondents. Finally we calculate a Coefficient of Reproducibility (CR).

$$\text{Reproducibility} = 1 - \frac{e}{n(N)}$$

where e is the number of errors, n is the number of items, and N is the number of cases. It is suggested that reproducibility should be 0.90 or better for a scale to be considered unidimensional.

The scalogram was a pioneering attempt to develop a homogeneous scale. While the claim for unidimensionality has been challenged, at worst, if a scale fails to meet the CR test, it would seem clearly to be too heterogeneous. The fact that the scale calls for a small number of items is another of its attractive features.

The major criticism of the method grows out of research that has shown that the CR is too permissive a criterion to assure unidimensionality. In one study, it was determined that a six-item Guttman scale could contain as many as three spuriously related items and still be statistically significant.[25] While other and better measures than the CR have been developed, critics still recommend against scalogram use. Typical is Robinson's view that ".... the Guttman model is simply inappropriate for describing the structure of all but a most limited subset of social research data."[26] He suggests that the most appropriate use for the scalogram is among behaviors that are highly structured—such as social distance, organizational hierarchies, and evolutionary stages.

Factor scales

The methods discussed up to this point are all efforts to define certain concepts or constructs and to devise a small set of variables or items by which to measure these concepts. The term *factor scales* is used here to identify a variety of techniques that have been developed to deal with two problems which have so far been glossed over. They are (1) how to deal more adequately with the universe of content which is multidimensional and (2) how to uncover underlying (latent) dimensions which have not been identified.

These techniques are designed to intercorrelate items in order to determine their degree of interdependence and in this way give meaning to the set of variables. There are many such approaches which the serious student will want to explore, such as latent structure analysis (of which the scalogram is a special case), factor analysis, cluster analysis, and metric and nonmetric

---

[25]Carmi Schooler, "A Note of Extreme Caution on the Use of Guttman Scales," *American Journal of Sociology* 29 (June 1966).

[26]John P. Robinson, "Toward a More Appropriate Use of Guttman Scaling," *Public Opinion Quarterly* 37 (Summer 1973), pp. 260–67.

multidimensional scaling. We restrict the discussion here to a major scaling technique, the semantic differential, which is based on factor analysis.[27]

Semantic differential (SD). This scaling method, developed by Osgood and his associates, is an attempt to measure the psychological meanings of an object to an individual.[28] It is based on the proposition that an object can have several dimensions of connotative meanings which can be located in multidimensional property space, in this case, called *semantic space*. While there is a substantial body of theory concerning this technique, the emphasis here is on its development and use.

The method consists of a set of bipolar rating scales, usually seven-point, by which one or more subjects rate one or more concepts on each scale item. The scale items appear as follows:

Good   _____:_____:_____:_____:_____:_____:_____ Bad

Passive _____:_____:_____:_____:_____:_____:_____ Active

The technique has been widely used in brand image and other marketing studies of institutional images, political issues and personalities, organizational morale, and others.

Osgood and his associates have produced a long list of adjective pairs useful for attitude research purposes. In a major study, they searched Roget's *Thesaurus* for such adjectives, locating 289 pairs. These were screened down to 76 pairs which were then formed into rating scales. They then chose 20 concepts with the psychological meaning they wished to probe. These concepts, which illustrate the wide applicability of the technique, were:

Person concepts—Adlai Stevenson, me, foreigner, my mother.

Abstract concepts—modern art, sin, time, leadership.

Event concepts—debate, birth, dawn, symphony.

Institutions—hospital, America, United Nations, family life.

Physical concepts—knife, boulder, snow, engine.[29]

By factor analyzing the data, they concluded that semantic space is multidimensional rather than unidimensional. Repeatedly they found that three factors contributed most to meaningful judgments by respondents. While the precise nature and importance of the factors varied, depending on the concepts being studied, the major factors that emerged were (1) *evaluation*, (2) *potency* or *power*, and (3) *activity*. The evaluation dimension usually accounted for one half to three fourths of the extractable variance. Potency and activity are about equal and accounted for a little over one fourth of the

---

[27]For more on the process of factor analysis, see Chapter 13.

[28]Charles E. Osgood, G. J. Suci, and P. H. Tannenbaum, *The Measurement of Meaning* (Urbana, Ill.: The University of Illinois Press, 1957).

[29]Ibid., p. 49.

extractable variance. In some cases the potency and activity dimensions combined into one labeled "dynamism." In other studies they also identified lesser dimensions which have been labeled "stability," "tautness," "novelty," and "receptivity."

Some major results of this *Thesaurus* study are shown in Table 9–4. Evidence was found for eight factors, but the three already mentioned were again the major ones. In addition, there was evidence that the evaluation factor might also be broken into subgroups based upon subsidiary loadings (correlations) on other factors:

Subfactor:

Meek goodness — Positive loading on evaluation plus a negative loading on the potency factor.

Dynamic goodness — Positive loading on evaluation plus a positive loading on activity factor.

Dependable goodness — Positive loading on evaluation plus a positive loading on a subsidiary factor identified as "stability."

TABLE 9–4   Results of *Thesaurus* study, unrotated square root factor analysis

Evaluation	Potency	Activity
good–bad	hard–soft	active–passive
positive–negative	strong–weak	fast–slow
optimistic–pessimistic	heavy–light	hot–cold
complete–incomplete	masculine–feminine	excitable–calm
timely–untimely	severe–lenient	
	tenacious–yielding	

Evaluation subcategories			
Meek goodness	Dynamic goodness	Dependable goodness	Hedonistic goodness
clean–dirty	successful–unsuccessful	true–false	pleasurable–painful
kind–cruel	high–low	reputable–disreputable	beautiful–ugly
sociable–unsociable	meaningful–meaningless	believing–skeptical	sociable–unsociable
light–dark	important–unimportant	wise–foolish	meaningful–meaningless
altruistic–egotistical	progressive–regressive	healthy–sick	
grateful–ungrateful		clean–dirty	
beautiful–ugly			
harmonious–dissonant			

Source: Adapted from Charles E. Osgood, G. J. Suci, and P. H. Tannenbaum, *The Measurement of Meaning* (Urbana, Ill.: The University of Illinois Press, 1957), Table 5, pp. 52–61.

| Hedonistic goodness | Positive loading on evaluation plus a positive loading on subsidiary factor which includes "pleasurable" and similar adjectives. |

While it is claimed that the *SD* scale is highly generalizable, it should be adapted to each research problem. The first step in scale development is to select the concepts to be studied. While concepts tend to be nouns or noun phrases, nonverbal stimuli such as visual sketches may also be used. The concepts are chosen by personal judgment and reflect the nature of the problem under study.

Once the concepts are chosen specific scale items must be selected. Here opinions diverge; some argue that the original bipolar word pairs should be used, while others argue that tailormade scales are better. If the traditional scale items are used, three criteria should guide their selection. The first criterion for selecting scale items is the factor(s) composition. If we use the traditional three of evaluation, potency, and activity, we should probably use at least three bipolar pairs for each factor. Scores on these individual items should be averaged, by factor, to improve their test reliability. The second selection criterion is the scale's relevance to the concepts being judged. It is important to choose adjectives that permit *connotative* perceptions to be expressed. Irrelevant concept-scale pairings tend to yield neutral midpoint values that have little information value. A third criterion is that scales should be stable across subjects and concepts. For example, a pair such as "large–small" may be interpreted by some to be denotative when judging a physical object such as "automobile" but be used connotatively in judging abstract concepts such as "management by objectives." Such variability would distort the measurement process. Scales should also be linear between polar opposites and pass through the origin. A pair that might fail this test is "rugged–delicate," which is nonlinear relative to evaluation; when used separately, both of these adjectives tend to have favorable meanings.[30] Finally, scales of unknown composition may be relevant to a particular problem and might be included.

To illustrate the use of the *SD*, assume that you are designing a scale to compare four candidates for the leadership position in an important industry organization. The scale is to be used by a panel of corporate leaders to rate candidates. The selection of concepts in this case is relatively simple; there are the four candidates, plus a fifth—the ideal candidate.

The nature of the problem influences the scale selection. First, shall we develop an instrument that has only evaluative scales, or shall we include scales for potency and activity? Since the person who wins this position must influence business leaders, it is decided to use all three factors. This person must deal with many people, often in a social setting; must have high integrity; and take a leadership role in encouraging more progressive policies in

---

[30]Osgood, *Measurement of Meaning*, p. 79.

FIGURE 9–2   *SD* scale for analyzing candidates for an industry leadership position

(E)	Sociable	(+3) : ___ : ___ : ___ : ___ : ___ : (−3)	Unsociable
(P)	Weak	(−3) : ___ : ___ : ___ : ___ : ___ : (+3)	Strong
(A)	Active	(+3) : ___ : ___ : ___ : ___ : ___ : (−3)	Passive
(E)	Progressive	(+3) : ___ : ___ : ___ : ___ : ___ : (−3)	Regressive
(P)	Yielding	(−3) : ___ : ___ : ___ : ___ : ___ : (+3)	Tenacious
(A)	Slow	(−3) : ___ : ___ : ___ : ___ : ___ : (+3)	Fast
(E)	True	(+3) : ___ : ___ : ___ : ___ : ___ : (−3)	False
(P)	Heavy	(+3) : ___ : ___ : ___ : ___ : ___ : (−3)	Light
(A)	Hot	(+3) : ___ : ___ : ___ : ___ : ___ : (−3)	Cold
(E)	Unsuccessful	(−3) : ___ : ___ : ___ : ___ : ___ : (+3)	Successful

FIGURE 9–3   Graphic representation of SD analysis

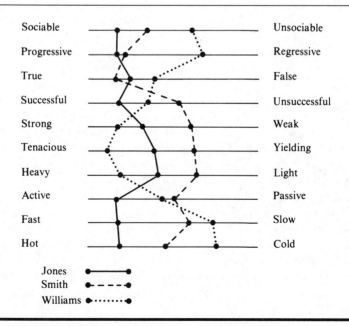

industry. The position will also involve high personal activity. On the basis of these requirements, we might choose 10 scales by which to score the candidates from $+3$ to -3. Figure 9–2 illustrates the scale makeup that might be used in this situation. The letters along the left side, which show the relevant factor, would be omitted from the actual scale, as would the numeric values shown. Note also that the evaluation, potency, and activity scales are mixed and that about one half are reversed in order to minimize the halo effect. In analyzing the results of this scaling, the set of evaluation values are averaged, as are those for the potency and activity scales.

One way to display data collected by such scales is illustrated in Figure 9–3. Here, the adjective pairs are reordered so that evaluation, potency, and activity descriptors are grouped together and profiles of three candidates are displayed.

Tailor-made *SD* scales.   Many researchers use ad hoc *SD* scales. For example, one such effort explored the problem with a retail store image using 35 pairs of words or phrases classified into eight groups. Excerpts from this scale are presented in figure 9–4.

FIGURE 9–4   Excerpts from an ad hoc scale for retail store image

---

CONVENIENCE OF REACHING THE STORE FROM YOUR LOCATION

near by __: __: __: __: __: __: __: distant

short time required
to reach store __: __: __: __: __: __: __: long time required to reach store

difficult drive __: __: __: __: __: __: __: easy drive

difficult to find
parking place __: __: __: __: __: __: __: easy to find parking place

convenient to other
stores I shop __: __: __: __: __: __: __: inconvenient to other stores I shop

PRODUCTS OFFERED

wide selection of different
kinds of products __: __: __: __: __: __: __: limited selection of different kinds of products

fully stocked __: __: __: __: __: __: __: understocked

undependable products __: __: __: __: __: __: __: dependable products

high quality __: __: __: __: __: __: __: low quality

numerous brands __: __: __: __: __: __: __: few brands

unknown brands __: __: __: __: __: __: __: well-known brands

Source: Robert F. Kelly and Ronald Stephenson, "The Semantic Differential: An Information Source for Designing Retail Patronage Appeals," *Journal of Marketing* 31 (October 1967), p. 45.

Other categories of scale items were general characteristics of the company; physical characteristics of the store; prices charged by the store; store personnel; advertising by the store; your friends and the store.

Since the scale pairs are closely associated with the characteristics of the store and its use, one could develop image profiles of various stores. Such data may be relevant at the manifest level, but in this form, represent an arbitrary scale development effort. There is little chance to interpret the results in terms of *SD* theory, nor can one uncover latent meanings unless the results are factor-analyzed.

On the other hand, recent research aimed at using the Osgood approach in the development of tailor-made *SD* scales looks promising.[31] There is also some evidence to suggest that the traditional scales do not work well in such research situations,[32] while other studies tend to confirm the value of the original scales.[33] In the light of this conflicting evidence, the verdict is still out on which approach is the more useful. Even so, there is evidence of a growing popularity for *SD*-type scales.

In summary, the *SD* has a number of specific advantages. It is an efficient and easy way to secure attitudes from a large sample. These attitudes may be measured in both direction and intensity. The total set of responses provides a comprehensive picture of the meaning of an object, as well as a measure of the subject doing the rating. It is a standardized technique that is easily repeated but escapes many of the problems of response distortion found with more direct methods.

A JOB SATISFACTION SCALE[34]

Brayfield and Rothe have developed a simple scale called "An Index of Job Satisfaction" which is frequently referenced in the management research literature. They began with the premise that job satisfaction could be inferred from individuals' attitudes toward their work. They formulated the following as desirable attributes for their attitude scale to possess:

1. It should give an index to overall job satisfaction rather than to specific aspects of the job situation.
2. It should be applicable to a wide variety of jobs.
3. It should be sensitive to variations in attitude.

---

[31]John Dickson and Gerald Albaum, "A Method for Developing Tailormade Semantic Differentials for Specific Marketing Content Areas," *Journal of Marketing Research* 14 (February 1977), pp. 87–91.

[32]Louis K. Sharp and W. Thomas Anderson, Jr., "Concept-Scale Interaction in the Semantic Differential," *Journal of Marketing Research* 9 (November 1972), pp. 432–34.

[33]William S. Peters and Richard Kuhn, "An Exploration in Store Measurement," *Decision Sciences* 1 (1970), pp. 113–28.

[34]Arthur H. Brayfield and Harold F. Rothe, "An Index of Job Satisfaction," *Journal of Applied Psychology* (October 1951), pp. 307–11.

4. The items should be of such a nature (interesting, realistic, and varied) that the scale would evoke cooperation from both management and employees.
5. It should yield a reliable index.
6. It should yield a valid index.
7. It should be brief and easily scored.

They initially considered both the Thurstone and Likert scale designs. They settled on the Thurstone technique chiefly because they had no readily available group of employed persons who could be used for the item analysis process. They did, however, have a class of 77 mature students in a course in Personnel Psychology, most of whom had several years of work experience.

The authors collected more than 1,000 statements that were edited down to 246. These were compiled into sets, and distributed to the students for judging. Sorting was done under supervision, using the Thurstone approach.[35] Scale values (medians) and Q values (interquartile ranges) for each statement were determined graphically.

Four specific criteria were used to judge which statements to include in the preliminary scale.

1. Select items that cover the entire continuum at approximately 0.5 step intervals, eliminating statements at the ends of the continuum as too extreme.
2. Choose only those statements that received consistent judgments as measured by Q scores of 2.0 or less. That is, on an 11-point scale, the middle one-half of the judgments were within a 2-point range.
3. Items referring to specific aspects of a job were eliminated, since an overall attitudinal factor was desired. For example, items regarding pay, working conditions, and so forth, were eliminated because they might have been too specific.
4. Acceptability to employees and management was judged. For example, the item "I am tempted to use illness as an excuse to stay home from this job" was rejected as reflecting unfavorably upon the individual worker.

A preliminary scale of 18 items was tested, using a rank correlation of odd and even items. This measure of reliability was low enough to prompt the authors to convert to a Likert scale, which evidence has shown typically products a higher reliability than does a Thurstone scale.

The final scale still consisted of 18 items, each with a five-point agreement-disagreement response category set. From the Thurstone scale value, it was known what direction to apply the scoring method to assure that a low total score would represent the dissatisfied end of the scale. The neutral

---

[35]For detailed instructions on using the Thurstone approach, see Allen L. Edwards, *Techniques of Attitude Scale Construction* (New York: Appleton-Century-Crofts, 1957).

FIGURE 9–5   Brayfield-Rothe index of job satisfaction

Some jobs are more interesting and satisfying than others. We want to know how people feel about different jobs. This page contains 18 statements about jobs. You are to cross out the phrase below each statement which best describes how you feel about your present job. There are no right or wrong answers. We should like your honest opinion on each one of the statements. Work out the sample item numbered (0).

0. There are some conditions concerning my job that could be improved.
    STRONGLY AGREE AGREE UNDECIDED DISAGREE STRONGLY DISAGREE

1. My job is like a hobby to me.
    STRONGLY AGREE AGREE UNDECIDED DISAGREE STRONGLY DISAGREE

2. My job is usually interesting enough to keep me from getting bored.
    STRONGLY AGREE AGREE UNDECIDED DISAGREE STRONGLY DISAGREE

3. It seems that my friends are more interested in their jobs.
    STRONGLY AGREE AGREE UNDECIDED DISAGREE STRONGLY DISAGREE

4. I consider my job rather unpleasant.
    STRONGLY AGREE AGREE UNDECIDED DISAGREE STRONGLY DISAGREE

5. I enjoy my work more than my leisure time.
    STRONGLY AGREE AGREE UNDECIDED DISAGREE STRONGLY DISAGREE

6. I am often bored with my job.
    STRONGLY AGREE AGREE UNDECIDED DISAGREE STRONGLY DISAGREE

7. I feel fairly well satisfied with my present job.
    STRONGLY AGREE AGREE UNDECIDED DISAGREE STRONGLY DISAGREE

8. Most of the time I have to force myself to go to work.
    STRONGLY AGREE AGREE UNDECIDED DISAGREE STRONGLY DISAGREE

9. I am satisfied with my job for the time being.
    STRONGLY AGREE AGREE UNDECIDED DISAGREE STRONGLY DISAGREE

10. I feel that my job is no more interesting than others I could get.
    STRONGLY AGREE AGREE UNDECIDED DISAGREE STRONGLY DISAGREE

11. I definitely dislike my work.
    STRONGLY AGREE AGREE UNDECIDED DISAGREE STRONGLY DISAGREE

12. I feel that I am happier in my work than most other people.
    STRONGLY AGREE AGREE UNDECIDED DISAGREE STRONGLY DISAGREE

13. Most days I am enthusiastic about my work.
    STRONGLY AGREE AGREE UNDECIDED DISAGREE STRONGLY DISAGREE

14. Each day of work seems like it will never end.
    STRONGLY AGREE AGREE UNDECIDED DISAGREE STRONGLY DISAGREE

15. I like my job better than the average worker does.
    STRONGLY AGREE AGREE UNDECIDED DISAGREE STRONGLY DISAGREE

16. My job is pretty uninteresting.
    STRONGLY AGREE AGREE UNDECIDED DISAGREE STRONGLY DISAGREE

17. I find real enjoyment in my work.
    STRONGLY AGREE AGREE UNDECIDED DISAGREE STRONGLY DISAGREE

18. I am disappointed that I ever took this job.
    STRONGLY AGREE AGREE UNDECIDED DISAGREE STRONGLY DISAGREE

Source: Arthur H. Brayfield and Harold F. Rothe, "An Index of Job Satisfaction," *Journal of Applied Psychology* (October 1951), p. 309.

response point was *undecided*. A copy of the final scale is presented in Figure 9–5.

The reliability of this scale has been measured by computing an odd-even item correlation which, when corrected by the Spearman-Brown formula, gives a reliability coefficient of 0.87. Validity was evaluated by correlating with the Hoppock job satisfaction scale. The product-moment correlation between these two scales was 0.92. In addition, the form was tested with a group of people who could not be separated into two groups—those employed in personnel occupations and those not employed in such occupations. It was hypothesized that those in personnel occupations would be more satisfied with their jobs than those not in personnel jobs. This hypothesis was confirmed by the data. On the basis of these tests, it was concluded that the index has adequate reliability and validity.

SUMMARY

Scaling describes the procedures by which one assigns numbers to various degrees of opinion, attitude, and other concepts. These procedures may be classified in six different ways:

1. Study objective—do we measure the characteristics of the respondent or the stimulus object?
2. Response form—do we measure by using a categorical or comparative scale?
3. Degree of preference—do we measure our preferences or make nonpreference judgments?
4. Scale properties—do we measure by using nominal, ordinal, interval, or ratio scales?
5. Number of dimensions—do we measure using a unidimensional or multidimensional scale?
7. Scale construction technique—do we develop scales by arbitrary decision, consensus, item analysis, cumulative scaling, or factor analysis?

In this chapter, two of these classifications—the response form and scale construction techniques were emphasized.

When one uses categorical scales, one judges an object in absolute terms against certain specified criteria. You can use either a graphic or an itemized rating scale. When you use comparative or ranking methods, you make relative judgments against other similar objects. Three well-known methods are the paired-comparison, the rank order, and successive intervals methods.

Arbitrary scales are designed largely through the researcher's own subjective selection of items. These scales are simple and inexpensive to construct and have a certain face validity for their designer, but it is generally not possible to judge their validity in any other way.

In the consensus method, a panel is used to judge the relevancy, ambiguity, and attitude level of scale items. Those items that are judged best are then included in the final instrument. The Thurstone method of equal-appearing intervals is developed by the consensus methods.

With the item analysis approach, one develops a number of items believed to express either a favorable or an unfavorable attitude toward some general object. These items are then pretested to determine which ones discriminate between persons with high total scores and those with low total scores on the test. Those items that best meet this discrimination test are included in the final instrument. Likert scales are often developed using this approach.

With cumulative scales, it is possible to estimate how a respondent has answered individual items by knowing the total score. The items are related to each other, on a particular attitude dimension, in such a way that if one agrees with a more extreme item, one will also agree with items representing less extreme views. Guttman's scalogram is the classic example of scale development.

Factor scales are developed through factor analysis or similar correlation techniques. They are particularly useful in uncovering latent attitude dimensions and approach scaling through the concept of multi-dimension attribute space. Semantic differential scales are an example.

SUPPLEMENTAL READINGS

1. Edwards, Allen L. *Techniques of Attitude Scale Construction.* New York: Appleton-Century-Crofts, 1957. Thorough discussion of basic unidimensional scaling techniques.
2. Kerlinger, Fred N. *Foundations of Behavioral Research.* 2d ed. New York: Holt, Rinehart & Winston, 1973. Chapters 29–34 cover various scaling and other data collection techniques, some of which are not discussed in this text.
3. Miller, Delbert C. *Handbook of Research Design and Social Measurement.* 3d ed. New York: David McKay Company, 1977. Presents a large number of existing sociometric scales and indexes, as well as information on their characteristics, validity, and sources.
4. Osgood, Charles E.; George J. Suci; and Percy H. Tannenbaum. *The Measurement of Meaning.* Urbana, Ill.: The University of Illinois Press, 1957. The basic reference on *SD* scaling.
5. Snider, James G., and Charles E. Osgood, eds. *Semantic Differential Technique.* Chicago: Aldine, 1969. A collection of 52 papers on *SD* technique plus a semantic atlas for 550 concepts.
6. Summers, Gene F., ed. *Attitude Measurement.* Chicago: Rand McNally, 1970. An excellent collection of papers on various aspects of scaling.

DISCUSSION QUESTIONS

1. Discuss the relative merits and demerits of:
   a Rating versus ranking scales.
   b Likert versus differential scales.
   c Unidimensional versus multidimensional scales.

2. Suppose some researcher gives you a scale to complete. It has as its subject the economic system currently found in the United States.
   a Describe the various measurement objectives that the researcher might have in mind in asking you to complete this questionnaire.
   b What would the scale be like and how would it be developed if it were a:
   Thurstone differential scale.
   Likert-type summated scale.
   Semantic differential scale.
   Scalogram.
   Multidimensional scale.
3. This chapter has been partially organized on the basis of five methods of scale construction. What are these methods and how do they differ? Is this difference of real importance? Explain.
4. You receive the results of a paired-comparison preference test of four soft drinks from a sample of 200 persons. The results are as follows:

	Koak	*Zip*	*Pabze*	*Mr. Peepers*
Koak	X	50*	115	35
Zip	150	X	160	70
Pabze	85	40	X	45
Mr. Peepers	165	130	155	X

*Read as 50 persons preferred Zip over Koak.

   a How do these brands rank in overall preference in this sample?
   b Develop an interval scale for these four brands.
5. One of the problems in developing rating scales is the choice of response terms to use. Below are samples of some widely used scaling codes. Do you see any problems with them?
   a Yes _____ Depends _____ No _____
   b Excellent _____ Good _____ Fair _____ Poor _____
   c Excellent _____ Good _____ Average _____ Fair _____ Poor _____
   d Strongly   Un-   Dis-   Strongly
      Approve ___ Approve ___ certain ___ approve _____ Disapprove _____
6. Assume that you are to judge a set of statements that will be used in developing a differential scale for an employee attitude survey. Score each of the below listed statements from 1 to 10, with 10 being the most positive favorable statement, and 1 the least favorable. After scoring these statements refer to page 254 to compare your judgment with the average judgments made in the actual study. How do you account for any substantial differences between your scores and the average scores?

   Score
   _____The pay in this company is terrible.
   _____I think the company goes outside to fill good jobs instead of promoting people who are here.
   _____The company is sincere in wanting to know what its employees think about it.

_____I think this company treats its employees better than any other company does.

_____I believe accidents will happen no matter what you do about them.

_____One can get ahead in this company if one tries.

_____The workers put as much over on the company as the company puts over on them.

_____My boss gives all the breaks to lodge and church friends.

_____Soldiering on the job is on the increase.

_____In the long run this company will "put it over" on you.

7. Below is a Likert type of scale that might be used to evaluate your opinion of the educational program you are in. There are five response categories: Strongly Agree through Neutral to Strong Disagree. If "5" represents the most positive attitude, how would the different items be valued?

   a This program is not very challenging.

   SA   A   N   D   SD

   b The general level of teaching is good.

   SA   A   N   D   SD

   c I really think I am learning a lot from this program.

   SA   A   N   D   SD

   d Students' suggestions are given little attention here.

   SA   A   N   D   SD

   e This program does a good job of preparing one for a career.

   SA   A   N   D   SD

   f This program is below my expectations.

   SA   A   N   D   SD

   Record your answers to the above items. In what two different ways could such responses be used? What would be the purpose of each?

8. Using the semantic differential scale below, record your impressions of the educational program you are in.

good ____	: ____	: ____	: ____	: ____	: ____	: ____	bad
weak ____	: ____	: ____	: ____	: ____	: ____	: ____	strong
active ____	: ____	: ____	: ____	: ____	: ____	: ____	passive
complete ____	: ____	: ____	: ____	: ____	: ____	: ____	incomplete
severe ____	: ____	: ____	: ____	: ____	: ____	: ____	lenient
fast ____	: ____	: ____	: ____	: ____	: ____	: ____	slow
cold ____	: ____	: ____	: ____	: ____	: ____	: ____	hot
meaningful ____	: ____	: ____	: ____	: ____	: ____	: ____	meaningless
heavy ____	: ____	: ____	: ____	: ____	: ____	: ____	light

   a Assuming 7 is a positive score, how would you score the response alternatives above?

   b Which of these items are evaluative? Activity? Potency?

   c What are your scores on the above three dimensions?

   d How does your answer compare to the answers you gave in question 7?

9. Using the above SD scale again, score your ideal educational program and calculate your evaluation, activity, and potency scales for this ideal program. How does this one compare with your answer in question 8?

10. What are the critical differences between a classical SD scale and an ad hoc SD scale? What are the advantages and disadvantages of each?

SAMPLING

10. Elements of sampling

Dick Ward walked out of class with Fred Thomas and both headed for the Rathskeller for lunch. They were hungry and in a hurry because their entrepreneurship class would begin in 45 minutes. As luck would have it, however, everyone else on the campus also seemed to be eating at the Rat.

"Looks like we go hungry again," moaned Fred.

"Won't Big U. ever get adequate eating facilities here?" Dick responded. "I tell you Fred, we really should implement our entrepreneurship project. Professor James thinks we have a real winner and I do, too. This campus could easily support a membership dining club on Forsythe street in the Wainwright building."

"You may be right, Dick, if I get much more of this long waiting for lunch every day, I may take you up. When I talked to Bill Johnson's father at the bank yesterday, he sounded like he could arrange the financing if we put together a good plan. By the way, where are you on the market research phase of this project?"

"Right now, I'm trying to learn how to draw a sample for the survey we want to run. We have written the questionnaire and tested it. Now we need to decide who we are going to interview and how many interviews should we take," was the reply.

"What kind of sample are you going to use?" asked Fred.

"I'm still considering that question," was Dick's response. "Ideally, I'd like to use a random probability sample, but nonprobability sampling is also a possibility. I've never studied statistics before so I am having to begin at the very beginning on this topic. Believe me! It is slow going. Right now I'm studying the nature of sampling and the basic concepts of both probability and nonprobability sampling."

THE NATURE OF SAMPLING

Most people intuitively understand the idea of sampling. One taste from a drink tells us whether it is sweet or sour. If we select a few employment

275

records out of a file of 4,000, we usually assume that this sample reflects the characteristics of the full 4,000. If some of our staff favor a four-day week, we infer that others will also. These examples vary in their representativeness, but each is a sample.

The basic idea of sampling is that some of the *elements* in a *population* provide useful information on the entire population. An element is the subject on which the measurement is being taken. It is the unit of study. For example, each office worker questioned about the four-day week is a population element, and each account analyzed is an element of an account population. Population is the total collection of elements about which we wish to make some inferences. All office workers in the local office may comprise the population of interest, and all 4,000 files may also define a population of interest.

Why sample?

The economic advantages of taking a sample rather than a census are massive. Consider the probable cost of taking a census. Why should we spend thousands of dollars interviewing all 4,000 employees in our company if we can find out what we need to know by asking only a few hundred?

Deming argues that the quality of a study is often better with sampling than with a census. He suggests, "Sampling possesses the possibility of better interviewing (testing), more thorough investigation of missing, wrong, or suspicious information, better supervision, and better processing than is possible with complete coverage."[1] Recent research findings substantiate this opinion. Assael and Keon found that more than 90 percent of the total survey error in one study was from nonsampling sources and only 10 percent or less was from random sampling error.[2] The U.S. Bureau of the Census demonstrates its confidence in sampling by making sample surveys to check the accuracy of its census.

Sampling also provides much quicker results than does a census. The speed of execution minimizes the time between the recognition of a need for information and the availability of that information. Then, too, some situations require sampling. For example, when we test the breaking strength of materials we must destroy them, a census would mean complete destruction of the materials. Sampling is also the only process possible if the population is infinite. For example, we must take a sample of dice throws since the population of dice throws is infinite.

The major problem is that any sample we draw may not be representative of the population from which it is drawn. The result would be that any value

---

[1] W. E. Deming, *Sample Design in Business Research* (New York: John Wiley & Sons, 1960), p. 26.

[2] Henry Assael and John Keon, "Nonsampling versus Sampling Errors in Survey Research," *Journal of Marketing Research*, Spring 1982, pp. 114–123.

we calculate from the sample (statistic) would be incorrect as estimates of the population value (parameter). When the sample is drawn properly, however, some sample items underestimate the parameters and others overestimate them. Variations in these item values tend to counteract each other; this counteraction tendency results in a statistic (sample value) that is generally close to the parameter (population value). For these offsetting effects to take place, however, it is necessary (1) that there be enough members in the sample and (2) they must be drawn in a way to favor neither the overestimating or the underestimating tendencies.

What is a good sample?

The ultimate test of a sample design is how well it represents the characteristics of the population it purports to represent. In measurement terms, the sample must be *valid*. Validity of a sample depends upon two considerations.

Accuracy.   First is the matter of *accuracy*—defined as *the degree to which bias is absent from the sample*. An accurate (unbiased) sample is one in which the underestimators and the overestimators are balanced among the members of the sample. There is no *systematic variance* with an accurate sample. Systematic variance has been defined as "the variation in measures due to some known or unknown influences that 'cause' the scores to lean in one direction more than another."[3] For example, it has been said that homes on the corner of the block tend to be larger and more valuable than those within blocks. Thus, a sample in which we select corner homes only will cause us to overestimate home values in the area.

The classic example of a sample with systematic variance was the *Literary Digest* presidential election poll in 1936 in which more than 2 million persons participated. The poll indicated that Alfred Landon would defeat Franklin Roosevelt for the presidency of the United States. Even the large size of this sample did not counteract its systematic bias. Later evidence indicated that the poll drew its sample from the middle and upper classes, while Roosevelt's appeal was heavily among the much larger working class.

Precision.   A second criterion of a good sample design is *precision of estimate*. No sample will fully represent its population in all respects. A sample statistic may be expected to differ from its parameter as a result of random fluctuations inherent in the sampling process. This is often referred to as *error variance* or *sampling error* and reflects the influences of chance in drawing the sample members. Error variance is that which is left over after all known sources of systematic variance have been accounted for. In theory, error variance consists of random fluctuations only, although some unknown systematic variance is often included.

---

[3]Fred N. Kerlinger, *Foundations of Behavioral Research*, 2d ed. (New York: Holt, Rinehart and Winston, 1973), p. 74.

Precision is measured by the *standard error of estimate,* a type of standard deviation measurement; the smaller the standard error of estimate, the higher is the precision of the sample. After giving due consideration to problems of overcoming bias, it is desirable that the sample design produce a minimum standard error of estimate. However, not all types of sample designs provide estimates of precision, and samples of the same size can produce different amounts of error variance.

Types of sample design

There are a variety of sampling techniques available. Which one is selected depends on the requirements of the project, its objectives, and funds available. The different approaches may be classified by their representation basis and the element selection techniques as in the accompanying table.

	Representation basis	
Element selection	*Probability*	*Nonprobability*
Unrestricted	Simple random	Convenience
Restricted	Complex random	Purposive
	Systematic	Judgment
	Cluster	Quota
	Stratified	
	Double	

Representation. The members of a sample are selected either on a probability basis or by some other means. Probability sampling is based on the concept of *random selection—a controlled procedure that assures that each population element is given a known nonzero chance of selection.*

In contrast, *nonprobability selection* is nonrandom. That is, each member does not have a known nonzero chance of being included. Allowing interviewers to choose sample members "at random" (meaning as they wish or wherever they find them) is *not random sampling.* Only probability samples provide estimates of precision.

Element Selection. Samples may also be classified by whether the elements are selected individually and directly from the population viewed as a single pool, or whether additional controls are placed on the process of element selection. When each sample element is drawn individually from the population at large, it is an *unrestricted sample. Restricted sampling* covers all other forms of sampling.

NONPROBABILITY SAMPLING

Any discussion of the relative merits of probability versus nonprobability sampling clearly shows the technical superiority of the former. In probability sampling, researchers use a randomization process of element selection in order to reduce or eliminate sampling bias. Under such conditions, one can have substantial confidence that our sample is representative of the population from which it is drawn. In addition, with probability sample designs, one can estimate an interval range within which to expect the population parameter to fall. Thus, not only can one reduce the chance for sampling error, but also estimate the range of probable sampling error present.

With nonprobability sampling, one can use a variety of approaches to choose which persons or cases to include in the sample. Often one even allows the choice of subjects to be made by field workers on the scene. Under such conditions, there is greater opportunity for bias to enter into the sample selection procedure and to distort the findings of the study. In addition, with nonprobability designs, one cannot estimate any range within which to expect the population parameter to fall. Given these obvious technical advantages of probability sampling over nonprobability sampling, why then would anyone choose the latter? It turns out that there are some practical reasons for using these less satisfactory methods.

Conditions of use

One may use nonprobability sampling because such a procedure satisfactorily meets the sampling objectives. For example, while a random sample will give us a true cross-section of the population, this may not be the objective of the research. If there is no desire or need to generalize to a population parameter, then there is much less concern about whether or not the sample fully reflects the population. Often, the researcher has more limited objectives; in fact, he or she may be looking only for a feel of the range of conditions, or for examples of dramatic variations. This is especially true in exploratory research where one may wish to contact only certain persons or cases that are clearly nontypical.

A second important reason why nonprobability sampling may be chosen over the probability sample is because of cost and time requirements. Probability sampling clearly calls for more planning and repeated callbacks to assure that each selected sample member is contacted. These activities are expensive. Carefully controlled nonprobability sampling often seems to give acceptable results, so the investigator may not even consider probability sampling.

Third, while the probability sampling may be superior in theory, there are breakdowns in its application. Even carefully stated random sampling procedures may be subject to careless application by the persons involved. Thus, the ideal probability sampling may be only partially achieved bacause of the human element.

It is also possible that nonprobability sampling may be the only feasible alternative. The total population may not be available for study in certain cases. For example, at the scene of a major event it may be infeasible to even attempt to construct a probability sample. A study of past correspondence between two companies must use an arbitrary sample because the full correspondence is normally not available.

In another sense, those who are included in a sample may select themselves. In mail surveys, those who respond may not represent a true cross-section of those who receive the questionnaire. The receivers of the questionnaire decide for themselves whether or not they will participate. There is some of this self-selection in almost all surveys because every respondent chooses whether or not to be interviewed. Unless great care is taken, a probability sample may be less precise than expected.

Sampling methods

Convenience. Nonprobability samples that are also unrestricted are called *convenience* samples. Such a sample is the least reliable design, but is normally the cheapest and easiest to conduct. In this case, researchers or field workers are given the freedom to choose whomever they find to be included into the sample. Hence, the name "convenience." Examples include informal pools of friends and neighbors, or the sample that might be secured by a newspaper that has invited its readers to state their positions on some public issue.

While a convenience sample has no controls to insure precision, it may still be a useful procedure. Often one will take such a sample to test ideas or even to gain ideas about a subject of interest. In the early stages of exploratory research, when you are seeking guidance, you might use this approach. Such samples may also give evidence that is so overwhelming as to make the more sophisticated sampling unnecessary. For example, in interviewing students on a campus concerning some issue of campus concern, one might talk to 25 students selected more or less by accident and find that the responses are so overwhelmingly one-sided that there is no incentive to interview further.

Purposive sampling. When one draws a nonprobability sample that conforms to certain criteria, it is called *purposive sampling*. There are two major types—judgment sampling and quota sampling.

Judgment sampling occurs when one handpicks sample members to conform to some criterion. For example, in a study of labor problems, you may want to talk only with those persons who have experienced some sort of on-the-job discrimination. Another example of judgment sampling occurs when election results are predicted from only a few selected precincts that have been chosen because of their predictive record in past elections.

When used in the early stages of an exploratory study, a judgment sample is quite appropriate. When one wishes to select a biased group for screening purposes this sampling method is also a good choice. For example, companies often try out new product ideas on their employees. The rationale is that one would expect the firm's employees to be more favorably disposed toward a new product idea than the general public. Thus, if the product does not pass this group it does not have prospect for success in the general market.

Sudman describes an inappropriate judgment sample whose use is of great economic importance in the United Sates.

> Many economists and statisticians feel that the sample now used for the Consumer Price Index (CPI) is both poorly drawn and too small to reflect accurately important price changes in the U.S. economy. Unlike the Current Population Survey, which is in 449 sample areas, the CPI is in only 56 cities and metropolitan areas selected judgmentally and to some extent on the basis of political pressure. In reality, these cities represent only themselves although the index is called the Consumer Price Index for Urban Wage Earners and Clerical Workers, and most people believe the index reflects prices everywhere in the United States. Within cities, the selection of retail outlets is done judgmentally so that the possible size of sample biases is unknown.[4]

The *quota sample* is the second type of purposive sampling. One uses it to try to assure that the sample is representative of the population from which it is drawn. The logic behind quota sampling is that certain relevant characteristics describe the dimensions of the population. If a sample has the same distribution on these particular variables, then one reasons that it is likely to be representative of the population with regard to other variables on which we have not controlled. For example, suppose the student body of BIG University is 65 percent male and 35 percent female. The sampling quota would call for sampling students at a 65–35 percent ratio between the sexes. This would eliminate distortions due to a nonrepresentative sex ratio.

In most quota samples, researchers specify more than one control dimension. Each that is chosen should meet two tests: (1) It should be one whose distribution in the population we can estimate; and (2) it is one which we should have reason to believe is relevant to the topic studied. For example, one may believe that response to a question should vary, depending upon the sex of the respondent. If so, seek proportional responses from both men and women. You may also feel that undergraduates differ from graduate students, so this would be a dimension. You may also choose dimensions such as the student's academic discipline, ethnic group, religious affiliation, and social group affiliation.

Only a small number of these controls can be used. To illustrate, suppose you would like to consider the following:

Sex—2 categories—male, female

Class Level—2 categories—graduate and undergraduate

College—6 categories—Arts and Science, Agriculture, Architecture, Business, Enginering, other

Religion—4 categories—Protestant, Catholic, Jewish, other

---

[4]Seymour Sudman, *Applied Sampling* (San Francisco: Academic Press, 1976), p. 10.

Fraternal affiliation—2 categories—Greek, independent

Family social class—3 categories—upper, middle, lower

In the extreme case, you might ask an interviewer to find a male, undergraduate, business student, who is Catholic, a fraternity member, and from an upper-class home. All combinations of these five factors would call for 288 such cells to consider. This type of control is known as precision control. It gives greater assurance that a sample will be representative of the population, but it is costly and too difficult to carry out when the variables exceed, say, three or so.

When you wish to use more than three control dimensions, you should depend on *frequency control*. With this control form, the overall percentage of those with each characteristic in the sample should match the percentage holding the same characteristic in the population. No attempt is made to find a combination of specific characteristics in a single person. In frequency control, we would probably find that the accompanying sample array is an adequate reflection of the population.

	Population	Sample
Male	65%	67%
Married	15	14
Undergraduate	70	72
Campus resident	30	28
Independent	75	73
Protestant	39	42
White	90	89

There are several weaknesses in quota sampling. First, the idea that quotas on some variables assume representativeness on others is an argument by analogy. It gives no real assurance that the sample is representative on the variables being studied. Often, the data used to provide controls may also be out of date, or in some other way inaccurate. Then, too, there is such a practical limit on the number of simultaneous controls that can be applied so that the quota may not be precise enough. Finally, the choice of subjects is still left to field workers to make on a judgmental basis. They may choose only friendly looking people, people who are convenient to them, and so forth.

In spite of the problems with quota sampling, it is widely used by opinion pollsters, marketing and other researchers. Probability sampling is usually much more costly and time consuming. Advocates of quota sampling argue that while there is some danger of systematic bias, the risks are usually not that great. Where predictive validity has been checked (for example, in election polls), quota sampling has generally been satisfactory. Then, too, while probability sampling may be theoretically superior, its technical requirements are often violated. Thus, the reasoning goes, "we might just as well begin with a good quota sample and save time and money."

PROBABILITY SAMPLING

The unrestricted or simple random sample is the simplest form of probability sampling. Recall that all probability samples must provide a known nonzero chance of selection for each population element. A simple random sample is the special case in which each population element has an equal chance of being selected into the sample; this type will be used here to explore the procedures for choosing probability samples.

Sampling procedure

There are a number of design decisions that must be made. Recall that Dick Ward and Fred Thomas are interested in starting a dining club near the campus of Big University. Their idea is to make its facilities available on a membership basis. To launch such a venture, they will need to make a substantial investment. In addition, there are a number of risks which they would like to minimize through research. One important research question might be, "Who would patronize such a club and on what basis?" More specifically, they might be interested in the following investigative questions:

1. How many would join the club under various membership and fee arrangements?
2. How much would the average member spend per month?
3. What meals and days would be the most popular?
4. What menu and service formats would be the most popular?

To find answers to these and other questions, the students might conduct a sample survey. What are the steps to take?

Steps in sampling design

Five decisions must be made in designing a sample. While they are presented here sequentially, their order is not fixed, and an answer to one question often forces a revision in an answer given earlier. The critical sampling questions are:

1. What is the relevant population?
2. What type of sample?
3. What sampling frame?
4. What are the parameters of interest?
5. What size sample is needed?

What is the relevant population? The definition of the population can be apparent from the management problem or the research objectives, but often is not. Is the population for the dining club at Big University to be defined as the full-time day students on the main campus of Big University? Or, should the population include all persons employed at Big University? Or, should townspeople who live in the neighborhood be included? Without knowing the service target chosen, it is not obvious which of these is the appropriate population.

There may also be a confusion as to whether the population consists of individuals, households or families, or a combination of these. If a study concerns income, then the definition of the population element as individual or household can make quite a difference. Good operational definitions are critical at this point.

In the dining-club example, assume that the club is to be solely for the students and employees on the main campus. Thus, they might define the population as "all currently enrolled students and employees on the main campus of Big University." However, this does not include family members. You may want to revise our definition to make it "current students, employees, and their families of Big University, main campus."

What type of sample? What method should be used? With the kind of personnel records available at a University, it would be easy to use a quota sample. But because the population is geographically concentrated, a probability sampling method is possible. University directories are generally available and the costs of using a simple random sample would not be great in this case. Then, too, since they are thinking of a major investment in the club, they would like to be confident that they have a representative sample.

Choosing a simple random sampling technique has several consequences. With this sample design the students can make probability-based confidence estimates of various parameters. In using this method they must also give careful attention to the execution of the sampling process. The selection must follow an appropriate procedure in which there is no chance for interviewers or others to modify the selections made. No one other than those selected can be included in the study; strong efforts must be made to include all of the elements in the original sampling frame. The students must exclude substitutions except as clearly specified and controlled according to predetermined decision rules.

In spite of all of this care, the actual sample achieved will not match perfectly the sample that is originally drawn. Some persons will refuse to participate and others will be difficult to find. The latter represent the well-known "not-at-home" problem and require that a number of callbacks be made to assure that they are adequately represented in the sample.

What sampling frame? The concept of *sampling frame* is closely related to the population. It is defined as the *list of elements from which the sample is actually drawn*. Ideally, it is a complete and correct list of population members only. As a practical matter, however, the sampling frame often differs from the theoretical population.

The Big University directory would be the logical choice as a sampling frame. Directories are usually published in the fall, but suppose the study is being done in the spring. The list will be in error because some new persons will have come to campus and others will have left since the directory was published.

You might use the directory anyway, ignoring the fact that it is not fully current. Just how much inaccuracy one can tolerate in choosing a sampling frame is a matter of judgment. Obviously, if the directory was a year old, the error might be unacceptable. One way to make the frame more representative would be to secure a supplemental list of the new students and employees.

A greater distortion would be introduced if there were a branch campus population included in the directory as well as those at the main campus. This would be an example of a too inclusive frame. That is, the frame includes elements other than the ones in which we are interested. (Students and employees who have left since the directory was published are another example.)

Often one has to accept a sampling frame that includes persons or cases in addition to those in whom we are interested. For example, you may have to use a telephone directory to draw a sample of business telephone numbers. Fortunately, this is an easy problem to deal with. You draw our sample from the larger population and screen out those who are not members of the group we wish to study.

The campus dining club survey is an example of a frame problem which is easily solved. Often one finds this task much more of a challenge. Suppose you need to sample the members of an ethnic group, say orientals in Chicago. There is probably no directory of this population; while you may use the general city directory, sampling from this too inclusive frame, it would be costly and inefficient. Orientals probably represent only a small fraction of Chicago's population and the screening task would be monumental. Since ethnic groups tend to cluster in certain neighborhoods one might identify these areas of concentration and then use a reverse area telephone or city directory to draw a sample. (City directories and reverse telephone directories are organized by street address.)

What parameters to estimate?   In determining the nature of the sample design, it is important that students determine what specific population parameters are of interest. Some of these will correspond to the investigative questions already asked. For example:

1. The proportion of persons who express an interest in joining the club.
2. The average expected expenditures per month per member.
3. Average number of weekday lunches that will be demanded.

There may also be important subgroups in the population about whom they would like to make estimates. For example, they might want to draw conclusions about the extent of club use that could be expected from married students versus single students, residential students versus in-town students, and so forth. Such questions have a strong impact upon the nature of the sampling frame they accept, the design of the sample, and its size.

Parameters of interest may also be classified as *variables* or *attributes* data. Variables, as used in this special statistical sense, are normally computed from ratio or interval scale data such as dollars, age, length, scores, and so on, and may be *continuous* or *discrete*. Continuous variables such as age and length, can take all possible values within the relevant ranges; discrete variables, such as family size and number of visits per month, can take only selected values. The most common measures of variable data are the arithmetic mean and the standard deviation.

Attribute measures are necessary for nominal data and are widely used for other measures as well. Examples of attribute measurements are the proportion of a sample that expresses an interest in joining the club, or the proportion of married students who report they now eat in restaurants at least five times a month. The most frequent concentration measure of attributes is the percentage; the variance measure is the *pq* ratio.

How large a sample? Much folklore surrounds this question. One false belief is that a sample must be large or it is not representative. This is much less true than most people believe. Remember the *Literary Digest* fiasco? A sample of more than 2 million voters failed to predict correctly the presidential election of 1936. In recent years, there has been controversy in congressional hearings about the representativeness of a national sample of TV listeners. Samples of 1,000 or more have been branded as totally inadequate by many critics but seldom, if ever, by a statistician. Sample size is only one aspect of representativeness. A sample of more than 2 million can be misleading while a sample of 1,000, drawn in the proper manner, can be more than adequate.

One way to determine the size of a probability sample is to follow what others have done. Sudman has reported on the sample sizes used in several hundred studies (see Table 10–1). He suggests that these are "a useful guide for planning."[5] He warns that they should be used by the inexperienced researcher only as a check of his or her judgment against that of others.

Often it is claimed that a sample should bear some proportional relationship to the size of the population from which it is drawn. One hears such views as, "a sample should be at least 10 percent or more of its population if it is to be credible." This is not true. The absolute size of a sample is much more important than its size relative to the population. How large a sample should be is a function of the variation in the population parameters under study, and the estimating precision needed by the researcher. A sample of 400 may be appropriate in some cases, while more than 2,000 is required in other circumstances, and in another case, perhaps only 40 is called for.

The basic formula for calculating sample size in probability sampling assumes an infinite population. Thus, a sample of 100 drawn from a popula-

---

[5]Sudman, *Applied Sampling*, p. 86.

TABLE 10–1 Typical sample sizes for studies of human and institutional populations

A. *By subject matter*

	National			Regional		
	Mode	*Q_3*	*Q_1*	*Mode*	*Q_3*	*Q_1*
Financial	1000+	—	—	100	400	50
Medical	1000+	1000+	500	1000+	1000+	250
Other behavior	1000+	—	—	700	1000	300
Attitudes	1000+	1000+	500	700	1000	400
Laboratory experiments	—	—	—	100	200	50

B. *Number of subgroup analyses*

	National		Regional or special	
	People/ Households	*Institutions*	*People/ Households*	*Institutions*
None or few	1000–1500	200–500	200–500	50–200
Average	1500–2500	500–1000	500–1000	200–500
Many	2500+	1000+	1000+	500+

Source: Sudman, Seymour, *Applied Sampling* (New York: Academic Press, 1976).

tion of 5,000 has roughly the same estimating precision as 100 drawn from a population of 200,000,000. The only problem with the sample from the larger population is the difficulty of actually drawing the sample.

The single most important factor in determining the size of sample needed for estimating a parameter of a population is the size of the population variance. The greater the dispersion or variance in the population, the larger the sample must be to provide a given estimation precision. For example, if we were asking opinions on a particular topic and everyone in the population held the same view, then a sample of one gives the complete picture of population opinion. If there are two different opinions possible, it takes a minimum of two in the sample to register them and it takes a larger sample to estimate the relative frequency of the two views in the population. If there are a dozen possible views, an even larger sample is needed to register them and estimate their frequency.

Just how large a sample Dick and Fred need for their dining club study depends upon how much precision they wish to secure. Since a sample can never reflect its population for certain, the researchers must determine how much precision they need. Precision is measured in terms of (1) interval range in which they would expect to find the parameter estimate; and (2) the degree of confidence they wish to have in the estimate. More on these items later.

The size of the probability sample needed can be affected by the size of population, but only when the sample size is large relative to the size of the population. This so-called "finite adjustment factor" enters the calculation when the sample is 5 percent or more of the population. The net effect of the adjustment is to reduce the size of sample needed to achieve a given precision.

Other considerations often weigh heavily upon the sample size decision. The conditions under which the sample is being conducted may indicate that only certain designs are feasible. For example, one type of sample may be the appropriate design because we have no lists of population elements and must therefore sample geographic units. Since various designs have differing statistical and economic efficiencies, the choice of design coupled with the other requirements mentioned above will also affect the size of sample.

The researcher may also be interested in making estimates concerning various subgroups of the population; then the sample must be large enough for each of these subgroups to meet the desired quality level. One achieves this in simple random sampling by making the total sample large enough to assure that each critical subgroup meets the minimum size criterion. In more complex sampling procedures, the smaller subgroups are sampled more heavily and then weighted.

Cost. Cost considerations have a major impact on decisions about the size and type of sample, as well as the data collection methods. Almost all studies have some budgetary constraint, and this can mean that a nonprobability sample must be used. Probability sample surveys incur callback costs, listing costs, and a variety of other costs which are not as important when more haphazard methods are used.

Costs often dictate the size of sample. For example, if there is a $2,000 budget for interviewing, and it costs an estimated $15 to complete a personal interview using a simple random sample, it is obvious that the sample cannot exceed 133 respondents. By changing the design to a geographic cluster sample, we might be able to reduce this to, say, $12 per interview, allowing a sample size of 167. A shift to a self-administered questionnaire might reduce costs to $8 per interview, giving a sample of 250.[6]

Cost factors may also dictate abandoning personal interviewing in favor of either telephone or mail surveys. Thus, telephone interviews might cost $4 each, allowing a sample of 500. In changing the type of data collection method, of course, the amount and type of data that can be obtained also changes.

Sampling concepts

There are a few basic concepts that everyone must understand in order to work with probability samples. Our treatment is largely intuitive, using

---

[6]All estimates of costs given here are hypothetical.

the dining club example at Big University. If the two students were to interview all of the students and employees in the defined population, asking them, "How many lunches would you eat per month at the new club?" they would get a distribution something like that shown in Part A of Figure 10–1.

The responses would range from zero to as many as 30 lunches per month, with an arithmetic mean (mu or μ) or, say, 9 per month. In addition, the students can measure the dispersion of the responses by the standard deviation (sigma or σ), also shown in Part A. However, they will not take a census and so they do not know what the mu and sigma are. Rather, they take a sample and use it to estimate the population parameters, getting something like the distribution in Part C of Figure 10–1.

Definitions of key concepts in Figure 10–1. The population distribution that will be found if one takes a census of all students concerning how many meals they would eat at the new club during a month is illustrated in Part A of the figure. Sample distribution.—If the sample is 64 students, there is a distribution of 64 frequencies of expected meals ranging from 0 meals to some number of meals reflecting high patronage. This distribution is illustrated in Part C and should approximate the same form as the population distribution. Distribution of sample means.—Assume we draw a random sample of 64 students, calculate their expected average usage, and return their names to the pool. Then draw a second and other repeated samples in the same manner, calculating a mean for each sample drawn. After calculating a number of these sample means, they can be plotted in a distribution which will approach the form of that shown in Part B.

μ = Mu, the arithmetic mean of the population member responses as to the number of meals per month that they expect to eat at the new club.

σ = The standard deviation of the population and a measure of the dispersion of individual responses about the mean.

$\overline{X}$ = The arithmetic mean of a particular sample drawn from the population.

s = The standard deviation of the particular sample drawn from the population.

$\sigma_{\bar{x}}$ = The standard error of the mean. It is a measure of dispersion of the distribution of sample means and is the standard deviation of this distribution.

Point estimate. Suppose a random sample of 64 students and employees of Big U. is asked how often lunch would be taken by them in the proposed dining room. Assume that the average answer ($\overline{X}$) is 10 lunches per person per month. This is a *point estimate* of the mean of the population for this question. If anyone asks Dick for his best estimate of the number of lunches per month that the average respondent would buy he would say, "10.0."

FIGURE 10–1   A comparison of the concepts of population distribution, sample distribution, and distribution of sample means.

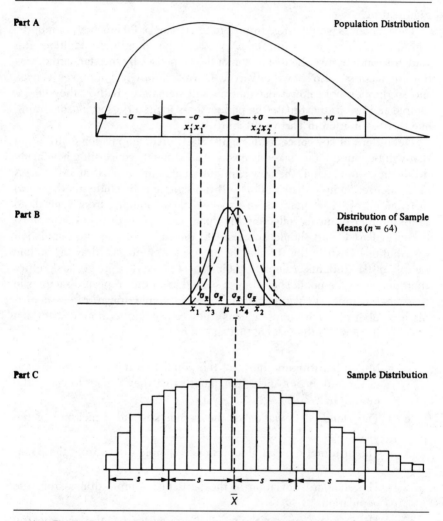

Note: The distributions in these figures are not to scale, but this fact is not critical to an understanding of the dispersion relationships depicted.

If Dick were to plot the distribution of responses from this sample, it would look like Part C of Figure 10–1. Note three points about this sample distribution. First, the sample distribution is shown as a histogram; it represents a frequency distribution of empirical data, while the smooth curve in Part A is a theoretical distribution of continuous data. Second, the sample distribution is much like the population distribution in appearance but not a perfect duplication. One would expect that it would not be; no sample is a perfect replication of its population. Third, the mean of the sample $(\overline{X})$ also differs from the mean of the population (μ). Again, this is expected because the mean of the sample is only an estimate of the population mean. The sample distribution in Part C also has its own standard deviation (here identified by s).

If Dick returns the 64 names to the pool and draws a second random sample of 64 would he get the same answer of 10.0? He might, but probably not. Suppose he gets 9.3 with the second sample of 64. If he takes yet a third sample of 64, he would probably get a different sample mean, say of 10.4, while a fourth sample might result in a mean of 8.1. Each of these is a separate point estimate of the population mean. But, you might ask, which one is the true mean? The answer is that we do not know. We can only know with certainty with a complete census.

Distribution relationships. If Dick were to draw a large number of random samples of 64, he could calculate and plot the means of each sample to secure the solid line distribution found in Part B of Figure 10–1. According to the *central limit theorem* in statistics, the sample means (or other statistics calculated from these samples) will be distributed around the population mean approximately in the form of a normal distribution. Even if the basic population is not normally distributed, the distribution of sample means will be normal if there is a large enough set of samples. We do not here go into how large is large enough, but suffice it to say that researchers generally accept and use this concept in sampling.

Understanding the relationship between the distributions in Parts A and B of Figure 10–1 is critical. First, distribution B is both more normal and has less dispersion than distribution A. This is so because the points in the population distribution represent individual responses while the points in distribution B represent means of samples (in this case means of samples of 64 responses each). Second, the dispersion of distribution B means will be narrower or wider depending on whether the sample sizes are larger or smaller, respectively.

One might guess that there is some functional relationship between a population distribution and a distribution of sample means drawn from that population. There is, and the relationship between these two distributions is critical for drawing inferences about parameters. Without going into the theory, the relationship between the dispersion of a population distribution and that of the sample mean can be stated in the following form:

$$\sigma_{\bar{x}} = \frac{\sigma}{\sqrt{n}}$$

$\sigma_{\bar{x}}$ = Standard error of the mean of a given sample size.
σ = Standard deviation of the population.
n = Sample size.

The standard error of the mean varies directly with the standard deviation of the population from which it is drawn. If the population standard deviation were smaller, say 2.0 rather than 4.0, the standard error of the mean would be only one half as large. *The standard error of the mean also varies inversely with the square root of the size of the sample.* If the square root of the sample size is doubled, the standard error is cut by one half if the standard deviation is constant. These relationships are:

A

$$\sigma_{\bar{x}} = \frac{\sigma}{\sqrt{n}}$$

C

$$\sigma_{\bar{x}} = \frac{2}{\sqrt{64}} = 0.25$$

B

$$\sigma_{\bar{x}} = \frac{4}{\sqrt{64}} = 0.5$$

D

$$\sigma_{\bar{x}} = \frac{4}{\sqrt{256}} = 0.25$$

Interval estimating. Researchers use the sample mean as a point estimate of the unknown population mean although we know that it is probably not exactly equal to the population mean. An important feature of probability sampling is that one can estimate how near the sample value probably is to the population value.

To illustrate this interval estimating feature, return to the illustration of the sample of 64. Any sample mean falls within the range of the extremes of the distribution shown in Part B of Figure 10–1. You also know that about 68 percent of the sample means in this distribution will fall between x_3 and x_4 and about 95 percent will fall within the interval ranging from x_1 to x_2.

If one projects points x_1 and x_2 up to the population distribution (Part A of Figure 10–1) at points x_1' and x_2', one sees the interval within which any given mean of a random sample of 64 is likely to fall about 95 times out of 100 samples drawn. There is about a 5-percent chance that any particular sample of 64 drawn would have a mean that falls outside the interval x_1' to x_2'.

Estimating the population mean. The only problem with using this reasoning to estimate the population mean is that it literally says the sample mean has a 95 percent chance of falling within two standard errors of the population mean. However, you do not know the population mean from which to measure the standard errors. You get around this problem by inferring that if there is a 95-percent chance that a sample mean is within two standard errors of the population mean, then there is also a 95-percent chance that the population mean is within two standard errors of a sample mean. This inference enables you to find a sample mean, mark off an interval of estimate around it, and state a confidence likelihood that the population mean is within this bracket.

In practice, one takes only one sample and calculates a mean $(\overline{X})$ of, say, 10.0 and an s of 4.1. One then infers that 10.0 is the best point estimate of the population mean and that there would be a distribution of means around this estimate. The dashed-line distribution in Part B of Figure 10–1 illustrates this distribution. The dashed-line projections from the distribution of sample means (B) to the population distribution (A) show the interval range of estimate about the sample mean. By this process, one estimates an interval range (x_1'' to x_2'') within which the population mean should fall. The point estimate of the population mean is the sample value of 10.0 times per month. Anything more about the parameter must be stated in probabilistic terms as an interval estimate.

Because Dick and Fred plan to invest heavily in this project, they would want some assurance that the population mean is close to the figure reported in any sample they take. To find out how close the population mean is to the sample mean, Dick must calculate the standard error of the mean ($\sigma_{\bar{x}}$) and estimate an interval range within which the population mean is likely to be. The basic relationship to use is:

$$\sigma_{\bar{x}} = \frac{\sigma}{\sqrt{n}}$$

Given a sample size of 64, he still needs a value for σ in order to compute $\sigma_{\bar{x}}$. Almost never will one have the value for the standard deviation of the population (σ), so we must use some proxy figure. The best proxy for σ is the standard deviation of the sample (s), in this case 4.1. Thus, the computation of the standard error of the mean is:[7]

$$\sigma_{\bar{x}} = \frac{s}{\sqrt{n-1}} = \frac{4.1}{\sqrt{63}} = \frac{4.1}{7.937} = 0.52$$

If one standard error of the mean is equal to 0.52 visits, then 1.96 standard errors are equal to 1.02 visits. That is, Dick can estimate with 95-percent confidence that the population mean of student visit expectations is within 10.0 ± 1.02 visits, or from 8.98 to 11.02 lunch visits per month.

Changing interval estimates. This estimation may not be satisfactory in two ways. First, it may not represent the degree of confidence that Dick wants in the interval estimate. For example, he might want a higher degree of confidence than the 95-percent level used here. This presents no problem. He can refer to a table of areas under the normal curve and determine various combinations of standard deviation and probabilities. The accompanying table summarizes some of those more commonly used. Thus, if he wants a greater confidence in the probability of including the population mean in the interval range he can move to a higher standard error, say, $\bar{X} \pm 3\sigma$. In this case, we would estimate that the population mean lies somewhere in the range of 10.0 ± 3(0.52) or from 8.44 to 11.56. Then 997 out of 1,000 times, he could expect this interval to include the population mean.

---

[7] To make the sample standard deviation an unbiased estimate of the population, it is necessary to divide the sample standard deviation by $\sqrt{n-1}$ rather than $\sqrt{n}$.

Standard error	Percent of area*	Approximate degree of confidence	Interval range
1.00	68.27	2 to 1	μ is between 9.48 and 10.52
1.65	90.10	9 to 1	μ is between 9.14 and 10.86
1.96	95.00	19 to 1	μ is between 8.98 and 11.02
2.00	95.45	21 to 1	μ is between 8.96 and 11.04
2.33	98.02	50 to 1	μ is between 8.78 and 11.21
3.00	99.73	270 to 1	μ is between 8.44 and 11.56

*Includes both tails in a normal distribution.

One might wish to have an estimate that will hold for a much smaller range, for example, 10.0 ± 0.2. To secure this smaller interval range of estimate, we must either (1) accept a smaller degree of confidence in the results; or (2) take a sample large enough to provide this smaller interval with adequate confidence levels.

You can calculate that if one standard error is equal to 0.52 visits, then 0.2 visits would be equal to 0.38 standard errors (0.2/0.52). If you refer to a table of area under the normal curve, we find that there is a 29.6-percent chance that the true population mean lies within a ± 0.38 standard error of 10.0.[8] That is, with a sample of 64, the sample mean would be subject to so much error variance that only 30 percent of the time could Dick expect to find the population mean between 9.8 and 10.2. This is such a small degree of confidence that he would normally move to the second alternative; he would increase the sample size until he could secure the desired interval estimate and degree of confidence.

The sample size decision

Dick Ward and Fred Thomas were meeting again to work on their dining club project. The more they thought about this idea, the more enthusiastic they became about it. On this Thursday night, they must choose the type and size of sample to take for their market survey.

Fred started off the discussion, "Look Dick, this sampling is your job, not mine. I don't know what we should do, or how big a sample we should take, but if we hope to get our financing we have to have one big enough to be convincing to the bankers. But if we take a sample larger than we need, we run up our costs."

Dick nodded in agreement, "You're right about that. I've looked at this sampling problem from several ways. If we are to do it both scientifically

---

[8] See Appendix B, Table B–1 at back of book.

and economically, we should use a simple random sample and we must take these steps:

1. Decide how to measure the precision we want.
2. Quantify this precision in terms of:
   —size of interval estimate
   —how confident we want to be of this estimate.
3. Determine the expected dispersion in the population for the questions used to measure precision.
4. Decide whether the finite population adjustment should be used.
5. Calculate the size sample needed.

How to measure precision? To measure precision, first select the key questions in the study. These are the ones whose right answers are critical to the decision. One then calculates how large a sample is needed to get adequate precision on these questions. For example, in our study, the two major questions that are really critical and for which we surely want solid numbers are:

1. What percent of the people in our population say they will join our club, based on our projected rates and services?
2. Given our price levels, how many times per month would each member patronize the club for lunch or dinner?

There are other important questions, but these two illustrate what to do.

How to quantify precision? One must make two subjective decisions in order to estimate the sample size needed. One is how much confidence to place in our population interval estimate; the other is how large this estimating interval should be. While one may think in terms of 95-percent confidence levels, this is not required. The 95-percent level is often used, but we may want more or less confidence in the estimate. You must set the level to express the degree of confidence wanted in the resulting interval estimate.

You must also decide on the size of the interval estimate in light of our particular needs. That is, take a sample to estimate a parameter for some purpose. Depending upon that purpose, choose a narrower or a wider interval. Both the degree of confidence and the desired interval of estimate are important determinants of the size of sample. They are important because they determine the standard error of the sample mean that is required to meet your needs.

What is the expected population dispersion? The next factor that affects the size of sample for a given precision is the dispersion of the population. The smaller the population dispersion, the smaller the sample needed to give a representative picture of population members. Suppose you are interested in determining the average age of a certain population. If the age ranges from 10 to 15 years, a small sample will give you a close estimate of the population's average age. If the population consists of persons ranging from less than 1 to 100 years of age, a larger sample is needed for the same degree of confidence in the estimates.

Is the finite population adjustment needed? A final factor that affects the size of a random sample is the size of the population. Where the size of the sample exceeds about 5 percent of the population, it is proper to recognize that the finite limits of the population put a constraint on the size of sample needed.

What size sample to draw? Suppose that you want to be 95-percent confident that the expected average monthly number of meals taken at the proposed campus dinner club will be within an interval of ± 0.1 meals. This means that if you take a sample of students and find the average number of expected meals to be 10.0, then you can be 95-percent confident that the entire student body average is within the range of 9.9 to 10.1 meals. This is a high degree of precision. The interval estimate of ± 0.1 meals must encompass a dispersion of ± 1.96 standard errors of the mean. Hence one standard error of the mean equals 0.051 (0.1/1.96). Assume further that you have reason to believe that you will find the sample standard deviation to equal about 4.1 meals. With these data, you can solve the sample size problem.

$$\sigma_{\bar{x}} = \frac{s}{\sqrt{n-1}} = 0.051 = \frac{4.1}{\sqrt{n-1}}$$
$$n = 6,464$$

if

± 0.1 = Desired interval within which the parameter is expected (subjective decision).

$1.96\sigma_{\bar{x}}$ = 0.95 confidence level for estimating interval within which to expect population mean (subjective decision).

$\sigma_{\bar{x}}$ = 0.051 = Standard error of the mean (0.1/1.96)

s = Standard deviation of sample (used here as estimate of population dispersion) = 4.1.

This is the appropriate sample size no matter how large the student body is if we want that high degree of precision. On the other hand, there are only 20,000 people in the population and 6,464 represents a sample of almost a third of them. Here is a case where the finite adjustment factor is called for. This adjustment corrects the sample size needed as follows:

$$\sigma_{\bar{x}} = \frac{s}{\sqrt{n-1}} \times \sqrt{\frac{N-n}{N-1}} = 0.051 = \frac{4.1}{\sqrt{n-1}} \times \sqrt{\frac{20,000-n}{20,000-1}}$$
$$n = 4,883$$

where

N = size of population
n = size of sample

Use of the finite adjustment reduces the size sample needed for a certain precision, but this reduction is insignificant unless the sample is at least 5 percent of the population.

Obviously, one does not need such precision in the mean count estimate as 0.1 meals per month per person. A more realistic estimate might be within a ± 0.5 meal. What sample size would one need to be 95 percent confident that the population mean is within a ± 0.5 meal of the sample mean?

$$\sigma_{\bar{x}} = \frac{s}{\sqrt{n-1}} = 0.256 = \frac{4.1}{\sqrt{n-1}}$$
$$n = 257$$

where

$$\sigma_{\bar{x}} = 0.256 \ (05/1.96)$$

If the finite population of 20,000 is considered, the sample size is 254 for an interval estimate of ± 0.5 meals. If we are willing to accept a ± 1 meal interval range, then an $n = 65$ is adequate.

Sampling of attributes

Up to this point, sample size needs have been discussed in terms of variables—measured as arithmetic means and standard errors of the mean. Just as often, however, one deals with attribute data. An example is when one measures the percentage of people who have a certain characteristic or feel a certain way. One of the two key questions concerning Dick and Fred's dining club study concerned: What percentage of the people in the population say they will join the dining club (based on certain projected rates and services)? This is an attribute question critical to their project decision.

Solution procedure. One chooses a sample to answer the above question using the same general procedure as before. With variables data, the measure of concern is the arithmetic mean ($\overline{X}$), while with attributes it is p (the proportion of the population that has a given attribute).[9] When the data involve variables, the population variance is measured by the standard deviation squared (σ^2), while with attributes, the variance is measured in terms of $p \times q$ (in which q is the proportion of the population not having the attribute, and $q = 1 - p$). The measure of dispersion of the sample statistic also changes from the standard error of the mean ($\sigma_{\bar{x}}$) to the standard error of the proportion (σ_p). The relationships compare as shown in the table on page 298.

Dick can calculate a sample size based on attributes data by making the subjective decisions concerning the acceptable interval estimate and the degree of confidence. Assume that 30 percent of the students say they will

---

[9] A proportion is the mean of a dichotomous variable when members of a class receive the value of 1, and nonmembers receive a value of 0.

	Variables data	Attributes data
Variance	$\sigma_{\bar{x}}^2 = \dfrac{\sigma^2}{n}$	$\sigma_p^2 = \dfrac{pq}{n}$
Standard error	$\sigma_{\bar{x}} = \dfrac{\sigma}{\sqrt{n}}$	$\sigma_p = \sqrt{\dfrac{pq}{n}}$

join the club. He decides that he wants to estimate the true proportion in the population within 10 percentage points of this figure ($p = 0.30 \pm 0.10$). Assume further that he wants to be 95-percent confident that the population parameter is within ± 0.10 of the sample proportion. The calculation of the sample size proceeds in the same manner as before:

$$\sigma_p = \sqrt{\frac{pq}{n-1}} = 0.051 = \sqrt{\frac{0.3 \times 0.7}{n-1}}$$
$$n = 82$$

± 0.10 = Desired interval range within which population proportion is expected (subjective decision).

$1.96\sigma_p$ = 0.95 confidence level for estimating interval within which to expect the population proportion (subjective decision).

σ_p = 0.051 = Standard error of the proportion (0.10/1.96)

pq = Measure of sample dispersion (used here as an estimate of population dispersion).

The sample size of 82 persons is based upon an infinite population assumption. If the sample size is less than 5 percent of the population, there is little to be gained by using the finite population adjustment.

In the examples used up to this point, the assumption is that prior information or preliminary questioning provided the variance estimate. Suppose this information is not available. Then what? With attributes data there is a feature concerning the variance that is not found with variables data. The pq ratio can never exceed 0.25. For example, if $p = 0.5$ then $q = 0.5$, and their product is 0.25. If either p or q is greater than 0.5, then their product is smaller than 0.25 (for example, $0.4 \times 0.6 = 0.24$, and so on). When we have no information regarding the probable p value, we can assume that $p = 0.5$ and solve for the sample size.

If we use the maximum variance estimate we find the sample needs to be 97.

$$\sigma_p = \sqrt{\frac{pq}{n-1}} = 0.051 = \sqrt{\frac{0.5 \times 0.5}{n-1}}$$
$$n = 97$$

The interpretation of data found with a sample of 97 chosen randomly from the student population would be: If it is found that 50 percent of the respondents say they will join the club with dues at $5 a month, then you can be 95-percent confident that, in a census, from 40 to 60 percent of all students would say they would join the club.

Actual sample precision. Suppose Dick takes a sample of 97 students and find that only 20 percent say they will join if the dues are $5 per month. Does he still estimate that the true population percentage is 0.50 ± 0.10, or does he estimate that the true percentage in the population is 0.20 ± 0.10? He does neither. He should recognize that the original variance estimate (pq) was too large; he recalculates the standard error of the percentage, using the actual sample size of 97 and the actual sample variance found. The result is:

$$\sigma_p = \sqrt{\frac{0.2 \times 0.8}{97 - 1}} = \sqrt{\frac{0.16}{96}} = \sqrt{0.001666}$$
$$\sigma_p = 0.041$$

He estimates, with a 95-percent confidence, that the population proportion falls within the range of 0.20 ± 0.08, or 12 to 28 percent.

Asymmetrical confidence regions. We have assumed thus far that confidence levels and interval ranges fall equally on both sides of a mean or proportion. Thus, we talk of a 95-percent confidence that the population proportion falls within 0.20 ± 0.08. With symmetrical confidence levels, as shown in A of Figure 10–2, we accept that there is a 0.025 chance that the population proportion is outside the estimated interval range on each tail of the distribution. However, what if Dick is only concerned about the *minimum level* of club acceptance? He can also put all of this 0.05 area in the lower tail of the distribution and ask the question, "What is the estimate of the minimum population proportion, with 95-percent confidence? This situation is illustrated in B of Figure 10–2.

FIGURE 10–2   Example of symmetrical and asymmetrical confidence regions

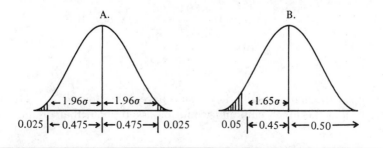

Reference to Appendix B, Table B–1 indicates that such an interval range would include 1.65 standard errors below 0.20 and all of the distribution above 0.20. Thus, we estimate, with a 95-percent confidence, that the population proportion is 0.132 or greater. In this case, the use of an asymmetrical confidence region enables us to estimate that the probable lower limit for p is 0.132 rather than 0.12.

The decision

Fred and Dick reviewed their budget estimates and the results of an exploratory survey they had taken of a few students and employees. Their budget estimates suggested that they needed to secure about $35,000 in meal revenue per month, at an average check of $3, plus another $5,000 in membership fees to make the club an attractive venture.

They agreed that the sample survey had to enable them to estimate whether or not these revenue levels could be reached. This can be done by securing answers to the two questions already used for illustrating sample size calculations. They are:

1. What percentage of the sampled say they will join the dining club if there is a $5 per month membership fee, with meal prices roughly equal to those in campus facilities?
2. Of those who say they will join, how many meals a month will they buy?

In an exploratory survey, Fred and Dick found only 10 percent who said they would join. Of those, the average meal use was estimated at 10 per month with a standard deviation of 4.1. Using these data, and other assumptions needed, Dick calculated the following sample size requirement:

Assume $p = .10$

Choose a 95-percent confidence level.

Interval estimate—one tailed test of .03. (That is, if they find $p = .10$, then they can be 95 percent confident that the population p is .07 or greater.)

$$\sigma_p = \sqrt{\frac{p \times q}{n - 1}} = .03/1.65 = \sqrt{\frac{.1 \times .9}{n - 1}}$$

$$018.18 = \sqrt{\frac{.09}{n - 1}}$$

$$n = 273$$

If they get the above results they would have 27 persons (273 × .10) who want to join the lunch club and would be asked about their frequency of use.

Assume $\overline{X} = 10$ and $s = 4.1$

Choose confidence level of 95 percent.

Interval estimate—one tailed test.

$$\sigma_{\bar{x}} = \frac{s}{\sqrt{n-1}} = \frac{4.1}{\sqrt{26}} = 0.8$$

I.E. $= 1.65 \times 0.8 = 1.3$

Lower limit $= 10 - 1.3 = 8.7$ (that is, if they find that the average number of meals is 10, with an $s = 4.1$, then they can be 95 percent confident that the population average is at least 8.7 meals per month).

The two students conclude that their figures look good. They can take a sample of 273 persons, randomly drawn from the latest university directory. If they find the expected 10 percent who say they will join, they can be confident that the population percentage is at least 7 percent or 1,400 (.07 $\times$ 20,000). If the subsample of 27 report expected usage of 10 times per month they can be confident that the population will report an expected usage of at least 8.7 times per month. These estimates would result in a revenue total of $43,453 per month or more than their projected need.

$$1400 \times \$5 \text{ per month} = 7,000$$
$$1400 \times \$3 \times 8.7 \text{ meals} = \underline{36,540}$$
$$\text{Total} \qquad\qquad\quad 43,540$$

One final point is that they may want to increase the sample size somewhat to give themselves a margin for error. For example, if the variance is actually larger than they expect, then their sample should be larger than that calculated. Just how much to increase sample size is a matter of judgment.

Summary

Sampling is based on two premises. One is that there is enough similarity among the elements in a population that a few of these elements will adequately represent the characteristics of the total population. The second premise is that while some elements in a sample underestimate a population value, others overestimate this value. The result of these tendencies is that a sample statistic such as the arithmetic mean is generally a good estimate of a population mean.

A good sample has both accuracy and precision. An accurate sample is one in which there is little or no bias or systematic variance. A sample with adequate precision is one that has an error variance of sampling error that is within acceptable limits for the study's purpose.

There are a variety of sampling techniques available. They may be classified by their representation basis and element selection techniques as shown in the accompanying table.

| | Representation basis | |
Element selection	Probability	Nonprobability
Unrestricted	Simple random	Convenience
Restricted	Complex random	Purposive
	Systematic	Judgment
	Cluster	Quota
	Stratified	
	Double	

Probability sampling is based on the concept of random selection—a controlled procedure that assures that each population element is given a known nonzero chance of selection. In contrast, nonprobability selection is "not random." When each sample element is drawn individually from the population at large, it is unrestricted sampling. Restricted sampling covers those forms of sampling in which the selection process follows more complex rules.

The simplest type of probability approach is simple random sampling. In this design, each member of the population has an equal chance of being included in a sample. In developing a probability sample, there are five procedural questions that need to be answered:

1. What is the relevant population?
2. What type of sample shall we draw?
3. What sampling frame shall we use?
4. What are the parameters of interest?
5. What size sample is needed?

In probability sampling, we make two kinds of estimates of a population parameter. First, you make a point estimate, which is the single best estimate of the population value. In addition, you make an interval estimate which covers the range of values within which you expect the population value to be, with a given degree of confidence. All sample-based estimates of population parameters should be stated in terms of such an interval with its attendant probability value.

The size of a probability sample is determined by the specifications of the researcher and the nature of the population. These requirements are largely expressed in the following four questions:

1. What is the degree of confidence we want in our parameter estimate?
2. How large an interval range will we accept?

3. What is the degree of variance in the population?
4. Is the population small enough that the sample should be adjusted for finite population?

Cost considerations are also often incorporated into the sample size decision.

Nonprobability sampling also has some compelling practical advantages that account for its widespread use. Often probability sampling is not feasible because the population is not available. Then, too, there are frequent breakdowns in the application of probability sampling that can vitiate its technical advantages. You find also that a true cross-section is often not the aim of the researcher, who may be seeking only some general idea of the range of conditions, and this limited objective does not require probability sampling. Finally, nonprobability sampling tends to be much less expensive to conduct than does probability sampling.

Convenience samples are the simplest and least reliable forms of sampling. About their only virtue is relatively low cost. One type of purposive sample is the judgmental sample in which one is interested in studying only selected types of subjects. The other type of purposive sampling is the quota sample. This can be the most sophisticated type of nonprobability sampling. Subjects are selected to conform to certain predesignated control measures to secure a representative cross-section of the population.

SUPPLEMENTAL READINGS

1. Deming, W. E. *Sample Design in Business Research*. New York: John Wiley & Sons, 1960. A classic by an author who has long been one of the major authorities on sampling.
2. Green, Paul, and Donald Tull. *Research for Marketing Decisions*. 4th ed. Englewood Cliffs, N.J.: Prentice Hall, 1978. Good discussion of both classical and Bayesian sampling.
3. Kish, Leslie. *Survey Sampling*. New York: John Wiley & Sons, 1965. A widely read basic reference on survey sampling.
4. Namias, Jean. *Handbook of Selected Sample Surveys in the Federal Government*. New York: St. John's University Press, 1969. A unique collection of illustrative uses of sampling for surveys carried out by various federal agencies. Of interest both for the sampling designs presented and the information on the methodology used to develop various government statistical data.
5. Sudman, Seymour. *Applied Sampling*. New York: Academic Press, 1976. An excellent source for procedures that are practical applications of probability techniques. Especially useful for students and nonexpert samplers.

DISCUSSION QUESTIONS

1. Distinguish between:
   a Statistic and parameter.
   b Sample frame and population.
   c Restricted and unrestricted sampling.

    d Standard deviation and standard error.
    e Simple random and complex random sampling.
    f Convenience and purposive sampling.
    g Sample precision and sample accuracy.
    h Systematic and error variance.
    i Variable and attribute parameters.
    j Symmetrical and asymmetrical confidence regions.
    k 0.05 and 0.01 confidence levels.

2. Under what kind of conditions would you recommend:
    a A probability sample? A nonprobability sample?
    b A simple random sample? A cluster sample? A stratified sample?
    c Using the finite population adjustment factor?
    d A disproportionate stratified probability sample?

3. You plan to conduct a survey using unrestricted sampling. What are the subjective decisions that you must make?

4. You draw a random sample of 300 employee records from the personnel file and find that the average years of service per employee is 6.3, with a standard deviation of 3.0 years.
    a What percent of the workers would you expect to have more than 9.3 years service?
    b What percent would you expect to have more than 5.0 years service?

5. Suppose you needed to interview a representative sample of undergraduate students but had concluded that there was no way to use probability sampling methods. You decide to use nonprobability methods. The university registrar can give you counts of the number of students who are freshmen, sophomores, juniors, or seniors, plus how many male and female students are in each class. How would you conduct a reasonably reliable nonprobability sample?

6. You wish to take an unrestricted random sample of undergraduate students at Cranial University to ascertain their levels of spending per month for food purchased off campus and eaten on the premises where purchased. You ask a test sample of nine students about their food expenditures and find that on

		Sample size			
		Infinite population confidence level		Finite population (N = 900) confidence level	
Standard deviation s	Desired interval range	2σ	3σ	2σ	3σ
$1,000	$300	—	—	—	—
	150	—	—	—	—
	100	—	—	—	—
$2,000	300	—	—	—	—
	150	—	—	—	—
	100	—	—	—	—

the average they report spending $20, with two thirds of them reporting spending from $10 to $30. What size sample do you think you should take? (Assume that your universe is infinite.)

7. You wish to adjust your sample calculations to reflect the fact that there are only 2,500 students in your population. How does this additional information affect your estimated sample size in question 6?

8. Suppose that you are going to take a sample survey and you want to estimate within a probable plus or minus 5 percent the proportion of people who have made a job change within the past year. What size of sample would you take if it was to be an unrestricted sample?

9. One way to visualize the relation of sample size requirements in unrestricted various combinations of four factors which affect sample size. Given the following information, calculate the sample sizes needed for the cells of the accompanying table.

APPENDIX   COMPLEX PROBABILITY SAMPLING

Simple random sampling is often impractical. For example, it requires a population list that is often not available. The use of this design may also be wasteful because it fails to use all of the information about a population; in addition the implementation of a simple random design may be expensive in time and money. These problems have led to the development of alternative designs that are superior to the simple random design in terms of statistical and/or economic efficiency.

A more efficient sample in a statistical sense is one that provides a given precision (standard error of the mean) with a smaller sample size. One achieves this largely by utilizing knowledge to stratify the population. A sample that is economically more efficient is one that provides a desired precision at a lower dollar cost. One achieves this with designs that enable you to lower the costs of data collecting, usually through reduced travel expense and interviewer time.

In the discussion that follows four alternative probability sampling approaches are considered: systematic, stratified, cluster, and double sampling.

Systematic sampling

The most widely used version of probability sampling is probably *systematic sampling*. In this approach, every *k*th element in the population is sampled, beginning a random start with an element from 1 to *k*. The major advantage of systematic sampling is its simplicity and flexibility. It is easier to instruct field workers to choose the dwelling unit listed on every *k*th line of a listing sheet than it is to use random sampling numbers tables. With systematic sampling there is no need to number the cards in a large personnel file prior to drawing a sample. Merely determine the total number of cards in the file, the sampling ratio to use, and the random start; then begin drawing a sample by choosing every kth card. Invoices or customer accounts can be sampled by using the last digit or a combination of digits of an invoice of customer account number. Time sampling is also an easy device.

While systematic sampling has some theoretical problems from a practical point of view, it is usually treated as a simple random sample. In fact, this design is statistically more efficient than a simple random sample when similar population elements are grouped on the list. This might occur if the list elements are ordered chronologically, by size, class, and so on. Under these conditions the sample approaches a proportional stratified sample. The effect of this ordering is more pronounced on the results of cluster samples than for element samples and may call for the use of a proportional stratified sampling formula.[1]

A major problem with systematic sampling is the possible periodicity in the population that parallels the sampling ratio. For example, in sampling days of the week, a one in seven sampling ratio would give biased results. A less obvious case might involve a survey in an area of apartment houses where the typical pattern is eight apartments per building. Many systematic sampling fractions, such as one in eight, could easily oversample some types of apartments and undersample others. The only protection against this is constant vigilance by the researcher.

Another type of problem may occur when there is a monotonic trend in the population elements. That is, the population list varies from the smallest to the largest element or vice versa. Even a chronological list may have this effect if a measure has trended in one direction over time. Whether a systematic sample drawn under these conditions provides a biased estimate of the population mean depends upon the initial random draw. Assume that a list of 2,000 commercial banks is created, arrayed from largest to smallest, from which a sample of 50 must be drawn for analysis. A sampling ratio of 1 to 20 and begun with a random start at 16 and drawing every 20th bank after that would exclude the 15 largest banks and would give a downward size bias to the findings. There are ways to deal with this. One might randomize the population before sampling, change the random start several times in the sampling process, or replicate a selection of different samples.

Stratified sampling

Most populations can be segregated into a number of mutually exclusive subpopulations, or *strata*. For example, university students can be divided by their class level, school, sex, and so forth. After a population is divided into the appropriate strata, a simple random sample can be taken within each stratum. The sampling results can then be weighted and combined into appropriate population estimates.

---

[1]Leslie Kish, *Survey Sampling* (New York: John Wiley & Sons, Inc., 1965), p. 118.

Why stratify? There are three reasons why a researcher chooses a stratified random sample. They are to (1) increase a sample's statistical efficiency; (2) provide adequate data for analyzing the various subpopulations; and (3) enable different research methods and procedures to be used in different strata.[2]

Stratification is almost always more efficient statistically than simple random sampling and at worst is equal to it. With the ideal stratification, each stratum is homogeneous internally and heterogeneous with other strata. This might occur in a sample that includes members of several distinct ethnic groups. In such a case, stratification makes a pronounced improvement in statistical efficiency.

Stratification is also useful when the researcher wants to study the characteristics of certain population subgroups. Thus, if one wishes to draw some conclusions about activities in the different classes of a student body, it would be useful to sample on a stratified basis.

Stratification is also useful when different methods of observation, sampling, or data collection are called for in different parts of the population. This might occur when we survey company employees at the home office with one method, but must use a different approach with employees scattered over the country.

How to stratify? Assuming that data are available on which to base a stratification decision, how shall one go about it?[3] There are three major decisions that must be made:

1. What stratification base or bases to use?
2. How many strata to use?
3. What strata sample sizes to draw?

The ideal stratification would be based on the principal variable under study. For example, if the major concern is to learn how many times per month students would use the dining club, then one would like to stratify on this expected number of use occasions. The only difficulty with this idea is that if one had this information, one would not need to do the study. We must, therefore, pick a variable for stratifying what we believe will correlate with the frequency of club use per month.

However, researchers often have several principal variables about which we want to draw conclusions. A reasonable approach to this problem is to seek some basis for stratification that correlates well with the major variables. It might be a single variable (class level) or it might be compound (class, by sex). In any event, you will have done a good stratifying job if the stratification base maximizes the difference among strata means and minimizes the within-stratum variances for the variables of major concern.

---

[2]Kish, *Survey Sampling*, pp. 76–77.

[3]Typically statification is carried out prior to the actual sampling but when this is not possible, it is still possible to post-stratify. Ibid., p. 90.

How many strata to use? There is no precise answer to this question, but theoretically the more strata, the closer you are likely to come to maximizing interstrata differences and minimizing intrastratum variances. You must base the decision partially on the number of subpopulation groups about which you wish to draw separate conclusions. Costs of stratification also enter into the decision. Cochran suggests that there is little to be gained in estimating overall population values when the number of strata exceeds six.[4]

What strata sample sizes to draw? The answer to this question falls in two areas. First is the matter of how large the total sample should be; the second question is how the total sample shall be allocated among strata. Answers to each of these questions depend on the answer to the other. For example, in deciding how to allocate a total sample among various strata, there are several alternatives—use either a proportionate or a disproportionate sample; if disproportionate, then is it based upon some optimization scheme, or is it primarily reflecting the need to have adequate coverage of various strata? We consider several of these variations.

Proportionate sampling. Common sense suggests that each stratum is properly represented if the sample drawn from it is in proportion to the stratum's share of the total population. This approach is more popular than any other stratified sampling procedure. Proportionate sampling will generally have higher statistical efficiency than will a simple random sample. The method is also much easier to carry out than other stratifying methods. A third advantage is that such a sampling procedure provides a self-weighting sample; the population mean can be estimated simply by calculating the mean of all sample cases. On the other hand, proportionate stratified samples will often gain little in statistical efficiency if the strata means and variances are somewhat similar for the major variables under study.

Disproportionate sampling. Any stratification that departs from the proportionate relationships is obviously disproportionate. There may be a large number of disproportionate allocation schemes. One type might be a judgmentally determined disproportion based upon each stratum being large enough to secure adequate confidence levels and interval range estimates for individual strata.

The logic of disproportionate sampling, however, usually is determined by three factors which affect how a sample will be allocated among strata. Cochran points out that

> In a given stratum, take a larger sample if
> 1. The stratum is larger.
> 2. The stratum is more variable internally.
> 3. Sampling is cheaper in the stratum.[5]

---

[4]W. G. Cochran, *Sampling Techniques*, 2d ed. (New York: John Wiley & Sons, 1963), p. 134.

[5]Cochran, *Sampling Techniques*, p. 96.

If one uses these suggestions as a guide it is possible to develop an optimal stratification scheme. When there is no difference in within-stratum variances and when the costs of sampling among strata are equal, this optimal design is a proportionate sample.

While disproportionate sampling is theoretically superior, there is some question as to whether it has wide applicability in a practical sense. If the differences in sampling costs or variances among strata are large then disproportionate sampling is desirable. Kish suggests that "differences of several-fold are required to make disporportionate sampling worth-while."[6]

The allocation problem. We can illustrate the differences in allocaton between proportionate and disproportionate samples by assuming that we take a sample of 226 students in the dining club study. Assume further that we take an exploratory sample and from this have estimated the means and standard deviations for the five strata as shown in Table 10A–1. These figures show substantial differences among classes, and suggest that disproportionate sampling might be more efficient. The allocation scheme to be used under assumptions both of proportionate and disproportionate sampling is now determined.

TABLE 10A–1   Average expected club usage per month

	Population N	Mean $\bar{X}$	Standard deviation s
Freshman	4,000	4	1.6
Sophomore	4,000	5	2.0
Junior	3,600	9	4.4
Senior	3,400	10	4.8
Graduate	5,000	12	6.0

In proportionate sampling the allocation among the five strata should satisfy the following equalities:[7]

$$\frac{n_1}{N_1} = \frac{n_2}{N_2} = \cdots = \frac{n_s}{N_s}$$

where

n_1 = Sample size in stratum 1.

N_1 = Population size in stratum 1.

---

[6]Kish, *Survey Sampling*, p. 94.

[7]Robert Ferber, *Statistical Methods in Market Research* (New York: McGraw-Hill, 1949), p. 75.

In disproportionate sampling the sample size for each stratum should be weighted by the stratum variance to satisfy the following equalities:

$$\frac{n_1}{N_1\sigma_1} = \frac{n_2}{N_2\sigma_2} = \cdots = \frac{n_s}{N_s\sigma_s}$$

where

σ_1 = Standard deviation of stratum 1.

In cost optimal disproportionate allocation, the size of the sample from each stratum should be weighted by the stratum variance as well as the cost of sampling and data gathering in that stratum to satisfy the following equalities:

$$\frac{n_1}{N_1\sigma_1 \sqrt{C_1}} = \frac{n_2}{N_2\sigma_2 \sqrt{C_2}} = \cdots = \frac{n_s}{N_s\sigma_s \sqrt{C_s}}$$

where

C_1 = Cost associated with data gathering in stratum 1.

TABLE 10A–2   Stratified sampling allocation for dining club study

	(1) Popu-lation relative W_i	(2) S_i	(3) W_iS_i	(4) $\sqrt{C_i}$	(5) $W_iS_i/\sqrt{C_i}$	(6) Propor-tionate	(7) Sample allocation Dis-propor-tionate	(8) Cost optimal
Freshman	0.20	1.6	0.320	2.0	0.16	45	19	22
Sophomore	0.20	2.0	0.400	2.0	0.20	45	23	28
Junior	0.18	4.4	0.792	2.449	0.3234	41	47	45
Senior	0.17	4.8	0.816	2.449	0.3332	38	48	46
Graduate	0.25	6.0	1.500	2.449	0.6125	57	89	85
Total	1.00		3.828		1.6291	226	226	226

Proportionate:
$n_i = W_iN$
$n_1 = W_1N = 0.20(226) \doteq 45$

Disporportionate:
$n_i = \dfrac{W_i\sigma_i}{\Sigma(W_i\sigma_i)} N$
$n_i = \dfrac{0.320}{3.828} (226) \doteq 19$

Cost Optimal:
$n_i = \dfrac{W_i\sigma_i/\sqrt{C_i}}{\Sigma(W_i\sigma_i/\sqrt{C_i})}$
$n_i = \dfrac{0.16}{1.6291} (226) \doteq 22$

Given the assumed data in Table 10A–1, the above relationships, and an expected survey cost in the freshman and sophomore strata of $4 per interview and a $6 cost in the other strata, the sample of 226 would be allocated as shown in Table 10A–2.

The results from Table 10A–2 indicate that the differences in strata variance are indeed large enough to affect allocations. Samples of the freshman and sophomore classes are reduced by one half or more by disproportionate sampling. The introduction of cost differences does not have much effect in this case. At first glance it might appear that the disproportionate samples are sometimes too small to draw class conclusions. However, calculation will show that the various stratum standard errors of the mean are more equal with the disproportionate than with the proportionate sample.

Total sample size. In the above example, the sample size was set at 226, but how was this obtained? Following the procedures described earlier, the

---

TABLE 10A–3 Stratified sample calculation for dining club study

	W_i	s_i^2	$W_i s_i^2$	$\bar{X}_i$	$(\bar{X}_i - \bar{X})^2$	$W_i(\bar{X}_i - \bar{X})^2$
Freshman	0.20	2.56	0.512	4	16.9744	3.39488
Sophomore	0.20	4.00	0.800	5	9.7344	1.94688
Junior	0.18	19.36	3.485	9	0.7744	0.13939
Senior	0.17	23.04	3.917	10	3.5344	0.60085
Graduate	0.25	36.00	9.000	12	15.0544	3.76360
Total	1.00		17.714			9.84560

$\bar{X} = \Sigma(W_i \bar{X}_i) = .8 + 1.0 + 1.62 + 1.7 + 3.0 = 8.12$

Disproportionate Sample:

$1.96\sigma_{\bar{x}} = 0.5$

$\quad \sigma_{\bar{x}} = 0.2551$

$$\sigma_{\bar{x}}^2 = \frac{\Sigma(W_i \sigma_i)^2}{n} \doteq \frac{\Sigma(W_i s_i)^2}{n-1}$$

$0.2551^2 \doteq \dfrac{(3.828)^2}{n-1}$

$\quad n \doteq 226$

Proportionate Sample:

$$\sigma_{\bar{x}}^2 = \frac{\Sigma W_i \sigma_i^2}{n} = \frac{\Sigma W_i s_i^2}{n-1}$$

$0.2551^2 \doteq \dfrac{17.714}{n-1}$

$\quad n \doteq 273$

Simple Random Sample:

$$\sigma_{\bar{x}}^2 = \frac{\Sigma W_i \sigma_i^2 + \Sigma W_i(\bar{X}_i - \bar{X})^2}{n} \doteq \frac{\Sigma W_i s_i^2 + \Sigma W_i(\bar{X}_i - \bar{X})^2}{n-1}$$

$0.2551^2 \doteq \dfrac{17.714 + 9.8456}{n-1}$

$\quad n \doteq 424$

researcher makes subjective decisions about the interval estimate and the level of confidence desired. Assume a 0.95 level of confidence with a total sample interval estimate of 0.5 visits per month. Given these requirements, and the calculations in Table 10A–3, the sample size is determined as shown. With the disproportionate approach, a sample of 226 is needed, while to secure the same precision calls for a proportionate sample of 273 and a simple random sample of 424.

It is clear in this case that stratification is more efficient than simple random sampling, and disproportionate stratified sampling is 21 percent more efficient than proportionate sampling. These results are secured because both of the means and the variances of the strata are substantially different.

Cluster sampling

In a simple random sample, each population element is selected individually. The entire population can also be divided into groups of elements and some of the groups for study randomly selected. This is *cluster sampling*. An immediate question might be: How does this differ from stratified sampling? They may be compared as follows:

Stratified sampling	*Cluster sampling*
1. We divide the population into a few subgroups, each with many elements in it. The subgroups are selected according to some criterion that is related to the variables under study.	1. We divide the population into many subgroups, each with a few elements in it. The subgroups are selected according to some criterion of ease or availability in data collection.
2. We try to secure homogeneity within subgroups and heterogeneity between subgroups.	2. We try to secure heterogeneity within subgroups and homogeneity between subgroups, but we usually get the reverse.
3. We randomly choose elements from within each subgroup.	3. We randomly choose a number of the subgroups which we then typically study in toto.

If properly done, cluster sampling also provides an unbiased estimate of population parameters. Two major problems foster the use of cluster sampling: (1) the need for more economic efficiency than can be provided by simple element sampling; and (2) the frequent unavailability of a practical sampling frame for individual elements.

Cluster efficiency. Statistical efficiency for cluster samples is usually lower than for simple random samples, chiefly because clusters tend to be homogeneous. Families in the same block (a typical cluster) tend to be similar in social class, income level, ethnic origin, and so forth. Thus, additional interviews in such a cluster provide less information about the population than a cluster that is more heterogeneous.

While statistical efficiency in most cluster sampling may be low, economic efficiency is often great enough to overcome this weakness. The criterion, then, is the *net relative efficiency* resulting from the tradeoff between economic and statistical factors. For example, it may take 690 interviews with a cluster design to give the same precision as 424 simple random interviews. But if it costs only $2 per interview in the cluster situation and $4 in the simple random case, it is obvious that the cluster sample is more attractive.

Area sampling. Much research involves populations that can be identified with some geographic area. When this occurs, it is possible to use *area sampling*, the most important form of cluster sampling. This method meets both the problems of high sampling cost and the unavailability of a practical sampling frame for individual elements. Area sampling methods have been applied to national populations, county populations, and even smaller areas where there are well-defined political or natural boundaries.

Suppose that you want to survey the adult residents of a city. You would seldom be able to secure a listing of such individuals. It would be relatively easy, however, to get a detailed city map which shows the blocks of the city. If you take a sample of these blocks, you are also taking a sample of the adult residents of the city, because as the saying goes, "Everybody has to be someplace."

Cluster design. In designing cluster samples, including area samples, there are a number of questions which must be answered. While these questions are interrelated, they are discussed separately:

1. How homogeneous are the clusters?
2. Shall we seek equal or unequal clusters?
3. How large a cluster shall we take?
4. Shall we use single-stage or multi-stage clusters?
5. How large a sample is needed?

1. Clusters tend to be homogeneous in many internal characteristics and this contributes to low statistical efficiency. One sometimes can improve this efficiency by constructing clusters in such a way as to increase intracluster variance. For example, in the dining club study, Dick and Fred might construct clusters that would include members from all classes. In area sampling, they might combine contiguous blocks that contain different income groups or social classes. Area cluster sections do not have to be contiguous but much of the cost savings are lost if they are not near each other.

2. A cluster sample may be composed of clusters of equal or unequal size. The theory of clustering is that the means of sample clusters are unbiased estimates of the population mean. This is more often true when clusters are equal. It is often possible to construct artificial clusters that are approximately equal, but natural clusters, such as households in city blocks, often vary substantially. While one can deal with clusters of unequal size, it may be desirable to reduce or counteract the effects of unequal size. There are several approaches to this.

One way to overcome the wide variation in cluster size is to combine small clusters and split large clusters until all approximate an average size. A second approach is to stratify clusters by size and choose clusters from each stratum. A third approach is size-stratified subsampling in which clusters are stratified by size and then subsampled, using varying sampling fractions to secure an overall sampling ratio. For example, one may seek an overall sampling fraction of 1/60 and desire that subsamples be about five elements each. One group of clusters might average about 10 elements per cluster. In the "10 elements per cluster" stratum you might choose 1 in 30 of the clusters, and then subsample each chosen cluster at 1/2 rate to secure the overall 1/60 sampling fraction. Among clusters of 120 elements, you might select clusters as a 1/3 rate and then subsample at a 1/20 rate to secure the 1/60 sampling fraction.[8]

3. The third question concerns the size of cluster. There is no a priori answer to this question. Even with single-stage clusters, say, of 5, 20, or 50, it is not clear which size is superior. Some have found that, in studies using single-stage clusters, the optimal cluster size tends to be no larger than the typical city block.[9] To compare the efficiency of the above three cluster sizes requires that one determines the different costs for each size and estimates the different variances of the cluster means.

4. The fourth question concerns whether to use a single-stage or a multi-stage cluster design. For most area sampling, especially large-scale studies, the tendency is to use multi-stage methods. Kish expresses the case well when he writes,

> There are four reasons that justify subsampling, in preference to the direct creation of smaller clusters and their selection in one-stage cluster sampling:
>
> (1) *Natural clusters* may exist as convenient sampling units, yet larger than the desired economic size . . . , (2) We can *avoid the cost of creating smaller clusters* in the entire population and confine it to the selected sampling units . . . , (3) The *effect of clustering* . . . is often less in larger clusters. For example, a compact cluster of four dwellings from a city block may bring into the sample similar dwellings, perhaps from one building; but four dwellings selected separately can be spread around the dissimilar sides of the block. (4) The sampling of *compact clusters may present practical difficulties*. For example, independent interviewing of all members of a household may seem impractical.[10]

5. How large a sample is needed? That is, how many subjects must be interviewed or observed? The answer to this question depends heavily upon

---

[8] For detailed treatment of these and other cluster sampling methods and problems, see Kish, *Survey Sampling*, pp. 148–247.

[9] J. H. Lorie, and H. V. Roberts, *Basic Methods of Marketing Research* (New York, McGraw-Hill, 1951), p. 120.

[10] Kish, *Survey Sampling*, p. 156.

the specific cluster design and these details can be complicated. Unequal clusters and multi-stage samples are the chief complications and their statistical treatment is beyond the scope of this book.[11] Here we will treat only single-stage samples with equal-size clusters (hereafter referred to as *simple cluster sampling*). It is analogous to simple random sampling.

The simple random sample is really a special case of simple cluster sampling. That is, one can think of a population as consisting of 20,000 clusters of one student each, or 2000 clusters of 10 students each, and so on. *The only difference between a simple random and a simple cluster sample is the size of cluster.* Since this is so, one should expect that the calculation of a probability sample size would be the same for both types. This is basically true; the only changes that one must make are to take into account that the number of elements in a cluster may vary.

You have calculated that a simple random sample of 424 individual students (that is, clusters of one) provides a 95 percent confidence that an estimate of expected monthly student visits to the club would be within ± 0.5. The task now is to estimate how many clusters, say of 10 elements each, must be studied to give a similar precision. Determine the number of clusters of 10 as follows.[12]

$$\sigma_{\bar{x}} = \frac{\sigma_c}{\sqrt{m}}$$

where

σ_c = The standard deviation of cluster means.

m = The number of sample clusters.

One should expect that the population standard deviation will be smaller for clusters of 10 than for clusters of one; just how much smaller depends upon the size of the clusters and the degree of homogeneity within the clusters.

An example. Consider again the dining club problem. Assume that all students must go through a registration at the beginning of the semester at a specific location. Assume further that you can conveniently sample them there in groups of 10, and that this procedure will cost only $2 per completed questionnaire, compared to $4 for a simple random sample. Would it be better to use cluster sampling or simple random sampling, assuming the same precision requirements?

You must first estimate the standard deviation of the means of clusters of 10 in the population. Since all classes register at the same time, these clusters of 10 should have more heterogeneity in them—and more homo-

---

[11]For specifics on these problems and how to solve them, the reader is referred to the many good sampling texts. Two that have already been mentioned are Kish, *Survey Sampling*, chapters 5, 6, and 7, and Cochran, *Sampling Techniques*, chapters 9, 10, and 11.

[12]In this discussion, we ignore the finite population correction, although it is more often needed in cluster than in simple random sampling.

geneity between clusters than is often the case. A small test sample might indicate that standard deviation of clusters of 10 may be about 2.1. With this information, plus the already-determined precision requirements, you can compute that you will need 69 clusters of 10 students each.

$$\sigma_{\bar{x}} = \frac{\sigma_c}{\sqrt{m}} = \frac{s_c}{\sqrt{m-1}}$$

$$0.2551 = \frac{2.1}{\sqrt{m-1}}$$

$$m = 69 \text{ clusters}$$

This would mean that a sample of 690 students, taken in clusters of 10, provides the precision of a simple random sample of 424. While the cluster sample requires 266 more interviews, it provides a cost saving of $316. The cluster sample has greater economic efficiency.

Double sampling

It may be more convenient or economical to collect some information by sample and then use this information as the basis for selecting a subsample for further study. This procedure is called *double sampling*, sequential sampling, or multiphase sampling. It is usually found in conjunction with stratified and/or cluster designs, and the calculation procedures are somewhat complicated and beyond the scope of this chapter.

Double sampling can be illustrated by the dining club example. You might use a telephone survey or some other inexpensive survey method to determine (1) the students interested in joining such a club, and (2) the degree of their interest. You might then stratify the interested respondents by degree of interest and subsample among them for intensive interviewing on expected consumption patterns, reactions to various service patterns, and so on. Whether it is more desirable to gather such information by one-stage or two-stage sampling depends largely upon the relative costs of the two methods.

ANALYSIS AND REPORTING

11. Elements of analysis

Once the field data begin to flow in, the attention is turned to data analysis. Actually, if the project has been done correctly, most of the analysis planning has already been done. Back in the research design stage, decisions should have been made about how to analyze the expected data. Dummy tables should have been set up in which to record the data. In spite of the logic of this approach, many researchers wait until the analysis stage to plan what to do. The flaw in this timing is the frequent discovery, too late, that some data were not collected, or collected in the wrong format for analysis.

This chapter is concerned with three major topics. First is *data preparation*, which includes the processes of editing, coding, and tabulation. These are activities to assure (1) the accuracy of data and (2) its conversion from raw form to classified and/or reduced forms more appropriate for the analysis and interpretation stages. Second, *analysis* involves breaking down and rearranging data into more meaningful groups to aid the search for significant relationships. A third topic, interpretation, somewhat overlaps analysis but is more concerned with drawing inferences from the study data using other information, hypotheses, and theories. The discussion here deals largely with data preparation and analysis.

DATA PREPARATION

Editing

The customary first step in analysis is to edit the raw data. One edits to detect errors and omissions, correct them when possible, and in other ways assure that minimum data quality standards are achieved. One edits to assure that the data are (1) accurate; (2) consistent with other information; (3) uniformly entered; (4) complete; and (5) arranged to facilitate coding and tabulation.

Field editing. During the stress of data collection, the interviewer often uses ad hoc abbreviations, special symbols, and the like. As soon as possible after an interview, field workers should review their reporting forms, complete what was abbreviated, translate personal shorthand, and rewrite illegible entries. Where needed to fill gaps, a callback should be made rather than guessing what the respondent "probably would have said." Such self-interviewing has no place in quality research.

In large projects, field editing review is a responsibility of the field supervisor. It, too, should be done as soon as possible after the data have been gathered. A second important control function of the field supervisor is to validate the field results. This normally means that he or she will reinterview some percentage of the respondents, at least on some of the major questions. Many commercial research firms will recontact 10 percent or so of the respondents.

Central editing. At this point, the research form should get a thorough editing. For a small study, the use of a single editor assures maximum consistency of work. In larger studies, the tasks may be broken down so that each editor can deal with one entire section. This approach will not identify inconsistencies between answers in different sections. However, this problem can be handled by identifying points of possible inconsistency and having one editor check specifically for them.

In some cases, it is obvious that an entry is incorrect, entered in the wrong place, or states time in months when it was requested in weeks. When replies clearly are inappropriate or missing, the editor can sometimes determine the proper answer by reviewing the other information in the schedule. This practice, however, should be limited to those few cases where it is obvious what the correct answer is. It may be better to contact the respondent for correct information, if time and budget permit. Another alternative is for the editor to strike out the answer if it is clearly inappropriate. Here an editing entry of "no answer" or "unknown" is called for.

Another editing problem concerns faking. Interviewer cheating can be a big problem. Arm-chair interviewing is difficult to spot, but the editor is in the best position to do so. One approach is to check responses to open-end questions. These are more difficult to fake. Distinctive response patterns in other questions will often emerge if faking is taking place. To uncover this, the editor must analyze the interview schedules by interviewer.

Some useful rules to guide editors in their work are:

1. Be familiar with instructions given to interviewers and coders.
2. Do not destroy, erase, or make illegible the original entry by the interviewer. Original entries should be crossed out with a single line so as to remain legible.
3. Make all entries on a schedule in some distinctive color and in a standardized form.
4. Initial all answers changed or supplied.
5. Place initials and date of editing on each schedule completed.

Coding

You code when you assign numerals or other symbols to answers so as to enable the responses to be grouped into a limited number of classes or categories. This classifying of data into a limited number of categories sacrifices some data detail but is necessary for efficient analysis. By this method, several thousand replies can be reduced to a few categories which contain the critical information needed for analysis. *A category is a partition of a set; and categorization is the process of using a set of rules to partition a body of data.* Four major rules should guide the establishment of category sets. Categories should be:

1. Appropriate to the research problem and purpose.
2. Exhaustive.
3. Mutually exclusive.
4. Derived from one classification principle.

Appropriateness. Categories must provide the best partitioning of data for testing hypotheses and showing relationships. Year-by-year age differences may be important to the question being researched. If so, wider age classifications hamper our analysis. If specific income, attitude, or reasons why categories are critical to the testing relationships, then we must assure that the best groupings are chosen. In particular, choose frequency class boundaries that match those being used for comparisons. It is disheartening, late in a study, to discover that age, income, or other frequency classes do not precisely match those of data with which we wish to make comparisons.

Exhaustiveness. If there are a large number of "other" responses, it indicates that our classificaton set may be too limited. In such cases, we may not be tapping the full range of information in the data. Failure to present an adequate list of alternatives is especially damaging when multiple-choice questions are used. Any answer that is not specified in the set will surely be underrepresented in the tally.

While the exhaustiveness requirement in a single category set may be obvious, there is a second aspect which is less apparent. Does the one set of categories fully capture all of the information in the data? For example, responses to an open-ended question about family economic prospects for the next year may originally be classified only in terms of being optimistic or pessimistic. It may also be enlightening to classify responses in terms of other concepts such as the precise nature of these expectations (income, jobs, or what), variations in responses between family heads and others in the family.

Mutual exclusivity. Another important rule is that category components should be mutually exclusive. This standard is met when a specific answer can be placed in one and only one cell in a category set. For example, in an occupation survey, the classifications may be (1) professional; (2) managerial; (3) sales; (4) clerical; (5) crafts; (6) operatives; and (7) unemployed. Some respondents will think of themselves as being in more than one of these groups. The man who views selling as a profession and who spends part of his time supervising others may feel that he fits under three of these categories. One of the functions of operational definitions is to provide categories that are composed of mutually exclusive elements. In this case operational definitions of the occupations to be classified under "professional," "managerial," and "sales" should clarify the situation. The problem of how to handle an unemployed salesman brings up a fourth rule of category design.

Single dimension. The need for a category set to follow a single classificatory principle means that every class in the category set is defined in terms of one concept. Returning to the occupation survey example, the man in the study might be both a salesman and unemployed. The "salesman" label expresses the concept of an *occupation type*, while the response "unemployed" is another dimension concerned with *current employment status* without regard to the respondent's normal occupation. When a category set employs more than one dimension it will normally not be mutually exclusive unless the cells in the set combine the dimensions (employed manager, unemployed manager, and so on).

A classification example. The problems of classification are especially marked with responses to open-end questions. Suppose the members of a factory work force are asked, "How can management-employee relations be improved?" Among the responses received from the workers might be the following:

1. Management should treat the worker with more respect.
2. Managers should stop trying to speed up the assembly line.
3. Working conditions in the shop are terrible. Managers should correct them.
4. Foreman "Z" should be fired. He is unfair in his treatment of workers.
5. Managers should form management-worker councils in the department to iron out problems and improve relations.
6. Management should stop trying to undermine union leadership.
7. Management should accept the union's latest proposals on new work rules.

In most surveys, there are many more than seven replies, but these are enough to illustrate the prolems of forming appropriate categories. First, the type of categories that are developed should reflect the objectives that the data are being collected to serve (be appropriate for the research problem and purpose). For example, the survey might be concerned largely with learning the general perceptions of the workers as to the locus or responsibility for improving company-employee relations. In this case, the categories might be as few and as general as in the table at top of next page.

This set of categories appears to be mutually exclusive and contains only one concept dimension. The provision of the "other" classification assures that the category set is exhaustive. If many responses suggest actions by the general public, government, or certain regulatory bodies, then to include all of these in "other" would ignore much of the richness of the data.

Who should initiate action?	Mentioned	Not mentioned
A. Management	_____	_____
B. Union	_____	_____
C. Worker (other than union)	_____	_____
D. Joint management-union	_____	_____
E. Joint management-workers	_____	_____
F. Other	_____	_____

If we used only the above set of categories for analysis, we would be ignoring most of the information in the answers. The comments often suggest specific actions, and most researchers would want to collect and analyze these suggestions. For this purpose the replies might be classified in terms of decision areas in which actions may be taken:

1. Human relations.
2. Production processes.
3. Working conditions.
4. Other action areas.
5. No action area mentioned.

How could we classify a response suggesting a combined production process-working condition action? This could be handled by adding combination alternatives. This decision area set of responses may also be used as subcategories under the first list, giving the accompanying joint set of classification possibilities:

	Mentioned	Not mentioned
A. Management		
1. Human relations	_____	_____
2. Production processes	_____	_____
3. Working conditions	_____	_____
4. Other action areas	_____	_____
5. No area mentioned	_____	_____
B.		
C.		
D.		
E.		
F. Other		
1. Human relations	_____	_____
2. Production processes	_____	_____
3. Working conditions	_____	_____
4. Other action areas	_____	_____
5. No area mentioned	_____	_____

Coding procedure

When codes are established early in the research process, it is possible to precode the questionnaire choices. Precoding, shown in Figure 11–1, is especially valuable for computer tabulation because one can usually key punch directly from the original questionnaires.

With hand coding, it is wise to use a standard method and code in the margin with a colored pencil. This procedure will reduce key punch and

---

FIGURE 11–1   Excerpts from a precoded questionnaire

How would you rate the *growth potential* of the following companies?
(Please check only *one* for each company.)

	Avco	Gulf + Western	Leasco	Litton	Textron
Excellent	11–1 ☐	12–1 ☐	13–1 ☐	14–1 ☐	15–1 ☐
Good	–2 ☐	–2 ☐	–2 ☐	–2 ☐	–2 ☐
Fair	–3 ☐	–3 ☐	–3 ☐	–3 ☐	–3 ☐
Poor	–4 ☐	–4 ☐	–4 ☐	–4 ☐	–4 ☐
Don't know	–5 ☐	–5 ☐	–5 ☐	–5 ☐	–5 ☐

FIGURE 11–2   Coding sheet for punch cards

Project __FSB__   __2/72__   ID __203__

Column	Code	Column	Code
1	0 ① 2 3 4 5 6 7 8 9	41	0 1 2 3 4 5 6 7 8 9
2	0 1 ② 3 4 5 6 7 8 9	42	0 1 2 3 4 5 6 7 8 9
3	0 1 2 3 ④ 5 6 7 8 9	43	0 1 2 3 4 5 6 7 8 9
4	0 1 ② 3 4 5 6 7 8 9	44	0 1 2 3 4 5 6 7 8 9
5	0 1 2 3 ④ 5 6 7 8 9	45	0 1 2 3 4 5 6 7 8 9

Column	Code	Column	Code
36	0 ① 2 3 4 5 6 7 8 9	76	0 1 2 3 4 5 6 7 8 9
37	0 1 2 3 4 5 6 7 8 9	77	0 1 2 3 4 5 6 7 8 9
38	0 1 2 3 4 5 6 7 8 9	78	0 1 ② 3 4 5 6 7 8 9
39	0 1 2 3 4 5 6 7 8 9	79	⓪ 1 2 3 4 5 6 7 8 9
40	0 1 2 3 4 5 6 7 8 9	80	0 1 2 ③ 4 5 6 7 8 9

tabulating errors, especially if the data are punched into cards directly from the questionnaire. Sometimes a safer method is to transcribe the data from the questionnaire to a coding sheet. An example of such a sheet to be used for computer tabulating is shown in Figure 11–2.

SPECIAL DATA PROBLEMS

"Don't know" responses

No matter how good a research instrument is, there are always some responses that are difficult to handle. Two common types are (1) the incorrect or incomplete answer and (2) the "don't know" (*DK*) response. The former has already been discussed in the section on editing, but the *DK* problem remains to be treated.

DK situations. When the *DK* response group is small, it is of little significance, but there are times when it is of major concern; and it may even be the most frequent response received. Does this mean that the question which elicited this response is useless? As is often true, the answer is, "It all depends." There are two categories into which most *DK* answers fall.[1] First, there is the legitimate *DK* response when the respondent actually does not know the answer and this response meets our research objectives (we expect a number of *DK* responses and consider them to be useful answers).

In the second situation, a *DK* reply illustrates the researcher's failure to get the appropriate information. Consider the following illustrative questions:

1. Who developed the Managerial Grid concept?
2. Do you believe the president's new fiscal policy is sound?
3. Do you like your present job?
4. Which of the various brands of chewing gum do you believe has the best quality?
5. How many times a year do you go to the movies?

It is reasonable to expect that some legitimate *DK* responses will be made to each of these questions. However, in the first question the respondents are asked for a level of information that they often will not have. There would seem to be little reason to withhold a correct answer if known. Thus, most *DK* answers to this question should be considered as legitimate.

DK response in the second question presents a somewhat different problem. It is not immediately clear whether the respondent is ignorant of the president's fiscal policy or knows the policy, but has not made a judgment about it. The researchers should have asked two questions: In the first, they

---

[1] Hans Zeisel, *Say It with Figures.* 4th ed. (New York: Harper & Row, 1957). p. 42.

would have determined the respondent's level of awareness of fiscal policy; if the interviewee passed the awareness test, then a second question would have secured judgment on fiscal policy.

In the remaining three questions, the *DK* response is more likely to be a failure of the questioning process, although some will surely be legitimate. The respondent may be reluctant to give the information. *DK* response to question 3 may be a way of saying, "I do not want to answer that question." Question 4 might also elicit a *DK* response in which the reply translates to, "This is too unimportant to talk about." In question 5, the respondents are being asked to do some calculation about a topic to which they attach little importance. In this case, the *DK* may mean, "I do not want to do that work for something that has so little importance."

Dealing with undesired *DK* responses. The best way to deal with undesired *DK* answers is to design better questions at the beginning. The interviewers, however, must deal with the problem in the field; prior to interviewing, they should identify the questions for which a *DK* response is unsatisfactory. Several actions are then possible. First, good interviewer-respondent rapport will motivate respondents to provide more usable answers. When interviewers recognize an evasive *DK* response, they can repeat the question or probe for a more definite answer. Finally, the interviewer may record verbatim any elaboration by the respondent and buck the problem on to the editor.

If the editor finds a number of undesired responses, he or she can do little unless the verbatim comments can be interpreted. About the only hope for understanding the real meaning rests on securing some clue from the respondent's other questions. One way to do this is to estimate the allocation of *DK* answers from other data in the questionnaire. It may be that the pattern of responses parallels the pattern of responses, say, of certain income, educational, or experience groups. For example, suppose that a question concerning whether the employee likes his present job elicited the answers in Table 11–1. The correlation between years of service and the "don't know" answers and the "no" answers would suggest that most of the "don't knows" are disguised "no" responses.

TABLE 11–1 Handling "don't know" responses

| | Do you like your present job? | | |
Years of service	Yes	No	Don't know
Less than 1 year	10%	40%	38%
1–3 years	30	30	32
4 years or more	60	30	30
Total	100%	100%	100%
n =	650	150	200

There are several ways to handle "don't know" responses in the tabulations. If there are only a few, it does not make much difference how they are handled, but they will probably be kept as a separate category. If the *DK* response is legitimate, it should remain as a separate reply category. If we are not sure how to treat it we should also keep it as a separate category and let the reader make the decision.

Another way to treat *DK* responses is to assume that they occur more or less randomly. Using this approach, we distribute them among the other answers in the same ratio that the other answers occur. This assumes that those who reply "don't know" are proportionally distributed among all of the groups studied. This can be achieved either by prorating the *DK* responses or by excluding all *DK* replies from the tabulation. The latter approach is better since it does not inflate the actual number of other responses. This proration can be risky in opinion polls, as was learned in the 1948 presidential election. The polls at that time indicated that Dewey was leading Truman but with a large *DK* opinion group. The pollsters assumed that this body of undecided voters would allocate themselves about as the decided voters had, but on election day, almost all of the uncommitted voted for Truman.

The use of percentages

Percentages serve two purposes in data presentation. They simplify by reducing all numbers to a range of from 0 to 100. Second, the use of percentages translates the data into standard form, with a base of 100, for relative comparisons. For example, in a sampling situation, the number of cases that fall into a category is meaningless unless it is related to some base. A count of 314 families with two or more autos has little meaning unless we know that this is from a total sample of 654. Using the latter as the base, we conclude that 48 percent of the families have two or more autos.

While the above calculation is useful, it is even more useful when the research problem calls for a comparison of several distributions of data. For example, assume that a similar study of auto ownership five years ago showed that 551 families out of a sample of 1,450 owned two or more autos. By using percentages, we can see the relative relationships and shifts in these data (see Table 11–2).

Tabular percentages. When two-dimension tables are used, there is a question in which direction the percentages should be calculated. Zeisel advocates the rule that "percentages should be computed in the direction of the causal factor" (use the total number of cases in each category of the independent variable as the base for calculating the percentages).[2] Thus we must decide which of the two factors will be considered to be the cause (independent variable) and which the effect (dependent variable). At times either may be considered the causal factor, although usually one is more

---

[2]Zeisel, *Say It with Figures*, p. 24.

TABLE 11–2   Percentage relationships

Family auto status	Five years ago No.	%	Today No.	%
No auto	290	20	98	15
One auto	609	42	242	37
Two or more	551	38	314	48
	1,450	100	654	100

Table 11–3   1972 unemployment in the United States by age (in thousands)

Age group	Unemployed	Employed	Total civilian labor force
16-19 years	1,017	6,158	7,175
20 years and over	2,867	66,916	69,783
Total	3,884	73,074	76,958

Source: *Monthly Labor Review* (April 1974), p. 92.

TABLE 11–4   1972 unemployment in the United States by age

Age group	Unemployed	Employed	Total civilian labor force
A.			
16–19 years	26%	8%	9%
20 years and over	74	92	91
Total	100%	100%	100%
B.			
16–19 years	14%	86%	100%
20 years and over	4	96	100
Total	5%	95%	100%

significant than the other. For example, consider the data in Table 11–3. In which direction should any calculated percentages run?

If the percentages run vertically, as in part A of Table 11–4, they imply that employment status has some effect on age. This is an illogical proposition. On the other hand, when the percentages run as shown in part B, the suggestion is that age has some effect on whether a person is employed. It is apparent from part B of Table 11–4 that the unemployment rate among the 16–19 year old group was more than three times as high, in 1972, as that of persons 20 years and older.

Problems in the use of percentages. Percentages are used by virtually everyone dealing with numbers, and in too many cases they are used incorrectly. Boyd and Westfall suggest the following rules.[3]

1. *Averaging percentages.* Percentages cannot be averaged unless each is weighted by the size of the group from which it is derived. Thus, in most cases, a simple average will not suffice and it is necessary to use a weighted average.
2. *Use of too large percentages.* This often defeats the purpose of percentages—which is to simplify. A large percentage is difficult to understand and tends to confuse. If a 1,000 percent increase is experienced, it is better to describe this as a tenfold increase.
3. *Using too small a base.* Percentages hide the base from which they have been computed. A figure of 60 percent when contrasted with 30 percent would appear to indicate a sizable difference. Yet if there are only three cases in the one category and six in the other, the differences would not be as significant as they have been made to appear through the use of percentages.
4. *Percentage decreases can never exceed 100 percent.* This is obvious, but this type of mistake occurs frequently. The higher figure should always be used as the base. For example, if a price was reduced from $1.00 to $0.25 the decrease would be 75 percent (75/100).

TABULATION

Tabulation is the process of summarizing raw data and displaying it in compact form for further analysis. It is another stage that should be considered early in the research sequence. Dummy tables, to illustrate the tabulations and comparisons that will be needed, should be set up before the final research design details are settled. Data from the pilot study may be entered in these tables to indicate whether the anticipated relationships are likely to be found in the main study.

Tabulation may be by hand or by computer. The choice is made largely on the basis of the size and type of study, alternative costs, time pressures,

---

[3]Harper W. Boyd, Jr. and Ralph Westfall, *Marketing Research*, 3d ed. IHomewood, Ill.: Richard D. Irwin, 1972), p. 540.

and the availability of computers and computer programs. If the number of questionnaires is small, and their length is short, hand tabulation is quite satisfactory. Electronic tabulation is more appropriate when the opposite conditions hold. If computer-based tabulation programs are available, it may be desirable to design the questionnaire to fit the computer program's requirements.

Hand tabulation

In hand tabulation, one uses (1) the direct tally; (2) the list and tally; or (3) the card sort method. When there are simple codes and few cross-tabulations, it is feasible to tally directly from the questionnaire. In the listing method, the code responses are transcribed onto a large worksheet, allowing a line for each questionnaire. Various counting and tallying methods may be used, depending upon personal preferences. One simple approach is to lay a ruler along a row or column and count the number of times each code, for a given question, has been entered on the worksheet.

The card sorting method is the most flexible hand tabulation approach. Any grouping can be broken out and tabulated, and a large number of cross-classifications can be made quickly and easily. Hand tabulation can be surprisingly fast if one develops a modest skill in card sorting. Figure 11–3 illustrates a simple card developed for tabulating a survey with about 40 variables.

FIGURE 11–3   Sample hand sorting card

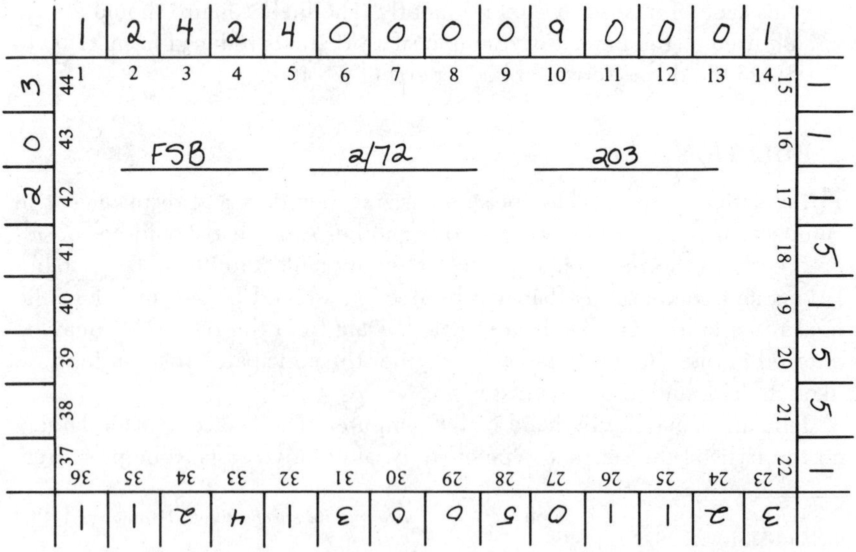

Computer tabulation

In recent years, some computer programs have been developed to simplify the researcher's tabulation and analysis task; this part of the research process can now be completed easily and quickly. In addition, these programs greatly increase the researcher's analysis repertoire. To avail ourselves of these versatile tools, we generally need only to (1) assure ourselves that the data can be used conveniently in the chosen computer program; (2) have a computer with the appropriate program available; and (3) be able to provide to the computer certain simple instruction and control messages, along with the data.

SPSS. One versatile statistical analysis package is the *Statistical Package for the Social Sciences* (SPSS).[4] It is an integrated set of computer programs that are invaluable to the business researcher. Included in this package are procedures for various types of regression and correlation analysis, analysis of variance, discriminant analysis, factor analysis, and canonical correlation. In addition, of course, it includes programs for simple descriptive statistics, scatter plots, cross-tabulations, and even a program for Guttman scalogram analysis.

While SPSS and similar programs provide massive power for statistical analysis, the feature of interest here is its contingency table program. When data are classified according to two or more characteristics, the resulting matrix is generally known as a *contingency table*. For example, an $r \times c$ contingency table describes a matrix with r rows and c columns. This data analysis form, also called a *cross-tabulation*, is probably the most commonly used analysis method in the social sciences.

The SPSS has a subprogram, CROSSTABS, which we can use to produce a two-dimensional table in the form shown in Figure 11–4. The data in this table represent the tabulation of responses to a four-point opinion scale which was administered to the employees of a commercial bank. In this particular table, the cross tabulation is between variables 001 and 012 in which:

001 = The department classification of the employees.

012 = The opinion responses to the statement "My supervisor gives me credit and praise for work well done."

In each cell of the table, are four values: (1) the actual frequency count of persons in each department who chose each of the four response alternatives to statement 012; (2) row percentages; (3) column percentages; and (4) percent of total responses for these frequencies.

---

[4]Norman H. Nie, C. Hadlai Hull, Jean G. Jenkins, Karin Steinbrenner, and Dale H. Bent, *SPSS*, 2d ed. (New York: McGraw-Hill, 1975), p. 1. Another powerful statistical analysis package is the SAS. In some ways, it is more versatile and easier to use than SPSS. For specifics, see Anthony J. Barr, James H. Goodnight, John P. Sall, and Jane T. Helwig, *A User's Guide to SAS 76* (Raleigh, N.C.: SAS Institute, 1976).

FIGURE 11–4 Two-dimensional table produced by subprogram CROSSTABS of SPSS

Variable 012 credit and praise

Var 001 Dept	Count Row pct Col pct Tot pct	Definite yes 1	General yes 2	General no 3	Definite no 4	No answer 5	Row total
Group 1		2 6.3 8.7 1.9	16 50.0 34.8 15.2	10 31.3 41.7 9.5	3 9.4 30.0 2.9	1 3.1 50.0 1.0	32 30.5
Group 2		7 23.3 30.4 6.7	11 36.7 23.9 10.5	9 30.0 37.5 8.6	3 10.0 30.0 2.9	0 0.0 0.0 0.0	30 28.6
Group 3		2 16.7 8.7 1.9	4 33.3 8.7 3.8	4 33.3 16.7 3.8	1 8.3 10.0 1.0	1 8.3 50.0 1.0	12 11.4
Group 4		12 38.7 52.2 11.4	15 48.4 32.6 14.3	1 3.2 4.2 1.0	3 9.7 30.0 2.9	0 0.0 0.0 0.0	31 29.5
	Column Total	23 21.9	46 43.8	24 22.9	10 9.5	2 1.9	105 100.0

Chi Square = 20.334 with 12 degrees of freedom, significance = .061
Cramer's V = 0.254

This two-dimensional table allows us to test for a hypothesized relationship between the department in which respondents are employed and their attitude toward their supervisor as measured by variable 012. A glance at the data in Figure 11–4 suggests that those persons in group 4 of department 001 have a more favorable opinion of their supervisor's "credit and praise" practices than do persons in the other three groups.

Another feature of the SPSS is that one can recode variables to make new combinations out of the original data. For example, one can combine the two "yes" and two "no" classes into single "yes" and "no" categories, drop the "no answer" responses, and even combine the members of groups 1, 2, and 3 into one classification and members of group 4 into a second classification.

In addition to this two-way analysis, one might also want to analyze the responses classified simultaneously by group and length of service. This requires a three-way tabulation, and CROSSTABS can provide for up to eight-way tabulations. Unless you have a large data file, however, seldom will we use tables more complex than three-way. Three-way tables are invaluable, as you will soon learn, for analyzing potential causal relationships between variables. This ability to provide three-way tables is one of the outstanding features of the CROSSTABS program. With it, you can analyze the relationship between attitude and employee group, while holding length of service constant.

Figure 11–4 also includes several statistical test values. The availability of such statistics can certainly be of great value to researchers, but their automatic inclusion in the printout points up an important danger of "canned" computer programs. The inclusion of test values suggests to the statistically unsophisticated user that such calculations must be appropriate for the data presented. This may clearly not be the case. These measures are merely mechanical computations applied blindly to whatever data are put into the program. The computer will calculate the measures, using proper calculational algorithms, but it is left to the user to determine whether the measures are appropriate to the situation. For example, chi square is computed for the contingency table in Figure 11–4, even though these data do not meet one of the basic conditions for the use of this test.

A second danger with a program such as the SPSS grows out of its power to generate output so quickly and easily. For example, merely by introducing a card in the CROSSTABS subprogram that states,

CROSSTABS Table = A to Z to A to Z

one can generate every two-way table for all variables from A to Z. The computer can produce these hundreds of tables in a matter of minutes. In addition, one might also ask for three-way tables, four-way tables, and so on. In fact, one can easily be swamped with output far beyond the capacity to use it effectively. This output deluge may also encourage some to engage in a sort of wholesale data-searching for relationships that are "statistically significant." Such searching, unguided by logic, runs counter to generally accepted research thinking. In any 100 contingency tables, one would expect to find about five sets of data that are "statistically significant" at the 0.05 level, merely by chance.

BMDP. Another widely available package of computer programs is the BMD series which was first published by the University of California Press in 1961. It has been replaced by the currently available BMDP series.[5] These programs provide a wide variety of analytical capabilities that range from plots and simple data description to advanced statistical techniques. Among the procedures are multi-way frequency tables, various regression programs, including nonlinear regression, and other types of multivariate analysis. This set of programs is frequently updated.

---

[5]W. J. Dixon and M. B. Brown, eds., *BMDP-79* (Berkeley, Calif.: University of California Press, 1979).

PC programs. With the greater use of personal computers (PCs), there is a growing interest in PC statistical packages. Among those currently on the market is Microstat.[6] It is available for computers using either CP/M and DOS operating systems. It is a library of statistical programs that perform most common statistical tests and procedures. Included are simple descriptive statistics, hypothesis testing, analysis of variance, regression analysis, time series analysis, and probability distributions.

DATA PRESENTATION

Data reduction

Many research studies result in a large volume of raw statistical information which must be reduced to more manageable dimensions if one is to see the meaningful relationships in it. This process of data reduction is the preserve of descriptive statistics.[7] One can do this reduction task manually, or use one of the computer-based statistical packages such as SPSS, BMDP, or SAS.

One assigns data to groups in order to reduce the number of classes to a more manageable number. If the data are numeric, these classifications form a set known as a frequency distribution. Table 11–5 presents two different frequency distributions of the same data. Deciding on the number and width of the frequency class intervals calls for skill and judgment. The objective, of course, is to display the data in such a way as to make it more meaningful for the analyst. Typically, one uses from 5 to 15 classes, and they may be of equal or unequal width.

The frequency distribution shown in section A of Table 11–5 has 11 equal-width intervals and 1 open-ended interval.[8] This distribution has one half of the accounts in one class in the distribution, making this class interval too gross for us to understand much about the real distribution of many accounts. The distribution in section B is an improvement in that it shows some of the small accounts' detail which might be helpful in our interpretation. It also reduces the number of accounts in the largest class to 32 percent of the total. On the other hand, it introduces frequency classes of different width that are somewhat more difficult to use. In both cases, there is a bimodal distribution with a second peak at around $10,000. At the time of this study, the maximum insured value of a savings account was $10,000. This appears to have placed a practical ceiling on the size of many accounts.

---

[6] Published by Ecosoft, P.O. Box 68602, Indianapolis, Ind. 46268-0602.

[7] There are two major areas of statistics—descriptive and inferential. Descriptive statistics concern the development of certain indexes from the the raw data, while inferential statistics are concerned with the process of generalization from small groups to populations.

[8] Open-ended intervals are generally not desirable, but often cannot be avoided. In the data shown in Table 11–5, this class was largely concentrated in the $10,000 to $14,999 class, but there was a scattering of holdings as high as $40,000.

TABLE 11–5 Two frequency distributions of savings accounts by size of account, 1968

A Account size	No. of accounts	B Account size	No. of accounts
1– 999	8,200	Under 10	1,000
1,000– 1,999	2,000	10– 99	2,000
2,000– 2,999	1,000	100– 999	5,200
3,000– 3,999	800	1,000– 2,999	3,100
4,000– 4,999	600	3,000– 4,999	1,400
5,000– 5,999	800	5,000– 6,999	1,200
6,000– 6,999	400	7,000– 8,999	600
7,000– 6,999	300	9,000– 10,999	1,500
8,000– 8,999	300	11,000+	300
9,000– 9,999	300		16,300
10,000– 10,999	1,200		
11,000+	300		
	16,300		

Source: Files of Suburban City Bank.

Summary statistics. The data in frequency distributions are transformed by the calculation of a number of statistical indexes which summarize the results even further. One major set of indexes are measures of central tendency, of which the three most important are the arithmetic mean, median, and mode. The geometric mean and harmonic mean are also sometimes used. With attributes data, the p is the equivalent of the arithmetic mean. A second important group of indexes are the measures of dispersion, of which the major ones are the variance and its square root—the standard deviation. Other measures such as the mean deviation, range, and interquartile range are also used. With nominal data, the pq ratio is the analogue of the variance. There are other classes of standard indexes to measure the skewness and kurtosis (or height) of distributions, but these will not be explored here. In addition, we often develop special indexes to reflect the constructs and concepts that are unique to our study. This process has already been discussed in Chapter 4.

DATA ANALYSIS

Descriptive analysis

Descriptive analysis is largely the study of distributions of one variable. This study provides us with profiles of companies, work groups, persons, and other subjects on any of a multitude of characteristics such as size, composition, efficiency, or preferences. These tabulations are especially useful when the approximate distribution of a variable is unknown. For example, in the Suburban City Bank study (see Table 11–5), the management has no precise idea of the size distribution of their savings accounts. Such descriptive data are important entries in their bank of data if they are thoroughly to understand their savers.

One-dimension analysis does more than merely show the size and shape of a distribution. In addition, it provides useful benchmark data for measuring the state or condition at any particular time. For example, it will tell us the average work performance level for new employees. Management decision-making effort is often directed toward changing the shape of the distribution of such variables (for example, raising the average or reducing the variance). In addition, distributions of one dimension facilitate prediction when they tell us, for example, that two thirds of the members of a camping club are usually absent from work on the Monday after a weekend excursion.

While unidimensional analysis is often a prelude to bivariate and multivariate analysis, even some of these more complex forms are chiefly descriptive in nature. For example, one might conduct a study of employees to determine who might be eligible for a proposed early retirement program. You might classify those of a certain age group by position, tenure, department location, skills classification, and other factors. In such an analysis, the objective would be to determine where and to what degree this new program would affect operations.

Causal analysis

The concern in causal analysis is with the study of how one variable affects, or is "responsible for," changes in another variable. The stricter interpretation of causation, found in experimentation, is that some external factor produces a change in the dependent variable. In much business research, however, one is interested in cases in which the cause-effect relationship is less explicit. In fact, you are more interested in understanding, explaining, predicting, and controlling relationships between variables than you are with determining causes per se.

One can seldom affect anyone's age, sex, club membership, religion, social class, education, and childhood history; yet these and similar factors influence people's attitudes, work, and consumption practices, as well as other dispositions and behaviors. One must deal with associations between these factors if one is to understand how such dispositions and behaviors come about. For example, do age differences explain consumption variations? What indicators predict who are the superior machinists? What factors lead a person to become a consistent saver? While the tools in ex post facto analysis research are less powerful than in experimentation, you can still use the experiment as the logic model; you can also employ the strong inference approach of establishing a number of hypotheses which you can then try to disconfirm.

Correlation. When two variables covary, researchers say they are correlated. Does this covariation mean that there is some connection between them? There are several ways by which one might determine whether such correlations do exist. You might informally observe events in which A occurs to see if B also occurs. In research, however, one usually wants a more orderly method. One way to approach the task is to classify each variable into two or more categories and then cross-classify the variables in these subcategories. This approach is especially useful when the data are in nominal form. If the data are ordinal, interval, or ratio, you can use more powerful forms of statistical correlation.

Cross-tabulation

A first stage in the search for asymmetrical relationships between two variables is to cross-classify each variable and present the results in a two-way table. In the examples that follow, we will use dichotomous classifications in the interests of simplicity of presentation. Obviously, however, more than two categories can be used for each variable. In an earlier chapter, the example of a factory with high absenteeism on Mondays was used. Observation suggested that many of the workers who were frequently absent on Mondays were also members of a camping club. Table 11–6 shows the club membership and Monday absentee pattern. Percentages are calculated in the direction which logic suggests is the more likely flow of influence.

While one might conclude from Table 11–6 that club membership is the cause of high absenteeism, consider the possible relationships that might be found in such a two-way table.

TABLE 11–6   Club membership and levels of Monday absenteeism (percent)*

Absentee status	Club member?	
	Yes	No
High	40	20
Low	60	80
Total	100	100
n =	(60)	(300)

*Data hypothetical.

Elaboration

The recognition of an asymmetrical relationship between two variables is only the first step of analysis. Even if one finds that there is a substantial covariation and are convinced there is an asymmetrical relationship, one may still want to ask two questions: why and under what conditions? One advances hypotheses to answer these questions and then use elaboration both to test the reasoning and serve as a tool of discovery.

By the process of *elaboration*, a third or test factor is introduced into the association through cross-classifying the three variables. We might introduce the age of the employees as a test factor in the absenteeism study and find the relationships shown in Table 11–7. Here we relate club membership and absenteeism while holding age constant. Obviously, age is not literally being held constant, but what is being shown are how absenteeism and club membership correlate within two different age groups.

TABLE 11–7 Club membership and levels of absenteeism by age of employee (percent)*

| Absentee status | Young | | Old | |
	Club member	Not a club member	Club member	Not a club member
High	48	46	14	15
Low	52	54	86	85
Total	100	100	100	100
n =	(46)	(50)	(14)	(250)

*Data hypothetical.

In Table 11–7, you stratify on age and through this process examine the contingent relationships between (1) age and club membership, (2) age and absenteeism, and (3) club membership and absenteeism. This elaboration indicates that there are associations between all three. First, persons classified as "young" are much more likely to be club members than are "old" workers. Second, there is clearly a much higher rate of absenteeism among young workers than among older ones. Third, as shown in Table 11–6, club members have higher absenteeism rates than do nonclub members. The elaboration shows, however, that the introduction of age virtually eliminates the effect of club membership on absenteeism. The original club-absenteeism correlation resulted from the high concentration of young workers in the club rather than from the effect of club membership itself.

When one analyzes associations through elaboration, there are different ways to logically relate the third variable to the two original variables. The third variables can be extraneous, component, intervening, suppressor, or distorter variables.[9]

Extraneous variables.   One may stratify on some third factor and find that the original relationship between two variables disappears. This is evident that the original *IV-DV* association is a spurious one. For example, in Table 11–7, club membership is *not* an important causal factor for explaining absenteeism among the workers. Thus, here is a highly plausible interpretation that is actually misleading.

On the other hand, this same process can be used to provide evidence that dubious interpretations are actually sound. That is, if the introduction of the third variable does not affect the original relationship, then there would be some support for the original relationship. This point is illustrated in Table 11–8 in which the newfound relationship between absenteeism and age is analyzed further by adding a test factor of job skill. This analysis indicates that the absenteeism-age relationship holds up; the skill variable appears to be largely extraneous. Each time what appears to be a relevant third variable is introduced and the relationship remains, the more confidence one can have in the relationship between age and absenteeism.

TABLE 11–8   Levels of absenteeism and age of worker by worker skill level (percent)

Absentee status	Unskilled		Skilled	
	Young	Old	Young	Old
High	47	16	46	14
Low	53	84	54	86
Total	100	100	100	100
n =	(59)	(104)	(37)	(160)

Component variables.   In business research, there may often be propositions which are true, but the *IV* is so global as to offer little real insight. In this case, if we break the *IV* concept down into its components we may be able to understand a great deal more about the relationship. For example, we might find that blue collar and white collar workers react differently to a training exercise. This is less enlightening than to track down that the difference is due more to specific work culture differences between the two

---

[9]Morris Rosenberg, *The Logic of Survey Analysis* (New York: Basic Books, 1968). The discussion in this section draws on the concepts advanced by Rosenberg.

groups. Or, it is one thing to find that expenditures for wine vary among families at different stages in the family life cycle, but it is something more if we can find the component within family life cycle which is controlling.

To illustrate the nature of the component variable, consider that it is often thought that successful salespeople have a certain type of personality. To test this hypothesis, assume that personality tests are given to 200 newly hired salespeople. After a period of time, one determines which people have been successful and which have not. Then, cross-classify them by their total scores on the personality tests. One may secure results like those found in Part A of Table 11–9. These hypothetical data indicate that scores on the personality battery are helpful predictors. On the other hand, such a global variable tells us little about the specific personality factors that may be operating.

TABLE 11–9   Personality and sales success (percent)*

Sales success	Part A Personality test scores		Part B Empathy test			
			High		Low	
	High	Low	High	Low	High	Low
Yes	60	30	68	55	32	23
No	40	70	32	45	68	77
Total	100	100	100	100	100	100
$n =$	(100)	(100)	(78)	(22)	(22)	(78)

*Data hypothetical

The hypothesis has also been advanced, however, that successful salespeople generally have a high empathy for others. One can test this by using the empathy component of the general personality test, securing the relationships shown in Part B of Table 11–9. This indicates that the empathy component of the test battery is an important contributor to the ability to predict which salespeople will be successful.

Intervening variables.   When one makes a causal analysis, especially of social phenomena. it is "tapping in" on an ongoing stream of events that proceed serially, and in some complexity, from causes to effects. In such a chain of connections there is a chance that the original *IV* affects the *DV* through some intervening factor. Thus B is a consequence of A and a determinant of C.

Suppose you observe that an increase in personal income seems to be followed by a higher rate of personal savings. You might conclude that there must be some link between these two. You hypothesize that there is an intervening variable of "motivation to save." This argument is:

Change in income → Change in motivation to save → Change in saving.

To illustrate the nature of this intervention, again consider the case in which younger workers show a much higher absenteeism rate than do older workers. However, it is hard to imagine that age, per se, brings about this absenteeism. There must be something in the relationship that we have yet to see. Much has been made in recent years of the decline of the "work ethic" in society. It is suggested that many of the younger generation do not accept this ethic. Therefore, one might hypothesize that the higher absenteeism from younger workers results from their greater rejection of the work ethic. Then, administer a scale to the workers which measures their attitudes toward work and find the relationships shown in Table 11–10.

TABLE 11–10: Worker age and absenteeism by work ethic attitude (percent)*

Absentee status	Reject work ethic		Accept work ethic	
	Young	Old	Young	Old
High	96	71	13	3
Low	4	29	87	97
Total	100	100	100	100
n =	(70)	(35)	(15)	(240)

*Data hypothetical

Suppressor variables.   When these variables are at work, there is no relationship between two variables while logic suggests that there should be one. One may be misled into thinking that an absence of correlation is true when actually the *IV-DV* relationship is blocked out or dampened by the suppressor variable. For example, you might expect that shoppers from lower-income families would be more responsive than middle-class shoppers to the introduction of unit pricing in grocery stores. Suppose, however, that you conduct a study and find little difference between lower-income and middle-income families in their response to unit pricing (see Part A of Table 1–11. You might hypothesize, however, that the expected higher responsiveness of lower-income families has been suppressed in the statistics because the better educated would respond more to unit pricing, but it is the more poorly educated who are concentrated in the lower income group. This revised hypothesis is tested in Part B of Table 11–11. The results show that the lower-income shopper does respond more than the middle-income shopper to unit pricing when education level is held constant.

TABLE 11–11: Shopper income class and use of unit pricing information by shopper education level (percent)*

| Use of unit price information | Part A Income class | | Part B | | | |
| | | | High education | | Low education | |
	Middle income	Lower income	Middle income	Lower income	Middle income	Lower income
High	30	30	34	50	18	23
Low	70	70	66	50	82	77
Total	100	100	100	100	100	100
n =	(200)	(200)	(150)	(50)	(50)	(150)

*Data hypothetical

Distorter variables. Distorter variables are those which, when accounted for, reveal that the correct interpretation is the reverse of that suggested by the original data. For example, it is often argued that families typically use the bank closest to their home. Suppose, however, that you conduct a study of 400 households, 200 of which are located within a mile of our client bank, while the other 200 are located more than a mile from the bank. The results indicate something unusual. It seems that a higher percentage of the more distant families are customers of the bank than is the case with the nearby families. These results are shown in Part A of Table 11–12. Since this does not seem reasonable we look for further information which might explain this anomaly. Introduce a third variable, the comparison of the distance from the family's home to the nearest competing bank. Then each family is classified as to whether the competing bank is closer or more distant to the family's home than is our bank. The results of this analysis, shown in Part B of Table 11–12, indicate that the correct interpretation is the opposite of the original. After adjusting for the nearness of the competing bank, we find that the closer a family's home is to the bank, the more likely it is to have an account with us.

In summary, there are two contributions which the introduction of test factors can make. In the first instance, elaboration may keep us from being misled. There are two such dangers from a two-variable relationship: (1) we

TABLE 11–12: Bank use and home-bank distance by distance of competition (percent)*

| | Part A | | Part B | | | |
| | | | Competition is farther | | Competition is closer | |
Have account?	0–1 Miles	1 Mile +	0–1 Miles	1 + Miles	0–1 Miles	1 + Miles
Yes	35	40	60	52	27	22
No	65	60	40	48	73	78
Total	100	100	100	100	100	100
n =	(200)	(200	(50)	(120)	(150)	(80)

*Data hypothetical

may accept a hypothesis which is false; and (2) we may reject a hypothesis which is true. When we consider extraneous variables we help avert the acceptance of a false hypothesis. Use of a suppressor variable analysis helps avoid the rejection of hypotheses which are true while the use of distorter variable analysis helps us avoid both of these cases.

A second contribution is to provide more precise and specific understanding of a two-variable relationship. For example, by using component variables, one can find out what it is in a general variable that is critical to the relationship. The use of an intervening variable may give a more precise understanding of the temporal and logical process of movement from *IV* to *DV*; the use of an antecedent variable may allow an extension of the causal sequence.

Conditional relationships. In the elaboration examples used up to this point, the introduction of a test factor has generally affected various subgroups in approximately the same way. It may be, however, that the impact of the test factor affects one subgroup more than another. These are *conditional relationships* and represent a situation where we wish to specify the conditions under which the original relationship is strengthened or weakened. For example, assume that in the absenteeism study, you used a test variable of worker seniority (rather than age) along with the original club membership-absenteeism relationship. This is illustrated in Table 11–13 and suggests that seniority is an important factor in explaining absenteeism. However, there is an interaction between seniority and club membership and their effects on absenteeism. With low seniority employees, club membership appears to stimulate added absenteeism. Among more senior employees, just the opposite occurs.

TABLE 11–13:   Club membership and levels of absenteeism by seniority (percent)

Absentee status	Less than 3 years seniority		3 Years or more seniority	
	Club Member	Not a club member	Club member	Not a club member
High	51	35	7	17
Low	49	65	93	83
Total	100	100	100	100
n =	(45)	(150)	(15)	(249)

Computerized analysis

Cross-classification is a cumbersome and time-consuming process, although the excellent computer-based tabulation programs such as SPSS have made it easier and more useful. In addition, a new multivariate approach gives promise of even more powerful classification analysis. One such program is the Automatic Interaction Detector (AID) program.[10]

AID is basically a sequential partitioning procedure that begins with a specified dependent variable and a set of predicting characteristics. It searches among up to 300 variables for the best single division according to each predictor variable, chooses one, and splits the sample into two subgroups so as to maximize the reduction in the unexplained sum of squares of the dependent variable. These two subgroups then become two separate samples for further analysis. The search procedure is repeated to find that variable which, when split into two parts, makes the next largest contribution to the reduction of unexplained variation in each subsample, and so on.

Figure 11–5 illustrates the analysis tree that resulted from an AID study of the do-it-yourself activities of families. The initial dependent variable is the annual hours spent in home production by heads of families and wives. The illustration indicates that the best binary split was between married couples and single persons. The latter spent substantially less time in do-it-yourself activities. The married couples sample was then analyzed against the remaining variables and the best binary split for reducing unexplained variance was the type of family dwelling. Further analysis indicated that larger families, with more education, who lived in rural areas and whose youngest child was between two and eight years of age, were the most active do-it-yourselfers, with an average of 1,168 hours per year per family.

---

[10]John A. Sonquist, Elizabeth L. Baker, James N. Morgan, *Searching for Structure* (Ann Arbor, Mich.: Institute for Social Research, The University of Michigan, 1971).

FIGURE 11–5: Hours of home production done in 1964 by heads of families and wives (for 2,214 families)*

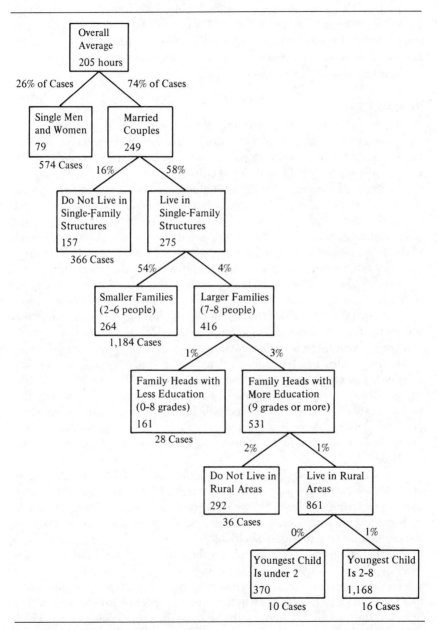

*Home production is defined as unpaid work other than regular housework, minus volunteer work, and minus courses and lessons.

Source: J. Morgan, I. Siageldin and N. Baerwaldt, *Productive Americans* (Ann Arbor, Mich.: Survey Research Center, University of Michigan, 1965), p. 128.

While this technique holds promise as an analysis tool, it has several limitations. Large samples are generally required, with some suggesting that 1,000 to 2,000 or more are needed. Then, too, AID takes no account of intercorrelated predictors. As a result, the order of appearance of variables is no indication of their relative importance; exclusion does not necessarily imply insignificance.[11]

SUMMARY

The first step in analysis is to edit the collected raw data to assure that they are accurate, consistent with other data, uniformly entered, as complete as possible, and ready for coding and tabulation. In survey work, it is common to use both field and central editing.

Coding is the process of assigning numerals or other symbols to answers so we can group the responses into a limited number of categories. These categories should be appropriate to the research problem, exhaustive of the data, mutually exclusive, and unidimensional. Since coding eliminates much of the information in the raw data, it is important that the researcher design category sets carefully in order to utilize the available data more fully.

"Don't know" replies are evaluated in the light of the nature of the question and the respondent. While many are legitimate *DK* responses, some result from a question that is ambiguous or an interviewing situation that is not motivating. It is generally better to report DK responses as a separate category, unless there is some compelling reason to treat them otherwise.

Survey results may be hand-tabulated if the study is small, if there are relatively few cross-tabulations, and if computer facilities are not available. There are three types of hand tabulation—the direct tally, the list and tally, and the card-sort methods. When studies involve large numbers or many cross-tabulations, there is a greater use of computers, since software programs have been developed. There are a number of statistical packages available.

Causal analysis is the term used to describe the study of how one or more variables affect, or are responsible for, changes in, one or more other variables. In experimental research, we interpret causal more strictly than we do with ex post facto studies. In that case, we must usually think in terms of the correlation or association of variables.

A first stage in the search for relationships between two variables often is to cross-classify each variable against one or more others and to look for interactions between them. The cross-classification procedure begins with a two-way table which indicates whether there is or is not an interrelationship between the variables. Continue the analysis through elaboration, in which a third variable, is introduced to form a three-way table. By this process, one often finds conditional relationships in which factor A appears to affect

---

[11]Peter Doyle and Ian Fenwick, "The Pitfalls of AID Analysis," *Journal of Marketing Research* (November 1975), pp. 408–13.

factor B, but only when factor C is held constant. There are many ways that we may logically relate the third variable to the two original variables. The third variable can be extraneous, a component, intervening, a suppressor, or a distorter.

Computer cross-tabulation programs have greatly facilitated the cross-tabulation type of analysis. In addition, special algorithms, such as the Automatic Interaction Detector program (AID), have been developed as a means for extending the powers to analyze data in terms of classifications.

SUPPLEMENTAL READINGS

1. Nie, Norman H.; C. Hull; Hadlai; Jean G. Jenkins; Karin Steinbrenner; and Dale H. Bent. *SPSS: Statistical Package for the Social Sciences,* 2d ed. New York: McGraw-Hill, 1975. The complete writing on the SPSS statistical package. It also contains excellence summaries on various statistical techniques and measures.
2. Phillips, Bernard S. *Social Research.* 2d ed. New York: Macmillan, 1971. See Chapters 13–16 for a good discussion on analysis of data.
3. Reichard, Robert S. *The Numbers Game.* New York: McGraw-Hill, 1972. A highly readable text on the use and abuse of managerial statistics. Worthwhile reading for every researcher.
4. Rosenberg, Morris. *The Logic of Survey Analysis.* New York: Basic Books, 1968. An excellent treatment of causal analysis using crossbreaks. Recommend the entire book.
5. Zeisel, Hans. *Say It with Figures.* 5th ed. New York: Harper & Row, 1968. Entire book is worth reading for its excellent discussion of numerical presentation and causal analysis.

DISCUSSION QUESTIONS

1. Define or explain
   a The purpose of coding
   b The rules for establishing category sets.
   c SPSS
   d Elaboration.
   e Asymmetrical relationship.
2. How should one handle "don't know" responses?
3. One of the problems facing the shoe store manager is that many shoes must eventually be sold at markdown prices. Suppose that this prompts us to conduct a mail survey of shoe store managements in which the question, "What methods have you found most successful for reducing the high markdowns' problem?" is asked. We are interested in extracting as much information as possible from these answers in order better to understand the full range of strategies that store managements use. Establish what you think is a sound group of category sets by which to code, say, 500 responses similar to the 14 below. Try to develop an integrated set of classifications that reflects your theory of markdown management. After developing the set, use it to code the 14 responses.

a Have not found the answer. As long as we buy style shoes we will have markdowns. We use PMs on slow merchandise but it does not eliminate markdowns. (PM is "push-money"—special item bonuses for selling a particular style of shoe.)

b Using PM before too old. Also reducing price during season. Holding meetings with salespeople indicating which shoes to push.

c By putting PMs on any slow-selling items and promoting same. More careful check of shoes purchased.

d Keep a close watch on your stock and markdown when you have to, that is, rather than wait, take, a small markdown on a shoe that is not moving at the time.

e Using the PM method.

f Less advance buying—more dependence on in-stock shoes.

g Sales—catch bad guys before it's too late and close out.

h Buy as much good merchandise as you can at special prices to help make up some markdowns.

i Reducing opening buys and depending on fill-in service. PMs for salespeople.

j Buy more frequently, better buying, PM on slow-moving merchandise.

k Careful buying at lowest prices. Cash-on-the-buying-line. Buying closeouts. FDs, overstock, "cancellations." (FD—factory discontinued style.)

l By buying less "chanceable" shoes. Buy only what you need, watch sizes, don't go overboard on new fads.

m Buying more staple merchandise. Buying more from fewer lines. Sticking with better nationally advertised merchandise.

n No successful method with the current style situation. Manufacturers are experimenting, the retailer takes the markdowns—cuts gross profit by about 3 percent—keep your stock at lowest level without losing sales.

4. Suppose you were preparing two-way tables of percentages for the following pairs of variables. How would you run the percentages?

a Age and consumption of breakfast cereal.

b Family income and confidence about the family's future.

c Marital status and sports participation.

d Crime rate and unemployment rate.

5. You do a study of the attrition between the students who enter college as freshmen and those who stay to graduate. You find the following relationships between attrition, aid, and distance of home from school:

	Aid?		Home near aid?		Home far aid?	
	Yes	No	Yes	No	Yes	No
Drop out	25%	20%	5%	15%	30%	40%
Stay	75	80	95	85	70	60

What is your interpretation? (In your interpretation consider all variables and relationships.)

6. Assume that you conduct a study of food usage practices and find that Catholics seem to spend more for cereal than do Protestants. You elaborate the relationship further by introducing size of family.

Total amount spent on cereal		5 or more		1–4	
Cath.	Prot.	Cath.	Prot.	Cath.	Prot.
$120	$75	$140	$118	$70	$60

How do you interpret this additional information?

7. At a local health agency, they are experimenting with two appeal letters, A and B, by which to raise funds. They send out 400 of the A appeal and 400 of the B appeal (divided equally among working class and middle class neighborhoods). They secured the following results:

	Appeal A		Appeal B	
	Middle class	Working class	Middle class	Working class
Contribution	20	40	15	30
No contribution	80	60	85	70
	100	100	100	100

a Which appeal is the best?
b Which class responded better?
c Is appeal or social class a more powerful independent variable? By how much?

8. Assume that you have collected data on employees of a large corporation in a major metropolitan area. You analyze the data by type of work classification, education level, and whether the workers were reared in a rural or urban setting. The results are as shown below. How would you interpret them?

Annual employee turnover per 100 employees

	Part A		Part B			
			High education		Low education	
	Salaried	Wage	Salaried	Wage	Salaried	Wage
Rural	8	16	6	14	18	18
Urban	12	16	10	12	19	20

12. Hypothesis testing

In Chapter 11, the problems and procedures for preparing data for analysis were discussed; also explored was some of the logic of analysis, especially as applied to classificatory data. That type of analysis may often be sufficient, but sometimes one wants to quantify the asymmetrical relationships and submit them to statistical testing.

Statistical inference is one of the two major categories of statistical procedures, the other being descriptive statistics. Within the topic of statistical inference, there are two problems. One of these, the estimation of population values, was discussed in Chapter 10 and will not be pursued further here. The second, the testing of statistical hypotheses, is the topic of this chapter. The first section includes a general treatment of the process of hypothesis testing, while later sections cover some specific types of parametric and nonparametric tests for statistical significance. Finally, measures of statistical association and techniques of multivariate analysis are reserved for Chapter 13.

HYPOTHESIS TESTING

Testing approaches

There are two approaches to hypothesis testing. The more established is the so-called *classical* or *sampling-theory* approach; the second is known as the Bayesian approach. The classical is the traditional approach; it is found in all of the major statistics books and is widely used in research applications. This approach represents an objective view of probability in which the analysis and decision making rest totally upon an analysis of available sampling data. A testing hypothesis is established which is then rejected or fails to be rejected, based on the sample data collected.

The Bayesian approach is an extension of the classical approach. It also uses sampling data for making decisions, but it goes beyond this to consider all other information that is available. This additional information consists of subjective probability estimates stated in terms of degrees of belief. These subjective estimates are based on general experience rather than on specific collected data. They are expressed as a prior distribution that can be revised after gathering sample information. The revised estimate, known as a posterior distribution, may be further revised by additional information, and so on. Various decision rules are established, cost and other estimates can be introduced, and the expected outcomes of combinations of these elements are used to judge decision alternatives.

The Bayesian approach, while based on the centuries-old Bayes theorem, has emerged as an alternative hypothesis-testing procedure since the mid-1950s. Many believe that this approach will eventually win a major place in applied statistical inference, but its acceptance in research practice has been slow. Further discussion of Bayesian procedures is beyond the scope of this text. The reader interested in learning more about Bayesian inference is urged to consult one of the references at the end of this chapter.

Statistical significance

Following the sampling-theory approach, one accepts or rejects a hypothesis on the basis of sampling information alone. Since any sample will almost surely vary somewhat from its population, one must judge whether or not these differences are statistically significant or insignificant. A difference is statistically significant if there is good reason to believe that the difference does not represent random sampling fluctuations only. For example, the controller of a large retail chain may be concerned about a possible slowdown in payments by the company's customers. She measures the rate of payment in terms of the average number of days receivables outstanding. Generally, the company has maintained an average of about 50 days with a standard deviation of 10 days. Suppose the controller has all of the customer accounts analyzed and finds that the average is now 51 days. Is this difference statistically significant from 50? Of course it is, because the difference is based on a census of the accounts and there is no sampling involved. It is a fact that the population average has moved from 50 to 51 days. While it is of statistical significance, whether it is of practical significance is another question. If the controller judges that this variation has no real importance, then it is of little practical significance.

Since it would be too expensive to analyze all of a company's receivables frequently, one normally resorts to sampling. Assume a sample of 25 accounts is randomly selected and the average days outstanding are calculated to be 54. Is this statistically significant? The answer is not obvious. It is significant if there is good reason to believe that the average age of the total group of receivables has moved up from 50. Since the evidence consists only of a sample, consider the second possibility, that this is only a random sampling error, and thus not significant. The task is to judge whether such a result from this sample is or is not statistically significant. To answer this question, one needs to consider further the logic of hypothesis testing.

The logic of hypothesis testing

In classical tests of significance, two kinds of hypotheses are used. The *null hypothesis* is used for testing. It is a statement that no difference exists between the parameter and the statistic being compared to it. In the controller example, the null hypothesis states that the population parameter of 50 days has not changed. A second, or *alternative* hypothesis, holds that there has been a change in average days outstanding (i.e., the sample statistic of 54 indicates that the population value probably is no longer 50). The alternative hypothesis is the logical opposite of the null hypothesis.

The accounts receivable example can be used further to explore how these concepts are used to test for significance. The null hypothesis (H_0) is: There has been no change from the 50 days average age of account outstanding. The alternative hypothesis (H_A) may take several forms, depending upon the objective of the researcher. The H_A may be of the not the same form. The average age of account has changed from 50 days. A second variety may be the more than or less than type. The average age of receivables has increased (decreased) from 50 days. These types of alternative hypotheses, known as two-tailed and one-tailed hypotheses, respectively, will be discussed again later. The hypotheses may be expressed in the following form:

Null, $\qquad H_0$: μ (mu) $= 50$ days

Alternative, H_A: $\mu \qquad \neq 50$ days (not the same case)

or, $\qquad H_A$: $\mu \qquad > 50$ days (more than case)

or, $\qquad H_A$: $\mu \qquad < 50$ days (less than case)

In testing these hypotheses, adopt the decision rule: Take no corrective action if the analysis shows that one cannot reject the null hypothesis. Note "not to reject" rather than "accept" the null hypothesis. It is argued that a null hypothesis can never be proved and therefore cannot be "accepted." Research gives only a chance to (1) disprove (reject) or (2) fail to reject the hypothesis. In spite of this view, it is quite common and certainly more convenient to say, "accept the null" rather than the clumsy, "fail to reject the null." In our discussion, "accept" means "fail to reject" the null hypothesis.

If one rejects the null hypothesis (finding a statistically significant difference), then you are accepting the alternative hypothesis. In either accepting or rejecting a null hypothesis, however, one can make incorrect decisions. You can accept the null hypothesis when it should have been rejected, or reject it when it should have been accepted. These problems can be illustrated in the following manner.

One of two conditions (states of nature) exists in the population—either the null hypothesis is true or it is false. There are also two decision alternatives—one either accepts or rejects the null hypothesis. Two of these situa-

	State of nature	
Decision	*H_0 is true* (*S_1*)	*H_0 is false* (*S_2*)
(*A_1*) *Accept H_0*	Correct decision Confidence level Probability = $1 - \alpha$	Type II error Probability = β
(*A_2*) *Reject H_0*	Type I error Significance level Probability = α	Correct decision Power of test Probability = $1 - \beta$

tions result in correct decisions, while the other two lead to decision errors. In the Type I case (α), a true hypothesis is rejected. The α value is called the level of significance and is the probability of rejecting a true hypothesis. With the Type II error (β), one accepts a null hypothesis that is false. Each of these errors is examined in more detail.

Type I error. Assume that the controller's problem is deciding whether or not the average age of accounts receivable has changed. Assume that the population mean is 50 days, the standard deviation of the population is 10 days, and the size of the sample is 25 accounts. With this information, one can calculate the standard error of the mean ($\sigma_{\bar{X}}$) (the standard deviation of distribution of sample means). This hypothetical distribution is pictured in Figure 12–1. The standard error of the mean is calculated to be 2 days.

$$\sigma_{\bar{X}} = \frac{\sigma}{\sqrt{n}} = \frac{10}{\sqrt{25}} = 2$$

If the decision is to reject H_0 at the 95-percent confidence level ($\alpha = .05$), a Type I error of .025 in each tail is accepted (assumes a two-tailed test). In part A of Figure 12–1, see the *regions of rejection* indicated by the shaded areas. The area between these two regions is known as the region of acceptance. The dividing points between rejection and acceptance areas are called critical values. Since the distribution of sample means is normal, the critical values can be computed in terms of the standardized random variable.[1]

$$z = \frac{\bar{X} - \mu}{\sigma_{\bar{X}}}$$

$$-1.96 = \frac{\bar{X}_{c_1} - 50}{2}$$

$$\bar{X}_{c_1} = 46.08$$

---

[1]The standardized random variable, denoted by z, is a deviation from expectation, and is expressed in terms of standard deviation units. The mean of the distribution of a standardized random variable is 0 and the standard deviation is 1. With this distribution, the deviation from the mean by any value of X can be expressed in terms of standard deviation units.

$$1.96 = \frac{\overline{X}_{c_2} - 50}{2}$$

$$\overline{X}_{c_2} = 53.92$$

where

z = significance level = 1.96
$\overline{X}_c$ = The critical value of the sample mean
μ = The population value stated in H_0 = 50
$\sigma_{\overline{X}}$ = The standard error of a distribution of means of samples of 25.

The probability of a Type I error is

$$P(A_2|S_1) = 0.05, \text{ or } 5 \text{ percent}$$

The probability of a correct decision if the null hypothesis is true is 95 percent. One can change the probability of a Type I error by moving critical

---

FIGURE 12–1   Probability of making a type I error given H_0 is true

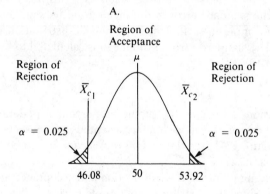

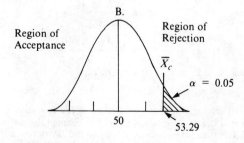

values either closer to, or farther away from the assumed parameter of 50. This can be done if a smaller or larger α error is accepted and critical values are moved to reflect this. One can also change the Type I error and the regions of acceptance by changing the size of the sample. For example, if one takes a sample of 100, the critical values that provide a Type I error of .05 are 48.04 and 51.96.

The alternative hypothesis concerned a change in either direction from 50, but the controller may be interested only in increases in the age of receivables. For this, one uses a one-tailed (more than) H_A and places the entire region of rejection in the upper tail of the distribution. One can accept a 5 percent α risk and compute a new critical value (X_c) by entering Appendix Table B–1 with the value of 0.05 to find the z value of 1.645. Substitute this in the z equation and solve for $\overline{X}_c$.

$$z = 1.645 = \frac{\overline{X}_c - 50}{2}$$
$$\overline{X}_c = 53.29$$

This new critical value, the boundary between the regions of acceptance and rejection, is pictured in part B of Figure 12–1.

Type II error. The controller would commit a type II error if he accepted the null hypothesis ($\mu = 50$) when in truth it had changed. The type II error is difficult to determine because its size depends on the α error specified, the size of sample used, and especially the new population parameter assumed. One secures a different β error if the new μ moves from 50 to 54 than if it moves only to 52. We must compute separate β error estimates for each of a number of assumed new population parameters and $\overline{X}_c$ values. To illustrate, assume that the μ has actually moved to 52 from 50. Under these conditions what is the probability of our making a type II error if the critical value is set at 53.29? This may be expressed in the following fashion:

$P(A_2|S_1) = \alpha = 0.05$ (assume a one-tailed alternative hypothesis)
$P(A_1|S_2) = \beta = ?$

If the new μ is 52 then

$$z = \frac{53.29 - 52}{10/\sqrt{25}} = .645 \qquad \begin{array}{c} \beta \\ \text{Probability} \\ = \quad .741* \end{array}$$

This condition is shown in Figure 12–2. With an α of 0.05, and a sample of 25, there is a 74-percent probability (shaded area) of a type II (β error) if μ is 52. If the μ was some other value the probability of the μ error would

---

*In reading Table B–1, in the Appendix in the back of the book, the values in the body of the table are the tail area values. Thus a z of 0.645 standard deviation in the μ_2 distribution gives a tail value of .259 (25.9 percent). To find the area to the left of the critical value of 53.29 when $\mu = 52$, compute $1 - .259$ or .741.

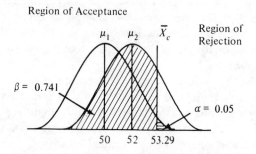

Region of Acceptance

$\beta = 0.741$

$\alpha = 0.05$

μ_1 μ_2 $\bar{X}_c$

Region of
Rejection

50   52   53.29

FIGURE 12–3   Power of test

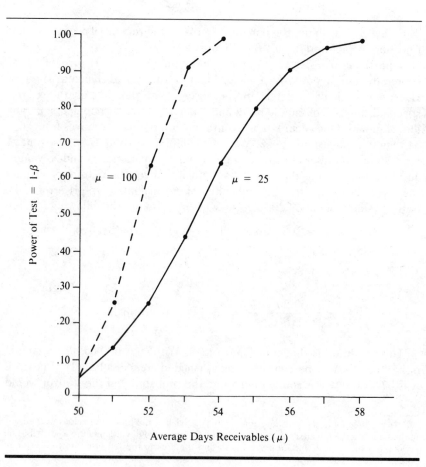

Power of Test $= 1 - \beta$

1.00
.90
.80
.70
.60
.50
.40
.30
.20
.10
0

$\mu = 100$

$\mu = 25$

50   52   54   56   58

Average Days Receivables (μ)

also be different. Actually, it is usual practice to speak of the Power of Test (or 1 − β) as the measure of type II error. Figure 12–3 shows the power of test values for various assumed changes in μ. For example, with *n* = 25, if μ changes from 50 to 52 there is a 26-percent chance that one will correctly reject the false null hypothesis. Note, however, this means that there is a 74-percent chance that μ could move from 50 to 52 and one would still fail to reject the null hypothesis and take any action that might be called for by the change.

There are several ways that one can improve this type II error. One can shift the critical value closer to the original μ of 50, but to do this, we must accept a bigger α. Whether to take this action depends on the evaluation of the relative α and β risks. In this case, it might be desirable to enlarge the acceptable α risk, because a worsening of the receivables situation would probably call for increased efforts to stimulate collections. Committing a type I error would mean only that one engaged in efforts to stimulate collections when the situation had not worsened. This act probably would not have many adverse effects even if the days of credit outstanding had not increased.

A second way to reduce the type II error is to increase the size of sample. For example, if the sample size were increased to 100, the power of test would be much stronger as shown by the dashed line in Figure 12–3. Actually, if a type II error is of great concern, one should use both of these improvement alternatives.

Statistical testing procedures

Testing for statistical significance follows a relatively well-defined pattern although authors differ in the number and sequence of steps. One six-stage sequence is as follows:

1. *State the null hypothesis.* While the researcher is usually interested in testing a hypothesis of change or differences, the null hypothesis is always used for statistical testing purposes.

2. *Choose the statistical test.* In order to test a hypothesis, one must choose an appropriate statistical test. There are many tests from which to choose, and there are at least four criteria that can be used in choosing a test. One is the power efficiency of the test. A more powerful test provides a given level of significance with a smaller sample than will a less powerful test. In addition, in choosing a test, one can consider the manner in which the sample is drawn, the nature of the population, and the type of measurement scale used. For instance, some tests are useful only when the sequence of scores is known, or when observations are paired. Other tests are appropriate only if the population has certain characteristics; still other tests are useful only if the measurement scale is interval or ratio. More attention is given to the problems of test selection in the next section.

3. *Select the desired level of significance.* The choice of the level of significance should be made before we collect the data. The most common level is 0.05, although 0.01 is also widely used. Other α levels such as 0.10, 0.025, or 0.001 are sometimes chosen. The exact level to choose is largely determined by how much α risk one is willing to accept and the effect that this choice has on β risk. The larger the α, the lower the β.

4. *Compute the calculated difference value.* After the data are collected, use the formula for the appropriate significance test to obtain the calculated value.

5. *Obtain the critical test value.* After we compute the calculated t, χ^2, or other measure, we must look up the critical value in the appropriate table for that distribution. The critical value is the criterion which defines the region of rejection from our region of acceptance of the null hypothesis.

6. *Make the decision.* For most tests if the calculated value is larger than the critical value we reject the null hypothesis and conclude that the alternative hypothesis is supported (although it is by no means proved). If the critical value is the larger we conclude that we have failed to reject the null.[2]

TESTS OF SIGNIFICANCE

Types of tests

There are two general classes of signifiance tests—the parametric and nonparametric. The parametric tests are more powerful and are generally the tests of choice if their use assumptions are reasonably met. The use of both the t test and the F test is based on the following assumptions:

1. The observations must be independent. That is, the selection of any one case should not affect the chances for any other case to be included in the sample.
2. The observations should be drawn from normally distributed populations.
3. These populations should have equal variances.
4. The measurement scales should be at least interval so that arithmetic operations can be used with them.

When one uses a parametric test, it is assumed that these conditions are met, although typically no special tests are made to assure this conformance. However, the assumptions have been tested empirically with artificial populations, and the indications are that the tests are quite robust. That is, they hold up well even though actual conditions depart substantially from those

---

[2]While differing in details, this procedure format was suggested by that found in Sidney Siegel, *Nonparametric Statistics for the Behavioral Sciences* (New York: McGraw-Hill, 1956), chapter 2.

theoretically required.[3] Therefore, it is common to find such tests being used in circumstances where, under a strict interpretation, only nonparametric tests are appropriate.

Nonparametric tests have fewer and less stringent assumptions. They do not specify normally distributed populations or homogeneity of variance. Some tests require independence of cases, while others are expressly designed for situations with related cases. Nonparametric tests are the only ones usable with nominal data; they are the only technically correct tests to use with ordinal data, although parametric tests are sometimes employed in this case. Nonparametric tests may also be used for interval and ratio data although they waste some of the information available. Nonparametric tests are also easy to understand and to use, although this is not a major scientific reason for their use. The parametric tests have greater efficiency when their use is appropriate, but even in such cases, nonparametric tests often achieve an efficiency as high as 95 percent. This means that the nonparametric test will provide the same statistical testing power with a sample of 100 as a parametric test with a sample of 95.

What test to use? Any attempt to choose a particular significance test requires that one consider the following three questions:

1. Does the test involve one sample, two samples, or k samples?
2. If two samples or k samples, are the individual cases independent or related?
3. Is the measurement scale nominal, ordinal, interval, or ratio?

Using these three criteria, one can classify the major nonparametric and parametric tests as shown in Figure 12–4. For example, if the testing situation involves two independent samples with interval or ratio measurements, one should use the t test of differences. In the remainder of this chapter, we will discuss only the most widely used of the tests listed in Figure 12–4. Most of the remainder of these tests are briefly illustrated in the Appendix to this chapter.

The one-sample case

The one-sample case occurs when one has a single sample and wishes to test the hypothesis that it comes from a specified population. In this case one encounters questions such as:

1. Is there a difference between observed frequencies and the frequencies one would expect, based on some theory?
2. Is there a difference between observed and expected proportions?

---

[3]See Fred N. Kerlinger, *Foundations of Behavioral Research* (New York: Holt, Rinehart & Winston, 1973), p. 287, for more on this point plus an extensive referencing of the studies on this question.

FIGURE 12–4   Recommended statistical techniques by measurement level and testing situation

Measure-ment level	One-sample case	Two-sample case		k-sample case		Measures of association
		Related samples	Independent samples	Related samples	Independent samples	
Nominal	Binomial χ^2 one-sample	McNemar	Fisher exact probability χ^2 two-sample	Cochran Q	χ^2 for k samples	Contingency Co-efficient C Cramer's statistic Lambda
Ordinal	Kolmogorov-Smirnov one-sample test Runs test	Sign test Wilcoxon matched pairs	Median test Mann-Whitney U test Kolmogorov-Smirnov Wald-Wolfowitz	Friedman two-way ANOVA	Median extension Kruskal-Wallis one-way ANOVA	Spearman rank correlation Kendall *tau* Kendall partial rank coefficient Kendall *W.*
Interval and ratio	t test*	t test of differ-ences*	t test*	Two-way ANOVA*	One-way ANOVA*	Pearson product-moment *r** Partial corre-lation* Multiple corre-lation*

*Parametric tests; all others are nonparametric.

3. Is it reasonable to conclude that a sample is drawn from a population with some specified distribution (normal, Poisson, and so forth)?
4. Is there a significant difference between some measure of central tendency ($\overline{X}$) and its population parameter (μ)?

There are a number of tests which may be appropriate in this situation. The parametric test is discussed first.

Parametric test.   The t test is used to determine the statistical significance between a sample distribution mean and a parameter. Typical of the one-sample applications of a t test are:

1. Comparison of the average burn life of a sample of light bulbs to determine if a production lot meets quality specifications.
2. A comparison of the proportion of persons who would join a dining club to an assumed population proportion.
3. Determination of whether the average performance of a sample of employees who have received special training has increased over the average past performance of all employees.

Example. To illustrate the application of the *t* test to the one-sample case, consider again the controller's problem mentioned earlier. With a sample of 100 accounts, one finds that the mean is 52.5 days outstanding receivables, with a standard deviation of 14. Do these results indicate that the population mean might still be 50 days?

In this problem, there is the more usual situation in which one has only the sample standard deviation (*s*). This must be used in place of the population standard deviation (σ). When one substitutes *s* for σ, use the *t* distribution, especially when the sample size is less than 30. Define *t* as:

$$t = \frac{\overline{X} - \mu}{s/\sqrt{n}}$$

As the sample increases past 30 observations, the *t* distribution approaches that of the standard normal curve. The distribution of *t* varies, depending on the degrees of freedom (defined here as $n - 1$).

This significance test is conducted by following the six-step procedure recommended earlier.

1. *Null hypothesis.* H_0: = 50 days

   H_A: > 50 days (one tailed test)

2. *Statistical test.* Choose the *t* test because the data are ratio measurements. Assume that the underlying population is normal, and that we have randomly selected the sample from the population of customer accounts.

3. *Significance level.* Let $\alpha = 0.05$, with $n = 100$.

4. *Calculated value.* $t = \dfrac{52.5 - 50}{14/\sqrt{100}} = \dfrac{2.5}{1.4} = 1.786$; d.f. $= n - 1 = 99$.

5. *Critical test value.* We obtain this by entering the table of the *t* distribution (Appendix B–2 at back of book) with 99 d.f. and a level of significance value of 0.05. One secures a critial value of about 1.66 (interpolated between d.f. = 60 and d.f. = 120).

6. *Decision.* In this case, the calculated value is greater than the critical value (1.786 > 1.66), so one rejects the null hypothesis and concludes that the average accounts receivable outstanding has increased.

Nonparametric tests. There are a variety of nonparametric tests that may be used in a one-sample situation, depending upon the measurement scale used and other conditions. If the measurement scale is nominal (classificatory only), it is possible to use either the binomial test or the χ^2 one-sample test. The binomial test is appropriate when the population is viewed as only two classes, such as male and female, buyer and nonbuyer, and successful and unsuccessful. Thus, all observations fall into one or the other of these categories. This test is particularly useful when the size of sample is so small that the χ^2 test cannot be used.

Chi square (χ^2) test. Probably the most widely used nonparametric test of significance is the χ^2 test. It is particularly useful in tests involving nominal data but can be used for higher scales. Typical are cases where persons, events, or objects are grouped in two or more nominal categories such as "yes-no," "favor-undecided-against," or class "A, B, C, or D."

Using this technique one tests for significant differences between the *observed* distribution of data among categories and the *expected* distribution based upon the null hypothesis. Chi square is useful in cases of one-sample analysis, two independent samples, or k independent samples. It must be calculated with actual counts rather than percentages.

In the one-sample case, establish a null hypothesis from which the expected frequency of objects in each category is deduced. Then compare the deviations of the actual frequencies per category with the hypothesized frequencies. The greater the difference between them, the less the probability that these differences can be attributed to chance. The value of χ^2 is the measure that expresses the extent of this difference. The larger the divergence the larger the χ^2 value.

The formula by which the χ^2 test is calculated is:

$$\chi^2 = \sum_{i=1}^{k} \frac{(O_i - E_i)^2}{E_i}$$

in which

O_i = Observed number of cases categorized in the ith category.

E_i = Expected number of cases in the ith category under H_0.

k = The number of categories.

There is a different distribution for χ^2 for each number of degrees of freedom (d.f.), defined here as $k - 1$. For example, if there are 10 categories, there are nine d.f., and so on. Depending on the number of d.f., you must be certain that the numbers in each cell are large enough to make the χ^2 test appropriate. When d.f. = 1, each expected frequency should be at least 5 in size. If d.f. > 1, then the χ^2 test should not be used if more than 20 percent of the expected frequencies are smaller than 5, or when any expected frequency is less than 1. Expected frequencies can often be increased by combining adjacent categories. For example, four categories of freshmen, sophomores, juniors, and seniors might be classified into upper class and lower class. If there are but two categories, and still there are too few in a given class, it would be better to use the binomial test.

Assume that a survey of student interest in the dining club that was discussed in Chapter 10 is taken. We have interviewed 200 students and learned of their intentions to join such a club if opened. We would like to analyze the results by living arrangement (type and location of student housing and eating arrangements). Classify the 200 responses into the four categories shown in the table below. Do these variations in intention indicate that there is a significant difference among these students or are these sampling variations only? Proceed as follows:

1. *Null hypothesis.* $H_0: O_i = E_i$

   That is, the proportion in the population who intend to join the club is independent of living arrangement: $H_A: O_i \neq E_i$. That is, the proportion in the population who intend to join the club is dependent on living arrangement.

2. *Statistical test.* Use the one-sample χ^2 to compare the observed distribution to a hypothesized distribution. The χ^2 test is used because the responses are classified into nominal categories and there are sufficient observations.

3. *Significance level.* Let $\alpha = 0.05$, $n = 60$.

4. *Calculated value.* $\chi^2 = \sum_{i=1}^{k} \dfrac{(O_i - E_i)^2}{E_i}$

   Calculate the expected distribution by determining what proportion of the 200 students interviewed were in each group. Then apply these proportions to the number who intend to join the club. Then calculate the following:

   $$\chi^2 = \frac{(16 - 27)^2}{27} + \frac{(13 - 12)^2}{12} + \frac{(16 - 12)^2}{12} + \frac{(15 - 9)^2}{9}$$
   $$= 4.48 + 0.08 + 1.33 + 4.0$$
   $$= 9.89; \text{d.f.} = 3$$

5. *Critical test value.* Enter the table of critical value for χ^2 (Appendix B–3) with 3 d.f. and secure a value of 7.82 for $\alpha = 0.05$.

6. *Decision.* The calculated value is greater than the critical value, so the null hypothesis is rejected.

Living arrangement	(1) Intend to join	(2) Number interviewed	(3) Percent ([2]/200)	(4) Expected frequencies ([3] × 60)
Dorm/fraternity	16	90	0.45	27
Apartment/rooming house, nearby	13	40	0.20	12
Apartment/rooming house, distant	16	40	0.20	12
Live at home	15	30	0.15	9
Total	60	200	1.00	60

Two-sample case

In this case, there are two samples and the task is to test whether or not they might have come from the same population. The null hypothesis is that any difference in the sample statistics or distributions is due to random sampling fluctuations only. Examples of such situations include studies of output of two samples of workers, different samples in a public opinion poll, the comparison of test and control groups in an experiment, and the like. Two major variations of the two-sample case—one in which the sample members are related and one in which they are independent are briefly discussed.

Two related samples. The two related sample cases concern those situations in which persons are closely matched (such as husband and wife) or where the same person is measured twice. For example, one might compare the output of specific workers before and after vacations, one might match persons before randomly assigning them to test and control groups in a tasting experiment. Both parametric and nonparametric tests that are applicable under these conditions are discussed.

Parametric test. The t test would normally be inappropriate for this situation because one of the t test's basic assumptions is that observations are independent. This problem is solved, however, by finding the difference between each matched pair of observations and thereby reducing the two samples into a one-sample case. That is, there is now a number of differences, each independent of the other, for which one can compute an arithmetic mean and other statistics. For example, one might secure the average units produced per day for each of 25 workers, both before and after a work rules change. By securing the before-after differences, you have reduced this to one sample of 25 independent observations.

McNemar test. This nonparametric test may be used with either nominal or ordinal data, and is especially useful with before-after measurement of the same subjects. Test the significance of any observed change by setting up a fourfold table of frequencies to represent the first and second set of responses:

Before	After	
	Do not favor	Favor
Favor	A	B
Do not favor	C	D

Since $A + D$ represents the total number of people who changed (B and C are no-change responses), the expectation under a null hypothesis is that $\frac{1}{2}(A + D)$ cases change in one direction and the same proportion in the other direction. The McNemar test uses the following transformation of the χ^2 test:

$$\chi^2 = \frac{(|A - D| - 1)^2}{A + D} \text{ with d.f. } = 1$$

The "minus 1" in the equation is a correction for continuity since the χ^2 is a continuous distribution and the observed frequencies represent a discrete distribution.

To illustrate this test's application, a survey is taken in a large corporation whose management decided to tell their employees of the "values of our economic system" in an internal education campaign. Assume that they took a random sample of their employees before the campaign, asking them to complete a questionnaire on their attitudes on this topic. On the basis of their responses, divide the workers into equal groups as to their favorable or unfavorable views of the economic system. After the campaign, the same 200 employees are asked again to complete the questionnaire. They are again classified as to favorable or unfavorable attitudes. The testing process is:

1. *Null hypothesis.* H_0: $P(A) = P(D)$
    H_A: $P(A) \neq P(D)$

2. *Statistical test.* The McNemar test is chosen because nominal data are used, and the study involves before-after measurements of two related samples.

3. *Significance level.* Let $\alpha = 0.05$, with $n = 200$.

4. *Calculated value.* $\chi^2 = \dfrac{(|10 - 40| - 1)^2}{10 + 40} = \dfrac{29^2}{50} = 16.82$; d.f. $= 1$

Before	After	
	Unfavorable	Favorable
Favorable	10	90
Unfavorable	60	40

5. *Critical test value.* Enter the table of the χ^2 distribution and find the critical value to be 3.84 with $\alpha = 0.05$ and d.f. $= 1$.

6. *Decision.* The calculated value is greater than the critical value ($16.82 > 3.84$) indicating that one should reject the null hypothesis. In fact, χ^2 is so large that it would have surpassed an α of 0.001.

Two independent samples. This testing situation is often found in research studies. For example, one compares the buying attitudes of a sample of subscribers from each of two magazines to determine whether they are from the same population. One tests output results from two different production methods or tests price movements of two samples of common stocks to see if they are from the same population.

Parametric test. The t test is the more frequently used parametric test for two independent samples, although the F test can be used. To use the t test in this case, however, one must make some adjustments to the calculation procedure. With two independent samples, you now have two sets of sample data with two separate estimates of the population mean. We are interested in the differences between means. If one could take a large number of similar pairs of samples, one would secure a distribution of *differences between means*, in which μ would be zero if the samples were from the same population. One could also calculate a standard error of the differences between two means. Since you are interested in the differences between two means, use the difference standard error as the denominator of our t equation:

$$t = \frac{(\overline{X}_1 - \overline{X}_2)}{\sigma_{\bar{x}_1 - \bar{x}_2}}$$

in which

$$\sigma_{\bar{x}_1 - \bar{x}_2} = \sqrt{\frac{s_1^2}{n_1} + \frac{s_2^2}{n_2}}$$

To illustrate this application, consider a problem that might face a manager who wishes to test the effectiveness of two methods for training new salespeople. The company selects 22 sales trainees who are randomly divided into two experimental groups—one receives type A, and the other type B training. The salespeople are then assigned and managed without regard to the training they have received. At the year's end, the manager reviews the performances of salespeople in these groups and finds the following results:

	A group	B group
Average weekly sales	$\overline{X}_1 = \$1,500$	$\overline{X}_2 = \$1,300$
Standard deviation	$s_1 = \$\ 225$	$s_2 = \$\ 251$

Use the standard procedure to determine whether one training method is superior to the other.

1. *Null hypothesis.* H_0: There is no difference in sales results produced by the two training methods.

   H_A: Training method A produces sales results superior to those of method B.
2. *Statistical test.* The t test is chosen because the data are at least interval in form and the samples are independent.
3. *Significance level.* $\alpha = 0.05$ (one-tailed test)
4. *Calculated value.*

$$t = \frac{1,500 - 1,300}{\sqrt{\dfrac{225^2}{11} + \dfrac{251^2}{11}}} = \frac{200}{101.6} = 1.97, \text{ d.f.} = 20$$

Without going into details, there are $n - 1$ degrees of freedom in each sample, so total d.f. $= (11 - 1) + (11 - 1) = 20$.

5. *Critical test value.* Enter the table of the t distribution with d.f. $= 20$, one-tailed test, $\alpha = 0.05$. The critical value is 1.725.

6. *Decision.* Since the calculated value is larger than the critical value $(1.97 > 1.725)$, reject the null hypothesis and conclude that training method A is probably superior.

Chi square test. The χ^2 test is applicable to cases in which one tests for a significant difference between samples. It is especially valuable with nominal data but can be used with stronger measurements. The general solution method is the same as presented earlier although the formula is a little more complex.

$$\chi^2 = \sum_{i=1}^{r} \sum_{i=1}^{k} \frac{(O_i - E_i)^2}{E_i}$$

in which

O_i = Observed number of cases categorized in the ith cell.

E_i = Expected number of cases under H_0 to be categorized in the ith cell.

$\sum_{i=1}^{r} \sum_{i=1}^{k}$ = The direction to sum all row-column cells.

Suppose that a manager who recently quit smoking has become interested in whether smoking has some deleterious effects on worker efficiency. He wonders, for example, whether smoking promotes accidents on the job. Since the company has complete reports of on-the-job accidents, he draws a sample of names of workers who were involved in accidents during the last year. He draws a similar sample from among workers who had no reported accidents in the last year. He then interviews members of both groups to determine if they are smokers or not. He finds the following relationship.

	Accident	No accident	Total
Heavy smoker	12 (8)	4 (8)	16
Medium smoker	9 (7.5)	6 (7.5)	15
Light smoker	6 (6.5)	7 (6.5)	13
Nonsmoker	13 (18)	22 (18)	36
Total	40	40	80

The expected values have been calculated and are shown in parentheses. The testing procedure is:

1. *Null hypothesis.* H_0: There is no difference in on-the-job accident occurrences between smokers and nonsmokers.

H_A: There is a difference in on-the-job accident occurrences between smokers and nonsmokers.

2. *Statistical test.* χ^2 is appropriate but may waste some of the data because the measurement appears to be ordinal.

3. *Significance level.* $\alpha = 0.05$, with d.f. $= (r - 1)(c - 1) = 3$

4. *Calculated value.* The expected distribution is provided by the marginal totals of the table. If there is no relationship between accidents and smoking there will be the same proportion of smokers in both accident and nonaccident classes. The numbers of expected observations in each cell are calculated by multiplying the two marginal totals common to a particular cell and dividing this product by n. For example,

$$\frac{40 \times 16}{80} = 8, \text{ the expected value in cell } (1, 1).$$

$$\chi^2 = \frac{(12 - 8)^2}{8} + \frac{(4 - 8)^2}{8} + \frac{(9 - 7.5)^2}{7.5} + \frac{(6 - 7.5)^2}{7.5} + \frac{(6 - 6.5)^2}{6.5}$$
$$+ \frac{(7 - 6.5)^2}{6.5} + \frac{(13 - 18)^2}{18} + \frac{(23 - 18)^2}{18} = 7.44$$

5. *Critical test value.* Enter Appendix Table B–3 and find the critical value 7.82 with $\alpha = 0.05$ and d.f. $= 3$.

6. *Decision.* Since the calculated value is less than the critical value, the null hypothesis is not rejected.

k sample case

One is often faced with the problem of testing for significance when three or more samples are involved. Under these conditions, determine simultaneously whether the samples might have been drawn from the same or identical populations. One is interested in testing for an overall difference among the samples. In this section, the k independent sample case is considered before the related sample case because parametric testing under independent sampling conditions introduces the simpler problem of variance analysis.

k independent sample case. As with the two sample cases, the samples are assumed to be independent of one another. This is the condition that one finds when a completely randomized experiment is carried out, or even a factorial design when the subjects are assigned to treatment groups in a simple random manner. One also wishes to compare more than two samples in ex post facto studies.

Parametric tests. When conditions are appropriate for parametric tests of more than two samples, use *analysis of variance* (ANOVA). As Kerlinger has pointed out, however, analysis of variance is ". . . not just a statistical method. It is an approach and a way of thinking."[4] In this testing procedure, the total variance in a set of data is analyzed by breaking it down into its component sources which can be attributed to various factors in the research. Theoretically, any number of component factors can be extracted, but as a practical matter, one seldom goes above three, and more usually one or two. One determines statistical significance of each of these factors by expressing the variance attributed to it as a ratio to the estimated sampling variance of the data. Do this by means of the F test which can be stated as:

$$F = \frac{\text{Variance due to factor } X + \text{Sampling variance}}{\text{Sampling variance}}$$

If the variance due to factor X is small, then the F ratio will be small. On the other hand, if the F ratio is large, factor X accounts for a large part of the total variance in the data.

The simplest form of ANOVA is the one-way model which is used with simple random samples to compare the impact of a single independent variable on the dependent variable. To simplify the discussion, consider only the case in which samples are of equal size and the fixed-effects model is assumed.[5] To illustrate one-way ANOVA, consider again the pricing example from the experimentation chapter (see page 123). The objective of that study was to determine the sales impact when the chain's private brand of canned green beans was priced at various discounts below the national brand of beans that the company carried. Assume that the traditional price discount has been one cent per can and that we wish to test this against differentials of three and five cents. The *IV* is the price differential used, and the *DV* is the monthly case sales, per store, of the store brands minus the case sales of the national brand.

In one-way analysis of variance, one can think of the value of a specific dependent variable measurement as being made up of three parts: the grand mean of all observations, the treatment or *IV* effect, and random error. This three-part partition can be expressed as:

$$X_{ij} = \mu + C_j + e_{ij}$$

in which

X_{ij} = The observation in row i, column j

C_j = The column or treatment effect in column j

e_{ij} = Random error or sampling effect

---

[4]Kerlinger, *Foundations*, p. 216.

[5]With the fixed-effects model, we assume that the test treatments are not randomly selected from a larger population of test treatments. Because of this assumption, our test results cannot be generalized to other levels of treatment. The alternative is the random-effects model.

The total variance (SS_T) can be broken into two components representing the last two items of the above equation. These components are usually referred to as "between columns" variance (SS_K) and "within columns" variance (SS_W). The former represents the effect of treatments while the latter represents the remaining variance. While we call the latter "sampling variance," it includes all other unidentified forms of variance.

To illustrate one-way ANOVA, assume that we conduct the pricing experiment using a total of 18 stores, randomly assigned to the three treatments (price discounts of one cent, three cents, and five cents per can). We follow the normal procedure:

1. *Null hypothesis.* H_0: There is no difference in sales response among the three price difference groups.

   H_A: There is a difference between sales response among the three price groups.

2. *Statistical test.* We use the F test with analysis of variance because there are k independent samples and we accept the assumptions underlying the parametric test.

4. *Calculated value.* $F = \dfrac{\text{Between-groups mean square}}{\text{Within-groups mean square}}$

   $= 3.62, \text{ d.f.} = (2, 15)$

   See calculation details in Table 12–1.

5. *Critical test value.* We enter Appendix Table B–9 with d.f. $= (2, 15)$, $\alpha = 0.05$, and secure a critical value for $F = 3.68$.

6. *Decision.* Since calculated F is less than critical value $(3.62 < 3.68)$, we fail to reject the null hypothesis and conclude that the differences in sales volume may be due to sampling variations only. Note, however, that the value is very close. The failure to reject the null hypothesis grows out of the fact that a large part of the total variance in the data remains unexplained and therefore is assumed to be due to random variation. The example appears again in a later section.

Chi square test. When there are k independent samples in which the data are nominal, the chi square test is the test of choice. While it can also be used for classificatory data of a higher measurement scale, it wastes some of the information found in the data. The k sample χ^2 test is merely an extension of the two-independent-samples case treated in an earlier section. It is calculated and interpreted in the same way and will not be elaborated here.

k related samples. When there are k samples in which observations or subjects are matched, or where the same subject is used more than once, the situation calls for a two-way analysis of variance. In the parametric case, again use the F test but with efforts made to extract additional variance. The price discount experiment illustrates the procedure.

TABLE 12–1   Calculation of a one-way analysis of variance (data hypothetical)

		Price differentials				
One cent		Three cents		Five cents		
X_A	X_A^2	X_B	X_B^2	X_C	X_C^2	
6	36	8	64	9	81	$N = 18$
7	49	9	81	9	81	$n = 6$
8	64	8	64	11	121	$k = 3$
7	49	10	100	10	100	
9	81	11	121	14	196	
11	121	13	169	13	169	
ΣX 48		59		66		$\Sigma x_T =$ 173
$\overline{X}$ 8		9.83		11		$\overline{X}_T =$ 9.61
ΣX^2	400		599		748	$\Sigma x_T^2 = 1{,}747$

Correction term $= \dfrac{(\Sigma x_T)^2}{N} = \dfrac{(173)^2}{N} = 1{,}662.72$

Total sum of squares $= SS_T = \Sigma X_T^2 - C = 1747 - 1{,}662.72$
$= 84.28$

Between columns sum of squares $= SS_K = \dfrac{(\Sigma X_A)^2}{n_A} + \dfrac{(\Sigma X_B)^2}{n_B} + \dfrac{(\Sigma X_C)^2}{n_C} - \dfrac{(\Sigma X_T)^2}{N}$
$= (384 + 580.16 + 726) - 1{,}662.72$
$= 1{,}690.16 - 1{,}662.72$
$= 27.44$

Within columns sum of squares $= SS_W = SS_T - SS_K$
$= 84.28 - 27.44$
$= 56.85$

Source	Sum of squares	d.f.	Mean square	F
Between columns	27.44	2	13.72	3.62
Within columns	56.84	15	3.79	
	84.28	17		

Recall that in the one-way ANOVA, it was impossible to reject the null hypothesis even at the $\alpha = 0.05$ level. Yet a look at the data in Table 12–1 suggests that there is some impact from the larger discounts. Another conclusion to draw from inspecting that data is that there is substantial variation within samples. Could it be that there are other variables operating within columns and that all of this variance is not random variation?

It might be reasonable to conclude, for example, that if the stores varied in size then the sales would also vary substantially because of this store size effect. If one could block on store size it might be possible to extract this source of variance. Recall again that this is the object of ANOVA—to break total variance down into its component parts to account for each and to judge its effect.

Assume that you do block on store size, developing six sets of three stores with approximately equal sales volume. You then randomly assign the stores in each of the six size sets to each of the three test sample groups. Assume further that when the experiment is run, the results are same as those shown in Table 12–1. Now, however, each row of that table represents a stratum of three stores matched for size. With this additional information, one can extract the variance that may be in the data because of store size differences. Do this extracting by calculating means for each row (stratum or block) and the "between rows" sum of squares and mean square. These calculations are shown in Table 12–2. The results of this two-way analysis are that the effects of store size and price discount are both highly significant ($p < 0.01$). We see further that most of the residual unexplained variance found in the one-way case has now been explained by the store size. Seldom in practice does one find a second blocking factor that has such a marked effect in removing additional variance, but it is not uncommon to find that randomized block designs such as this can substantially improve the ability to account for variance and determine statistical significance.

TABLE 12–2   Two-way analysis of variance

Size group	Price differences			ΣX_R	$\overline{X}$	X^2
	One cent X_A	Three cents X_B	Five cents X_C			
X_1	6	8	9	23	7.67	181
X_2	7	9	9	25	8.33	211
X_3	8	8	11	27	9	249
X_4	7	10	10	27	9	249
X_5	9	11	14	34	11.33	398
X_6	11	13	13	37	12.33	459
ΣX	48	59	66	173		1,747

Between-row sum of squares $= SS_R = \dfrac{(\Sigma X_1)^2}{n_1} + \dfrac{(\Sigma S_2)^2}{n_2} + \dfrac{(\Sigma X_3)^2}{n_2} + \dfrac{(\Sigma X_4)^2}{n_4} + \dfrac{(\Sigma X_5)^2}{n_5} + \dfrac{(\Sigma X_6)^2}{n_6} - \dfrac{(\Sigma X_T)^2}{N}$

$= [176.33 + 208.33 + 243 + 243 + 385.33 + 456.33] - 1,662.72$

$= 1,712.32 - 1,662.72$

$SS_R = 49.6$

Source	SS	dt	MS	F
Between columns	27.44	2	13.72	19.05
Between rows	49.6	5	9.92	13.78
Residual	7.24	10	0.72	
	84.28	17		

SUMMARY

There are two approaches to hypothesis testing—the *classical* or *sampling theory* and the *Bayesian*. With the sampling theory approach, one establishes a null hypothesis and then gathers sample information with which to test the hypothesis. The Bayesian approach also employs sampling data but as an additional element of information by which to improve the decision maker's prior objective judgment based on other information.

A difference between two or more sets of data is statistically significant if it actually occurs in a population. In sampling, however, to define a result as statistically significant, sample evidence must indicate a difference so great that there is little chance that it could result from random sampling fluctuations.

Hypothesis testing can be viewed as a six-step procedure:

1. Establish a null hypothesis as well as the alternative hypothesis. It is a one-tailed test of significance if the alternative hypothesis states the direction of difference. If no direction of difference is given, it is a two-tailed test.

2. Choose the statistical test on the basis of the assumption about the population distribution and measurement level. The form of the data can also be a factor. In the light of these considerations, one typically chooses that test that has the greatest power efficiency or ability to reduce decision errors.

3. Select the desired level of confidence. While $\alpha = 0.05$ is the most frequently used, many others are also used. The α is the significance level that we desire and is typically set in advance of the study. Alpha is the risk of rejecting a true null hypothesis and represents a decision error. The β or type II error is the decision error that results from accepting a false null hypothesis. Usually, one determines a level of acceptable α error, then seeks to reduce the β error by increasing the size sample, shifting from a two-tailed to a one-tailed significance test, or both.

4. Compute the actual test value of the data.

5. Obtain the critical test value, usually by referring to a table for the appropriate type of distribution.

6. Make the decision by comparing the actual test value with the critical test value.

In this chapter, and its appendix, a number of parametric and nonparametric significance tests are discussed that are applicable under various conditions. They are summarized in Figure 12–4.

SUPPLEMENTAL READINGS

1. Hays, William L., and Robert L. Winkler. *Statistics: Probability Inference, and Decision*, 2d ed. New York: Holt, Rinehart & Winston, 1975. Chapter 12 is a good summary of nonparametric statistics.

2. Huck, Schuyler W.; William Cormier; and William G. Bounds. *Reading Statistics and Research,* New York: Harper and Row, 1974. A unique book that briefly explains the meanings of various statistical inference concepts and tests found in scholarly research journals. A book for the reader of research who is overwhelmed by the statistics in journal articles.

3. Kerlinger, Fred N. *Foundations of Behavioral Research.* New York: Holt, Rinehart & Winston, 1973. See especially chapters 13–16 on analysis of variance.

4. Mosteller, Frederick, and Robert E. K. Rourke. *Sturdy Statistics.* Reading, Mass.: Addison-Wesley, 1973. Excellent discussion on significance testing.

5. Siegel, Sidney. *Nonparametric Statistics for the Behavioral Sciences.* New York: McGraw-Hill, 1956. The classic book on nonparametric statistics.

DISCUSSION QUESTIONS

1. Distinguish between:
    a   Parametric and nonparametric tests.
    b   Type I and Type II errors.
    c   Null hypothesis and alternative hypothesis.
    d   Acceptance region and rejection region.
    e   F test and t test.
    f   One-tailed and two-tailed tests.
2. a   How can the probability of a Type I error be reduced? A Type II error?
    b   How does practical significance differ from statistical significance?
    c   Suppose you interview all members of the freshman and senior classes and find that 65 percent of the freshmen and 62 percent of the seniors favor a certain ecological proposal. Is this difference significant?
3. You conduct a survey of a sample of 25 members of this year's graduating class and find that their average GPA is 3.2. The standard deviation of the sample is 0.4. Over the last 10 years, the average has been 3.0. Is this year's class significantly different from the long-run average? At what alpha level would it be significant?
4. You are curious about whether the professors and students at your school are of different political persuasions. So you take a sample of 20 professors and 20 students drawn randomly from each population. You find that 10 professors say they are conservative while only 6 students claim that they are conservative. Is this a statistically significant difference?
5. You contact a random sample of 36 graduates of Western University and learn that their starting salaries were $18,000 last year. You then contact a random sample of 40 graduates from Eastern University and find that their average starting salary was $18,800. In each case, the standard deviation of the sample was $1,000. Test the hypothesis that there is no difference between average salaries received by the graduates of these two schools.
6. A random sample of students is interviewed to determine if there is an association between class and attitudes toward corporations. With the following

results, test the hypothesis that there is no difference among students on this attitude.

	Favorable	Neutral	Unfavorable
Freshmen	100	50	70
Sophomore	80	60	70
Junior	50	50	80
Senior	40	60	90

7. You do a survey of business school students and liberal arts school students to find out how many times a week they read a daily newspaper. In each case, you interview 100 students. You find the following.

$$\overline{X}_b = 4.5 \text{ times per week}$$

$$s_b = 1.5$$

$$\overline{X}_{1a} = 5.6 \text{ times per week}$$

$$s_{1a} = 2.0$$

Test the hypothesis that there is no significant difference between these two samples.

8. The management of the One-Koat Paint Company has developed a new type of porch paint that it hopes will be the most durable on the market. They test their product against the two leading competing products by using a machine that scrubs until it wears through the coating. One-Koat runs five trials with each product and secures the following results (in thousands of scrubs).

Trial	One-Koat	Competitor A	Competitor B
1	37	34	24
2	30	19	25
3	34	22	23
4	28	31	20
5	29	27	20

Test the null hypothesis that there is no difference among the means of these products.

9. In problem 8, assume now that the five trials were made with five different types of primer. Perform a two-way ANOVA.

APPENDIX   NONPARAMETRIC SIGNIFICANCE TESTS

In addition to the χ^2 nonparametric test, there are many others that are quite useful in particular cases. Some of these are listed in Figure 12–4, and are discussed briefly here.

One sample case

The Kolmogorov Smirnov (KS) test is a frequent test of choice when the data are at least ordinal, and the research situation calls for a comparison of an observed sample distribution with a theoretical distribution. Under these conditions, the KS one-sample test is more powerful than the χ^2 test and can be used for small samples when the χ^2 test cannot. The KS is a test of goodness-of-fit in which we specify the *cumulative* frequency distribution that would occur under the theoretical distribution and compare that with the observed cumulative frequency distribution. The theoretical distribution represents our expectations under H_0. We determine the point of greatest divergence between the observed and theoretical distributions and identify this value as D (maximum deviation). From a table of critical values for D, we determine whether such a large divergence is likely on the basis of random sampling variations from the theoretical distribution. The value for D is calculated as follows:

$$D = \text{maximum}|F_O(X) - F_T(X)|$$

in which

$F_O(X)$ = The observed cumulative frequency distribution of a random sample of n observations. Where X is any possible score, $F_O(X)$ = k/n, where k = the number of observations equal to or less than X.

$F_T(X)$ = The theoretical frequency distribution specified under H_0.

We illustrate the *KS* test, with an analysis of the results of the dining club study, in terms of various class levels. Take an equal number of interviews from each class but secure unequal numbers of persons interested in joining. Assume that class levels are ordinal measurements. The testing process is as follows: (See accompanying table.)

1. *Null hypothesis.* H_0: There is no difference among student classes as to their intention of joining the dining club.

   H_A: There is a difference among students in various classes as to their intention of joining the dining club.

2. *Statistical test.*   Choose the *KS* one-sample test because the data are ordinal measured, and we are interested in comparing an observed distribution with a theoretical one.

3. *Significance level.* $\alpha = 0.05$, $n = 60$.

4. *Calculated value.* $D = \text{maximum } |F_O(X) - F_T(X)|$

	Freshman	Sophomore	Junior	Senior	Graduate
Number in each class	5	9	11	16	19
$F_O(X)$	5/60	14/60	25/60	41/60	60/60
$F_T(X)$	12/60	24/60	36/60	48/60	60/60
$|F_O(X) - F_T(X)|$	7/60	10/60	11/60	7/60	0

$D = 11/60 = 0.183; n = 60$

5. *Critical test value.* We enter the table of critical values of D in the KS one-sample test (Appendix B–4 at the back of the book) and learn that with $\alpha = 0.05$ the critical value for D is

$$D = \frac{1.36}{\sqrt{60}} = 0.175$$

6. *Decision.* The calculated value is greater than the critical value, indicating that we should reject the null hypothesis.

Two-sample case

Two related samples. The sign test is used with matched pairs when the only information is the identification of the pair member that is larger or smaller or has more or less of some characteristic. Under H_0, one would expect that the number of cases in which $X_A > X_B$ to equal the number of pairs in which $X_B > X_A$. All ties are dropped from the analysis and n is adjusted to allow for these eliminated pairs. This test is based on the binomial expansion and has a good power efficiency for small samples.

Wilcoxon Matched-Pairs Test. When one can determine both *direction* and *magnitude* of difference between carefully matched pairs, use the Wilcoxon matched-pairs test. This test has excellent efficiency and can be more powerful than the t test in cases where the latter is not particularly appropriate. The mechanics of calculation are also quite simple. Find the difference score (d_i) between each pair of values and rank order the differences from smallest to largest without regard to sign. The actual signs of each difference are then added to the rank values and the test statistic T is calculated. T is the sum of the ranks with the less frequent sign. Typical of such research situations might be a study where husband and wife are matched, where twins are used, where a given subject is used in a before-after study, or where the output of two similar machines is compared.

Two types of ties may occur with this test. When two observations are equal, the d score becomes zero and we drop this pair of observations from the calculation. When two or more pairs have the same d value, average their rank positions. For example, if two pairs have a rank score of 1, assign the rank of 1.5 to each and rank the next largest difference as third. When n

< 25, use the table of critical values (Appendix B–5 at the back of the book). When $n > 25$, the sampling distribution of T is approximately normal with:

$$\text{Mean} = \mu_T = \frac{n(n + 1)}{4}$$

$$\text{Standard deviation} = \sigma_T = \sqrt{\frac{n(n + 1)(2n + 1)}{24}}$$

$$\text{The formula for the test is } z = \frac{T - \mu_T}{\sigma_T}$$

Suppose that you conduct an experiment on the effect of brand name on quality perception. Recruit 10 subjects and ask them to taste and compare two samples of product, one identified as a well-known drink and the other as a new product being tested. In truth, however, the samples are identical. The subjects are then asked to rate the two samples on a set of scale items judged to be ordinal. Test these results for significance by the usual procedure.

1. *Null hypothesis.* H_0. There is no difference between the perceived qualities of the two samples.

   H_A: There is a difference in the perceived quality of the two samples.

2. *Statistical test.* The Wilcoxon matched-pairs test is used because the study is of related samples in which the differences can be ranked in magnitude.

3. *Significance level.* $\alpha = 0.05$, with $n = 10$ pairs of comparisons minus any pairs with a d of zero.

4. *Calculated value.* T equals the sum of the ranks with the less frequent sign. Assume that we secure the following results:

Pair	Branded	Unbranded	d_i	Rank of d_i	Rank with less frequent sign
1	52	48	4	4	
2	37	32	5	5.5*	
3	50	52	−2	−2	2
4	45	32	13	9	
5	56	59	−3	−3	3
6	51	50	1	1	
7	40	29	11	8	
8	59	54	5	5.5*	
9	38	38	0	*	
10	40	32	8	7	$T = 5$

*There are two types of tie situations. We drop out the pair with the type of tie shown by pair 9. Pairs 2 and 8 have a tie in rank of difference. In this case, we average the ranks and assign the average value to each.

5. *Critical test value.* Enter the table of critical values of T with $n = 9$ (Appendix B–5 at the back of the book) and find that the critical value with $\alpha = 0.05$ is 6. Note that with this test, the calculated value must be smaller than the critical value in order to reject the null hypothesis.

6. *Decision.* Since the calculated value is less than the critical value, reject the null hypothesis.

Two independent samples. When a researcher has two independent samples of ordinal data, the Komolgorov Smirnov (KS) two-sample test is useful. Like the one-sample test, this two-sample test is concerned with the agreement between two cumulative distributions, but both represent sample values. If the two samples have been drawn from the same population, the cumulative distributions of the samples should be fairly close to each other, showing only random deviations from the population distribution. If the cumulative distributions show a large enough maximum deviation D, it is evidence for rejecting the H_0. In order to secure the maximum deviation, one should use as many intervals as are available so as not to obscure the maximum cumulative difference. The two-sample KS formula is:

$$D = \text{maximum } |F_{N_1}(X) - F_{N_2}(X)| \text{ (two-tailed test)}$$
$$D = \text{maximum } [F_{N_1}(X) - F_{N_2}(X)] \text{ (one-tailed test)}$$

D is calculated in the same manner as before, but the table for critical values for D (two-sample case) is presented in Appendix Table B–5 when $n_1 = n_2$ and is less than 40 observations. When n_1 and/or n_2 are larger than 40, Appendix Table B–7 should be used. With this larger sample it is not necessary that $n_1 = n_2$.

Here, use the smoking-accident study (see page 367). Suppose that the smoking classifications represent an ordinal scale and you test these data with the KS two-sample test. Proceed as follows:

1. *Null hypothesis.* H_0: There is no difference in on-the-job accident occurrences between smokers and nonsmokers.
   H_A: The more a person smokes, the more likely that person is to have an on-the-job accident.

2. *Statistical test.* The KS two-sample test is used because it is assumed that the data are ordinal.

3. *Significance level.* $\alpha = 0.05$, $n_1 = n_2 = 40$

4. *Calculated value.*

	Heavy smoker	Medium smoker	Light smoker	Nonsmoker
$F_{n_1}(X)$	12/40	21/40	27/40	40/40
$F_{n_2}(X)$	4/40	10/40	17/40	40/40
d_i	8/40	11/40	10/40	0

5. *Critical test value.* We enter Appendix Table B–6 with $n = 40$ to find that $D = 11$ when $p \leq 0.05$ for a one-tailed distribution.

6. *Decision.* Since the critical value equals the calculated value, we reject the null hypothesis. Note in this case that the KS test has found the results to be statistically significant while the χ^2 test of the same data did not.

Mann-Whitney U test. This test is also used with two independent samples if the data are at least ordinal; it is an alternative to the *t* test without the latter's limiting assumptions. When the larger of the two samples is 20 or less, there are special tables for interpreting U; when the larger sample exceeds 20, a normal curve approximation is used.

In calculating the U test, treat all observations in a combined fashion and rank them, algebraically, from smallest to largest. The largest negative score receives the lowest rank. In case of ties, assign the average rank as in other tests. With this test, you can also test samples that are unequal. After the ranking, the rank values for each sample are totalled. Compute the U statistic as follows:

$$U = n_1 n_2 + \frac{n_1(n_1 + 1)}{2} - R_1$$

or

$$U = n_1 n_2 + \frac{n_2(n_2 - 1)}{2} - R_2$$

in which

n_1 = Number in sample 1
n_2 = Number in sample 2
R_1 = Sum of ranks in sample 1

With this equation, one can secure two U values, one using R_1 and the second using R_2. For testing purposes, use the smaller U.

An example may help to clarify the U statistic calculation procedure. Let's consider the sales training example with the *t* distribution discussion. Recall that salespeople with training method A averaged higher sales than salespeople with training method B. While these data are ratio measured, one still might not want to accept the other assumptions which underly the *t* test. What kind of a result could be secured with the U test? While the U test is designed for ordinal data, it can be used with interval and ratio measurements.

1. *Null hypothesis.* H_0: There is no difference in sales results produced by the two training methods.
    H_A: Training method A produces sales results superior to the results of method B.

2. *Statistical test.* The Mann-Whitney U test is chosen because the measurement is at least ordinal, and the assumptions under the parametric t test are rejected.

3. *Significance level.* $\alpha = 0.05$ (one-tailed test)

4. *Calculated value.*

Sales per week per salesperson

Training method A	Rank	Training method B	Rank
1,500	15	1,340	10
1,540	16	1,300	8.5
1,860	22	1,620	18
1,230	6	1,070	3
1,370	12	1,210	5
1,550	17	1,170	4
1,840	21	1,770	20
1,250	7	950	1
1,300	8.5	1,380	13
1,350	11	1,460	14
1,710	19	1,030	2
	$R_1 = 154.5$		$R_2 = 98.5$

$$U = (11)(11) + \frac{11(11 + 1)}{2} - 154.5 \qquad U = (11)(11) + \frac{11(11 + 1)}{2} - 98.5$$

$$= 32.5 \qquad\qquad\qquad = 88.5$$

5. *Critical test value.* Enter Appendix Table B–8 with $n_1 = n_2 = 11$, and find a critical value of 34 for $\alpha = 0.05$, one-tailed test. Note that with this test, the calculated value must be smaller than the critical value in order to reject the null hypothesis.

6. *Decision.* Since the calculated value is smaller than the critical value ($34 > 32.5$), reject the null hypothesis and conclude that training method A is probably superior.

Thus, one would reject the null hypothesis at $\alpha = 0.05$ in a one-tailed test using either the t or the U test. In this example, the U test has approximately the same power as the parametric test.

When $n > 20$ in one of the samples, the sampling distribution of U approaches the normal distribution with

$$\text{Mean} = \mu_U = \frac{n_1 n_2}{2}$$

$$\text{Standard deviation } \sigma_U = \sqrt{\frac{(n_1)(n_2)(n_1 + n_2 + 1)}{12}}$$

and

$$z = \frac{U - \mu_U}{\sigma_U}$$

Other nonparametric tests. Other nonparametric tests are appropriate under certain conditions when testing two independent samples. When the measurement is only nominal, the Fisher exact probability test may be used. When the data are at least ordinal, use the median and Wald-Wolfowitz runs tests. When the data are interval, use the randomization test for two independent samples.[1]

K sample case

You can use tests more powerful than χ^2 with data which are at least ordinal in nature. One such test is an extension of the median test mentioned earlier. We illustrate here the application of a second ordinal measurement test known as the Kruskal-Wallis one-way analysis of variance.

The Kruskal-Wallis test is a generalized version of the Mann-Whitney test. With it, we rank all scores in the entire pool of observations from smallest to largest. The rank sum of each sample is then calculated, with ties being distributed as in other examples. One then computes the value of H as follows:

$$H = \frac{12}{N(N - 1)} \sum_{j=1}^{k} \frac{T_j^2}{n_j} - 3(N + 1)$$

in which

T_j = Sum of ranks in column j
n_j = Number of cases in jth sample
$N = \Sigma w_j$ = Total number of cases
k = Number of samples

When there are a number of ties, it is recommended that a correction factor (C) be calculated and used to correct the H value as follows:

$$C = 1 - \left\{ \frac{\sum_{i}^{G} (t_i^3 - t_i)}{N^2 - N} \right\}$$

in which

---

[1]For details on these and other nonparametric tests, see Siegel, *Nonparametric Statistics;* Linton C. Freeman, *Elementary Applied Statistics* (New York: John Wiley & Sons, 1965); or Frederick Mosteller and Robert E. K. Rourke, *Sturdy Statistics* (Reading, Mass.: Addison-Wesley, 1973).

G = Number of sets of tied observations
t_i = Number tied in any set i
H' = H/C

To secure the critical value for H', use the table for the distribution of χ^2 (Appendix B–3), and enter it with the value of H', and d.f. = $k - 1$.

To illustrate the application of this test, use the price discount experiment problem. The data and calculations are shown in Table 12A–1 and indicate that, by the Kruskal-Wallis test, one again barely fails to reject the null hypothesis with $\alpha = 0.05$.

TABLE 12A–1   Kruskal-Wallis one-way analysis of variance (price differentials)

One cent		Three cents		Five cents	
X_A	Rank	X_B	Rank	X_C	Rank
6	1	8	5	9	8.5
7	2.5	9	8.5	9	8.5
8	5	8	5	11	14
7	2.5	10	11.5	10	11.5
9	8.5	11	14	14	18
11	14	13	16.5	13	16.5
	T_i = 33.5		60.5		77

$T = 33.5 + 60.5 + 77$
  $= 171$

$$H = \frac{12}{18(18 - 1)} \left[\frac{33.5^2 + 60.5^2 + 77^2}{6} \right] - 3(18 + 1)$$

$$= \frac{12}{342} \left[\frac{1,122.25 + 3,660.25 + 5,929}{6} \right] - 57$$

$$= 0.0351 \left[\frac{10,711.5}{6} \right] - 57$$

$H = 5.66$

$$C = 1 - \left(\frac{3[(2)^3 - 2] + 2[(3)^3 - 3] + [(4)^3 - 4]}{18^3 + 18} \right)$$

$$= 1 - \frac{18 + 48 + 60}{5814}$$

$$= 0.978$$

$$H' = \frac{H}{C} = \frac{5.66}{0.978} = 5.79$$

d.f. = $k - 1 = 2$

  $p > 0.05$

Nonparametric tests. In the *k*-related sample case, in which the measurement is only nominal, we can use the Cochran *Q* test, an extension of the McNemar test discussed earlier. When the data are at least ordinal, you may also use the Friedman two-way analysis of variance test, an extension of the Wilcoxon matched-pairs test discussed earlier. Details on the calculation procedures for these tests are found in many statistics references.[2]

---

[2]See Siegel, *Nonparametric Statistics,* or W. L. Hays, *Statistics for the Social Sciences* (New York: Holt, Rinehart & Winston, 1973).

13. Data analysis—measures of association

Chris Riley could hear the clatter of an electric typewriter in the next room as she looked down at the page and began to read; she had two hours to answer the three problems before her.

She felt good about the interviews that morning. Now she had to demonstrate that she could apply multivariate analysis to business research situations. If she did this well, she felt she would get the staff research job with this famous consulting firm in whose office she now was sitting. The problem statements were brief but she could see that they would take some careful thought. The questions were:

1. It is reasonable to hypothesize that household income has an effect on household food expenditures. How might you statistically test this hypothesis? If there is such a relationship, how would you measure it? What other variables might influence household food expenditures and how might these be introduced into the income-food expenditure relationship?

2. Develop a statistical analysis by which to screen MBA graduates for employment. The client is a firm that has had unsatisfactory experience hiring MBAs and would like a statistical model to help them improve their selection.

3. You are the director of the MBA program at Big University and have been reviewing the grade sheets for the first-year students. The data appear to support a hypothesis of yours that some people do well in certain allied courses while others do better in a different set of courses. You decide to use these data to test this hypothesis. What would you do and how would you do it?

Before dealing with these questions, Chris decided to review some of the concepts which she thought were appropriate here.

ASSOCIATION MEASUREMENT

Several research purposes can be served by associating statistical data. First, one can determine whether there appears to be any relationship between two or more sets of data. For example, are certain employee attitudes related to the types of jobs the employees hold? By such analysis, one can develop a better understanding of how variables are related. It is possible to estimate the relative importance of correlations among variables. For example, does method A or method B produce the better results in variable Z?

A second research purpose served by the analysis of association is that of prediction. Knowing the dimensions of one readily available variable, it is possible to predict the size of another variable that is not as available. For example, leading indicators are widely used in economics to forecast business conditions, and scores on tests are used to predict worker success.

The third value of association analysis is that one can sometimes statistically control the influence of certain variables in order to study the impact of other variables. For example, one can study the relationship between family food expenditures and family income, holding constant the effect of family size.

There are two basic types of association problems—those involving *dependency* and those with *interdependency relationships*. A dependency relationship is one in which there are both independent and dependent variables. In an interdependency situation, there are two or more variables whose relationships are of interest, but none is assumed to depend on or be influenced by the others. For each of these cases, there are a number of statistical techniques available. Among the dependency association techniques are correlation, regression, and discriminate analysis. For the interdependency relationship, factor analysis is discussed.

CORRELATION

With correlation analysis, one calculates a coefficient by which to measure the closeness of association between variables. With regression, one develops an estimating equation by which to use data from one or more independent variables to estimate values for a dependent variable. Both correlation and regression are affected by the assumptions made about the measurement levels involved and the distributions that underlie the data. For example, when associating two nominal variables, only certain types of procedures are appropriate. Other procedures apply when ordinal variables are used and still others when higher measurement levels are used. In each case, however, one is interested in calculating a summary statistic or equation that expresses the association of different levels of one variable with different levels of one or more other variables. Correlation for nominal measurement levels is presented first.

Nonparametric correlation

Nominal data. There is no fully satisfactory measure of association for categorical data. The most widely known measure is C, the contingency coefficient, but it suffers from the defect that its upper limit may not be 1. Two measures that are more useful are Cramer's statistic and the index of predictive associations, or lambda.

Cramer's statistic.[1] This association measure is based on first calculating a chi square (χ^2). Cramer's statistic (V) is then computed from the equation

$$V = \sqrt{\frac{\chi^2}{mn}}$$

where n is the size of sample and m is the number of rows or columns minus 1.0, whichever is less ($r - 1$ or $c - 1$). For example, from the hypothetical example on the incidence of smoking and accidents (see page 367), we found a χ^2 of 7.44. Cramer's V for this example is:

$$V = \sqrt{\frac{7.44}{(1)80}} = 0.30$$

This indicates that there is a moderate statistical relationship between workers who smoke and accidents on the job, but there is no suggestion from this statistic that one causes the other, nor is there an indication of direction to this association. The range of this statistic is from zero (no association) to as high as 1.0 (complete association) when the row totals give a frequency distribution identical to the column totals. In other cases, however, the upper limit approaches 1.0.

Lambda. The coefficient *Lambda* (λ) is a second and different approach to measuring the degree of association between two nominal variables. It is based on how well the frequencies of one nominal variable offer predictive evidence about the frequency of the second nominal variable. Thus, it is not based on chi square. The lambda coefficient is also asymmetrical; one can calculate the direction of prediction or association.

Lambda is computed in a straightforward way. Assume, for example, that the results shown in Table 13–1 came from an opinion survey among a sample of 400 adults.

Assume for the moment that only 180 out of the 400 (or 45 percent) favor the tax liberalization, while 220 (or 55 percent) do not favor it. With this information alone, if asked to predict the opinions of the individuals in the sample, one would achieve the best prediction record by always choosing the model opinion of "do not favor." By so doing, however, you would be wrong 180 times out of 400.

Now suppose one had prior information about respondent occupation status and then was asked to predict opinion. Would it improve the predic-

---

[1] For more details, see W. L. Hays and R. L. Winkler, *Statistics: Probability, Inference and Decision*, 2d ed. (New York: Holt, Rinehart & Winston, 1975), pp. 835–37.

TABLE 13–1 What is your opinion about a proposal to liberalize the capital gains tax?

Occupation class	Favor	Do not favor	Total
Managerial	90	20	110
White collar	60	80	140
Blue collar	30	120	150
Total	180	220	400

tions? Of course, it would! You would make the predictions in the accompanying table.

	Our prediction score	
	Corrct	Error
If managerial, choose "favorable"	90	20
If white collar, choose "do not favor"	80	60
If blue collar, choose "do not favor"	120	30
Total	290	110

By this tally, one can see that the additional information reduced the error prediction from 180 to 110. In terms of the lambda criterion, the results are:

$$\lambda = \frac{\text{Number of errors in first case } - \text{ Number of errors in second case}}{\text{Number of errors in first case}}$$

$$= \frac{180 - 110}{180} = 0.39$$

Lambda is interpreted as the percent improvement in prediction of opinion as a result of knowing the respondent's occupation category.

The general formula calculating lambda is:

$$\lambda_{D|I} = \frac{\Sigma f_{KI} - F_D}{n - F_D}$$

where

f_{KI} = The maximum frequency found within each subclass of the independent or prior variable.

F_D = The maximum frequency among the marginal totals of the dependent variable.

n = Size of sample.

If one wishes to estimate occupation categories from opinions on the proposed capital gains liberalization, that is, start with opinions as the prior or independent variable, one would secure the following:

$$\lambda_{D|I} = \frac{(90 + 120) - 150}{400 - 150} = 0.24$$

This is interpreted as meaning 24 percent of the error in predicting respondent occupation class is eliminated by knowing the person's opinion on the capital gains tax question. Lambda varies between zero (no ability to eliminate errors) and 1.0 (ability to eliminate all errors).

Ordinal data.   When data are at least ordinal measurements, one has the choice of two excellent rank order correlation methods, both of which possess a power efficiency of about 0.9 when compared with parametric measures. Neither requires the assumption of a bivariate normal distribution. The most widely used is Spearman's rank-order correlation coefficient (r_s). The second nonparametric correlation method is the Kendall *tau*. It is somewhat more complicated in calculation but can be generalized to partial correlation coefficients while the Spearman cannot. Finally, there is the Kendall coefficient of concordance (W), a nonparametric measure of association that may be used with k sets of rankings.[2] Here, Spearman's coefficient is discussed.

Spearman's rank correlation.   Spearman's *rho* (as it is often called) is actually a special form of the Pearsonian correlation coefficient (r) which is introduced next. It is a relatively easy statistic to compute. The major deficiency of *rho* is said to be its sensitivity to distortion from ties in ranks. When this is a problem, one can use a slightly more complicated formula with a tie correction factor. (See Table 13–2.)

To illustrate the use of *rho*, consider a situation where the Big Corporation is recruiting new management trainees. Assume that the field has been narrowed to 10 applicants for the final evaluation. They all come to company headquarters, go through a battery of tests, and are interviewed by a panel of three executives. The test results are evaluated by a psychologist who then ranks the 10 in terms of the test evidence. The executive panel also ranks the applicants on the basis of their interviews. In assessing the results of these measurements, you decide to compare how well these two sets of rankings agree.

You list the applicants, and beside each applicant's name, you enter his/her ranks by each evaluation method. Where scores are tied, you assign the

---

[2]Sidney Siegel, *Nonparametric Statistics for the Behavioral Sciences* (New York: McGraw-Hill, 1956), pp. 202–38.

TABLE 13–2　　Spearman rank correlation

| | Rank by | | | |
| | Panel | Psychologist | | |
Applicant	x	y	d	d²
A	3.5	6	−2.5	6.25
B	10	5	5	25.00
C	6.5	8	1.5	2.25
D	2	1.5	0.5	0.25
E	1	3	−2	4.00
F	9	7	2	4.00
G	3.5	1.5	2	4.00
H	6.5	9	2.5	6.25
I	8	10	2	4.00
J	5	4	1	1.00
				57.0

average of the ranks that would have been assigned if no ties had occurred. Then you determine the difference (d) between the two ranks, square these differences and total the squared values as follows:
The computation of *rho* is

$$r_s = 1 - \frac{6\Sigma d^2}{n^3 - n} = 1 - \frac{6(57)}{(10)^3 - 10} = 0.654$$

where

　　n = the number of subjects being ranked.

This computation confirms that there is substantial correlation between the two measurements and suggests that they are reasonably valid. There may be some question as to the effect of the three pairs of ties in the data. You may choose to guard against this distortion by recalculating the results with the tie correction factor.[3] In this case, the correction factor reduces r_s from 0.654 to 0.651. It would appear that a few ties have little effect on the value of *rho*.

Parametric correlation

Recall the problems facing Chris Riley at the beginning of this chapter. She immediately recognized the problem concerning the relationship of

---

[3]See Siegel, *Nonparametric Statistics,* pp. 207–10, for computation details.

household income to food expenditures as one involving parametric correlation and regression.

Bivariate correlation. When one uses sample information, the parametric correlation measure is the Pearson product-moment coefficient r. It is a summary statistic that represents the linear relationship between two sets of variables. For example, assume that you want to measure the relationship between family food expenditures and family income.[4] There are data for 30 families drawn from the files of a larger study. Correlate these data and secure a Pearsonian coefficient (r) of 0.73. What does this mean? The r statistic can range from $+1$ (perfect positive correlation) through 0 (absence of correlation) to -1 (perfect inverse correlation). These and other relationships are shown graphically in Figure 13–1.

The precise average relationship between income and expenditures is given in Figure 13–1 by the solid line called the regression line of best fit. It is expressed by the equation:

$$Y = a + bx$$

in which

$a =$ the regression coefficient or amount of Y when $X = 0$. It is also known as the Y intercept.

$b =$ the regression coefficient or amount that Y varies, on the average, with a change of one unit of X.

The regression line is fitted to the data by the least squares technique and measures how the dependent variable changes with variations in the independent variable. It is that line about which the squared deviations of the Ys are at a minimum, and the algebraic sum of the deviations equals zero. It is analogous to calculating an arithmetic mean of the relationship between the X and Y variables. In fact, the line of best fit goes through the point of means of X and Y as shown by the dashed lines on the figure. It is apparent also from the scatter of points that family income can explain much of the deviations of family food expenditures from the average.[5] It is a characteristic of r that its square (the coefficient of determination) is an estimate of the explained deviation of individual items from $\overline{Y}$. For example, if $r = 0.73$ for the data in Figure 13–1, then 0.73^2 or about 53 percent of the total deviation from $\overline{Y}$ of these 30 paired observations can be explained in terms of family income.

Hypothesis testing. Up to this point, only the descriptive application of correlation has been mentioned, but it is also used for statistical inference.

---

[4]Computation of these measures by hand is somewhat tedious and the calculation specifics are not covered here. We use the various SPSS computer programs for these chores.

[5]"Explain" used here is not in terms of causation, but rather it means that the regression line statistically correlates with, on the average, a certain proportion of the total deviation of observations from the mean of Y.

FIGURE 13–1   Scatterplot of annual household income and household
food expenditures

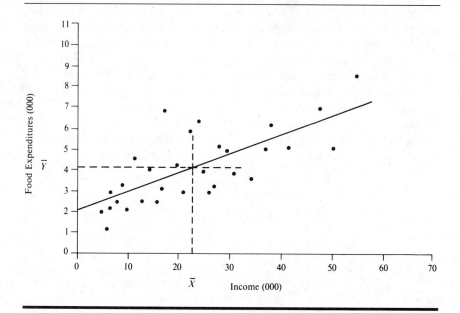

For example, one might test the null hypothesis that $\rho = 0$.[6] Use the t test
and the following equation to secure the calculated value.

$$t = \frac{r\sqrt{n-2}}{\sqrt{1-r^2}} = \frac{.73\sqrt{28}}{\sqrt{1-.73^2}}$$

$$t = 5.6 \qquad d.f. = 30 - 2 = 28$$

Assume that you establish a critical value based on a one-tailed test of $\alpha = $
.05. We enter the t table (Appendix B–2 at back of book) and find that one
can reject the null hypothesis, if the calculated t value is greater than 1.701
(one tailed test) with d.f. = 28. Clearly $t = 5.6$ is statistically significant,
even beyond $\alpha = .0005$.

While it is reasonable to expect that family income affects food expenditures, it is apparent from the scatterplot in Figure 13–1 that income alone
does not explain all variations in food expenditures. In addition, you might
hypothesize that size of family also influences food spending. Again use an

---

[6]ρ = rho = the population coefficient of correlation for which r is a sample-based
estimate.

SPSS program for simple correlation to calculate the relationship between family size and family food expenditures, securing an $r = .50$. This also is statistically significant. The r^2 of .25 indicates that 25 percent of the variation in food expenditures in this sample of 30 families is statistically accounted for by variations in family size.

But now another question arises. Is there any overlap in the explanatory power of these two independent variables? That is, how much impact might family income have if you were able to study families all of the same size? The correlations calculated to this point have ignored any interaction between the effects of income and family size on food expenditures. One can "control" one of these variables statistically while measuring the effect of the other variable on food expenditures through the technique of partial correlation.

Partial correlation. The effect of this technique is analogous to the elaboration, using nominal data, discussed in Chapter 11. Using the partial correlation program in SPSS, first calculate the following so-called zero order correlation matrix.

Variable	(1) Food expenditures	(2) Income	(3) Family size
(1) Food expenditures	1.00	.73	.50
(2) Family income		1.00	.12
(3) Family size			1.00

One can also calculate the partial correlation between food expenditures and family income, holding family size constant, as $r_{12.3} = 0.77$.[7] This compares to .73 when the influence of family size was ignored. Thus, in this sample, knowing family size does not improve much the ability of family income to predict food expenditures. However, one more question arises. How well can you estimate food expenditures if one uses both independent variables? This is a problem for multiple correlation.

Multiple correlation. With multiple correlation, one can introduce, simultaneously, the effect of two or more independent variables and calculate their net impact on a dependent variable. The coefficient of multiple correlation for a sample is known as R, and its square (R^2) is the coefficient of multiple determination. While R can be hand-calculated, we use the SPSS multiple regression program to calculate $R = 0.83$, and $R^2 = 0.69$.

---

[7] $r_{12.3}$ should be read as the correlation between variables 1 and 2, holding the effect of variable 3 constant.

To summarize, the coefficients used in this example may be interpreted as follows:

Interpretation

$r_{12}^2 = (0.73)^2 = 0.53$ About 53 percent of the variation in family food expenditures is explained by variations in family income, with other factors not considered.

$r_{13}^2 = (0.50)^2 = 0.25$ About 25 percent of the variation in family food expenditures is explained by variations in family size, with other factors not considered.

$r_{12.3}^2 = (0.77)^2 = 0.59$ About 59 percent of the variation in family food expenditures is explained by variations in family income when the effects of family size are held constant.

$R_{1.33}^2 = (0.83)^2 = 0.69$ About 69 percent of the variation in family food expenditures is explained by a combination of family income and family size.

The above statistics show that combining the two independent variables simultaneously does improve our ability to estimate family food expenditures. We return to this example in the next section.

MULTIVARIATE ANALYSIS

Up to this point, the emphasis has been on associating two variables in a paired relationship. In recent years, however, there has been a rapid development and application of multivariate statistical tools to business research problems. These developments have been stimulated by the increased availability of large-scale computers.

One author defines multivariate analysis as "those statistical techniques which focus upon, and bring out in bold relief, the structure of simultaneous relationships among three or more phenomena."[8] The major point in this definition is that multivariate analysis is a shift away from the paired relationships between two variables to the simultaneous relationships among three or more variables.

Since there are many multivariate techniques, it may be helpful to classify them in some orderly fashion. One widely used classification is based on the nature of the relationships among the variables. In this sense, the analysis may involve either dependence or independence assumptions. The dependence condition is found when one or more of the variables are criterion variables (DVs) and one or more are predictor variables (IVs). Multiple regression and discriminate analysis are popular examples of dependence

---

[8]Jagdish N. Sheth, ed., *Multivariate Methods for Market and Survey Research* (Chicago: American Marketing Association, 1977) p. 3.

FIGURE 13–2 Recommended association measurement techniques by use situation*

ANALYSIS OF DEPENDENCE

Situation	Variable	Number of variables	Measurement level	Technique
1	Dependent	1	Metric	Simple regression or ANOVA
	Independent	1	Metric	
2	Dependent	1	Metric	Multiple regression
	Independent	>1	Metric	
3	Dependent	1	Metric	1. Dummy variable multiple regression
	Independent	>1	Nonmetric	2. Multiple classification analysis (MCA)
				3. Automatic interaction detection (AID)
4	Dependent	1	Nonmetric	Discriminant analysis
	Independent	>1	Metric	
5	Dependent	1	Nonmetric	MCA with 0-1 DV
	Independent	>1	Nonmetric	
6	Dependent	>1	Metric	Canonical analysis
	Independent	>1	Metric	
7	Dependent	>1	Metric	Multivariate ANOVA
	Independent	>1	Nonmetric	
8	Dependent	>1	Nonmetric	Convert to canonical analysis
	Independent	>1	or Metric	

ANALYSIS OF INDEPENDENCE

Situation	Number of variables	Measurement level	Grouping	Technique
1	Several	Metric	Variables	R-factor analysis
2	Several	Metric	Objects (e.g., people)	1. Q-factor analysis
				2. Cluster analysis
				3. Multidimensional scaling
3	Several	Nonmetric	Variables	1. Nonmetric factor analysis
				2. Latent structure analysis
4	Several	Nonmetric	Objects	1. Nonmetric MDS
				2. Latent class analysis
				3. Nonmetric cluster analysis

*Thanks to J. Paul Peter for suggesting this organization scheme. Partially adapted from T. C. Kinnear and J. R. Taylor "Multivariate Methods in Marketing Research: A Further Attempt at Classification," *Journal of Marketing* (October 1971), p. 57.

techniques. With the independence condition, the variables are interrelated without the assumption that some are predictors and others are criterion measures. Factor analysis, cluster analysis, and multidimensional scaling are examples of these procedures.

A second classification scheme is based on the measurement scale levels of nonmetric (nominal or ordinal scales) and metric (interval or ratio scales). Finally, if criterion and predictor variables are used, the appropriate technique will depend upon the number of each variable type. A combination of these three considerations, with suggestions for the appropriate technique to use for each, is shown in Figure 13–2.

Multiple regression

This is the best known and most widely used multivariate statistical technique. An extension of the bivariate least squares model presented earlier in the chapter, it assumes at least interval level data although there is a frequent use of dummy variables as predictors.[9] The generalized equation for multiple regression is:

$$Y = a + b_1X_1 + b_2X_2 + b_3X_3 \ldots b_nX_n$$

where

a = The value of Y when all X values are zero.

b_i = The regression coefficient associated with each unit of X_i

The b values are stated either in raw score units (the actual X values) or as standardized scores (X values restated in terms of their standard deviations). In either case, the value of the regression coefficient states the amount that Y varies with each unit change of the associated X variable when the effects of all other X variables are being held constant. When the regression coefficients are in standard terms, they are called beta weights (β) and their values indicate the relative importance of the associated X values. for example, in an equation where $\beta_1 = 0.60$ and $\beta_2 = 0.20$, one concludes that X_1 has three times the influence on Y as does X_2.

Multiple regression is used as a descriptive tool in three types of situations. First, it is used often to develop a self-weighting estimating equation by which to predict values for a criterion variable (DV) from the values for several predictor variables (IVs). Thus, we might try to predict company sales on the basis of new housing starts, new marriage rates, annual disposable income, and a time factor. Another prediction study might be a regression in which one estimates a student's academic performance in college from the variables of (1) rank in high school class; (2) SAT verbal scores;

---

[9]A dummy variable is a binary 0–1 variable and is often used to introduce nominal dichotomies such as sex, race, and so on, as predictor variables.

(3) SAT quantitative scores; and (4) a rating scale reflecting impressions from an interview.

A second descriptive application is to control for confounding variables in order to evaluate better the contribution of other variables. For example, one might wish to control the brand of a product, and the store in which it is bought in order to study the effects of price as an indicator of product quality.[10] A third use of multiple regression as a descriptive tool is to test and explain causal theories. In this approach, often referred to as path analysis, regression is used to describe an entire structure of linkages that have been advanced a priori from some causal theory.[11] In addition to being a descriptive tool, a multiple regression is also used as an inference tool to test hypotheses and to estimate population values from simple data.

An example. Return to the food expenditure problem to illustrate multiple regression with the following variables:

Y = Annual family food expenditures

X_1 = Annual family income

X_2 = Family size

X_3 = Family location (0 = rural, 1 = urban)

Use the multiple regresson package from SPSS to compute the correlation values and the regression coefficients. The major elements of the printout from this package are shown in Figure 13–3. The inclusion of the three independent variables correlates well with family food expenditures (R = 0.878). The R^2 of 0.771 indicates that about 77 percent of the variation in family food expenditures for this sample of 30 families can be accounted for by differences in family income, family size, and whether they live in urban or rural areas.

The other reported statistics have the following interpretations:

1. Adjusted R square = 0.7445—R square is adjusted for the number of independent variables. The net effect of this adjustment is to reduce the R square slightly but to make it comparable to other R squares from equations with a different number of independent variables.

2. Standard error = 0.8697—This is the standard deviation of actual values of Y about the regression line of estimated Y values.

3. Analysis of variance—This analysis measures whether or not the equation represents a set of regression coefficients which, in total, are statistically significant from zero. The critical value for "F" is found in Appendix B–2 with degrees of freedom of 3,26. The Appendix Table B–9 indicates a

[10]Benson Shapiro, "Price Reliance: Existence and Sources," *Journal of Marketing Research* 10 (August 1973), pp. 286–89.

[11]For a discussion of path analysis, see Fred Kerlinger and E. Pedhazer, *Multiple Regression in Behavioral Research* (New York: Holt, Rinehart & Winston, 1973), chapter 11.

FIGURE 13–3 Multiple regression analysis of family income, family size and location on family food expenditures

MULTIPLE REGRESSION

FILE   NONAME   (CREATION DATE = 07/20/84)

07/20/84   PAGE 19

************************ MULTIPLE REGRESSION ************************

VARIABLE LIST 1
REGRESSION LIST 1

DEPENDENT VARIABLE . .   V2   FOOD

VARIABLE(S) ENTERED ON STEP NUMBER 1 . .   V5   LOCATION
                                            V3   HOUSEHOLD INCOME
                                            V4   HOUSEHOLD SIZE

			ANALYSIS OF VARIANCE	DF	SUM OF SQUARES	MEAN SQUARE	F
MULTIPLE R	0.87804		REGRESSION	3.	66.19259	22.06420	29.17050
R SQUARE	0.77095		RESIDUAL	26.	19.66607	0.75639	
ADJUSTED R SQUARE	0.74452						
STANDARD ERROR	0.86971						

------- VARIABLES IN THE EQUATION -------   ------- VARIABLES NOT IN THE EQUATION -------

VARIABLE	B	BETA	STD ERROR B	F	VARIABLE	BETA IN	PARTIAL	TOLERANCE	F
V5	1.102366	0.27560	0.38594	8.159					
V3	.7582867D-01	0.61723	0.01189	40.659					
V4	.6076182	0.44860	0.12890	22.221					
(CONSTANT)	-.1899372								

ALL VARIABLES ARE IN THE EQUATION

STATISTICS WHICH CANNOT BE COMPUTED ARE PRINTED AS ALL NINES.

Source: Data are hypothetical.

critical value of 2.98 for an $\alpha = .05$. Clearly the equation is statistically significant.

4. The column headed B indicates the computed regression coefficients for the regression equation of:

$$Y = -.1899 + .0758X_1 + .6076X_2 + 1.1024X_3$$

5. The column headed Beta gives the regression coefficients expressed in standardized format, i.e., in terms of standard deviations. When these are used, the regression Y intercept is zero. These beta weights also show the relative contribution of the three independent variables to the explanatory power of this equation. It shows, for example, that household income explains more than do either of the other two variables.

6. Standard error of B is a measure of the sampling variability of each regression coefficient. That is, .01189 is the standard deviation of the sampling variability of .0758, the regression coefficient for family income.

7. The column F measures the statistical significance of each of the regression coefficients. Again compare these to the table of F values in Appendix B, using degrees of freedom of 1, and $(n - k - 1)$ or 26. All three regression coefficients are judged to be significantly different from zero.

Regression problems. One difficulty with multiple regression is that of multicollinearity—the situation where some or all of the independent variables are highly correlated. When such a condition exists, the estimated regression coefficients can fluctuate widely from sample to sample, making it risky to use the coefficients as an indicator of the relative importance of predictor variables. Just how high can acceptable correlations be between independent variables? There is no definitive answer, but correlations at a 0.8 or greater level should be dealt with in one of two ways: (1) choose one of the variables and delete the other, or (2) create a new variable that is a composite of the highly intercorrelated variables and use this new variable in place of its components. In the example just presented, the matrix of simple correlations indicates that there is no correlation between any two independent variables greater than 0.20, indicating that multicollinearity is no problem here.

Another problem with regression is that users of this technique too often fail to cross-validate their equation with data beyond those that were used to calculate the equation originally. The most practical approach is for the researcher to set aside a portion of the data (say, a fourth to a third) and use only the remainder to compute the estimating equation. One then uses the equation on the set-aside data to calculate an R^2 for the held out data. This can then be compared to the original R^2 to determine how well the equation predicts beyond its data base.

Discriminant analysis

Often researchers wish to classify persons or objects into two or more groups. For example, one might need to classify persons as either buyers

or nonbuyers, good or bad credit risks, or superior, average, or poor per-
formers in some activity. The problem here is to establish a procedure by
which to predict into which category various subjects fall. Discriminant
analysis provides a means by which such categorization can be carried out
statistically.

Discriminant analysis is a technique in which a nominally scaled criterion
or dependent variable is related to one or more independent variables which
are usually interval or ratio scaled. Once the discriminant equation is found,
it can be used to predict into which class a new observation should be
placed. This is done by calculating a linear function of the form:

$$D_i = d_{i1}Z_1 + d_{i2}Z_2 + \cdots + d_{ip}Z_p$$

which

D_i is the score on discriminant function i

The d are weighting coefficients

The Zs are the standardized values of the discriminating variables used in
the analysis.

A single discriminant equation is required if the categorization calls for
two groups. If three groups are involved in the classification, it requires two
discriminant equations. If more categories are called for in the dependent
variable, it is necessary to calculate a separate discriminant function for each
pair of classifications in the criterion group.

While the most common use for discriminant analysis is to classify persons
or objects into various groups, it can also be used to analyze known groups
to determine the relative influence of specific factors for determining into
which group various cases fall. For example, one might have supervisor
ratings that enable one to classify administrators as successful or unsuccessful
on administrative performance. One might also be able to secure test results
on these people concerning the three measures of Ability to Work with
Others (Z_1), Motivation for Administrative work (Z_2), and General Professional Skill (Z_3). Suppose the discriminant equation is:

$$D = 0.06Z_1 + 0.45Z_2 + 0.30Z_3$$

Since a feature of discriminant analysis is that it uses standardized values for
the discriminant variables, one can conclude from the coefficients that Ability to Work with Others is less important than the other two in classifying
administrators as being successful or unsuccessful.[12]

An example. The management of your company has been hiring MBAs
for some years, but with indifferent success. They ask you to develop a
procedure by which to improve their selection batting average. This looks
like a problem for discriminant analysis, so you gather information on 30
MBAs who have been hired in recent years. Fifteen of these have been

---

[12]Fred Kerlinger, *Foundations of Behavioral Research*, 2d ed. (New York: Holt Rinehart
& Winston, 1973), p. 651.

successful employees while the other 15 were unsatisfactory. The personnel files provide the following information which can be used to conduct the discriminant analysis.

Z_1 = Years of prior work experience

Z_2 = GPA in graduàte program

Z_3 = Employment test score

The SPSS package on discriminant analysis is used to determine how well these three independent variables will correctly classify those who are judged successful from those judged unsuccessful. The classification results are shown in Table 13–3. This indicates that 25 of the 30 cases were correctly classified using these three variables.

TABLE 13–3   Discriminant analysis classification results

Actual group		No. of cases	Predicted group membership	
			0	1
Group Unsuccessful	0	15	13 86.7%	2 13.3%
Group Successful	1	15	3 20.0%	12 80.0%
Percent of "grouped" cases correctly classified: 83.33%				

The standardized and unstandardized discriminant function coefficients are as follows:

	Unstandardized	Standardized
Z_1	.36084	.65927
Z_2	2.61192	.57958
Z_3	.53028	.97505
(constant)	12.89685	

These results indicate that Z_3 (the employment test) has the greatest discriminating power. Several significance tests are also computed in this package. One, chi square, indicates that the equation is statistically significant at the α = .0004 level.

Other dependence measures. Multiple classification analysis (MCA) is a form of multiple regression in which the predictor variables are nominally scaled while the criterion variable is metric.[13] Another dependence measure

---

[13]For details on MCA, see F. M. Andrews, J. N. Morgan, J. A. Sonquist and L. Klein, *Multiple Classification Analysis*, 2d ed. (Ann Arbor, Mich.: Institute for Social Research, 1973).

is automatic interaction detection (AID). A discussion and example of this technique is found in Chapter 11. A final dependence technique to be mentined here is canonical analysis. It also is an extension of regression analysis, in this case, to predict simultaneously a set of criterion variables from their joint covariance with a set of predictor variables.[14]

Factor analysis

Factor analysis is a general description for a number of specific computational techniques. All of these techniques, however, have the objective of reducing a large number of measures to some smaller number by telling us which belong together and which seem to measure the same thing. The predictor-criterion relationship that was found in the dependence situation is replaced by a matrix of intercorrelations between a number of variables, none of which is viewed as being dependent upon the others. For example, one may have data on 100 employees in terms of scores on six attitude scale items. One should begin factor analysis by correlating each pair of scale items.

The second step in factor analysis is to construct a new set of variables on the basis of relationships in the correlation matrix. While this can be done in a number of ways, the most frequently used approach is *principal component analysis.* By this method, a set of variables is transformed into a new set of composite variables or principal components that are not correlated with each other. These are *factors.* This is done by finding the best linear combination of variables as far as accounting for the variance in the data as a whole. Such a combination makes up the first principal component and is the first factor. The second principal component is defined as the best linear combination of variables in terms of explaining the variance *not* accounted for by the first factor. In turn, there may be a third, fourth, and so on, components, each being the best linear combination of variables in terms of explaining the variance not accounted for by the previous factors.

This process can continue until all of the variance is accounted for, but as a practical matter, it is usually stopped after a small number of factors have been extracted. The output of a principal components analysis might look like the hypothetical data shown in the unrotated factors section of Table 13–4. (For the moment, ignore the rotated factors section of the table.) The values in the table are correlation coefficients between the factor and the variables (0.7 is the r between variable A and factor I). These correlation coefficients are called *loadings.* Two other elements in Table 13–4 need explanation. Eigenvalues are the sum of the variances of the factor values (for factor I the eigenvalue is $0.7^2 + 0.6^6 + 0.6^2 + 0.5^2 + 0.6^2 + 0.6^2$).

---

[14]For details on canonical analysis, see P. E. Green, M. H. Halbert, and P. J. Robinson, "Canonical Analysis: An Exposition and Illustrative Application," *Journal of Marketing Research* 3 (February 1966), pp. 32–39.

When divided by the number of variables, it yields an estimate of the amount of total variance explained by the factor. For example, factor I accounts for 36 percent of the total variance. The column headed h^2 gives the *communalities* or estimates of the variance in each variable which is explained by the two factors. With variable A, for example, the communality is $0.7^2 + (-0.4)^2 = 0.65$, indicating that 65 percent of the variance in variable A is statistically explained in terms of factors I and II.

TABLE 13–4   Factor matrices

Variable	A Unrotated factors			B Rotated factors	
	I	*II*	*h²*	*I*	*II*
A	0.7	−0.4	0.65	0.79	0.15
B	0.6	−0.5	0.61	0.75	0.03
C	0.6	−0.35	0.48	0.68	0.10
D	0.5	0.5	0.50	0.06	0.70
E	0.6	0.5	0.61	0.13	0.77
F	0.6	0.6	0.72	0.07	0.85
Eigenvalue	2.18	1.39			
Percent of variance	36.3	23.2			
Cumulative percent	36.3	59.5			

In this case, the unrotated factor loadings are not enlightening. What one would like to find is some pattern in which factor I would be heavily loaded (have a high r) on some variables and factor II on others. Such a condition would suggest rather "pure" constructs underlying each factor. You attempt to secure this less ambiguous condition between factors and variables by *rotation*. This procedure can be carried out by either orthogonal or oblique methods, but only the former will be illustrated here.

To understand the rotation concept consider that you are dealing only with simple two-dimensional rather than multidimensional space. The variables in Table 13–4 can be plotted in two-dimensional space as shown in Figure 13–4. Two axes cut this space, and the points are positioned relative to these axes. The location of these axes is arbitrary, and they represent only one of an infinite number of reference frames that could be used to reproduce the matrix. As long as one does not change the intersection points and keeps the axes at right angles, when an orthogonal method is used, one can rotate them to find a better solution or position for the reference axes. "Better" in this case means a matrix that makes the factors as pure as possible (load each variable with as few factors as possible and as many zeros or near zeros as possible). From the rotation shown in Figure 13–4, it can be seen

FIGURE 13–4   Orthogonal factor rotations

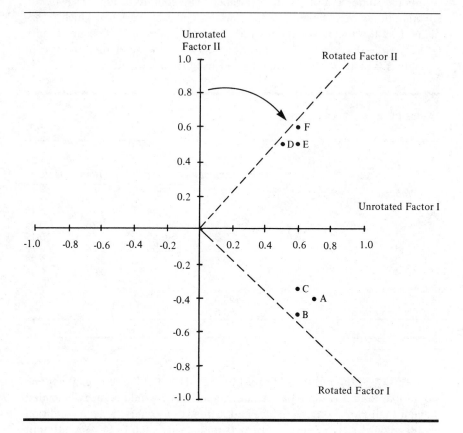

that the solution is improved substantially. Using the rotated solution suggests that the six scales actually reflect only two underlying factors (see the rotated factors section of Table 13–4).

Interpreting factors.   The interpretation of factor loadings is largely subjective. It is at this point that factor analysis becomes interpretive art. *There is no way to calculate the meanings of factors; they are what one sees in them.* For this reason, factor analysis is largely used for exploration. One can detect patternings of latent variables with the aim to discover new concepts and/or reduce data. Factor analysis is also used to test hypotheses, although this is a less well-developed use and more controversial than the exploration.

An example.   One of the problems posed to Chris Riley at the start of this chapter was:

You are the director of the MBA program at Big University. You have been reviewing the grade sheets for the first year students and are struck by the grade patterns in the data. You have long thought that there were a few distinct types of people when it came to management study and you decide to test this idea. What would you do and how would you do it?

If Chris knows her multivariate analysis, she would recognize this as a problem for factor analysis to be answered as follows. Suppose the director chooses a sample of 21 grade reports for students in the middle of the GPA range. To factor analyze them, she performs three major steps:

1. Calculates a correlation matrix between grades for all pairs of the 10 courses for which she has data.
2. Factor analyzes the matrix of correlations by the principal components method.
3. Uses a rotation procedure in an effort to clarify the factors so as to improve their interpretation.

She uses the factor analysis package of SPSS to perform these steps. Table 13–5 shows a portion of the correlation matrix. These data represent zero order correlation coefficients between the 10 courses. For example, grades secured in V1 (Financial Accounting) correlated rather well (0.56) with grades received in course V2 (Managerial Accounting). The next best correlation with VI grades is an inverse correlation ($-.44$) with grade in V7 (Production).

TABLE 13–5   Correlation coefficients, student grade data

Variable	Course	V1	V2	V3	V10
V1	Financial accounting	1.00	0.56	0.17	−0.01
V2	Managerial accounting	0.56	1.00	−0.22	0.06
V3	Finance	0.17	−0.22	1.00	0.42
V4	Marketing	−0.14	0.05	−0.48	−0.10
V5	Human behavior	−0.19	−0.26	−0.05	−0.23
V6	Organization design	−0.21	−0.00	−0.56	−0.05
V7	Production	−0.44	−0.11	−0.04	−0.08
V8	Probability	0.30	0.06	0.07	−0.10
V9	Statistical inference	−0.05	0.06	−0.32	0.06
V10	Quantitative analysis	−0.01	0.06	0.42	1.00

Using the correlation matrix, she can compute the principal components factor analysis shown in Table 13–6. While the program will produce a table with as many as 10 factors, you choose, in this case, to stop the process after

TABLE 13–6 Factor matrix using principal factor with iterations, student grade data

Variable	Course	Factor 1	Factor 2	Factor 3	Communality
V1	Financial accounting	0.41	0.71	−0.23	.73
V2	Managerial accounting	0.01	0.53	−0.16	.31
V3	Finance	0.89	−0.17	0.37	.95
V4	Marketing	−0.60	0.21	0.30	.49
V5	Human behavior	0.02	−0.24	−0.22	.11
V6	Organization design	−0.43	−0.09	−0.36	.32
V7	Production	−0.11	−0.58	−0.03	.35
V8	Probability	0.25	0.25	−0.31	.22
V9	Statistical inference	−0.43	0.43	0.50	.62
V10	Quantitative analysis	0.25	0.04	0.35	.19
	Eigenvalue	1.83	1.52	.95	
	Percent of variance	18.3	15.2	9.5	
	Cumulative percent	18.3	18.5	43.0	

three factors have been extracted. Several features in this table are worth noting. She recalled that the communalities indicated the amount of variance in each variable that is being "explained" by the factors. Thus, these three factors accounted for about 73 percent of the variance in grades in the financial accounting course. It should be apparent from these communality figures that some of the courses are not explained well by the factors selected. Which are they?

TABLE 13–7 Varimax rotated factor matrix, student grade data

Variable	Course	Factor 1	Factor 2	Factor 3
V1	Financial accounting	0.84	0.16	−0.06
V2	Managerial accounting	0.53	−0.10	0.14
V3	Finance	−0.01	0.90	−0.37
V4	Marketing	−0.11	−0.24	0.65
V5	Human behavior	−0.13	−0.14	−0.27
V6	Organization design	−0.08	−0.56	−0.02
V7	Production	−0.54	−0.11	−0.22
V8	Probability	0.41	−0.02	−0.24
V9	Statistical inference	0.07	0.02	0.79
V10	Quantitative analysis	−0.02	0.42	0.09

The eigenvalue row in Table 13–6 is a measure of the explanatory power of each factor. For example, the eigenvalue for factor 1 is 1.83 and is computed as follows:

$$1.83 = (0.41)^2 + (0.01)^2 + \cdots + (0.25)^2$$

The percent of variance accounted for by each factor in Table 13–6 is computed by dividing eigenvalues by the number of variables. When this is done, one sees that the three factors accounted for about 43 percent of the total variance in course grades.

In an effort to clarify the factors more, employ a varimax rotation to secure the matrix shown in Table 13–7. The heavy factor loadings for the three factors are as follows:

Factor 1		Factor 2		Factor 3	
Financial accounting	.84	Finance	.90	Marketing	.65
Managerial accounting	.53	Organization design	−.56	Statistical inference	.79
Production	−.54				

Interpretation. The varimax rotation appears to clarify the relationship among course grades, but as pointed out earlier, the interpretation of the results is largely subjective. Chris might interpret the above results as showing three kinds of students, classified as the accounting, finance, and marketing types. What other interpretations might you make?

Chris saw that there were a number of problems that influenced the interpretation of these results. Among the major ones are:

1. The sample is small and any attempt at replication might well produce a different pattern of factor loadings.
2. Using the same data, extracting five or some other number of factors rather than three can result in different patterns.
3. Even if the findings are replicated, it may be that the differences are due to the varying influence of professors or the way they teach the courses rather than the subject content.
4. The labels may not truly reflect the latent construct which underlies any factors which we extract.

Chris points out, therefore, that factor analysis is a difficult tool to use. It is powerful but the results achieved must be interpreted with great care. For these reasons it has been used more for exploration than for analysis. In many research settings it is, however, highly useful as a data reduction device.

SUMMARY

Several research purposes can be served by associating statistical data. First, one can determine whether there is correlation between two or more data sets. If there is a correlation, one can often use one data set to predict another. One might be able to statistically "control" the influence of certain variables in order to study the impact of others.

There are two basic types of association problems, those involving dependencies and those involving interdependencies. In the former the variations in one data set are said to depend upon the variations in one or more sets of independent variables. In the interdependency situation, no variable is assumed to depend on another.

For situations involving nonparametric statistics, the correlation measures of Cramer's statistic and lambda are presented, as well as Spearman's rank correlation. Parametric bivariate, partial, and multiple correlations are also illustrated.

Multivariate analysis describes those statistical situations in which there is a need to study simultaneously the relationships among three or more variables. The particular technique to be employed depends upon several considerations: Is the relationship one of dependency or interdependency? Are the variables expressed in parametric or nonparametric form? In some cases, the number of variables involved is also a factor in the choice of technique.

Detailed examples are presented for multiple regression, discriminant analysis, and factor analysis.

SUPPLEMENTAL READINGS

1. Cohen, Jacob, and Patricia Cohen. *Applied Multiple Regression/Correlation Analysis for the Behavioral Sciences*. 2d ed. Hillsdale, N.J.: Lawrence Erlbaum Associates, 1983.
2. Cooley, W. W., and P. R. Lohnes. *Multivariate Data Analysis*. New York: John Wiley & Sons, 1971.
3. Kerlinger, Fred N. *Foundations of Behavioral Research*. New York: Holt, Rinehart & Winston, 1973. Especially chapters 35–37 on multiple regression and factor analysis.
4. Kim, Jae-On, and Charles W. Mueller. *Introduction to Factor Analysis*. Beverly Hills, Calif.: Sage Publications, 1978. No. 13 of the Quantitative Applications in the Social Sciences Series.
5. Klecka, William R. *Discriminant Analysis*, Beverly Hills, Calif.: Sage Publications, 1980. No. 19 of the Quantitative Applications in the Social Sciences Series.

DISCUSSION QUESTIONS

1. Distinguish between:
   a Dummy variable and dependent variable.

    b   Regression coefficient and correlation coefficient.

    c   Dependency and interdependency.

    d   Discriminant analysis and regression analysis.

2. What is the meaning of the following:

    a r^2_{yz}

    b $r^2_{xy.z}$

    c $R^2_{x.yz}$

3. A research team conducted a study of voting preferences among 130 registered Democrats and 130 registered Republicans prior to an election on a specific tax proposal. They secured the following results:

	Favor	Against
Democrats	50	80
Republicans	90	40

    Calculate an appropriate measure of association.

4. An analyst sought to predict the annual sales for a home-furnishing manufacturer using the following predictor variables:

    X_1 = Marriages during the year

    X_2 = Housing starts during the year

    X_3 = Annual disposable personal income

    X_4 = Time trend (first year = 1, second year = 2, and so forth)

Using data for 24 years, they calculated the following estimating equation:

$$Y = 49.85 - 0.068X_1 + 0.036X_2 + 1.22X_3 - 19.54X_4$$

They also calculated an $R^2 = .92$ and a standard error of estimate of 11.9. Interpret the equation and the statistics above.

5. What type of multivariate methods do you recommend in each of the following and why?

    a   You want to develop an estimating equation that will be used to predict which applicants will come to your university as students.

    b   You would like to predict family income using such variables as education, stage in family life cycle, and so forth.

    c   You wish to estimate standard labor costs for manufacturing a new dress design.

    d   You have been studying a group of successful salespeople. They have taken a number of psychological tests. You want to bring meaning out of these test results.

6. A researcher was given the assignment of predicting which of three courses of action would be taken by the 280 employees in the Desota plant that was going to be sold to its employees. The alternatives were:

    a   Take severance pay and leave the company.

    b Stay with the new company and give up severance pay.

    c Take a transfer to the plant in Chicago.

She gathered data on employee opinions, inspected personal files, and the like, and then did a discriminant analysis. Later, when the results were in, she found the following results:

	Predicted decision		
Actual decision	A	B	C
a	80	5	12
b	14	60	14
c	10	15	70

How successful was the researcher's analysis?

7. Referring to the example in the chapter concerning student grades, answer the following questions:

    a How are the factor loadings interpreted?

    b What is the meaning of a communality of .11 found in Table 13–6?

    c Give another interpretation of the three factors extracted in Table 13–7.

14. Research reporting

It may seem unscientific, and even unfair, but the intrinsic value of a study can be easily destroyed by a poor final report or presentation. Research technicians may appreciate the brilliance of a study that is badly reported, but most will be heavily influenced by the quality of the reporting. This fact should prompt researchers to make special efforts to communicate clearly and fully.

This chapter covers two final major topics that face researchers. First is the writing of the formal report that sets forth the findings, conclusions, procedures, and other details of the study. A second task is to make an oral presentation to key persons who wish to be briefed on the research and its results.

THE WRITTEN RESEARCH REPORT

The research report contains findings, analysis of these findings, interpretations, conclusions, and sometimes recommendations. You, as the researcher, are clearly the expert on the topic covered. You know the specifics in a way no one else can. Because a research report is an authoritative one-way communication, it imposes a special obligation on you to maintain objectivity. Even if your findings seem to point to a certain course of action, for example, you should demonstrate restraint and caution when proposing that course.

Reports may be defined in terms of their degree of formality and design. The formal report tends to be long and follows a well-delineated format. This contrasts to the more informal or short report.

Short reports

Short reports are appropriate for studies in which the problem is well-defined, of limited scope, and for which methodologies are simple and

411

straightforward. Most information reports, progress, and interim reports are of this sort. For example, you may write up an investigation into cost-of-living changes that is needed for upcoming labor negotiations. Or, you might report on a preliminary exploration of the feasibility of filing "dumping" charges against a foreign competitor.

Short reports usually are five pages or less. At the beginning, there should be a brief statement on the authorization of the study, the problem examined, and its breadth and depth. Next, are the conclusions and recommendations, followed by the findings that support the conclusions. Section headings should be used.

The letter is one form of a short report. Its tone tends to be informal. The format follows that found in any good business letter and should not exceed a couple of pages. A letter report is often written in personal style (we, you) although this depends on the situation.

Memorandum reports are another variety and follow the *To, From, Subject* format. The following suggestions may be helpful in writing such a report:

1. Tell the reader why you are writing this report (it may be in response to a request).
2. If the memo is in response to a request for information, remind the reader of the exact point raised, answer it, and then follow with any necessary details.
3. Write in an expository style, emphasizing brevity and directness.
4. If time permits, write the report today and leave it for review tomorrow, before sending it.
5. Attach detailed materials as appendixes where needed.

Long reports

Long reports are of two types, the technical or base report, and the popular report—which of these to use depends chiefly on the audience and the researcher's objectives. While some researchers try to write a single report that satisfies both needs, this complicates the task and it is seldom satisfactory.

The technical report. This report should include full documentation and detail. It will normally survive all working papers and original data files and so will become the major source document. It is the report that other researchers will want to see because it has the full story of what was done and how it was done.

While completeness is a goal in a technical report, you must guard against including nonessential material. One good guide is that sufficient information of a procedural nature should be included to enable others to replicate the study. This should include sources of data, research procedures, sampling design, data gathering instruments, index construction, data analysis methods, and other technical matters. Most of this information should be attached in an appendix.

A technical report should also include a full presentation and analysis of significant data. Conclusions and recommendations should be clearly related to specific findings. Technical jargon should be minimized and defined when used. There can be brief references to other research, theories, and techniques. While you may expect the reader to be familiar with these references, it is useful to include some short explanations, perhaps as footnotes or endnotes.

The popular report. In some cases, the client has no research background, and may be interested in results rather than methodology. The major communication medium in this case is the popular report. It may still be helpful to have a basic report, in case the client may later wish to have a technical appraisal made of the study.

The fact that the popular report is designed for a nontechnical audience presents the researcher with some special problems. Readers are less concerned with methodological details but more interested in learning quickly the major findings and conclusions. They want help in making decisions. Sometimes, the report is developed for a single person and needs to be written with that person's individual characteristics and needs in mind.

The style of the popular report should encourage rapid reading, quick comprehension of major findings, and prompt understanding of the implication and conclusions. While the report tone is journalistic, it must still be accurate. Headlines and underlining for emphasis should be used; pictures and graphs often replace tables. Sentences and paragraphs should be short and direct. There should be liberal use of white space and wide margins. It may even be desirable to put only a single finding on each page. It also helps to have a theme running through the report and even graphic or animated characters designed to vary the presentation. The popular report is shorter than the basic report and follows the psychological format explained below.

RESEARCH REPORT FORMAT

There is no one best format for all long reports. Two arrangements are typically found:

1. *Logical.* In this format, the introductory information covering the purpose of study, methodology, and limitations is followed by the findings. The findings are analyzed and then followed by the conclusions and recommendations.
2. *Psychological.* This is largely an inversion of the logical order. The conclusions and recommendations are presented immediately after the introduction, with the findings coming later. This is probably the most widely used format, especially in popular reports. Readers are quickly exposed to the most critical information—the conclusions and recommendations. Then if they wish to go further, they may read on into the findings which support the conclusions already given.

Report format details

A long report has clearly defined parts. While some may be dropped, others added, and their order varied from one situation to another, the following outline is in the logical format typical of technical reports and many student reports.

Report Outline

Prefatory pages	A.	Title page
	B.	Letters of transmittal and authorization
	C.	Tables of contents, charts, and illustrations
	D.	Synopsis
Body of report	E.	Introduction
	F.	Findings
	G.	Summary and conclusions
	H.	Recommendations
Appended sections	I.	Appendix
	J.	Bibliography

There seems to be a growing preference for using the psychological format in student reports. If the above outline were changed to reflect this, we would place the recommendations, summary, and conclusions before the findings.

Title page. The title page should include four items: the title of the report, the date, for whom prepared, and by whom prepared. A satisfactory title should be brief, but should include the following three elements: (1) the variables included in the study; (2) the type of relationship between the variables; and (3) the population to which the results may be applied.[1]

Redundancies such as, "A Report of . . . . A Discussion of . . . ." merely add length to the titles but little else of value. Single word titles are also generally of little value. Several acceptable ways of stating report titles are:

Descriptive study:	The Five-Year Demand Outlook for Plastic Pipe in the United States
Correlation study:	The Relationship between the Value of the Dollar in World Markets and Relative National Inflation Rates
Causal study:	The Effect of Various Motivation Methods on Worker Attitudes among Textile Workers

[1]Paul E. Resta, *The Research Report* (New York: American Book Company, 1972), p. 5.

Table of contents. As a rough guide, any report of several sections that totals more than six to ten pages should have a table of contents. If there are many tables, charts, or other exhibits, they should also be listed after the table of contents in a table of illustrations.

Letters. For many intraorganizational projects, it is not necessary to have a letter of transmittal. Such a letter should be included if the study is for a specific client (e.g., the company president or an outside organization) or the relationship between the parties is formal. The letter should refer to the authorization for the project and any specific instructions or limitations placed on the study. The letter should also state the purpose of the study and its scope.

For public reports for external organizations (for example, the federal government), it is common to include a letter of authorization to show the authority and the charge that was given.

Synopsis. The synopsis (or Executive Summary) can serve two purposes. It may be a report in miniature in which case it may, but need not be, in the same organizational format as the body of the report. It could be a concise summary of the major findings and conclusions but should not exceed one or two pages. The second version of a synopsis represents little more than a prose table of contents indicating the major topics in the study or the major actions taken. Such a presentation, often called an abstract, is found most often in engineering and scientific reports. Abstracts are usually restricted to 150 words or less.

In either case, the synopsis should be written after the rest of the report is finished. It should not mention any new information and normally has no graphics. In writing the synopsis, you should expect to have a high density of significant words since the essence of synopses is that they are concise summaries.

Introduction. This section of the report normally contains several major subsections. Patterns vary, but one common model consists of three parts—the problem, the methods, and the limitations.

Problem. The statement of the problem usually comes first and contains three parts—the background, the problem statement itself, and the hypotheses. In the background, researchers should introduce the major variables and relate them to previous research and theory. In applied research studies, the background statements relate the study to a management problem and/or organizational situation which have led to the study. If some of the relevant variables are not studied, this fact should also be mentioned.

The background discussion leads into a statement of the specific problem which the research addresses. Often this might best be discussed in terms of a research question and its associated investigative questions. Such concepts as "investigative questions" may confuse the reader unless they are defined. In the problem statement, it is important to state clearly the variables of concern, the type of relationship between them, and the target group which is being studied. Operational definitions of critical variables should also be included. In correlational or causal studies you might also include hypotheses statements.

Methods. This section should cover at least five items. First, explicitly define the target population that is being studied and any sampling methods used. If explanations are called for, and they usually are, make them brief. A second part of this section should cover the research design used and the rationale for using it. Third, briefly discuss the materials and instruments. Copies of such materials, as well as any detailed discussion of them, should be placed in an appendix. The fourth portion of the methods section should deal with the specific data collection methods. If there are detailed materials, such as field worker instructions, place them in the appendix. Fifth, there should be a summary discussion of the data analysis methods. Identify only statistical tests, computer programs, and the like, but relegate details to the appendix.

Limitations. The topic of limitations is often handled in an ambivalent fashion. Some people wish to ignore the matter, feeling that mentioning limitations detracts from the impact of the study. Such an attitude is unprofessional and borders on the unethical. Others seem to adopt a masochistic approach of putting down their own study in detail. Balance is called for; this section should be a thoughtful presentation of significant methodology or implementation problems. An even-handed approach is one of the hallmarks of an honest and competent investigator. All research studies have their limitations, and the sincere investigator recognizes that readers need aid in judging their validity.

Some authorities on research reporting recommend that statements of limitations should be placed along with the discussion of findings and conclusions. In some cases this may be better, but it is not common practice in business research.

Findings. This is generally the longest section of the report. It should be an organized presentation of results and not a clutter of prose, charts, and tables. The objective here is an exposition of the data rather than drawing interpretations or conclusions. When quantitative data can be presented, it should be done in as simple a way as possible. This means simple charts and tables, not complex ones.

The data need not include everything that you have collected. The criterion for inclusion is, "Is this material important to the reader's understanding of the problem and the findings?" However, make sure to show that which is unfavorable to your hypotheses as well as that which supports them.

It is useful to present findings in numbered paragraphs or to present one finding per page with the quantitative data supporting the findings presented in a small table or chart on the same page (see Figure 14–1). While this practice adds to the bulk of the report, it presents data in a convenient way for the reader.

Summary and conclusions. The summary is a brief restatement of the essential findings. Sectional summaries may be used if there are many spe-

---

FIGURE 14–1   Example of a findings page in a commercial bank
market study

Findings: 1.   In this city, *commercial banks are not the preferred savings medium.* Banks are in a weak third place behind Savings and Loans Associations and government bonds.

       2.   Customers of the Central City Bank have a *somewhat more favorable attitude towards bank savings,* and less of a preference for government bonds.

Question: Suppose that you have just received an extra $1,000 and have decided to save it. Which of the savings methods listed would be your preferred way to save it?

Savings method	Total replies	Central City customers	Other bank customers
Government bonds	24%	20%	29%
Savings and loan	43	45	42
Bank	13	18	8
Credit union	9	7	11
Stock	7	8	5
Other	4	2	5
Total	100%	100%	100%
	$n = 216$	105	111

---

cific findings. These may then be combined into an overall summary. In simple descriptive research, a summary of findings may complete the report, as conclusions and recommendations may not be required.

Findings state facts while conclusions represent inferences drawn from the findings. A writer is sometimes reluctant to make conclusions and leaves the task to the reader. If you do this, it is an abdication of research responsibility. As the researcher, you are the one person best informed on all of the factors of the study which critically influence both findings and conclusions.

Conclusions may be presented in a tabular form for easy reading and reference. Summary findings may be subordinated under the related conclusion statement. These may be numbered and coded in a way to refer the reader to related pages or tables in the findings sections.

Recommendations. There are usually a limited number of the writer's opinions on suggested future actions. The nature of these actions depends on the study. If it is academic research, the recommendations are likely to be for further study to test, deepen, or broaden understanding in the subject area. In applied research for decision making, the recommendations will usually be for managerial actions rather than research actions. In this instance, the writer may offer several alternative actions but probably should assess them.

Appendix. Here put complex tables, statistical tests, supporting documents, copies of the forms used, detailed descriptions of the methodology, instructions to field workers, and any other evidence that may be important backup detail. The reader who wishes to learn about the technical details of the study and/or look at the more detailed breakdowns of the statistics will usually want a complete appendix.

Bibliography. There should be a bibliographic section, if the study makes heavy use of secondary research sources. For specific references, use footnotes or end-notes placed at the conclusion of each major section rather than referring to the bibliography. Proper bibliographic formats are illustrated by the references at the end of this chapter.

Popular report format

Popular reports are usually presented in psychological order, but the differences between popular and technical reports are much greater than mere sequence. As pointed out earlier, the detail, depth, writing style, and communication forms also differ. A typical popular report follows.

1. Title page. Indicate the subject, date of the report, for whom prepared, and by whom prepared.

2. Table of contents. Needed if the report is more than a few pages long.

3. Objectives of the study. A brief summary that explains the factors that brought about the study, including any hypotheses to be tested or research questions to be answered.

4. Methodology. A brief nontechnical statement of the methods used, the type of sample and its size, the limitations of the study and its methods, and something of the manner in which the study was carried out. In all cases, these should be mostly nontechnical in nature. Any supporting data should go into an appendix.

5. Conclusions and recommendations. Highlights of the major findings are presented here in summary form. If recommendations or implications are called for, they should also be placed here.

6. Findings. These should be a simplified presentation of the basic factual data found in the study. Statistical data should be presented in charts or simple tables. Each graph or table should present only one or a few basic points. Commentary on the specific findings and their relationships should also be briefly presented near the graphic. Presentation density (the amount of material per page) should be low. Often it is desirable to allow one page per single graph or table with its attendant commentary.

7. Appendix. The appendix should be much shorter than in the technical report, but include a copy of the measuring instrument, information on the sampling design, reference materials, detailed statistical tables, and the like.

Other formats

An organization may have its own special reporting format. This is often the case with professional journals. It is important to determine in advance whether a publication has specific format requirements. For example, the *Journal of Applied Psychology* publishes the results of many research studies carried out in businesses and other organizations. From a perusal of some copies of this journal, it would appear that the editors encourage a format along the following lines:

1. Introduction. A statement of the nature of the problem studied and a brief discussion of previous studies that are pertinent to the development of the specific question or hypothesis to be tested.

2. Method. A brief statement of what was done, where it was done, and how it was done. Included is mention of the specific techniques and tools used.

3. Results. A combined tabular or graphic presentation of salient findings with a discussion of these findings. The discussion is both a statement of the relationships found and a comparison of these findings with the hypotheses or questions originally posed.

4. Conclusion. A brief recapitulation of the results and sometimes some comments about broader implications of the findings.

Regardless of the type of report or the format followed, however, the problems of writing tend to be the same.

WRITING THE REPORT

Students often give inadequate attention to reporting their findings and conclusions. This is unfortunate because a well-presented study can often impress the reader more than another study with greater scientific quality but a weaker presentation.

Report writing skill is especially valuable to the junior executive or management trainee who aspires to rise in an organization. Reporting skill may be overrated, but the executive who can write a good report often finds his/her career prospects enhanced.

Prewriting concerns

There are a few general considerations that are useful to keep in mind before writing. One should ask again, "What is the purpose of this report?" Writing a reply to this question is one way to make sure that the problem is clearly in mind.

A second prewriting question is, "Who will read the report?" This suggests that thought be given to the needs, temperament, and biases of the audience. You should not distort facts to meet these needs and biases, but consider these factors in developing the presentation. Knowing who reads the report may suggest its appropriate length. Generally, the higher the report destination in an organization, the shorter the report should be; the decision on how much to write is related to how much the client is willing to read.

Another important reader consideration is the ignorance distance—the gap in knowledge on the subject between the reader and the writer. The greater the ignorance distance, the more difficult it is to convey the full findings meaningfully and concisely.

A third prewriting question is, "What are the circumstances and limitations under which you are writing?" Is the nature of the subject highly technical? Do you need statistics? Charts? What is the importance of the topic? An important subject justifies more effort than a minor one. What should be the scope of the report? How much time is available? Deadlines often impose limitations upon the type of report that can be written.

A final prewriting question is, "How will the report be used?" Try to visualize the reader using the report. Will it be read by more than one person? If so, how many copies should be made? How can the report be made more convenient to use? What is the "direction of travel"? How much attention must be given to getting the attention and interest of the reader?

The outline. Once the researcher has made the first analysis of the data, drawn tentative conclusions, and performed statistical significance tests, it is time to develop a writing outline. One widely used outlining system employs the following organization structure:

I. *Major Topic Heading*
   A.   Major subtopic heading
      1.   Subtopic
         a.   Minor subtopic
           (1)   Further detail
              (a)   Even further detail

Two styles of outlining are widely used—the topic outline and the sentence outline. In the topic form, a key word or two is put down; the assumption is that the writer knows its significance and will later remember the nature of the argument represented by that point. It is also used when the outliner knows that a given point should be covered but is not yet sure how to do it.

The sentence outline expresses the essential thoughts that are associated with the specific topic. This approach leaves less development work for later writing, other than elaborations and explanations that may improve report readability. It has the obvious advantages of pushing the writer to make the decisions on what to include and how to say it. It guards against forgetting certain specific points that one wanted to make. It is probably the best outlining style for the inexperienced researcher, because it specifies the writing job into its two major components—what to say, and how to say it. An example of the type of detail found with each of these outlining formats is:

Topic outline	Sentence outline

I. Demand
  A. How measured
    1. Voluntary error
    2. Shipping error
      a. Monthly variance
	I. Demand for refrigerators
	  A. Measured in terms of factory shipments as reported to the U.S. Department of Commerce
	    1. Error is introduced into year-to-year comparisons because reporting is voluntary.
	    2. A second factor is variations from month to month because of shipping and invoicing patterns.
	      a. Variations up to 30 percent in 198X depending upon whether shipments were measured by actual shipment date or invoice date

Presentation considerations

Well-written reports are not as common as one might think, but help exists for those who wish to improve their writing results. There are excellent manuals on report writing, and every serious researcher should have one. The general message in such manuals is that reports should be physically inviting, easy to read, and match the comprehension abilities of the designated audience. Some key elements of these three considerations will be summarized here.

Physical presentation. One frequent problem is poor report appearance. Duplicated reports may be difficult to read because of poor reproduction. The organization of the report (or lack of it) may suggest a slapdash approach. Student reports, in particular, suffer from dirty typewriter type, typing print that is barely legible (old ribbon), or very smudgy (new ribbon). Students writing team reports often use several typewriters with different type faces, and this contributes to an amateurish appearance.

Incorrect spelling and poor punctuation will also destroy a report's credibility. Indeed, probably no single element detracts more from a report's quality image than spelling errors. Many of these are simple typographic mistakes, suggesting careless report preparation. There is no substitute for careful proofreading, preferably by several people.

Overcrowding of text represents a third appearance problem. Readers need the visual relief provided by ample white space. We define "ample" as one inch of white space at the top, bottom, and right-hand margins. On the left side, the margin should be at least one and one-fourth inches to provide room for binding or punched holes. Even greater margins will often improve report appearance and highlight key points or sections. Overcrowding also occurs when the report contains page after page of large blocks of unbroken text. This produces an unpleasant psychological effect on readers because of its formidable appearance. The problem of overcrowded text may be overcome if writers will:

1. Use shorter paragraphs. As a rough guide, any paragraph longer than half of a page should be suspect. Remember that each paragraph should represent a distinct thought.
2. Indent parts of text that represent listings, long quotations, or examples.
3. Use headings and subheadings to divide the report and its major sections into homogeneous topical parts.
4. Use vertical listings of points (such as this list).

Inadequate labeling is another physical problem. Each graph or table should contain enough information to be self-explanatory. Text headings and subheadings also help with the labeling problem. They function as signs for the audience, telling it the organization of the report and indicating the progress of discussion. They also help readers to skim the material and to return easily to particular sections of the report.

Readability. Sensitive writers consider the reading ability of report recipients to assure that they get high readership. One can achieve high readership more easily if the topic interests the readers and is in their field of expertise. In addition, one can show the usefulness of the report by pointing out how it might help the readers. Finally, we can write at a difficulty level that is appropriate to the recipients' reading abilities. To test writing for difficulty level, use one of the standard readability indexes.

Gunning Fog Index.[2]   Research on the readability of prose has led to the development of measuring formulas by which to estimate reading difficulty. One such system is the Gunning Fog Index. Gunning maintains that the reading difficulty of a piece of prose can be measured by (1) the average length of sentence and (2) the percentage of words of three syllables or more per 100 words of text. He suggests the following procedure for testing readability levels:

1. Find the average number of words per sentence. Use a sample at least 100 words long. Divide the total number of words by number of sentences. This gives the average sentence length.
2. Count the number of words of three syllables or more per 100 words. Don't count (a) words that are capitalized; (b) combinations of short easy words—like bookkeeper, butterfly; (c) verbs that are made three syllables by adding ed or es—like created or trespasses.

---

[2]Robert Gunning, "How to Improve Your Writing," reprinted with permission from the June 1952 issue of *Factory*. A Morgan-Grampian publication, page 132.

3. Add the two factors above and multiply by 0.4. This will give you the Fog Index. It corresponds roughly with the number of years of schooling a person would require to read passage with ease and understanding (The Fog Index of this entire passage is 6.7).

Advocates of readability measurement do not claim that all written material should be at the simplest level possible. They argue only that the level should be appropriate for the audience. They point out that comic books score about six on the Gunning scale (that is, a person with a sixth-grade education should be able to read that material). *Time* usually scores at about the 10 level, while *The Atlantic* is reported to have a score of 11 or 12. Material that scores much above 12 becomes difficult for the general public to read comfortably.

Such measures obviously give only a rough approximation of the true readability of a report. One should not try to write by formula alone. The use of a readability measurement can help match a report to its audience, but good writing calls for a variety of other skills to assure reading comprehension.

Comprehensibility. Good writing varies with the writing objective. Research writing is designed to convey information of a precise nature. It should contain none of the multiple meanings and elegant allusions that are prized in fiction or poetry. Writing should not be dull, but it should be without frills. With plain discourse, it is easier to avoid ambiguity. Take care to choose the right words—words that convey thoughts accurately, clearly, and efficiently. There is a special problem when concepts and constructs are used and not clearly defined, either operationally or descriptively.

At a detail level, there is a problem of how words and sentences are related. Misplaced modifiers run rampant in carelessly written reports. Subordinate ideas are mixed with major ideas in such a way as to make the mass confusing to readers. Readers must sort out what is important and what is secondary when this should have been done for them by the writer.

Finally, there is the matter of pace. Rathbone defines this as:

> "the rate at which the printed page presents information to the reader. . . . The proper pace in technical writing is one that enables the reader to keep his mind working just a fraction of a second behind his eye as he reads along. It logically would be slow when the information is complex or difficult to understand; fast when the information is straightforward and familiar. If the reader's mind lags behind his eye, the pace is too rapid; if his mind wanders ahead of his eye (or wants to) the pace is too slow.[3]

If the text is overcrowded with concepts, there is too much information per sentence. By contrast, sparse writing has too few significant ideas per sentence. Writers use a variety of methods to adjust the pace of their writings.

---

[3]Robert R. Rathbone, *Communicating Technical Information* (Reading, Mass.: Addison-Wesley Publishing Company, © 1966), p. 64. Reprinted with permission.

Many of these have already been mentioned but their importance bears repeating here for emphasis:

1. Use ample white space and wide margins to create a positive psychological effect on the reader.
2. Break large units of text into smaller units with headings to show organization of the topics.
3. Relieve difficult text with visual aids when possible.
4. Emphasize important material and deemphasize secondary material through sentence construction and through judicious use of italicizing, underlining, capitalization, and parentheses.
5. Choose words carefully, opting for the known and the short rather than the unknown and long. Graduate students, in particular, seem to revel in using jargon, pompous constructions, and long or arcane words. Naturally, there are times when technical terms are appropriate. It is also true that scientists communicate efficiently with jargon, but in most applied business research, the audiences are not scientifically trained and need more help than many writers supply.
6. Repeat and summarize critical and difficult points and ideas to assure that readers have time to absorb them.
7. Make strategic use of service words. Rathbone identifies these words as those that "do not represent objects or ideas, but show relationship. Transitional words, such as the conjunctions, are service words. So are phrases such as 'on the other hand,' 'in summary,' and 'in contrast.' "[4]

Presentation of statistics.[5] The presentation of statistics in research reports is a special challenge to writers. Four basic ways to present such data are (1) include them in a text paragraph; (2) place in semitabular form; (3) put in tables; or (4) show graphically.

Text presentation. This is probably the most common approach when there are only a few statistics used as simple comparisons. The writer can direct the reader's attention to certain numbers or comparisons or can place an emphasis on specific points. However, statistical data too often are submerged in the body of the text, requiring the reader to scan the entire paragraph to get the meaning of the figures. For example, the following material, while including only a few simple comparisons, becomes more complicated when text is combined with statistics.

> A comparison of the three major competing firms in our industry shows that Ajax Ltd. has the best sales growth record over the five years 1979–1983. They averaged an annual sales growth, in constant dollars, of 8.3 percent as compared to a 4.7 percent sales increase for the Beta Corp.

---

[4] Rathbone, *Communicating*, p. 72.

[5] The material in this section draws heavily on chapters 3 through 6 of Frederick E. Croxton, Dudley J. Cowden, and Sidney Klein, *Applied General Statistics*, 3d ed. (Englewood Cliffs, N.J.: Prentice-Hall, 1967).

Cotter Co. was third with a 1.6-percent sales increase. Ajax also turned in the best average return on investment among the three companies for the same time period. The average annual ROI for Ajax was 19.6 percent as compared to 12.1 percent for Beta, and 8.5 percent for Cotter Co.

Semitabular presentation. When there are only a few simple figures in a discussion, they may be taken out of the text and set up in a simple listing. This method makes reading and understanding quantitative comparison much easier than when the statistics are imbedded in the text. An example of semitabular presentation is shown in the accompanying table.

A comparison of the three major competitors over the five-year period, 1979 through 1983, indicates that Ajax Ltd. performed better than the other two companies, both on sales growth and ROI. Beta Corp. had the second best performance on both scores.

	Average annual sales growth (constant dollars)	Average annual return on investment
Ajax Ltd.	+9.3%	+19.6%
Beta Corp.	+4.7	+12.1
Cotter Co.	+1.6	+ 8.5

Tabular presentation. Tables are generally superior to text for presenting statistics, although they should be accompanied by comments directing reader attention to important figures. Tables facilitate quantitative comparisons and provide a concise, efficient way to present numerical data.

Tables are either general or summary in nature. General tables tend to be large, complex, and detailed. They serve as the general repository for the statistical findings of the study and usually are in the appendix of a research report.

Summary tables contain only a few key pieces of data closely related to a specific finding. To make these tables inviting to the reader (who often tends to skip them), the table designer should omit unimportant details and collapse multiple classifications into only those few that are clearly relevant. Averages, percentages, indexes, and other computed measures should often be substituted for the data in original units.

Any table should contain enough information for the reader to understand its contents. The title should explain the subject of the table, how the data are classified, the time period, and other relevant coverage statements. A subtitle is sometimes included under the title to explain something about the table; most often this is a statement of the measurement units in which the data are expressed. The contents of the columns should be clearly identified by the column heads, and the contents of the stub should do the same for the rows. The body of the table contains the data, while the footnotes contain any needed explanations. Footnotes should be identified by letters or symbols such as asterisks, rather than by numbers, in order to avoid confusion with data values. Finally, there should be a source note if the data do not come from your original research. Table 14–1 illustrates the various parts of a table.

TABLE 14–1 U.S. production of shoes and slippers, by class, 1965 and 1975 (millions of pairs)* } **Title**

Class	1965	1975 } **Column heads**
Total	626.7	433.7
Footwear, except slippers	536.0	365.2
Men	118.2	104.8
Youth and boys	25.6	17.7
Women	280.0	173.5
Misses	36.5	15.2 **Body**
Children	33.5	17.2
Infants and babies	32.5	21.9
Athletic shoes	7.0	11.4
Other footwear	2.8	3.5
Slippers	90.7	68.5

Stub {

Footnote {* Excludes Alaska and excludes rubber footwear.
Source Note {Source: U.S. Bureau of Census, *Current Industrial Reports*, M31A.

Graphic presentation. Compared to a table, graphs show fewer pieces of information and only approximate values. They generally take more time and effort to construct than do tables. Their great advantage, however, is that they can more easily convey general quantitative values and comparisons than tables. Readers are more likely to read graphs than tables.

There are many graphic forms, but only line diagrams and bar charts are discussed here. Others, such as area charts, volume charts, and statistical maps are also used. Bar charts involve one-dimensional comparisons, while line diagrams and area charts make two-dimensional comparisons. Volume charts seem to show three dimensions. Three-dimensional charts easily confuse and should be used sparingly.

1. Line diagrams. Line diagrams are used chiefly for time series and frequency distributions. While there are no agreed upon presentation standards, there are several problems that affect the way readers perceive line diagrams. The first is the use of a zero base line. Since the amount of a statistic is indicated by distance on a chart (length of a bar or distance above a base line), it is important that graphs give accurate visual impressions of values. One good way to achieve this is to include a zero base line on the scale on which the curves are plotted. To set the base at some other value is to introduce a visual bias. This can be seen by comparing the visual impressions in parts A and B of Figure 14–2. Both are accurate plots of the Gross National Product of the United States from 1972 through 1977. In part A, however, using the base line of zero places the curve well up on the chart and gives a better perception of the relation between the absolute size of GNP and the changes from year to year. The graph in part B, with a base line at $1,000 billion, can easily give the impression that the growth was at a more rapid rate. When space or other reasons dictate using shortened scales, the zero base point should still be used, but with an added break in the scale as shown in part C of Figure 14–2. This will warn the reader that the scale has been reduced.

Another presentation problem is the balance of size between vertical and horizontal scales. There is no correct answer to this problem, but the problem can be seen by comparing parts B and C in Figure 14–2. In part C, the horizontal scale is twice that in part B. This changes the slope of curve, creating a different perception of growth rate.

A third problem with line diagrams occurs when relative and absolute changes among two or more sets of data are shown. In most charts, we use arithmetic scales where each space unit has identical value. This shows the absolute differences between variables, as in part A of Figure 14–3 which presents the total U.S. population and that of the three Pacific states. This is an arithmetically correct way to present these data; but if we are interested in rates of growth, the visual impressions from a semilogarithmic scale are more accurate. A comparison of the line diagrams in parts A and B of Figure 14–3 shows how much difference the use of a semilogarithmic scale makes. Each is valuable and each can be misleading. In part A, notice that both areas have been growing in population and that the population of the Pacific states is only a small portion of total U.S. population. One can even estimate what this proportion is. Part B gives insight into growth rates that are not clear from the arithmetic scale. Part B shows that the Pacific states population has grown at a much faster rate than for the United States in total.

2. *Bar charts.* There are a few guidelines and customary practices important in bar chart construction. Vertical bars are generally used for time series and for quantitative classifications, for example, different age and income groups. In drafting charts, one usually leaves a space between bars equal to one half or more of the width of the bar. An exception to this separation rule is the histogram (a bar chart of a continuous data that have been grouped into a frequency distribution). A second exception is with a multiple variable chart (see part A of Figure 14–4). Scale guidelines on bar charts are also valuable for reader convenience.

FIGURE 14–2   U.S. Gross National Product, 1972–1977 ($ billions)

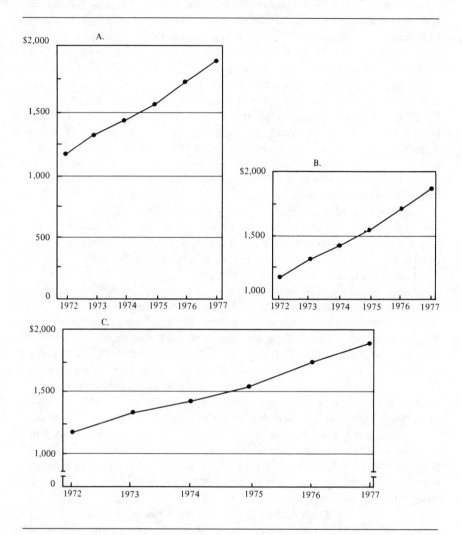

Source: U.S. Department of Commerce.

Bar charts come in a variety of patterns. Some widely used designs are illustrated in Figure 14–4. They include (a) multiple variable charts, (b) two direction charts, (c) component part charts, and (d) 100-percent component part charts. The pie chart (a form of area chart) is illustrated in part E of Figure 14–4.

FIGURE 14–3   Population of the United States and Pacific states area, 1920–1970 (millions)

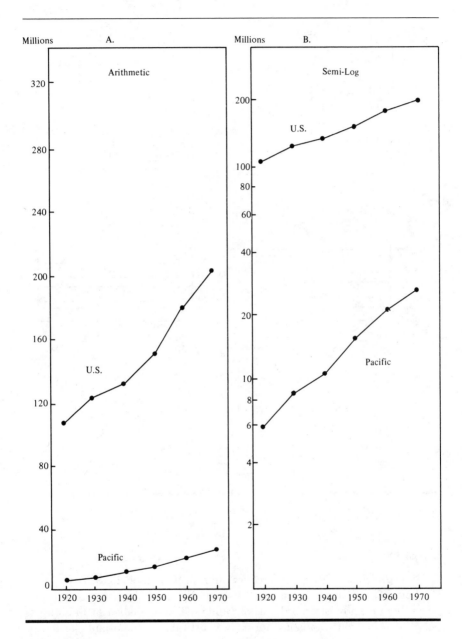

FIGURE 14–4   Examples of various types of bar charts

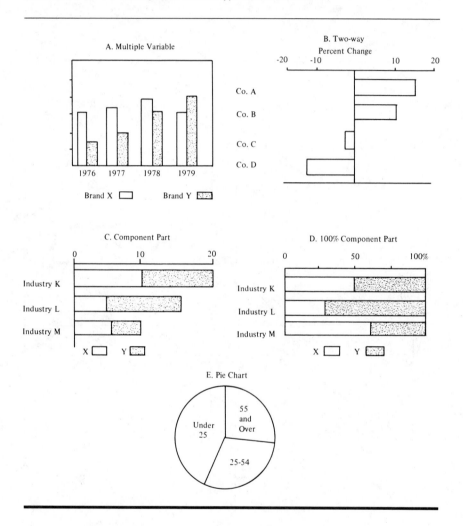

A. Multiple Variable

Brand X   Brand Y

B. Two-way
Percent Change

Co. A
Co. B
Co. C
Co. D

C. Component Part

Industry K
Industry L
Industry M

X   Y

D. 100% Component Part

Industry K
Industry L
Industry M

X   Y

E. Pie Chart

Under 25

55 and Over

25-54

BRIEFING

Nature of briefings.   Researchers often present their findings orally in briefings. These presentations have some unique characteristics that distinguish them from most other kinds of public speaking. Only a small group of people is involved. Statistics normally constitute an important portion of topic. The audience members usually are managers with an interest in the topic but want to hear only the critical elements. Speaking time will often be as short as 10 to 20 minutes, but may run longer than an hour. The presentation is normally followed by questions and discussions.

Preparation.   A successful briefing typically requires a condensation of a lengthy and complex body of information. Since speaking rates should not exceed 100 to 150 words per minute, a 20-minute presentation limits one to about 2,000 to 2,500 words. If one is to communicate effectively under such conditions, one must plan carefully. Begin this by asking two questions: first, how long should you plan to talk? Usually there is some indication of the acceptable presentation length. It may be the custom in an organization to take a given allotted time for a briefing. If the time is severely limited, then the need for topical priorities is obvious. This leads to the second question: What are the purposes of the briefing? Is it to raise concern about certain problems which have been uncovered? Is it to add to the general knowledge of members of the audience? Is it to give them conclusions and recommendations that contribute to their decision making? Questions such as these illustrate the general objectives of the report. After answering these questions, one should develop a detailed outline of what you are going to say. Such an outline should contain at least the following major parts.

1. Opening.   A brief statement, probably not more than 10 percent of the allotted time, designed to set the stage for the body of the report. The opening should be direct, attention-arresting, and indicate the nature of the discussion to follow. It should explain the nature of the project, how it came about, and what it attempted to do.

2. Findings and conclusions.   While either logical or psychological formats may be followed in the briefing, it is more common to use the psychological format or a combination logical-psychologic approach. In the latter case, the conclusions may be stated immediately after the opening remarks, with each conclusion followed by the findings which support it.

3. Recommendations.   Where appropriate, these are stated as the third stage; each recommendation may be followed by references to the conclusions leading to it. Presented in this manner, they provide a natural climax to the report. At the end of the presentation, it may be appropriate to call for questions from the audience.

Early in the planning stage you need to make two further decisions. The first concerns the type of audio-visuals (A/V) that will be used and the role they will play in the presentation. A/V decisions are important enough that they are often made *before* the briefing outline and text is developed. More will be said about A/V later.

The second important decision concerns the type of speaking aids to use. Will you give a memorized speech, read a paper verbatim, use notes, or what? Most find that memorization is a risky and time-consuming course to follow. Any memory slip during the presentation can be a catastrophe. It is not recommended. Nor is reading a written text advised, in spite of the fact that this is widely done at professional meetings. Most people do not read that well, and to try it is to burden the audience with a plodding performance. Notwithstanding this advice, it may be a good idea to write out a complete draft. In this way, one can try out lines of argument, experiment with various ways of expressing thoughts, and develop particular phraseology.

It is probably best to depend on notes. Audiences accept them and their presence does wonders in allaying speaker fears. Even if one never uses them, they are there for psychological support. Many prefer to use 5- × 8-inch cards for their briefing notes because they hold more information and the fewer cards require less shuffling than do the smaller 3- × 5-inch size. Card contents vary widely but some general guides for their design are:

1. Place title and preliminary remarks on the first card.
2. Use each of the remaining cards to carry a major section of presentation, with the amount of detail depending on the needs for statement precision and the speaker's desire for supporting information.
3. Include key phrases, illustrations, statistics, dates, particular turns of phrase, and pronunciation guides for difficult words. Include also quotations and ideas that bear repeating.
4. Along the margin place instructions and cues, such as SLOW, FAST, EMPHASIZE, TRANSPARENCY A, TURN CHART, GO BACK TO CHART 3, and the like.

After the outline and the A/V aids, comes the final stage of preparation— the rehearsal. Rehearsal is a prerequisite to effective briefing but *it is a stage too often slighted*, especially by inexperienced speakers. Giving a briefing is an artistic performance, and nothing improves it more than for the speaker to demonstrate mastery of the art. First rehearsal efforts should concentrate on those parts of the presentation that are awkward or poorly developed. After the problem areas have been worked out, there should be at least a couple full-scale practices under simulated presentation conditions. At this stage all parts should be timed and edited until the time target is met. Throughout this process a videotape recorder is an excellent diagnostic tool.

Delivery. While the content of a report is obviously the chief concern, the speaker's delivery is also an important variable. A polished presentation adds to the receptiveness of the audience, but there is some danger that the presentation may overpower the message. Fortunately, the typical research audience knows why it is assembled, has a high level of interest, and does not need to be entertained. Even so, the briefer faces a real challenge in communicating effectively. The delivery should be restrained. Demeanor, posture, dress, and total appearance should be appropriate to the occasion. Speed of speech, clarity of enunciation, pauses, gestures all play their part. Voice pitch, tone quality, and inflections are proper subjects for concern. There is little time for anecdotes and other rapport developing techniques, yet the speaker must get and hold audience attention.

Speaker problems. Inexperienced speakers have many difficulties in making presentations. They often are nervous at the start of a presentation and may even find breathing difficult. This is natural and should not be of undue concern. It may help in this case to take a deep breath or two, holding each for a brief time before exhaling as fully as possible. This might be done inconspicuously on the way to the podium.

There are a number of other problems that are frequently observed with inexperienced speakers. These may be summarized as follows:

1. Vocal problems
   a Do you speak so softly that someone cannot hear you well? It is helpful to have someone in the back of the room who can signal if your voice is not carrying far enough.
   b Do you speak too rapidly? Remind yourself to slow down. Make deliberate pauses before sentences. Speak words with precision without exaggerating. However, some people talk too slowly and this tends to make the audience restive.
   c Do you vary volume, tone quality, and rate of speaking? Any or all of these can be used successfully to add interest to the message and engage audience attention. Speakers should not let their words trail off as they complete a sentence.
   d Do you use overworked pet phrases, repeated "uhs," "you know," and "in other words"?
2. Physical problems
   a Do you rock back and forth on your heels or roll or twist from side to side or lean too much on the lectern?
   b Do you hitch or tug on clothing, scratch, fiddle with pocket change, keys, pencils, or other devices?
   c Do you stare into space? This lack of eye contact is particularly bothersome to listeners and is common with inexperienced speakers. Many seem to choose a spot above the heads of the audience and continue to stare at this spot except when looking at notes. *Eye contact is important.* The audience members need to feel that you are looking at them. It may be helpful to pick out about three persons or spots in the audience (left, right, and center) and practice looking at each spot successively as you talk.
   d Do you misuse visuals by fumbling, putting them on in incorrect order or upside down? Do you turn your back to the audience to read from visuals?

Audio/visuals. There is a variety of A/V media that researchers can use with good effect. While there is some use of sound and video players, sound movies, and sound filmstrips, the discussion here is limited to *visual aids* that are relatively simple and inexpensive to make. Six such techniques are:

1. Chalkboards—These are flexible, inexpensive, and require little specific preparation. On the other hand, they are not novel, and do not present much of a professional appearance. Furthermore, they reduce speaking

time to the extent that the speaker is writing. If you use the chalkboard, be sure to write legibly or print, leave space between lines, and do not talk to the board with your back to the audience.

2. Handout materials—These are inexpensive and can give a professional look if done carefully. Handouts can include pictures and graphic materials which might be difficult to display otherwise. The disadvantages include the time needed to produce them and their distracting impact if not properly used. You may give them out when the audience leaves, but a better use is to refer to them during your talk. If you use them this way, *do not hand them out until you are ready to refer to them.*

3. Flip charts—You can show color, pictures, and large letters with these. They are easy and inexpensive to make; they can focus listener attention on a specific idea. If not well-made, they can be distracting. Unless they are large, they should be restricted to small groups and to types of material that can be summarized in a few words.

4. Opaque protection—This allows you to project regular printed material on a screen. This is sometimes a great advantage, but the machine is bulky and its magnification is small. It requires more darkness than other methods and is useful only for small groups.

5. Overhead transparencies—These may be different sizes, but the most common is about the same as an 8½- × 11-inch page. They are easy to make with color markers or with a copy machine. They are inexpensive and the projectors are widely available. You can also show overlays and buildups. If carelessly made, they look amateurish, but they can be attractive with careful printing. In using transparencies, be sure they are in correct order, and right-side up when you put them on the projector.

6. Slides—Most are 35 mm, but larger sizes are sometimes used. They are relatively inexpensive, can show color, and present a professional-looking image if well done. They are somewhat more difficult to make than the others. When using them, be sure the slides are loaded into the projector properly and in sequence.

The choice of speaking aids is largely determined by what you wish them to do, by meeting room conditions, by time and budget constraints, and by available equipment.

Why use them? Visual aids can serve a number of important functions in a research presentation. The most obvious is to present materials that cannot otherwise be communicated efficiently. For example, statistical relationships are difficult to describe verbally, but a picture or graph communicates well. How better to describe some object or material than to show it or picture it?

Visual aids help the speaker to clarify major points. Through the visual reinforcement of something said verbally, the speaker can stress the importance of certain points. In addition, the use of two channels of communication (hearing and sight) enhances the probability that the listener will understand and remember the message.

Visual aids also improve the continuity and memorability of the speaker's message. Verbal information is so transient that any slight lapse of listener attention results in losing the information thread. The failure fully to comprehend a given point cannot be remedied by going back to hear again for the speaker has gone on. With a visual aid, however, there is more opportunity to review the point, relate it to earlier comments by the speaker, and in this way improve retention.

What to put in them? There are differences of opinion as to the proper contents for visual aids. One view is that there should be only a few visuals and they should be largely restricted to pictures and statistics with a minimum of words.[6] Advocates of this position claim that words make visuals dull and uninformative. Too often, this argument goes, visuals are only groups of abstract nouns such as "Objectives, Operations, Preparation, Planning, Productivity, or Progress," and that these are of little communications help.[7] Of course, it is possible to develop dull and uninformative visual aids, but this should not be used as a blanket condemnation of word visuals. The weight of informed opinion seems to be that a well-conceived visual can be made up totally of words. The criterion is "Does it contribute to the effective transmission of a message from speaker to audience?" This requirement can be met with visuals which are all words or all pictures, or a combination; but obviously a set of single abstract nouns does not contribute much.

Some writers on the subject of visual presentations suggest that visuals should be used to present the full outline of a report. One offers the following suggestions as to how a set of visual aids might appear in a briefing on "How to Conduct a Briefing."[8]

1. PLAN YOUR BRIEFING

(Transparency 1)   1.1   Decide why you are giving the briefing.

               1.2   Study your expected audience.

               1.3   Anticipate problems, questions, objections.

               1.4   Get facts about time, place, etc.

2. DEVELOP YOUR PRESENTATION

(Transparency 2)   2.1   Select your main ideas.

               2.2   Make sure they are vital to the audience.

               2.3   Assemble factual support.

               2.4   Organize your material.

               2.5   Prepare needed visual aids.

---

[6]For this view see Anthony Jay, *Effective Presentation* (London: British Institute of Management, 1970).

[7]Ibid., p. 45.

[8]Reprinted by special permission from Robert Hays, *Practically Speaking—in Business, Industry, and Government* (Reading, Mass.: Addison-Wesley, 1969), pp. 149–53.

3. PRACTICE YOUR BRIEFING

(Transparency 3) 3.1 Use your notes for practice.
3.2 Practice entire briefing at least three times out loud.
3.3 Cut material to stay within time limit.
3.4 Rehearse opening and closing especially.
3.5 Check to see that all material is ready.

4. DELIVER YOUR BRIEFING

(Transparency 4) 4.1 Arrive ahead of time.
4.2 Start on time and end on time.
4.3 Keep eye contact with audience.
4.4 Save some time for questions.
4.5 Summarize main points.

5. HOW TO CONDUCT A BRIEFING

(Transparency 5) 5.1 Plan your briefing.
5.2 Develop your presentation.
5.3 Practice your briefing.
5.4 Deliver it.

SUMMARY

The quality of the presentation of research findings can have an inordinate effect on a reader's or listener's perceptions of the quality of the study. Recognition of this fact should prompt a researcher to make special efforts to communicate skillfully and clearly.

Research reports contain findings, analysis, interpretation, conclusions, and sometimes recommendations. They may follow the short informal format typical of memoranda and letters, or they may be longer and more complex. Long reports are organized in either a logical or psychological sequence. In the former the problem is presented, followed by the findings, conclusions, and recommendations. In the psychological sequence, the conclusions and recommendations precede the findings. The logical sequence is more frequently used in reports designed for the technical reader. The psychological format is for the lay reader or manager.

The writer of research reports should be guided by four questions: (1) what is the purpose of this report? (2) who will read it? (3) what are the circumstances and limitations under which it is written? and (4) how will the report be used? Reports should also be clearly organized, physically inviting, and easy to read. Writers can achieve these goals, if they are careful with mechanical details, writing style, and comprehensibility. There is a special problem with presenting statistical data. While some may be incorporated in the text, most statistics should be placed in tables or graphs. The table or graph form to use depends on the specific data and presentation problem.

Briefings on research study findings are common and should be developed with concern for the communication problems that are unique to oral presentation situations. Briefings are usually under time constraints; good briefings require careful organization and preparation. Visual aids are a particularly important aspect of briefings but are too often ignored or treated inadequately.

Whether written or oral, poor presentations do grave injustice to what might otherwise be excellent research. Good presentations, on the other hand, add luster to both the research and the reputation of the researcher.

SUPPLEMENTAL READINGS

1. Berenson, Conrad, and Raymond Colton. *Research and Report Writing for Business and Economics.* New York: Random House, 1971. Chapters 8 through 17 cover report writing.
2. Howell, William S., and Ernest G. Borman. *Presentational Speaking for Business and the Professions.* New York: Harper & Row, 1971. Thorough treatment of the problems and processes of designing and delivering presentations to business and professional audiences.
3. Lesikar, Raymond V. *How to Write a Report Your Boss Will Read and Remember.* Homewood, Ill.: Dow Jones-Irwin, 1974. Stresses report writing in a business setting. Appendixes present illustrations of various reports.
4. *MLA Handbook for Writers of Research Papers, Theses, and Dissertations.* New York: Modern Language Association, 1977. This is a widely used guide in colleges and universities for the written preparation of research results. Lucid recommendations for mechanics and formatting of academic research results. It does not take up questions of writing style.
5. Moyer, Ruth; Eleanor Stevens; and Ralph Switzer. *The Research Handbook for Managers and Executives in Business, Industry, and Government.* New York: John Wiley & Sons, 1981. A comprehensive source on the preparation of reports, their documentation, sources of information, and writing style.
6. Spear, Mary Eleanor. *Practical Charting Techniques,* New York. McGraw-Hill, 1969. A thorough coverage of the principles of graphic presentation.
7. Strunk, William, Jr., and E. B. White. *The Elements of Style.* New York: Macmillan, 1959. A classic on the problems of writing style.
8. Welsh, James J. *The Speech Writing Guide.* New York: John Wiley & Sons, 1968. A short, highly readable guide for business and professional people who need a practical reference tool for writing a presentable speech.

DISCUSSION QUESTIONS

1. Distinguish between:
   a Informational and research reports.
   b Logical and psychological research report formats.
   c Technical and popular reports.
   d Topic and sentence outlines.
2. What should you do about:
   a Putting information in a research report concerning the study's limitations?
   b The size and complexity of tables in a research report?

    c The physical presentation of a report?

    d Pace in your writing?

3. What type of report would you suggest be written in each of the following cases:

    a The president of the company has asked for a study of the company's pension plan and its comparison to those of other firms in the industry.

    b You have been asked to write up a marketing experiment, which you recently completed, for submission to the *Journal of Marketing Research.*

    c Your division manager has asked you to prepare a forecast of cash requirements for the division for the next three months.

    d The National Institute of Health has given you a grant to study the relation between industrial accidents and departmental employee morale.

4. Begin on one of the following listed pages with the first complete paragraph and calculate the Fog Index for the text of 100 or more words. Rewrite the material to reduce the index by at least two points.

    a Page 243

    b Page 277

    c Page 337

    d Page 412

5. Research reports often contain much statistical materials of great importance, but are often presented poorly. Suggest five important shoulds that a research report writer ought to know.

6. The typical student research report has many deficiencies in presentation in addition to its limitations in project design and content. Make a list of what you believe to be the major presentation problems with student written research reports. With student oral research reports.

7. What are the major problems that you personally have with writing good reports? What can you do about these problems?

8. Outline a set of visual aids that you might use in an oral briefing on:

    a How to write a research report.

    b The outlook for the economy over the next year.

    c The major analytical article in the latest *Business Week.*

9. There are a number of graphic presentation forms. Which would you suggest using to show each of the following? Why?

    a A comparison of changes in average annual per capita income for the United States and the Soviet Union from 1970 to 1980.

    b The percentage composition of average family expenditure patterns, by the major types of expenditures, for families whose heads are under 35 years with families whose heads are 55 years or older.

    c A comparison of the change, between December 31, 1978, and December 31, 1979, of common stock prices of six major electronics firms.

APPENDIXES

APPENDIX A

Business Reference Tools

INTRODUCTION

The purpose of this guide is to describe the most important bibliographies and other reference works in the field of business. These are some of the tools which business students should know before they attempt to write a paper or thesis. They are divided into three main groups: (1) guides to reference materials; (2) bibliographies; (3) miscellaneous reference works.

I. GUIDES TO REFERENCE MATERIALS

Because this list of reference tools describes only the major works, students should examine one or more of the guides described below. They describe the varied sources of information available in the field of business, tell the purposes for which these sources may be used, and give directions on their use. There are also guides to more specialized topics, such as the guides to statistics listed in the section on that subject.

Encyclopedia of Business Information Sources: A Detailed Listing of Primary Subjects of Interest to Managerial Personnel, with a Record of Sourcebooks, Periodicals, Organizations, Directories, Handbooks, Bibliographies, and Other Sources of Information on Each Topic. 4th ed. Detroit: Gale Research, 1980.

The entries are designed to identify the "right place to begin" an information search rather than to answer specific questions. The first volume is arranged alphabetically by general topic; the second, by geographic source.

Johnson, Herbert Webster. *How to Use the Business Library.* 4th ed. Cincinnati: Southwestern Publishing, 1972.

This manual serves as a good introduction to such materials as handbooks, yearbooks, directories, and government publications that are most useful to business executives.

Sheehy, Eugene P. *Guide to Reference Books.* 9th ed. Chicago: American Library Association, 1976.

This standard bibliography of reference works includes many titles in business and related fields. This guide will refer to Sheehy occasionally as a source of additional references. There are supplements to the 9th edition, 1980.

Universal Reference System. Vol. 3: Political Science, Government, and Public Policy Series. Vol. 8: Economic Regulation: Business and Government. Princeton, N.J.: Princeton Research Publishing, 1969.

This multivolume set presents "an annotated and intensively indexed compilation of significant books, pamphlets, and articles, selected and processed by the Universal Reference System—a computerized information retrieval service in the social and behavioral sciences."

White, Carl Milton. *Sources of Information in the Social Sciences: A Guide to the Literature.* 2d ed. Chicago: American Library Association, 1973.

Chapter 3 is entitled, "Economics and Business Administration."

II. BIBLIOGRAPHIES

Briefly defined, a bibliography is a list of books or other printed materials. Most bibliographies are arranged either by author or by subject. The card catalog, one of the most important bibliographies, lists only books available in a given library, while other bibliographies list books that may not be in the collection. Some bibliographies list only certain types of publications, such as dissertations or government publications. In order to collect all the important references on a subject, it is necessary to know and use a wide variety of bibliographies.

A. The public catalog

The catalog is a bibliography of books in a library. Cards for books are filed under author, title, and subject. Subject headings are a frequent cause of difficulties in using the catalog, and the following suggestions may help you save time. When you are searching for material by subject and are not sure of the correct subject heading, consult the following work:

U.S. Library of Congress. Subject Cataloging Division. *Library of Congress Subject Headings*. 2 vols. 9th ed. Washington, D.C.: Government Printing Office, 1980.

This list tells what headings are used in the catalog and also provides cross-references from headings that are not used to ones that are. For example, if you should look for the subject *Business Arithmetic*, this list will tell you that the subject heading used in the catalog is *Business Mathematics*.

The Library of Congress list also suggests related subjects to consult. For example, under *Office Management*, you find the related headings *Business Records*, *Credit Managers*, *Office Procedures*, and so forth. Similar cross-references are made on cards filed in the public catalog.

A point to remember is that subject headings are usually specific. When looking for material on *marketing*, try that subject first, not the more general subject *business*. Cross-references usually will help lead you from the general headings to more specific ones. For example, the cross-references under *Business* refer to special fields of business, such as *Accounting, Advertising, Marketing*, and so on. If you do not find enough material under your specific topic, try the next broader topic that includes it.

Subject headings are made only for the three or four most prominent subjects treated in a book; you cannot count on finding subject cards for every topic mentioned. You must use your ingenuity in determining what categories of books could conceivably treat your topic. If you do not find a subject entry for a particular technique used in advertising, try the subject heading Advertising.

You will save time if you learn to recognize the information given on the catalog cards. The following items are included: author; title; publisher; date of publication; number of pages or volumes; series; notes listing the contents; notes describing special features, such as illustrations, maps, or bibliographies; and a list of subject headings assigned to that book. The description of the book on the catalog card may tell you whether or not it is worth examining.

A library's public catalog does not record every publication received by that library. Among the types of materials often excluded from the catalog are the following:

1. Most U.S. government publications. (See the later sections of this guide which describe government document bibliographies.)
2. Most United Nations publications.
3. Reports from companies. (For example, corporation annual reports.)

Another point to keep in mind about a library's public catalog is that it records only the books in that library. If you are engaged in serious research, you cannot afford to limit yourself to the books in one library. Any single collection is limited by the funds available and by the interests of those who influence the book ordering. Instead of depending on the catalog alone, you should turn also to other types of bibliographies.

B. Single-subject bibliographies

Unfortunately, there is no single comprehensive bibliography of business literature, but there are many bibliographies covering specific areas, such as production, marketing, and accounting.

The student might find it advantageous to examine the important bibliographies written on the subject. Books which are primarily bibliographies may be found in the public catalog under the appropriate subject heading, for example, *Accounting—Bibliography.*

C. General bibliographies

If you cannot find a bibliography on your subject, or if you feel that the bibliographies you have located are incomplete or out-of-date, you should consult the general bibliographies. This category includes the catalogs of the great national libraries and national and trade bibliographies. The most important American general bibliographies with a subject approach are described below:

American Book Publishing Record, BPR. New York: R. R. Bowker, 1960—. Vol. 1—, Monthly.

This periodical aims to be a complete record of American books published in the month preceding its date of issue. It is arranged by the Dewey Decimal Classification, with author and title indexes. There is also an annual accumulation.

Association for University Business and Economic Research. *Bibliography of Publications of University Bureaus of Business and Economic Research,* AUBER bibliography. V22—, 1977—. Morganton, W. Va.: Bureau of Business Research, West Virginia University.

This is a selective index to reports, bulletins, and monographs published by bureaus of business research affiliated with universities. The supplements also list selected articles appearing in periodicals published by these bureaus. There is an author and subject index.

Bibliographic Index: A Cumulative Bibliography of Bibliographies. New York: H. W. Wilson, 1937—.

Bibliographies printed in books and periodicals as well as separately published bibliographies are listed by subject.

Cumulative Book Index: A World List of Books in the English Language. New York: H. W. Wilson, 1928—.

Books published in the English language in the United States, and since 1930, in other parts of the world are recorded by author, title, and subject in this comprehensive bibliography.

Subject Guide to Books in Print. New York: R. R. Bowker, 1957—.

Currently available American trade books are listed by subject.

Subject Guide to Forthcoming Books. New York: R. R. Bowker, 1967—. Vol. 1—.

This bimonthly publication "aims to list all books expected to be published in the U.S.A. during the next five months."

Most of the general bibliographies are arranged by author. If you know the name of the author who has written on your subject, you may use these bibliographies to find out the titles of other books he or she has written. These general bibliographies are also used to verify and complete references when you know the author's name but are not sure of the title, date, or publisher.

Books in Print. New York: R. R. Bowker, 1948—.

This is an annual author, title, and subject index to the collection of publishers' catalogs known as *The Publishers' Trade List Annual.* It can be used as quick identification of a recent American work when only the author or title or subject is known, as well as to determine whether a particular book is available for purchase. For information about books published after this annual appears (also published semiannually), use *Forthcoming Books* listed immediately below or the *Cumulative Book Index and American Book Publishing Record,* described above.

Forthcoming Books. New York: R. R. Bowker, 1966—. Vol. 1—.

This publication is an author-title list, including new books in print.

The National Union Catalog, Pre-1956 Imprints; a Cumulative Author List Representing Library of Congress Printed Cards and Titles Reported by Other American Libraries. London: Mansell, 1968–1981. 754 vols.

The National Union Catalog: A Cumulative Author List Representing Library of Congress Printed Cards and Titles Reported by Other American Libraries. New York: Roman and Littlefield. Various sets from 1958.

These companion works and monumental bibliographical tools are especially valuable for providing locations of books in major American libraries. Libraries with special collections occasionally publish their catalogs in book form, thus expediting the search for hard-to-find material.

Cornell University. New York State School of Industrial and Labor Relations. Library. *Library Catalog.* 12 vols. & Supplements. Boston: G. K. Hall, 1967–69.

This library is especially strong in labor management relations, human relations in industry, personnel, social insurance and employee welfare, labor economics, labor union organization and administration, labor industry, and international labor conditions and problems.

D.   U.S. government publications

Publications issued by the U.S. government contain information of real value to students of business. Some of the bibliographies already described, such as the *National Union Catalogs* list government publications, as does "PAIS" (described below with the periodical indexes). But in order to be sure of locating all of the relevant materials, you should use the special document bibliographies. The most important ones are listed below. Consult also *Sheehy's Guide to Reference Books.*

Guide to U.S. Government Publications. McLean, Va.: Documents Index, 1973—.

This invaluable tool provides access to U.S. government serials and periodials by issuing agency, title, or documents number.

Monthly Catalog of United States Government Publications. Washington, D.C.: U.S. Government Printing Office, 1895—.

Entries in the Monthly Catalog are indexed for access by author, title, subject and series/report. Cumulative indexes are published semiannually and annually. Titles in all indexes are followed by the text entry number where more detailed information is available.

Remember that the public catalog does not list the majority of government publications. *The Monthly Catalog* serves as a printed catalog to the documents collection because it gives the call numbers (Superintendent of Documents numbers) used to arrange and shelve these publications, just as the public catalog gives Library of Congress numbers.

U.S. Department of Commerce. *Publications Catalog of the U.S.* Washington, D.C.: U.S. Government Printing Office, 1979—.

This is a catalog and subject index based on the Commerce Department's biweekly *Commerce Publication Updates.* Material is included from the Office of Technical Services, the Area Redevelopment Administration, the Business and Defense Services Administration, the Bureau of International Commerce, the National Bureau of Standards, and the Bureau of the Census. The Census Bureau also issues its own catalog along with a basic list which covers publications issued from 1790 to 1972.

U.S. Congress. *Congressional Record.* Washington, D.C.: Government Printing Office, 1873—.

This constitutes "the public proceedings of each House of Congress as reported by the Official Reporters thereof. . . . Published each day that one or both Houses are in session, excepting very infrequent instances when two or more unusually small consecutive issues are printed at one time." The weekly index contains many subject headings directly related to business and possibilities of intended or accomplished congressional action, remarks, speeches, and discussion.

Congressional Information Service. CIS Index 1970—. Washington, D.C.: Government Printing Office.

Acts as an index to publications of the U.S. Congress published monthly with quarterly and annual accumulations. CIS provides current, comprehensive access to the contents of the entire spectrum of congressional working papers.

E. United Nations publications

United Nations Documents Index. UNDOC. New York: United Nations, Dag Hammarskjold Library, 1979—.

The UN publishes extensively in the field of international economic problems, for example, finance, natural resources, technical development, and trade. Publications are listed in this index by issuing body, and indexed by subject. The monthly issues are superseded by an annual cumulation. Be sure to note the four-volume cumulative index for the years 1950–1962.

As with U.S. government documents, most UN publications are not listed in the public catalog.

F. Dissertations and research in progress

Dissertations are not systematically listed in any of the sources already described. The following specialized bibliographies list completed dissertations and other research projects which are in progress. January issues of the *Journal of Business* include a list of recently completed doctoral dissertations in the field of business.

American Doctoral Dissertations. Ann Arbor, Mich.: University Microfilms, 1955–56.

This annual publication provides "a complete listing of all doctoral dissertations accepted by American and Canadian universities. This is published on a school-year basis and is arranged by subject categories and institutions. An author index is an integral part of each publication." Business-related topics may be found under *Business Administration* and *Economics, Commerce—Business.* The title varies, and there are comparable publications covering earlier periods.

Dissertation Abstracts International. Ann Arbor, Mich.: Xerox University Microfilms, 1938—.

Abstracts of doctoral dissertations that are available for purchase in complete form in microfilm or Xerographic reproduction are listed here. The abstracts are arranged by broad subject areas with an author index. Beginning with Volume 27 (1966), *Dissertation Abstracts* was divided into two sections: A: the Humanities and Social Sciences, and B: the Sciences and Engineering. Both sections have indexes which are issued separately. With Volume 30 (1969), Dissertation Abstracts became *Dissertation Abstracts International* to reflect the addition of European universities. The coverage of universities has increased in recent years and now includes a section C: *European Abstracts.* For the most complete list of dissertations, use the *Comprehensive Dissertation Index 1861–1972,* with the annual supplements.

G. Indexes to periodicals, newspapers, and serials

The latest information on most subjects is found in periodicals and newspapers. Some information may never be published in any other form. To locate these articles, it is necessary to use indexes designed for that purpose.

Applied Science and Technology Index (formerly *Industrial Arts Index*). New York: H. W. Wilson, 1913—.

This is a cumulative subject index to English language periodicals which analyzes more than 300 periodicals relevant to the applied sciences. Many of the periodicals indexed have a direct bearing upon business activities and carry business information in the form of reports, articles, news notes, and special issues. Subject headings include *Budget—United States, Business Management, Business Charts, Finance, Stocks,* and so on.

Business Periodicals Index. New York: H. W. Wilson, 1958—.

Approximately 260 business and economics periodicals in the English language are cumulatively indexed by subject. This index is particularly good for the practical aspects of business operations and specific businesses, industries, and trades. For material before 1958, see the *Industrial Arts Index,* 1913–57.

Index to Legal Periodicals. New York: H. W. Wilson, 1908—.

These monthly indexes, which contain subject headings from many areas of human activity, are published for the American Association of Law Libraries.

New York Times Index. New York: New York Times Co., 1851—.

This most comprehensive newspaper index published is also valuable for establishing dates of articles in other newspapers.

PAIS—*Bulletin.* New York: Public Affairs Information Service, Inc., 1915—.

A large number of English language periodicals from all over the world are selectively indexed and many books, government publications, and pamphlets are listed by subject in this bibliography which covers business, banking, and economics, as well as subjects in the area of public affairs. It is often cited as *PAIS*. Note the cumulative indexes for 1915–74. The *Foreign Language Index* covers materials in French, German, Italian, Portuguese, and Spanish beginning with 1968.

Selected Rand Abstracts. Rand Corporation, Santa Monica, Calif.: 1963—, Vol. 1—.

The Rand Corporation, established in 1948 as an independent, nonprofit organization is engaged in a program of research concerned with the security and public welfare of the United States. This research is financed by the U.S. Air Force, by other government agencies, and by the corporation. *Selected Rand Abstracts*, a complete guide to current unclassified publications of the Rand Corporation, is published four times each year. The volume is cumulative through the year. Issue Number 4 (December) is the permanent record for the year. Documents issued during the period 1946–62 are listed in the *Index of Selected Publications*.

Social Sciences Citation Index: An International Interdisciplinary Index to the Literature of the Social Sciences. Philadelphia: Institute for Scientific Information, 1969—.

This lists references to publications cited during the period covered as well as original articles. It is especially valuable for tracing a given author's influence in a specific field.

Vertical File Index: A Subject and Title Index to Selected Pamphlet Materials. New York: H. W. Wilson, 1935—. Monthly (except August).

This is a useful source for locating ephemeral material, much of it free. The *Monthly Catalog* listed above should be consulted for references to pamphlets issued by the U.S. government. Most pamphlets are not cataloged.

The Wall Street Journal Index. Princeton, N.J.: Dow Jones Books, 1957—.

This monthly index is divided into two sections, one for corporate news (arranged by the name of the firm) and one for general news (arranged by subject).

Students whose topic overlaps other fields, such as psychology or sociology, should consult *Sheehy's Guide to Reference Books* for the titles of indexes in those fields.

H. Lists of periodicals

Students working with periodicals will occasionally need the kind of information found in the two kinds of periodical lists described below. The first type, represented by the first four directories, indicates what titles are currently being published, and gives their addresses, subscription prices, and similar information. The second type, represented by the last two titles, is primarily intended to inform the user in what libraries the periodicals can be found.

Ayer Directory of Publications. Philadelphia: Ayer Press, 1880—.
This annual list of American newspapers and periodicals is arranged by state and city, and gives detailed information (editor, publisher, address, circulation figures, subscription price) for each title. It has an alphabetical index of the periodical titles and a classified list of trade, technical, and professional journals.

Business Marketing. "Guide to Special Issues." Chicago: Crain Communications, Inc., monthly.
This directory is currently included in every third issue. Publications are listed within primary market classifications and are listed for up to three months prior to the advertising closing date. Data include the name of the special issue, date of publication, a brief description of the issue, advertising closing date, and associated services, for example, reader inquiry card.

Standard Periodical Directory. New York: Oxbridge Publishing Company, 1964/65—.
This directory provides a subject arrangement of over 65,000 U.S. and Canadian periodicals, with an alphabetical title index. Entries include such information as publisher, editor, address, frequency, price, circulation, and special features. It covers every type of periodical with the exception of suburban weekly and small daily newspapers.

Ulrich's International Periodicals Directory: A Classified Guide to Current Periodicals, Foreign and Domestic. New York: R. R. Bowker, 1932—.
This bibliography is particularly useful for finding comprehensive lists of periodicals in various subject fields and for determining in what indexes a periodical is analyzed. It also identifies periodicals containing bibliographies and book reviews.

Union List of Serials in Libraries of the United States and Canada. 3d ed., 5 vols. New York: H. W. Wilson, 1965.
This is the most comprehensive list of periodicals available. It gives a brief bibliographical description of each title and indicates holdings in American libraries. It is a basic tool for identifying periodical titles and for locating specific volumes.

New Serial Titles. Washington, D.C.: Library of Congress, 1950—.

This serves as a supplement to the *Union List of Serials;* it includes much the same type of information and is used for the same purposes.

III. MISCELLANEOUS REFERENCE SOURCES

The emphasis in the preceding sections was bibliographical; that is, most of the works cited are used to find information about published materials. The books described in this section, with few exceptions, are primarily compilations of facts and figures arranged for ease of consultation. Some of these books will refer you to further, more detailed sources, but all contain explicit answers to many questions. The following are samples of the type of questions answered by these works:

What was the gross national products of the United States for the last five years?
What companies manufacture clay pipe?
What is a voucher register?
How many persons are employed in manufacturing in St. Louis, Missouri?

A. Atlases

Atlases are useful to executives in many areas, especially to those concerned with marketing, exporting and importing, and transportation. No reference is made here to any of the numerous excellent general atlases, descriptions of which can be found in *Sheehy's Guide to Reference Books*. One atlas designed for business use is described below:

The *Commercial Atlas and Marketing Guide*. Chicago: Rand McNally, annual.

This atlas contains reference maps for foreign countries, U.S. states, and Canadian provinces. Special maps cover transportation, communications, population distribution, retail trade and manufacturing, time zones, and airline distances. There are many tables of statistical and factual information useful to executives.

B. Biographical works

American Assembly of Collegiate Schools of Business. *Faculty Personnel: A Directory of the Instructional Staffs of Member Schools*. St. Louis, Mo.: American Assembly of Collegiate Schools of Business, 1925—.

This directory lists more than 16,200 faculty members from approximately 470 universities and colleges. Included is selected background information on full-time faculty with the rank of instructor and above at both accredited and nonaccredited schools. Faculty members are alphabetically grouped under their current university or college affiliation.

Dun & Bradstreet Reference Book of Corporate Managements. New York: Dun & Bradstreet, 19—.

This book lists more than 30,000 officers and directors in the 2,400 companies of greatest investor interest. The entries are arranged alphabetically by the name of the corporation and there is an index to principal officers.

The International Who's Who. London: Europa Publications Ltd., 1935—.

The book contains biographies of people from almost every country in the world and in almost every sphere of human activity.

Standard and Poor's Register of Corporations, Directors, and Executives. New York: Standard and Poor's Corp., 1928—.

This publication lists the directors and other important executive personnel of over 38,000 industrial corporations. Biographical information for each person includes the following information: business affiliations, business address, home address, fraternal membership, education, and date of birth. This directory also provides the following data for the companies: address of the home office, the principal products, number of employees, and annual sales range. A geographical index lists the corporations by state and city.

Who's Who in Finance and Industry. Chicago: Marquis Who's Who, 1936—.

This work provides a complete summary of the background of individuals who have distinguished themselves in areas of commercial activity. It includes many more executives than are found in *Who's Who in America* and gives considerably more detail than is given in Standard & Poor's *Register.* It lists business affiliations, education, clubs and organizations, and addresses for over 18,000 American and foreign leaders in business administration, production, technology, sales, and business-related professions.

C. Business services

Because business is a field that changes so rapidly, most reference works soon become out of date. The latest factual information on many subjects, such as commodity prices, foreign exchange, securities, and tax regulations, is contained in business service publications, which are kept up-to-date by supplements or loose-leaf revisions.

Directory of Business and Financial Services. New York: Special Libraries Association, 1924—.

This guide describes 1,051 services, including newsletters, bulletins, reports, and other publications, and represents 421 publishers.

Consumerism; New Developments for Business. Chicago: Commerce Clearing House, 1971—.

This publication is a weekly service that briefly explains new developments regarding consumerism in legislation and rulings by government agencies.

Commodity Year Book. New York: Commodity Research Bureau, 1938—.

This annual volume is "designed to help clarify the great changes taking place in the world of commodities" by means of graphs, charts, tables, and text. It is updated three times yearly by the *Commodity Year Book Statistical Abstract Service.*

Moody's Industrial Manual. New York: Moody's Investors Service, 1909—.

This annual book presents the history of the company, a description of the business and its products, a list of principal plants, a list of officers and directors, and financial data, such as the firm's dividend record. It is updated by the semiweekly *Moody's Industrial News Reports*, a loose-leaf service with cumulative indexes. Other Moody's Manuals are devoted to banks, investments, municipalities, public utilities, and transportation firms.

Prentice-Hall Federal Taxes. Englewood Cliffs, N.J.: Prentice-Hall, 1921—.

This complete and authoritative service reprints federal tax laws, regulations, rulings, and decisions, along with extensive editorial comment.

Standard & Poor's Trade and Securities Statistics (loose-leaf). New York: Standard & Poor's, 1941—.

This service is issued in three parts: Current Statistics; Business and Finance; and Security Price Index Record.

Two other Standard & Poor's loose-leaf services that can be valuable to the investor or the researcher into individual companies are:

Stock Reports; Over-the-Counter Regional Exchanges. 4 vols. New York: Standard & Poor's (loose-leaf, updated regularly).

This contains the Standard N.Y.S.E. Stock Reports, Over-the-Counter and Regional Exchange Reports, Standard A.S.E. Stock Reports, Standard Convertible Securities Reports, and Definitions of Terms.

Daily Stock Price Record: New York Stock Exchange. New York: Standard and Poor's, 1961—.

This quarterly publication is divided into two parts. Part I, "Major Technical Indicators of the Stock Market," is devoted to market indicators widely followed as technical guides to the stock market. Part II, "Daily and Weekly Stock Action," gives the daily and weekly record of stocks listed either on the NYSE, the ASE, or the OTC Market.

The Value Line Investment Survey. New York: Arnold Bernhard, weekly.

This publication is divided into four parts: They are the (1) Summary and Index; (2) Selection and Opinion; (3) Ratings and Reports; and

(4) Miscellaneous. This is a valuable source for regularly updated financial information on hundreds of companies.

University libraries may also have a microfiche file or annual business reports, 10Ks filed with the SEC and prospectuses of companies listed on the American and New York Stock Exchanges.

D. Dictionaries and encyclopedias

For definitions of business terms not found in general dictionaries, consult the following specialized reference works.

Moore, Norman D. *Dictionary of Business, Finance and Investment.* Dayton, Ohio: Investor's System, 1975.
> This volume defines terms used in the fields of accounting, advertising, banking, commodities, credit, imports, retailing, the stock market, and other areas of interest to students and executives.

Altman, Edward I. *Financial Handbook.* 5th ed. New York: The Ronald Press, 1981.
> This volume is a compendium of information needed by bankers, investors, and financial managers. Topics are presented in brief outline accompanied by many examples and tables.

Heyel, Carl, ed. *The Encyclopedia of Management.* 3d ed. New York: Van Nostrand Reinhold, 1982.
> This work summarizes the major areas of management and provides references for further reading.

International Encyclopedia of the Social Sciences. 17 vols. New York: Macmillan, 1968.
> This basic reference source for the social sciences includes such topics as economics, industrial organization, labor economics, money and banking, public finance, and certain aspects of business management. Bibliographies at the end of each article and a detailed index in the final volume lead to additional sources of information. Its predecessor, *The Encyclopedia of the Social Sciences,* 1930, is still valuable for historical and biographical material.

Munn, Glenn G. *Encyclopedia of Banking and Finance.* 7th ed. Boston, Mass.: Bankers Pub., 1973.
> This one-volume encyclopedia includes definitions of words and phrases used in business, as well as encyclopedic articles with bibliographies covering the fields of money, credit, and banking.

Tver, David F. *The Gulf Publishing Company Directory of Business and Science.* 3d ed. Houston, Texas: Gulf Publishing, 1974.
> This dictionary "comprises specialized terminology from such disciplines as medicine, law, psychology, and geology; the rapidly developing jargon on computers, aerospace, and electronics; and such business

essentials as labor and personnel, advertising and printing, accounting, finance, business law, and insurance."

E.   Directories

Business directories are lists of organizations or companies, systematically arranged, giving addresses, officers, and other data. Many directories dealing with specific industries and trades contain factual and statistical data. Because many of these directories are revised frequently, they are valuable sources of current information.

Klein, Bernard. *Guide to American Directories: A guide to the major directories of the United States covering all Trade, Professional and Industrial Categories.* 11th ed. Coral Springs, Fla.: B. Klein Publications, 1982.

This guide lists directories published by business reference publishers, magazines, trade associations, chambers of commerce, and government agencies.

Thomas Register of American Manufacturers and Thomas Register Catalog File. New York: Thomas Publishing, 1905—.

This directory lists approximately 75,000 different products, giving for every product the companies which manufacture it. The main section groups company names by state and city under the product. One volume is an alphabetical list of companies; another contains a brand names index; the final volumes are devoted to catalogs of companies.

Missouri Directory of Manufacturing and Mining. St. Louis, Mo.: Informative Data, 1982.

Manufacturing and mining firms are listed separately in three sections: alphabetically by the name of the establishment; geographically by city; and by product according to the Standard Industrial Classification Number.

Metro St. Louis Directory of Manufacturers. St. Louis, Mo.: St. Louis Regional Commerce and Growth Association, 1976—.

"The *Metro St. Louis Directory of Manufacturers* lists manufacturing establishments (as defined by the Standard Industrial Classification Manual, 1972) located in the following counties of Missouri and Illinois: Missouri—City of St. Louis, Franklin, Jefferson, St. Charles, St. Louis: Illinois–Clinton; Madison, Monroe, St. Clair." Comparable directories are published for many states and cities of the United States.

Wasserman, Paul. *Consultants and Consulting Organizations Directory; A Reference Guide to Concerns and Individuals Engaged in Consultation for Business and Industry.* 5th ed., Detroit: Gale Research, 1982.

This is a reference guide to concerns and individuals engaged in consultation for business and industry.

Consumer Sourcebook, 2 vols., 3d ed. Detroit: Gale Research, 1981.

> The subtitle of this book provides a thorough description of this book: "A Directory and Guide to Government Organizations; Associations; Centers and Institutes; Media Services; Company and Trademark Information; and Bibliographic Material Relating to Consumer Topics, Sources of Recourse, and Advisory Information." The entries for agencies, organizations, and for publications are annotated.

Encyclopedia of Associations. Detroit: Gale Research, 1956——.

> Directories of associations can be very useful in subject approaches to problems.
>
> United States and selected international associations are listed in three volumes: (1) *National Organizations of the United States;* (2) *Geographic and Executive Index;* (3) *New Associations and Projects.* Brief descriptions of the associations, dates, addresses, officers, meetings, size, and publications are among the details provided.

F. Statistical works

Guides and bibliographies. So many publications contain statistics that it is sometimes difficult to find precisely the data you need. *Sheehy's Guide to Reference Books,* the *Business Periodicals Index,* "*PAIS,*" and *The Wall Street Journal* are useful for locating sources for statistics on various subjects. When U.S. government statistics are needed, the relatively new *American Statistics Index* is especially helpful.

American Statistics Index. Washington, D.C.: Congressional Information Service, 1973——.

> The cover of this regularly updated service reads, "A comprehensive guide and index to the statistical publications of the U.S. government."

Guide to U.S. Government Statistics. Arlington, Va.: Documents Index, 1956——.

> This volume may be used for the quick location of statistical sources by subject and for a description of all of the statistical publications of U.S. government agencies. It is arranged by government agency.

Statistical Reference Index, 1980. Washington, D.C.: Congressional Information Service. Published monthly with annual accumulation.

> A selective guide to American statistical publications from private organizations and state government sources.

U.S. Office of Management and Budget. *Statistical Services of the United States Government.* Rev. ed. Washington, D.C.: U.S. Government Printing Office, 1975.

> This "is designed to serve as a basic reference document on the statistical programs of the federal government." It is divided into three parts: I. The Statistical System of the Federal Government; II. Principal Social and Economic Statistical Programs; and III. Principal Statistical Publications of Federal Agencies.

Statistics Sources: A Subject Guide to Data on Industrial, Business, Social, Educational, Financial, and Other Topics for the United States and Internationally. 7th ed. Detroit: Gale Research, 1981.

U.S. Bureau of the Census. *Directory of Federal Statistics for Local Areas: A Guide to Sources, 1976.* Washington, D.C.: U.S. Department of Commerce, Bureau of the Census, 1978.

This directory provides table-by-table descriptions of statistical reports on areas smaller than states. Only reports issued by federal departments or agencies prior to January 1, 1977, are included. To be included in this directory, a table must provide statistics on a type of local area for the entire United States.

Compilations of statistics. The following works are useful compilations of statistics.

U.S. Bureau of the Census. *Statistical Abstract of the United States, 1878—*. Washington, D.C.: U.S. Government Printing Office, 1879—.

This annual compendium of summary statistics on political, social, industrial, and economic organizations of the United States should be the starting point in gathering figures on any topic relating to business subjects. Information is included on federal regions, states, and metropolitan areas. The source notes for the tables and the appended bibliography of sources of statistics lead to more detailed publications of the federal government and of private organizations.

There are several supplements to the *Statistical Abstract. The County and City Data Book* provides recent figures for counties, cities, standard metropolitan statistical areas, and urbanized areas. The *State and Metropolitan Area Data Book* gives figures for these areas. *The Congressional District Data Book* presents a variety of statistical information for districts of the 93d Congress. *Historical Statistics of the United States: Colonial Times to 1970,* 2 vols., has a broad range of data for historical research. This book also provides valuable leads to other sources.

U.S. Office of Business Economics. *Survey of Current Business.* Washington, D.C.: U.S. Government Printing Office, 1921—.

Each issue of this periodical contains statistical series on national income, personal income, and expenditures; expenditures for new plants and equipment; production and prices of commodities; and other figures on various aspects of the nation's economy. Historical data for many of the series carried in the monthly issues are available in several supplements, the most important of which is *Business Statistics.* Published in odd-numbered years, this volume is designed to be a handy, comprehensive work. For a list of other supplements to the *Survey of Current Business,* see *Statistical Services of the U.S. Government* or *Guide to U.S. Government Publications.*

APPENDIX B
Selected Statistical Tables

TABLE B–1   Proportion of the area under the normal curve with values as extreme as the observed values of z

z	.00	.01	.02	.03	.04	.05	.06	.07	.08	.09
.0	.5000	.4960	.4920	.4880	.4840	.4801	.4761	.4721	.4681	.4641
.1	.4602	.4562	.4522	.4483	.4443	.4404	.4364	.4325	.4286	.4247
.2	.4207	.4168	.4129	.4090	.4052	.4013	.3974	.3936	.3897	.3859
.3	.3821	.3783	.3745	.3707	.3669	.3632	.3594	.3557	.3520	.3483
.4	.3446	.3409	.3372	.3336	.3300	.3264	.3228	.3192	.3156	.3121
.5	.3085	.3050	.3015	.2981	.2946	.2912	.2877	.2843	.2810	.2776
.6	.2743	.2709	.2676	.2643	.2611	.2578	.2546	.2514	.2483	.2451
.7	.2420	.2389	.2358	.2327	.2296	.2266	.2236	.2206	.2177	.2148
.8	.2119	.2090	.2061	.2033	.2005	.1977	.1949	.1922	.1894	.1867
.9	.1841	.1814	.1788	.1762	.1736	.1711	.1685	.1660	.1635	.1611
1.0	.1587	.1562	.1539	.1515	.1492	.1469	.1446	.1423	.1401	.1379
1.1	.1357	.1335	.1314	.1292	.1271	.1251	.1230	.1210	.1190	.1170
1.2	.1151	.1131	.1112	.1093	.1075	.1056	.1038	.1020	.1003	.0985
1.3	.0968	.0951	.0934	.0918	.0901	.0885	.0869	.0853	.0838	.0823
1.4	.0808	.0793	.0778	.0764	.0749	.0735	.0721	.0708	.0694	.0681
1.5	.0668	.0655	.0643	.0630	.0618	.0606	.0594	.0582	.0571	.0559
1.6	.0548	.0537	.0526	.0516	.0505	.0495	.0485	.0475	.0465	.0455
1.7	.0446	.0436	.0427	.0418	.0409	.0401	.0392	.0384	.0375	.0367
1.8	.0359	.0351	.0344	.0336	.0329	.0322	.0314	.0307	.0301	.0294
1.9	.0287	.0281	.0274	.0268	.0262	.0256	.0250	.0244	.0239	.0233
2.0	.0228	.0222	.0217	.0212	.0207	.0202	.0197	.0192	.0188	.0183
2.1	.0179	.0174	.0170	.0166	.0162	.0158	.0154	.0150	.0146	.0143
2.2	.0139	.0136	.0132	.0129	.0125	.0122	.0119	.0116	.0113	.0110
2.3	.0107	.0104	.0102	.0099	.0096	.0094	.0091	.0089	.0087	.0084
2.4	.0082	.0080	.0078	.0075	.0073	.0071	.0069	.0068	.0066	.0064
2.5	.0062	.0060	.0059	.0057	.0055	.0054	.0052	.0051	.0049	.0048
2.6	.0047	.0045	.0044	.0043	.0041	.0040	.0039	.0038	.0037	.0036
2.7	.0035	.0034	.0033	.0032	.0031	.0030	.0029	.0028	.0027	.0026
2.8	.0026	.0025	.0024	.0023	.0023	.0022	.0021	.0021	.0020	.0019
2.9	.0019	.0018	.0018	.0017	.0016	.0016	.0015	.0015	.0014	.0014
3.0	.0013	.0013	.0013	.0012	.0012	.0011	.0011	.0011	.0010	.0010
3.1	.0010	.0009	.0009	.0009	.0008	.0008	.0008	.0008	.0007	.0007
3.2	.0007									
3.3	.0005									
3.4	.0003									
3.5	.00023									
3.6	.00016									
3.7	.00011									
3.8	.00007									
3.9	.00005									
4.0	.00003									

TABLE B–2   Table of critical values of *t*

df	Level of Significance for One-Tailed Test					
	.10	.05	.025	.01	.005	.0005
	Level of Significance for Two-Tailed Test					
	.20	.10	.05	.02	.01	.001
1	3.078	6.314	12.706	31.821	63.657	636.619
2	1.886	2.920	4.303	6.965	9.925	31.598
3	1.638	2.353	3.182	4.541	5.841	12.941
4	1.533	2.132	2.776	3.747	4.604	8.610
5	1.476	2.015	2.571	3.365	4.032	6.859
6	1.440	1.943	2.447	3.143	3.707	5.959
7	1.415	1.895	2.365	2.998	3.499	5.405
8	1.397	1.860	2.306	2.896	3.355	5.041
9	1.383	1.833	2.262	2.821	3.250	4.781
10	1.372	1.812	2.228	2.764	3.169	4.587
11	1.363	1.796	2.201	2.718	3.106	4.437
12	1.356	1.782	2.179	2.681	3.055	4.318
13	1.350	1.771	2.160	2.650	3.012	4.221
14	1.345	1.761	2.145	2.624	2.977	4.140
15	1.341	1.753	2.131	2.602	2.947	4.073
16	1.337	1.746	2.120	2.583	2.921	4.015
17	1.333	1.740	2.110	2.567	2.898	3.965
18	1.330	1.734	2.101	2.552	2.878	3.922
19	1.328	1.729	2.093	2.539	2.861	3.883
20	1.325	1.725	2.086	2.528	2.845	3.850
21	1.323	1.721	2.080	2.518	2.831	3.819
22	1.321	1.717	2.074	2.508	2.819	3.792
23	1.319	1.714	2.069	2.500	2.807	3.767
24	1.318	1.711	2.064	2.492	2.797	3.745
25	1.316	1.708	2.060	2.485	2.787	3.725
26	1.315	1.706	2.056	2.479	2.779	3.707
27	1.314	1.703	2.052	2.473	2.771	3.690
28	1.313	1.701	2.048	2.467	2.763	3.674
29	1.311	1.699	2.045	2.462	2.756	3.659
30	1.310	1.697	2.042	2.457	2.750	3.646
40	1.303	1.684	2.021	2.423	2.704	3.551
60	1.296	1.671	2.000	2.390	2.660	3.460
120	1.289	1.658	1.980	2.358	2.617	3.373
∞	1.282	1.645	1.960	2.326	2.576	3.291

Source: Abridged from Table III of Fisher and Yates, *Statistical Tables for Biological, Agricultural, and Medical Research*, 6th ed., published by Oliver and Boyd Ltd., Edinburgh, 1963. By permission of the publishers.

TABLE B–3   Critical values of chi square (χ^2)

df	Probability under H_0 that $\chi^2 \geqq$ Chi Square					
	.99	.98	.95	.90	.80	.70
1	.00016	.00063	.0039	.016	.064	.15
2	.02	.04	.10	.21	.45	.71
3	.12	.18	.35	.58	1.00	1.42
4	.30	.43	.71	1.06	1.65	2.20
5	.55	.75	1.14	1.61	2.34	3.00
6	.87	1.13	1.64	2.20	3.07	3.83
7	1.24	1.56	2.17	2.83	3.82	4.67
8	1.65	2.03	2.73	3.49	4.59	5.53
9	2.09	2.53	3.32	4.17	5.38	6.39
10	2.56	3.06	3.94	4.86	6.18	7.27
11	3.05	3.61	4.58	5.58	6.99	8.15
12	3.57	4.18	5.23	6.30	7.81	9.03
13	4.11	4.76	5.89	7.04	8.63	9.93
14	4.66	5.37	6.57	7.79	9.47	10.82
15	5.23	5.98	7.26	8.55	10.31	11.72
16	5.81	6.61	7.96	9.31	11.15	12.62
17	6.41	7.26	8.67	10.08	12.00	13.53
18	7.02	7.91	9.39	10.86	12.86	14.44
19	7.63	8.57	10.12	11.65	13.72	15.35
20	8.26	9.24	10.85	12.44	14.58	16.27
21	8.90	9.92	11.59	13.24	15.44	17.18
22	9.54	10.60	12.34	14.04	16.31	18.10
23	10.20	11.29	13.09	14.85	17.19	19.02
24	10.86	11.99	13.85	15.66	18.06	19.94
25	11.52	12.70	14.61	16.47	18.94	20.87
26	12.20	13.41	15.38	17.29	19.82	21.79
27	12.88	14.12	16.15	18.11	20.70	22.72
28	13.56	14.85	16.93	18.94	21.59	23.65
29	14.26	15.57	17.71	19.77	22.48	24.58
30	14.95	16.31	18.49	20.60	23.36	25.51

Source: Abridged from Table IV of Fisher and Yates, *Statistics for Biological, Agricultural, and Medical Research,* published by Oliver and Boyd Ltd., Edinburgh, 1963. By permission of the publishers.

TABLE B–3   *(concluded)*

.50	.30	.20	.10	.05	.02	.01	.001
.46	1.07	1.64	2.71	3.84	5.41	6.64	10.83
1.39	2.41	3.22	4.60	5.99	7.82	9.21	13.82
2.37	3.66	4.64	6.25	7.82	9.84	11.34	16.27
3.36	4.88	5.99	7.78	9.49	11.67	13.28	18.46
4.35	6.06	7.29	9.24	11.07	13.39	15.09	20.52
5.35	7.23	8.56	10.64	12.59	15.03	16.81	22.46
6.35	8.38	9.80	12.02	14.07	16.62	18.48	24.32
7.34	9.52	11.03	13.36	15.51	18.17	20.09	26.12
8.34	10.66	12.24	14.68	16.92	19.68	21.67	27.88
9.34	11.78	13.44	15.99	18.31	21.16	23.21	29.59
10.34	12.90	14.63	17.28	19.68	22.62	24.72	31.26
11.34	14.01	15.81	18.55	21.03	24.05	26.22	32.91
12.34	15.12	16.98	19.81	22.36	25.47	27.69	34.53
13.34	16.22	18.15	21.06	23.68	26.87	29.14	36.12
14.34	17.32	19.31	22.31	25.00	28.26	30.58	37.70
15.34	18.42	20.46	23.54	26.30	29.63	32.00	39.29
16.34	19.51	21.62	24.77	27.59	31.00	33.41	40.75
17.34	20.60	22.76	25.99	28.87	32.35	34.80	42.31
18.34	21.69	23.90	27.20	30.14	33.69	36.19	43.82
19.34	22.78	25.04	28.41	31.41	35.02	37.57	45.32
20.34	23.86	26.17	29.62	32.67	36.34	38.93	46.80
21.24	24.94	27.30	30.81	33.92	37.66	40.29	48.27
22.34	26.02	28.43	32.01	35.17	38.97	41.64	49.73
23.34	27.10	29.55	33.20	36.42	40.27	42.98	51.18
24.34	28.17	30.68	34.38	37.65	41.57	44.31	52.62
25.34	29.25	31.80	35.56	38.88	42.86	45.64	54.05
26.34	30.32	32.91	36.74	40.11	44.14	46.96	55.48
27.34	31.39	34.03	37.92	41.34	45.42	48.28	56.89
28.34	32.46	35.14	39.09	42.56	46.69	49.59	58.30
29.34	33.53	36.25	40.26	43.77	47.96	50.89	59.70

TABLE B–4 Critical values of D in the Kolmogorov-Smirnov one-sample test

Sample Size N	Level of Significance for $D = Maximum \; |F_0(X) - S_N(X)|$				
	.20	.15	.10	.05	.01
1	.900	.925	.950	.975	.995
2	.684	.726	.776	.842	.929
3	.565	.597	.642	.708	.828
4	.494	.525	.564	.624	.733
5	.446	.474	.510	.565	.669
6	.410	.436	.470	.521	.618
7	.381	.405	.438	.486	.577
8	.358	.381	.411	.457	.543
9	.339	.360	.388	.432	.514
10	.322	.342	.368	.410	.490
11	.307	.326	.352	.391	.468
12	.295	.313	.338	.375	.450
13	.284	.302	.325	.361	.433
14	.274	.292	.314	.349	.418
15	.266	.283	.304	.338	.404
16	.258	.274	.295	.328	.392
17	.250	.266	.286	.318	.381
18	.244	.259	.278	.309	.371
19	.237	.252	.272	.301	.363
20	.231	.246	.264	.294	.356
25	.21	.22	.24	.27	.32
30	.19	.20	.22	.24	.29
35	.18	.19	.21	.23	.27
Over 35	$\dfrac{1.07}{\sqrt{N}}$	$\dfrac{1.14}{\sqrt{N}}$	$\dfrac{1.22}{\sqrt{N}}$	$\dfrac{1.36}{\sqrt{N}}$	$\dfrac{1.63}{\sqrt{N}}$

Source: F. J. Massey, Jr., "The Kolmogorov-Smirnov Test for Goodness of Fit," *Journal of the American Statistical Association,* 46, p. 70. Adapted with the kind permission of the publisher.

TABLE B–5   Critical values of T in the Wilcoxon matched-pairs test

N	Level of Significance for One-Tailed Test		
	.025	.01	.005
	Level of Significance for Two-Tailed Test		
	.05	.02	.01
6	0	—	—
7	2	0	—
8	4	2	0
9	6	3	2
10	8	5	3
11	11	7	5
12	14	10	7
13	17	13	10
14	21	16	13
15	25	20	16
16	30	24	20
17	35	28	23
18	40	33	28
19	46	38	32
20	52	43	38
21	59	49	43
22	66	56	49
23	73	62	55
24	81	69	61
25	89	77	68

Source: Adapted from Table I of F. Wilcoxon, *Some Rapid Approximate Statistical Procedures* (New York: American Cyanamid Company, 1949), p. 13, with the kind permission of the publisher.

TABLE B–6 Critical values of *D* in the Kolmogorov-
Smirnov two-sample test (small samples)

N	One-Tailed Test*		Two-Tailed Test†	
	α = .05	α = .01	α = .05	α = .01
3	3	—	—	—
4	4	—	4	—
5	4	5	5	5
6	5	6	5	6
7	5	6	6	6
8	5	6	6	7
9	6	7	6	7
10	6	7	7	8
11	6	8	7	8
12	6	8	7	8
13	7	8	7	9
14	7	8	8	9
15	7	9	8	9
16	7	9	8	10
17	8	9	8	10
18	8	10	9	10
19	8	10	9	10
20	8	10	9	11
21	8	10	9	11
22	9	11	9	11
23	9	11	10	11
24	9	11	10	12
25	9	11	10	12
26	9	11	10	12
27	9	12	10	12
28	10	12	11	13
29	10	12	11	13
30	10	12	11	13
35	11	13	12	
40	11	14	13	

*Source: Abridged from I. A. Goodman, "Kolmogorov-Smirnov Tests for Psychological Research," *Psychological Bulletin* 51, 1951, p. 167, copyright (1951) by the American Psychological Association. Reprinted by permission.

†Source: Derived from Table 1 of F. J. Massey, Jr., "The Distribution of the Maximum Deviation Between Two Sample Cumulative Step Functions," *Annals of Mathematical Statistics* 23, 1951, pp. 126–27, with the kind permission of the publisher.

TABLE B–7   Critical values of D in the Kolmogorov-Smirnov two-sample test for large samples (two-tailed test)

Level of Significance	Value of D So Large As To Call for Rejection of H_0 at the Indicated Level of Significance, Where $D = $ Maximum $\|S_{n_1}(X) - S_2(X)\|$
.10	$1.22 \sqrt{\dfrac{n_1 + n_2}{n_1 n_2}}$
.05	$1.36 \sqrt{\dfrac{n_1 + n_2}{n_1 n_2}}$
.025	$1.48 \sqrt{\dfrac{n_1 + n_2}{n_1 n_2}}$
.01	$1.63 \sqrt{\dfrac{n_1 + n_2}{n_1 n_2}}$
.005	$1.73 \sqrt{\dfrac{n_1 + n_2}{n_1 n_2}}$
.001	$1.95 \sqrt{\dfrac{n_1 + n_2}{n_1 n_2}}$

*Adapted from N. Smirnov, "Table for Estimating the Goodness of Fit of Empirical Distributions," *Annals of Mathematical Statistics* 18, 1948, pp. 280–81, with the kind permission of the publisher.

TABLE B–8   Partial table of critical values of U in the Mann-Whitney test

Critical Values for One-Tailed Test at $\alpha = .025$ or a Two-Tailed Test at $\alpha = .05$

n_1 \ n_2	9	10	11	12	13	14	15	16	17	18	19	20
1												
2	0	0	0	1	1	1	1	1	2	2	2	2
3	2	3	3	4	4	5	5	6	6	7	7	8
4	4	5	6	7	8	9	10	11	11	12	13	13
5	7	8	9	11	12	13	14	15	17	18	19	20
6	10	11	13	14	16	17	19	21	22	24	25	27
7	12	14	16	18	20	22	24	26	28	30	32	34
8	15	17	19	22	24	26	29	31	34	36	38	41
9	17	20	23	26	28	31	34	37	39	42	45	48
10	20	23	26	29	33	36	39	42	45	48	52	55
11	23	26	30	33	37	40	44	47	51	55	58	62
12	26	29	33	37	41	45	49	53	57	61	66	69
13	28	33	37	41	45	50	54	59	63	67	72	76
14	31	36	40	45	50	55	59	64	67	74	78	83
15	34	39	44	49	54	59	64	70	75	80	85	90
16	37	42	47	53	59	64	70	75	81	86	92	98
17	39	45	51	57	63	67	75	81	87	93	99	105
18	42	48	55	61	67	74	80	86	93	99	106	112
19	45	52	58	65	72	78	85	92	99	106	113	119
20	48	55	62	69	76	83	90	98	105	112	119	127

Critical Values for One-Tailed Test at $\alpha = .05$ or a Two-Tailed Test at $\alpha = .10$

n_2 \ n_1	9	10	11	12	13	14	15	16	17	18	19	20
1											0	0
2	1	1	1	2	2	2	3	3	3	4	4	4
3	3	4	5	5	6	7	7	8	9	9	10	11
4	6	7	8	9	10	11	12	14	15	16	17	18
5	9	11	12	13	15	16	18	19	20	22	23	25
6	12	14	16	17	19	21	23	25	26	28	30	32
7	15	17	19	21	24	26	28	30	33	35	37	39
8	18	20	23	26	28	31	33	36	39	41	44	47
9	21	24	27	30	33	36	39	42	45	48	51	54
10	24	27	31	34	37	41	44	48	51	55	58	62
11	27	31	34	38	42	46	50	54	57	61	65	69
12	30	34	38	42	47	51	55	60	64	68	72	77
13	33	37	42	47	51	56	61	65	70	75	80	84
14	36	41	46	51	56	61	66	71	77	82	87	92
15	39	44	50	55	61	66	72	77	83	88	94	100
16	42	48	54	60	65	71	77	83	89	95	101	107
17	45	51	57	64	70	77	83	89	96	102	109	115
18	48	55	61	68	75	82	88	95	102	109	116	123
19	51	58	65	72	80	87	94	101	109	116	123	130
20	54	62	69	77	84	92	100	107	115	123	130	138

Source: Abridged from D. Auble, "Extended Tables from the Mann-Whitney Statistic," *Bulletin of the Institute of Educational Research* at Indiana University 1, no. 2, reprinted with permission. For tables for other size samples consult this source.

TABLE B–9   Critical values of F distribution for alpha (α) equal to 5 percent

n_2	n_1 Degrees of Freedom (Greater Mean Square)																		
	1	2	3	4	5	6	7	8	9	10	12	15	20	24	30	40	60	120	∞
1	161.4	199.5	215.7	224.6	230.2	234.0	236.8	238.9	240.5	241.9	243.9	245.9	248.0	249.1	250.1	251.1	252.2	253.3	254.3
2	18.51	19.00	19.16	19.25	19.30	19.33	19.35	19.37	19.38	19.40	19.41	19.43	19.45	19.45	19.46	19.47	19.48	19.49	19.50
3	10.13	9.55	9.28	9.12	9.01	8.94	8.89	8.85	8.81	8.79	8.74	8.70	8.66	8.64	8.62	8.59	8.57	8.55	8.53
4	7.71	6.94	6.59	6.39	6.26	6.16	6.09	6.04	6.00	5.96	5.91	5.86	5.80	5.77	5.75	5.72	5.69	5.66	5.63
5	6.61	5.79	5.41	5.19	5.05	4.95	4.88	4.82	4.77	4.74	4.68	4.62	4.56	4.53	4.50	4.46	4.43	4.40	4.36
6	5.99	5.14	4.76	4.53	4.39	4.28	4.21	4.15	4.10	4.06	4.00	3.94	3.87	3.84	3.81	3.77	3.74	3.70	3.67
7	5.59	4.74	4.35	4.12	3.97	3.87	3.79	3.73	3.68	3.64	3.57	3.51	3.44	3.41	3.38	3.34	3.30	3.27	3.23
8	5.32	4.46	4.07	3.84	3.69	3.58	3.50	3.44	3.39	3.35	3.28	3.22	3.15	3.12	3.08	3.04	3.01	2.97	2.93
9	5.12	4.26	3.86	3.63	3.48	3.37	3.29	3.23	3.18	3.14	3.07	3.01	2.94	2.90	2.86	2.83	2.79	2.75	2.71
10	4.96	4.10	3.71	3.48	3.33	3.22	3.14	3.07	3.02	2.98	2.91	2.85	2.77	2.74	2.70	2.66	2.62	2.58	2.54
11	4.84	3.98	3.59	3.36	3.20	3.09	3.01	2.95	2.90	2.85	2.79	2.72	2.65	2.61	2.57	2.53	2.49	2.45	2.40
12	4.75	3.89	3.49	3.26	3.11	3.00	2.91	2.85	2.80	2.75	2.69	2.62	2.54	2.51	2.47	2.43	2.38	2.34	2.30
13	4.67	3.81	3.41	3.18	3.03	2.92	2.83	2.77	2.71	2.67	2.60	2.53	2.46	2.42	2.38	2.34	2.30	2.25	2.21
14	4.60	3.74	3.34	3.11	2.96	2.85	2.76	2.70	2.65	2.60	2.53	2.46	2.39	2.35	2.31	2.27	2.22	2.18	2.13
15	4.54	3.68	3.29	3.06	2.90	2.79	2.71	2.64	2.59	2.54	2.48	2.40	2.33	2.29	2.25	2.20	2.16	2.11	2.07
16	4.49	3.63	3.24	3.01	2.85	2.74	2.66	2.59	2.54	2.49	2.42	2.35	2.28	2.24	2.19	2.15	2.11	2.06	2.01
17	4.45	3.59	3.20	2.96	2.81	2.70	2.61	2.55	2.49	2.45	2.38	2.31	2.23	2.19	2.15	2.10	2.06	2.01	1.96
18	4.41	3.55	3.16	2.93	2.77	2.66	2.58	2.51	2.46	2.41	2.34	2.27	2.19	2.15	2.11	2.06	2.02	1.97	1.92
19	4.38	3.52	3.13	2.90	2.74	2.63	2.54	2.48	2.42	2.38	2.31	2.23	2.16	2.11	2.07	2.03	1.98	1.93	1.88
20	4.35	3.49	3.10	2.87	2.71	2.60	2.51	2.45	2.39	2.35	2.28	2.20	2.12	2.08	2.04	1.99	1.95	1.90	1.84
21	4.32	3.47	3.07	2.84	2.68	2.57	2.49	2.42	2.37	2.32	2.25	2.18	2.10	2.05	2.01	1.96	1.92	1.87	1.81
22	4.30	3.44	3.05	2.82	2.66	2.55	2.46	2.40	2.34	2.30	2.23	2.15	2.07	2.03	1.98	1.94	1.89	1.84	1.78
23	4.28	3.42	3.03	2.80	2.64	2.53	2.44	2.37	2.32	2.27	2.20	2.13	2.05	2.01	1.96	1.91	1.86	1.81	1.76
24	4.26	3.40	3.01	2.78	2.62	2.51	2.42	2.36	2.30	2.25	2.18	2.11	2.03	1.98	1.94	1.89	1.84	1.79	1.73
25	4.24	3.39	2.99	2.76	2.60	2.49	2.40	2.34	2.28	2.24	2.16	2.09	2.01	1.96	1.92	1.87	1.82	1.77	1.71
26	4.23	3.37	2.98	2.74	2.59	2.47	2.39	2.32	2.27	2.22	2.15	2.07	1.99	1.95	1.90	1.85	1.80	1.75	1.69
27	4.21	3.35	2.96	2.73	2.57	2.46	2.37	2.31	2.25	2.20	2.13	2.06	1.97	1.93	1.88	1.84	1.79	1.73	1.67
28	4.20	3.34	2.95	2.71	2.56	2.45	2.36	2.29	2.24	2.19	2.12	2.04	1.96	1.91	1.87	1.82	1.77	1.71	1.65
29	4.18	3.33	2.93	2.70	2.55	2.43	2.35	2.28	2.22	2.18	2.10	2.03	1.94	1.90	1.85	1.81	1.75	1.70	1.64
30	4.17	3.32	2.92	2.69	2.53	2.42	2.33	2.27	2.21	2.16	2.09	2.01	1.93	1.89	1.84	1.79	1.74	1.68	1.62
40	4.08	3.23	2.84	2.61	2.45	2.34	2.25	2.18	2.12	2.08	2.00	1.92	1.84	1.79	1.74	1.69	1.64	1.58	1.51
60	4.00	3.15	2.76	2.53	2.37	2.25	2.17	2.10	2.04	1.99	1.92	1.84	1.75	1.70	1.65	1.59	1.53	1.47	1.39
120	3.92	3.07	2.68	2.45	2.29	2.17	2.09	2.02	1.96	1.91	1.83	1.75	1.66	1.61	1.55	1.50	1.43	1.35	1.25
∞	3.84	3.00	2.60	2.37	2.21	2.10	2.01	1.94	1.88	1.83	1.75	1.67	1.57	1.52	1.46	1.39	1.32	1.22	1.00

Reprinted by permission from *Statistical Methods* by George W. Snedecor and William G. Cochran, sixth edition © 1967 by Iowa State University Press, Ames, Iowa.

TABLE B–10   Table of random digits

97446	30328	05262	77371	13523	62057	44349	85884	94555	23288
15453	75591	60540	77137	09485	27632	05477	99154	78720	10323
69995	77086	55217	53721	85713	27854	41981	88981	90041	20878
69726	58696	27272	38148	52521	73807	29685	49152	20309	58734
23604	31948	16926	26360	76957	99925	86045	11617	32777	38670
13640	17233	58650	47819	24935	28670	33415	77202	92492	40290
90779	09199	51169	94892	34271	22068	13923	53535	56358	50258
71068	19459	32339	10124	13012	79706	07611	52600	83088	26829
55019	79001	34442	16335	06428	52873	65316	01480	72204	39494
20879	50235	17389	25260	34039	99967	48044	05067	69284	53867
00380	11595	49372	95214	98529	46593	77046	27176	39668	20566
68142	40800	20527	79212	14166	84948	11748	69540	84288	37211
42667	89566	20440	57230	35356	01884	79921	94772	29882	24695
07756	78430	45576	86596	56720	65529	44211	18447	53921	92722
45221	31130	44312	63534	47741	02465	50629	94983	05984	88375
20140	77481	61686	82836	41058	41331	04290	61212	60294	95954
54922	25436	33804	51907	73223	66423	68706	36589	45267	35327
48340	30832	72209	07644	52747	40751	06808	85349	18005	52323
23603	84387	20416	88084	33103	41511	59391	71600	35091	52722
12548	01033	22974	59596	92087	02116	63524	00627	41778	24392
15251	87584	12942	03771	91413	75652	19468	83889	98531	91529
65548	59670	57355	18874	63601	55111	07278	32560	40028	36079
48488	76170	46282	76427	41693	04506	80979	26654	62159	83017
02862	15665	62159	15159	69576	20328	68873	28152	66087	39405
67929	06754	45842	66365	80848	15262	55144	37816	08421	30071
73237	07607	31615	04892	50989	87347	14393	21165	68169	70788
13788	20327	07960	95917	75112	01398	26381	41377	33549	19754
43877	66485	40825	45923	74410	69693	76959	70973	26343	63781
14047	08369	56414	78533	76378	44204	71493	68861	31042	81873
88383	46755	51342	13505	55324	52950	22244	28028	73486	98797
29567	16379	41994	65947	58926	50953	09388	00405	29874	44954
20508	60995	41539	26396	99825	25652	28089	57224	35222	58922
64178	76768	75747	32854	32893	61152	58565	33128	33354	16056
26373	51147	90362	93309	13175	66385	57822	31138	12893	68607
10083	47656	59241	73630	99200	94672	59785	95449	99279	25488
11683	14347	04369	98719	75005	43633	24125	30532	54830	95387
56548	76293	50904	88579	24621	94291	56881	35062	48765	22078
35292	47291	82610	27777	43965	31802	98444	88929	54383	93141
51329	87645	51623	08971	50704	82395	33916	95859	99788	97885
51860	19180	39324	68483	78650	74750	64893	58042	82878	20619
23886	01257	07945	71175	31243	87167	42829	44601	08769	26417
80028	82310	43989	09242	15056	48250	04529	96941	48190	69644
83946	46858	09164	18858	12672	55190	02820	45861	29104	75386
00000	41586	25972	25356	54260	95691	99431	89903	22306	43863
90615	12848	23376	29458	48239	37628	59265	50152	30340	40713
42003	10738	55835	48218	23204	19188	13556	06610	77667	88068
86135	26174	07834	17007	97938	96728	15689	77544	891ρ6	41252
54436	10828	41212	19836	89476	53685	28085	22878	71868	35048
14545	72034	32131	38783	58588	47499	50945	97045	42357	53536
43925	49879	13339	78773	95626	67119	93023	96832	09757	98545

Source: The Rand Corporation, *A Million Random Digits with 100,000 Normal Deviates*, Glencoe, Ill. The Free Press, 1955, p. 225.

Index

This book has been set in 10 and 9 point Caledonia, leaded 2 points. Section numbers are 36 point Caledonia Bold and section titles are 24 point Caledonia Bold CAPS. Chapter numbers and titles are 18 point Caledonia Bold. The overall type area is 27 picas by 47 picas.